Ireland, Sweden
and the
Great European
Migration
1815–1914

Ireland, Sweden
and the
Great European
Migration
1815–1914

DONALD HARMAN AKENSON

LIVERPOOL
UNIVERSITY PRESS

First published 2011 by
Liverpool University Press
4 Cambridge Street
Liverpool
L69 7ZU

British Library Cataloguing-in-Publication data
A British Library CIP record is available

ISBN 978-1-84631-661-6 cased

Typeset in Caslon and Franklin Gothic by BBR (www.bbr-online.com)
Printed in the UK by Bell and Bain Ltd, Glasgow

To the memory of the Åkesons,
and to all who sailed with them

CONTENTS

1. Introduction 1

2. Were They in the Same Boat? 4

3. Shouldn't They Be Leaving in Droves? 27

4. Leading Sectors: Sweden 65

5. Leading Sectors: Ireland 93

6. Deprivation and Famine 136

7. After Axial Stress 168

8. Convergence as Success 188

9. A Most Controlled Country 200

10. Open Verdicts 227

11. Epilogue 257

Select Bibliography 264

Index 284

TABLES

2.1. European populations (in thousands)   17

3.1. Population of Ireland (in millions)   31

3.2. Irish agricultural enterprises, c. 1845, in statute acres   38

3.3. Swedish agricultural enterprises, 1800 (categorized by adult male head-persons)   46

3.4. Swedish agricultural enterprises, 1805–60 (categorized by adult male head-persons)   53

7.1. "World" Irish Population (in thousands), 1871–1921   172

7.2. "World" Swedish Population (in thousands), 1850–1920   172

7.3. Age grouping of emigrants, 1861–1910, Sweden and Ireland as percentage of total emigration   173

8.1. Swedish agricultural enterprises, 1860–1900 (categorized by adult male head-persons)   191

FIGURES

2.1. Åkerman's European emigration curve as generalized for Europe   5

2.2. Pre-Christian Sweden (modern place-names)   11

2.3. Swedish geographical units   12

2.4. Irish counties   13

2.5. Gustav Sundbärg's model for late-nineteenth-century Swedish socio-demographic regions   15

3.1. Irish agricultural security, pre-Famine   37

3.2. Swedish agricultural security, c. 1800   48

7.1. A socio-cultural reading of Åkerman's emigration curve   170

Chapter One

INTRODUCTION

ONE

Jacob Burckhardt, the Renaissance art and cultural historian (1818–97) is said to have observed that "Everywhere in the past we encounter things which remain unexplained only because they were completely self-understood in their time, and like all daily matters, were not thought necessary to write down."[1] Some knowledge that is common in one generation becomes virtually unknown in the next or the next or later. This knowledge usually touches on things people are not either proud or ashamed of—just everyday things about making a living or keeping a family in order. But sometimes things that everyone in a community knows—such as who actually is the father of which child—goes unrecorded because of an agreed communal self-censorship. Either way, one generation's knowledge frequently is a later generation's amnesia.[2]

If that is what Burckhardt meant, then most days of the week I would agree with him. The odd few decades of writing Irish history, working on creating an evidence-based story of the Irish worldwide, and on the evolution and impact of the Jewish-Christian scriptures have made me acutely aware of how little we historians know of the lives of the people about whom we write, and whom we increasingly "theorize." There is no shame in admitting to doubts, to lacunae in our knowledge, and to the need for intelligent guessing, but we rarely do so.

To our collective embarrassment and perhaps shame, we often forget the work of earlier generations of scholars, many of whom knew things that we now have forgotten. Read the "historiographic" survey in a few PhD theses, and it immediately becomes clear that some very good minds are being badly tainted in attitude. We force our postgraduates to write self-vaunting introductory pieces that show how important their work is and how significant an improvement it is over all past efforts. Occasionally that posture is right, but usually not. As a general rule, I think that historians (of all people) ought not to will into silence the voices of past historians. This comes to mind in the present context, because as I have read migration histories of the various European nations written in the last 30 years, it has been striking how many of them are so tightly nation-focused that they forcibly elide something that, as historians, we once knew: that the nineteenth and early twentieth-century migrations from Europe were integral units of a larger Great Migration. Granted the out-migration pattern of every nation (indeed every region, every parish) has its own singular characteristics, but in the "true" nineteenth century—1815 to 1914—much of what seems noteworthy as being unusual or even unique in the case of individual nations is more significant as a commonplace. Outstanding scholars in earlier generations knew this and I will refer to some of their individual work in later chapters. So, one of the reasons that I relate to each other the migration history of Ireland and of

Sweden is simply to bring back some knowledge we once knew. These two cases are not presented as entities in themselves, but as samples (not statistical samples: more like the core samples that geophysicists employ) of the larger Great European Migration of the nineteenth century.

TWO

B ecause this book is a study in transnational history, readers will need to accept a set of compromises as far as the rubrics and protocols of presentation are concerned, especially in the documentary notes. Thus, Swedish readers will have to put up with more capital letters and punctuation marks than they are accustomed to. And they will note that some of the items cited are somewhat archaic linguistically. That is hardly surprising, given how quickly the Swedish language has changed during the past century and a quarter. Readers in the British Isles will note that the mode of documentation and citation is resolutely North American, including the usage of double quotation marks and the inclusion of introduced punctuation within any given reference. Probably, readers in the USA will be a little niggled by my use of English Standard spelling, while their counterparts in the British Isles may not like my belief that the Americans are grammatically correct when it comes to collective nouns. Canadian readers, however, will be quite accepting of all these things, this being their amiable nature.

Those items are essentially cosmetic. However, fundamental to an understanding of the Great European Migration is a matter that most mainline historians will accept, rather like an eighteenth-century Anglican bishop affirming the Athanasian Creed— meaning that their lips may mouth their words, but that their hearts may not be in it. Specifically, most historians in academic history departments will say, yes, paying attention to economic historians is useful and, yes, indeed, numbers certainly are important in historical exposition: but, in fact, in the English-speaking world, the last three decades have seen a general retreat from engagement with systematic quantitative information as a necessary component of historical work. And fewer and fewer economic historians are now employed in history departments, and those who work in departments of economics are usually viewed as being part of a separate intellectual universe. (The case in Europe, particularly in Sweden, is not so dramatic, but the trend is there also.)

Within the world of academic historians, the gains that have been made latterly by incorporating various forms of critical theory into everyday historical work are immense, and one embraces them with cautious enthusiasm. However, the excesses of critical theory have led to a questioning in many quarters of all quantitative evidence and of all social-science-based thinking. This seems to me to be a major mistake because, while one must grant that the full objective reality of any social phenomenon can never be fully known, there are varying levels of approximation of reality, and in the case of the Great European Migration, several million people whose actions need collective description. And those migrants certainly were not simply part of some ideologically derived construction pressed upon the data by the hegemonic imagination of a ruling caste.

If I show an unfashionable admiration for economic historians (of a certain sort) and an appreciation of numbers (again, of a certain sort), this is in part because each of those components helps to provide the intellectual freedom to think about matters I find fasci-nating. Systematic sets of numbers that cover the entire range of behaviour of a large body of people (systematic, careful numbers, not the ones many historians of migration pull out of the air—or elsewhere) of course are valuable in themselves. And, equally important, the numbers emancipate the historian's imagination so that he or she can deal with individual cases. There is a nice secure-making circle here: broad-based data sets tell one where an individual or a small group fits within the larger picture; and the small cases illustrate central matters of the big-number data set or show where important outliers are located and how they work. Thus, broad-based numerical description and tight narrative exposition are part of the same process. An historical discussion of the transnational flux of the nineteenth century that had only one of these would be like casting a massive cathedral bell, but neglecting to cast and affix a sounding hammer.

The numbers in this book are broad based, but very simple. They are the product of accounting, not mathematics in any sophisticated sense. They are employed in most cases to define parameters of experience and to fit into an expositional logic tree. Anyone who can reconcile his or her own bank statement can follow them.

As for the references to economic historians, these are often presented in admiration. However, I do not believe that academic historians have any less powerful tools of analysis than do econometricians, merely different ones, and my goal is to learn, not to worship. Where Cliometric material is used, it is translated into English: I hope, accurately.

NOTES

1   Martin E. Marty, *A Nation of Behavers* (Chicago: University of Chicago Press, 1976), p. xi.
2   For a discussion of cultural amnesia in the linguistic sphere, see K. David Harrison, *When Languages Die: The Extinction of the World's Languages and the Erosion of Human Knowledge* (New York: Oxford University Press, 2007).

Chapter Two

WERE THEY IN THE SAME BOAT?

ONE

I f scholars of the Great European Migration of 1815–1914[1] have one thing in common, it is the desire to see pattern. And almost all would suggest that pattern implies repetition and regularity, even if only in regularity of development. At minimum, this desire for comforting regularity is understandable, and at best it involves an heroic effort to find order in a flood tide of information.

For, indeed, the sea of information is vast: the usual estimates are that about 55 to 60 million Europeans left the European continent (including the British Isles) between the end of the Napoleonic Wars and the beginning of World War I.[2] They fetched up, at least for a time, in one of the several New Worlds that seemed suddenly to have opened to them.[3] This is an extraordinary number and it represents a diffusion over huge patches of the globe: South America, New Zealand and Australia, the West Indies, Africa and North America. To keep the diffusion from degenerating into mere confusion, the common procedure is to wall off as much as possible the period between the Great European War that ended in 1815 from what came before and to build a similar barrier between the Great European War that began in 1914 and the period that came after. This construction—sometimes called "the true nineteenth century"—fits well with the actual migration data, and is justified as long as the time barriers are not totally impermeable to suggestions that there are some continuities between the Great Migration and its predecessors and successors.

A fine example of the desire to find regularity in the face of flood is Sune Åkerman's often-reproduced schematic (figure 2.1). He employed the figure to indicate the Swedish flow from 1850 to 1915, but in fact the model is transportable and is widely used by economic historians of migration to illustrate an Ideal Type of European out-migration. By sliding the curve a bit left or right on the timeline, it will represent the smoothed curve of emigration for most European countries, and when projected on a larger screen, it does a good job of describing total migration out of Europe.

There is comfort in this sort of perceived regularity, and even more in the confidence of scholars, such as the pioneering Cliometricians, who see the Great European Migration as being a nicely regularized phenomenon that at heart was simply a convergence of western national economies. Thus, acting like good Milton Friedmanesque molecules, European workers moved to places where their wages were better (only the USA is seriously considered as a possible destination in this model). And, voilà, the world became more like the US.[4] Long before the new econometric history evolved, Walter Lippman, as a piece of World War II propaganda entitled *The US War Aims* (1944),

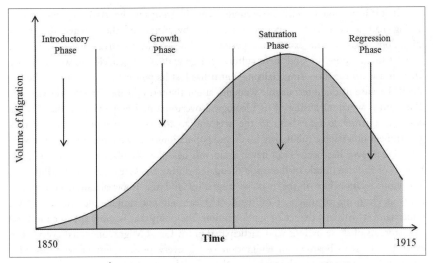

Figure 2.1. Åkerman's European emigration curve as generalized for Europe.

Source: Kevin O'Rourke and Jeffrey G. Williamson, *Globalization and History. The Evolution of a Nineteenth-Century Atlantic Economy* (Cambridge: MIT Press, 1999), p. 128, based on Harald Runblom and Hans Norman (eds.), *From Sweden to America. A History of the Migration* (Minneapolis: University of Minnesota Press, 1976), p. 25.

publicized the phrase "the Atlantic Community" and ten years later, Frank Thistlethwaite was summarizing the Great European Migration as follows:

> The hegira which conquered and settled the North American Continent was part of a great folk movement which embraced the whole Atlantic basin. American growth was part of the growth of a wider community on both sides of the Atlantic, a community which included not only Canada and the West Indies, but the British Isles and later North Germany and Scandinavia. *This Atlantic community was perhaps the greatest achievement of the expansion of Europe* ... [emphasis mine].[5]

These and scores of similar attempts at showing the Great European Migration to be a regular and, indeed, normal phenomenon are necessary. They are perhaps arrogant—sometimes overweeningly self-confident—but are necessary because they are emotionally comforting.

Comforting: why would that be desirable in scholarly examinations of a set of social occurrences? Because by excluding the hideously distressing worldwide context in which the Great European Migration took place, the events appear to be not just regular, but normal. The Great European Migration seems to be predictable, to be based upon the rational self-interest of the participants, and thus in some sense to have been democratic and therefore moral. In reality, it was anything but.

Far from being normal, the Great European Migration was one of the truly freak phenomena in human history. It was not simply a case of Ravensteinian hydraulics working smoothly in the Atlantic Community (although those forces played their part), but mostly of human beings scrambling up shingle beaches amidst boiling surf.

That it is possible to celebrate accurately certain groups in the "Atlantic Community" having had a beneficial economic experience by virtue of the nineteenth-century migrations, rests on the exact same period of time—1815 to 1914—having been the greatest single period of land theft, cultural pillage and casual genocide in world history. There is a word for this—imperialism—but it has lost its power to engage most scholars, chiefly because of the interminable wrangles about the term during the late Marxian era. The word is worth cleansing of its ideological overtones and employing in the classical descriptive sense: to refer both to the acts and to the spirit of empire. That is: to a government or a people ruling over lands and populations that were not initially its own.

There never has been—and never again will be—the colonization of "empty" New Worlds of the magnitude of those subinfeudated during the Great European Migration. The basic relationship of the massive migration and the imperialization and ethno-religious cleansing of much of the world is clear, but not simple, and we do not yet understand it with any degree of sophistication. The point that is most apt to be resisted by historians of those nations who participated in the Great Migration is that everyone— every person who boarded an emigration vessel, every peasant farmer who cashed a remittance order from his children in a New World, every labourer, priest, farmer, civil servant and hawker of ballads and newspapers from the old homeland was part of a single system. This system—call it capitalism, call it democratic market economics, it really does not matter—joined together in a single network the societies of nineteenth and early twentieth-century Europe and the marching army ants who were conquering the New Worlds. It is undeniable that many of the migrants from Europe left deplorable conditions and that many had themselves been victims of several forms of exploitation and abuse. Yet, these same individuals, when in a New World, themselves became oppressor and exploiters, sometimes directly, sometimes only systemically, but always inevitably. The better life for Europe's migrants was paid for in part by a worse life for those they dispossessed. At some distant point, the disjuncture in each European nation's history between the pain so many migrants experienced at home and the pain they inflicted, however indirectly, in their new land will be joined into a single narrative. For the present, keeping the dissonance between those two portions of the story continually in the back of our minds, an ever-present drone-bass in our consciousness, is the best we can do.

TWO

I n practice, the single biggest decision in any attempt to illuminate the character of the Great European Migration is this: what does one do with nations and with their frequent embodiment as states? That there is not any primordial relationship between state and nation or between either one of them and the construction of regional, local or personal identities is well recognized among historians. One can justifiably question, as does Donna Gabaccia, "the tyranny of the national in the discipline of history."[6] And this tyranny, if anything, is stronger in the social sciences. However, as Rogers Brubaker asks, once we accept that "nation-state" is not equivalent to "society," then "what follows from this critique?" His caution is worth attention:

... If the methodological critique is coupled—as it often is—with the empirical claim about the diminishing relevance of the nation-state, and if it serves therefore to channel attention away from state-level processes and structures, there is a risk that academic fashion will lead us to neglect what remains, for better or worse, a fundamental level of organization and fundamental locus of power.[7]

Where the nation-state is frequently most useful to the historian is in its function as a collector of data. States do not collect information for the convenience of historians, but without the curatorial function of the state, not much deep social history would be written. (Privately financed social surveys, though by no means unknown in the nineteenth century, were rare.) Of course, one uses state-assembled data cautiously and with a set of intentions that are often different from those of the original collectors.[8]

Yet, even the most dedicated skeptic of national history has to admit the possibility that at times the borders which the state employs for data collection are coterminous with the boundaries of an integral social system. Ireland, from 1801 to 1922, is one such unit. Most emphatically, this is not to say that all the major sectors of the Irish populace got along famously with each other—who would suggest that? But the divisions within Irish society in the "true" nineteenth century were divisions within a single, larger socio-economic system, and the dimensions of that system were those of the geographic island of Ireland. Undeniably, Ireland was in a colonial or semi-colonial relationship with Great Britain (this is still a live and lively issue in Irish historiography and, to a lesser degree, Irish politics), but even the imperial constitutional nomenclature of the period—"the United Kingdom of Great Britain and Ireland"—made clear that Ireland remained a separate, albeit not independent, unit.

Here we are at the nub of a significant issue—that of intention. Given that I am an historian of Ireland, what do I hope to do in situating Ireland in the matrix of the Great European Migration? My goal is to help to remove from the historiography of the Irish diaspora the dead hand of a literary tradition that depicts Ireland as a story unto itself. The Irish diaspora's narrative is an engrossing and sometimes wrenching history, but Irish exceptionalism has too long been an unexamined doctrine. Actually, much of what happened in Ireland occurred elsewhere in Europe as well, and most of the things that Irish migrants did were done by other Europeans also.

The most efficient way to make these points—and at the same time to raise some new questions for historians of Ireland and of its diaspora—is to engage in a tight, but not rigidly taxonomic, comparison with a similar European nation during the "true" nineteenth century. The best comparator for this particular exercise is Sweden.

THREE

If, in mid-twentieth century that suggestion had been made, it would have been met with derision. Sweden in the two decades immediately after World War II was seen as the antipole of Ireland: highly industrialized (in a civilized way), socialist (in a vague sense), expanding in numbers (within reason) and allegedly preferring sex to alcohol as a primary means of social diversion. Just the opposite of Ireland.

Now, in the twenty-first century, the two nations are much closer together in their societal patterns, so it is easier to acknowledge that in the nineteenth century the two nations were also quite alike economically, that they had parallel patterns of out-migration, and therefore that they are justifiably comparable. Not identical—what would be the point of that?—but similar enough to make their differences suggestive. The most important adjustment that has to be made is to remove Norway from the Swedish data-catchment area. Norway was an internal colony of Sweden (under a regnal union) from 1814 to 1905.[9] If one works historically within the borders of Sweden-sans-Norway, one has a state data-collection area that has the same boundaries as the socio-economic system of the Swedish populace.

Sweden is particularly useful as a comparator to Ireland, because, as Kevin O'Rourke and Jeffrey Williamson have pointed out, the two nations in the nineteenth and early twentieth centuries were part of a constellation of states that comprised the "poor European periphery." Obviously, Sweden and Ireland both are geographically peripheral in Europe, being among the northern outliers that benefit from the Gulf Stream. But what O'Rourke and Williamson are referring to is a group of states that in the mid-nineteenth century was distinguished by poverty, little industrialization and low labour productivity: Sweden, Denmark, Norway, Italy, Portugal, Spain and Ireland. They form a set.[10] (One could justifiably add most of Scotland and rural pre-1851 England to that same group, save that reliable site-specific data are lacking.) So treating Sweden and Ireland as part of a single set is creditable. Each provides a core sample of a larger set of phenomena.

Within this set, Ireland was distinguished from the 1840s onward by having the nineteenth century's highest gross out-migration rate—that is, out-migration expressed as a proportion of the home population. Norway was second and in some years had proportionately more out-migration than did Ireland. And only Ireland and Norway had consistently higher out-migration rates than did Sweden.[11] We will deal with the actual numbers later: here what counts is Swedish and Irish comparability. In the second half of the nineteenth century, they were in the same league, although Ireland was streets ahead.

A graphic way to put a human face on the historical situation is to expand David Fitzpatrick's summary of later nineteenth-century Irish culture—"growing up in Ireland meant preparing oneself to leave it"[12]—to include Sweden's being in a parallel condition. Thus, almost one-fifth of the Swedish males born in the period 1861–75 had emigrated by the early 1890s.[13] According to H. Arnold Barton, by 1910 "it was commonly estimated that about one out of every five Swedes was living in America."[14] The Swedish proportions are not as high as those of the Irish—in 1890, roughly 40 per cent of those persons born in Ireland were living overseas[15]—but they point to a similar cultural condition. Although neither the majority of Swedes nor the majority of Irish actually emigrated, the possibility of leaving meant that growing up in each country in the latter decades of the nineteenth century inevitably became a preparation for leaving it. In these two Gulf Stream countries, everyone knew the way the tides ran, even if they did not themselves choose to take to the sea.

One of the marked advantages of comparing Ireland and Sweden is that each society possesses an integral set of contemporary data on population, migration and related matters. None of these data sets is perfect, but they are much more useful than those that have to be put together by later aggregation in several other European nations. For example, the information on Italy before 1861 and Germany before 1851 must be cobbled together from separate and often idiosyncratic sources. For Ireland and for Sweden proper (sans Norway and Finland, which the Russians had acquired in 1809), the boundaries of information collection were stable, quite unlike the situation in central Europe, where state boundaries were frequently rearranged by military force.

Also, because after 1815 Sweden and Ireland were only indirectly affected by the European wars of the nineteenth century, they provide a nice clean set of laboratories for viewing migration as a largely voluntary process. During the period 1815–1914 there was almost no physical expulsion or forced resettlement of population through military conquest in either country. Equally importantly, the population history of both nations was not directly affected by the high mortality that wars so often bring. (This was the problem for France, wherein the demographic pattern was singular in Europe and its emigration history so atypical as to form an outlier in the overall picture.) Thus, Ireland and Sweden provide clean case studies of population growth and of the expansion of emigration among poor agricultural nations. That granted, one is fortunate that in each nation one is dealing with large-magnitude migration information. The absolute numbers are big enough to preclude any random determination of the overall patterns. Of course, the smaller one makes the cells of analysis (counties, parishes, townlands), the more the chance of hitting epiphenomenal occurrences increases. Even so, the consistency in the definition of the subunits over the long periods of time by which the data were collected means that *longue durée* time series can control for wobble that might otherwise occur if one only had a picture of a small unit at a single moment in time. Further, in both Ireland and Sweden, the past two decades have witnessed an impressive amount of high quality work in microstudies of small geographic and social groups and these studies often impact directly on the way historians view the regional and national emigration patterns.

Of course no data set is ever completely trustworthy, and one of the big advantages of both Ireland and Sweden is that during the high period of out-migration, the internal documentation for each country can be checked against the independently collected information from the receiving countries. Sometimes this cross-checking is a bit unsettling.

And, finally, though justifiably comparable in terms of being European peripherals and being characterized by high out-migration, Sweden and Ireland are useful comparators because they did not interact very much. Hardly at all, actually: so each country is an independent observational unit. One would have to stretch very hard indeed to put together a portfolio of Old World intersections of any significance. There is no equivalent in Swedish literature to the German phenomenon: a mixture of scholarly devotion to ancient Irish texts and of soppy-eyed romanticism among German novelists and poets about the singular Irish soul. And for their part, Irish adventurers preferred to walk to Jerusalem (as did Buck Whalley in 1789), not to Stockholm.[16] Granted, while Sweden was an imperial power, Irish mercenaries were recruited for Swedish service. For example, in the period 1609–13, after the Desmond and Tyrone Wars and the Flight of the Earls, as many as two thousand Irish Catholic soldiers were recruited to serve the Crown in Sweden, Russia and Finland. It was not entirely a happy experience: desertion rates were high and those Irish soldiers who absconded in Russia were killed by the local populace.[17] A century later, the Anglo-Irish captain, James Jefferyes, did rather better. He served as a volunteer, 1707–09, during Sweden's Russian campaign and the British and the Swedish governments used him as a backstairs conduit of information. Jefferyes was later employed as a diplomat in the Baltic region, eventually became governor of Cork City and made an advantageous second marriage to the daughter of Viscount Middleton.[18] The other eighteenth-century intersection of note was consequent upon the Irish financier John Jennings gaining a concession in 1762 in the province of Västerbotten for a blast furnace and forge on a river that emptied into the Baltic Sea. The operation began production in 1764, but despite these being good years for the Swedish iron industry, Jennings had not made any profit by the time of his death in 1772.[19] Doubtlessly, there were many more individuals of Irish and of Swedish origins whose lives intersected, but they do not add up to a pattern of cultural or economic interaction of any great weight—certainly not enough to influence either nation's pattern of migration.

The one place Swedish and Irish lives often crossed was after the individual decision to engage in long-distance migration. In the nineteenth and early twentieth centuries, the intersection was literal, directly physical and often visually memorable. The place that most Irish people first saw a real-life Swede, and Swedes saw a live Irishman, was in Liverpool, England. This was a hub of transworld human shipment that has no parallel in our own time. Heathrow Airport of today is small beer in comparison, for it is easy to move around the world and still avoid Heathrow. In the mid-to-late nineteenth century, it was very difficult to migrate from Europe to any place—North America, Australia, New Zealand, parts of Africa—without going through the port of Liverpool as one's long-distance embarkation point. For most Europeans, as well as for the Irish and British, it was cheapest and safest to get to Liverpool by boat and train, stay in lodgings for a while, and then board transoceanic transport. (The chief exception was India and sometimes Africa, for which the south coast of England was the most common embarkation point.) For Irish and Swedish emigrants, the stay in Liverpool, the fraught and noisy embarkation, the scramble of ships out of the Mersey, was a parallel, albeit not a shared experience.

FOUR

Both Sweden and Ireland benefit significantly from the Gulf Stream (Ireland rather more so), which historically has made possible much more dense settlement of the population than otherwise would have been the case. (The obvious comparison is to inland regions in Russia of the same degrees of latitude.) As far as maps are concerned, the chief points that an historian needs to cope with are, first, that in each case during most of the era of the Great Migration, the population of each nation was predominantly rural and even most "urban" inhabitants lived in hamlets or villages. This dictates that the historian will necessarily describe most patterns and events in the same way that people of the time did: by placing them on a grid that is not focused on cities, but which gives fairly large swatches of rural land a single designation. And, secondly, in each country an array of traditional names existed alongside official designations for a given area or region. Often these had no governmental or juridical meaning, but they were used in contemporary documents and, indeed, many of the terms are still alive today.

Begin with a traditional map of the pre-Christian settlement of Sweden. Figure 2.2 indicates the approximate line of settlement between the warring *Svear* (Swedes)

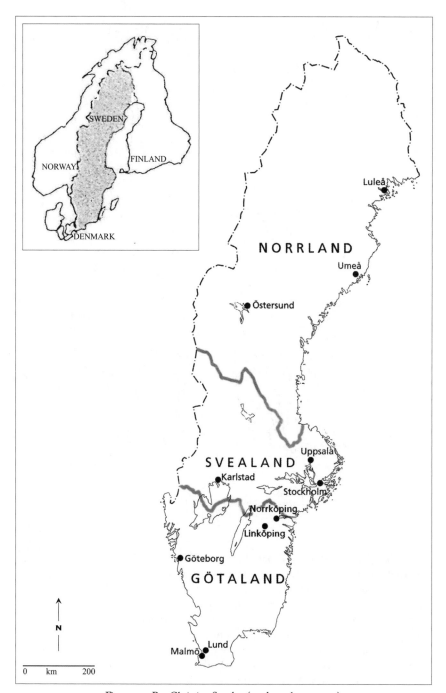

Figure 2.2. Pre-Christian Sweden (modern place-names).

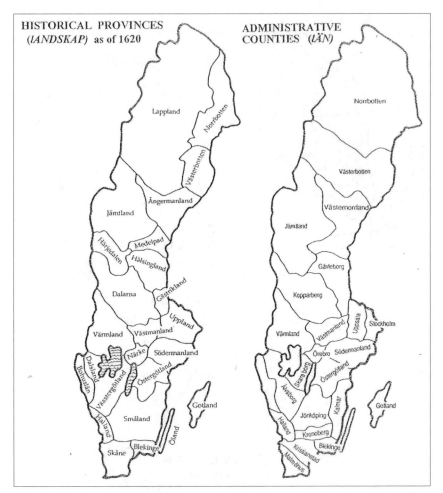

Figure 2.3. Swedish geographical units.

and *Göthar* (Goths) in pre-Christian times. The Goths held the south, the Swedes the middle of the land, and the far north was not much worth fighting over. By the time the land we recognize today as Sweden was Christianized, the Goths and Swedes were ruled under a united, if fractious, monarchy. The point is, that although the terms Svealand and Götaland are nearly a millennium out of service, they appear in nineteenth-century writings and, indeed, even in twenty-first century travel literature.

Less archly antiquarian, but much more confusing, are the names for the historical provinces (*landskap*). These were of medieval provenance and served as a terminological umbrella over large tracts of territory that either shared common geographic characteristics or, more often, were part of a semi-autonomous economic and social system. These names were part of the social identity of most inhabitants and are in common usage to the present day and are frequently found as reference terms in modern historical literature that deals with the nineteenth century. Fine: the problem is that in the 1620s, during the reign of Gustav II Adolphus, a rearrangement was affected whereby the 24 or 25 landskap (traditions varied) were converted into 23 administrative counties (*län*). (The number of these counties varied slightly over time.) The whole business remains slightly vexing to historians because in most cases the län had borders that were almost—but not quite—the same as those of the old landskap. And, while most people of the nineteenth and twentieth centuries used the old names for their locales, the Swedish state collected information according to the new boundaries and new names.

This is manageable, but in English-language writing one must guard against using

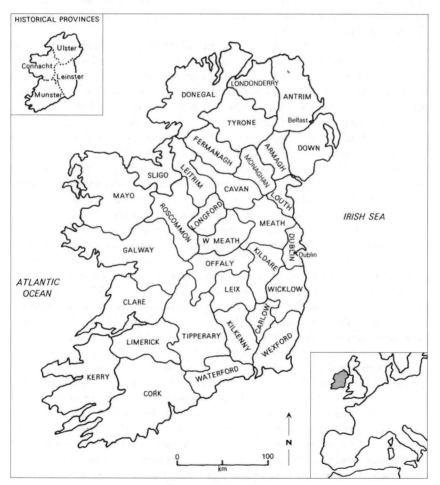

Figure 2.4. Irish counties.

"province" or "county" in reference to Sweden in a way that might equate the terms with the same words as employed in Ireland. Figure 2.4 shows both the historical four provinces of Ireland and the 32 Counties. (The post-1922 names of Counties Leix and Offaly are employed as they were of ancient origin and not simply patriotic relabellings.) Now, the crucial fact is that, unlike Sweden, the Irish counties nested together under the provinces, and thereby the provinces and counties formed a single unified system of geographical designation. In everyday nineteenth-century life in Ireland, most self-identity was with the county rather than the province, but collections of social statistics usually stacked each county within its appropriate province, and then produced national summaries on a province-by-province basis. I think it is reasonably simple to keep the Irish and Swedish meanings separate simply by using "län" rather than "county" each time the reference is to Sweden. Since there are only four Irish provinces (Munster, Connacht, Leinster and Ulster), it should be fairly easy to know when an Irish province or a Swedish one is being referred to—always with the caveat that they are not at all the same thing. And when in doubt, take a look at the map.[20]

Fortunately, certain basic units can be equated. The Irish parish, or parishes, is so close in its form and function to the Swedish *socken/socknar* that the English word fits. In both countries, this was the fundamental unit for collecting information on each individual, the foundation of all demographic and migration studies. As for a unit between the parish and the county (in Ireland) or the län (in Sweden), the utility term "district" will suffice. In Ireland, early in the nineteenth century, the barony served as the intermediate entity, but mid- and late-century governmental reforms made them obsolete by replacing them with rural district and urban district councils. Nevertheless, as late as the 1901 census, Irish enumerations were organized and reported on a barony basis. The Swedish equivalent of the barony in the nineteenth century was the *härad* which, however, was mostly a judicial unit. Later, in the twentieth century, "kommun" or "commun" became the term for a functioning administrative unit between the parish and the län.[21]

Given the basic outlines of the administrative boundaries of the two countries, brief comment on the socio-economic geography of each nation is in order. Considering Ireland, the distinguished geographer J. H. Andrews suggested that two themes should be visualized as an overlay to the outline map. The first is that a gap existed between the east and the west of Ireland. Andrews defined an "eastern triangle" that had its base points at Dundalk in the north and a bit south of Dublin in the south and which ran about 50 miles inland. This included the best land in the country and the area's communication network was highly developed. In sharp contrast, in the era of the Great European Migration, the far west had the worst land, a high incidence of abject poverty, and much of it was remote and difficult of access. The second theme is that the north of Ireland always has been set apart from the rest of the country. Because of the mixture of drumlins, lakes, deep forest and low mountains, Ulster was the most difficult part of the country for foreigners to conquer and it remained the most "Gaelic" until the early seventeenth century. Then, finally broken, the north was subinfeudated with English and Scottish Protestant settlers and therefore became the only part of Ireland with a substantial non-Catholic population. These two overlays, therefore, provide the basic social contours with which to interpret Irish regional characteristics. The socio-physical characteristics affected emigration rates, but not in ways that are intuitively obvious.[22]

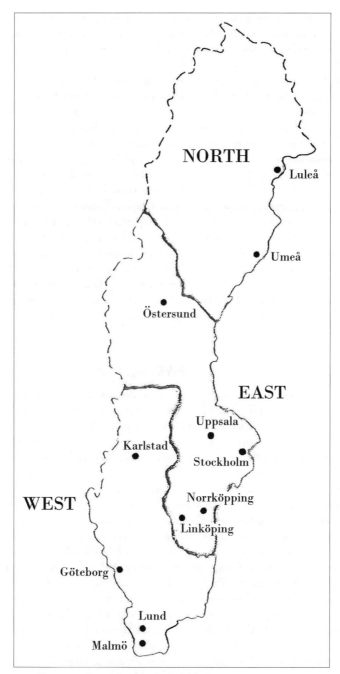

Figure 2.5. Gustav Sundbärg's model for late-nineteenth-century
Swedish socio-demographic regions.

The Swedish situation is a bit harder to describe topographically. A standard early twentieth-century Swedish government handbook defined four regions—the highlands of northern Sweden, the lowlands of central Sweden, the Småland highlands and the plains of Skåne[23]—but that does not tell us very much about the human geography. This difficulty explains why the first editor of that same official handbook—the great, if somewhat idiosyncratic, Swedish social statistician, Gustav Sundbärg—later devised a map of Sweden's demographic regions. These are shown in figure 2.5 and were keyed primarily to the degree the population within each län exhibited a propensity for long-distance migration. This propensity, in turn, related in some degree to demographic matters (particularly marital fecundity), and to the availability of agricultural resources.

The basic points were (1) the "North" (as defined by Sundbärg's social criteria) was characterized by high marital fertility, but low international out-migration rates, and presumably by high rates of internal migration. (One says "presumably" because Sundbärg did not accept as reliable the available data on migration within Sweden itself); (2) the West, which had high marital fertility and a high incidence of external migration; and (3) the East, where marital fecundity was moderate, as compared to the other two regions, and in which the propensity to migrate internationally was markedly lower than in the West, but higher than in the North.[24] Sundbärg's demographic framework is useful, but it is merely one of several possible ways of describing the human geography of the nineteenth century. Both contemporaneous and later scholars put forward alternative schema.[25]

FIVE

Since this book is in many ways a response to decades of reading books that either promulgate or take for granted Irish exceptionalism, one central fact must be made clear: Ireland during the era of the Great European Migration indeed was unique in a significant fashion in that at the end of the period it had a lower population than at the beginning. Whether or not this is an intellectually fatal exception that voids the comparison of Ireland to other European histories (and of course to the Swedish experience) is something that the reader will have to adjudge.[26]

In order to place Irish and Swedish migration into a meaningful perspective, we need to look at some crude numbers: "crude" because they are necessarily cartoon-like in simply drawing outlines and not filling in any fine shadings. The first series (table 2.1) is the set of estimates (and, indeed, very rough estimates they are before mid-nineteenth century) for the total population of Europe and for Sweden and Ireland within that general population. This, during the era of the Great European Migration.[27]

This population set could easily be taken to suggest that because of the trauma of the Great Famine (1845–49), Irish society embraced a form of family limitation that resulted in the natural increase in the population being not increase (!), but decrease. Certainly that pattern, if engaged by societal choice, would have been unique in pre-twentieth-century European history, but that is not what happened. Granted, it became much harder after the Famine to form a family (that will be discussed in a later chapter), yet in fact Ireland had an overall pattern of natural increase in the post-Famine years. If we

Table 2.1. European populations (in thousands).

Year	European total	Swedish population	Irish population
1820	212,768	2,585	
1821			6,802
1830		2,888	
1831			7,767
1840	250,972	3,139	
1841			8,175
1850		3,482	
1851			6,552
1860	282,893	3,860	
1861			5,799
1870		4,169	
1871			5,412
1880	331,745	4,566	
1881			5,175
1890		4,785	
1891			4,705
1900	400,577	5,136	
1901			4,459
1910	447,299	5,522	
1911			4,390

define "natural increase" as the excess of live births over deaths of all sorts, then we have a revealing set of juxtapositions of the Irish and the Swedish situations. These show that for the years 1841–1900, inclusive, the two nations had the following levels of absolute natural increase:[28]

Sweden	2,845,000
Ireland	1,880,000

This is particularly striking because by including the Famine decade, 1841–50, in the data, the numbers actually understate the natural increase of the post-Famine years in Ireland.

As mentioned earlier, Ireland's singularity in the era of the Great European Migration was worthy of note. Ireland was the only European country to lose population from the mid-nineteenth century onwards because it was the only nation in which net out-migration exceeded natural increase. Ireland became the most intensive edge of the European migration pattern, but not an exception to the pattern.

The actual numbers for pre-1850 European migration look rather more authoritative on paper than they are in reality, and those for the second half of the century are only better by degree. Still, they oscillate around some level of reality, and keep being found in various standard sources, so one must be aware of them. One of the earliest is Gustav Sundbärg's work. It is as follows for *net* transoceanic (mostly transatlantic) out-migration from Europe.[29]

Period	Net transoceanic European out-migration
1816–20	160,000
1821–30	340,000
1831–40	1,000,000
1841–50	2,500,000
1851–60	3,550,000
1861–70	3,550,000
1871–80	3,536,000
1881–90	7,104,000
1891–1900	6,288,000
1901–10	13,336,000

Within very wide tolerances, this sets down parameters of rough utility, and in its indirect mode of calculation is actually preferable to later more directly derived estimates.

For later periods (post-1850), a direct estimation of *gross* out-migration from Europe to the various New Worlds is that of 1929 compiled by Imre Ferenczi and Walter F. Willcox for the National Bureau of Economic Research. It remains basic to subsequent revisions of European migration estimates. Their numbers are as follows:[30]

Period	Gross European migration to non-European destinations
1851–60	2,716,000
1861–70	2,844,000
1871–80	3,275,000
1881–90	7,326,000
1891–1900	6,653,000
1901–10	12,208,000

Obviously, something is amiss if these estimates of gross out-migration (post-1850) are less than Sundbärg's for net for most decades! The chief (although far from the only) problem is that the Willcox and Ferenczi numbers were drawn primarily from the often-incomplete reports of the whole range of European and New World governments and no attempt was made to compensate for the undercounting that occurred in every country, both through illegal migration and through return migration.[31]

As in court cases, sometimes indirect evidence is better than direct. Here we could chase down every subsequent estimate and still be only grasping handfuls of fog. I have no trouble accepting O'Rourke and Williamson's recent (1999) guess that *gross* European migration in the period 1820–1920 was about 60 million[32] or Sundbärg's calculations (done in 1910/13), which put net out-migration at about 41 million for 1820–1910. Those are compatible net/gross numbers and fit with possible return migration rates. As a broad European context for specific national discussions, they have utility.

When one turns to defining the Irish and the Swedish curves, the material is slightly maddening. Before mid-nineteenth century, and even thereafter, neither country did much of a job of tallying out-migration. Thereafter, although the numbers were reported with clarity, this was the clarity of the illusionist. In both cases, the real dimensions were a blurry backdrop to the false precision of the governmental tallies. Surprisingly (given the high reputation of Swedish historical statistics), the Irish material pre-1851 is more trustworthy, because Ireland, as part of the United Kingdom, had some records maintained by direction of the imperial authorities that Sweden did not. Then, in 1851–52, an effort was begun to keep track of permanent migrants who left from Irish ports, but the count was episodic at best: it missed most individuals who went to Great Britain for a time and then emigrated from there. In 1876, a more strenuous effort at tabulating Irish out-migration was attempted, and one finds nicely precise tables, county-by-county, but the results still are undercounts.

With all those qualifications in mind, the following is my approximation of the pattern of gross overseas emigration from Ireland from the mid-1820s until 1910.[33]

Period	Total gross overseas emigration
1825–30	129,182
1831–40	437,753
1841–50	1,298,394
1851–60	1,216,265
1861–70	818,582
1871–80	542,703
1881–90	734,475
1891–1900	460,917
1901–10	485,461

The details of the Swedish pattern before 1851 (when Sweden began to collect out-migration data) are even more fuzzy than are those of the Irish. An indirect way of calculating *emigration to all non-Swedish destinations* (not merely overseas) is to note the base population in 1801, the natural population increase between 1801 and 1850, inclusive, and then define the amount by which this exceeds the actual population in 1850. This number, 26,602, is then taken to be the actual *net* emigration to all extraterritorial destinations. Now, since in this same time period, 1801-50, there were in-migrants to Sweden, and since these in-migrants and returned migrants were supposed to be recorded by local pastors, then one can add their number to the population diminution number to obtain *gross emigration*, 1801–50, namely 76,602. This is the method employed by Gustav Sundbärg[34] and it has a broad-shouldered robustness, but it depends on (a) an accurate record of immigrants being kept—does the number 50,000 not seem just a bit back-of-the-envelope?—and also (b) on there being accurate data on birth and death rates—numbers that at an aggregate level, Sundbärg had to generate himself (aided by his employees) from primary data that had only been half-processed by previous statistical authorities. So, I think the best way to summarize the situation is as follows: an educated guess, by Gustav Sundbärg, who knew intimately the limited primary sources, is that total Swedish net emigration for 1801–50 was about 25,000, and gross emigration about 75,000. But where those emigrants actually went is a mystery. They certainly did not go to North America: the 1850 United States census showed 3,559 Swedes.[35] The only reasonable suggestion is that most Swedish out-migration in the first half of the nineteenth century was to other European countries. (And, indeed, the emphasis upon transoceanic migration in the nineteenth century's historiography obscures the European labour mobility that was much more characteristic of the era than is usually recognized.)

After 1851 the focus is tighter. In that year, official emigration statistics were collected, at first from parish priests, and then (from 1856) were augmented by data from secular authorities based on passport data and, later, on shipping manifests. There were hiccoughs in the record-keeping as late as the mid-1890s.[36]

To start with a set of baseline figures, the following are the numbers of governmentally registered Swedish migrants to non-European countries:[37]

Period	Registered emigration to non-European countries		Contemporary official numbers, gross out-migration to all destinations	
1851–60		14,915		16,900
1861–70		88,831		122,447
1871–80		101,996		150,269
1881–90		319,211		376,401
1891–1900		204,513		246,772
	1900–10	224,043	1901–05	147,677
Total	**1851–1910**	**953,509**	**1851–1905**	**1,060,466**

When, before the First World War, the Swedish government investigated emigration, the statisticians realized that these numbers were too low. Gustav Sundbärg made two attempts at correcting them. One of these yielded a total for *net* emigration to all places (something that is different from either column above) as being a total of 843,281 for the period 1851–1900, and *gross* emigration to all places being 1,008,825.[38] He later updated these estimates to 1910, giving a gross out-migration total of 1,297,108 for gross emigration, 1851–1910, and 1,035,195 for net.[39] Manifestly, these are considerably bigger numbers than are the registered numbers, but they should, in fact, be still larger. Studies of specific locales in the latter third of the nineteenth century reveal either parish-origin undercounting or fumbling when information was collected by central authorities, ranging from between 0.4 per cent of registered migrants to 39.2 per cent.[40] Some of this comes from the systemic undercounting of transoceanic migration (a person who re-emigrated in less than two years was not counted as ever having emigrated).[41] However, the greater source of undercounting involved labour migration to other countries in Europe which often went unrecorded. All that granted, the sharpest study of the undercounting issue concludes that one simply cannot multiply the official figures by some compensatory percentage—for the local variations in undercounting were too large to permit this form of error correction.[42]

So, in their individual eras of emigration flood, more Swedish and more Irish migrants left their homeland than governmental officials realized. This is the way of information in a migration flood: officialdom never quite catches up with reality.

SIX

In the next chapters, four points will be made. The first is that, in relation to the high degree of economic and epidemic risk involved in living in each culture, the propensity to migrate was remarkably low. Secondly, in both countries a specific leading sector nevertheless developed and in each case this was as much a cultural as an economically stimulated entity. And, thirdly, each nation eventually was fuelled by a massive accelerant of out-migration: the Irish Famine, certainly, but also the Swedish Deprivation of 1867–68. One uses "accelerant" in the same way that fire marshals refer to petrol. It is something that puts matters beyond immediate control. So, fourth, once that accelerant had its effect, emigration became an everyday and integral part of the way each nation functioned: something that had to be lived with, year in, year out.

NOTES

1   I am not here denying the reality of the major migrations in Europe—the other "Great Migration"—that occurred in the fourth through seventh centuries of the Common Era.

2   One can easily compile a list of more than a hundred books and articles that incorporate this estimate. They run from Frank Thistlethwaite's paper that began the modern era of European diaspora research to state-of-the-art econometric histories by Jeffrey Williamson. See Frank Thistlethwaite, "Migration from Europe Overseas in the Nineteenth and Twentieth Centuries," in *Rapports V. Histoirée Contemporaine* (Stockholm: Sixteenth International Congress of the Historical Sciences, 1960), p. 35 and Timothy J. Hatton and Jeffrey G. Williamson, *The Age of Mass Migration: Causes and Economic Impact* (New York: Oxford University Press, 1998), p. 3, where the number is 55 million, 1850–1914. See also Kevin O'Rourke and Jeffrey G. Williamson, *Globalization and History. The Evolution of a Nineteenth-Century Atlantic Economy* (Cambridge: MIT Press, 1999), p. 119, where the number is 60 million, 1820–1920, a comparable figure.

3   Whether or not the 55–60 million figure is adequately cited, the widely used estimates are extrapolated from one of the amazing scholarly productions of the early twentieth century, Walter F. Willcox and Imre Ferenczi, *International Migration*, vol. 1, *Statistics* (New York: National Bureau of Economic Research, 1929). The second volume (1931), which was not a seminal work, was a collection of interpretive essays by various scholars and Willcox was sole editor.

4   Jeffrey Williamson's work is a good example of this perspective (see note 2 above for Williamson's most relevant books.). Other leaders in the field are cited in later chapters.

5   Frank Thistlethwaite, "Atlantic Partnership," *Economic History Review*, 2nd ser., vol. 7, no. 1 (1954), p. 1. Thistlethwaite explicitly recognized his indebtedness to Lippman's book (Boston: Little Brown and Co., 1944), especially pp. 73–88. Thus, the following statement by Lippman (p. 87) is noteworthy: "The national differences within the Atlantic region are variations within the same cultural tradition. For the Atlantic Community is the extension of Western or Latin Christendom from the Western Mediterranean into the whole basin of the Atlantic Ocean."

6   Donna R. Gabaccia, "Is Everywhere Nowhere? Nomads, Nations and the Immigrant Paradigm of United States History," *Journal of American History*, vol. 86 (Dec. 1999), p. 1116. A similar point, based on a much smaller database than is Gabaccia's work, was Charlotte Erickson's judgement that the Great Migration was not really "national in scope," but instead was "constituted by particular streams from one village and region to a particular country or city elsewhere." Charlotte Erickson, *Leaving England: Essays on British Emigration in the Nineteenth Century* (Ithaca: Cornell University Press, 1994), p. 5.

7   Rogers Brubaker, "In the Name of the Nation: Reflections on Nationalism and Patriotism," *Citizenship Studies*, vol. 8 (Jun. 2004), p. 119.

8   For an excellent example of freeing migration data from the restrictive (and often changing) boundaries of state data collection, see Dirk Hoerder, *Cultures in Contact. World Migrations in the Second Millennium* (Durham: Duke University Press, 2002).

9   For a study of the cultural interaction of the two nations during the period of regnal union, see H. Arnold Barton, *Sweden and Visions of Norway. Politics and Culture, 1814–1905* (Carbondale: Southern Illinois University Press, 2003).

10 See the following by Kevin O'Rourke and Jeffrey G. Williamson: "Around the European Periphery 1870–1913: Globalization, Schooling, and Growth," *NBER Working Paper No. W5392*, developed under the same title in *European Review of Economic History*, vol. 1 (Sep. 2006), pp. 153–90; and *Globalization and History*, esp. table 2.2, p. 19 and table 14.2, p. 276.

11 Lars Ljungmark (tr. Kermit B. Westerberg), *Swedish Exodus* (1965; Carbondale: Southern Illinois University Press, 1979), pp. 10–13. The Norwegian migration is an extraordinary phenomenon. Historians of the United States are well aware that one of the pioneering texts in US immigration history is Theodore C. Blegen, *Norwegian Migration to America, 1825–1860* (Northfield: Norwegian-American Historical Association, 1931; 2nd rev. ed., 1940). Scottish scholars will note that I have left Scotland out of the discussion of gross emigration rates, despite the fact that they are known to have been high. The reason is that no one really knows how large, since the border with England and Wales was so easily permeable; the overseas migration of Scots mostly took place from English ports and was poorly tallied; and the place-of-birth data in nineteenth-century English censuses were often unreliable. As for the English case, that too is indeterminate because England was a transshipment point for much of continental Europe's out-migration, as well as that from Ireland.

12 David Fitzpatrick, *Irish Emigration, 1801–1921* (Dundalk: Dundalgan Press Ltd, for the Economic and Social History Society of Ireland, 1984), p. 30.

13 Briant Lindsay Lovell, *Scandinavian Exodus. Demography and Social Development of 19th-century Rural Communities* (Boulder: Westview Press, 1987), p. 63.

14 H. Arnold Barton, *The Old Country and the New: Essays on Sweden and America* (Carbondale: Southern Illinois University Press, 2007), p. 75. This commonplace estimate is somewhat high as it includes both emigrants and their US-born children.

15 Fitzpatrick, *Irish Emigration*, p. 5.

16 H. Arnold Barton's charming and assiduous *Northern Arcadia. Foreign Travelers in Scandinavia, 1765–1815* (Carbondale: Southern Illinois University Press, 1998) is sparse to the vanishing point on Hibernian-Swedish travel literature.

17 Steve Murdoch and Alexia Grosjean, "Irish Soldiers in Swedish Service, 1609–13," *The Irish Sword*, vol. 24 (Winter 2004), pp. 161–63.

18 Ragnhild Hatton (ed.), *Captain James Jefferyes's Letters from the Swedish Army, 1707–1709* (Stockholm: P. A. Norstedt and Söner, 1954).

19 Stiftelsen Olosfors Bruksmuseum, web page, "The History of Olofsfors," 14 February 2008.

20 Swedish spelling of the provinces and counties has changed over the past two centuries. I have silently modernized spelling except in direct quotations. The Swedish literary practice of Latinizing several of the provincial names is avoided.

21 The most accurate translation of *härad* into English is Florence Edith Janson's suggestion that "hundred" is appropriate. She is correct that härad is similar to the old English term (and, in fact, it corresponded in medieval times to the barony in Ireland). The trouble is, unless one is an English historian of the medieval or early modern period, the term "hundred" is alien in meaning. Florence Edith Janson, *The Background of Swedish Immigration, 1840–1930* (Philadelphia: University of Pennsylvania, 1931), p. 30n2.

    The reason for staying with "district" as a utility term is that "kommun," when used in the late nineteenth century, sometimes meant merely a parish, but at other times it denoted a larger encompassing municipality.

22 J. H. Andrews, "A Geographer's View of Irish History," in T. W. Moody and F. X. Martin (eds.), *The Course of Irish History* (Cork: Mercier Press, 1967), pp. 17–29. It is worth noting that this volume, edited by Moody and Martin, was the first successful attempt to have Irish historians speak to a general audience in a fashion that did not play to popular prejudices in either the political or religious spheres. The achievement was all the more remarkable because it began as a series of 21 programs as part of the celebration of the fiftieth anniversary of the 1916 Rising.

23 Gunnar Andersson, "Configuration and Water-system," in Gustav Sundbärg, *Sweden. Its People and its Industry. Historical and Statistical Handbook* (Stockholm: KB, 1904), pp. 5–22, revised and reprinted as "Configuration," in Axel Johan Josef Guinchard (ed.), *Sweden. Historical and Statistical Handbook. First Part. Land and People* (Stockholm: KB, 1914), pp. 4–19. Because this handbook is a rather slippery bibliographic item, three comments are in order. First, it should be noted that it went through several editions. The first edition—edited by Gustav Sundbärg, at that time First Actuary of the Royal Swedish Central Bureau of Statistics—was published in French for the Paris Exhibition of 1900, in Swedish in 1901 and in English for the St Louis World's Fair in 1904. The second edition—edited, revised and considerably expanded by Johan Guinchard, director of the Municipal Bureau of Statistics for Stockholm—was published in Swedish in 1913 and came out in a German edition in the spring of 1914, keyed to the Baltic Exhibition of that year, and later in 1914 an English edition, intended for the San Francisco Exhibition of 1915 was published. Second, in English-language historical writing one sometimes sees the second edition being misleadingly cited as "Guinchard," as if it were a monograph, not an edited collection. And, most misleadingly, one misses the fact that it is a revised edition. This would be a picky point except for a third observation: that the hand of Gustav Sundbärg not only lay behind the selecting and editing of the articles in volume one (several of which he wrote himself), but that it became an invisible hand in the second edition. Although Sundbärg died in November 1914, the majority of the material in the second edition comprised items he had commissioned for the first edition.

24 Government of Sweden [author: Gustav Sundbärg], in *Emigrationsutredningen, Bilaga V, Bygdestatistik* (Stockholm: KB, 1910), p. 5 (map) and discussion, pp. 4–9. Map reprinted in Government of Sweden [author: Gustav Sundbärg], *Emigrationsutredningen, Betänkande* (Stockholm: KB, 1913), p. 223, with slightly modified discussion, pp. 224–29. Sundbärg's map is presented as only a general guide. He had limited resources and there are some obvious problems. He worked only on a district (härad), rather than a parish basis. Because of the availability of data, he focused on the last years of the nineteenth century and the early twentieth century. His basic data set dealt only with the rural regions and, as will be mentioned in the text, he did not accept the available data on internal migration. Whether or not one should see marital fertility and emigration as being as closely bound together as Sundbärg implied, is still a subject of debate among Swedish historians, especially those doing microstudies of specific parishes and districts.

   A bibliographic footnote: although his full name was Axel Gustav Sundbärg, all his public work and the bibliography of his writings elide the first name.

25 For example, Jonas Ljungberg, in a modern article "The Impact of the Great Emigration on the Swedish Economy," *Scandinavian Economic History Review*, vol. 45, no. 2 (1997), pp. 159–89, suggested that emigration and economic data were best conceptualized as occurring in six distinct regions: South, Småland, West, East, Central and North.

26 I wish that there were a large bibliography of trustworthy popular books on European (including Swedish and Irish) population and migration patterns, but there is not. There are, however, relevant scholarly items that are readable and provide an introduction to their respective topics without becoming so technical as to lose the general historian. On pre-1800 migration, see Nicholas Canny (ed.), *Europeans on the Move. Studies on European Migration, 1500–1800* (Oxford: Clarendon Press, 1994). Dudley Baines' booklet in the Economic History Society series is succinct and has a useful bibliography: Dudley Baines, *Emigration from Europe, 1815–1930* (London: Macmillan, 1991). The best intentionally popular English-language book on Swedish out-migration is Westerberg's translation of Ljungmark's *Swedish Exodus*. Fitzpatrick's *Irish Emigration* is still fundamental. A very useful discussion of Swedish population patterns is Erland Hofsten, *Svensk beforkningshistoria. Några grunddrag i utvecklingen från 1750* (Stockholm: Raben and Sjögren, 1986). Concerning Ireland, Cormac Ó Gráda's "Poverty, population, and agriculture, 1801–45," is a tiny masterpiece, found in W. E. Vaughan (ed.), *A New History of Ireland*, vol. 5, *Ireland under the Union, I, 1801–70* (Oxford: Clarendon Press, 1989), pp. 108–33. There is no popular book on the Swedish Diaspora as a worldwide phenomenon. The only single-author study of the Irish diaspora is D. H. Akenson, *The Irish Diaspora. A Primer* (Belfast: Institute of Irish Studies, the Queen's University of Belfast, and Toronto: P. D. Meany Co., 1993). There are, however, multiauthored collections of essays. One of these is Patrick O'Sullivan (ed.), *The Irish World Wide* (Leicester: Leicester University Press, 1992–97), 6 vols. Also containing valuable essays is Andy Bielenberg (ed.), *The Irish Diaspora* (London: Longman, 2000).

27 Before the unification of Italy and the integration of the Prussian censuses into those of the rest of the Germanies in the 1860s, total figures are somewhat unreliable, with most authorities believing that, in general, early state censuses underestimated total population. For a conservative set of series for each European country, based on each country's twentieth-century official publications, see B. R. Mitchell, *European Historical Statistics, 1750–1970* (New York: Columbia University Press, 1975), pp. 17–27. The

Swedish material here (and in Mitchell) is based on the work of Gustav Sundbärg in *Emigrationsutredningen, Bilaga IV, Utvandringsstatistik* (Stockholm: KB, 1910), pp. 40, 76–77 and 92–99, and subsequently revised in Guinchard, *Land and People*, p. 111. The Irish figures are from the printed censuses of the United Kingdom census authorities. The 1821 enumeration probably was an underestimate and that of 1831 an overestimate.

28   Sundbärg, *Utvandringsstatistik*, table 15, p. 92.

29   Sundbärg, *Betänkande*, table 219, p. 596. Some qualifications are necessary. The first is that it is impossible to infer where Sundbärg obtained the pre-1851 data for any country (direct national records being lacking even for Sweden), and for several nations (Bulgaria, Italy, Hungary and several others) for periods after midcentury. Sundbärg has detailed calculations in *Utvandringsstatistik*, table 2, pp. 76–77 and notes, pp. 133–34, but the numbers do not quite parse; however, he did admit that he was engaged in educated guesswork, so he can be granted some leeway. Second, and crucially, although he does not label his table as "net," it certainly is. This follows from his basic method, which was to define out-migration as that portion of total natural increase between two enumeration periods which could not be accounted for in the subsequent census. (As I say, where he found the equivalent of censuses for most pre-1851 entries is a mystery.) Then, he somehow divided that amount of total inferred out-migration between transoceanic and "other removal." This latter number was usually relatively small. Third, despite its obvious problems, his material has one major virtue: his method potentially managed to circumvent the apparent cul-de-sac formed by holes in the direct data, something no later work using only direct out-migration registration ever achieved. His implicit-net method takes into account unrecorded emigration and also the sharp rise in return migration in the 1890s and early twentieth century. (See Sundbärg, *Betänkande*, table 220, p. 597.)

      Readers of Swedish emigration history written since, roughly, the early 1960s will note that I am more respectful of Gustav Sundbärg than is usual and that I find the 1907–13 Emigration Commission that he designed and directed to be considerably more useful than is usually accepted as the case. A good example of the distancing from, and occasional direct distrust of Sundbärg, is found in the monographs and the two major summary volumes put out by the monumental Uppsala Migration Research Project of the 1960s and 1970s. And that tone continues to the present day. Now, in fact, there are good reasons for scholars not to like Sundbärg and his commission's reports. (1) The 1907–13 Emigration Commission comprises 20 separate book-length "Appendices" and a meandering, nearly 900-page reflective report by Sundbärg and by a few independent scholars. The whole business is very messy and hard to use: the interconnections between volumes are not well marked and, also, one must watch for contradictions and elisions as between volumes. (2) At several points, since he is engaged in pioneering work, Sundbärg interpolates and interprets data in ways that clearly are not defensible. (3) Sundbärg introduced into this great body of information—and into his own independent writings—a set of Romantic beliefs concerning the basic nature and character of the Swedish folk that are uncomfortably close to the sort of thinking about the northern European character that caused more than a little trouble in European history in the twentieth century.

      Yet, where possible, one prefers to work with this body of 1907–13 data because here, unlike later revisions done by the Swedish central Bureau of Statistics, one can see where the primary data sits and what the problems with them are. In their smoothness, later revisions give the user a sense of confidence that really is not justified. And, some of the work of the Emigration Commission is brilliant in its accounting detail, originality and national level of historical context, qualities that are lost in later rewrites. In particular, most of the work of Nils Wohlin is superb.

30   Willcox and Ferenczi, *International Migration*, vol. 1, *Statistics*, table 1, pp. 230–31.

31   Because I may here seem to be running against my subtheme—namely, the appreciation of work done long ago and subsequently undeservedly ignored—a bit of clarification is necessary. Ferenczi (especially, as the real researcher) and Willcox did indeed do heroic work for their time, putting together for the International Labor Organization and the National Bureau of Economic Research all the known official government-published data from the sending and receiving countries. And yet their work is that rarity, an old study (the late 1920s) that is highly *over*-appreciated. For a discussion of some of the many flaws in the Willcox and Ferenczi material, see J. D. Gould, "European Inter-Continental Emigration, 1815–1914: Patterns and Causes," *Journal of European Economic History*, vol. 8 (Winter 1979), pp. 593–679.

      Now, to give one example of the exceptionally long shelf-life of the Willcox and Ferenczi material, let me point to a front-edge study of the 1990s, Timothy J. Hatton's "A Model of UK Emigration, 1870–1913," *Review of Economics and Statistics*, vol. 77 (Aug. 1995), pp. 407–15. In common with most econometricians, he simply took the Willcox and Ferenczi data as gospel and then worked out an explanatory mathematical model. He, like so many of his econometric colleagues, had no apparent interest in the quality of his input data. In this case, it is quite striking that he was unacquainted with the major corrective sources on UK migration, namely the massive work done in the post-World War II years by N. H. Carrier and J. R. Jeffery for the General Register Office of the United Kingdom; nor any acquaintance with William Forbes Adams' work in the early 1930s that corrected much of Willcox and Ferenczi on Irish migration (which was part of the UK in this period). (Full references to these works are given in note 33, below.) The corrections in the empirical database that these works demanded was major, yet Hatton's model has been uncritically built into several subsequent books on European out-migration.

32 O'Rourke and Williamson, *Globalization and History*, p. 119. As other work by Williamson indicates, they are relying on some revision of Willcox and Ferenczi. See Hatton and Williamson, *The Age of Mass Migration*, pp. 3–12.

33 The basic data for the table are taken from Government of Ireland, *Commission on Emigration and other Population Problems, 1948–1954* [Pr.2541] (Dublin: Stationery Office, 1955), p. 124, as is the data for 1851–1920. However, for the years before 1851, this commission's report left several holes which are filled in by N. H. Carrier and J. R. Jeffery in Government of the United Kingdom, *External Migration: A Study of the Available Statistics, 1815–1950* (London: HMSO, 1953), p. 95. In turn, the Carrier and Jeffery material has been corrected for undercounting for sailings to the USA and to British North America, according to the work of William Forbes Adams, *Ireland and Irish Emigration to the New World from 1815 to the Famine* (New Haven: Yale University Press, 1932), pp. 413–14. For 1836, for which Adams made no estimate, I have interpolated the data myself. For the years 1846–50 (for which Adams made no corrections for undercounting), I have used his formula. See D. H. Akenson, *The Irish in Ontario. A Study in Rural History* (Montreal and Kingston: McGill-Queen's University Press, 1984; 2nd ed., 1999), pp. 14, 15, 29–30. For summary tables, see my *The Irish Diaspora*, table 11, p. 56. These figures, which revise upward the reports of Irish transoceanic migration are, in my estimate, as far as one should go in augmenting official Irish out-migration records. Such a caution is necessary because the "High Counting" syndrome has recently hit Irish migration studies and there are wholly conjectural estimates floating about that raise Irish out-migration numbers (especially pre-Famine numbers) beyond credibility, as they do so without comprehensive or replicable data.

34 Sundbärg, *Utvandringsstatistik*, pp. 46–47.

35 *Statistical History of the United States from Colonial Times to the Present* (New York: Basic Books, 1976), table C.228–95, p. 118.

36 Lars-Göran Tedebrand, "Sources of the History of Swedish Emigration," in Harald Runblom and Hans Norman (eds.), *From Sweden to America. A History of the Migration* (Minneapolis: University of Minnesota Press, 1976), pp. 76–93. In a source-critical examination of church registers (which provide the basis of the Swedish emigration count) for 21 urban areas and seven rural parishes, Rolf Johansson found that, especially before the 1870s, there was a bureaucratic carelessness in the transfer of emigration information to the Central Bureau of Statistics. And, in some jurisdictions, a systemic error was in operation: only information on transoceanic migration was fully collected and that on intra-European migration was often ignored. Rolf Johansson, "Registrering av Flyttare. En Källkritisk Granskning av Svensk Kyrkobokboksmaterial, 1840–1890," *Scandia Tidskrift för Historisk Forskning*, vol. 42 (1976), pp. 167–92.

37 Compiled from Sten Carlsson, "Chronology and Composition of Swedish Emigration to America," table 5.1, pp. 117–18, in Runblom and Norman, *From Sweden to America*. Carlsson's source is *Bildrag till Sveriges Officiella Statistik*, Serie A, 1851–1900 [Population Mobililty, 1901–1930]. There is a very slight variance between these numbers and the series, also based on official Swedish statistical office reports, found in Willcox and Ferenczi, *International Migration*, table 1, p. 756.

38 Sundbärg, *Utvandringsstatistik*, p. 47. The numbers for each decade of net emigration are found in tables 17–21, pp. 94–98. By comparing his own figures to registered migration, Sundbärg concluded that the *unreg*istered proportion of emigration to all destinations was the following proportion of the registered movement: 1850s (119 per cent); 1860s (20 per cent); 1870s (12 per cent); 1880–84 (10 per cent); 1885–93 (1 per cent); 1894–1900 (8 per cent); 1901–10 (7 per cent). See: Tedebrand, "Sources of the History of Swedish Emigration," pp. 84 and 86.

39 Sundbärg, *Betänkande*, p. 591. Incidentally, this reporting of the underregistration of emigrants varies somewhat from that he used in his earlier work: notably, the new suggestion is that the underregistration in the 1860s was 32 per cent, not 20 per cent (p. 593). I suspect this reflects a greater appreciation of the degree to which the Swedish famine of the late 1860s had spurred an emigration surge that was not well recorded by the clergy of the period.

40 Johansson summarizes previous studies; the numbers in the text come from his own "Registrering av Flyttare," table 3, p. 173 and table 8, p. 189.

41 Tedebrand, "Sources of the History of Swedish Emigration," pp. 87–88.

42 Johansson, "Registrering av Flyttare," p. 189. The reader may note that earlier I indicated some admiration for Gustav Sundbärg's attempt at a wide-angle estimation of Europe-wide net emigration in the "true" nineteenth century, and yet that I am skeptical of his recalibrations of the post-1851 Swedish data. These two opinions hinge primarily (but not solely) on a single issue: unrecorded migration from one European nation to another. If one is making indirect calculations for Sweden, as Sundbärg did, the unrecorded out-migration to other European countries vitiates the estimates for Sweden as an individual nation. But if one works with Europe as a whole (as he did in his meta-calculation of pan-European migration), the problem is self-cancelling and thus disappears. A person lost to one national population simply pops up in another, but the total European data stays the same.

Chapter Three

SHOULDN'T THEY BE LEAVING IN DROVES?

ONE

O ne of the shrewdest and most talented observers of Irish economy and society tied together two observations concerning Irish out-migration before the Great Famine. The first of these was "That emigration was already substantial in the years between Waterloo and the Famine is nowadays universally conceded." And, secondly: "Yet the reluctance or inability of the Irish to leave in still greater numbers for distant lands before 1845 remains an important historiographic theme, and the image of peasant multitudes clinging to home, 'like sailors to the mast or hull of a wreck' is given point by the numbers that died during the Famine." Thus, Cormac Ó Gráda,[1] and these two observations—honour them by calling them the *Ó Gráda Paradox*—provide the frame for our discussion of the period before massive stress initiated a migration flow that gained a life of its own and that seemed to be a rejection of the clinging to home that characterized life before the Great Famine.

In order to come to terms with the Ó Gráda Paradox, three pragmatic conventions are here necessary. (1) We will leave aside until later chapters the actual numbers and sorts of emigrants who did indeed leave before the Famine. We accept that they were many, very many, by contemporary European standards (that is the first arm of the Ó Gráda Paradox). But one cannot document everything at once. The numbers can wait, for here we are mostly concerned with the nature of the risk that living in Irish society entailed: this is the second arm of the Ó Gráda Paradox. Were they really clinging to the hull of a foundering vessel? (2) We will treat Sweden in this chapter a bit unfairly: as a case study whose chief function is to show that the high-risk nature of Irish society was not unique, nor was the reluctance to leave home, despite the vagaries of life within rural society. Indeed, in the Swedish case, the reluctance was extreme. And (3) we will clear the board of one word that cannot be used in any comparative discussion involving both Ireland and Sweden: "peasant."

Does this last convention not seem perverse? Certainly the word was employed in the nineteenth century in Ireland—witness the writings of the master observer of the rural Irish, William Carleton. His *Traits and Stories of the Irish Peasantry* (1830)[2] was masterful tale-spinning and is not only hyper-accurate, but has the advantage of having been crafted by a native, not by one of the outside observers who tramped through pre-Famine Ireland as if they were on a photo-safari for rare mammals. Also, the term "peasant proprietorship" was used as a desideratum in the parliamentary debates that surrounded the passage of the Irish Land Acts of 1903 and 1909 which led eventually to Irish farmers obtaining freehold of their land. And, in the mid-twentieth century, to take a single example, one of the best studies of nineteenth and early twentieth-century Irish demotic culture, Kenneth H. Connell's *Irish Peasant Society* (1968),[3] bore its title with neither ambiguity nor implied opprobrium. Everyone knew what he was talking about and historians and historical anthropologists of the same period continue to use the word. Mind you, one would not have used the term "peasant" directly to the face of those it described—the contemporary Irish terms were "labourer" (meaning landless, or nearly landless, hired worker); and "small farmer" (small in acreage, that is)—but the term peasant is widely used today in Irish historical work.

Of course, neither Ireland nor Sweden ever had feudalism in the full and formal European sense so, technically, they never had peasants. That, however, would be too precious a reason for avoiding the term. Words, after all, are often redefined.

The real problem (if one is writing in English) is the Swedish term *bonde* (singular; *bönder*, plural). Its meaning varies considerably over time and place, but it usually is translated as "peasant." This is fine, except that in most cases it refers to an historical set of arrangements that are fundamentally incompatible with the term "peasant" in Irish studies. Unlike the Irish case, the nineteenth-century Swedish peasant usually was a freeholder and frequently employed servants. This is not to confuse them with rural gentry—but the Swedish "peasant" was way above the economic, legal and social status of the Irish "peasant." Since we cannot use the same word for two antithetical situations, "peasant" disappears. In the discussion that follows, a vocabulary will be used that bridges the Irish and the Swedish situations, without, I hope, putting too much torque on either one.

TWO

The pre-Famine Irish economy was growing, but in a peculiar and risky way. There is nothing that even resembles national accounts for Ireland in the first half of the nineteenth century, and even if there were, they would be of limited analytic power, because no set of national accounts includes either goods that are produced and consumed in the home or other income-in-kind. Still, we can be quite confident that Ireland in the pre-Famine years was not in economic decline.

Mind you, certain activities were in trouble, mostly those comprising the industrial sector. Irish economic historians have argued about whether actual deindustrialization occurred in the first half of the nineteenth century, or merely stagnation. (Significant growth, everyone agrees, is not on the table.) There exists no direct breakdown of Gross National Product, so one looks at socially constructed surrogates. For example, if one makes the assumption that "real" industrial activities take place in population centres, then the data are ambiguous. Below are the percentages of the Irish population living in towns and cities of ten thousand or more persons.[4]

Year	Percentage
1750	7.0
1800	7.4
1821	7.6
1841	7.8

Given that the total population was increasing, that leaves room for some mild urban movement, or even, if one were Pollyannaish, slightly increased industrial production. It could more sensibly be taken as an indication of immiserated rural dwellers who were desperately seeking refuge in the cities. In any case, if one considers that in 1841 only one-fifth of the population was found in villages and towns of more than 20 houses,[5] it would be hard to see industry as a strong sector. Granted, one must note that much of the activity that we would classify as industrial—spade manufacture and linen production being the best examples—was conducted primarily on individual farmsteads or crossroads manufactories. Direct data on actual individual employment is ropey; however, for 1821 and 1841 some useful material comes from the censuses. If one defines as widely as possible the number of persons engaged in industrial and commercial activities (as did the census officials, turning farriers into industrial workers and corner hawkers into commercial agents), the number so engaged declined from 1,170,044 in 1821 to 1,115,572 in 1841.[6] (Approximately two-thirds of the Irish labour force relied on agriculture as a mainstay of their livelihood.)[7]

My own view is that some deindustrialization actually occurred between 1815 and 1845, and this primarily because of extreme syncopation in the development of the Belfast region. Belfast and its surroundings was the one locale in Ireland that was an industrial hub. Up to the end of the Napoleonic Wars, it was an example of the first stage of the industrial revolution, the melding of cottage industries with increasing concentration of production, mostly in textiles. And, in the second half of the nineteenth century, Belfast, with the evolution of a robust heavy manufacturing sector, was a healthy part of the mature British industrial revolution. The years 1815–45 were another matter entirely. In that period, the war-generated demand for textiles suddenly dropped and thereafter competition from British textiles was hurtful. The two forms of textiles that were affected were linen, which was only slightly injured, and cotton, which was nearly ruined. As it developed in the second half of the eighteenth century, the Ulster linen industry, centred on the Lagan valley, was not a "putting out" system whereby capitalists provided the materials and the workers operated on a piece-work basis in their own cottages. Instead, the various stages of the process—retting, scutching, hackling, thread spinning, brown linen, white linen and final product—were produced by small independent entrepreneurs and were sold in open (competitive) markets. The independence of the small producers was backstopped by their being part of a social fabric: the fabric of rural communities. The families of most weavers, for example, also farmed. Only in the 1830s did it become technically possible to spin mechanically the very fine linen threads needed in the Irish linen trade and in 1839 there were 35 such mills in Ulster, employing 7,768 workers.[8] This undercut the social system of rural spinning and weaving, but the total employment probably did not diminish greatly, as Ulster still dominated the fine linen market of the British Isles.

The real problem was cotton, where the British factories simply crushed the Irish. In 1811, approximately 50,000 persons in the Belfast region were engaged in cotton spinning in factories and large numbers (certainly over 10,000) in cotton weaving. The census of 1841 show that just over 500 cotton spinners were left and a few more than 3,600 cotton weavers.[9] That was deindustrialization.

Now, if we accept that the overall Irish economy was growing in the half century before the Famine (data on that in a moment), is there any chance that heavy investment in capital projects—either industrial or agricultural—was laying a foundation for future growth, if not for immediate production? The simple answer is no. The one thing Irish historians of the nineteenth century have always agreed upon is that Ireland was under-invested. Perhaps they have agreed too easily, but in the 1980s Joel Mokyr devoted a major quantitative volume to the pre-Famine Irish economy and came to the conclusion that by any reasonable standard (most especially in comparison to Great Britain), capital accumulated very slowly in Ireland. The only two exceptions were forms of social capital investment: the development of one of Europe's best road systems and a system of mass primary education.[10] The road and waterway systems were cheap and extensive and, according to Cormac Ó Gráda, on the eve of the Famine "could have carried several times more passengers and goods without pressure or rise in cost."[11] The school system, called the "Irish national system of education," was built upon the enthusiasm of the Irish people of all classes for schooling, a cultural characteristic too often unremarked. The 1831 decision of the United Kingdom government to create a system of mass education predated similar systems of popular education in the rest of the British Isles by almost four decades.[12] It will be obvious that the communications network and the educational system, when combined with a rapidly reformed banking and monetary system after 1801,[13] were exactly the kind of things that made the migration of Irish persons into modernizing countries progressively less difficult. Perhaps Mokyr may have somewhat underestimated the capital investment occurring in Ireland, chiefly because the small-unit financial investment that occurs farm by farm, where smallholders put in their own drainage schemes or improved livestock productivity through breeding programmes, defies measurement.[14] Nevertheless, it is beyond possibility that large capital flows came from outside of Ireland to boost the economy through immediate capital projects.

So, one is left with the obvious: Ireland's economy was growing in the half century before the Famine because agricultural production was increasing sharply. The best estimate is that agricultural output rose 80 per cent between 1801 and 1845.[15] Irish exports of agricultural goods quadrupled in the same period[16] and about one-quarter of total output was exported in 1845.[17] Indeed, if one aggregates export and domestic markets, it is clear that the Irish farmer in 1845 had something approaching two-thirds of output available for sale in Irish or in international cash markets.[18] Even if this portion were (to be conservative) only one-half of total production, it was a large surplus of production over subsistence needs. Seemingly, the Irish economy, agricultural to its core, exporting steadily to serve the needs of the British industrial revolution, was healthy. In the present-day futures market, a corporate stock with this profile would be a definite buy.

Except for two hitches. One of these was the possibility that without significant new investment in agriculture, the system was destined to hit the slough of diminishing returns. This may already have been happening in the early 1840s. Second, only about 25–30 per cent of Irish farmers were involved in the surplus-to-subsistence markets.[19] So, our futures analyst would have hesitated to buy, because without considerable capital investment, future production well might drop in relation to annual input costs and, also, the diminishing returns would involve increasing numbers of the cash farmers falling back into subsistence farming. Actually, no, don't buy.

The causal factor holding this contradictory situation together—the overall growth of the Irish economy in the 40 years before the Famine, and the unease any attentive contemporary observer would have had about it—was of course population growth. The reader will notice that, unlike the usual discussion of Ireland before the Famine, I have not started with the population explosion. That is because I wish to break the accepted rhetorical mode. That accepted mode communicates the belief (as often implied or silently assumed as directly stated) that Irish population growth was an exogenous force and that once this topic is described, everything else follows, like a line of dominoes falling over once the first one is tipped. Actually, the Irish population explosion was part of a massive, slowly spiralling feedback system, and economics and social arrangements and population all interacted with each other constantly. This interaction need not have produced a catastrophe and the fact that disaster on an unpredictable scale ultimately occurred was not rationally foreknowable.

The population numbers, however, are easy enough to apprehend, although getting them almost right was a major triumph of mid-twentieth-century scholarship. In an extraordinary union of historical imagination and of heavy individual work, Kenneth Connell in *The Population of Ireland* (1950) provided realistic population estimates back to the early eighteenth century and presented an explanation of the pattern.[20] Both the pattern and the explanation have been cleaned and polished by recent historians, but they remain standard and seem to have a long future shelf-life. Before 1821 the government of the United Kingdom had no realistic idea of how many individuals lived in Ireland. (The first English census was 1801.) An effort to count the Irish populace in 1813–15 failed as a result of bad administration. Various individuals in the eighteenth and early nineteenth centuries had made concerted efforts at ascertaining the population at a specific date, but these provided no time series and no consistency of method as between estimates.[21] Connell's big leap of method was to see that one could use the hearth-tax returns to calculate pre-census population. As its base, this meant that if one could know the number of families in Ireland and also the average family size, the overall population could be calculated. Behind this simple formulation lay an immense amount of primary research and technical virtuosity by Kenneth Connell. Given below are the estimates of Connell and also the numbers of the official census and the revisions suggested by David

Table 3.1. Population of Ireland (in millions).

Date	Connell census estimate	Dickson revision	Clarkson revision	Lee revision
1687	2.2	2.0	1.7	
1712	2.8	2.0–2.3		
1725	3.0	2.2–2.6	2.2	
1753	3.2	2.2–2.6	2.3	
1791	4.8	4.4	4.2–4.6	
1821	6.8			7.2
1831	7.8			7.9
1841	8.2			8.4

Dickson, *et al.*,[22] L. A. Clarkson,[23] and Joseph J. Lee,[24] as summarized by Liam Kennedy and Leslie A. Clarkson.[25]

The upward march of these absolute numbers means that Ireland between 1751 and 1841 was probably experiencing an annual growth rate (on average) of 1.4 per cent. This is not a rapid rate by the standards of present day low-income countries where rates of over 2.0 per cent are common.[26] Considered over the contemporary range of time, however, the annual average of 1.4 per cent was probably the highest rate of population increase in Europe.[27] Crucially, the rate of population increase seems to have peaked sometime in the late eighteenth or early nineteenth century, and moved downward so that between 1821 and 1841 it averaged annually under 1.0 per cent[28] and probably was dropping even more quickly in the early 1840s. Nevertheless, although the statistical rate of increase may have been dropping, the number of real-world individuals still was rising.

The outline of this long segment of Irish population history, from the late seventeenth century through the 1841 census, can be taken as a solid and enduring monument to Kenneth H. Connell. His definition of the phenomenon would still stand, even if his explanation for it were crazy. But it is not, and with certain adjustments, it still works well.

To his great credit, Connell understood the logical simplicity of demographic machinery and did not mystify his readers. The fundamentals of the demographic machine are these: (1) Only change can explain change. When Population A becomes Population B, it can only be because something that affects Population A has changed and thereby turns it into a new population. Births exceeding deaths, for example. (2) What we want intellectually, however, is not the raw numbers of births and deaths, but *rates*. These make it possible to build a demographic machine that can be compared to those of other countries and also can be intertwined with social history to develop a comprehensive social description of, for example, family systems, over long time periods. (3) Connell discovered that sometime during the early eighteenth century, the rate of population increase in Ireland rose significantly. (4) Assuming the absence of external forces—such as large scale in-migration—there were only three logical alternatives: either the birth rate was rising, the death rate was dropping, or both. (5) Although at the time of his writing, the dominant theory in England was that eighteenth-century population growth occurred because of dropping death rates, Connell rejected this for Ireland. Thus, the explanation for accelerated population increase had to be in something that increased the birth rate. (6) More specifically, Connell stated that "the central argument of this work has been that an unusually rapid growth of population must be attributed very largely to the increase of fertility ..."[29] (7) Fertility, he recognized, was as much a result of cultural conventions as of biology and thus children are produced according to certain social rules. Connell, despite (or perhaps because of) his being a serious Marxian, had an appreciation for the power of the Catholic church. (He did not comment much on other denominations.) The church, even in the days of the penal laws, had sufficient social control that, with the concurrence of the laity, family formation outside of marriage was not widespread. (8) Hence, any increase in the fertility rate in the Irish culture had to do with increasing fertility *within* marriage. To complete the sentence quoted above, Connell argued that "rapid growth of population must be attributed very largely to the increase of fertility that followed earlier marriage."[30] In other words, something made marriage easier. (Connell believed this occurred around 1750 or somewhat earlier, but that degree of precision is not necessary for his logical machinery to work.) Fertility rates jumped. Notice here that (a) it is taken as axiomatic that the Irish populace was not practising birth spacing and this has never realistically been challenged; (b) that for Connell's demographic machine to work, it is not required that women marry at some shockingly early age, but merely that they marry *earlier* than previously and (c) that although Connell does not make much of it, reducing the difficulty of getting married— that is, increasing the marital rate—inevitably reduced the number of unmarried women who went through life in voluntary childlessness. (9) *Therefore*, change (increase) in marital fertility yielded change (increase) in successive Irish populations.

This is an elegant, successful and economical effort in intellectual machine construction. With a few improvements on the minor components,[31] it has stood for well over a half century and there is no challenger in sight. This, despite the fact that, although Connell's theory explains the acknowledged empirical phenomenon of the Irish population explosion, quantitative verification of its central cog—a drop in the marriage age—is impossible. Rather, the model is so durable because it fits so many social and economic aspects of pre-Famine Irish history.

The complex religio-social arrangement that is marriage in a Christian (largely Catholic) country did not change for merely frivolous reasons. Something big had to have happened. Given that one of the primary social rules in rural Ireland was that a woman and a man could marry, and start to procreate, only when they had control of enough land to support a family, something had to have happened to make it easier to "obtain a living." The acceptance of the potato as an ancillary crop in the early eighteenth century was grudging: it was a winter food for the poor and an animal food in substantial farming families. However, it had the advantage of effectively adding more land to Ireland's agricultural base: it tolerates damp and acid soils and thus is suitable for waste reclamation and, on normal ground, it produces four to eight times the caloric total of grain crops. Later, the potato became more and more a central fact of the daily nutrition of most small farmers. P. M. Austin Bourke's studies show this occurring around 1750, which melds nicely with Connell's demographic machinery.[32] The argument is quite broad: among the labouring and small farmer classes, it became easier to find a living, because smaller and/or less salubrious pieces of ground were required to support a family and to produce children.

Emphatically, we should not caricature the situation. What emerged was a complex, socially efficient interweaving of economic practices, religious beliefs and botanical possibility. Even on the eve of the Famine, Ireland was not a subsistence economy in which the potato was the sole food or even the main nutrition of everybody. As noted earlier, by the early 1840s, two-thirds of the nation's agricultural produce was surplus over subsistence. The potato figured in almost every farmer's and labourer's life, but in a range of ways: from virtually sole food, to a portion of a broader diet, to being reserved for animals.

Recall here that the national rate of population increase was slowing down in the period 1821–41. This correlates interestingly with Bourke's independent documentation that from roughly 1810 onwards, biological degeneration was affecting the potato crop. This took the form of the more nutritious and storable forms of potato losing their vigour—"the sinister trend towards monoculture"—and being replaced by big, watery, flavourless species—especially the "lumper"—which previously had been fed only to cattle.[33] The diminishing returns of potato cultivation, then, coincided with a moderation of Ireland's rate of population increase. Such a trend raises the possibility that, given two or three decades of breathing room, Ireland would have continued to adjust, and would have gradually escaped its population bubble without tragedy by limiting population growth and moving away from the degenerating potato monoculture.

THREE

Accepting that in, say, 1841, patterns in Ireland showed both a promise of gradual improvement in the general quality of life and also hints that things could become less acceptable, how does one approach the behaviour of the people on the ground? There are several useful approaches, but here I think there is profit in introducing a concept that is anachronistic in its technical form, but was actually something that most rural people of the time understood. The modern form of the concept is the assessment of *risk* or of its converse, *security*. It has a great deal to do with Irish (and Swedish) emigration.

Risk assessment (the conventional term for present-day security assessment) is a complex technical activity that affects most commercial and governmental activities, from running the chemical industry to insurance underwriting to deciding how many lifeguards are required at a public swimming bath. The basic technical terms and processes are easily accessible in the publications and electronic information on risk assessment put out by the various national regulatory bodies, such as the British Standards Association. Although probability statisticians sometimes talk in terms of "risk" being the probability that any defined event will happen—such as the "risk" of winning the lottery—in risk management usage, the basic term refers to an unpropitious event, just as it does in everyday speech.

Risk assessment conventionally stacks two independent thoughts on top of each other. The first is an *if-then concept* that defines how much pain there would be if something nasty happened. This is the *hazard* and it is a statement that if Hazard X occurs, then Result Y will follow. Such as: "if a small nuclear device is detonated in the centre of Liverpool, 10,000 people will die" The second thought is the *probability statement* of how likely Hazard X is to occur. Such as: "the chances of a small nuclear device being detonated in the centre of Liverpool in any given year is one in two million." With these two concepts stacked on top of each other, the risk to any given citizen of being vaporized in Liverpool within the next year is formulated.

Modern actuarial risk assessments are very complex and can be very precise—if not always correct. But, in fact, they are the same basic calculations that were made by farmers throughout the nineteenth century and thereafter (and I suspect since the human practice of agriculture began): for example, what happens if the weather turns really foul, and how likely is that to happen?, and so on. Now, I think we can heuristically replicate at a general level (local conditions varied, granted) a risk assessment that the Irish farmer and the Swedish farmer would have accepted as representing the state of their respective agrarian economies.

The reason for doing this is that risk assessment will help to lead to an understanding of both aspects of the Ó Gráda Paradox—the recognition that a lot of people left pre-Famine Ireland for prudent economic reasons, and the implication that nevertheless too few people emigrated before the period of agricultural crisis. In themselves, restating these two points would not be any great intellectual advance, since we all know about the Irish Famine and the Swedish Deprivation. What I hope to suggest in this chapter and in subsequent chapters is that farmers of the time knew what they were doing, and for the most part they chose to embrace certain cultural values rather than those of neoclassical economic rationality. I hope that in the way the material is presented allows an escape from the keener Malthusians who have a very simple formulation that Irish starvation was an inevitability.[34]

Here then is the Hazard: a one-year crop failure. That was something well known in both Irish and Swedish societies, as I will show later. At present, we do not make any suggestion as to the probability of such a hazard becoming a reality in any given year.

Because it makes graphic presentation easier, we can approach the matter of rural risk by using its antonym—security. Let us ask a straightforward question: what did it take to make an Irish farmer secure? The query would have been easily understood by any smallholder or land agent or cattle drover in pre-Famine Ireland. The answer, I think, would be "enough land and a decent lease."

Or, to put it in analytic terms: rural security was a function of two factors, the amount of land a person operated and the conditions under which it was held. Consider first the conditions of land-holding. They were amazingly complex. The key fact is that, as articulated by Samuel Clark: "It is no exaggeration to say that most landlords in pre-Famine Ireland were not landowners; they were tenants with large land-holdings."[35] The Irish land system resembled a pyramid constructed by a crew of drunks who had never encountered either a plumb line or a level. It was not infrequent to have four or five levels of landlord between the freeholder and the person who farmed the land. Here is my own summary of the sometimes overlapping levels of the banjaxed pyramid, starting at the top with the most secure forms of land-holding and running down to the least secure:

- freeholders. There were approximately ten thousand of these in pre-Famine Ireland. Most were large landowners, and often they were absentees, but some freeholders had estates of less than 100 acres.
- copyholders and holders of other archaic forms of land rights. These were technically not as secure as freeholds, but they often ran for hundreds of years—the 999-year period being a common form—and effectively the holders were as secure as freeholders, although they sometimes had to pay symbolic annual rentals.
- long renewable leaseholds. These ran for decades and sometimes for more than a century. Usually there was a minimal annual rental. The heavy cost was upon renewal when a "fine," usually equivalent to a year's full market rental value, was required, subject to negotiation.
- leases for "lives," usually three lives. These generally were renewable. The particular three lifetimes were specified in the lease and there was an annual rental and usually a fine of a year's full market rental value (subject to negotiation) to insert a new name into the lease when one of the three lives expired.[36]
- long leaseholds that were not renewable.
- leases for 31 years.
- leases for 21 years. These being more common than the 31 year lease.
- "tenant-right," or "Ulster Custom" holding. As the name implies, this was mostly found in Ulster, but it was not universal there. Its bare bones were that a tenant had

a right to occupancy as long as he paid his annual rent. And when the tenant left, he had the right to compensation from his successor for the right of occupancy.[37]

- annual leases stated in writing.
- annual leases based on oral agreements. In practice, these were tenancies-at-will that ran for a single year.
- conacre. The least desirable of all arrangements from the tenant's point of view, these were tenancies-at-will which ran for less than a year.

Cloaked in this simplified schema of land-holding practices were two non-juridical realities. (1) The higher up on the ladder, the more likely it was that the land-holder, if resident on the land (a big "if") would improve it by such things as drainage, manuring, marling and the addition of serviceable farm buildings. That held, roughly, for the tenant-right holders on the scale and upward. (2) It will surprise no one who is acquainted with European rural history, that as one dropped further down the ladder, the size of the holdings became smaller and smaller and rents per acre usually rose. It did not pay to be poor.

Now, the second base variable determining agricultural security was the size of the holding. Here we have to be less sophisticated than were contemporaries and we must be satisfied with numerical descriptions of farm size. Actually, land quality is highly uneven, so a five-acre holding in Leinster probably was considerably more productive than one in Connacht. Indeed, in post-Famine Ireland it was common to describe a holding as having "the grass of four cows," or six cows, or whatever. This was a way of equilibrating different qualities of land, and there is no reason that the same shrewd eye was not operative before the Famine. Tenants were not idiots; indeed, no matter how small the holding, they were experts on the carrying capacity of each plot. So, having lost the knowledge our forebears possessed, we are forced to operate with numbers that assume an acre is the same as an acre any place else in Ireland. That admitted, the following is a ladder that contemporaries would have accepted in most parts of Ireland as being descriptively accurate of farm size. It reads from top downwards:[38]

Large (or "strong") farmers	50 acres and above	Hired help.
Medium farmers	20–50 acres	Modestly comfortable to substantial. Some hired help.
Small farmers	10–20 acres	Just getting by. Sometimes work off-farm.
	5–10 acres	Poor. Usually labour off-farm or do domestic crafts.
	1–5 acres	Poverty. Almost always required to labour off-farm.
	landless–1 acre	Land usually held in conacre. Extreme poverty.

So, we have two ladders—call each an axis—which, when taken together, yield an heuristic that we can use to help to describe risk security in pre-Famine Irish agricultural society.

The two variables permit the definition of two "Security Isobars." Isobar A is my own estimate of the minimum conditions in land and in terms-of-tenure that would allow a farm family to survive as a continuing economic unit for a single year of high distress: the Hazard of a failure of at least one crop, a major livestock epidemic, a long run of extremely bad weather. This Security Isobar A posits that there is some trade-off

between the security of tenure (good leases, among other things, permitted improvements and their benefits) and the amount of land held. Isobar B is my estimate of the
point at which a year of high distress would probably lead not only to the failure of the
economic enterprise, and to one or more deaths due to the family's falling well below the
subsistence line. In this region of risk there is little or no trade-off between farm size and
conditions of tenure: a family on five acres with no outside income would be immiserated
no matter how long a lease they might have had. Although these estimates are solely my
own, independent evidence suggests that I am not wandering in the wilderness.[39]

This is a *condominium of risk*. One must make it clear that this visual figure in itself
has no quantitative dimensions. Think of it as a cross-section of a slightly wonky three-
storey building. What we now want to know is, "given this structure, what were the
numbers of persons on each of the levels?" P. M. Austin Bourke provided a tabulation of
the various quantitative levels of land-holding in Ireland as of 1845. (Unhappily, there is
no similar calculation of the proportions of the farm enterprise that were held under the

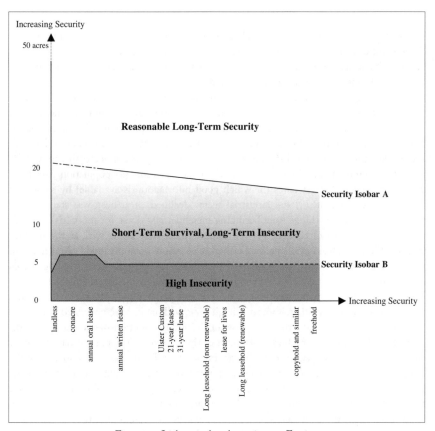

Figure 3.1. Irish agricultural security, pre-Famine.

Table 3.2. Irish agricultural enterprises, c. 1845, in statute acres.

Category	Number	Percentage of total	Cumulative percentage (poorest to richest)
Landless or less than one acre in conacre	650,921	41.0	41.0
Less than one acre (not conacre)	135,314	8.5	49.5
1–5 acres	181,950	11.5	61.0
5–10 acres	187,909	11.9	72.9
10–20 acres	187,582	11.8	84.7
20–50 acres	141,819	8.9	93.6
over 50 acres	70,441	4.5	98.1
undefined	30,433	1.9	100.0
Total	**1,586,369**	**100.0**	**100.0**

various forms of tenure; this was a real variable, certainly, but not nearly as important as the amount of land held.) These can be restated, as shown in table 3.2. As is the case with all pre-Famine data, the numbers look somewhat more precise than they really are, but they are fully adequate for the purpose at hand.[40]

Assuming that the average enterprise of five acres and under supported a single family, roughly 60 per cent of the pre-Famine population lived in poverty and were at significant risk from even one year of distress. (For those tiny farms that were dual or multiple-family, the risk of course was even greater; for farmers with no family, less.) To review the situation in the first four-and-a-half decades of the nineteenth century: (1) agricultural production, 1801–45, rose by about 80 per cent; (2) population rose from 1791 to 1841 (the closest dates for which good information is available) by somewhat more than 90 per cent; (3) the industrial sector declined, or at best, was stagnant; (4) there is no doubt that things were becoming incrementally worse for most Irish agricultural workers and small farmers; (5) yet, some farmers were doing well, as the increase in agricultural surpluses available in the market economy demonstrated.[41] And many of those doing well seem to have readjusted their land-holding practices (avoiding subdivision), married later and facilitated emigration among family members. This had reduced the annual increase in population to 0.5–0.6 per cent per annum in the early 1840s[42] and was a long-term strategy that, if given enough time, well might have prevented famine.

Obviously, major distribution-of-wealth and distribution-of-income problems existed, as they do in many high-risk societies right down to the present day. The poor were growing poorer, yet overall average incomes probably rose.[43] To focus on the high-risk end of the distribution, some empirical observations make the position of the poor clear. For example, the 1841 census enumerated 1,471,739 families nationally. Of these, 516,931 (35.1 per cent) were living in one-room rural mud cabins or one-room town tenements. And a further 566,659 (38.5 per cent) were housed in two-to-four room mud cabins and their town equivalent.[44]

As for diet, every class consumed potatoes to some degree—the per capita national average was over six pounds per day—but it was at the bottom of the socio-economic scale that they became virtually the only food. Bourke calculated that just prior to the Famine, 39 per cent of the Irish population ate 12 to 14 pounds of potatoes daily, and little else. An additional 16 per cent used it for their main food, supplemented by milk and sometimes fish. This was nutritionally adequate, being less than modern-defined dietary requirements only in vitamins A and D. Considered as a national nutrition strategy this was dicey, but not quite as risky as it first appears: half the potatoes grown were used for animal feed, mostly pigs and chickens and, further, potatoes were usually grown as part of the rotation of crops.[45] In theory, the failure of half a year's crop could be covered by diversion from animals.

In terms of risk assessment, a lot was going on at once: prospects for improved life for the top 15 per cent or so were visible; survival risks for the bottom 60 per cent in the case of a single-year period of distress were clear; and the remainder in-between could see the future as holding either more and more risk or, perhaps, their becoming medium-farmers, with milk on the table daily and a meat meal at least once a week.

FOUR

I n turning to Sweden, and to comparisons of that country before 1867 to Ireland before 1846, one is put in mind of Samuel Taylor Coleridge's beautifully bent story that he heard from one Dan Hennesay, who reported:

> Passing over Black Friars' whom should I see (coming from t'other end of the Bridge) but my old Chum, Pat Mahoney—and at the same moment he saw me—We ran towards each, & when we met, just in the middle of the Bridge—by Jasus!—it was neither of us.[46]

Cross-national comparisons between Ireland and Sweden can be like that: although not necessarily.

As was the case with pre-Famine Ireland, nothing like national accounts exists for pre-Deprivation Sweden. The basic problem is that the agricultural statistics for the country were inadequate until 1865, when the reporting responsibilities were taken from the governments of the län (who had been compiling data only every five years) and mandated as an annual duty of the national agricultural associations.[47] Still, among the three or four things that Swedish economic historians agree on, are the views that the national income grew considerably in the first two-thirds of the nineteenth century and that the average family income rose.[48]

And, like Ireland, Sweden was a nation-beyond-towns:[49]

Year	Rural percentage of total population
1800	90.2
1820	90.2
1840	90.3
1860	88.7

Until roughly mid-nineteenth century, then, Sweden was 90 per cent rural. Even then, as the rural proportion of the entire populace dropped slightly, it still was rising in absolute numbers.[50] In a world in which most people lived in small communities, surrounded by large swatches of countryside, it is not surprising that a significant segment of the agricultural population carried on its activities in what were officially defined as towns and cities: in 1860, an estimated 5.3 per cent of town populations was composed of agrarian persons and their dependents.[51]

Conversely, in the same year, 16.1 per cent of the populace in rural areas was not agrarian.[52] This was largely because most Swedish industry of the first two-thirds of the nineteenth century was conducted in rural locales. (Of course there were some activities that were neither agrarian nor industrial which were carried on in rural areas, so non-agrarian is not quite a synonym for industrial.) Much of the rural industrial work was small-scale handicrafts, the most important being textiles. Some of the textile products were for home or local trade by barter, but some entered the commercial market. More clearly identifiable as commercial products from "cottage industries" were clocks, grindstones, products of human and animal hair, carved or machined wood products, and finished metal products such as scythes. The final product in these cases often was the result of specialization, one craftsperson engaging in a single process and then passing the work on to someone down the road; to some observers, these arrangements resemble a piece-work factory system with the work benches far apart. There exists an argument among economic historians about the usefulness of the concept of "proto-industry"—the big question is whether or not the concept is teleological, meaning that proto-industry existed historically only if it led to full-blown industrialization.[53] Certainly some proto-industries evolved into industries in the modern sense, although the transformation was not a linear one based upon the logic of technology so much as a multilevel response to market forces. For example, the Swedish mining and iron industry went through a series of overlapping structural shifts from household economies to something that resembled in its core elements a modern production process, and some of this was accomplished by the mid-1860s.[54]

The most curious aspect of Swedish industrial development in the first 40 years of the nineteenth century was the late development of the timber industry. "To a great extent the explanation consists precisely in the importance of the forests to the iron industry," was Eli Heckscher's formulation.[55] He was referring to the fact that iron required charcoal, and several Crown and governmental restrictions captured most commercial timber for the iron market. After the Napoleonic Wars, however, the Crown hived off many of its timber holdings to private owners, but some cutting restrictions still applied and also limitations on the creation of sawmills. Thus, the newly private property was not worth much until the late 1840s when the United Kingdom and its empire turned to free trade. The Swedish cutting restrictions having been removed in 1842, the export trade became profitable and, when the final restrictions on erecting sawmills were eliminated in 1863, the trade grew swiftly.[56]

The crucial point about Sweden before the Deprivation is that, unlike Ireland before the Famine, Sweden was not experiencing deindustrialization: indeed, the industrial sector (broadly defined) was keeping pace with the growth of the industrial population and probably helping slightly to buoy general living standards. However, neither was

Sweden quickly becoming an industrial nation. The 1860s may have been a platform for the swift later development of industry, but the country was still massively agricultural and not changing that orientation very quickly, as the following figures confirm:[57]

Year	Percentage of population dependent upon industry, mining and commerce
1800	20.92
1810	17.58
1820	17.40
1830	17.90
1840	19.10
1850	22.06
1860	n/a

If anything, these figures exaggerate the position of industry, since they include all commercial activities, many of which are hardly industrial (such as local peddlers in needles, thimbles, thread) and also the domestic servants of persons in the industrial sphere.

Although anything approaching precise figures is unavailable, both in industry and agriculture, capital investment was greater than in Ireland. The industrial investment came quite late, with foreign capital figuring strongly only in the mid-1860s. It is clear that a significant domestic investment occurred in agriculture, most of it on a farm-by-farm level—land reclamation projects, new crops and new field systems—of which we will speak in a moment. As in Ireland, the biggest form of social investment was in education: a national school system was mandated in 1842, and ultimately, if unintentionally, facilitated emigration. The Swedish educational system was grafted onto a pre-existing responsibility of the Swedish state clergy to assure a basic level of catechetical knowledge and, by 1850, Sweden had the highest literacy rate in Europe.[58] In sharp contrast to pre-Famine Ireland, however, Sweden did not invest heavily in transport facilities. For example, the first railroads became operational only in 1856 and, in general, it was much harder to get around Sweden than to travel about Ireland. To put it another way, it was easier to get out of Ireland than out of Sweden.

The pivotal set of social data, in Sweden no less than in Ireland, was the rate of population growth. In absolute terms, Swedish population was as follows:[59]

Year	Population in thousands
1800	2,347
1810	2,377
1820	2,585
1830	2,888
1840	3,139
1850	3,482
1860	3,860

The Swedish average annual growth rate in population between 1800 and 1851 was 0.8 per cent.[60] This compares with an Irish average rate from 1751 to 1841 of 1.4 per cent (very high for European nations), which had, however, dropped below 1.0 per cent after 1821. The standard explanation for Swedish population growth is just the opposite of that for Ireland: Sweden's growth is usually ascribed entirely to a reduction in the death rate, rather than anything to do with fertility. At a descriptive level, the Swedish explanation is certainly correct: death rates did significantly exceed fertility rates in rural areas, which is to say, amongst the bulk of the population.[61]

In order to adjudge what the developments in the structure of the family, the economy and, more specifically, in agriculture meant to the majority of the population, we need a base picture that transforms the abstract data into more human terms. The overwhelming majority of the populace was engaged in agriculture and for any given family, or any individual who acted as a corporation-sole, the key question was: how much in the way of agricultural resources did each control and under what terms? That matter can be approached by employing a somewhat anachronistic concept, namely that each freehold farm, each tenanted holding and each individually contracted labourer was a separate economic enterprise and faced risk and reward as such. This suggestion would not have been generally embraced by the populace as an abstract concept in, say, 1800, but in fact it describes their world: at the bottom end, the alternatives were to find a master or a small holding or starve; in the middle, it was to pay the rent and the loans or be turfed onto the road; and at the top it was to make money or have the moneylenders camped in the front hall. The head of every enterprise encountered risk and sought security.[62]

Unlike Ireland (where we know fairly precisely the land controlled by each operator, but not the terms of tenancy), for Sweden we can be specific about the terms of economic control apportioned to each operator, but not of the actual resources that person had under hand. Still, I think it will be clear that we can develop a form of pre-Deprivation risk assessment that is comparable to the one we drew for pre-Famine Ireland.

The Swedish system of land tenure and of agricultural service was just as messy as was the Irish, but in a different way. Unlike Ireland (and rather closer to early eighteenth-century England),[63] the Swedish system in the late eighteenth and early nineteenth centuries consisted of two patterns: (1) those of large estates that ran as self-enclosed units (in England these were "manors," but that is a term we will not use as it carries a feudal resonance that is misleading in Sweden), and (2) those of the freehold villages, most of which in the late eighteenth century still were nucleated settlements. In fact, however distinct these two patterns were in statute law, they described cognate pyramids of resource control. Thus, the two can be melded into a single assessment of the risk of deprivation to which each socio-economic segment of the Swedish agricultural population was exposed.

That this is possible is in large degree because of the extraordinary work of Nils Wohlin. As part of the massive early twentieth-century governmental study of Swedish emigration, he produced three monographs and one volume of statistics that categorize and discuss the power position (that is, essentially a security/risk assessment) of persons in the Swedish agricultural sector.[64] Wohlin was the equivalent of an ambitious, hard-charging MIT assistant professor. He received his doctorate in 1912 at age 31, very young for the Swedish system. He had a deep, somewhat romantic interest in Swedish agrarian society and became the nation's leading expert on the historical documentation of the development of rural society. He worked as the secretary of the Emigration Commission from 1907–10, before having a bust-up with Gustav Sundbärg. In 1919 he became a Farmer's Union member of parliament, minister of commerce in 1923 and finance minister in 1928. That was the apogee of his political career, although he remained in parliament until 1942.

In his scholarly work, notably the historical studies done for the Emigration Commission, Nils Wohlin held the rare view that the Swedish church-produced records were useless as far as national-scale work on pre-nineteenth-century rural social structure was concerned.[65] And he had only marginally more faith in the nineteenth-century parish-level material. When doing his nineteenth-century work, he concentrated on two goals. The first of these was to define the meaning within Swedish society of the various categories that the central census authorities had employed. These changed during the century, so his challenge was to work out modes of equilibrating definitions as between time periods and also to assay how these protean definitions fit into the socio-economic power structure. Wohlin's second task was to fill in the numerical blanks in these now-comparable historical census categories. What he achieved is not perfect, but it is quite amazing.

What is especially valuable for our purposes is that Wohlin defined a ladder of agrarian power that is useful as a component for establishing a condominium-of-risk comparable to the one we developed for Ireland. This ranks the various types of agricultural enterprises. The schema starts at the top of the ladder and is as follows:

- Large estates owned in freehold, almost entirely by nobility or gentry. Crown estates are left out of direct calibration entirely.[66] This is the weakest part of Wohlin's work, but one suspects that it was hardly of his own choosing that this was the case. The entire Emigration Commission of 1907–13 was careful not to step on the toes of the rich and powerful, so Wohlin, in his socio-economic work for the commission, left the number of nobility and gentry estates undefined except for the year 1800, and even then they were singled out only in a side note. (This, despite these groups being included as part of a residual lump of unspecified farm operators in all of his totals.) These individuals (*godsägare*, landed property owner[s]), controlled what were superficially similar to medieval England's "manors." In fact, their origin in Sweden was mostly from the era of Sweden's becoming a great power on the European stage, when the Crown transferred big pieces of land to the nobility in exchange for tax revenues and military support. These large nobility and gentry estates were not the majority of Swedish land at the beginning of the nineteenth century (smaller freeholds predominated), but they were disproportionately significant in socio-political terms because they were strongest in two crucial areas: within 200 kilometres of Stockholm, the centre of political power, and in the rich arable land of the south, especially the province of Skåne.[67] These large estate "enterprises" (so they were, although their owners would have hated the vulgarity of the term) were typically self-enclosed. They usually included a big house (in the Irish sense) and a farm run directly by a farm manager and his staff. Also included in the normal case was a set of activities separate from the home farm: a number of subtenancies, with leases of varying terms and, at the bottom of the ladder, smallholders who mostly worked away from their own holding, and servants. Sometimes the entire estate was turned over to a single lessee and the owner became an absentee. In this case, the lessee had all the managerial powers of the owner, so in fact the social system was fundamentally the same. In the seventeenth and eighteenth centuries, the large landed estates of the nobility and most gentry had a cushion of legal privilege that allowed them to be less efficient than others: some estates (*frälse*) were in large part tax-relieved and others (*säteri*) were hyper-relieved, having no financial obligations to the state whatsoever. At the beginning of the nineteenth century, there were roughly 16,000 partly untaxed estates and approximately 6,000 without any tax obligations. These special breaks were leached away during the course of the nineteenth century, but did not entirely disappear until 1892.[68] That Wohlin did not deal directly with nobility-gentry estates is vexing but, in fact, even if they were left out entirely, the sum total of the Swedish population that was at most risk from a one-year catastrophe would not be greatly affected: the nobility and the gentry were hardly in danger of nutritional deprivation.[69]

- Freehold farms, most of whose origins were either in allodial colonization of formerly unfarmed land, or in Crown grants made during the seventeenth century intended to bond to itself the lower orders. These freehold farms (*hemman*) were held by owner-operators (*hemmansägare*, or *bönder*)—a group that we are here not calling "peasants," as has been previously explained. They are a complicated bunch. For two reasons: first, at the start of the nineteenth century most of the freehold owner-operators lived in nucleated villages and held scattered strips of land. As in a classic medieval open-field village, the cropping pattern was set communally and the farmers had a share of common waste land and usually of timber rights. During the course of the nineteenth century, most of the scattered strips were converted into consolidated holdings ("enclosures" in the vocabulary of English agriculture), and there were winners and losers in this process. The most successful of the freeholders rose to controlling more land than did some of the down-sliding nobility and gentry; the least successful saw their children become landless labourers. Secondly, although not actually freeholders, about one-quarter to one-fifth of farm operators leased lands in sufficient quantity and security to make the holders the socio-economic equivalent of freeholders.[70] Their leases could be from large freeholders, from the gentry and nobility, or from the Crown. These lessees were the *arrendator/arrendatoren* (meaning renters generally in the first two-thirds of the nineteenth century—a term that from roughly 1870 onwards is used in official documents and enumerations to mean a very big renter from a large estate). More specifically, in Wohlin's vocabulary the renters whose holdings were large and tenancies secure were denominated as the equivalent of the everyday freeholders (but not of the gentry freeholders) in the term *hemmansbrukare*.

- Short-term tenancies. The typical unwritten tenancy agreement, whereby a modest farm (*torp*) was rented, usually held for a four-to-eight-year period. Sometimes it was renewed to a single family across two or three generations. Torp could be rented either from large estates or, increasingly in the nineteenth century, from freehold farmers who were doing well. The distinguishing feature of this kind of tenancy was that, in addition to any crop or cash payments that were part of the lease, the *torpare* and family were required to put in day labour for their landlord. The amount was highly variable, ranging from a few days for a small holding to most of a family's work-time for a large one, and also varying widely by the custom of the region of the country.[71] They were not, however, servants, and the torp was recognized as an independent, albeit necessarily small, enterprise. And the conditions of day labour were specified in the oral contract and were to some degree protected by statute law. (We will continue to use the term "torp" and "torpare"—the singular and the plural are the same in each case—instead of the usual English translation—"croft" and "crofter"—since these have connotations in the agricultural history of the British Isles that are misleading.)

- Landless farm labourers, some of whom had reasonable expectations of the future, and others no hope. This heterogeneous category, as constructed by Wohlin, consisted of (A) the children, over age 15, of the operator of a freehold or its equivalent who worked at home. They were very much subordinate, but one of them (usually the eldest male) had a fair hope of inheriting the holding. And (B) it was common for the children of freeholders to sign on with other farmers at about age 15 as a male servant, a *dräng* (plural, *drängar*), or as a female farm servant, a *piga* (pl. *pigor*). They earned their room and board and perhaps a little cash. When this path was successful, it was a form of agricultural apprenticeship that prepared the young lad to inherit his father's freehold or to take a torp of his own; and the young girl learned house and animal management, the latter being especially important in a system where the animals were mostly a female responsibility. If the system did not work, it became a dead-end for the individual: year after year of hard work for almost no money.[72]

- Marginal individuals who had virtually no economic purchase. These consisted of: (A) *Stattorpare*, married men and women who became, as a household unit, servants on large estates. They usually were in a terminal position; unlike the unmarried young men and women, many of whom became servants as part of a life cycle, they could not be at all sanguine about obtaining a torp. In the usual case, these families had a house and small garden and worked virtually full time for the freeholder, with little or no cash or other payment. Although this group was small (Wohlin found it to be numerically significant only in the 1820s and thereafter), it was a labour category just waiting to be filled by those who were displaced by agricultural modernization. (B) Dependant lodgers, the men and women (*inhyseshjon/inhyseshjoner*) who were permitted to live in the house outshots or the outbuildings of a freeholder or larger torpare and to help with chores. They were essentially unpaid dogsbodies, often broken in health, and their keep was as much a matter of farmers' charity as of economics. (C) Persons who were beyond making any economic contribution besides an occasional day or two in the casual labour force as, for example, at haying time. They sometimes were housed by the parish poor officers and sometimes by estate owners and freeholders as part of an unspoken social contract. They were given a cottage (sometimes no more than a dugout hole with a rudimentary roof) on the most marginal land. Hence their classification as *backstugusittare* (occupiers of back-of-beyond hovels.) Here the sometimes-employed English word "cottager" is wildly misleading; the Swedish term is brilliantly clear and we will use it. (D) The people whom Wohlin called the "lösa daglönareklassen" and which we might well name the

Economically Walking Wounded. They were the rootless day labourers who had not even a sod hut to count on. Their numbers were not large—19,978 males in 1800. But they would be a useful litmus group of immiseration; unfortunately, however, Wohlin lumped them together with children under 15 in his tables and one can disaggregate them only for the year 1800.

- One category that Wohlin's work employed we will excise entirely from consideration: fishermen. These ran from 5,535 in 1800 to 8,820 in 1900 and, though conscientiously tallied, they do not fit into a discussion of agricultural land holding.

In table 3.3 we have the distribution of agricultural enterprises in the year 1800. Ironically, the categorization in that year is one of the most revealing for the entire century, as thereafter Wohlin's recalibration of the Swedish censuses loses track of the nobility-gentry estates and of the rootless day labourers.

Note that in table 3.3 we are *not* here dealing with the entire population, but with something that is more revealing of the actual structure of the agricultural sector: the configuration of *male* heads of enterprises as a surrogate for the entire agrarian structure. This focus deals with historical reality: overwhelmingly rural economic units were headed by men. Thus, although table 3.3 in the strictest sense uses male heads of enterprises as a surrogate for the entire structure, it is a surrogate that is so large as to be a hand inside a slightly larger glove. (And, not so incidentally, this employing of agricultural enterprises as our unit of analysis fits with our earlier unit of analysis of Irish agricultural enterprises and makes cross-national comparison easier.) Of course there were some farms and estates with women in charge: widows, especially, but also a few farms that had passed by inheritance to a daughter in a family with no male heirs.[73] Unfortunately, in the Swedish census data on which Wohlin's analysis is based, it is impossible to detach, consistently,

Table 3.3. Swedish agricultural enterprises, 1800 (categorized by adult male head-persons).

Category		Number	Percentage of total	Cumulative percentage (richest to poorest)
Independent landed classes	1. Noble-gentry estates operated by owners	4,491	0.8	0.8
	2. Commoner freeholders & substantial tenants	199,645	34.8	35.6
	3. Estates, freeholds and substantial tenancies of unspecified headship	5,591	0.9	36.5
Semi-independent	4. Torpare	64,644	11.3	47.8
Landless	5. Male unmarried servants & freeholder/substantial tenants (sons over age 15)	235,393	41.0	88.8
	6. Backstugusittare and dependent lodgers	44,467	7.7	96.5
	7. Rootless day labourers	19,978	3.5	100.0
	Total	**574,109**	**100.0**	

census-after-census and for all class levels, these female-run enterprises from the much more common statistical subsumation of women into male-headed enterprises. So one obtains a more accurate national profile by dealing only with male heads of enterprises, whether familial or corporations-sole.[74]

Nils Wohlin, in constructing the database for his monographs, was a highly responsible scholar, but he had an agenda: he was worried about the apparent, or alleged, long-term decline of the "independent" classes as the agricultural revolution of the nineteenth century careered along, and he tied to this apparent phenomenon the rise of emigration. Without buying into his entire agenda, we can honour his scholarship and eventually can join the implications of his data sets to our earlier approach to Ireland. One can use Wohlin's categories of status (legal and economic) to produce a condominium-of-risk levels among the pre-Deprivation Swedish agrarian population that turns out to be similar in structure to that of pre-Famine Ireland. (Of course, we are here using "risk" in the everyday sense of probability of something bad happening, and not in the narrow statistical sense of the term.)[75]

In terms of security/risk in the face of a one-year extreme crop failure, the risk was the chance of losing one's farm (in the case of smaller freeholders and various renters) and of increased incidence of disease and mortality for those lower on the scale. For Sweden, we lack detailed records of the size of individual holdings. There is nothing comparable to Ireland's 1841 census, but it would not be much use even if it did exist. This because (1) the agricultural land of Sweden was much more variable than that of Ireland, due both to climatic extremes and to large mountainous regions. An average hectare in Skåne and one in northern Dalarna might as well have been on separate continents.[76] (2) The average size of Swedish holdings at any time tells little unless one also knows: the average access to timber commons, and also the split between arable fields (*åker/åkrar*) and meadows (*äng/ängar*). And one does not: the earliest clear delineation of the size of agricultural holdings that the Emigration Commission could present was for 1904.[77]

So, give Wohlin his day: even though he could not cross-thatch size of land holdings with status categories, the relationship was so close, he believed, as to form an adequate statement of socio-economic position. I think that if one puts Wohlin's recalibration of the census data for 1800 together with his verbal exposition of the material, one has the visual heuristic concerning economic security and status of land-holding found in figure 3.2.[78]

As indicated in figure 3.2, Wohlin understood that some torp were in the high-insecurity zone and some were a level above that (hence, Transition Point A). Similarly, he recognized that some of the commoner-freeholders and their equivalent among the renters were less secure because of small holdings than were the better-off of the torpare. At least half, though, were in the zone of reasonable long-term security. (The border between these gradations is marked as Transition Point B.) Now, exactly how those theoretical transition points translated into hectares-held is indeterminate and highly variable by region, but that does not make Wohlin's vision any less telling.[79]

So, as an exercise in operating within Nils Wohlin's massive knowledge-base (he was probably the best-informed person about the historical socio-demography of rural Sweden in his era), let us ask: in 1800, in the case of a one-year crop failure, what proportion of the agricultural enterprises (including sole male workers) were in high jeopardy either of

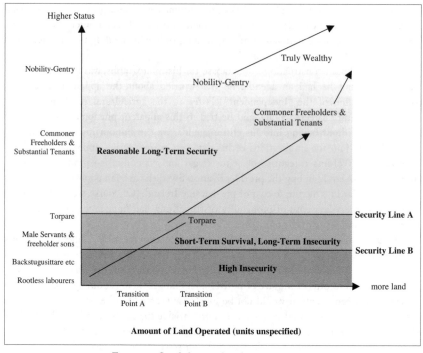

Figure 3.2. Swedish agricultural security, c. 1800.

complete economic collapse or, worse, of exposing the persons dependent upon them to severe health and mortality effects?

Start at the bottom, the high-insecurity zone. Certainly the rootless day labourers and the dependent lodgers and the backstugusittare, about 11 per cent of Wohlin's 1800 database ("about" because false precision would be misleading) were virtually destitute. And assume (it is an inference from Wohlin's discussion) that half of the torpare were stuck on the high-insecurity level and so too were half of Wohlin's category of farm servants and freeholders' and substantial tenants' sons. This is reasonable: many of the sons were effectively insured against complete calamity by their fathers' economic position; while, on the other hand, servants who came from lower down the scale, and those who were old and rheumatic and limited in strength were at great risk. This moiety fits with the census data. These were not the only poor people in the country, merely those in dire risk.

At the other end of the spectrum, the nobility and the gentry had roughly one per cent of the owner-supervised enterprises (but of course much, much more of the actual proportion of land). Let us assume that the largest commoner-freeholders, very well off but not of gentry status, probably reached one per cent of the holdings (such was the case at the end of the century). This amidst a freeholder-cum-substantial tenant group of which slightly more than half were in the long-term reasonable-security zone. Taken together, that would yield the following overall profile:

Long-term security	Nobility and gentry	1%	
	Very well-off freeholders	1%	
	Freeholders and equivalent tenants	18%	=20% subtotal
Short-term survival, long-term insecurity	Freeholders and equivalent tenants	17%	
	Torpare	5.5%	
	Male unmarried servants & freeholder (& equivalent) sons	20.5%	=43% subtotal
Highly insecure	Torpare	5.5%	
	Male unmarried servants & freeholder (& equivalent) sons	20.5%	
	Backstugusittare/dependent lodgers	8%	
	Rootless day labourers	3%	= 37% subtotal

Now, assuming that I am reading Nils Wohlin's intentions correctly,[80] the picture still is no more than a cloud pattern without some verification outside of the internal consistency of Wohlin's argument: that consistency is a necessary precondition for accepting his vision, but not sufficient in itself. Fortunately, in 1805 the Swedish government introduced into its regular enumerations a wonderfully peculiar question. It asked the parish clergymen, who were required to keep running population records and to compile the periodic census reports, to categorize the families in their districts according to four categories: (1) the rich, having at least 500 riksdalar (the Swedish currency until 1873 when the krona-öre system replaced it; equal to 5 shillings sterling in 1800) in excess of their annual needs; (2) the somewhat-rich, who have less annual surplus than that, but who do not need to incur any debts; (3) the poor who manage to keep life together, albeit with difficulty, including property owners who have greater liabilities than assets; and (4) the destitute, who are sustained only by virtue of gifts and charity. Although this question would drive a strict empiricist spare wild in its subjectivity, in its confusion of income and of assets, and in the absence of any controls for comparability from one clergyman to another, its answers nevertheless are revealing. The clergy were necessarily interested in the economic level of their flocks (which, by law, was everyone in the parish), as their dues depended upon local economic conditions. The 1805 results for rural households were:[81]

Rich	2.6
Moderately rich	25.8
Poor	55.6
Destitute	16.0
	100.0%

This is interesting in itself, and in relation to our reading of Wohlin's vision, it is heartening. If one takes the poor and destitute in the 1805 census as a single group, it encompasses nearly 72 per cent of the Swedish households. In figure 3.2, the combined categories of highly-insecure and getting-by-but-long-term-insecure, as estimated in the condominium-of-risk, is 80 per cent. That is as close to agreement between two independent sources as one could expect. Both pictures suggest that: (1) the destitute (16 per cent in the 1805 census, 11 per cent in Wohlin's 1800 data) undeniably were a serious slice of the rural population; (2) that roughly three-quarters of the rural families were either poor or without any long-term security. And (3) that probably only the top quarter (28 per cent in the 1805 data, 20 per cent in the 1800 schema) could look at their socio-economic future with confidence.

The trouble with the four categories in the 1805 clergy estimate of wealth is that they provide threshold levels, but do not tell how much on average was held by a household in each category. Fortunately, Lee Soltow located a previously untabulated wealth and tax inventory for 1800. He drew off a sample of 6,309 households and came to the conclusion that *non*-real estate wealth as between the four 1805 categories was:[82]

Rich	6,000 riksdalar
Moderately rich	300
Poor	15
Destitute	less than one daler

This indication of the levels of wealth is revealing only for the bottom two levels, as the rich were permitted to file a secret declaration of wealth.[83] (State complicity in tax avoidance by the rich is certainly not a new invention.) The useful point is that the bottom three-quarters of the population owned assets worth less than £4 sterling at contemporary rates.[84]

So, we have the base picture for the year 1800. What occurred in the Swedish agrarian world that could have altered that picture?

A lot, actually, and it is often called the Swedish agricultural revolution. In its simplest terms: (1) major amounts of land were claimed from waste or from forest and put into tillage or pasturage; (2) a series of technological improvements, ranging from crop rotation to improved seed and animal varieties increased output; and (3) a massive reorganization of the countryside occurred—"enclosure" is the cognate process in English agricultural history. The first two processes were overwhelmingly a benison—few losers and lots of winners, but the third was another matter.

The amount of cultivated land (arable crops and tame grasses) in the country grew from roughly 1.5 million hectares to 2.5 million between 1800 and 1850.[85] That is roughly a 73 per cent increase in farmable land.

But here is the conundrum. There are no really solid figures on Swedish crop production before 1861. The agricultural population from 1800 to 1860 grew by a bit less than 55 per cent.[86] Historians of Swedish agriculture agree that, considered nationally over the first six decades of the nineteenth century, production of vegetable products, especially grains and potatoes, grew faster than did the agrarian population. For the sake of argument, set the figure at 75 per cent—it could have been somewhat higher, but not much lower.[87] How did the agricultural workers achieve this—raising production while at the same time engaging the arduous process of land reclamation? Perhaps they worked harder. That is not a flippant suggestion, for underemployment is characteristic of subsistence farming and breaking out of the subsistence mode may have been a tonic for some. Perhaps they acquired better tools. Nothing elaborate: just better scythes, serrated sickles, spades with hard-finished faces, and mould-boarding for ploughs so that they scoured cleaner. All these things were being adopted, along with grain varieties that required fewer heat units.

And potatoes became the new vade-mecum of the kitchen garden. But, the biggest part of the reason that Swedish farming, considered as an entire sector, became more efficient was that the farmer, labourer, servant, hind, wasted less time walking.

That is what the enclosure movement was really about, saving steps. Granted, enclosure is always presented in more lofty conceptual terms and is discussed as a stage in the conquest of the rural environment by rational, market-based agriculture, and there is much in that. But for the people who were farming, the primary attraction of enclosure was not having to drag self and tools to 20 or 30 (or more)[88] different strips of land. And the second attraction was like unto it: not having to spend endless hours listening to blowhards and old fools and crabbit widows debate why sowing had to take place six weeks after Lady's Day, or was it Lady's Day Eve? And, as for getting the drooling village sumph to join in scything the common meadow on the agreed day, why that was enough to drive an ambitious farmer to conclude a pact with the devil.[89] Which, for some, enclosure turned out to be.

There is no definitive tally of how much of Sweden's land was reorganized during the enclosure era, nor can there be. The heart of the process was the destruction of the communal freehold village, with its two-or-three field system and multiple scattered strips of land; and its replacement by a set of individual freeholds with no more than two or three plots of land for each farm. And on each farm there was to be a house and outbuildings, everything now being distanced from the neighbours. That is the cartoon-clear version. On the ground, enclosure was sometimes half-done, and more communal farming remained than was anticipated by the promoters of enclosure. Moreover, although enclosure in the strict legal sense affected freehold communal villages, in fact the owners (or the chief tenants) of large "manor farms" often effected something very similar: they cleared off small subtenants and organized the leased holdings into blocks. Though different in law from village enclosure, the resulting final patterns would have been hard to distinguish in an aerial photograph.

What we can see most clearly of the village enclosure process is a succession of laws. The "big-redistribution acts" (*Storskiften*) of 1749 and 1757 were not actually such a big deal quantitatively, but they set a precedent for change. One landowner could request a consolidation of the village holdings into larger units; the acts were limited, however, by requiring consent of the majority of landowners and, in any case, no attack was made on the existence of the old common field hamlets. In contrast, an ordnance dealing only with the province of Skåne in 1803 permitted a single landowner to force a redistribution and consolidation of the village fields and, equally important, to force a dissolution of the villages around which each set of common fields had radiated. This was judged to work well, and was extended to Skaraborgs län in 1804 and to the entire country (in theory, but in practice to the southern half) in 1807. This single-person redistribution act (*Enskiftet*) caused a good deal of resentment and some opposition because if a single landowner petitioned the respective län's governor, and the petition was granted, all of the other freeholders (and Crown tenants) would have their holdings rearranged and their local village suppressed. Still, over a 20-year period it achieved its end in the southern parts of the country. The nearly final stage was the national purparty (*Lagaskiftet*) of 1827 which yielded a quasi-judicial reapportionment of lands into a maximum of two or three contiguous parcels for each freehold; village suppression was part of the process. In most areas the proceedings took two or three decades to complete and in certain areas much longer—the province of Dalarna being the site of intransigent resistance well into the twentieth century.[90] One can accept the historiographic consensus that, unlike enclosure in England, the process was generally conducted fairly and without loading towards the interests of the rich, and still understand why even some "progressive" farmers might have reservations about having their local villages destroyed and their farm lands reallocated by the decision of strangers in frock coats.[91]

Only a partial tally of enclosures for the period covered by the present discussion is available, but even so it yields an enormous number. Between 1828 and 1860, inclusive, nearly 8.7 million hectares of rural real estate (most of it non-arable) were redistributed. That excludes prior enclosures and those done without recourse to the enclosure law.[92]

Because there is no trustworthy score-card of most of the central features of the agricultural revolution of the first two-thirds of the nineteenth century—no precise production data, no reliable tally of incidence and chronology of enclosure, no census of innovation—Swedish economic historians have concentrated on case studies of localities for the first half of the nineteenth century and for national material have skipped to the story that unfolds with considerable precision for the last third of the century: solid production data began to be generated in 1865 and were retrospectively projected to 1861. That is sensible, but for our purposes in comprehending the physics of Swedish emigration, we require some fairly precise national indication of what the agricultural revolution did to the rural social structure.

Here the real genius of Nils Wohlin shines through. He understood full well that the individual line items in the nation's historical accounts simply were not there. But, like a good forensic auditor, he constructed a realistic narrative of the company history by arranging in sequence the handful of bottom-line entries that were available—at least available to someone with a shrewd eye for deciphering the meandering categories of the Swedish census authorities and possessing an historical knowledge of things that, to use Jacob Burckhardt's phrase, "were completely self-understood in their own time, and, like all daily matters, were not thought necessary to write down."

Given below is Nils Wohlin's vision of agrarian Sweden's evolving socio-economic categories from 1805 until the eve of the Great Deprivation. The material is by no means perfect: the censuses for 1855 and 1860 required interpolations in some major categories; there is no true census when one really wants it, in 1865. And, for technical reasons, the whole table makes Swedish rural society considered as a whole seem somewhat better off than it actually was. But Wohlin's work has the great advantage of showing the quanti-tative evolution of each of the major socio-economic groups and thus permitting each segment *to be measured over time as against itself*.[93] Thus, winners and losers become clear.

Table 3.4 is necessarily slightly different in categories from table 3.3 (the census authorities changed methods) but, like that table, it deals with agricultural enterprises as defined by the status of the male head of the enterprise, whether the enterprise involved several score people, a family, or only a solitary individual. It does not matter if one thinks of these enterprises as business units or as Chayanovian kernels or anything in-between: each had the same fundamental problem, namely how to cope with the risk of crop failure.[94]

The simple things shown by table 3.4 are the most important. In a period wherein the amount of farmable land has increased by roughly 73 per cent, the following level of increase in the major rural social groups had occurred:

Table 3.4. Swedish agricultural enterprises, 1805–60 (categorized by adult male head-persons).

Year	Commoner freeholders	Equivalent substantial tenants	Subtotal: "freeholder class"	Unspecified substantial holders	Subtotal: all freeholders & equivalent tenants	Torpare	Male servants & sons of "freeholder class" (over 15 years)	Stattorpare	Backstu-gusittare & dependent lodgers	Total enterprises
1805	151,021	53,051	204,072	31,877	235,949	63,163	204,860	n/a	43,317	547,289
1810	153,797	52,158	205,955	32,594	238,549	63,641	199,196	n/a	40,631	542,017
1815	147,971	50,292	98,263	24,778	223,041	69,228	204,241	n/a	40,863	537,373
1820	147,719	49,627	197,346	26,529	223,875	76,637	220,704	n/a	43,400	564,616
1825	148,432	50,385	198,817	19,475	218,562	81,394	213,637	9,239	48,383	571,215
1830	154,238	46,931	201,169	17,626	218,795	86,114	220,862	10,398	54,513	590,682
1835	157,670	47,190	204,860	18,512	223,372	91,331	235,531	12,691	59,525	622,450
1840	156,868	44,309	201,177	15,398	216,575	98,364	307,863	14,154	65,226	692,182
1845	161,749	42,438	204,187	13,592	217,779	94,252	333,653	15,609	78,376	739,669
1850	166,308	40,621	206,929	14,272	221,201	96,810	344,665	17,026	89,215	768,917
1855	171,231	37,866	209,097	11,758	220,855	95,214	309,011	18,706	100,391	744,177
1860	186,880	36,229	223,109	7,792	230,901	99,815	320,879	23,815	96,514	771,924

Category	Percentage increase
Commoner freeholders	23.7
Torpare	58.0
Male servants & sons of "freeholder class" (over 15 years)	56.6
Backstugusittare & dependent lodgers	122.8

Now, unless one wishes to posit a major (and thus far historically unrecorded) increase in the size of holdings granted to torpare and an equally significant improvement in the wages and living conditions of farm servants and also in the benisons granted to the economically marginal and dependent, then a clear conclusion is unavoidable: the agricultural revolution of the first two-thirds of the nineteenth century was primarily a direct benefit to the landowners, especially the commoner freeholders. Perhaps the non-landed caught a few crumbs from the table, perhaps not. That is unclear.

Undoubtedly, a greater proportion of heads-of-enterprises (meaning, mostly, heads of families) were in the high-insecurity zone as far as vulnerability to crop failure was concerned in the years just before the Deprivation than had been the case in the early years of the nineteenth century. As a rough estimate, assume that all the stattorpare and backstugusittare and dependent lodgers were in the high-insecurity zone and that half the torpare and male farm servants and adult sons of the freeholder class and its equivalent also were (this is the same heuristic we used earlier): then just under 43 per cent of the agrarian population was at high risk in the 1860s. Both as a portion of the population and as an absolute number, the vulnerable were increasing.

Nils Wohlin's data indicate that a rapid process of *rural social differentiation* was occurring. That is Lars Magnusson's term,[95] and it is preferable to the concept of "rural proletarianization," which is teleological and precludes the possibility that social differentiation might leave the bottom groups better off than previously.

Still, in this period, it is clear that two tectonic plates were moving in opposite directions. For freeholders, not only was the amount of land in their ownership increasing markedly, but the security of their land titles was increased because all newly allocated holdings were embedded in a set of legal processes as defined by the various enclosure commissions. Although at a philosophical level, all land is a usufruct, both freeholders and their social inferiors recognized that the world of the landowner was becoming less risky.

The opposite tectonics encompassed non-owners. The radical growth of the non-owners is quantitatively undeniable.[96] Equally importantly, this change was *qualitatively* magnified. Recall that one of the implications of the enclosure movement was the destruction of the myriad small villages that were the pivot of the common-field system. Thus, the process of social differentiation not only increased the gap between land-owners and all others in the agricultural population, it quite literally (meaning physically) displaced from their custom-defined locales the lower social orders. Moving and rebuilding a farmstead was one thing for a freeholder (there was profit to be made and power over resources to be gained) but for the landless there was no profit in being forced to move. Instead, their removal meant not only cost and inconvenience, but the diminution of the social safety network that had been an ameliorator of rural poverty. When freeholders and their servants had lived cheek by jowl in hamlets surrounded by the common fields, it was hard for the better-off to avert their eyes from the marginal, sick, or unlucky. With the dispersal of farmsteads, the moral economy that had been enforced by propinquity was weakened.

Undeniably, the agricultural revolution in general and the enclosure movement in particular was part of a major *mentalité* shift in Swedish rural culture. (Of course the mind-shift was both a cause and a result of the changes on the ground, parsing of which is impossible.) This shift can be easily conceptualized by thinking of the pre-enclosure village as if it were a single farm and, in terms of cultivation patterns, so it was. On that "farm" it was impossible to differentiate rents and wages and profit and thus to maximize profit in the way that, say, a shipping firm could. So, instead of maximizing profit, the village as an entity sought to secure a certain standard of life, mostly defined by consumption of food, at some communally defined level. Everyone knew what a good year and a bad year was, and the workers on the "farm" pretty much had a good or a bad year together.[97] In sharp contrast, once individual freeholds were separated as physically bounded entities by the enclosure process, a freeholder could know exactly what his own costs and revenues were and he could maximize profit the same way that an urban business could. No longer did the village act as a single farm, and no longer were good and bad years necessarily shared. In the long run, the new market orientation undoubtedly increased agricultural production. In the short run, it was a social dissolvent.

FIVE

Thus, a reasoned estimate is that approximately 60 per cent of the Irish rural population and more than 40 per cent of the Swedish population were at high risk, in mid-nineteenth century, from a single year's severe crop failure. This, despite improvements in agriculture in each society and promises of future adjustments that would align more comfortably the rural population and its resources. Of course, almost everyone in those societies would be affected adversely by the severe economic crimp that would follow a widespread crop failure, but the high-insecurity portion of the populace risked more: health and life and, at minimum, loss of immediate livelihood. I suspect that the hardest point for historians steeped in Irish history to take in is that Ireland, though hideously poor, was not alone. Sweden in, say, 1840, was nearly as badly off and nearly as vulnerable to disaster. For that year, Joel Mokyr completed a revealing set of calculations in which he concluded that the number of cultivated acres per person in the Irish population was 1.65. The number for Sweden was 1.54.[98]

In both cases, it is clear that one-half of the Ó Gráda Paradox is germane. If mere (or if one prefers, pure) economic self-interest was concerned, the Irish and Swedish peasantry should have been leaving each country in droves. That they did not do so I shall argue was not primarily the result either of economic constraints (such as transport costs or the lack of knowledge of opportunities) nor of indolence or backwardness, but stemmed from cultural values that for most persons made micro-economic calculations a matter of secondary relevance.

NOTES

1   Cormac Ó Gráda, "Poverty, population and agriculture, 1801–45," in W. E. Vaughan (ed.), *A New History of Ireland*, vol. 5, *Ireland under the Union, I, 1801–70* (Oxford: Clarendon Press, 1989), p. 120.

2   William Carleton, *Traits and Stories of the Irish Peasantry*, 2 vols. (Dublin: William Curry, 1830), expanded version, 3 vols. (Dublin: W. F. Wakeman, 1833). After Carleton's death (1869), publishers chopped and rearranged the stories in several subsequent editions.

3   Kenneth H. Connell, *Irish Peasant Society. Four Historical Essays* (Oxford: Clarendon Press, 1968).

4   Liam Kennedy and Leslie A. Clarkson, "Birth, Death and Exile: Irish Population History, 1700–1921," in B. J. Graham and L. J. Proudfoot (eds.), *An Historical Geography of Ireland* (London and New York: Harcourt Brace, Jovanovich, 1993), table 5.5, p. 161.

5   T. W. Freeman, *Pre-Famine Ireland. A Study in Historical Geography* (Manchester: Manchester University Press, 1957), p. 25. Freeman's book is one of the classics that is grossly underappreciated. It is remarkably comprehensive in its command of raw data, tightly organized, and has very little in the way of an ideological agenda.

6   Derived from Joel Mokyr, *Why Ireland Starved: A Quantitative and Analytical History of the Irish Economy, 1800–1850* (London: George Allen and Unwin, 1983), table 2.2, p. 14.

7   Cormac Ó Gráda, *Black '47 and Beyond. The Great Irish Famine in History, Economy, and Memory* (Princeton: Princeton University Press, 1999), p. 24.

8   For an admirable socio-economic analysis, see W. H. Crawford, "The Evolution of the Linen Trade in Ulster before Industrialization," *Irish Economic and Social History*, vol. 15 (1988), pp. 32–43. The data cited are found on p. 42. W. H. Crawford's lifetime bibliography of work on the linen and related textile industries is fundamental to any study of eighteenth and nineteenth-century Irish economic history. See "W. H. Crawford. A Bibliography," in Brenda Collins, Philip Ollerenshaw and Trevor Parkhill (eds.), *Industry, Trade and People in Ireland, 1650–1950. Essays in Honour of W. H. Crawford* (Belfast: Ulster Historical Foundation, 2005), pp. 277–80. Confirmation that the technical changes in the textile industry were the major (perhaps the only) instance of pre-Famine deindustrialization is found in Frank Geary, "The Act of Union. British-Irish Trade and Pre-Famine Deindustrialisation," *Economic History Review*, new ser., vol. 48 (Feb. 1995), pp. 68–88.

9   Freeman, *Pre-Famine Ireland*, p. 275.

10   Mokyr, *Why Ireland Starved*, esp. pp. 182–83.

11   Cormac Ó Gráda, "Industry and Communication, 1801–45," in Vaughan, *A New History of Ireland, 1801–70*, p. 150.

12   See D. H. Akenson, *The Irish Education Experiment. The National System of Education in the Nineteenth Century* (London: Routledge and Kegan Paul and Toronto: University of Toronto Press, 1970).

13   Ó Gráda, "Industry and Communication, 1801–45," pp. 150–55.

14   Liam Kennedy, "Why Ireland Starved: An Open Verdict," *Irish Economic and Social History*, vol. 11 (1984), p. 101. The entire article, pp. 101–06, is worth attention. See also Peter Solar, "Why Ireland Starved: A Critical Review of the Econometric Results," *Irish Economic and Social History*, vol. 11 (1984), pp. 107–15. See also Mokyr's reply, *Irish Economic and Social History*, vol. 11 (1984), pp. 117–21, which discusses Solar's criticisms but does not confront Kennedy's.

15   Ó Gráda, "Poverty, population and agriculture, 1801–45," p. 127. For an explanation of this estimate, see Cormac Ó Gráda, *Ireland. A New Economic History, 1780–1939* (Oxford: Clarendon Press, 1994), p. 162.

16   Ó Gráda, *Ireland. A New Economic History*, p. 162.

17   Ó Gráda, *Ireland. A New Economic History*, p. 127.

18   Ó Gráda, *Ireland. A New Economic History*, p. 123, table based on his *Ireland before and after the Famine: Explorations in Economic History, 1800–1925* (Manchester: Manchester University Press, 1988), pp. 47–50 and 70.

19   Cormac Ó Gráda, *Ireland's Great Famine. Interdisciplinary Perspectives* (Dublin: University College Dublin Press, 2006), p. 45, revising a 1988 article co-authored with Joel Mokyr, "Poor and Getting Poorer?," published in the *Economic History Review*, vol. 37, no. 2 (1988), pp. 209–35.

20   Kenneth Connell, *The Population of Ireland* (Oxford: Clarendon Press, 1950). For a full bibliography of Connell's work and a memorial assessment, see R. M. Hartwell, "Kenneth H. Connell: An Appreciation," *Irish Economic and Social History*, vol. 1 (1974), pp. 7–14. See also Leslie A. Clarkson, "Introduction: K. H. Connell and Economic and Social History at Queen's University, Belfast," in J. M. Goldstrom and Leslie A. Clarkson (eds.), *Irish Population, Economy, and Society. Essays in Honour of the late K. H. Connell* (Oxford: Clarendon Press, 1981), pp. 1–11.

21 The best of these individual estimates were by Arthur Young (1780), Daniel A. Beaufort (1792) and Thomas Newenham (1804). Their estimates are found in Freeman, *Pre-Famine Ireland*, table 1, p. 15. The table also includes the failed 1813 census.

22 David Dickson, Cormac Ó Gráda and Stuart Daultrey, "Hearth Tax, Household Size and Irish Population Change, 1671–1821," *Proceedings of the Royal Irish Academy*, sec. C, vol. 82 (1982), pp. 125–81.

23 Leslie. A. Clarkson, "Irish Population Revisited, 1687–1821," in Goldstrom and Clarkson, *Irish Population, Economy, and Society*, pp. 13–35.

24 Joseph J. Lee, "On the Accuracy of the pre-Famine Irish Censuses," in Goldstrom and Clarkson, *Irish Population, Economy, and Society*, pp. 37–56.

25 Kennedy and Clarkson, "Birth, Death and Exile," table 5.1, p. 160. I have inserted official census numbers and Lee's revision, which are missing in the original table, from Lee, "On the Accuracy of the pre-Famine Irish Censuses," p. 53.

26 Timothy W. Guinnane, "The Great Irish Famine and Population: The Long View," *American Economic Review*, vol. 84 (May 1994), pp. 303–04.

27 Ó Gráda, "Poverty, population, and agriculture, 1801–45," p. 118.

28 Kennedy and Clarkson, "Birth, Death and Exile," table 5.2, p. 160; Ó Gráda, *Ireland. A New Economic History*, table 1.1, p. 6.

29 Connell, *Population of Ireland*, p. 248.

30 Connell, *Population of Ireland*, p. 248.

31 The chief of these is that Connell may have been too closed-minded about the possibility of a concomitant (albeit secondary) drop in the death rate. Improved nutrition may have dropped the incidence of infant mortality. This of course would have played into the increase in marital fertility. Secondly, the system he describes may have held for the bulk of the population, but not for substantial farmers and those above them on the social scale. It is possible that Ireland had two systems of family formation and that these were separated by social class.

32 P. M. Austin Bourke, "The Visitation of God?", in Jacqueline Hill and Cormac Ó Gráda (eds.), *The Potato and the Great Irish Famine* (Dublin: Lilliput Press for *Irish Historical Studies*, 1993), p. 16. This volume, edited as an homage to a major, but previously underestimated scholar, continues Bourke's seminal work not only on potato culture but on the accuracy of Irish agricultural statistics before the Famine.

33 Bourke, "The Visitation of God?", pp. 20–25. The material is from Bourke's unpublished 1967 PhD, granted by the National University of Ireland, via University College, Cork. Quotation from p. 20.

34 Let me be clear. The problem is not with the Rev. Thomas R. Malthus, whose writings are too rarely read. Actually, he was one of the fine minds of the nineteenth century and, as Darwin asserted, a foundational thinker on the effect of population pressure in competitive societies. The problem is that (as any electronic search will quickly reveal) he has quite unfairly become an icon of a number of groups who discountenance compassion in dealing with humanitarian crises and somehow manage to use the Irish Famine as an example of societal irresponsibility.

35 Samuel Clark, *Social Origins of the Irish Land War* (Princeton: Princeton University Press, 1979), pp. 35–36. Although this study is focused on the land war of the last quarter of the nineteenth century, its discussion of the pre-Famine social structure (pp. 22–64) is a tour de force.

36 There was enormous variation in the "lives" employed. Sometimes they were successive monarchs, sometimes successive bishops of the Established Church, or often local worthies who were alive at the time of signing. Leaseholds with successive lives were usually more desirable than non-renewable long leaseholds but, when simultaneously living individuals were named, the degree of security was reduced.

37 Freeman reports that on the eve of the Famine the incoming tenant paid in the range of £10–25 an acre (*Pre-Famine Ireland*, p. 140). In some locales, compensation for improvements made to the land was paid to the outgoing tenant by the new one; in others, by the landlord; in others, not at all. For an excellent conspectus, see W. H. Crawford, "Landlord-Tenant Relations in Ulster, 1609–1820," *Irish Economic and Social History*, vol. 2 (1975), pp. 5–21. For an explanation of how these arrangements could be of benefit to the landlord as well as the tenant, see Timothy W. Guinnane and Ronald I. Miller, "Bonds without Bondsmen: Tenant-Right in Nineteenth-Century Ireland," *Journal of Economic History*, vol. 56 (Mar. 1996), pp. 113–42.

38 This ladder follows that implied by Bourke, "The Visitation of God?", pp. 79 and 99.

39 Although this is my own schematic depiction of a long reading of the contemporary material, I am heartened by its being roughly consonant with one aspect of work done by Cormac Ó Gráda and Joel Mokyr. In a study conducted in the 1980s, they developed a "Subjective Impoverishment Index" which indicated that "the critical threshold size was about twenty acres …," in reference to second-level assessments of whether or not the condition of the poor was deteriorating, as of the mid-1830s. (Ó Gráda, *Ireland's Great Famine*, p. 29.) In

other words, 20 acres was perceived by contemporaries as a break-line in social structure. Secondly, Ó Gráda (*Ireland's Great Famine*, p. 27) suggests that 50–60 per cent of the agricultural population lived in poverty, and this coincides with the proportion of the agricultural population with under five acres, the group that falls into the High Insecurity group in my analysis.

40 Table 3.2 is a restatement of data in Bourke, "The Visitation of God?", pp. 75, 79, 98. The chief change is that Bourke had an inferred number (quite a large one) for the number of landless labourers and those who held less than one acre in conacre, whom he put together (quite justifiably) as a single group. He did not include this number in his tabulation of agricultural categories (p. 98), although he did include those with under one acre who held land for a year or more (i.e., not in conacre). To be quite clear about the necessity of thinking of these numbers as somewhat rough, the following are relevant: (1) Bourke, unlike most users of the 1841 census data, realized that most of the raw data were collected in Irish acres (=1.62 statute acres) or in Cunningham acres (=1.29 statute acres) and had to be read accordingly. (2) as Bourke pointed out, what a farm unit was varied somewhat as between census takers, so the concept of farm size was blurred; (3) his tabulation of the data is labelled "c.1845," as it was done for the Poor Law Commissioners, and "the only statement that can be made with assurance is that they related to the immediate pre-Famine situation." (p. 194n21); (4) I am defining as a single agricultural enterprise the land held by an individual. This, as Bourke points out, is not quite the same thing as a holding (pp. 78–79). One individual could have more than one holding as part of a single enterprise. For our purposes, estimating risk, this definition is better than using holdings, since the number of holdings would somewhat magnify the apparent risk.

41 Cormac Ó Gráda suggests that 25 to 30 per cent of those in the agricultural sector were dealing in the wider market economy of the British Isles (*Ireland's Great Famine*, p. 45.) This does not mean that they were waxing rich, but that they had some surplus in a normal year. This proportion would be roughly equal to the 10-acre-and-above farmers. For a tight microstudy of the shift to surplus-producing, see Kevin O'Neill, *Family and Farm in Pre-Famine Ireland. The Parish of Killaashandra* (Madison: University of Wisconsin Press, 1984).

42 Ó Gráda, *Black '47*, p. 29.

43 Ó Gráda, *Ireland's Great Famine*, p. 26.

44 Freeman, *Pre-Famine Ireland*, table 7, p. 151.

45 Bourke, "The Visitation of God?", pp. 52–73. See also Joel Mokyr, "Irish History with the Potato," *Irish Economic and Social History*, vol. 8 (1981), pp. 8–29.

46 From Samuel Taylor Coleridge's Notebook for the year 1833, reproduced in Allan Clayson, "Coleridge and Wordsworth in the South East of England," *Coleridge Bulletin*, new ser., no. 28 (Winter 2006), quoted in Richard Holmes, "The Passionate Friendship," *New York Review of Books* (12 April 2007), p. 47.

47 "The Staff of the Institute for Social Sciences, University of Stockholm," *Wages, Cost of Living and National Income in Sweden 1860–1930*, vol. 3, *National Income of Sweden, 1860–1930* (London: P. S. King and Son, 1937), part 2, pp. 10–13. Two comments. (1) the original pre-1865 material was collected by local agricultural societies, each of which worked out its own methods. (2) the Central Bureau of Statistics projected data, crop by crop, back to 1861. For a history of the county agricultural societies, as they developed under the aegis of the Royal Swedish Academy of Agriculture from 1811 onward, see Jan Stattin, *Hushållningssällskapen och Agrarsamhällets Förändring—utveckling och verksamhet under 1800-talets första hälft* (Uppsala: Acta Universitatis Upsaliensis, 1980).

48 Much of the high quality of Swedish economic historiography is consequent upon the formative platform laid down by Eli F. Heckscher (1870–1952). For an appreciation of Heckscher, see Alexander Gerschenkron's preface to the 1963 English edition of Heckscher's *An Economic History of Sweden* (tr. Göran Ohlin) (Cambridge: Harvard University Press, 1963), pp. xiii–xlii. See also Yiva Hasselberg, "Networks and Scientific Integrity: Eli Heckscher and the Construction of Economic History in Sweden, 1920–1950," *Scandinavian Economic History Review*, vol. 54 (2006), pp. 273–90. Somewhat more critical are Carl-Axel Olsson, "Eli Heckscher and the Problem of Synthesis," *Scandinavian Economic History Review*, vol. 40 (1992), pp. 29–52, and Benny Carlson, "Eli Heckscher and Natural Monopoly: The Nightmare that Never Came True," *Scandinavian Economic History Review*, vol. 40 (1992), pp. 53–79. Heckscher's biggest contribution to bridging economic theory and economic history—the Heckscher-Ohlin theory concerning the convergence of international factor prices consequent upon the convergence of international commodity prices—is assayed in the chapter, "Were Heckscher and Ohlin right?" in *Globalization and History. The Evolution of a Nineteenth-Century Atlantic Economy*, by Kevin O'Rourke and Jeffrey G. Williamson (Cambridge: MIT Press, 1999), pp. 57–75. The answer to the question is, yes, they were right.

49 Gustav Sundbärg (revised by E. Arosenius), "Demography," in Axel Johan Josef Guinchard (ed.), *Sweden. Historical and Statistical Handbook. First Part. Land and People* (Stockholm: KB, 2nd ed., 1914), table 13, p. 119.

50 In the Swedish censuses, the definition of urban was a legal and archaic one. It included as urban sites only those defined by law, not by the number of people in the settlement. Thus, to take 1850 as an example, Haparunda, with 554 inhabitants, was a discrete urban area. (See Sundbärg, "Demography," table 14, p. 120.) However, several areas with populations above two thousand were excluded since they were not juridically recognized. Sundbärg guessed that in the early twentieth century, if it had been possible to obtain data on numbers of persons living in aggregations of two thousand and above, the number would have been about ten per cent higher than the number living in statutorily defined towns. (Sundbärg, "Demography," p. 119.) However, in the mid-nineteenth century, before anything close to urbanization had begun, there would have been fewer people in unrecognized aggregations of two thousand and above. A reasonable guess is that in midcentury the tiny statutory towns and the unrecognized aggregations balanced each other. So, in the table above and in subsequent discussion, "rural" numbers are taken to mean the probable proportion of the total population living in communities of under two thousand persons—usually a great deal smaller. Obviously, this mode of dealing with the national situation cannot be applied to any specific locale.

51 Staff of the Institute, *National Income of Sweden, 1860–1930*, part 2, p. 6. The 1860 number is an estimate because only from 1870 onwards did census authorities tally the agrarian population as an entity.

52 Staff of the Institute, *National Income of Sweden, 1860–1930*, part 2, p. 6.

53 Thus, Peter Gårestad"s analysis of changes in the tax system is analytically dependent upon proto-industrialization leading after the 1860s to an industrial economy based on international trade. Peter Gårestad, *Industrialisering och Beskattning i Sverige, 1861–1914* (Uppsala: Acta Universitatis Upsaliensis, 1987). On the other hand, Matts Isacson and Lars Magnusson recognize the problems with the concept of proto-industrialization, but apply it skillfully to a sphere of market-driven activities that is distinguished by being interregional in product placement, yet still is conducted as less-than-full-time activity by farmers and agrarian workers. Thus, proto-industry as a concept is situated in a rural social context that did not necessarily have to become fully industrial to be a significant economic reality. Maths Isacson and Lars Magnusson, *Proto-industrialisation in Scandinavia. Craft Skills in the Industrial Revolution* (Hamburg: Berg, 1987). The development of centres of pre-industrial work into subsequent forms was especially complex and required special social customs as an analgesic. Lars Magnusson has shown how certain forms of theft and embezzlement and illegal dealing by craftsmen in Eskilstuna at the start of the nineteenth century became part of an invisible social code that lubricated the frictional relationships between social classes. Lars Magnusson, "Försnilling, Smyghandel och Fusk. Förlaggssystem och hantverkskultur i Eskilstuna vid början av 1800-talet," *Historisk Tidskrift*, vol. 86 (1986), pp. 161–85. In another study of Eskilstuna, which in 1771 had become a free-city without guild regulations, the male workers, most of whom were engaged in metal work, showed very different marriage patterns, depending on their status as apprentices, journeymen or masters. See Anne Hörsell, *Borgare, Smeder och Änkor. Ekonomi och Beforkning i Eskilstuna gamla stad och fristad, 1750–1850* (Uppsala: Acta Universitatis Upsaliensis, 1983). Perhaps the most unusual interaction of semi-industrial activities and of town social patterns was in Falun, where widows of copper miners in the Stora Kopperberg were given the right to open taverns. At one time, 200 thus-licensed premises were in operation. (Roger Miller and Torvald Gerger, *Social Change in Nineteenth-Century Swedish Agrarian Society* (Stockholm: Acta Universitatis Stockholmiensis, 1985), p. 20n4).

54 Anders Floren and Göran Ryden, "Protoindustri och tidigkapitalism," *Historisk Tidskrift*, vol. 112 (1992), pp. 1–31.

55 Eli F. Heckscher, "The Place of Sweden in Modern Economic History," *Economic History Review*, vol. 4 (Oct. 1932), p. 17.

56 E. F. Söderlund, *Swedish Timber Exports, 1850–1950. A History of the Swedish Timber Trade* (Stockholm: Almqvist and Wiksells, 1952), pp. 3–9.

57 Nils Wohlin in Government of Sweden, *Emigrationsutredningen, Bilaga IX, Den Jordbruksidkande Befolkningen i Sverige, 1751–1900* (Stockholm: KB, 1909), table A, p. 3.

58 Kevin O'Rourke and Jeffrey G. Williamson, *Open Economy Forces and the late 19th-century Scandinavian Catch-up* (Cambridge: National Bureau of Economic Research, HIER Discussion Paper, no. 1709, 1995), p. 10. An interesting debate exists on whether or not the relatively high reading skills of the Swedish general population made the agrarian population more willing to accept innovation. For the case that the freeholders who were literate were more apt to favour the enclosure revolution than were those who were not literate, see Lars Pettersson, "Reading and Writing Skills and the Agrarian Revolution: Scandinavian Peasants during the Age of Enclosure," *Scandinavian Economic History Review*, vol. 44 (1996), pp. 207–20. The classic comparative literacy study is Carlo M. Cipolla, *Literacy and Development in the West* (Harmondsworth: Penguin Books, 1969).

59 See table 2.1 and associated note.

60 *Statistisk Årsbok 1952*, table 39, cited in Heckscher, *An Economic History of Sweden*, table 9, p. 135.

61 See the birth and death rate table in Sundbärg, "Demography," p. 113. The major exception to the excess of birth rate over death rate was in Stockholm, which was among the filthiest cities in Europe. Into the 1850s its average annual death rate was above 4.0 per cent. G. A. Montgomery, *The Rise of Modern Industry in Sweden* (London: P. S. King, 1939), p. 2. Christer Winberg has forcefully argued that although it is undeniable that birth rates exceeded death rates for almost all years in the eighteenth and nineteenth centuries, this is an empirical observation and may hide evolving social configurations. In a rural culture in which birth control and birth spacing were beginning to be widely practised, and in which there was not limitless room for more children, a drop in the death rate (especially a decline in infant mortality) should simply have resulted in a compensatory increase in birth limitation and ultimately in something approaching equilibrium. This did not happen: manifestly, something was occurring beyond a simple autonomous fall in the death rates. See Christer Winberg, *Folkökning och Proletarisering. Kring den sociala Structuromvandlingern på Sveriges landsbygd under den agrara revolutionen* (Göteborg: Historiska Institutionen i Göteborg, 1975).

62 The focus upon agricultural enterprises as entities in themselves allows us to avoid the vexed and indeterminate discussion concerning the size and character of the pre-industrial Swedish household. On this problem, see the extended research note by Lennart Palm, "Household Size in Pre-Industrial Sweden," *Scandinavian Economic History Review*, vol. 47 (1999), pp. 78–90.

63 Here one must pay tribute to what is still the clearest description of the two basic English land patterns (similar, but not quite the same as Sweden, as the nucleated villages were usually leasehold), *English Villagers of the Thirteenth Century*, by George C. Homans (Cambridge: Harvard University Press, 1941).

64 Nils Wohlin in *Den Jordbruksidkande Befolkningen*; in Government of Sweden, *Emigrationsutredningen, Bilaga X, Bondeklassens Undergräfvande* (Stockholm: KB, 1910); and in Government of Sweden, *Emigrationsutredningen, Bilaga XI, Toppare, Backstugu- och Inhysesklasserna* (Stockholm: KB, 1908). The statistical volume is *Emigrationsutredningen, Bilaga XII, Jordstyckningen* (Stockholm: KB, 1911). The most concise definition of his categories is found in *Den Jordbruksidkande Befolkningen*, p. 17 which, however, is peculiar in detailing only the socio-economic classes below the nobility and gentry, despite their holdings being included in Wohlin's overall tabulations (albeit unlabelled as such). The best English-language discussion that I have encountered of the Swedish land system(s) is found in Miller and Gerger, *Social Change in Nineteenth-Century Swedish Agrarian Society*.

65 In making various necessary comments and corrections when Wohlin's material is being engaged, I do not wish to obscure the fact that one must hold his work in something close to awe. He recalibrated the Swedish censuses from mid-eighteenth century onwards and created a statistical narrative and commentary that covered more than 150 years of national history. He did so before calculators, much less computers, were available, and in the face of the Swedish enumerations being much messier and more given to inconsistency in category definitions than is usually recognized.

Wohlin's work should not, however, be approached innocently. It is a primary source in the sense that it is not replicable by any modern researcher. One cannot just dive into a given table and cite it. He worked with data whose definitions changed over time, and usually he fully points to this in his text notes at the end of each batch of tables. However, Wohlin's labels on the actual tables often do not communicate those changed meanings, or how he combined subcategories into larger ones. So, on matters of any importance, one has to go to the lowest level among his data sets and then observe how the information is aggregated in successive calculations. At points, his time series are too rubbery in definition to be completely trusted. (Basically, there are three somewhat different sets of data that cover the nineteenth century: those derived for 1800; those from 1805 running up to 1860; and those starting in 1870. They really should not be merged without due notice.)

For a less appreciative approach to Wohlin's work, see Margareta Larsson, "1800-talets Sociala Förändringar ur Folkmängdstabellens Perspectiv," *Historisk Tidskrift*, vol. 109 (1989), pp. 516–49. Leaving aside Larsson's individual calculations that involve Wohlin's data (her work is not replicable on the basis of the information provided, but is within the range of reasonable possibility), Larsson makes one very shrewd observation and then gums it to death. The observation is that the thinking behind the original Swedish census categories of the Tabellverket of 1749 was tripartite—as was the Lutheran thinking about ecclesiastical estates. Fine, so was much of classic Roman and ancient Christian thought. Larsson is right that Wohlin had to work with census categories whose variables were potentially archaic, but in seeing them as frozen in time she misses the points that (1) the censuses actually changed a lot and in fact Wohlin's real problem was not with frozen categories but with ones that were disconcertingly plastic; and (2) the variables that she specifically treats dismissively—age, civil status and sex—are among the central things one wants to know about almost any civil or demographic community.

66 Counter-intuitive though it may seem, leaving the Crown estates out of direct enumeration has little effect: (1) taken as a corporation-sole, the Crown was only one landowner and in any case not an owner-operator in the sense that Wohlin employed the concept. And, more importantly (2) the Crown lands entered Wohlin's inventory of agricultural enterprises when they were leased to tenants.

67 In the extreme case, in the far south, around Ystad, 80 per cent of land in 1825 was held in large nobility-gentry estates. Jens Moller, "The Landed Estate and the Landscape: Landownership and the Changing Landscape of Southern Sweden during the 19th and 20th Centuries," *Geografiska Annaler. Series B. Human Geography*, vol. 67 (1985), pp. 45–52.

68 Florence Edith Janson, *The Background of Swedish Immigration, 1840–1930* (Philadelphia: University of Pennsylvania, 1931), p. 45.

69 A good indication of the touching-the-forelock that characterized the Emigration Commission was that the calculation of the extent of tax-free land was buried in a statistical appendix, undiscussed and, unlike Wohlin's usual precision, did not even carry a date. See Wohlin, *Jordstyckningen*, table C, "Frälsejordens Omfattning," pp. 20–22.

70 Wohlin, *Jordstyckningen*, Tabellbilaga A, pp. 6–7. See also table 3.3 below.

71 A recent study of 43 estates in southern Sweden showed that the average number of workdays per tenant in 1800 was 118 and that this had increased to 314 in 1850. This was easily the most demanding in Sweden and in fact was among the heaviest labour obligations in Europe. Mats Olsson, "Manorial economy and *corvée* labour in southern Sweden, 1650–1850," *Economic History Review*, new ser., vol. 49 (2006), p. 490.

72 Data in Börke Harnesk's *Legofolk. Drängar, Pigor och Bönder i 1700- och 1800-talens* (Umeå: Acta Universitatis Umensis, 1900) indicate that offspring of landholders who took jobs as servants often were considered déclassé and their chances of inheriting or marrying a farm-inheritor dropped. The real question is that of intra-family pecking order: some potential inheritors were put into servants' jobs as apprenticeships, while others were sent away as being unlikely ever to be needed on the home farm, especially younger sons and daughters. See review of Harnesk by Lars Edgren, *Historisk Tidskrift*, vol. 111 (1991), pp. 104–15.

73 Up to 1845, under Swedish law men inherited twice as much land as women. However, to avoid subdivision of freeholds, the recipient of the largest portion of the freehold (almost always a male) had the right to buy out the others. In 1845 women were granted equal inheritance rights, but brothers had the right to buy out sisters. Christer Winberg, "Familj och Jord in tre Västgötasocknar. Generationsskiften bland självägande bönder, c. 1810–1870," *Historisk Tidskrift*, vol. 101 (1981), pp. 275–310.

74 The sources for table 3.3 are Wohlin, *Den Jordbruksidkande Befolkningen*, table H, p. 26; with the numbers of nobility-gentry estates from table E, p. 12; and with rootless day labourers disaggregated from "Råtabeller," pp. 224–27, with notes, pp. 307–11. As a footnote on the nobles and gentry, it is worth observing that in 1805 the nobility and gentry and their families formed 3.3 per cent of the Swedish total population. This, combined with their proportion as actual direct managers in table 3.3, suggests that most nobility and gentry estates (two-thirds to three-quarters) were managed by estate managers or rented to large tenants. Of course, many of the upper class had more than one estate. In the entire population (men, women, children), the numbers of the upper classes and their proportions of the entire population were as follows:

Nobility & baronetage	1805	9,503	0.39%
	1830	10,458	0.36%
	1855	11,742	0.32%
Gentry	1805	69,348	2.88%
	1830	70,091	2.44%
	1855	79,441	2.24%

Source: Sundbärg, *Betänkande*, table 16, p. 82.

75 I am encouraged to encounter the excellent work of Tommy Bengtsson and Martin Dribe. They use Wohlinian categories (slightly altered) to study the demographic response to short-term economic stress in four parishes in western Skåne. To accomplish this, they completely reconstituted the family structure of these parishes. Economic stress was measured primarily by prices for food grains: high grain prices reflect bad harvests and are proxies for low food supply. For our present purposes, the point is that fertility and mortality both were affected in times of high prices and that this varied by Wohlinian class levels. Which is to say that Bengtsson and Dribe's work validates the use of Wohlin's categories as a form of security/risk analysis related to rural deprivation. See Tommy Bengtsson and Martin Dribe, "New Evidence on the Standard of Living in Sweden during the Eighteenth and Nineteenth Centuries: Long-Term Development of the Demographic

Response to Short-Term Economic Stress," in Robert C. Allen, Tommy Bengtsson and Martin Dribe (eds.), *Living Standards in the Past* (Oxford: Oxford University Press, 2005), pp. 341–69.

76   The reader may note that I am not employing the *mantal* as a unit of land equivalence. This was an early modern unit of taxability and it had been inflexible since the seventeenth century. It was supposed to be the amount of land in a given locality required to carry a single family. While the unit may be useful in the high-farming areas of the south and near Stockholm, where the land use pattern had changed little since the seventeenth century, in other regions there was enough reclamation and new freeholds so as to render the unit invalid as a national descriptor—and certainly not for the period of the nineteenth-century agricultural revolution. Even in constant-arable regions, the meaning of "mantal" bent greatly over time. In Skåne in the early 1800s, one-half mantal was enough to produce a farm surplus and one-sixteenth to one-half mantal could feed a family under normal weather conditions. (See Patrick Svensson, "Peasants and Entrepreneurship in the Nineteenth-Century Agricultural Transformation of Sweden," *Social Science History*, vol. 30 (Fall, 2006), esp. pp. 406–09.) Just how far away from reality the mantal was as referring to a merely sustainable family holding is shown in the 1820s: at Ström in Jämtland, the average size of a mantal was 13,000 acres of timber. (Söderlund, *Swedish Timber Exports*, p. 6.)

77   Wohlin, *Jordstyckningen*, table F, pp. 193–202. These are governmental statistics drawn up independently of the Emigration Commission and they do not quite match Wohlin's total numbers, as Gustav Sundbärg tells the readers in the preface to Wohlin's volume.

        That said, and readily admitting that the 1904 numbers should not be projected backwards, they still are interesting. (There were earlier censuses of land holdings, but they were not as precise.) The 1904 data show that of the *cultivated* land (i.e., not counting waste, commonage, meadow) in the definable agricultural holdings, 25.1 per cent were less than two hectares; 64.4 per cent were 2–20 hectares; 0.3 per cent were 20–100 hectares; and 0.9 per cent were over 100 hectares. As was the frequent case with the Swedish government at that time, there was an unexplained 4,075 holdings missing from the table (of a total number of holdings of 350,851). One suspects that these were nobility-gentry estates which were small in number but large in extent.

78   Two comments for persons accustomed to seeing everything always being displayed on the same X-Y axes, especially in classical economics. (1) At this point, no quantities of individuals are involved in the figure. This is a schematic of the abstract concept of risk. (2) For expository reasons, the axis is reversed from that in figure 3.1. This makes it easy to observe that the basic form of the condominium-of-risk was the same in Sweden and Ireland.

79   An informed *guess* (nothing more than that) is that, on a national average, at the start of the nineteenth century Point A was 5 hectares and Point B was 15 hectares. (In the province of Skåne at the time, the minimum amount of land required to be considered a freehold agriculturalist (bonde) was 6 hectares.) Below that level, even if one held land that was legally freehold, one dropped to a status equal to the better-off torpare. (See Bengtsson and Dribe, "New Evidence on the Standard of Living in Sweden," pp. 352–53.) The equivalent number would have been higher in less fertile regions.

80   Nils Wohlin published a number of articles in *Ekonomisk Tidskrift* in the first two decades of the twentieth century, and these allow a fair degree of triangulation on his attitudes and methods as they appear in his work in the Emigration Commission. Especially relevant is "Jorddelningsväsendet i Sverige och statistiken," *Ekonomisk Tidskrift*, vol. 9 (1907), pp. 415–54 and "Torpkommissionens Betänkande," *Ekonomisk Tidskrift*, vol. 13 (1911), pp. 359–79.

81   Lee Soltow, "The rich and the destitute in Sweden, 1805–1855: a test of Tocqueville's inequality hypotheses," *Economic History Review*, new ser., vol. 42 (Feb. 1989), table 2, p. 50. The proportion of the households in each category changed little, 1805–20. Thereafter the definitions of each category were sharply altered twice—in 1825 and in 1840—so that comparison over time becomes invalid.

        The instructions to the clergy (taken from a handwritten protocol for the 1810 census because Soltow could find no copies of the 1805 instructions) are found in Lee Soltow, "The Swedish Census of Wealth at the beginning of the 19th Century," *Scandinavian Economic History Review*, vol. 33 (1985), p. 1.

82   Soltow, "The Swedish Census of Wealth," pp. 2, 17.

83   Soltow, "The Swedish Census of Wealth," pp. 5 *n*6, 10 *n*13.

84   I hope that by this point the reader is seeing why Nils Wohlin's work for the Emigration Commission is so valuable. He recognized that some of the census and related data were of limited utility. (For example, secret wealth declarations do not make for good public records.) And he was aware of the changes in definitions in census categories over time. (Thus: the drop in the rural destitute from a bit above 16 per cent in the years 1805–20, to just over 3 per cent in 1855 is a reflection of changing census methods, not of changing social structure.) That is why Wohlin's avoiding the flotsam in the censuses and working with empirically verifiable social categories was so important. As long as he reaggregated the categories correctly, census by census, he

provided a meaningful statistical narrative. At points one may niggle at details, but fundamentally he got things right. Even skeptics should grant that by virtue of all this having been done by a single personality, whatever framework bias one may detect for, say, 1800, is there for 1900, so correction of the entire narrative (if that indeed is necessary) is readily accomplished—quite a different situation from dealing with a socio-economic device cobbled together by a series of committees.

85   Lars Magnusson, *An Economic History of Sweden* (London: Routledge, 2000), p. 8, citing the work of David Hannerberg.

86   See Wohlin, *Den Jordbruksidkande Befolkningen*, table A, p. 3. Wohlin did not trust the 1860 census, so he limited his table to 1850 (46.3 per cent agricultural population increase from the 1800 base) and then moves to 1870 (61.3 per cent). The year 1860 can be strictly interpolated (as a mean) at 53.8 per cent increase from the 1800 base, but that is probably a touch low because the Deprivation of the late 1860s probably reduced somewhat the 1870 figure.

87   The proposed annual rates are surveyed in Magnusson, *An Economic History of Sweden*, pp. 3–7. Three points: (1) the growth in crop production was quite uneven over time and may actually have declined 1820–50, with growth spikes at either end of the timeline, albeit for quite different reasons; (2) the big increases were in grain crops and in potatoes. The latter crop took hold much later in Sweden than it had in Ireland. Gustav Sundbärg estimated that potato cultivation increased from 6,000 hectares in 1800 to 136,000 hectares in 1860. (Sundbärg, *Betänkande*, table 21, p. 22). The production census for 1861 showed that slightly less than half of the potato crop was for human consumption. See Staff of the Institute, *National Income of Sweden, 1860–1930*, part 2, Appendix B, table 66, p. 46; (3) it is hard to know what to do with animal production figures, as they are very incomplete. The following are the numbers for the agricultural species for which there is information of some sort for 1805 and 1865:

		1805	1865
Work animals	Horses	395,000	428,000
	Oxen	216,000	283,000
Dairy/meat	Cows	820,000	1,186,000
	Heifers & steers	436,000	417,000

Source: Gustav Sundbärg, in Government of Sweden, *Emigrationsutredningen, Bilaga XIII, Allmänna Ekonomiska Data Rörande Sveriga* (Stockholm: KB, 1912), p. 46.

88   Janson (*The Background of Swedish Immigration*, pp. 49–51) chronicles the successive enclosure of a village in Skaraborgs län from an average of 53 separate pieces of land belonging to each villager in 1700 down to three of fewer parcels per farm after the enclosure in the mid-1830s.

89   The impression that small freeholders were generally economically conservative which, in Swedish historiography owes much to Eli Heckscher, has been fairly thoroughly discredited. Some were actively in favour of enclosure, some against, and no generalization is possible. See Svensson, "Peasants and Entrepreneurship," pp. 387–97 and 419–21.

90   Janson, *The Background of Swedish Immigration*, pp. 48–52; Magnusson, *An Economic History of Sweden*, pp. 15–17; Svensson, "Peasants and Entrepreneurship," pp. 401–02.

91   The classic *cri de coeur* about the injustices of the English enclosure proceedings was J. L. and Barbara Hammond, *The Village Labourer* (London: Longmans Green and Co., 1912). Although now seen as overwrought, it identifies clearly the potential points of abuse in the process. A fascinating Swedish enclosure chronicle is Gunnar Svensson, *Folket i Nasareths* (Väröbacka: Häralds, 1993). This deals with the suppression and relocation of two tiny hamlets in Halland and the moving of nine farms and their associated crofts under the 1827 act. The entire process took almost 20 years and caused a good deal of local enmity and, eventually, decay of the social fabric.

92   Government of Sweden, *Historisk Statistik för Sverige*, vol. 2, *Väderlek, Lantmäteri, Jordbruk, etc.* (Stockholm: Statistiska Centralbyrån, 1955), table D.4, pp. 16–17.

93   That quite elementary procedural point is emphasized because I have encountered studies that miss what Wohlin was showing. Either (1) they read the data entirely synchronically instead of longitudinally or (2) they converted the socio-economic categories for each year into a derived number (usually a percentage of that year's total) and then compared those derived numbers across time. This greatly understates the degree of social change because the total agrarian sector was growing markedly.

94   Table 3.4 is derived from Wohlin, *Den Jordbruksidkande Befolkningen*, table H, p. 26, and "Råtabeller," pp. 227–65 and notes, pp. 312–18, and *Jordstyckningen*, Tabellbilaga A, pp. 4–7, with the associated

commentary and table notes. Some relevant comments. First, table 3.4 makes the agricultural population seem somewhat better off than it really was, because Wohlin could not consistently disaggregate from the Swedish census the number of rural people who were totally broken physically or mentally. These he terms used-up, or wasting—in the sense similar to someone who wastes away from tuberculosis. *Faute de mieux*, he includes them with children under the age of 15 in an omnibus category of individuals who require more in economic cost than they produce in benefit. This is an accounting solution, but the hyper-poor are not fungible and certainly not in this way: a two-year old child at the family hearth and a spavined old worker are not in the same niche in the socio-economic world. Therefore, I have excluded that whole omnibus category from table 3.4, with a loss from view of an unknown number of the functionally destitute. Second, the "unspecified" landowner category must have been a nightmare to someone as rigorous as Wohlin. Recall that in table 3.3 (for 1800) there were roughly 4,500 self-managed nobility and gentry estates and also about 5,500 estates that were unspecified, meaning that they were distributed in some fashion as between nobility and gentry, commoner freeholders and holders of substantial tenancies. The census authorities changed their reporting from 1805 onwards, but not in a way that was helpful: "Unspecified"—a residual which Wohlin did not label in his tables and which I have here calculated—jumped suddenly to nearly 32,000 landed enterprises in 1805, which is 13.5 per cent of all self-managed landed holdings. The number drops consistently after 1810, down to 7,792 in 1860, when it represents 3.4 per cent of the database on landed holdings represented in table 3.4. One must feel some sympathy for Wohlin, for he was working with spongy census material. For example, he points out in his text that one cannot even infer a number for nobility-gentry estate self-operators from 1805–35 and that for 1840–55 the figure averages 5,220 nobles, a figure that he has had to derive indirectly. One almost hears his head hit the table in frustration. (*Den Jordbruksidkande Befolkningen*, pp. 11–12.) Thirdly, although not here presented, Wohlin has excellent cross-tabulations of his material by län.

95   Magnusson, *An Economic History of Sweden*, p. 27.

96   The above data show that in the first two-thirds of the nineteenth century all of the major non-owner strata increased nationally in number. However, that may be only the first wave of a series of effects that followed enclosure. In particular, it may be that the increase in torpare was a transitional effect and that when the full impact of enclosures worked themselves out, the torpare were forced down into the completely landless labour force. That is the hypothesis of Kalle Bäck and it is tentatively confirmed, at least in places with a high level of removal for enclosure and where the average acreage of the village was relatively low. The test area was 25 villages in Östergötland, which is taken as being a predictive locale. Kalle Bäck, "Lagaskifte och torpbebyggelsen i Östergötland, 1827–65," *Historisk Tidskrift*, vol. 108 (1988), pp. 321–39.

97   I am here adapting as metaphor the brilliant work on the Russian rural economy by Alexander V. Chayanov. See *The Theory of Peasant Economy*, a collection of translations of Chayanov's most important work, edited by Daniel Thorner, *et al.* (Chicago: Irwin, 1966).

98   Mokyr, *Why Ireland Starved*, table 2.6, p. 42.

Chapter Four

LEADING SECTORS: SWEDEN

ONE

"The general notion that the likelihood of migration is related to projected differences in economic well-being has been made operational in several recent econometric investigations." So wrote John Michael Quigley, of Harvard University and the National Bureau of Economic Research in 1972 in the *Quarterly Journal of Economics*.[1] He continues: "In the abstract, individual migration decisions are made by evaluating monetary differences in amenity relative to 'tastes' or to the 'psychic costs' of relocation."[2] This is a useful model for late nineteenth-century Europe, but is a non-disprovable theory. And, what was front-edge econometric history in 1972 is today close to being cast-iron orthodoxy. Concerning Ireland for the period 1850–1914, Quigley's formulation is convincing, just as it is for Sweden from 1870–1914 (Sweden being the focus of Quigley's own research). *If* one is limited to only one explanatory factor (phrased in however many variegated ways) behind the Great European Migration in the latter half of the nineteenth century, then projected differences in economic well-being wins the prize.

But, as far as Ireland is concerned, this nicely polished instrument from neo-classical economics does not seem to work very well before the Great Famine; nor for Sweden before the Great Deprivation. Although both Sweden and Ireland had more out-migration than is captured in official estimates, neither had anything approaching an appropriate response to the risk that individuals were exposed to (and, being sentient beings, full well knew they were exposed to) by remaining at home—at least if "appropriate" is measured by the same economic-monetary criteria that are employed to explain why they did indeed migrate in the late nineteenth century—the period in which most historians of the Great Migration choose to make their living.

Obviously, here we are dealing with matters of culture, but noting that it should be clear to readers that the word is contextually determined in the present study. It is, in many specific contexts, used the way that many economic historians do: whatever their formal brief, "culture" usually covers almost all non-economic inputs into decision making. Further, the term frequently implies "non-rational" means of thought and behaviour, with the standard of rationality being defined by what economic man would do. Clearly, I do not condemn this sort of irrational or non-rational behaviour; in my view, it often is to be admired. In other contexts, "culture" in the present study refers to the congeries of ideas, values and behaviours that define how people in a given society knit their lives together. These are "soft" matters, not amenable to empirical measurement, but no less real for that fact. Especially important in this soft world are ideational matters, some complex, others very straightforward. Religion is crucial here (and its formal advocate, theology, can be very complicated indeed), but so too are simple ideas such as who is boss in the family and what the proper role of each family member is. If, ultimately, I do not see the Great European Migration as fully explicable as an economic exercise, but rather view it equally as a cultural one, I am not gainsaying the reality of economic matters in the process. But economic motives operated differently in different eras; were always mediated by culture; were often trumped by aspects of soft culture that makes some decisions engaged by historical groups seem irrational; and finally, even in the late nineteenth century, when monetary calculations seem to explain most of the migration patterns, the increasing hegemony of economic motives was part of a cultural transformation. Thus, at times one employs "culture" to mean the sum total of soft and of economic strands in a given society, and therefore we can talk sensibly about Sweden and Ireland metamorphizing in the second half of the nineteenth century from intensely localized cultures into emigration-cultures. My overarching hope is to help to restore culture (widely interpreted) to the story of why so many people left Europe and, conversely, why so many did *not* leave.

TWO

First, to Sweden. Recall that in chapter two we cited Gustav Sundbärg's ingenious calculation that between 1801–50 net out-migration from Sweden to all destinations, both within Europe and extra-European, was a total of about 25,000 persons and that the gross out-migration total was 75,000. That, probably, is as close as anyone has been able to get in an era when records where absent. (And, probably, more accurate than were the early years of Swedish migration statistics, 1851–66.)

As far as adjudging the degree of out-migration as a coping response to the social and economic risk of living in Sweden in the first half of the nineteenth century, the most *mis*leading way of looking at the situation would be to do what is frequently done in historical studies of migration: compare total migration *over* a span of time with a population base enumerated at a *single* point in time. When this is done over a short span of time—say, comparing the population at the beginning of a specific calendar year with out-migration during that year—it usually is not a problem unless one is doing very precise demographic work, but longer spans of time can become distorting. What we would really like to compare is the total number of individuals who left Sweden, 1801–50—in Gustav Sundbärg's estimation, a sum total of gross out-migration of 75,000—and the total number of individuals who had at any time during the period 1801–50 lived in the Swedish socio-economic system. This is impossible to do with much precision in the present state of the evidence, but it is revealing to compare the average annual population of Sweden in that half-century, 1801–50, with the average annual level of out-migration. Specifically, the average annual population was roughly 2,806 million and the average annual number of out-migrants was 1,500—which is an impressively low level: 0.05 per cent. Indeed, in a society in which approximately 40 per cent of the population was under serious risk of economic deprivation from a single-year crop failure (deprivation not in abstract terms, but in terms of empty stomachs for many persons and small-farm bankruptcy for others), the number is astoundingly small. And, whatever parallax there may be in the Swedish data, the overall picture is clear.

Of course there is any amount of special pleading one can do to try to get back into synch with theoretical predictions of economic well-being as the main driver of emigration. For example, it is fair to note that economically able adults were the persons most likely to leave, so perhaps one should use their proportion of the population as the reference point. The Swedish population profile allows the derivation of the population in the 15–50 years-of-age group as follows:[3]

1801–25	50.3%
1826–50	49.7%

So, one could plead that the out-migration rate I am referring to should be doubled to 0.1 per cent. Let us momentarily grant that idea, while ignoring the fact that the only tight tally of individuals—that of Nils William Olsson and his associates—shows that from 1820–45 children under age 15 made up 10.1 per cent of migrants to the United States;[4] that there was an indeterminate, but roughly equal number of individuals over 50 years; and that from 1845 onwards the proportions of each increased markedly. Then, simply to indulge the denial of my main point, let us even permit the argumentative suggestion that half the population was female and also we shall accept the counterfactual assertion that they did not migrate so, really, emigration should only be calculated as a proportion of the male population in the 15–50 year age group. That would redouble to 0.2 per cent. This at a time when 40 per cent were at risk of deprivation. (In fact, the US sample shows that between 1820 and 1845 14.6 per cent of the out-migrants from Sweden were adult women,[5] and the proportion rose quickly thereafter.) So, even granting every argumentative exaggeration against the case we are here presenting, in the first half of the nineteenth century the Swedes stayed home with, if not enthusiasm, nearly unbending stoicism.[6]

The point where the pattern might seem to change is the second half of the 1840s. It appears to alter (at least if the US shipping lists are any indication) in the direction of increased family migration. And, certainly, the total outflow increased.

As discussed in chapter two, Gustav Sundbärg, using the same methods of calculation as for 1801–50, estimated the total (both to countries within Europe and outside) *net* out-migration from Sweden as 26,954 from 1851–60 and as 149,948 from 1861–70. Three problems arise from those figures—one is potentially correctable, one is difficult and one insurmountable: (1) the numbers, most recent experts agree, are too low, but (2) nevertheless they are rendered uselessly high for our purposes for 1861–70 because they include the flood years of 1867–70, which is beyond our present ambit. If the transoceanic data are representative, the out-migration from 1851–65 was only one-quarter of that for the whole period 1851–70.[7] And (3) for this period Sundbärg seems not to have had faith in the governmental data on in-migration and return migration, so he did not calculate gross out-migration figures—and those are the numbers that we need.[8] So, all that one can say with certainty is that Swedish out-migration increased markedly from 1845 to 1865, but that it still was not anything approaching a level commensurate with societal risk levels.[9]

THREE

Generally, it is not very profitable for an historical discussion to revolve around something that did *not* happen, and here we do not wish to do so any longer than is absolutely necessary. Nevertheless, one can point to circumstances in Swedish economic and political life that made out-migration difficult, at least as compared to the case of Ireland. For instance, land transport in Sweden was not very well developed in the first half of the nineteenth century, although rivers, lakes and canals were effective, especially the system between Stockholm and Göteborg. Railroads came late to Sweden. Topography was difficult. That said, most of the population lived within 200 km of salt-water ports that were open all—or almost all—year round. The bulk of these were small harbours that tied into the ocean-going network of the Baltic Sea on the east of Sweden or to Göteborg and to Danish ports on the western side. As early as the mid-1840s, a regular link between Göteborg and Liverpool operated (usually via a land link based at Hull), so that Swedish migrants to North America could piggyback on the economies of large-scale migration from the British Isles. British ports carried the bulk of transoceanic European migrants from the 1840s onwards, and by 1851 Liverpool was the leading emigration port for all of Europe.[10] Even for boats that made the run directly from Göteborg or Gävle to Montreal or to New York, the price ceiling was set by the competitive sailings from Liverpool.

Probably the most plausible candidate for an inhibitor of Swedish out-migration was the Swedish government. At the level of the central state, the doctrine that a nation's population numbers was the single greatest source of national power was not widely challenged until mid-nineteenth century. In the context of the massive and attenuating European wars of the late eighteenth and early nineteenth centuries, this was an intuitively satisfactory doctrine: big populations permitted big armies. At the domestic level, the view of a large population as being a Good Thing served the interests of the large land holders: human beings were still the most productive draught animals in Swedish agriculture. Hence, for these reasons, the governing classes were opposed to emigration and they made it difficult to leave—the difficulty being limited chiefly by their desire not to spend too much money in enforcing restrictions.

In our present world, where in most cases it is easier to migrate out of a given country than into another one, it is necessary to remember that until the middle one-third of the nineteenth century just the opposite held for most European jurisdictions. Specifically in the case of Swedish out-migrants, they required a formal passport to get out legally, but not one to enter most of their preferred destinations, particularly the United States. The Swedish laws were complicated because certain groups (such as skilled artisans, merchant seamen and men liable to military service) had special limitations.[11] Even for the average rural Swedish farm or farm-labouring family, the requirements were complicated and potentially humiliating. The following excerpts are from the reminiscences of a migrant who left Östergötland in 1849:

> In the winter between 1848–49 my father resolved to emigrate to America ... [He sold his property] ... The next move was to get a certificate of good character from the parish Rector, which was of utmost importance, as without one a person could not get a passport,

and consequently could not leave the Kingdom, but it was an undertaking that anyone would shrink from as the Rector was known to be a bitter opponent to [e]migration …

Nothing would do, however, but the Rector must issue the certificate which set forth the following points: "That the within named person having decided to remove from the parish is hereby certified that he was born [here insert date and year], that he was baptized according to the rites of the Evangelical Lutheran church. That he has been vaccinated and that he can read and write, that he has been confirmed in the church and has served his term in the militia, has been a good and law-abiding person heretofore, and has good and sufficient knowledge of the Christian religion according to the ritual of the Evangelical Lutheran church of this realm."

… The next move was to present the above to the Bailiff of the district, and get the following endorsement from him: "That the above-named person being to me personally known, this is to certify that he has paid his taxes for the previous year; he has no law suits pending in any of the courts in the kingdom, leaves no unpaid debts behind, and is a person of eminent and exalted respectability."

And then this most weighty document had to be presented to the Governor of the province in order to receive a passport from that august personage and to do this was a serious affair as a person heard nothing but jeers and insults from the time one entered the anteroom and gave his name and business to the liveried flunky, until one had safely got outside again of the executive mansion.[12]

Finally, the governor provided a Royal passport and the family could emigrate in peace.

Obviously, in such a localized system, the ease or difficulty of obtaining a passport could vary immensely. (And things were much simpler for short-term labourers to other European countries.) But notice the importance of obtaining the approval of the local parish priest who, in his combined role as civic official and spiritual leader, could be immensely difficult. Not only was he apt to articulate the civil establishment's view of the civically etiolating character of emigration, but this was also his last chance to land hard on those of whom he disapproved on religious grounds. When backed up by the local governor, this could be insurmountable: in the late 1850s, the governor of Västmanlands län, who was dead-set against Baptists and Mormons, refused three Mormons permission to migrate to the United States, apparently solely on grounds of his religious prejudice.[13]

Now, the last thing one should do is to see the civic inhibitions on emigration as an equivalent to the Berlin Wall. Most of those who wanted passports eventually received them and, in any case, Sweden's borders were extremely porous and slipping to the German states, Denmark, or the co-kingdom of Norway was not a breakout from behind an Iron Curtain. Moreover, from the early 1830s onwards, Sweden was under pressure from the example of the United Kingdom, Denmark and the German states to reduce its restrictions on out-migration. This pressure can in part be interpreted as a general European movement towards increasing the civil rights of citizens, but it became as much part of the tide of mid-nineteenth-century economic liberalism that trended towards free trade in goods, capital and labour. In the Swedish case, the entire business became enmeshed in the question of whether or not subdivision of small freeholds should be made easier (this being an alternative to more out-migration in the view of some). In any case, in 1860, the Swedish requirement for passports to leave the country was abolished. Restrictions continued for those with military obligations, and there still were departure forms and taxes, but these were now routine. After 1860, most control of emigration was for the protection of those who travelled, involving shipping regulations and supervision of emigration agents.[14]

Yet, if the restrictions on out-migration never were insuperable barriers and even if almost all of the restrictions disappeared in 1860, the long period of Swedish state inhibition of emigration was an important cultural marker. The desideratum of the preservation of state power via population power, the upper classes' need for a cheap and plentiful labour force, the instinctive willingness of the clergy of the state church to discourage emigration on both moral and social grounds, and the deference of the lower orders to the arcade of powers that towered above them—all these things formed an architecture of cultural hesitancy concerning emigration.

It is accurate to say that in the pre-Deprivation era, the cultural values of Swedish society, broadly considered, greatly reduced the proclivities of the population to emigrate. That is not a tautology—we are not saying that the Swedes did not out-migrate very much because the Swedes did not out-migrate very much. The society in general filtered information concerning emigration skeptically. There is no question that the Swedish population, at least from the 1830s onwards, was widely informed (if not always well informed) about the possibility of emigration to a New World, especially to the United States. The difference between the pre-Deprivation era and the last one-third of the nineteenth century is that in the 1840s to early 1860s, the golden glow of the New World propagandists was balanced by a spectrum of warnings that the new Eldorado well might be an unhappy place. (Nils Runeby's masterful 1969 volume is clearly demonstrative of a mid-nineteenth-century European skepticism toward America that has yet to be built sufficiently into the historiography of US immigration.)[15]

To get an idea of the informational conflict, consider the following reports that circulated in 1846. On the one hand, a letter written home from the United States described laconically the arrival in the USA of an emigrant ship. "This day the ship 'Wilhelmina' arrived from Gävle, carrying 118 passengers, of whom 7 adults and 21 children have died. One family lost five children."[16] News of that sort travels quickly, but so too does the opposite kind. The *Jönköpingsbladet* (26 May 1846), passed on another emigrant report: "A beggar girl from Kisa … is said to have described America in much more attractive colours than Joshua's returning spies described the Promised Land for the children of Israel. 'In America,' she is supposed to have said, 'the pigs go and eat themselves full of raisins and almonds, which everywhere grow wild, and when the pigs are thirsty, they drink from the ditches, where nothing but wine flows.'"[17]

If the actual emigration flows are any indication, before the Deprivation, the overwhelming bulk of the Swedish populace either distrusted the siren call from America, or at least discounted it enough that they did not consider emigration a normal part of their own society's menu of possibilities; after the Deprivation, just the opposite was true. I do not think that in either case we are observing anything close to economic rational choice theory in action. Instead, it is more realistic to posit that as far as information assessment and the projection of alternative futures were concerned, the default setting of the society radically changed as between the pre-Deprivation and post-Deprivation eras. This was a matter of cultural factors interacting with societal traumas that were independent of, or often superordinate to, everyday economic calculations.

FOUR

Here we will halt our attempt to explain directly a negative, the striking absence of large-scale Swedish out-migration when it would have made economic sense for hundreds of thousands of the populace to exit. Instead, we will focus on what indeed *did* happen, namely that certain types of people indeed chose to migrate well before the Deprivation. These people were heavily over-represented by individuals who were social deviants within Swedish society—in the non-pejorative sense of the term. That is: individuals who deviated markedly from the normal expectations of how an individual of a given station should spend his or her life. Another way of putting it is that the pre-Deprivation emigrants were strongly tinctured by persons who were in some sense countercultural.

That does not mean they were revolutionaries, simply that they did not fully buy into the mainstream culture. Their emigration was the culminating expression of that fact, but most certainly not its sole cause. A key characteristic of countercultural individuals or groups is that they are just as apt to be deeply conservative as they are to be sharply innovative. When countercultural cohorts leave a society, sometimes it is to find or establish a new world; other times to recreate an older, lost world, either real or imagined. These people were different and that difference was defined clearly and independently of the eventual emigration decision. The fact that it can be demonstrated that the pre-Deprivation emigrant stream was loaded towards countercultural groups in Swedish society works like a reflective lens. It confirms that the dominant culture embraced a heavy tilt against out-migration: if that were not the case, then "normals" and "deviants" should have left in equal proportions to their numbers in the general population. That inference is confirmed by positive evidence (data on what indeed did happen) rather than on assertions of negation (and of speculative postulates of why certain things did not happen), so we can work confidently with what otherwise would be whopping generalizations about what-society-believes, and we can also observe wide-scale changes in those beliefs as they effected migration patterns. And by focusing on those social deviants who so strongly influenced out-migration before the Great Deprivation, we can observe that they acted as a limited, but crucial series of *cultural punctures*. Interesting in themselves, these early emigrants are necessary of more than curious notice if we are to have any real understanding of why, after the Deprivation, the emigration pattern of Sweden flowed in kills and floods of humanity in the pattern that it did. When, in the later nineteenth century, the potentiality of out-migration was transformed from cultural deviation to cultural norm, it was along trace-lines that we will have seen already and noted.[18]

Although historians of Sweden do not use the term, the period 1810–73 can be characterized as the Penal Era in Swedish cultural history.[19] That is a term borrowed from Irish historiography. It is intended to highlight the fact that despite the popular impression that Sweden in those years found its way to enlightenment and toleration in a smooth and Whiggish fashion, the legislative, ecclesiastical and judicial choke-chain that enforced cultural conformity bit most harshly in the first two-thirds of the nineteenth century. That is because this was the only time in Sweden since the Reformation that a religious minority of any significant size arose that challenged religio-cultural orthodoxy. Early eighteenth-century Pietists had scared the establishment, but they had been no real challenge. In contrast, the congerie of nineteenth-century dissidents was at first quiet and almost furtive; but, as the nineteenth century progressed, it became clear they were both perduring and very good at complaining. And they were shrewd in their attachment to international allies. If, by 1873, the most aggravating portions of the Swedish penal code had been removed from the statute books, this removal was as much a monument to the dissidents being a troublesome lot as to Swedish culture in general becoming sweetly tolerant.

The Swedish penal code as it operated in the nineteenth century was sharply different from the Irish penal code as it functioned from, say, 1690 to 1829. The differences are worth noting at this point as they are relevant for understanding the early stages of both Swedish and Irish out-migration patterns.[20] The first, and most striking difference is one that Sweden shared with all of *ancien régime* Europe: namely, that the penal codes of Europe were inflicted on behalf of a majority of the population upon a minority. Ireland is the only place where a minority religion legislated a penal code against the religion of the majority of the population. Second, whereas the Irish code was mostly a matter of the Protestant Established Church disadvantaging Catholics, the Swedish code was primarily a case of the Protestant Established Church attempting to suppress other Protestant groups. There were not enough Roman Catholics in Sweden to worry about (although, of course, they were demonized), but in the later eighteenth and nineteenth centuries Protestant dissenters became another matter entirely. Third, the Swedish penal code was effective much later in time than was the Irish. The Irish code had mostly been erased by the 1790s, with the exception of the right of Catholics to sit in parliament (acquired in 1829), some minor impediments for the Catholic church on land trusts and similar matters—and the very big complaint that an Established Church still existed and was dependent upon several forms of public financing. The Church of Ireland (Anglican) was disestablished as of the beginning of the year 1871. Thereafter, religion in Ireland was a voluntary activity, with neither formal civic function nor direct state financial support.[21] Fourth, and most important: whereas the Irish code was much more venal and financially punitive than was the Swedish, it really did not go to the heart of the matter—namely, the suppression of individual conscience. By this I mean that the Irish code, after its first vitriolic spasm in the early eighteenth century, did not operate with the intent of converting the bulk of the Irish people to Protestantism. Instead, Catholics' property rights were sharply abridged, Catholics were excluded from most remunerative professions, and every effort was made to make the ecclesiastical administration of their faith difficult. However, the last thing anyone but a few zealots wanted was for the Irish Catholics to become adherents of the Established Church. That would have limited the transfer of pelf to the Anglican minority. The Swedish code, while much less nasty on the surface, was a spear thrust at the human soul. Or so its victims believed: for its intention was the suppression of religious beliefs not consonant with those of state Lutheranism.

Actually, there was good—or at least understandable—reason for the character of the Swedish code. It was medieval in mode, if not in immediate origin. The operational concept of citizenship was a denial of any hint of secularism. An individual's rights as a citizen were dependent upon his or her being part of the religious polity. In practical terms this was state church Lutheranism that, in liturgy, architecture and theology was notably "high," to borrow a term from the history of the Church of England. (To be clear: the Church of Sweden did not carry the word "Lutheran" in its official title, but it followed unabashedly the Augsburg Confession of 1530; and, though it rejected the Roman Catholic theology on the sacraments, its officiants were "priests" and the Lord's Supper was "Mass.") For most of the population, living in rural areas, any differentiation between civil and religious spheres was blurred at best since, at the start of the nineteenth century, topological definitions of the ecclesiastical parish and the civil parish in most cases were the same. The rector of each parish was a state functionary—it was a state church, after all—and was charged with assisting in the maintenance of law and order, in overseeing the education of the young, with performing all rituals surrounding birth (christening), marriage and death, and in keeping the vital records of the population. (The first broadly trustworthy census in Europe, compiled in the first half of the eighteenth century, was one of the great achievements of the clerical monitoring of the populace.) At its best, on the local level the everyday life of the farm and labourer-families was a melding of observations about life in the present world with a set of beliefs and values, most clearly articulated by the parish's Lutheran rector. It all fits.

This socio-religious web was not vulnerable to philosophic unbelief (Voltaire was not much discussed in byres), but it was highly vulnerable to hyper-belief. Specifically, any set of votive deviants who identified themselves with the "primitive church" of early Christian times and who devoutly held to the concept that what one owed to Caesar was sharply distinct from what one owed to God,[22] were trouble. This vulnerability to devout Christians who claimed to take their faith more seriously than did the function-aries of the state church was common to all the Lutheran state churches of Scandinavia and the Germanies and enthusiasts were viewed with the same distrust in the Lutheran lands as early Protestants had been viewed by the Catholic church. The form of hyper-religiosity that initially frightened the Swedish church establishment was Pietism which developed in the Germanies in the later seventeenth century and was distinguished by (1) lay persons holding meetings involving prayer, Bible reading and theological study in their homes and (2) by their insisting that they were not forming a separate church but were vivifying the official structure. Note that "Pietism" as a proper noun refers to those who insisted doggedly that they still were entirely within the Lutheran fold; "pietistic," the adjectival form, refers to a wider group—those who were keen on lay devotion, some of whom became separatists and who advocated cutting ties with the Established Church, others of whom did not. In its Swedish forms, Pietism was never very widespread.[23]

But it scared the authorities and in 1726 the *Konventikelplakat*—the Anti-Conven-ticle Act—was passed. That this penal measure was introduced during Sweden's so-called "Age of Freedom," 1718–72, is both irony and commentary. The statute is worth attention because in the nineteenth century it had considerable impact upon pietistic laity who were not part of Pietism in the strict sense. "Conventicles"—here meaning private meetings conducted by the lay people for private Bible study, the reading of Luther, singing of hymns and (potentially) the celebration of one or more of the sacraments—were banned. The leaders of the conventicles—which were modelled on the "house churches" of the early Christian church—were subject upon first conviction to a fine of 50 riksdalar. The same fine held for a second conviction and those who could not, or would not pay the fine were imprisoned on bread and water for two weeks. A third conviction resulted in banishment from Sweden. Penalties also were prescribed for participants in the services, but these were limited to those who took part in a service of Communion in which no Lutheran priest officiated. In practice, the Anti-Conventicle Act was moderated by the necessity (introduced by an act of 1762) of offences being prosecuted by the secular judicial authorities and in most cases the Controller of the Administration of Justice preferred to look the other way, providing the lay enthusiasts kept their heads down and did not publicly challenge the Lutheran rector.[24]

By their very nature, covert movements usually do not leave behind much in the way of written records and often one is reduced to documents produced by their state prosecutors. That granted, it does not appear that the penal measures were very significant until the early nineteenth century, when conventicles came above ground (became brazen, the state clergy claimed) and began to challenge directly the Lutheran establishment. That is when the real penal era started.

Nevertheless, a snapshot of the situation in the relatively quiet era in the middle of the eighteenth century is valuable, because it indicates that the Anti-Conventicle Act was not just an attempt at limiting certain fugitive religious practices but, more importantly, part of the control of the definition of citizenship. The Anti-Conventicle Act was embedded in the following practices and beliefs (some of which it explicitly repeated): that a child must be baptized, preferably soon after birth, by a cleric of the state church; a person who was not baptized was not legitimate and had limited rights of inheritance and of civic participation; adults were required to attend the state church at reasonable intervals; baptized children were to be instructed catechetically; from 1749 onwards the local priest was charged with conducting an annual interrogation of each household, paying particular attention to whether or not the children were being taught the Lutheran catechism (from this practice came the *husförhörslängd*, household catechetical registers that are the basis of the eighteenth-century Swedish censuses); confirmation (after 1810 a separate ritual) and first communion were to take place about age 15 (the age when adulthood began); only those who had taken first communion were eligible for civic benefits, ranging from access to parish poor relief to the right to hold public office and to enter the professions; to be legally married, one had to be joined to one's spouse by a state priest and this ritual was open only to those who had been baptized and confirmed in the state church; if a couple was not married by the state church, rights of inheritance upon spousal death were abrogated and any children of the marriage were illegitimate; burial services could only be carried out by a Lutheran rector; and the state church was supported in part by local taxation on the entire community.

The remarkable characteristic of all this is that it was unremarkable. Yes, it actually defined who was a person and who was an unperson. Yes, records on the beliefs of everyone in the population were kept in a Stalinist-like fashion (remember: national censuses, despite their statistical beauty, began in an attempt by the respective state to define and control its population). And, yes, present-day citizens of most western nations would chafe under similar restrictions. Yet, for the overwhelming mass of the Swedish people, the penal practices were not only natural, but necessary. After all, the basic Ecclesiastical Law of 1686 made absolutely clear that to be Swedish was to be Lutheran and that was that. It really did not require comment.[25]

Earlier I suggested that the penal era in Swedish history did not begin until the early nineteenth century and that it lasted roughly two-thirds of a century before tapering into mere inconvenience for its victims. This is not to deny that a form of penal code existed from the date of the Ecclesiastical Law of 1686. However, to have an effective penal era, one has to have someone to penalize, and the necessary target groups did not exist in numbers sufficient to produce the binary dialectic of state-v.-subversives as a national phenomenon until after 1800. Or so it appears: the matter is doubly messy and has not attracted many recent historians. One aspect of the problem is that the dissenting religious groups that begin to pop up after the turn of the century were highly localized, varied greatly by doctrinal shading, evolved in staccato fits and starts, and produced little in the way of internal institutional records—quite the opposite of the Swedish Established Church. They are best referred to under the term *Läsare* (plural or male singular), meaning Readers. The reference is to their core activity—reading the Bible and sometimes the works of the major Protestant theologians, especially Martin Luther, and discussing, praying and worrying the text in house meeting.[26] The complexity here is that the Readers filled a spectrum of belief running from an almost Romantic attachment to a golden age of truly pure Lutheranism which (if it ever existed) had disappeared by the end of the Napoleonic wars, all the way to extreme religious dissenters who were willing to found alternative denominations in opposition to the state church (in later parlance, these became the Free Churches). A very complex, very hard-to-document phenomenon.

The second, related messiness concerning the Readers is that most of the discrimination they faced was local, was embedded in community social sanctions, and when they were formally prosecuted it was in a very uneven fashion. An extraordinarily adept unwrapping of the complexities of the matter in one locale is Allan Sandewall's study of Readers in upper Norrland in the first half of the nineteenth century.[27] There, the separate vectors of emotion-filled revivalism and of acute liturgical conservatism combined in an unpredictable way to yield strong separatism in some parishes; all of which was made even less predictable by the interaction of hardline local Lutheran clergy and local law enforcement officers with their objects of attack, the Readers; and the countervailing attempts by national judicial authorities to calm everyone down and avoid court cases. Here is the background. Upper Norrland was the home of several revivalist lay-men and -women teachers: emotional, charismatic, but initially willing to stay just-barely within the state church. The unlikely exogenous event that set the north alight was the introduction nationally of a three-fold set of church reforms that affected everyone who ever sat in a pew. Between 1810 and 1819 the Lutheran church replaced three late-seventeenth-century standards of the faith—the Catechetical Handbook, the Order of Divine Service and the Church Hymnal. The revised Hymnal, introduced in 1819 was widely disliked, not just in Norrland but throughout Sweden, and it took decades before it was fully accepted; still, it was a minor matter. The new Catechism of 1810 tended towards Arianism and unsettled Readers, some of whom viewed it as heretical. But the deeper problem was the new Order of Divine Service, introduced in 1811. The intensely conservative nature of many of the Readers who eventually were labelled as being "radicals" is that they were highly upset to lose the old Lutheran services as they had been defined in 1693. And, surprisingly, the service they initially focused upon was not Holy Communion, but baptism. This was because the Sign of the Cross was not used in the new service, nor was the devil-and-all-his-pomp exorcized. Some Readers took to baptizing infants and young children within their faith-communities according to the 1693 book and refusing to let the Lutheran rector near. This was on the grounds that unless exactly the right words were said, as in the 1693 form, baptism was null and void and thereby the child's soul was endangered. During the 1820s, the liturgical revolt resulted in 17 recorded cases in upper Norrland of charges being brought by the judicial authorities, not a great number.

However, more frequent was a slightly bizarre Battle of the Duelling Re-Baptizers, fought out in isolated parishes. In this contest, Readers re-baptized, according to the form of the 1693 service book, children who had been baptized by the state clergy in the form of the new service book. And, Lutheran clergy, with the sheriff and his constables as enforcement officers, took to entering homes and forcibly re-baptizing children and infants whom the Readers had already dedicated using the 1693 ritual. Understandably, the central judicial authorities wished to avoid becoming involved in this unseemly business and modified the legal statutes so as to make prosecution in the civil courts of the Readers difficult.[28]

The next stage was harder for the civil authorities to ignore: after decades of tension with the Established Church, several conventicles of Readers separated from the state church. The key date was 1848 and the key ritual at issue now was Holy Communion, although the other services still were important points of dispute. Crucially, when these Norrland "radicals" took to operating as congregations separate from the state church, and in direct competition with it, they used the old Hymnal of 1695 and the Order of Divine Service of 1693, and they conducted the Communion service. The majority of Readers in upper Norrland stayed uneasily within the church, but in the 1850s, between one and two thousand Readers in Norrland had separated from the Established Church. This is not a large number, but represented too big a set of challenges to the church for the civil authorities to ignore. The Anti-Conventicle Act was used against the separatists, as well as new penal measures introduced in the 1850s (more of those later).[29]

Amongst the array of contrarieties and paradoxes that surround the religious upwelling of the nineteenth century was the surprisingly long leash given by the Swedish authorities to the British Wesleyan Methodist missionary, George Scott. In 1817, at age 23, Scott had been admitted to the board of Methodist preachers in London and in 1830 was challenged by the head of the English Wesleyans to become a missionary in Sweden. Why would the Swedish authorities allow a foreign proselytizer to operate in the country—especially given the history of Methodism in the British Isles, where it had started out as a ginger movement within the Church of England, but had evolved into a separate denomination with its own form of the sacraments? Because, indeed, he was foreign. Under an act of 1781, immigrants from foreign countries who were skilled in trades and belonged to a Christian denomination (excluding Roman Catholicism) were allowed to set up their own congregations.[30] Thus, George Scott came to Sweden as chaplain to a group of tradesmen employed in a Stockholm manufactory. His official title was "Pastor of the English Congregation, Stockholm." Scott picked up Swedish quickly and within a year was preaching to crowds of the locals. Scott combined a revivalist's energy with a strong social sense. He, as much as anyone indigenous, was the founder of the Swedish temperance movement. This probably explains why in 1837 he was granted permission to use monies donated by English Methodists to build a large chapel in Stockholm. Scott himself was a paradox. He had an aggressive personality and embodied the Methodist principle of the priesthood-of-all-believers. Yet, he was not in sympathy with those Readers who wished to set up their own congregations outside the Lutheran establishment and, indeed, his most able disciple, Carl Olov Rosenius, became the midcentury leader of a movement to energize and reform the state church from within. Nevertheless, Scott became the bête noir of rival Stockholm clergy of the Established Church and something of a whipping boy in the public press. During a fund-raising trip to the USA in 1841 he made some disparaging remarks about religious and social conditions in Sweden and thus stepped into trouble: when he returned to Sweden he was met with death threats. During the Lenten season of 1842 his chapel was attacked by a mob during Sunday service and he barely escaped with his life. He was forced back to England, but he left behind a wide band of influential figures (both within and outside the state church) and, significantly, several strands of ties to English-language religious leaders who showed in their own work that it was possible to have an effective Protestant church outside of state religion.[31]

In mentioning the upper Norrland and the Stockholm religious devotes,[32] I am in part using them as synecdoches. Undeniably, the Reader movement and related efforts were intensely local: the congregations were self-formed and autochthonous. Yet, by the 1840s there was no province in which the Readers were not present.[33] That is explicable in minor part by many of the lay preachers becoming peripatetic and encouraging local faith groups to coalesce, but in larger part it is the thousand-candles phenomenon: at some point it becomes clear that a myriad of local signals forms a national pattern.

This national pattern had three institutional impacts upon the Swedish religious structure, broadly considered. First, some phenomena, such as the temperance movement[34] and the Homeland Evangelical Mission Society founded in 1856 to vivify the church,[35] bridged the Readers and the Established Church. However, secondly, as the Readers became more and more self-confident during the 1840s, one wing developed into the Free Church Movement (*Frikykorörelsen*) that pressed directly for a reduction of the monopoly sphere of the Established Church and implicitly for a redefinition of both church and state, no small matter.[36] Bible Readers who took seriously the affirmation of St Paul—"For our homeland is in heaven" (Philippians 3:20)—thrust a sword at the entire Lutheran-State concordat. Effectively they were saying that either they, as followers of God's word, could not be Swedish in their deepest loyalty (for God's heaven, not any earthly land was where their citizenship lay) or, that they were indeed true Swedes, but that the Swedish Established Church was not really a legitimate institution, since the Almighty's kingdom never was on this earth. Not a subtle argument: but one that goes all the way back to the uneasiness about the earliest covenant cut between the Christian church and a state—that between the Emperor Constantine and the Christian bishops of the Western Church in the fourth century.

Thus, thirdly, as the more animated Readers pressed for greater religious freedom, the traditional wing of the Lutheran establishment fought back with greater enforcement of existing penal legislation and with new measures. (All this was complicated by mild reformers within the state church seeking for measures that would reduce the church's openness to state interference in matters that were purely pastoral or theological.) Much of the nastiness happened at the local level, where priests again began using the local sheriff for forced baptisms, and now increasingly refused to proclaim the banns of marriage for persons who had not been taking Communion according to the full

Lutheran rite. More pointedly aimed at leaders of the Readers' congregations was a decision in some areas to invoke a portion of the Anti-Conventicle Act that long had lain disused—the Profanation Clause (*Gäckeriparagrafen*) of the 1726 act. This treated as a punishable action the reading of scriptures, preaching and engaging in church-like liturgical acts as being a direct profaning of the holy sacraments as defined by the Lutheran church.[37]

With the benefit of hindsight, it is clear that from the year 1848 onwards the suppression of the Readers was impossible. In that year the Readers in Norrland, who had been arch-conservative in their ecclesiolatry, broke with the state church. And, crucially, in that same year myriad scattered Readers began to crystallize formally into the Baptist church which was anything but conservative in churchmanship. In September 1848 a Danish pastor, acting on behalf of Baptist congregations in Hamburg formed in the province of Halland the first Baptist congregation in Sweden. The indigenous Swedish leadership was taken up by Fredrik Olaus Nilsson, a Halland native who had travelled to the United States as a young man and been influenced by American Methodists and who, in 1849, was ordained a Baptist minister in Hamburg. This introduction of the formal Baptist church acted as a reagent: those Readers who were already inclined towards separation from state Lutheranism were rapidly precipitated into declaring themselves to be Baptists.[38]

The Baptists were serious trouble for the state church. They articulated a theology based on the responsibility of each individual before the Almighty, thus bypassing the state church and its mediation of divine grace through the sacraments. Indeed, the Baptists had no sacraments in the sense that they existed in the medieval Christian tradition. Each ritual—including their distinctive practice of adult baptism—was considered a testimony to a spiritual state, but not in any way a conduit of grace. Unlike the hierarchical state church, the Baptists' loose (and often argumentative) congrega-tional form was ideal for adaptation to the conditions of each locality. And, unlike most of the early Readers, the Baptists refused to truckle in any way to the state church. They challenged the church and became the cutting edge of the Free Church movement. In the 1850s, the Swedish Baptists developed strong ties with the Baptist churches in the United States. This gave them leverage that the early Readers never possessed, and it associated the Baptists with republicanism and extreme (for the times) political democracy.

The authorities of the state church quickly recognized the problem, but were unresolved as to whether to go hard or soft on these religious dissidents—and as a result followed both courses inefficiently. The early experience of F. O. Nilsson is illustrative of the hard line. Complaints lodged against him by a Lutheran rector in the diocese of Göteborg brought him to public notice and on New Year's Day, 1850, a mob broke up a service he was leading and beat him up quite badly. He was turned over to the local sheriff who held him in an unheated gaol cell for seven days. Then, at Jönköping later in the year, he was charged with a thought-crime: of holding doctrines contrary to the "true evangelical faith," of the Lutheran church. By his own words before the court, he clearly was guilty and he was sentenced to banishment from Sweden. (Moderate banishment, actually, as his property was left intact and his right of inheritance not abrogated.) This case went all the way to the supreme court and to a plea for royal clemency and then to banishment. Nilsson was dignified, refused to recant his beliefs and thus became a martyr, albeit not at mortal cost. (In 1860 Charles XV, not long on the throne, pardoned him.)[39]

In a similar way, the prosecution of Readers-turned-Baptists in the province of Dalarna in 1852 illustrates the danger of blow-back if local lay leaders were handled with inept harshness. As background, one should note that three environs were naturals for the Baptist movement in the 1850s: (1) Stockholm, by virtue of its relatively large population; (2) those seacoast areas of southern Sweden that were most in contact with foreign influences; and (3) certain inland areas that had traditions of local cultural independence, especially Småland, Närke (Örebro län) and Dalarna. It is not stereotyping to note that Dalarna was associated with the most viscerally democratic and contumacious populace in the country, at least since the era of Gustav Vasa. The nineteenth-century Dalarna economy was characterized by a highly articulated craft system, mining, and by a recalcitrance in the face of the enclosure laws. Nevertheless, by midcentury, both in agrarian and in mining districts, the customary rights of the small farmers and labourers were being eroded by a series of state enactments that tilted the formal legal system against the poor and middling.[40] Thus, the province was a natural hotbed for Readers and in the area around Lake Siljan an especially emotional form of lay piety had developed—the "Orsa-Läseriets"—and this ran directly into the unbending disciplinary propensity of the long-serving Lutheran priest, Olof Ulrik Arborelius, who held the Orsa benefice from 1831–68.[41] The first fully separate congregation in Orsa was formed in 1852 and then the local friction between state church and Readers passed beyond mere unpleasantness. A prosecution of two of the separatist Readers was instituted and they were fined, with the alternative that, should they not pay, one was to serve 23 days on bread and water and the other, more obdurate, 28 days. Learning of this in Stockholm, the Baptist leader Per Palmqvist wrote, "How long will this carry on? God help us!"[42] Such a heavy-handed approach only stiffened the resolve of the locals. The next year, 73 prosecutions were brought under the terms of the Profanation Clause of the Anti-Conventicle Act and 66 were convicted: they were given the choice of paying a fine of 20 riksdalar or 16 days gaol-time.[43] In 1853, more than 100 separatists (read: Baptists) were convicted for celebrating Holy Communion outside the confines of the parish church and one of their leaders was fined 100 riksdalar.[44] Again, in 1855, a prosecution was instituted and this time the guilty were put on bread and water and required publicly to acknowledge that they accepted the "true faith" of the Fatherland.[45] One could go on: the sum total of the efforts at pressuring the Dalarna religious dissidents was to weld them into a band of implacable opponents of the Swedish state-and-church covenant.

Manifestly, on the matter of religious freedom, something was occurring in the mid-nineteenth century that runs counter to the usual gloss on Swedish legal-political history: that in the first two-thirds of the century, the kingdom became gradually and ineluctably more liberal. In many ways it is true that from the inauguration of the constitutional monarchy with the Bernadotte hegemony in 1809, Sweden followed other European countries in freeing landed property from ancient restraints; it opened itself to more foreign trade and investment; granted women limited property rights (from 1858, single, but not married women, could hold property as a corporation-sole); eased restraints on Jews; erased most passport-to-emigrate requirements in 1860, and in 1867 replaced the old Four Estates with a bicameral parliament. And, conventionally, the repeal of the Anti-Conventicle Act in 1858 (effective in 1860) is treated as a major step towards the establishment of freedom of conscience. Indeed, the year 1958 was celebrated as the centenary of the beginning of the era of religious freedom.

Wrong. Such a celebration missed both the context of religious legislation in the 1850s and the redefinition, rather than the abolition, of the religious penal code. Allan Sandewall in 1957 poured scorn on this particular celebration by pointing out that the 1858 repeal of the Anti-Conventicle Act was preceded in 1855 by a new Sacramental Law that actually sharpened penal definitions. In effect, it was a prophylactic against repeal. Its most pointed section clarified the Profanation Paragraph of the Anti-Conventicle Act and raised the fines to 300 riksdalar for celebrants of the Lord's Supper and 50 riksdalar for communicants. This led to an increased legal campaign against separatists—mostly Baptists—which lasted until repeal of this new statute in 1864.[46] Coincident with this newly energized penal activity, the forced baptism of children—now mostly the children of Baptists who rejected infant baptism as superstitious—increased. Sandewall found that this activity, which depended upon the local law enforcement authorities cooperating with the church, quietly ceased in the north in the mid-1860s;[47] but that it continued sporadically elsewhere into the 1880s.[48]

Granted, the disappearance of the 1726 Anti-Conventicle Act in 1860 was a step toward religious toleration, but it was grudgingly granted. In the same year, 1860, the First Dissenter Act was decreed. Under it, a group of non-Lutheran Christians could apply for royal approval as a licit denomination. (No Catholics or Mormons needed apply, however.)[49] And individuals could apply for permission not to be Lutherans. In that case, before they were granted this permission by their local Lutheran priest, they were to be read a formal final exhortation to turn away from their apostasy. Not many took this dubious privilege and in 1873 the Second Dissenter Act dropped the requirement.[50] More importantly, the 1873 act rescued Baptists and other Free Church adherents from having their children defined as illegitimate: marriage ceremonies no longer required a Lutheran baptismal certificate as a prerequisite for marriage or that a state church priest officiate.[51]

There can be no tally sheet of the impact of the Swedish penal code upon everyday people in the first two-thirds of the nineteenth century. Most of its effects were local and unrecorded. As intended by its framers, the code induced everyday people to do things that they really did not wish to do—such as have their children baptized or receive first communion according to the form of the state church—for the prudential reason that a child's legitimacy and thus inheritance rights were thereby preserved; and it inhibited them from doing things they really wished to do—such as attend local groups that studied industriously the Bible and religious literature, sang psalms joyously and prayed intensely. Thought control always is beyond quantitative assessment. Even most of the formal enforcement—Lutheran priests and local sheriffs operating in small hamlets in the back of beyond—was neither recorded nor memorialized by the operatives or the victims. Recorded formal prosecutions were few in relation to the ubiquity of the Reader phenomenon, but that slenderness can be read as an index of the success of the code in making the Croppies lie down (to use an Irish analogy), as much as an indication of leniency. Only the Baptists completed an accounting of what the penal code has cost them: up to 1873 it was 28,000 Swedish crowns (they converted the fines into new money equivalent); a total of 98 years and 8 months prison-time for adherents; and ten believers deported from Sweden.[52] Not a huge total, but memorable.

(To complete the overview of the Swedish penal laws as they existed in softer form up to 1914, the following are the main facts. Under the 1873 Second Dissenter Act, a person over 18 years of age could formally withdraw from the Lutheran church and do so without a humiliating lecture on apostasy. If this right were not invoked, every adult citizen was automatically a member of the state church. A Protestant religious denomination could ask for sanction-of-legitimacy from the state. However, this so ran against the grain of the Free Church tradition that by 1910 only the Methodists and the Catholic Apostolic Church (the "Irvingites," not to be confused with the Roman Catholic church) had requested and received certification by the state. Civil marriage (that is, non-religious unions) became available in 1908. In 1910, tithes for the state church were abolished, but state funds still were paid to the Lutheran establishment. To take 1910 as a summary point, at that time the two main Free Church denominations were the Baptists (c. 53,000 members) and the Methodists (c. 17,500). The remainder of the twentieth century saw a gradual diminishing of the position of the state church. On 1 January 2000, the Lutheran church was disestablished, bringing to Sweden the degree of religious freedom achieved in Ireland on 1 January 1871).[53]

FIVE

H ere, let me be clear. In the context of examining the tie between the early Swedish emigration movement and cultural dissidents, I am not saying that a tranche of Readers and of the more formal Free Church adherents eventually left Sweden simply because the penal era made them thoroughly and righteously pissed off. Indeed it did, but there was more to the transaction than the dissidents reacting mechanically to the equivalent of a wad of parking tickets issued by the thought police.

The key is that *becoming a Reader was to enter a counterculture characterized by inner-migration.* For all Readers, taking over the study, and thus the definition, of some part of one's religious life was to move in some degree away from official Swedish culture. Most Readers probably remained uneasily within the state church (no definitive tally is possible), but the logic of the Readers' position led many to become full-bore independents. With the rejection of the hierarchical ecclesiastical structure of the Lutheran state church, the next stage was virtually inevitable: a severe questioning of the necessity and justice of the Swedish social hierarchy. It is hardly accidental that the Readers generally and the separatists especially, were fascinated with the reports they received from the USA, of a land that allegedly had an open social structure and was governed by a form of democracy. And, in a nice closing of the circle, it was believed that the crowning virtue of that far New World was complete religious freedom. The canonical date for the initial departure of what, in the late 1860s became the Great Swedish Migration, is 1845. In that year, Peter Cassel, a freehold farmer from Kisu in Östergötland led a group of 21 persons to settle in Jefferson County in what is now Iowa.[54] This was not a primarily religious migration, although the group was inclined toward Readerism. Cassel himself converted to Methodism after four years in North America and his letters home (designed to be read as public documents) praised American religious freedom, temperance and social equality.[55]

A truly religious, if somewhat exotic, migration was that of the "Eric Janssonists," which began in 1846. Jansson was a farmer's son from north of Uppsala who in his youth had a series of ecstatic visions that turned him into a prophet. His revelation—especially the liberating view that faith in Jesus Christ not only freed a person from past sins, but precluded future actions being sinful—attracted a following in Hälsingland, in the farther portions of Norrland and in parts of Dalarna. He spent a good deal of time in the early 1840s hiding from prosecution. In the summer of 1846, a well-executed illegal withdrawal of approximately 1,000 of his followers to the Illinois prairie was effected. There a communitarian utopian community was created, named Bishop Hill. By the time of the last migrants in 1854, roughly 1,500 persons had been part of the Janssonist exit. The Prophet himself was murdered in 1850, and the colony slowly crumbled, but not before its members had flooded Swedish newspapers and the elders among the Readers with American news.[56] A further, somewhat quixotic, group migration of the faithful was that led by Fredrik Gabriel Hedberg. A Finnish Lutheran priest, he energized a wide segment of northern Lutherans who wanted to keep the old (pre-1810) service books and hymnals. He favoured separatism, but still was loyal to Luther's teaching, which meant that his followers were prosecuted under the Anti-Conventicle Law for being too adherent to what they believed was true Lutheranism. In the summer of 1850 a group of about 100 sailed from Gävle, although Hedberg stayed home. The emigrants settled in Goodhue and Kandiyohi Counties in what would soon be Minnesota. There, in the later nineteenth century, among larger numbers of Swedish Baptists and Lutherans, they stayed apart, preserving in increasingly thin and reedy voices the late seventeenth-century Swedish Lutheran rituals.[57]

The migration of self-selected, tightly boundaried religious sects was the dominant feature of the later 1840s, but in the next decade a looser form of "group migration" most often dominated.[58] Co-religionists from several different locales would intermix with their neighbours from another sect or from the state church and become a temporary cohort moving towards a port city. Six, ten, a dozen of these gaggles would be aggregated by a shipping agent or by a harbour master and they would begin their long journey: either they sailed directly from one of the big Swedish ports to North America, or they went by smaller vessels to Hull in England, then by land to Liverpool and then to either Quebec City or Montreal or to a northern US port. By the end of the 1850s, the stream of out-migrants had become steady and predictable enough for families to migrate on their own without requiring a moveable community for security and support. That summary of course is schematic, but the undeniable point is that before the Great Deprivation, most Swedish migration was in family groups. The large scale migration of men and women on their own was in the future.

In the mid-1850s, an English traveller reported a conversation with a man near Karlskrona. The man said that hundreds of emigrants had gone from his home village. He explained: "It is the cursed Readers ... They turn everyone upside down."[59] If one uses "Readers" in the inclusive sense to comprehend both separatists and those Lutherans who were restive but remained formally in the state church,[60] then the sector of the Swedish population most susceptible to the "American fever" undoubtedly was the Readers.

Among the Readers, in the 1850s the Baptists were not just hosts of the fever, but the primary vectors of its spread. This occurred largely because of their international ties. Some of the leaders of the Baptist movement in the northern USA saw the position of the Readers in Sweden, especially the separatists, as a double opportunity: to provide a just refuge for those who suffered for the Gospel, and in so doing, to augment their own numbers in North America.

The pivotal link to the New World was Anders Wiberg, a storm of energy and in some ways a piece of ideological blotting paper: he seems to have been in communication with every major strand of the Reader movement, including those who stayed within the church. Wiberg, born in Norrland, was influenced by the Methodist pioneer George Scott and by C. O. Rosenius. Adopting at first their opposition to separatism, Wiberg was priested in the state church in 1843 and served a parish in Hälsingland, where he dealt on peaceable terms with local Eric Janssonists. He was active in the temperance field and he was also in correspondence with F. G. Hedberg. In the autumn of 1849, Wiberg left his benefice and became an itinerant preacher of separatist views, but was not yet possessed of tight formulations for an alternative to the state church. That changed under the influence of exiled Baptists in Denmark and in July 1852 Wiberg was baptized by the banished F. O. Nilsson. He then sailed to the USA and did a whirlwind job of promotion and fund-raising among northern American Baptists for their beleaguered brethren in Sweden. Wiberg learned English quickly and could tell colourful stories well. The American Baptist Publication Society employed him in the US as a proselytiser and then as a translator. The Americans were willing to bankroll Wiberg as a colporteur back in Sweden, officially as a representative of the American Baptist Publication Society as "Superintendent of Colportage in Sweden." The US Baptists also underwrote the printing of tracts and hymns for Swedish distribution and, almost incidentally, two argumentative books by Wiberg—the first of which, when it arrived in Dalarna in 1854, set off the initial major public baptism ceremony in that province, in Orsa parish.[61] Anders Wiberg arrived back in Sweden in 1855 and, until he returned to the USA in 1863 (for more fund-raising), somewhere in the vicinity of 800 to 1,000 persons per year formally converted to being Baptists—a significant number because the Baptists required a high degree of commitment, involving personal conversion, scrutiny by elders, public baptism and an ascetic lifestyle. Wiberg was assisted by scores of volunteers, mostly drawn from the ranks of Readers, and American money allowed the movement to pay the expenses of several local evangelists, and to found in 1856 a newspaper, *Evangelisten*, designed to put the Free Church case before the broader audience of Readers.[62] All this occurred against the backdrop of a national propaganda battle being fought, mostly in newspapers, about emigration. Readers and political radicals and some commercial interests promoted a rosy view of the USA. Anders Wiberg wrote to the Readers in Orsa, province of Dalarna, that he believed it would be a very good thing, and pleasing unto the Almighty, if the largest portion of Dalarna's population emigrated to the United States.[63] In contrast, many civil and most state church authorities viewed emigration as a way-station to Gomorrah.[64]

A moment ago, I mentioned that the state church of Sweden was clumsy in its prosecution of the religious separatists—this has been demonstrated adequately, I hope—and also that when it took the soft route it had the wrong touch. That second characterization is illustrated by the Kristianstad Tract Society. This was the product of concerned and conscientious Lutheran clergymen in Skåne, including the distinguished liberal, T. N. Hasselquist—later one of the founders of the Augustana Synod of the Lutheran churches in the USA. They began meeting in the late 1840s to discuss reform within the church establishment and ways to provide something that would satisfy the Readers and keep them within the state religious orbit. In 1855 this took the form of a tract society that published material and paid colporteurs to work in southern Sweden. Skåne was a sensible place to start, because it was especially permeable to foreign religious influences, by simple virtue of its coastline. From the early 1850s onwards, American influences had become prevalent and, not surprisingly, the Baptist movement took hold swiftly. The trouble with the Kristianstad Tract Society was that by appealing to the Readers in general, it inadvertently acted as a sounding board for some of the very same views that produced separatism. The Jane Austen Moment, the one that in a single incident illustrates that seducing the Readers was as difficult as was persecuting them, occurred in 1858: two colporteurs appointed by the society converted themselves to being Baptists and started teaching that faith.[65]

Among those attracted by the New World sheen of the Baptists, it is impossible to determine to what degree the lustre of America as a place of religious freedom was mixed with the concept of America as a place of economic opportunity. And, to approach that question and to continue to deal with Skåne, the remarkable figure of Hans Mattson appears: destined to be an almost honest migration promoter who at one time had nearly half the settleable land of the state of Minnesota on offer. He was born into a prosperous freeholder family (his parental household had 40–50 persons in it) in Omnestad parish, near Kristianstad. He was very well educated, partly in local schools, partly by tutors, including T. N. Hasselquist, who would have given him a more-than-rudimentary religious education. After Latin school in Kristianstad, young Mattson had entered the military as an artillery cadet with the plan of joining some northern army in the Schleswig-Holstein matter. Peace having been concluded, however, Mattson realized that there was little use for his talents and in the spring of 1851, he shipped to the USA. This was a young Swede-on-the-make. There is no hint that he had any religious ideals except those he kept with his mess kit, and he was after adventure and money. Full stop. Still, notice that as a preparation for his building a migrant-empire in the New World, in the spring of 1853 he converted to the Baptist faith and was immersed by the influential pioneer Baptist pastor, Gustaf Palmquist.[66] Soon thereafter, Mattson staked out an area in Goodhue County, Minnesota, about 12 miles west of Red Wing. He called it "Mattson's Settlement" and the next year attracted enough followers to make it a viable colony. The name was changed to "Vasa" in 1855, which made it sound less proprietorial and more patriotic. Mattson advertised in newspapers on both sides of the Atlantic and by the close of 1856, he had 200 settlers and had made enough money to move on to his next venture.[67] In Skåne he became something of a favourite son and his Baptist contacts helped him to attract migrants. This was increasingly the case in the late 1850s and then, after the American Civil War, in the late 1860s. (One should not be surprised that in later life when it became useful to cease being a Baptist and again to be a Lutheran, he did so.) Ultimately, Mattson did well financially by taking advantage of the network of dissent. And, manifestly his web of influence and that of the implacably religious Anders Wiberg overlapped.[68]

How the two webs that Wiberg and Mattson represented—the spiritual and the banausic—interacted is rarely visible on a microbasis. One of the few replicable observations of the interactions is found in Robert C. Ostergren's brilliant and thorough study of the physics of nineteenth- and early twentieth-century out-migration from the Lake Siljan region in central Dalarna and subsequent settlement in North America. Ostergren found that the epicentre of the emigration movement was in the parishes of Orsa and Våmhus on the north of the lake, areas that in the mid-1850s had come under the influence of Wiberg and the Baptist movement. In the early 1860s, few of the Baptists had bowed their heads to formally ask for permission to secede from the state church and hence they were being harshly treated by the civil authorities. There is no question that their motivation to leave Sweden was based on religious imperatives. These were what historical geographers call "first-migrators," meaning those that initiate a pattern. And the pattern that follows is fascinating, for the propensity to emigrate spread southwards and westwards around Lake Siljan and within two years was deeply affecting parishes in the region that had a much lower proportion of religious dissenters. As far as leaving Sweden was concerned, cultural dissent often triggered economic self-interest.[69]

Therefore, three points are worth emphasis. (1) In suggesting that the religious dissenters—Readers and various separatists, especially Baptists—were the cultural puncture that set the precedent for later widespread Swedish emigration, one does not have to engage in the tiresome and ultimately bogus exercise of arguing that the early religiously keen migrants possessed an unmixed holiness. They did not. All that we have to accept is that they did their personal bookkeeping in a way that is only in part amenable to the rational-economics school of emigration theory. These people took seriously the injunction "Lay not up for yourselves treasures upon earth ...[70] and the supplication, "So teach us to number our days that we apply our hearts unto wisdom,"[71] and they calculated both money and time in their own fashion. It was a very precise accounting system, but one that was in part invisible to the mortal eye. They engaged in a felicific calculus that had less to do with Bentham than with Bethlehem. Inconvenient as it may be and difficult as it is to assess historically, culture counts.

(2) In asserting the significance of the Readers and the separatists, one is not suggesting that in any theological sense they were holier than the adherents and clergy of the state church: merely that they were different and that they served as a catalytic cultural minority in a much larger polity.

And (3) one does not need to argue that the separatists and still-Lutheran Readers were the majority of Swedish migrants up to the time of the Great Deprivation. They were the cutting edge and, in the case of the Baptists, demonstrably the vector in large swathes of Sweden whereby the idea of overseas migration passed from parish to parish. The irony is that they encouraged members of the general society to make the prudential and material calculations of whether to remain living at the foot of an economic avalanche zone, or move to someplace safer.[72]

NOTES

1   John Michael Quigley, "An Economic Model of Swedish Emigration," *Quarterly Journal of Economics*, vol. 86 (Feb. 1972), p. 114. Quigley's model of Swedish emigration covered 1876–1908.

2   Quigley, "An Economic Model of Swedish Emigration," p. 114.

3   Derived from Gustav Sundbärg (revised by E. Arosenius), "Demography," in Axel Johan Josef Guinchard, *Sweden. Historical and Statistical Handbook. First Part. Land and People* (Stockholm: KB, 2nd ser., 1914), table 15, p. 125.

4   Calculated from Nils William Olsson, *et al.* by H. Arnold Barton, *The Old Country and the New: Essays on Sweden and America* (Carbondale: Southern Illinois University Press, 2007), pp. 19 and 23. This is the appropriate place to point to the monumental work of Olsson, US diplomat and eventual director of the American Swedish Institute in Minneapolis. He transcribed all known arrivals at US ports 1820–50 and then pursued these names through Swedish and US records. See *Swedish Passenger Arrivals in New York, 1820–50* (Chicago: Swedish Pioneer Society, 1967); *Swedish Passenger Arrivals in US Ports (except New York)* (Stockholm: Acta Stockholmiensis, 1979) and a combined edition, done with the aid of Erik Wiken, *Swedish Passenger Arrivals in the United States, 1820–1850* (Stockholm: Acta Stockholmiensis, 1995.) As in any ambitious work, there are errors and omissions in his citation of individual cases. And the US records were quite incomplete as entry via Pacific Ocean ports was excluded until 1850 (see *Statistical History of the United States from Colonial Times to the Present* (New York: Basic Books, 1976), discussion of statistical series C 89–331, p. 97) and European entry via the Canadas was totally unreported in this period. Thus there are questions of how representative the data are. Nevertheless, what Olsson was able to accomplish in the pre-digital era, by simple hard slogging, is extraordinary.

5   Barton, *The Old Country and the New*, pp. 19 and 23, based on Olsson's work. I realize that one could argue that the migrants to the United States were not representative of the entire flow of out-migrants in the first half of the nineteenth century. Doubtlessly that is true, but the divergence strengthens my argument against special pleading. Merely ask: would it be more difficult for an adult male to take a child, a wife, or a 55-year-old parent across to Denmark or to the USA? If anything, the US data, if regarded as a sample, overstates the domination of single males, aged 15–50, in the total out-migration flow from Sweden.

6   Ideally we could compare, at least notionally, the gross number of out-migrants with the total number of persons who at any time in the period 1801–50 became, say, 15 years of age or over. This would give a sharper assessment of the proportion of persons who, being capable of leaving Sweden on their own initiative, actually chose to do so. Unfortunately, the demographic data are not strong enough to make this estimate possible. (And, to presage the next chapter: such an assessment is even less feasible for Ireland.)

7   Calculated from Gustav Sundbärg in Government of Sweden, *Emigrationsutredningen, Bilaga IV, Utvandringsstatistik* (Stockholm: KB, 1910), table 25, p. 109.

8   Sundbärg, *Utvandringsstatistik*, pp. 55–56 and note lacunae in table 52, p. 162.

9   If one wants a very crude guess about the total gross out-migration, assume that (a là extra-European migration), three-quarters of the total 1851–70 emigration occurred in our time period (that is, excluding the Deprivation era): namely a total of net emigration of roughly 44,250 to all destinations. Even if one takes the generous step of tripling that number to translate net into gross out-migration, the proportion of the Swedish population that was out-migrating before the Deprivation was extremely small.

The US census for 1860 showed 18,265 persons born in Sweden living in the USA. The next census (1870: 97,332) was taken after the Deprivation flow had occurred, so it is not of direct value in the present discussion. Depending upon what assumptions one makes about deaths of immigrants, re-emigration rates, and about the flow between 1860 and 1866, one gets estimates of Swedish gross migration to the USA of Swedish persons, 1850–66, in the 30,000-plus range. (For census data, see *Historical Statistics of the United States*, Cambridge University Press online edition, Series C228–95, "Foreign-Born Population.")

10   Merseyside Maritime Museum, *Liverpool and Emigration in the 19th and 20th Centuries* (Sheet no. 64, 2008); Sundbärg, *Utvandringsstatistik*, table 29, p. 114. From the viewpoint of Irish history, the writings of John Belchem on Liverpool are the most insightful. Among the wide range, see especially, *Irish, Catholic and Scouse. The History of the Liverpool-Irish, 1800–1930* (Liverpool: Liverpool University Press, 2007.)

11   Nils Wohlin in Government of Sweden, *Emigrationsutredningen, Bilaga I, Utvandringslagstiftning öfversikt af dess utveckling och nuvarande beskaffenhet i Europas olika stater* (Stockholm: KB, 1908), pp. 7–10.

12   D. A. Peterson, "From Östergötland to Iowa," in the *Ford Dodge [Iowa] Messenger* (____, 1880), reprinted in *Swedish Pioneer Historical Quarterly*, vol. 22 (1971), pp. 138–42, subsequently reprinted in H. Arnold Barton, *Letters from the Promised Land. Swedes in America, 1840–1914* (Minneapolis: University of Minnesota Press,

1975), pp. 53–56. Barton's collection of primary material differs from most such enterprises by being a nicely crafted literary work that can be read for pleasure.

13   Report of the governor of Västmanland, 1860, p. 10, cited in Florence Edith Janson, *The Background of Swedish Immigration, 1840–1930* (Philadelphia: University of Pennsylvania, 1931), p. 201.

14   Ann-Sofie Kälvemark, "Swedish Emigration Policy in an International Perspective, 1840–1925," in Harald Runblom and Hans Norman (eds.), *From Sweden to America. A History of the Migration* (Minneapolis: University of Minnesota Press, 1976), pp. 94–105; Wohlin, *Utvandringslagstiftning*, pp. 10–12, 15–25.

15   Nils Runeby, *Den Nya Världen och den Gamla. Amerikabild och Emigrationsuppfattning i Sverige, 1820–1860* (Uppsala: Studia Historica Upsaliensia, 1969).

16   Anna Söderblom, "Läsare och Amerikafarare på 1840-talet," *Julbelg* (Uppsala, 1925), quoted in John S. Lindberg, *The Background of Swedish Emigration to the United States. An Economic and Sociological Study in the Dynamics of Migration* (Minneapolis: University of Minnesota Press, 1930), p. 17n19. A comment: Lindberg's book is a pioneering effort that has received much less respect than it deserves. The socio-economic theory has not aged well, but Lindberg had a strong sense of evidence and he collected some quantitative data that are not conveniently available elsewhere.

17   Quoted and translated in Barton, *Letters from the Promised Land*, p. 33. The newspaper report, obviously satirical in tone, added that "the governor's officials get no sleep at night from preparing emigrant passes. More than a hundred of these are supposed to have been issued." This entire article probably was a jab at Peter Cassel's settlement in Iowa.

18   The reader of reviews in thoughtful periodicals will know that it has become requisite for reviewers to note any potential conflict of interest concerning the items that they are reviewing (old school chums, shared employers, long-time quarrels, etc). This is a useful piece of ethical policing and it serves as a fair warning to the reader to be wary. In the usual case, it makes the writer hyper-scrupulous, but not always. Any road, I think that a similar notice should be required of the authors of scholarly books.

    In this case, the heads-up to the reader is this: given the author's own family background, be watchful of his assertion of the importance of early migrators, especially those who were religious dissidents in their own homeland. There are three family strands in my background that are here relevant. These are: (1) my father's people, families who left Sweden for Minnesota before the Deprivation of the nineteenth century. They were strong religious dissidents. (2) On my mother's side, one of the two families was the Harmans, who were not particularly early migrators in the German context—three brothers, shoe and leather workers, left Württemberg in the upper Rhine lands in the first decade of the nineteenth century and eventually located in Lycoming County, Pennsylvania. They were from a pietistic tradition that had, at best, been tolerated by the state church, and sometimes harassed. In America, our line became enthusiastically Methodist, both for the theology and the music (naming a child Charles Wesley Harman says it all). They drifted westward, farm by farm, during the nineteenth century, and finally settled in Minnesota, Wisconsin and Iowa, becoming Independent Congregationalists of a remarkably cheerful sort. And (3) on my mother's side, the other family was the Kenyons from near Oldham, Lancashire. They arrived in Rhode Island in the last quarter of the seventeenth century. They later married with the Greenes who had emigrated to Salem, Massachusetts in 1635 and had only managed to make it two years among the Puritans before leaving, after considerable aggravation, to form the Baptist colony of Rhode Island under Roger Williams. Our branch of the family drifted into upstate New York in the early nineteenth century and then went stepwise westward, before settling in northern Iowa.

19   I am putting aside two secondary matters that do not impinge greatly on the cultural characteristics of Swedish out-migration before the Deprivation. One of these is the question of how large the flow of intra-European migration by Swedes was. My suspicion is that it has been both underestimated statistically and undervalued historiographically because of the understandably intense fascination with long-distance migration. The second matter is the diverting picture of individual Swedes-on-the-make. These include the Delaware Colony, "New Sweden," of 1638 to 1655 (when it was taken over by the Dutch); the faintly ridiculous attempt at West Indian colonization, St Bathelemy (St Barts), that Sweden bought in 1784 and barely managed to give away in 1878; and, one of my favourite Swedes-on-the-make, Henric Gahn. Son of a rector from Ore in north-eastern Dalarna, Gahn became a cadet functionary in the diplomatic service and then went prospecting for opportunity in the USA. In mid-1794 he arrived in New York and had the good fortune soon to meet Joseph Priestley, Unitarian theologian, scientist (he is credited as being the first to fathom the existence of oxygen) and, more recently, the victim of mob violence in London. Young Mr Gahn, barely 20 years of age, offered to become a junior partner with Priestley and to supply him with stout Dalarna lads to work Priestley's 40,000 acres on the Susquehanna—African slaves being out of the question. The great man declined, but Gahn went on to be a successful businessman and the first Swedish consul in New York.

See Olof H. Selling, "Dahlkarlar skulle kunne med nytta tages i stort från Sverige," *Dalarnas Hembygdsbok, 1966* (Falun: Dalarnas Fornminnes och Hembygdsförbund, 1968), pp. 19–23.

20 The historiography of the Irish penal code reflects the high degree of challenge that the subject presents. The classic discussion of the "code," by Ireland's greatest historian of the post-Reformation era, is William E. H. Lecky (1838–1903), *History of Ireland in the Eighteenth Century* (London: Longmans, 1892; 2nd ed., 1913), vol. 1, pp. 136–69, 252–79. Lecky's scholarship still dominates the subject. In the 1950s Maureen [née McGeehin] Wall began a reassessment of the subject. Her work is conveniently available in *Catholic Ireland in the Eighteenth Century: Collected Essays of Maureen Wall*, edited by Gerard O'Brien and Tom Dunne (Dublin: Geography Publications, 1989). Since her death in 1972 there have been sporadic forays into the field, but not the root-and-branch study that the topic requires. When that fundamental restudy eventually is undertaken, it will need to employ as foundational context the compellingly original work of Sean J. Connolly, *Religion, Law, and Power: The Making of Protestant Ireland, 1660–1760* (Oxford: Clarendon Press, 1992.)

21 For the details of the retreat of the Anglican church from a state establishment to a voluntary religious body, see D. H. Akenson, *The Church of Ireland. Ecclesiastical Reform and Revolution, 1800–1885* (New Haven: Yale University Press, 1971).

22 Luke 20:25.

23 I am grateful to my friend and colleague, Professor James Stayer, an authority on the sixteenth and seventeenth-century forms of German Protestant enthusiasm, for guiding my reading on the matter. As far as Sweden is concerned, Pietism was split into two main forms. The early one, which frightened the church and government, followed A. H. Francke (1663–1727) in a strict system of guilt-penance-conversional rebirth. It had less long-run influence than did a second fragment, founded by Count von Zinzendorf (1700–60) that tried to bring the individual into a mystical union with Christ, who was interpreted as not merely saviour, but as creator and underwriter of the world. This form (known under various names—Herrnhutism, Bohemian Brethren, Moravian Brethren) had a longer life in Sweden than did A. H. Francke's version of Pietism, in part because its emphasis upon personal emotionality and upon high culture to aid that emotionality played well with a segment of the aristocracy and haute bourgeoisie.

24 Allan Sandewall, *Separatismen in Övre Norrland, 1820–1855* (Uppsala: Svenska Kyrkhistoriska Föreningen, 1952), pp. 61–68; George M. Stephenson, *The Religious Aspects of Swedish Immigration. A Study of Immigrant Churches* (Minneapolis: University of Minnesota Press, 1932), pp. 11–12. Stephenson's writings were underappreciated at the time and since then, although I suspect his work is due for a revival. He was three-quarters of a century ahead of his time in recognizing the generative power of religious beliefs and institutions in Swedish out-migration. And he worked on difficult groups—Free Church bodies, whose records are episodic at best—not merely the established state church. See Kevin Proeschold, "The Prolific Pen of George M. Stephenson: An Annotated Bibliography," *Swedish-American Historical Quarterly*, vol. 52 (Apr. 2002), pp. 106–35. The text of the Anti-Conventicle Act is available on http://konventiklar.blogspot.com/2008/01/bilaga-konventikeplaketets-lydelse.html. For the context that produced the 1726 act, see Carola Nordbäck, *Samvetets Röst. Om mötet mellan Luthersk ortodoxi och konservativ Pietism i 1720-talets Sverige* (Umeå: Department of Historical Studies, Umeå University, 2004).

25 Although the central argument here deals with Protestant dissenters, one should note that the Swedish antipathy to Catholics produced some very long-lasting penal enactments, and that the position of Jews, though better than that of the Catholics, was marked by their being distrusted and limited in their civil rights.

Jews were banned from Sweden until 1782, when commercial and skilled migrants were allowed to settle in four cities: Stockholm, Göteborg, Norrköping and Karlskrona. They were allowed to practice their religion privately, but were prohibited from joining guilds, owning landed estates and marrying Christians. An 1838 effort to grant Jewish persons greater freedoms produced anti-Jewish rioting and only a mild measure of relief was effected. In 1873, over some popular opposition, most of the restrictions on Jews were removed and the Jewish faith became a state-recognized religion. In 1910, there were 4,400 Jewish persons in Sweden. See: Neil Kent, *A Concise History of Sweden* (Cambridge: Cambridge University Press, 2008), pp. 145–46; Franklin D. Scott, *Sweden. The Nation's History* (Minneapolis: University of Minnesota Press, 1977), pp. 384–86; K. B. Westman, "Church and Religion," in Guinchard, *Land and People*, pp. 335–36.

Catholicism, being the founding hatred of Lutheranism, was long penalized in Sweden. Citizens of Sweden were forbidden from becoming Roman Catholics and as late as the 1850s two male converts to Catholicism were attainted of their property and banished from Sweden and in 1858 six adult female converts were expelled from the country. From the Reformation until 1781, Catholic Mass was forbidden except in foreign embassies. From 1781 onwards foreign workers in Sweden were allowed to practice the

Roman Catholic faith, but chapels were limited to unobtrusive structures that did not attract attention or public animus and, in fact, the first non-embassy Catholic church in Stockholm was built in 1837. Only in 1873 were Catholics granted almost full civil rights, but even then regular orders of nuns, priests, or brothers were banned and so were monasteries and convents and this continued until mid-twentieth century. There were about 2,600 Catholics in Sweden in 1910 and about 59,000 in the early 1970s. It is fair to say that the penal code affected the Catholics (and, indeed, all non-Lutherans) in a residual fashion until the disestablishment of the Lutheran state church in Sweden at the beginning of the twenty-first century. See: Kent, *A Concise History of Sweden*, pp. 145, 189; Scott, *Sweden. The Nation's History*, p. 573; Westman, "Church and Religion," pp. 330–36, and "Stockholm" entry in *The Catholic Encyclopedia* (1913).

26 A slightly arch term, *Läsarinna* referred to a fetching or a bourgeois female devote. *Läsarpräst* in some contexts meant a layman who took up hot-gospelling. In other circumstances it was a reasonably respectful term for a Lutheran clergyman who threw in with the local Readers and used their activities as a way of bolstering the Established Church.

27 To refer again to Allan Sandewall, see *Separatismen in Övre Norrland*. This is one of the splendid earlier works that is now overlooked almost entirely in Swedish nineteenth-century studies. An historian of Ireland can only be envious: we do not as yet have a study in comparable depth of the operation of the penal laws and their interaction with local social and religious sensibilities in even a single Irish county.

28 Sandewall (*Separatismen in Övre Norrland*, pp. 287–96) reproduces the text of the legal decrees introduced 1817–44 that directly affected Norrland. For a discussion of the Readers' movement in Norrland as a contest over ownership of the public sphere, the Readers being an attack on the Church-State monopoly of acceptable public discourse, see Tom Ericsson and Börje Harnesk, "'Disputationsmöten och öfningsfält för tankekrafter.' Läseriet i övre Norrland in 1800-talets början," *Historisk Tidskrift*, vol. 113 (1993), pp. 582–610.

29 The reader will observe that I am refusing to give a capsule explanation of why the religious animation of the nineteenth century occurred. It can hardly be irrelevant that the Readers became assertive in a time when the agency of the rural labourers and some freehold farmers was being undercut by the enclosure movement; nor that Europe had just experienced a war that revolved, in part, around the legitimacy of ancient forms of authority. Nor that similar movements of religious animation were occurring elsewhere in Europe and in North America. Still, given the state of the literature, I think it is best as a temporary expedient, to take the Readers as an independent phenomenon and to hope that they will someday be explained adequately.

30 E. Kenneth Stegeby, "An Analysis of the Impending Disestablishment of the Church of Sweden," *Brigham Young University Law Review*, vol. 51 (1999), p. 710.

31 Scott's ministry is closely documented in an impressive biography by Gunnar Westin, *George Scott och hans Verksamhet i Sveriga* (Stockholm: Svenska Kyrkans Diakonistyrelses Bokförlag, 1928–29), vol. 1, *Akademisk Avhandling* and vol. 2, *Handlingar, Tal och Brev*. See also Stephenson, *The Religious Aspects of Swedish Immigration*, pp. 13–15.

32 Among the potentially useful terms that are not available for application in the discussion of the Readers is "evangelical." The problem is that as early as 1544 the state church had declared itself to be the Evangelical Lutheran Church (Stegeby, "Impending Disestablishment of the Church of Sweden,", p. 710) and the term was employed sufficiently frequently thereafter concerning the state church to render it useless as an historical descriptor of the nineteenth-century Reader movement. If one could employ the term the in the same general way that it is used in English historiography to denominate the nineteenth-century English religious revival (both within and outside the Church of England), that would be fine. However, it is less confusing just to avoid the word. That practice has the secondary advantage of not merging the Readers into the much-different twentieth-century form of American evangelicalism.

33 Stephenson, *The Religious Aspects of Swedish Immigration*, p. 33.

34 Founded with royal approval in the 1830s, the Temperance Society was a cross-section of the "good and the gracious" and of religious leaders. At its peak, in the mid-1840s, the society had more than 100,000 members. Like many such organizations, it aimed at reducing drinking among the lower orders. This was not merely an effort at social control, but at medical improvement. In 1829 there were 173,000 private stills operative in Sweden. Annual consumption of *brännvin* (vodka being the closest present-day equivalent, or, if flavoured, gin or aquavit) was estimated at 40 litres per man, woman and child. That, however, is hard to verify because home distilling also involved home consumption. See Haldan Bengtsson, "The Temperance Movement and Temperance Legislation in Sweden," *Annals of the American Academy of Political and Social Sciences*, vol. 197 (May 1938), p. 134. In a more controlled urban-based estimate, in the artisans' town of Eskilstuna, in 1854 the Medical Officer of Health estimated that per each adult male 2.6 litres of vodka were consumed weekly, plus beer, cheap brandy, etc. (P. C. Malm, quoted in Lars Magnusson, "Drinking and the Verlag System, 1820–1850: The Significance of Taverns and Drink in Eskilstuna before Industrialisation," *Scandinavian*

Economic History Review, vol. 34 (1986), p. 2. What constitutes excessive alcohol consumption is a contested matter, but it has been clearly demonstrated that the reduction in alcohol consumed per person, 1861–1913, had a direct impact in reducing mortality, as well as an indirect effect in extending life through improvement in real wages. Thor Norström, "Real Wages. Alcohol Consumption and Mortality in Sweden, 1861–1913," *European Journal of Population*, vol. 4 (1988), pp. 183–96.

35 Given our discussion of the Readers' movement in Norrland, the following study of the Evangeliska Foster-lands-Stiftelsens (the Homeland Evangelical Mission Society) is revealing: Stefan Gelfgren, "Väckelse och Sekularisering. Exemplet Umeås Evangelisk-Lutherska Missionsförening, 1850–1910," *Historisk Tidskrift*, vol. 123 (2003), pp. 373–94.

36 Historians sometimes distinguish between the Old Readers (*Gamalläsare*) who, like the original Norrland dissidents at heart were hyper-orthodox, and the New Readers (*Nyaläsare*) who were stronger on salvation-by-grace without the need of an hierarchical church and who were more open to separatism. The distinction is not consistently drawn, however, and, given the plasticity and swift evolution of the faith-communities, the general term Reader is preferable.

37 Allan Sandewall, "Konventikelplakatets upphävande—ett gränsar i Svensk Religionsfrihetslagstifning?" *Kyrkohistorisk Årsskrift*, vol. 58 (1957), pp. 138–40.

38 The early "heroic" period in the Swedish Baptist community is attractively memorialized in *Svenska Baptism genom 100 År: En Krönika i Ord och Bild* (Stockholm: privately printed, 1958), pp. 1–25. A more densely documented appreciation is A. G. Hall, *Svenska Baptisternas Historia under en Tid af femtio År, 1848–1898*, vol. 1 (Chicago: A. G. Halls, Förlag, 1900).

39 Stephenson, *The Religious Aspects of Swedish Immigration*, pp. 77–78.

40 Maria Ågren, *Jord och Gäld: Social skiftning och rättslig konflikt i södra Dalarna c. 1650–1850* (Uppsala: Acta Universitatis Upsaliensis, 1992), pp. 90ff.

41 Helmer Fält, *Separatismen i Orsa, 1850–1860* (Stockholm: Diakonistyrelsens Bokförlag, 1967), pp. 66–79, 129–35.

42 Per Palmqvist to Anders Wiberg, 24 December 1852, letter reproduced in Gunnar Westin, *Emigranterna och Kyrkan. Brev från och till svenskar i Amerika, 1849–1892* (Stockholm: Svenska Kyrkans Diakonistyrelses Bokförlag, 1932), p. 63.

43 Fält, *Separatismen i Orsa*, p. 215.

44 D. Forsell to Anders Wiberg, 27 July 1853, reproduced in Gunnar Westin (ed.), *Ur den Svenska Folkväckelsens Historia och Tankevärld. Brev fran och till den Svenska Baptismens Banbrytare, 1850–1855* (Stockholm: B.M:s Bokförlags, 1933–34), vol. 2, pp. 22–27.

45 Scott, *Sweden. The Nation's History*, p. 359.

46 Sandewall, "Konventikelplakatets upphävande," p. 140.

47 Sandewall, "Konventikelplakatets upphävande," pp. 140–41.

48 Stephenson, *The Religious Aspects of Swedish Immigration*, p. 91.

49 The Swedish state's attitude towards Roman Catholics is referred to above, note 25. The Swedish frisson on the Mormon question is culturally diagnostic, but is beyond the scope of the present discussion. Suffice it to note that the Mormons joined the Catholics as the great Thou-Shalt-Nots. A mixture of a voyeur-istic interest in the marriage customs of the Latter-day Saints, conjoined with fear of the Mormons' organi-zation of migration from the Scandinavian countries to the American West, kept them in the public eye much more than their thin numbers might seem to justify. Thus, when the massive Emigration Commission report was published 1907–13, there was a detailed statistical and verbal discussion of only one denomi-nation, the Mormons: Government of Sweden [editor: Gustav Sundbärg], *Emigrationsutredningen, Bilaga III, Mormonvärfningen* (Stockholm: KB, 1910). In 1900 there were 2,294 Latter-day Saints in Sweden, including children (table C, p. 49.) The commission calculated that between 1852 and 1909, LDS missionaries had baptized 17,529 persons in Sweden. Of course death and lapsing from the faith affected their numbers, but 7,822 had emigrated (table A, p. 48). That is a remarkably high percentage, much more than for any other denomination of any size. Unlike other groups of religious dissenters (a) the Mormon faith was not in any sense indigenous to Sweden and (b) by virtue of their tight tie to LDS settlements in the American West (mostly Utah), the Mormons did not induce the emulation that was engendered by out-migration of other dissenting groups. See William Mulder, *Homeward to Zion. The Mormon Migration from Scandinavia* (Minne-apolis: University of Minnesota Press, 1957) and LeRoy R. Hafen and Ann W. Hafen, *Handcarts to Zion. The Story of a Unique Western Migration, 1856–1860* (Glendale, CA: Arthur H. Clark Co., 1976). Curiously, although the LDS strand of Swedish out-migration patterns has been heavily studied, a countervailing cultural transaction actually deserves more attention: namely the impact of Scandinavian mythology and forms of genealogical narrative upon the theology and practice of the LDS church which, among other goals,

seeks to chart the genealogical relationships of the entire human race. See D. H. Akenson, *Some Family. The Mormons and how Humanity keeps track of itself* (Montreal and Kingston: McGill-Queen's University Press, 2007).

50 Jonas Alwall, "Religious Liberty in Sweden: An Overview," *Journal of Church and State*, vol. 42 (2000), p. 151.

51 Stephenson, *The Religious Aspects of Swedish Immigration*, pp. 90–91.

52 Lindberg, *Swedish Emigration to the United States*, p. 41.

53 Alwall, "Religious Liberty in Sweden," pp. 166–71; Westman, "Church and Religion," pp. 330–35; Stegeby, "Impending Disestablishment of the Church of Sweden," pp. 704–07, 712–67.

54 This is a trifle hard on the splendid haute-bourgeois Romantic, Gustaf E. M. Unionius (1810–1902). A Swedo-Finn, son of a lawyer, he entered military college, but lost interest and subsequently studied law and then medicine and then became a government clerk and then in 1841 led a small party of all-too-genteel pioneers to "New Uppsala"—soon renamed Pine Lake, Wisconsin. They did badly at best and in 1845 he became an Anglican priest and spent the next 13 years ministering to immigrant Swedes in the Midwest. His migration letters (at first strongly pro-American, later less so) had a strong newspaper readership in the home country and he wrote a widely read memoir of his time in the USA. There he was caught between the dissenters from the old country and the Lutherans and in 1858, chastened by the lack of response to his ministry, he returned to Sweden. (See Runeby, *Den Nya Världen och den Gamla*, pp. 344–56, and Stephenson, *The Religious Aspects of Swedish Immigration*, pp. 210–13). His widely read memoir is *Minnen från en sjuttonårig vistelse i nordvästra Amerika*, 2 vols. (Uppsala: W. Schultz, 1861–62).

55 The standard discussion is H. Arnold Barton (ed.), *Peter Cassel and Iowa's New Sweden* (Chicago: Swedish-American Historical Society, 1995). See also Runeby, *Den Nya Världen och den Gamla*, pp. 200–14. This includes a reprint of George Stephenson's 1929 pamphlet of translated letters and documents relating to New Sweden, Iowa.

56 For an evocative biography, see Paul Elmen, *Wheat Flour Messiah. Eric Jansson of Bishop Hill* (Carbondale: Southern Illinois University Press, 1976). The most discriminating scholarly discussion is Barton, *The Old Country and the New*, pp. 31–50. See also Stephenson, *The Religious Aspects of Swedish Immigration*, pp. 49–73. The clearest New World comparator to Eric Jansson is Joseph Smith, Jr, the Prophet of Mormonism. The sequence of their careers is similar: rural childhood, youthful ecstatic visions, redefining of Christianity, preaching in religiously "burnt over" districts, acquisition of devotes, exodus under persecution into a new land, communitarian life, death by assassination. The time periods in which each man operated are remarkably close. Of course, one ultimately succeeded, the other did not.

57 Runeby, *Den Nya Världen och den Gamla*, pp. 300–01; Stephenson, *The Religious Aspects of Swedish Immigration*, pp. 28, 82; Westin, *Emigranterna och Kyrkan*, p. 17.

58 The best-known story of a group of religiously motivated migrants—Vilhelm Moberg's semi-fictional emigrants from the province of Småland in the early 1850s—illustrates this transitional form of group migration. Moberg's tetralogy is a magnificent achievement: *Utvandrarna [The Emigrants]* (1949), *Invandrarna [Unto a New Land]* (1952), *Nybyggarna [The Settlers]* (1956) and *Sista Brevet till Sverige [Last Letter Home]* (1959). The set of books made Moberg the most translated and widely read Swedish novelist in the years between Selma Lagerlöf and Henning Mankell. The popular interest that he stimulated in the nineteenth-century Swedish migration story was shrewdly and productively focused by the scholars of the Uppsala Project during the 1960s and 1970s. Yet, as one encounters the historical migration literature of the past 20 years or so, one becomes aware that Moberg has become He Who Cannot be Named.

Why? One can only guess, but there are some potential reasons. First, Vilhelm Moberg was fairly cranky, especially in his sunset years, and he was not beyond pointing out an inconvenient truth: that he had done what Swedish academic scholars should have done, namely, tell a big story to a general audience. As compared to the English-speaking world (and especially to the community of Irish historians), Swedish historians have not often taken responsibility for communicating their findings to the larger community. Second, Moberg, an instinctive if unpredictable populist, knew a lot of things that the professional scholars had forgotten. Basic things: about renting land and getting food and tugging the forelock, things like that, which are a bit vulgar and do not map elegantly in a scholarly monograph. Some of these things he had learned from ethnologists and folklore collectors, but a lot came from his having listened to old people. Third, and most unsettling, Moberg's tetralogy unavoidably raises the question that from other sources has come to bedevil the present-day historical profession. Namely: were the Greeks right in believing that Clio was one muse, not two?

59 Charles L. Brace, *The Norse-Folk; or, a Visit to the Homes of Norway and Sweden* (London, 1857), pp. 406–07, quoted in George M. Stephenson, "The Background of the Beginnings of Swedish Immigration, 1850–1875," *American Historical Review*, vol. 31 (Jul. 1926), p. 713.

60   A nice case which illustrates the permeable boundary between various sorts of Readers is that of the Norelius brothers from Norrbäck in Hassela Parish in northern Hälsingland. Both were predisposed to strong piety. They emigrated to the USA in the summer of 1850. There, Andrew Norelius became a Baptist and was ordained in 1856; Erik Norelius was ordained as a Lutheran clergyman and was a founder of the Augustana Lutheran Synod which was closer to the Readers' definition of a proper religious polity than it was to the terms of the state church in Sweden. For the bare biographical facts, see Olsson, *Swedish Passenger Arrivals in New York*, p. 255.

61   The Swedish book, *Det Kristliga Dopet* (1855) was published almost immediately thereafter in the USA as *Christian Baptism: set forth in the Words of the Bible* (Philadelphia: American Baptist Publication Society, 1855). The English version (311 pp.) was written by Wiberg himself. He also introduced his *Hvilken bör döpas?* which he had published earlier (Stockholm, 1852). Wiberg was closely informed about the Orsa Readers and manifestly recognized the area as a target-point. Communications concerning Orsa are preserved and are reproduced in full in Westin, *Ur den Svenska Folkväckelsens Historia*: D. Forsell to Anders Wiberg, 27 July 1853 (vol. 2, pp. 24–27), 14 September 1864, Forsell to Wiberg (vol. 2, pp. 229–39).

62   Hall, *Svenska Baptisternas Historia*, vol. 2, pp. 465–73; Stephenson, *The Religious Aspects of Swedish Immigration*, pp. 79–87; *Svenska Baptism genom 100 År*, pp. 25 and 47.

63   Anders Wiberg to "Orsa-läsarna," 3 May 1852, reproduced in Westin, *Ur den Svenska Folkväckelsens Historia*, vol. 1, pp. 117–18.

64   Runeby, *Den Nya Världen och den Gamla*, pp. 214ff. and 359–89.

65   Stephenson, *The Religious Aspects of Swedish Immigration*, pp. 44, 86, 168; Westin, *Emigranterna och Kyrkan*, pp. 23–24.

66   Hans Mattson to T. N. Hasselquist, 14 April 1853, cited in Westin, *Emigranterna och Kyrkan*, pp. 21–22. Mattson's own later report is found in his memoir, *Reminiscences. The Story of an Emigrant* (Saint Paul: D. D. Merrill Co., 1892), pp. 31–32.

67   Lars Ljungmark (tr. Kermit B. Westerberg), *Swedish Exodus* (Carbondale: Southern Illinois University Press, 1979), pp. 22–23.

68   One would like to know if Mattson and Wiberg ever explicitly interacted. There is some indication that Wiberg was kept indirectly informed of Mattson's progress. On one occasion, Gustaf Palmquist in Rock Island, Illinois, let Wiberg know when Mattson was bringing westward from Boston a band of Swedes, mostly from Skåne. See Gustaf Palmquist to Anders Wiberg, 24 August 1853, reproduced in Westin, *Ur den Svenska Folkväckelsens Historia*, vol. 2, p. 47.

69   Robert C. Ostergren, *A Community Transplanted. The Trans-Atlantic Experience of a Swedish Immigrant Settlement in the Upper Middle West, 1835–1915* (Madison: University of Wisconsin Press, 1988), pp. 121–22. Ostergren refers (p. 121) to the people of the Orsa and Våmhus parishes as follows: "The original infection of 'American Fever' came from outside the region and seems to have been associated with individuals who had outside contacts of a revolutionary nature, namely the large numbers of religious nonconformists living in Orsa and Våmhus." Ostergren's book, while well respected, deserves much more attention than it has received. It is part of a very rare genre: the fully successful scholarly tracing of a community from a site in Europe to its full settlement in a New World. Most studies (my own included) are limited by their dealing with one group of people getting on the boat and a whole different set getting off. Tracing full communities of individuals is extremely hard and I know of only three successful scholarly attempts to do so concerning Northern Europe or the British Isles: Ostergren's, and Jon Gjerde, *From Peasants to Farmers. The Migration from Balestrand, Norway, to the Upper Middle West* (Cambridge: Cambridge University Press, 1985) and Catharine Anne Wilson, *A New Lease on Life. Landlords, Tenants, and Immigrants in Ireland and Canada* (Montreal and Kingston: McGill-Queen's University Press, 1994). The latter reconstructs the migration and adaptation of communal patterns from the Ards Peninsula in Ireland to Amherst Island in Ontario.

70   Matthew 6:19, partly doubled in Luke 12:21 (AV).

71   Psalm 90:12 (AV).

72   Perhaps I should reiterate here evidentiary matters that are threaded through earlier portions of this chapter. (1) There are no reliable numbers for Swedish out-migrants in the two decades before the Great Deprivation. (2) Swedish domestic censuses of the time did not tally dissenters and (3) the portion of Readers within the Lutheran church is entirely unknown. Therefore it follows that the argument made concerning the potency of cultural dissenters as a lead sector in the pre-Deprivation out-migration is made on circumstantial evidence, context, logic, and upon judgments of positive probability. The case, I think, is quite strong. I would not emphasize this point except that Swedish emigration studies that deal with transoceanic migrants generally have shied away from dealing with intangibles, especially religion. Although I am very keen on seeing that matters of accounting be done accurately, there is a danger in moving from counting things to believing that the only things that really count are those that can be counted.

Chapter Five

LEADING SECTORS: IRELAND

ONE

Ireland: another matter certainly? Certainly a lot different from Sweden: one cannot mechanically transfer specific conclusions from Sweden to Ireland, so why bother? Here we should once again remind ourselves why we are engaged in comparative history. Mostly it is an exercise in enlarging our sensitivities to things we might otherwise not notice or to help us avoid believing that what we see in one country is necessarily particular to it. Were Ireland and Sweden to be perfect cognates for each other, then (rather like the early Chomsky on language) we would need only to study one of them closely in order to know both of them intimately. That is hardly the case, yet we ought to consider the possibility that the two main conclusions drawn from looking at emigration from pre-Deprivation Sweden has some resonance when we take a parallel look at emigration flows from pre-Famine Ireland. Not identity, resonance. And the Swedish conclusions were simple: (1) that the numbers of out-migrants was small (actually miniscule) in relation to the numbers in the population under severe economic risk and (2) that a cultural minority, acting for reasons far separated from simple economic calculation, set down a pattern of out-migration that eventually was to be followed by a massive outflow.

Hence, we should first look at the numbers of out-migrants from Ireland. Nothing complicated is involved here, because the Irish historiography has come to a reasonable equilibrium in discussing the character and limits (a key word) of our knowledge of the migrant flow in the pre-Famine years.

The historiographic trail is simple. There are no reliable numerical series of out-migration from Ireland, 1800–45, because none of the several jurisdictions involved (Ireland, Great Britain, British North America, the United States of America and Australia being the most important) kept consistent or comprehensive records. The major—and thoroughly underappreciated—plinth on which modern scholarship is founded is William Forbes Adams's 1932 monograph on Irish migration to North America from 1815–45.[1] This is an heroic slog through a train-load of government documents, everything relevant that could be found. Adams had an excellent sense of evidence, especially for contradictions in various reports of the same phenomena and also an instinct for recognizing holes in what were supposed to be complete data sets. And, within reason, he interpolated missing numbers and adjudicated between conflicting ones. A degree of non-North American context was added to Adams's work by the Republic of Ireland's commission on emigration which met from 1948–54, published in 1955.[2] Much more useful was a study that the Irish commission was unable to make use of because the Irish report was mostly completed by 1952 but was delayed in publication for political reasons. This is the invaluable compendium on external migration from the United Kingdom, assembled by N. H. Carrier and J. R. Jeffery for the General Register Office of the United Kingdom (1953.)[3] In 1973, Cormac Ó Gráda made a guesstimate that even the best figures concerning Irish out-migration in the second half of the nineteenth century were one-quarter too low. Implicitly, this was a challenge concerning the numbers for the whole nineteenth century. We needed to do better.[4] In 1984, I published an updating and expansion of William Forbes Adams's work as it affected British North America and the United States of America.[5] The composite series, 1825–1910 (given in the present study in abbreviated form in chapter two, is found in my primer on the Irish diaspora (1993).[6] What has emerged from this sequence (in which there are more players than space permits my discussing) is that most scholars in the field take Irish emigration to all transoceanic destinations from 1800 to 1845, inclusive, to have been approximately one million, and that is not High Counting.[7]

But that is the easy half of the equation: for we also need to have a sensible speculation of how many Irish persons migrated to Great Britain before the Famine. The records are not hopeless, but nearly so. We do, however, have one fulcrum point: the 1841 census of Ireland and the impressionistic, but not uninformed, reflections of the census commissioners on what the most likely case was before 1841. Suffice it to say that the accepted number among present-day scholars is that "about half a million Irish migrants"[8] had migrated and settled in England and Scotland, 1801 to 1845, inclusive, and this turns out to be sensible, even if the mode of getting there sometimes seems to be via a crystal ball. (My own estimate is 450,000, but for the purposes of the present exercise, we can accept the standard estimate, as it loads things against the case I am about to make.)[9]

So, we can take 1.5 million as the total gross emigration from Ireland, 1801–45, of persons who were intending to spend the bulk of their life outside of Ireland. What a big number. What a small number!

That, of course, is the *Ó Gráda Paradox*, which we first encountered in chapter three. Cormac Ó Gráda is deadly accurate in presenting the two seemingly conflicting judgements that are in fact the two arms of a paradox that is the base reality of Irish migration history "By contemporary [European] standards, the pre-Famine exodus was unparalleled and it was probably unprecedented." And yet "the reluctance or inability to leave in still greater numbers before 1845 remains an important historiographic theme ..."[10]

The key to reconciling these two strands of the Ó Gráda Paradox—each of which is true both to the historical data and to the social and cultural context of the data—is to recognize that the Irish migrant flow prior to the Famine (a) though large compared to other European populations (b) nevertheless was remarkably small in relation to the size of the Irish population that knowingly exposed itself to serious risk of malnutrition and disease by staying in Ireland, each of these risks of staying in Ireland being chiefly a function of available economic resources and of their allocation and (c) hence, one can infer that out-migration prior to the Famine, although it made excellent economic sense, was not an everyday and acceptable item on the cultural horizon of the Irish population. It was strongly in opposition to cultural norms. The situation was very far from being identical with that in pre-Deprivation Sweden, but the Swedish experience makes us sensitive to the often-ignored facts: that (a) the bulk of the Irish population, though aware of the risks they faced, expressed a strong preference for cultural continuity over prudential and economic shrewdness and escape; (b) those who did choose to exit were in some sense expressing exception to the dominant values of Irish society; ultimately, taken together, the pre-Famine out-migrants effected a set of cultural punctures that made possible the quick and efficient transition to a society-wide emigration tradition after the massive shock of the later 1840s.

As was the case with Sweden, the key to evaluating the meaning of the magnitude of migration is to compare the average annual population of Ireland, 1801–45, with the average annual out-migration. In the roundest numbers (all that the data permit), a total of 1.5 million persons emigrated in 1801–45, meaning 33,300 average annually. In the period 1801–45, the average size of the Irish population was approximately 7.1 million (again, only an approximation, given the sketchy data). That is: the average annual emigration rate was about 0.47 per cent. This, by comparative standards, was high: nearly ten times the Swedish rate. Almost certainly the migration rate was rising as the nineteenth century wore on. To take the single year for which the data are best—1841—the population of Ireland by census figures was 8.175 million, total gross transoceanic out-migration was nearly 32,500,[11] and migration to Britain for long-term settlement approximately 18,500,[12] a total of 51,000. Thus, in that year, 0.62 per cent of the population migrated out of Ireland. This in a society in which, as detailed in chapter three, about 60 per cent of the populace was at risk from a single-year crop failure.

Were the Irish fools? Absolutely not. Admittedly, there has long been a school of semi-racist thought that has stereotyped the bulk of the Irish population as hopelessly backward, impercipient, feckless and unable to assess the market economy or engage in a sensible calculation of the risk level of various alternative life courses. That is not a mode of thought that in the present discussion is worth direct refutation or, indeed, identification of its purveyors. Instead, I wish to present as an affirmative argument, these points: (1) that the Irish agricultural sector had a history of being highly risk prone and that this was so endemic to the agricultural economy that anyone who put a spade in the ground was acquainted with that baleful fact; (2) that communication of information concerning misfortune (that is, of risk becoming actual calamity) within even the lowest strata of society was swift: there was no blackout on knowledge; and (3) in the first half of the nineteenth century, the bulk of the Irish adult population was well acquainted with money economies and markets, and with how to navigate them. Therefore (4), it will be concluded that it was not a failure of information or a lack of *nous* that kept the overwhelming majority of the Irish population from acting upon a "rational" and "objective" assessment of the risk they were engaging, but a set of cultural values—positive affirmations—that made them do their sums in a way that is forever mysterious to the merely econometric.

To be clear, in presenting an affirmative argument (not just a residual collection of negative factors) that appertain to the perplexing half of the Ó Gráda Paradox—that only a surprisingly small fraction of the Irish population left home, instead of being economically "rational" and seeking higher living standards elsewhere—I am rejecting two ideas as not being helpful. I do not accept that the concept of cultural inertia or backwardness, however it may be rhetorically packed, is helpful. Although the market economy had penetrated all but the most obscure nooks and crannies of Ireland by the early nineteenth century, the market economy did not have the powers over human decision-making which is generally accepted as being operative and determinative in the great migration flows of the second half of the twentieth century. These were local communities, but money and markets worked within them with great clarity (rents were calculated in money and paid in specie) and if the market mentality did not rule these worlds, it was not because the people were primitive, but because they had alternate ways of thinking.

Further, the idea that the low level of pre-Famine migration from Ireland (and of pre-Deprivation migration from Sweden) is explained by invoking an undefined "poverty trap" is facile and misleading. Granted, some people, in some parts of the country had no hope of leaving if they so wished—too many children, too little land, no off-farm employment—but those are individual cases and what we are seeing in the national case of low out-migration before the Famine is a pattern that ran across almost the entire society. (Certain exceptions will be discussed later.) The fact that the poverty-trap explanation for low pre-Famine out-migration is specious is massively obvious: the Great Famine itself is the disproof. A society that was much, much poorer in, say, 1847, than it was in 1841 could, by some extraordinary means, finance out-migration in vast numbers. This is not a pleasant argument to make, but it is necessary. In a moment, I will show that a parallel logic involving the cost of transportation out of Ireland reinforces my point that on a national scale, the poverty-trap explanation is a distraction.

TWO

The most rhetorically compelling illustration of the fact that Irish agriculture was endemically risk-prone is found in a remarkable compendium put together in mid-nineteenth century by Sir William Wilde—pioneer eye surgeon, romantic antiquarian, pioneer statistician, Dublin libertine and, not incidentally, father of Oscar Wilde.[13] In the wake of the Great Famine, the United Kingdom government directed the Irish census commissioners to analyse what had occurred. And the commissioners did so in their report on the 1851 census—ten massive volumes—in a level of detail unprecedented in the British Isles, if not in all of Europe. Sir William was appointed an assistant commissioner of the Irish census and his task was both to analyse the deaths that occurred in Ireland between 1841 and 1851 and, more importantly for our present purposes, to survey the pre-Famine occurrence of major death-causing catastrophes. His *Table of Cosmical Phenomena, Epizootics, Ephiphitics, Famines and Pestilences in Ireland* was everything its title proclaimed it to be: an amazingly detailed chronology that ran to 292 folio pages and was preceded by a source-discussion and followed by nearly a full volume of analysis, including a discussion of the epidemiology of the Great Famine. The second half of the work became dated quickly, but the chronological listing in *Table of Cosmical Phenomena* … remains invaluable, provided it is taken on its own terms. It provides a checklist of what pre-modern texts said about disasters in Ireland and, for the modern period, a catalogue of events whose broad outlines would have been known in the general folk culture in the first half of the nineteenth century.[14] The early material is fascinating in its own right (Wilde cites mythic bad-events in the third millennium BCE), but it is in the material for the 1580s that he begins to catalogue situations that still had a resonance in the folk-memory of his own time: the Desmond Wars of the 1580s, combined with vicious weather, produced a decade of off-and-on famine in Munster and parts of Connacht. Material in the Annals of the Four Masters implicitly confirmed the memorability (if not necessarily the precise accuracy) of the famous observation by Edmund Spenser concerning the sufferers: "Out of every quarter of the woods and glynnes, they came creeping forth upon their hands, for their leggs could not beare them; they looked like anatomies of death; they spake like ghosts crying out of their graves; they did eat the dead carrions, happy were they could find them."[15] During the civil wars of the mid-seventeenth century, the combined effects of war, local famines and epidemics was extensive. Sir William Petty estimated that between 1641 and 1652, 504,000 persons had died in Ireland, "wasted by the sword, plague, famine, hardship, and banishment."[16] Even if Petty's estimate is too large, recall of real catastrophe survived a full two centuries later, for the Cromwellian conclusion to the wars was a memory peg that was nearly universal in Ireland. But were ordinary people at risk in peacetime? Silly question. The middle years of the eighteenth century were visited by notably bad weather, as Wilde's chronology testifies. The winter of 1739–40 was very cold and wet and the summer only seasonally better. Potatoes and grains failed in large areas and modern estimates are that 300,000 to 480,000 died in 1740–41—meaning 13 per cent to 21 per cent of the populace.[17] "*The famine of 1741 was the worst in Irish history*," adjudged A. T. Q. Stewart [emphasis mine], and in terms of the proportion of the population that starved or died from deprivation-related diseases, he is right.[18] This 1740–41 famine was hardly an obscure event: Wilde cites a score of printed reports, beginning with the first major potato rot in Ireland in 1739, and the printed reports were a pale reflection of the wider experience. The public memory of this risk-turned-catastrophic was only erased after 1845, for then the memory of the Great Famine of 1845–49 became a blinder which, being held close to the eye, blocked vision of similar events further back in time. And there was more. Wilde's chronology shows a partial potato failure in 1800–01, and in 1816–19 grain and potato failures, and associated diseases were regional, intermittent and fatal, although in undetermined numbers.[19] Those are the major points in Wilde's chronology of risk-turned-real, in the early modern and modern era, but one could fill in a hundred or more smaller smash-ups mentioned in his threnody and still be incomplete. The conclusion is compelling and simple: there was plenty of knowledge of the various risks to which the Irish agrarian society was vulnerable, enough to go around.

But could it indeed go around?—meaning, could the news of such risks be communicated efficiently across locales and regions? Or were these pain-events usually sealed occurrences, happening in one locale and buried there behind walls of silence? We have one case from the first half of the nineteenth century that answers this question the same way a definitive experimental result answers a laboratory question. In an elegant and innovative study, Professor Sean J. Connolly dealt with the diffusion of a putative antidote to cholera. The situation was as follows. Cholera had been slouching towards the British Isles from India all during the 1820s. The first case was reported in Belfast in March 1832 and by May had found purchase in 14 of the 32 Counties. The moment whence Connolly is able to turn this catastrophe into a sharp historical experiment was 9 June 1832 when it is recorded that the Virgin Mary was believed to have appeared and offered a charm that would ward off cholera: ashes from blessed-turf that would protect a householder from cholera, when a portion was placed in the cottage rafters. And there was a commandment for communication: each householder was to mix a bit of the blessed-turf with his own hearth's ashes and give them in a cloth parcel to four other householders. In other words, a pyramid of communication was involved, each piece of sacred medical knowledge being multiplied by a factor of four at each iteration. (This limitation makes Connolly's experiment nicely conservative: if people were simply passing bits of knowledge from one person to another, they could do so more quickly and engage a large number of transmissions with no bother.) The results were striking: in the course of only six days the parcels of sacred medicine, in slightly varying versions, had gone all the way from Cork to Donegal and had spread over at least three-quarters of Ireland. The only limitations were that natural barriers, especially the mountainy parts of Connacht, were an impediment. Notably, however, in areas of alleged economic backwardness that were not barricaded by physical obstacles, communication was fluid. In the present context, what this train of events says is clear: in one of those rare moments when one can actually observe communication in Irish demotic culture, we see that news could travel rapidly and with reasonable accuracy.[20]

Now we can adduce another natural experiment, one somewhat less definitive, but nevertheless strongly indicative. We would like to have some test evidence that the Irish farm labourers were (or were not) responsive to market fluctuations if they—not later observers, they—felt it was in their primary self-interest to be so. The reason the agricultural labourers are important is that if they were responsive to markets that worked in terms of money when it suited their interests to be so, then *mutatis mutandis*, those above them were. Here is the experiment: it was conducted for us by vessels that plied the Britain-Ireland sea lanes; the subjects were Irish seasonal labourers; and the data were collected by the Irish census commissioners. The event in question was the British harvest season of 1841. In order to obtain some sense of how many Irish agricultural labourers worked the British harvests, the census commissioners put tally-men from 1 May to 1 August at the ports from which packets sailed to and from England and Scotland and they tried to ascertain the county from which each person originated. Unintentionally, this exercise became part of a natural experiment. (That none of these participants thought of themselves as being part of an experiment adds to its value.) To make sense of what occurred, one has to accept that the easiest port for labourers to reach from most parts of Connacht was Dublin harbour. The labourers were mostly on foot and an extra two days on the march was no small matter, especially given that they were in a race to get to English harvest areas, from whence they usually would work northwards. Yet, that is not what happened. According to the census commissioners, "the singular thrift and foresight which has frequently been remarked as characterizing these people, is curiously illustrated by [our] table, in which it will be seen that no less than 12,256 Connaught labourers embarked at Drogheda, and only 8,308 at Dublin." The commissioners continued: "This unusual circumstance is attributed to a small reduction in the fare from Drogheda, a few weeks before the season commenced, which reduction was industriously made known in all the towns through which the stream of labourers was likely to pass in its progress from the west."[21] Of course one can niggle at the edges of this result, but what remains unmuted is the informed admiration that the Irish census commissioners (never a notably sentimental bunch) had for these labourers—the spalpeens knew the difference between a ha'penny and a farthing and would tramp miles for the difference.

There is one point worth repeating that stands in contrast to the Swedish experience in the parallel time period: namely, that there was no legal impediment to Irish persons migrating out of the country, at least not in terms of passports or other civil inhibitions on exiting. (The chief inhibition was that if a person was being sought on a felony charge, he or she was to be apprehended and kept in the United Kingdom for trial: where, curiously, if the felony were of the right sort, the felon would then be sentenced to one of the colonies. Thus, for some felons, transportation became the preferred mode of emigration.) And, as I have shown already and will illustrate again, out-migration of some sort was just barely possible financially for most physically able adults, at least from the end of the Napoleonic wars onwards.

More importantly, it was within the financial ability of a significant proportion of the Irish population, poor though it generally was, to make an economically induced migratory move, if that had been desired.

Consider the situation. (1) From 1815 onwards, several New Worlds were open for filching. Doing so was hard work, but so too was supporting life any place. The end of the Napoleonic Wars in 1815 terminated a period of danger for long-distance migrants. Within half a dozen years, Australia, the Canadas, Newfoundland all became fair game, as did newly independent parts of South America, such as Argentina, Brazil, Venezuela, Chile and Mexico. Equally, it finally became clear, with the United States' victory over the United Kingdom at the Battle of New Orleans, and with the final defeat of Bonaparte, that the heart of the North American continent—"the Trans-Appalachian frontier"— would be controlled by the United States and would not be subject to wide-scale international warfare.[22] Whole worlds, therefore, were open. (2) Crucially, intercontinental travel became quite cheap in terms of money, if not of time. Near the end of the Napoleonic Wars, a steerage ticket from Liverpool to a US port cost £10–12 per adult, but by 1821 this had dropped to a bit over £4 to Quebec City and £5 to New York City. By the 1830s, the rates for steerage (with food rations) from Liverpool to North America ran from £3.10s to £5. Crucially (and rather surprisingly), this rate structure stayed roughly the same for the rest of the century. So, if the cost of emigration was affordable in the heavy years of out-migration later in the century, *mutatis mutandis* it was affordable earlier.[23] Note that the mode of demonstration here, based on J. D. Gould's observations, allows an escape from the tendentious matter of trying to ascertain the putative wages of an agricultural labourer in the pre-Famine era—most estimates hover around £5 annually, but on very slippery evidentiary ground and are not here directly relevant, and how much those above them on the scale grossed is purely speculative. The effect of Gould's data is to suggest that (a) since fare prices were stable over long periods of time, and (b) undeniably, hundreds of thousands of very poor people booked transatlantic passages in the Famine era, therefore (c), unless one wants to argue that the Famine migrants were financially better off that those of, say, the 1820s and 1830s, then it is clear that transoceanic migration was financially possible from at least the early 1820s onward for the bulk of the population. That they chose not to leave is another matter entirely and this points to the heart of the Irish migration decision which, in the pre-Famine era, was more of a cultural than an economic matter. And (3), finally to demonstrate this point in really simple terms. As will be shown in a moment, from the mid-1820s onward, one could get out of Ireland—at least to Great Britain—for a fare of a shilling at most.

To clarify. I am not attempting to prove directly that the clear and unambiguous refusal of the great mass of the Irish populace to engage in out-migration in the pre-Famine era was a function of their cultural values—using "cultural" in this instance the way most economic historians do, to cover almost all non-economic inputs into decision-making. Nor do I think one could ever directly demonstrate it. However, at some point, we have to go down one of two branching and unreconcilable lines of explanation: (1) Either the pre-Famine Irish refused to act on the widespread information they possessed about the risks of continuing to live in their society and thus they were in some ways backward, lazy and affrighted, or (2) they were adequately informed about risk, money and how to escape Ireland, but chose not to do so. Obviously, alternative "1" is merely reductive, because it forces one to define all instances of collective non-responsiveness to market calculations as evidence of societal retardation, thus leaving one with the definition that the only normal society is an "efficient" market society. This means that societies that largely reject the hegemony of "rational" calculations are pigeon-holed as being backward and their citizens as being adolescent and impercipient. That may be the paradigm for the International Monetary Fund in the twenty-first century, but it is bad history. Instead, alternative "2" is much more sensible, not least because we have historical documentation of several hundred non-market-dominated societies that have operated quite well. And, alternative "2" has the considerable advantage of treating pre-Famine Irish society on its own terms, not on lines-of-judgement set externally to the culture. Thus, what has been viewed as fatalism in the face of the *tremendum* in pre-Famine culture, I see as faith by the people that they would make it through; and what other observers have defined as passivity, I interpret as affirmation. That is, these tough, knowledgeable, able people took in the risk and, in effect, said: right, got that. But we're staying. And they did.

THREE

By opting for alternative "2," we are implicitly saying that in pre-Famine Ireland, as in pre-Deprivation Sweden, the idea of permanently leaving the homeland was not part of the thought-menu of the general culture. It was more often on the menu in Ireland than in Sweden, but nevertheless it was very much a minority alternative. Hence, we should follow a similar historical path as that we engaged in the case of pre-Deprivation Sweden: look for the significant minority (actually, here, minorities) whose actions and/or beliefs eventually caused them to act as a cultural puncture—the functional precursors of the post-Famine flood.

Here, in the first instance, we can move quickly back to a group that we have just left: the Irish seasonal agricultural labourers who worked in Great Britain. From the viewpoint of Irish demotic culture, one can view them as colporteurs of migration: they listened to the message of wages-to-be-won in England and Scotland; they went, did well enough, and returned home to share their earnings and inevitably their knowledge. Certainly Irish migrant labourers had long been part of the agricultural cycle of the neighbouring kingdoms: when the English parliament tried to expel all Irishmen in 1413, vagrants, a code-word for migratory workers, were specifically mentioned.[24] However, only after the Napoleonic Wars did the numbers become large. This was indirectly the result of one of those technological changes that everyone recognized at the time and now is almost forgotten: the improvement in steam engines that allowed them to be used in rough seas. In June 1816, the legendary *Rob Roy* made the first steam navigation from the Clyde to Belfast and opened the era of steam shipping to and fro across the Irish Sea. Within ten years, regular services ran from several east-coast ports in Ireland to the major British west-coast harbours. Previously there had been a motley flotilla of sailing vessels that carried passengers on the same voyages, and they were only gradually displaced and turned into carriers of low-priority cargos. The admirable characteristic of the steam vessels was their predictability. "Before the application of steam made its duration a matter of certainty, the voyage [between Ireland and Britain], which usually occupied but three or four days, could occupy three or four weeks."[25] In decent weather, the steam packets made Liverpool from Dublin in twelve hours and Holyhead in six. For potential seasonal labourers, the actual sailing time required was of less importance than the high degree of certainty the steam vessels promised. This made all the difference; the labourers could plan their tramp and know that within a given amount of time they almost certainly would be in Britain, moving towards work. At first the fares were very high—14 shillings for steerage—but they quickly dropped, to a shilling one-way, or slightly more. In 1824 and in 1833, the Cork-Bristol run offered passage for five or six pence and there were times when the passage was entirely free to the Clyde or to Bristol, because coal boats, having emptied their holds in Ireland, needed ballast to return to Britain. Irish migrants as ballast had the great advantage of being able to jump on and off the boat, unlike beach-shingle or other of the usual forms of ballast. The really strong flow of Irish seasonal migrants thus dates only from the 1820s when, in the words of a parliamentary report, a "floating bridge" was put in place between Ireland and Britain.[26]

The actual numbers that used the floating bridge are a mystery. Having become a large platoon in the 1820s, the numbers grew and in 1841 were large enough (as already mentioned) to attract the attention of the Irish census commissioners. They tallied 57,651 persons leaving Ireland for Great Britain between 1 May and 1 August 1841.[27] This was certainly an undercount as some seasonal labourers shipped earlier in the year to work at tasks such as completing the previous year's threshing. And, as the commissioners themselves admitted, the census staff totally lost boatloads of migrants who boarded vessels that anchored off the coast, rather than docked at harbour. As for the movement back to Ireland, the census commissioners' intentions were good: they planned to enumerate in the Irish ports all persons who had sailed from a British port to an Irish one. But, "on their return to Ireland they land in such haste, that all attempts to count them were abandoned."[28] In a counsel-of-despair, the census commissioners guessed that 40,000 seasonal migrants made the round trip and between 17–18,000 stayed on in England and Scotland.[29] This guess of 17–18,000 permanent migrants to Britain during the four specified months of 1841 is not crazy, for it comes close to their estimated permanent flow for the period of about 18,500 a year.[30] But it is irrelevant to the main point: that their summer-of-frenetic-counting has made it easy for historians to walk away from the matter. And, what I suspect really is the case is that the actual number of temporary Irish workers in Britain was considerably greater than the "40,000" the Irish census people gave us as net, or the 57,000-plus as gross, and that the number of Irish-born persons in Britain who were permanently "settled" is correspondingly less than is usually thought.[31]

What is certain is that the seasonal labourers came back to Ireland with money in their pockets. The Irish census commissioners believed that each male labourer brought back in hand about £5 from his time in Britain.[32] This paid the rent on the family holding and bought necessities. Consider what this meant from a cultural viewpoint. However unintentionally, each returned labourer was a missionary from a strange land. Each one brought detailed knowledge of how to travel from the remotest part of Ireland to the land of the world's first industrial revolution; and how to tie into a transportation network that circled the globe. Indeed, the majority disembarked at Liverpool, the centre of the worldwide transshipment of human beings. For the most part, the migrant workers were preserving by their economic support the society of rural Ireland; simultaneously, they were inducing a series of cultural punctures. Each time a returned spalpeen told the story of his travels, he was unintentionally, but unavoidably, leading his auditors to rip up their old map of the world and redraw it. The pragmatic knowledge of how to get out of Ireland was not acted upon by the majority of those to whom it was retailed. Yet, it did not vanish: the knowledge was stored as facts, as tools not at present needed, but there when the time came.

By now, we are starting to suspect that the Ó Gráda Paradox is rather like a Russian doll: within it are further subsets of historical paradox. One of these we have been illustrating when looking at the travel pattern of Irish migrant workers to Great Britain: (a) even among the most economically mobile—20 to 35-year-old males—the overwhelming bulk of the population did not do the economically rational thing and sell their labour in one of the higher markets outside of Ireland; (b) however, those who did indeed decide to do so, passed over a major threshold in *mentalité* and quickly adopted the model of "economic man" so long as they were in the labour market. As the Irish census commissioners noted, the spalpeens were highly responsive to cost incentives and committed to turning their earnings into domestic savings.

A nice confirmation of this last observation is found by looking at the overall pattern of permanent out-migration from Ireland. The decade, 1831–41, is the only one for which we have reasonably solid information, but it is highly revealing. Given below are the choices of destination for permanent out-migrants, 1831–40:[33]

Destination	Number in thousands	Total out-migration (%)
British North America	262	42.2
United States of America	171	27.5
Australasia	5	0.8
Great Britain	183	29.5
Total	**621**	**100.0**

The key question these data raise is: why was British North America (not the USA) strongly preferred as a destination by transoceanic migrants? The answer is glaringly simple. These people, once they had decided to migrate overseas, acted with calculation and economic shrewdness—and sailing to Canada (that is, British North America) in most cases was cheaper, even for those heading to the northern parts of the USA. The business of shipping migrants to North America was highly competitive and the system of imperial preferences enforced in the British Empire provided an invisible subvention for each transoceanic passenger. Squared timber and certain commodities came into the United Kingdom from British North America under tariff protection and the ships had to take something back across the Atlantic. Among the useful cargoes were human beings. The overall transaction was that, because there was not free trade in certain items produced by the colonies, the UK public paid more for some goods, while the emigrants from the UK paid less to leave the country than the true cost of transport. (There is, of course, also a distance factor that favoured the Maritimes and Quebec.) "In 1832 steerage passage from Ireland to New York cost 90 shillings ... three times the fare from Irish ports to Quebec."[34] Even if the differential was not that great in every year, it was substantial, and Irish migrants calculated carefully.

A parenthesis. Note: (1) that the pattern-of-preference for destinations shown for 1831–40—British North America, then Great Britain, then the USA—can be taken as representing the overall pattern, 1801–45; (2) however, also note that preferred places of disembarkation are not to be confused with places of permanent settlement, since sailing to British ports for a permanent "settlement" was often part of a multistep journey to some New World, and in North America there was a good deal of cross-border traffic, both from BNA to the USA and vice versa.; (3) and that, concerning the North American traffic, one should not lazily assume that the Irish migrants to Canada automatically dropped into the US and therefore that the history of the Irish in North America can be written simply as the history of the Irish in the USA.[35]

FOUR

Out-migrants rarely were typical of their home society and it is merely a commonplace to note this. In the case of Ireland, however, they were much more different from the stay-at-homes before the Famine than they were after: which is only reasonable if, as I am arguing, the pre-Famine out-migrants were in some sense deviant from the culture of the majority and, in contrast, after the Famine, emigrants were acting in conformity with dominant cultural values.

Still, we have yet to survey several of the sorts of people who provided the cultural punctures that made later emigration so quick and obvious a course of action to be followed. Granted, the seasonal Irish labourers were important as lamplighters of the paths out of the remoter parts of Ireland, yet they were the least deviant of out-migrants, for they left Ireland temporarily so that they could remain in it permanently.[36]

The pre-Famine Irish situation was much messier than was that of pre-Deprivation Sweden. That, though, is one reason why we engage in comparative studies: sometimes one gets a clearer hint of what the character and dimensions of a fundamental historical process may be by looking at an instance where that process is sharply focused. In Sweden, the Readers in general and the Baptists in particular were clearly silhouetted as being ideological deviants within Swedish culture; and the ties of the Baptists to transatlantic co-religionists was so clear that one can locate confidently the pre-Deprivation punctures in Swedish society. So, we might well look for similar, but less easily identifiable, cohorts within Irish society.

The Irish situation is a very slippery eel to wrestle with, because multiple groups were involved. Most of the emigrating cohorts had behavioural roots set down well before 1800. This means, among other things, long before comprehensive and non-reactive accounting of out-migrants began. Yet, most (emphatically, not all, most) of the sets of pre-Famine out-migrants that we will survey had one thing in common: each cohort came out of a tense sectarian world and felt that in some ways life was stacked against them.

In the previous chapter, I summarized the Irish penal code of the eighteenth century. Here that eighteenth-century code has to be placed along a wider horizon. In matters related to Irish out-migration of the post-Reformation era, a triad of patterns existed. (1) From the submission of the Great O'Neill to Queen Elizabeth's deputy in the spring of 1603 to the signing of the Treaty of Limerick in the autumn of 1691, there indeed existed penal statutes enacted by one side upon the other (depending on who was dominant), but the real situation was one of civil war. If the war sometimes raged hot and sometimes was merely smouldering, civil war still it was. (2) Usually Irish historians date the penal code in its high form as running from the early 1690s (some prefer 1703) until a series of repeal measures, 1781–93. That is fine as long as one accepts (3) that a shadow-code continued until 1871 when the Anglican church ceased to be a government-financed state church. Within that third period the main event was Catholic Emancipation (that is, the right to sit in the United Kingdom parliament without taking a noxious oath) in 1829. However, also signally important, although rarely understood as a matter of Catholic-relief, were the Encumbered Estates Acts of 1848 and 1849 which finally permitted the breaking of entail on landed property. This quickly made a large amount of landed property, most of which was formerly held by dead-broke Protestant gentry and aristo-crats, available to anyone in the Irish economy with enough cash or credit.[37] Given the eighteenth-century penal code, the sectarian wars that preceded it, and the shadow-code that followed on, we should first look at the primary (but not the only) victims of this situation—the Roman Catholics. Our interest here is in matters that directly influenced the Irish portion of the Great European Migration of the nineteenth and early twentieth centuries.[38] And the general pattern is once again one of the Russian dolls that are enhulled within the Ó Gráda Paradox—this one being that the curious nature of the Irish religious tensions forced the majority of the population to act as if it were the minority. This follows from the sectarian power being mostly in the hands of the adherents of the Church of Ireland, Anglicans in modern usage, who comprised roughly one-in-ten of the population of Ireland.

Now, to look at out-migration, take first the case of Newfoundland.[39] Whatever its attractions, no one should ever confuse Newfoundland with Eldorado. That certainly was the lesson learned by the first Catholic colonizer, Sir George Calvert (created Lord Baltimore, 1625). Calvert was English and a Catholic, albeit of a blurred hue. Reports are that he had embraced Catholicism in 1621, but kept it quiet. Certainly he had done so by 1625. He had already received grants of lands in County Longford and, later, in County Wexford, which had been taken from Irish Catholics. As required by the terms of the grants, he had tried to fill these lands with Protestants, but did not do very well. He had, however, acquired a speculative grant in 1621 for a Newfoundland colony and then for the entire Avalon Peninsula in 1623. In line with the official government line, he publicly talked about planting Protestant settlements in Newfoundland, but his real market was Irish Catholic gentry (in this case Old English) who had been displaced by the sectarian wars and wanted to recoup their social position. And they would supply their own retainers, meaning impoverished Catholic tenantry. Lord Baltimore sent out agents in 1625 and himself visited in 1627 and then arrived with his family in 1628. The colony had three priests and perhaps 100 settlers. His lordship spent the winter in agonies of cold and rheum and wrote piteous letters to his monarch and to anyone who might help him. The colony, Ferryland, survived; Lord Baltimore looked for more salubrious grounds. He sailed to Virginia and tried to plant a colony there: the Virginia Company blocked that effort. But shortly before his death in 1632 Lord Baltimore received a grant for the Maryland colony, rather richer pickings.[40]

Newfoundland, in the eyes of contemporary royal courtiers, represented only the crumbs of empire, but these could add up. Although the Irish settlements in Newfoundland grew very slowly for the next century and a half (and were submerged in an English- and Scots-controlled commercial system), a fascinating circular trade emerged—Waterford-Newfoundland-Waterford, with side-loops to English ports—that ran from the 1690s until the 1820s. And mostly it was run by Catholic merchants and overwhelmingly it employed Catholic labour. The fundamentals of the trade were that fishers and shore labourers were sent from Ireland to Newfoundland and that provisions were dispatched, sometimes to England, sometimes elsewhere, but eventually vessels with provender and other supplies sailed to Newfoundland; on the return journey, massive amounts of dried cod were carried back and, at season's end, most of the transhumant workers. In the 1730s, the mostly temporary population taken to Newfoundland was around 1,000 persons. This rose to about 5,000 a year in the era of the American Revolution. That out of a total summer population, mostly from England, of roughly 30,000.[41] Permanent settlement in Newfoundland was discouraged by the imperial government—in 1763 there were only around 12,000 resident settlers of all nationalities—but it was 21,975 in 1805 and 40,568 in 1815, and growing. How many of these were Irish Catholics is unclear, but the colonial governor's office estimated that in St John's there were 2,000 Irish persons in 1794 and this had increased to about 14,000 when a census was taken in 1836.[42]

John Mannion's study of the trade makes it clear that during the eighteenth century, a slight majority of the Irish merchants in the Newfoundland business were Roman Catholics.[43] Given the Irish penal code, how did they get away with it? In part this was possible because the Irish circular trade was covered by a much larger trade with Newfoundland that was run by west-of-England merchants, and focused on Bristol. The Irish Catholic shipping owners kept their head down, and frequently made an outward call to an English port, thus merging in the general moil of English shipping. Irish provisions often were offloaded in an English port and carried on English bottoms to Newfoundland. Still, that does not explain how the Catholic merchants escaped the economic penalties visited upon their rural gentry counterparts. One suspects that they were canny, avoiding applying for membership in corporations or guilds that required an anti-Catholic test; also it was landed property, not trading establishments, that the penal code moved from Catholic to Protestant hands. Besides, it paid the Irish authorities and the Ascendancy to ignore the Catholic trading activities: exported salt beef and salt pork paid money directly back into the agricultural sector, with a bit taken off for customs duties. However veiled in discretion some of these trading activities were, and however small the actual number of Irish permanent settlers in Newfoundland, the cultural sum total of all these activities was unmistakable. In the orbits of Waterford, Wexford City, Youghal and Cork City, a strand of experience and knowledge was kept alive among the Irish Catholic population that ran against the tight adhesion to home and hearth: half-way across the Atlantic was an unpleasant but remunerative site for seasonal work. This message thus kept alive in south Munster and south-east Leinster was similar in tone and effect to that which the seasonal migrants to Great Britain carried back to Connacht and north-western Ulster. As permanent settlers increased in Newfoundland in the first half of the nineteenth century, for many families along the south-east Irish coast, a cousin on the near coast of North America became an ordinary part of the family furnishings.[44]

FIVE

Another, almost fugitive, aspect of the mental map of a thin slice of the Irish Catholic populace concerned the West Indies.[45] It is easily forgotten that in the seventeenth and eighteenth centuries a network of Catholic gentry families from around Cork, Limerick and Galway used the West Indies as a way of preserving their positions as the sectarian tectonics of Irish society rocked back and forth and, mostly, hurt the Catholics. These are well-known families with gentry associations: Blake, Cotter, Farrell, Galway, Kirwan, Nangle, Roche, Shiell, Skerret, Stapleton, Sweetman, Tuite and Walsh, among others. The Irish Catholic connection ran from the 1630s to the 1830s at the gentry/merchant-adventurer level. The ties to the Caribbean were sharply two-tiered and a lower level of young men and women, recruited in Munster and south-east Leinster as indentured servants, provided the initial draught of brute human strength: until African slaves became readily available. The Irish Catholic component in the West Indian slave system was wrapped in the larger demographics of the English empire; and the Caribbean islands were Beyond the Line, in the sense of being places where the usual rules did not apply.[46] Good places for Irish Catholics of all classes to preserve their status or improve their prospects.

Three characteristics stand out concerning the hugely variegated Irish Catholic migrants to the Caribbean. The first is that they were white. This otiose observation is necessary only because a strange strand has straggled into Irish historiography: it tries to present Irish Catholic migrants as forever-victimized and therefore innocent of hard dealing with indigenous peoples and with African slaves—and thus as not-white in the sense that whiteness carries a moral burden in these matters. As far as this idea is sited in the West Indies and in the Irish homeland, it has been definitively knocked on the head by Nini Rodgers, *Ireland, Slavery and Anti-Slavery: 1612–1865* (2007). In the Caribbean, the Irish of all religions and classes participated willingly in the dispossession of the Arawak and Carib; and they were only too pleased when the Africans were debouched to do the heavy labour. And many Catholic families back in Ireland quietly prospered by way of the slave economy.[47]

Indeed, the second characteristic is equally clear: that over time, almost everyone involved in the West Indian business, from merchant prince down to indentured labourer, had a chance in the Big Casino, an opportunity to win. Not that the conditions were salubrious and not that everybody won, but the odds were better than being a Catholic at home. Mind you, even for the planter class, life expectancy in the West Indies was short: a study of Jamaican and Barbadian tombstones for 1650–1750 shows that for white males who reached the age of 20, the median age of death was 45, and for women it was 36.[48] The most obvious winners among the Irish Catholics were those who entered the slave-islands' game with the most status, if not necessarily the most money, to wager. The classic case is that of William Stapleton who was appointed governor of Montserrat in 1668 and used this as the basis for a Leeward Islands empire. He was the second son of an Old English family in Tipperary that had lost its lands in the civil wars through loyalty to the Royalist cause. He was, therefore, an estateless soldier-of-fortune; but Stapleton had served with distinction at the rank of Lieutenant-Colonel and deserved reward. His aptitude for colonial government was considerable, and he was highly adept at manoeu-vring around the awkward fact that he—and several members of his administration—did not affirm the Established Church and would not renounce the Catholic faith. When he died in 1686 he left behind a baronetcy (created in 1679), several square miles of choice plantations on four islands, hundreds of slaves, and lands in England.[49]

At the other end of the social spectrum, the indentured labourers had little hope of acquiring plantations and their life could be cruel. Yet, for them the Caribbean was also a casino, and they too could win, albeit on a smaller scale. The key to understanding West Indian indentured labour is that it revolved around defined-term contracts that were entered into by young men and woman who were desperately short of opportunity in Ireland, but were not willing to jump onto just any boat. The clearest illustration is the difficulties of Captain Thomas Anthony who in 1636 tried to fill his vessel with young servants at Kinsale, a key out-point for the under- and unemployed young adults of Munster. The trouble for Captain Anthony was not only that there was competition for the young indenturees (a Dutch merchant captain had already scooped up the best of the lot and another Dutch vessel already was in port), but that the potential migrants knew too much about alternative futures—they refused to go to Virginia, where Captain Anthony was originally contracted, and would only go to St Christopher, where wage rates were higher.[50] Equally important for an understanding of indentured labour is a recognition that it was a fixed-term contract—between four and six-and-three-quarter years in the West Indies in the mid-seventeenth century. At the end of that time the former servants received "freedom dues" of £10–12 sterling (often paid in equivalents in local currency or in sugar or tobacco).[51] At that point, they were free agents in a chroni-cally labour-short market. This is where their West Indian gamble either paid off or went bust. Some sank into inert poverty (Jamaica and Barbados developed a poor-white ethclass); some became plantation managers and slave overseers; others, probably the majority, moved from island to island, searching opportunity, and migrating eventually to the North American mainland, especially to the Delaware Valley. It is crucial to recognize that for these Irish Catholic youths, mostly from Munster, indentured labourers were not considered chattel slaves or anything close to it. It is estimated that between 1630 and 1780, 50 to 60 per cent of the "labour flow" to the British colonies in the Caribbean and North America were either formally indentured or were persons whose status was virtually the same as that of indentured servants.[52] Thus, from the mid-1650s onward, when their terms had been fulfilled, the white labouring population in the English portion of the western hemisphere was made up mostly of free persons. Unpleasant, arbitrary, risky and sometimes cruelly exploitative, yes; but indentureship was not slavery.[53]

The third primary characteristic of the band of Irish Catholic migrants to the Caribbean is that many of them were both by social inclination and political necessity notably plastic in their religious adhesion. Brian McGinn has observed that "the religious status of the early settlers was in fact flexible and equivocal. Rather than professing either a Catholic or a Protestant faith, many Irish planters adhered to both—either at separate times or, in some cases, simultaneously."[54] To take one small case: on Montserrat, the most Irish and the most Roman Catholic of the British empire's Caribbean islands, of the 17 largest Catholic land- and slaveholding families, 11 (roughly 53 per cent) turned Protestant between the family's seventeenth-century arrival on the island and 1729.[55] As for the lower end of the social spectrum, there are no direct Caribbean data that I am aware of. It is not useful to draw any inference from the fact that neither the Established Church nor the Catholic church provided much in the way of resources and competent personnel until well into the nineteenth century. That noted, as we will see in a moment, a related situation in the mainland American colonies resulted in a large rollover of Irish Catholic frontier settlers to Protestantism. This seems to have been mostly for convenience (there were more Protestant clergy about and births, marriages and funerals usually require sacral celebration) and also to reduce friction with the majority of their neighbours, Protestants.

The Irish Catholics in the West Indies were not a big-number case, but they were far more consequential historically than they might at first appear. One must remember that for most of the seventeenth century the West Indies were the really valuable colonies in the Empire, and, further, that with stepwise migration, the Irish migrants to the Caribbean subsequently became part of the foundation population of North America. But in what numbers? Louis Cullen estimates the seventeenth-century Irish migration to all the Americas as roughly 30,000.[56] W. J. Smyth calculates 100,000,[57] while Fitzgerald and Lambkin in their recent survey opt for 60,000.[58] (This, in comparison to an English flow in the same period of roughly 190,000.)[59] Manifestly, no one knows with much precision how many Irish migrants went to the Americas, much less about the Caribbean proportion.[60] However, Cullen is convincing in arguing that the seventeenth-century migration to the Americas was strongly from the south and east of Ireland, the very areas in which warfare and subsequent famine had knocked loose both Catholic gentry and their retainers and tenantry.[61] So, purely conjecturally, if a slight majority of the seventeenth-century Irish migrants to the Americas were Roman Catholics when they left Ireland and if the West Indies was the most common first point of settlement, it still is hard to get much more than 25,000 seventeenth-century Irish Catholics as migrating as settlers to the West Indies, even using W. J. Smyth's upper overall estimate.[62] No big deal, apparently, except that demographically they became consequential over time, because they and their descendants became a sizeable chunk of the demographic base of the American mainland. As for Ireland itself, direct Catholic migration to the West Indies dropped in the 1690s as the London government exerted more direct control on its sugar colonies and pushed local governors and their assemblies to enforce exclusions on Catholics in civic offices. This worked for a while, but by mid-eighteenth century, the white population on several of the islands was so thin on the ground that penal measures had to be abandoned: London came to fear African slaves more than Irish Catholic slave owners. By then, labour migrants were bypassing the islands and going directly to North America. What continued was a network of trade relationships of several prosperous Catholic families of Cork, Limerick, Galway and, increasingly Dublin, dealing in sugar, rum, provisions and sometimes in off-shore slaves and West Indian plantation ownership. This spilled into general Irish commerce and politics. "The ubiquity of Irish contacts with the Caribbean islands in the eighteenth century is impressive; supplies for and produce from slave plantations impacted upon town and countryside, quickening the pace of social and political change."[63] Thus, the expanding Irish commercial relationships with the slave economy in the eighteenth century fuelled urban growth in Munster and around Dublin (meat packing and sugar refining) and they buoyed the rural hinterlands with increased demand for animal products. And this, in the swirling floods and eddies of pre-Famine Irish migration history leads to another irony within the overall Ó Gráda Paradox: to some degree, the penal legislation against Catholics was counteracted by the imperial enslavement of black Africans, as both Catholic and Protestant merchants did well out of the West Indian trade. And, ironically, this helped hold together the alliance of liberal members of the all-Protestant Irish parliament and the leaders of the Catholics who sought penal relief: for, after the American Revolution, Irish "patriots" demanded free trade for Ireland, by which they meant the right to participate fully in the spoils of the slave system, via sugar, molasses, rum, provisions and human bodies. Thus, most of the substantial Catholic sugar refiners who signed a petition supporting the interests of their industry in 1780 were also fund-raisers for the Catholic Committee. Indeed, one of them, Edward Byrne, the wealthiest Catholic merchant in Ireland, was given special responsibility for getting the Roches of Limerick and Cork on side for Catholic penal relief.[64] And, later, Roche's Bank of Cork City, founded in the early nineteenth century, was the first Catholic-owned bank in Ireland and its base was three generations of extensive commerce in the slave islands.[65]

If, in the nineteenth century, slave emancipation meant that few Irish persons, whatever their rank, were interested in migrating to the Caribbean, the long-standing trade relationships with the Caribbean running throughout much of Munster, and parts of Connacht and Leinster, left a residual knowledge that was especially salient for a small cross-section of the Catholic population: it ran from country drovers to abattoir workers, to sugar boilers, to clerks in factoring firms, to substantial Catholic businessmen and merchant-adventurers. They knew they were part of a larger world, even if, for the moment, they prosecuted their personal well-being at home.

On the eve of the Great Famine, the Catholic relationship with Newfoundland and the residual knowledge of the hectic (albeit sometimes covert) comings and goings that had pivoted around the slave islands were small blocks of information. But each case was a puncture point in the dominant cultural value of staying at home, despite the avalanche of risk that was poised above the Irish populace. Neither of these puncture points should be overemphasized, but, when tied to a third instance—the experience of the pre-Famine Irish Catholic migration to North America—a perforation was in place, one that facilitated the fundamental cultural shifts of the Famine era's proceeding with startling swiftness.

SIX

One mentions the pre-Famine Irish Catholic migration to North America and then takes a deep breath: like almost all historical phenomena, we know a good deal less about it than we would wish. That is not the problem. The real problem is that as historians we know a great deal less than we think we do, and are loath to accept the indeterminacy that necessarily veils the subject. Here, is the nub of the difficulty: there are no direct systematic data on the number of Catholic migrants from Ireland at any time. Full stop: anytime, even the twentieth century. Nor are there direct systematic data on the religious persuasion of Irish migrants in any of the significant places of their pre-Famine arrival. And only in Upper Canada (now Ontario) are there convincing proxy data. Until the early 1980s the dominant practice was simply to present a set of assertions (or, to imply them and skip nimbly away) that posited: (a) the only Irish migration that counted was the transatlantic migration to the USA (British North America was excluded, Great Britain ignored, and the rest of the world virtually unmentioned); (b) the migration of Irish persons to the Thirteen Colonies before the American Revolution was taken as being almost entirely Ulster Presbyterian; (c) the post-Famine migration that counted was to the USA and this was so overwhelmingly Roman Catholic that "Irish-American" was thought to be a synonym for "Irish Catholic"; and (d) the long period between the Revolution and 1845 was virtually ignored. There were honourable exceptions, but I am not here guying the then state of affairs in general. Since then, a good deal of admirable work has decentred the world of Irish diaspora studies, particularly by suggesting that destinations other than those that are at present in the USA were of significance. (The most influential items of this collective work are clearly identified in the present volume.) Nevertheless, a central twin conundrum remains: what part did Catholics play in the Irish flow to colonial America?; and what part in the larger flow, 1800–45, to North America generally? Not easy questions, for although the United States began federal enumerations in 1790, the census authorities did not begin asking people where they were born until the 1850 census—and never, to this day, have they enquired into religious allegiance.

So, there are only disconnected observations and heroic guessing. That is not said dismissively, for the willingness to go up on a high wire without a safety net beneath is rare among historians. David Noel Doyle has been the most intrepid in this regard and I present his intuitions with the belief that they are probably realistic in their major implications and undoubtedly are inaccurate in their details. (I imagine he would agree.) In Doyle's interpretations, the 1790 US census can be read as revealing a distribution of the multigenerational ethnic/national groups population (that is, the first, and all subsequent

generations according to whence they originally out-migrated) among a total population
of about 3.17 million white persons:

	Doyle's 1981 estimates[66]	Doyle's 1989 estimates[67]
Roman Catholic	139,400	4–5% of US total [c,143,000]
Anglican	31,600	?
Ulster-Presbyterian	276,000	350,000-plus
Total Irish	**447,000**	**440,000–517,000**

An admirable aspect of Doyle's willingness to provide varying sets of guesses is that
it confirms that any semi-quantitative statements about eighteenth-century migration
patterns have to be followed by a clear caveat—that they should be taken as being (in
my view) in a maximum range of plus-or-minus 25 per cent of any suggested number.[68]
Doyle's work says that Irish Catholics were a minority of pre-1790 migrants to the USA,
but a significant one.

For most of the eighteenth century, one necessarily talks not about the migrant
stream to all of North America, but merely to the former Thirteen Colonies (up to 1776
the non-French flow of European migrants to the Maritimes, New France, and areas
west, was so small that ignoring it does not distort the general picture). However, towards
the end of the eighteenth century and thereafter, British North America (as it was usually
termed between the final separation of the USA in 1783 and Canadian confederation in
1867) was a strong alternative to the USA as a primary destination. From 1815 until the
mid-Famine years it undoubtedly was the destination-of-choice for migrants, wherever
in eastern North America they eventually planned to settle.[69] And there is no evidence of
any significant segregation of Irish Catholics and non-Catholics in this matter, although
it has been suggested that Protestants, being better off, generally tended to go to Philadelphia and other US ports and the poorer Catholics to Quebec and New Brunswick.[70]
The entire east coast of North America north of Florida was open to Irish Catholics, not
just the old Thirteen Colonies, and they knew it.

The only systematic information available on the actual Catholic proportion of
the overall Irish migrant flow to North America originates in British North America.
It is proxy data that come out of the 1842 census of Upper Canada (Ontario). These
data have their limits, but possess the advantage of dealing with the entire population
of the province. And Upper Canada, being by far the "most Irish" jurisdiction in North
America in ethnic terms, has a wide sample of a large number (for the times) of Irish
migrants. Among the Irish-born and among the first generation born of Irish parentage
who were resident in Upper Canada in 1842, 34.5 per cent were Roman Catholic.[71]
Of course a census is taken at one point in time and does not represent a summary of
migrant flows over time (early migrants die off; and on the key cultural issue of religion,
conversions to the faith of the majority may reduce the minority religious estimates). That
granted, I would be more comfortable taking as a statement of Irish migration to North
America that, from 1800 through 1841, somewhat over one-third of all Irish migrants
were Catholics, than I would with any of the other guesses I have seen. In addition, I
suspect that in the heavy outflow of 1842–45 they were at least half.[72] This is to reinforce

one of the basic straight-ahead points that I have been here arguing in this chapter: that the Ó Gráda Paradox—which underscores the large absolute numbers of total Irish out-migrants as compared to other European countries and simultaneously highlights the striking reluctance of the people to leave in relation to the risk they experience in staying—does not indicate ignorance, economic backwardness, fecklessness, or indolence on the part of the Irish Catholic population. No, every person who out-migrated, whether to Great Britain or North America or Australasia, whether seasonally, as was the case with many migrants to Newfoundland and to Britain, or permanently, had processed a good deal of information and acted upon it. And they themselves became information beacons. Sometimes they returned home, sometimes they wrote,[73] always they were talked about. Their behaviour in emigrating, though strongly deviant from dominant cultural values, was a set of punctures in the cultural norms. They became predicates of a future change in cultural norms.

To conclude in a very compressed fashion our conspectus of the Irish Catholic migrants to North America before the Great Famine: first, one must again state, they were white Europeans. They were not chattels and, like all other Europeans in North America, they benefited from, and indirectly participated in, the sack and reduction (in the Cromwellian sense) of the indigenous population, and they also benefited from the enslavement of Africans. Second, they settled mostly in rural areas and participated in an economy that was primarily agricultural. So did every other nationality, and the point would not need stating except that a strong tradition in Irish diaspora scholarship emphasizes that after the Famine, the migrants to the USA were city people. This may or not be true; but certainly before the Famine the Irish Catholic migrants were rural. Third, it appears probable that in the eighteenth century most Irish Catholic migrants to the Thirteen Colonies came as indentured servants, but in the first half of the nineteenth century they shipped under the newly dominant system of prepaid fares.[74] And, fourthly, the proportion of Irish Catholics in North American society was almost certainly less than their proportion in the migration stream. Or, more bluntly: conversion to some form of Protestantism was far from rare. This is a vexed topic, not least because until recently it has been viewed through the lens of later nineteenth-century Irish Catholicism which was deeply devoted to keeping the faithful, faithful. The religious blurring that occurred in eighteenth and early portions of the nineteenth centuries was not something that historians within the Irish Catholic community wished to dwell on, especially if they were accustomed to the compounding of Irish nationalism and Irish Catholicism as inter-twined virtues. Yet it was a reality. John England, the first Catholic bishop of Charleston, South Carolina, was using numbers the way the biblical prophets did, metaphorically, when he suggested in 1839 that three million Irish Catholics had been lost in the almost priestless inland areas of the USA;[75] metaphorical, indeed—there had not been that many total Irish Catholics to all of North America by that date, but serious nonetheless: until at least the early 1840s, the Catholics were for turning. No great spiritual schism was involved, merely ordinary social physics. Most Irish Catholics were living in rural and small-town settings where they were surrounded by Protestants. They were less well-served by their church than were the Protestant denominations, most of which, especially the Baptist, Methodist and other congregationally organized groups, mobilized more easily in frontier and new farming areas. During the eighteenth century most of the colonies had some form of penal legislation against Catholics and the residuals continued well into the nineteenth century. These realities require recognition, for unless one wears sectarian blinders, it is hard to accept an historical perception that a former Irish Catholic was any the less Irish because, in America, he or she became a Protestant.[76]

SEVEN

Within Ireland, Catholics in the penal era and its aftermath were a majority group that, because of the singular nature of the Irish state religious settlement, was disadvantaged the way religious minorities were on the European continent: thus, the fact that they in many ways acted like an aggrieved minority is hardly surprising. But what about the demographic minority within the Irish population, the Protestants?[77] In the eighteenth century and the pre-Famine years, they were fairly sharply split between the Anglo-Irish (Anglicans) and Dissenters (mostly, but not entirely, Ulster Presbyterians). The penal code of the eighteenth century and the privileged position of the Church of Ireland until its disestablishment in 1871 was constructed for the Anglicans' benefit. The first religious census of Ireland, that of 1834, provides the following religious breakdown:[78]

Denomination	Number	Percentage
Roman Catholic	6,427,712	81
Anglican	852,064	11
Presbyterian	642,356	8
Other Dissenters	21,808	–

As far as Irish out-migration before 1845 is concerned, the Ulster Presbyterians were the lead sector among the Protestants.[79] (Other smaller Protestant groups will be mentioned below, but the Presbyterians are the ones who were most influential.) The Ulster Presbyterians were all too aware of being defined in Ireland as a distinct and discountenanced minority.[80] To take only the most obvious results of their position in Ireland, in the homeland they were generally sympathetic to the American Revolution, were overwhelmingly for Irish political reform, and a robust minority took part in the 1798 Rising; in the Thirteen Colonies a sizeable minority of the Ulster-Scots and their descendants took an active part in the American Revolution. An entire universe of causality lies behind their attitudes and behaviour, running from what Sean Connolly called "the dour incivility of the Presbyterians," that could be traced to their lowland Scottish roots,[81] to their biblical world-view on many issues and Enlightenment emphasis upon literacy and logic. All this produced "a classic milieu for the development of late-eighteenth century popular radicalism."[82] Natural dissidents, indeed.

That being true, it nevertheless is a good idea to focus fairly tightly on the smaller causalities that produced the most migration-inclined minority in Ireland. And the key here is that they felt themselves to be caught in a *kulturkampf* with the Established Church. Religion is far from the whole story of Ulster Presbyterian cultural dissidence, but it is the pivot upon which all the other aspects of their attitude hinge.[83]

Their collective perspective, in which they often defined themselves as being politically slighted and economically cheated, was produced by the several forms of discrimination (including political and economic) being perceived through the prism of the state church's early attempts to victimize them religiously. It is easy enough to argue that the Presbyterians' "oppressions" were based on questions of authority,[84] not on narrow matters of religious dogma or liturgical practice, but that misses the point that religion itself is about beliefs in the nature of authority: divine authority. More germane is the caveat that in the earlier decades of the seventeenth century, Presbyterian clergy in Ireland had been perfectly willing to occupy empty churches and glebes in Ulster and to collect tithes. At first the Church of Ireland was too weak to resist, so a *faute de mieux* toleration of the early Presbyterians existed, these Dissenters being preferable to Roman Catholics. When Thomas Wentworth (earl of Strafford, 1640) became lord deputy of Ireland in 1632, he appointed vigorous high church bishops to the northern sees and the culture-war with the Presbyterians was on—and not to cease until 1871. Near the end of the civil wars of the mid-seventeenth century, the Presbyterians, though they had earlier been persecuted by Cromwell who had drawn up plans to send their leaders beyond the Shannon,[85] had made an uneasy alliance with the Cromwellians. They were too attached to monarchy to be entirely trusted by the Cromwellians, but they were preferable to Anglicans, so their seizure of several score parishes and of their revenues was approved. And then, following the Restoration of Charles II in 1660, the Presbyterian clergy were turned out of 61 parishes and the battle with the state church was directly re-engaged. Clearly indicative of how the fight for authority pivoted around religion was four Presbyterian ministers being imprisoned in the years 1660–70 for refusal to respond to a summons from a bishop of the state church.[86] In 1681, the Laggan Presbytery declared a public day of fasting and prayer for the Christian church in Ireland and Britain. This was taken as being an interference with Crown prerogatives, and another four Presbyterian clerics were summoned to the Privy Council in Dublin, interviewed and fined £20 each: they refused to pay and spent almost a year under house arrest.[87]

Yet, the Restoration Settlement, while kicking the Presbyterian clergy, simultaneously held out a sweetener or at least a bit of compensation. In 1672 the Crown instituted the *regium donum*. This royal gift provided £600 per annum towards the payment of Presbyterian clergy. Subsequently, the grant had a staccato history. It was abolished by James II, restored at the rate of £1,200 per year by William III, abolished again in 1714, then restored in 1715 and in 1718 raised to £1,600 annually. It continued in various forms until 1871, when all direct subventions to religion in Ireland ceased.[88] The eye-blinking ambiguity that an historian has to deal with here—that the state and its adjuvant, the state church, simultaneously penalized and financially underwrote Presbyterianism in Ireland—is nothing as to the maddening uncertainty that was felt at ground level. One does not have to read much experimental psychology to know that a random mixture of reward and beating will produce a snarling dog; or an emotionally incontinent adolescent; or, as here, a synod of unpredictable, unsettled and snappish Presbyterians.

The profoundly upsetting ambiguity in the Irish penal code is well illustrated when one moves from purely ecclesiastical matters to the religiously focused social situations. The joint actions of civil and state-church authorities were rarely completely in step with each other, but they had the effect of reminding the Ulster-Scots that they were perceived by state and state church as bearing the mark of Cain: just as their clergy could not be trusted ecclesiastically, the entire polity of Ulster Presbyterians could not be fully trusted in civil affairs. For a social group that believed strongly that they were a covenanted people—covenanted both to the Almighty and to each other[89]—this disjuncture between themselves and the surrounding authorities meant that their own self-perception was always sacral. Their being treated badly confirmed their own rightness.[90] The key eighteenth-century example of the entire Presbyterian minority (not just its ministers) being defined with the same juddering and distrustful ambiguity that was shown to the clergy is this: in 1704, during the drafting for passage through the Irish parliament of the Test Act, a very nasty piece of anti-Catholic legislation, the English privy council insisted that anti-Dissenter provisions be added. Thus, everybody had to take the "Test" of receiving Holy Communion according to the form of the Established Church as a prerequisite for holding any public office in Ireland. The Presbyterians, like the Roman Catholics, could not in good conscience perform this act, so they were cut out of the municipal corporations (where they were well represented in the north of Ireland), grand juries (the closest thing Ireland had to rural local government bodies) and militia officerships. The Presbyterians' "political importance was lowered, and another deep line of disqualification was introduced into Irish life. The Test Act was another great step in the path of division, and it did much to make Protestant co-operation impossible."[91] Now, in fact, the state in Ireland could not afford to throw away any non-Catholic allies, so in the Jacobite disturbance of 1715, Presbyterians were quietly permitted to serve as militia officers. More importantly, in 1719 a narrow toleration act made Presbyterianism a licit religion and, in the civil sphere an awkward dance was introduced: the Presbyterians took civil office and then were forgiven for not having taken the Test by an Act of Indemnity which gave them an extended period of time to take the Test. This went on year after year until 1780 when they were granted permanent relief. So, for most of the eighteenth century, the Ulster Presbyterians were told that because of their religion they were not really full citizens, but that they were expected to be grateful and loyal anyway.[92] The deeply contradictory message the Presbyterians received from their governors was rooted in a conflict within the ruling Anglican elite: some really wished sweeping societal cleansing of both Catholics and Dissenters, and others believed such an attempt would be pyrrhic at best. Sean Connolly suggests that the "likely picture is of an official commitment to achieving sweeping social change, which was taken seriously only by a dedicated minority, but which a more pragmatic majority felt politically unable to disown, and towards which from time to time it felt obliged to make positive gestures."[93]

Religiously based identity politics of a confused, vexing and unpredictably discriminatory nature were visited upon the Presbyterians right down to the family level, in this case the matter of marriage. The Established Church's view was that marriage was, and must continue to be, an ecclesiastically controlled sacrament. This was thought necessary because of a tight little logic trap: (a) marriage was a divinely ordained sacrament; (b) only a divinely appointed custodian of this sacrament could administer it; (c) in Ireland, the Established Church bishops asserted that their church was entrusted by God with administering and protecting this sacrament; so (d) if the officials of the church admitted the validity of marriages conducted by Presbyterian ministers, then by implication those clergy were recognized as having spiritual legitimacy and (e) the whole premise of the state church as the only authentic church would have been undercut, and "in the eccle-siastical turmoil of the early eighteenth century, that was unthinkable."[94] This line of reasoning would have held any time after the Protestant reformation, but in practice it was only in the 1690s and the early decades of the eighteenth century that the Church of Ireland felt secure enough to attack on this front. Unlike other areas of the penal code, aggression here required no special legislative action: marriage fell under the jurisdiction of the church's ecclesiastical courts. Thus, for marrying a Presbyterian man and woman, a Presbyterian minister was liable to prosecution in the courts of the state church, and this became common. Moreover, the couple thus joined had to worry about the direct implication that their children would be illegitimate. For the growing merchant class and small freeholders this immediately implied a worry with inheritance, even if their estates were small. As J. C. Beckett observed, "obscure men and women ... continued to endure indignity, inconvenience and expense through having been married by their own ministers."[95] Prosecutions continued into the 1730s, and only in 1738[96] were Presbyterian marriages given legal status and even so an oath of loyalty was required, a small indication of second-class status. This finally was removed in a Dissenters relief act in 1782 (over the opposition of the bishops in the Irish House of Lords). That noted, there remained one continuing source of salt in the wound. The 1782 relief act had given full legal status to marriage within the Presbyterian community—but what about the legitimacy of a marriage of, say, an Anglican man and a Presbyterian woman conducted by a Presbyterian cleric? No major matter, one might think; yet it was a source of considerable Presbyterian bitterness right up until the eve of the Famine, for until the matter was clarified, the Presbyterian clergy still were second class and mixed marriages celebrated by them were of questionable legal validity. (The safest position for a mixed Protestant couple was to go to the local Church of Ireland rector for his sanction, and this was ritual subordination.) Only in 1844 was the matter put to rest by an act of the United Kingdom parliament that made such mixed marriages unassailable in law.[97]

Now, I am *not* arguing that the actions and attitudes of the Ulster-Scots were only a function of their religious beliefs—and certainly not that religion was the sole, or even chief motive for the out-migration of a large number in the eighteenth and first half of the nineteenth centuries. But religion was the prism by which they were viewed by authorities of the state and of the state-church, and perforce it was the prism by which the Ulster-Scots viewed the larger society. And one cannot understand very much about the Ulster Presbyterians unless one acknowledges the primary mode through which they understood themselves. Well-documented cases of entire congregations and of the majority of clergy in certain presbyteries migrating to the Thirteen Colonies run from 1684 to 1773,[98] but theology should not be seen as the primary reality: religiously based identity was a much broader bolt of cloth than the narrow issue of church forms and traditions.

Take economic matters: the Presbyterians were deeply aggrieved at times in the eighteenth and early nineteenth centuries by their economic position. To simplify greatly, in rural society a family's position depended upon weather and markets (determining revenue) and on the prices of seed and, most importantly, on land rents and taxes (deter-mining costs). When things went badly, there is no question that the Presbyterians inter-preted the situation as being in considerable part a result of their position as a religiously discriminated group. This was not as big a reach as it might first appear, because they were cued by the state itself to look at land costs through a religious lens. A first charge upon the produce of the land was owed to the Established Church as tithes. From an accounting point of view, tithes were merely land taxes and such taxes are ubiquitous worldwide. However, in the eighteenth and nineteenth centuries, not only was this a tax imposed to support a rival and condescending denomination (and thus a grievance to both Catholics and Presbyterians), but tithes were a maximally obnoxious mode of taxation. In their usual form (which held until the 1830s), tithes were collected by direct social harassment. During the summer months, before harvest, a tithe-proctor (basically a professional debt collector) entered the local farm, valued the crops and tried to strike a bargain with the occupier. If that worked, payments were in cash, but it was possible to pay in kind. In any event, one either agreed to pay one's tithes or the matter went to the local magistrates for settling. The tithe-proctor, being a subcontractor, had every motive to gouge the occupier of land, as had the farmer to be obstructive: a perfect system for building grievance.[99]

The Ulster Presbyterians frequently identified their landlords by religious labels, virtually epithets. This is hardly surprising, given the distribution of land holding. "In the province of Ulster, Archbishop Synge [bishop of Raphoe 1714–16, archbishop of Tuam. 1716–41] assures us that there were not in his time more than 40 Protestant Dissenters of the rank of gentlemen, nor more than four who were considerable landowners ..."[100] Another contemporary estimate set the number of Dissenters (read: Presbyterians) who possessed landed estates worth more than £200 a year in Counties Antrim, Down and Tyrone at about 60.[101] Patrick Griffin has documented a signal phenomenon in the year 1717–29, a rough era both religiously and economically for the Ulster-Scots: "Presbyterians did not distinguish between the hardships of 1717–29 and the problems they experienced in the church. Ulster Dissenters believed the economic challenges they confronted had religious origins, that their 'many sins ... provoked a holy and righteous God to visit us with scarcity of bread.'"[102] That was when they were in a self-flagellating mode. Alternately, the Presbyterians blamed the iniquitous Episcopacy-backing landlords. An apparently widespread belief in the eighteenth century was that in the Williamite era, Anglican landlords had given preferential treatment to adherents of the state church and that when leases fell "this was a favourable opportunity with them for venting their miserable spleen on their unfortunate tenants who had the boldness to keep consciences of their own."[103] That was the folk stereotyping their economic betters. However, an accurate observation by the Ulster Presbyterians was that they had a set of landlords to deal with which included several who were unusually unpredictable and incompetent, even by general Irish standards. The largest of these, and the one who had the most Presbyterian tenants, were the successive earls of Donegall, collateral descendants of Sir Arthur Chicester, who had been the Lord Deputy of Ireland at the time of the plantation of Ulster. The Donegall estate in the early eighteenth century ran to 90,000 acres in Antrim and Down, including all of Belfast, and 160,000 acres in County Donegal. The relevant landlords in the present case were: the third earl, who died in the siege of Barcelona in 1706 and left the estate with a debt equal to five times its annual rental; the fourth earl, who succeeded as a child and lived to 1757 and was very close to being an idiot (a chancery investigation in 1750 found him incapable of subtracting 60 from 100, but decided this did not disqualify him from being an Irish landlord); and the fifth earl, who was determined to make up for his predecessors' incompetence by wringing every penny he could out of his lands. The wholesale re-leasing of Belfast in 1767 was only a start.[104]

In the early 1770s a large swatch of the rural Donegall leases in Counties Antrim and Londonderry fell in, and the fifth Lord Donegall either exacted high renewal fines or he replaced smallholders with large holders who in turn either put the land to pasture-farming or became rack-renting middlemen. Several thousand tenants lost their livelihood, and in response they formed a violent body, the Steelboys, who in the years 1771–73 visited violence on agents of the new landholders, upon grabbers and often upon their homes and livestock. The group, overwhelmingly Presbyterian, were strong enough that when several of them were had on felony charges at Carrickfergus, there was no hope of a jury convicting them and the government had to move the trials to Dublin. The Steelboy movement subsided in 1773. In tradition, it is held that many of them escaped to the Thirteen Colonies and found their way into the revolutionary army.[105]

All these matters relate to the marker of Ulster-Scots identity being the Presbyterian religion in the eighteenth century, but they will add little to our understanding of pre-Famine migration to New Worlds if we are not cognizant of a further fact: neither the centrality of religious identity among the Ulster-Scots, nor their perduring self-assertion as a distinct minority community, moderated after the American Revolution or after the 1798 Rising in Ireland. The form changed early in the nineteenth century, but not the substance. This assertion runs counter to most of the historical literature on eighteenth-century radicalism which, as far as the Ulster-Scots are concerned, prefers to see them as having been part of something advanced and a bit *chic* up until the '98 Rising and then backward and insular thereafter. In modern terms, they are seen as going from revolutionary to counter-revolutionary, or, to be highly anachronistic, as moving from the progressive radical left to the troglodytic right. One can admire the advanced intellectual positions within Irish national thought taken by the Belfast merchants in the 1780s and 1790s, without conflating their intellectual nimbleness with the rural populism of the small farmers, weavers and hired labourers, many of whom for their own local reasons supported a rising that briefly seemed to take the form of a modern international revolutionary movement.[106] Indeed, I think the key to recognizing the striking bedrock constancy of *mentalité* of the Ulster-Scots in the eighteenth and nineteenth centuries is found in its deep, unbreakable cultural self-assertion at the local level, with all abstract ideologies, *except religion*, being a temporary overlay. At the risk of being tiresomely obvious, the Presbyterian ecclesiastical system was both a visual representation of the collective Ulster-Scots cultural framework and a functional part of that framework. Presbyterian organization starts at the bottom, the congregation, and authority builds upward—quite the reverse of military systems or of hierarchical churches. That was as true in 1845 as it was in 1745. What Marianne Elliott accurately identified as the "disdain by Presbyterianism for authority,"[107] was not a negative characteristic, but the result of their Presbyterian faith in the loci of legitimate authority being either in the local sphere or in the spiritual; between heaven and hearth there was precious little to which they yielded unconditional authority.

Here is a brief exhibit that illustrates the continuity within the Ulster-Scots community, before and after the '98 Rising. It comes from Ballycarry (sometimes called Broadisland) and from its neighbour, the peninsula of Islandmagee. Taken together they formed the cockpit of Ulster Presbyterianism. They are very close to being an historical Ideal Type in Max Weber's sense: they show Ulster Presbyterianism in an environment that is almost laboratory pure. Few Anglicans and even fewer Catholics were resident in the eighteenth and nineteenth centuries and the locals kept themselves to themselves. Ballycarry had the first permanent Presbyterian clergyman in Ireland, the Rev. Edward Brice. He arrived (probably) in 1611 and preached in Ballycarry and also in Islandmagee, 1613–36, in a church that once had been Catholic.[108] Because of its location—a day's sail from points on the lowland Scottish coast—this was a primary invasion site for that portion of the Protestant settlement of Ulster that occurred spontaneously rather than by state planning. Places such as Ballycarry-Islandmagee were settled by frontier-seizures that only later were recognized in law: this was not quite an autochthonous community, but very close. Now, in the late eighteenth century, many of the inhabitants of this small Presbyterian world were in severely bad temper. They were paying tithes to the Established Church (with scarcely any Anglicans in the locale, save one landlord and the coast-watchers, whose anti-smuggling brief did not make them terribly popular); they had been hurt by the violence that surrounded the Donegall estates (the splash was only indirect, as they were on a portion of the Donegall estate that was long-leased to rather saner Ulster nobles); they long had been in communication with former neighbours and with relatives now resident in the United States, and they admired the individual rights formulated in the USA and espoused in French-derived revolutionary literature: they could not vote as, until the Irish Franchise Act of 1850, only freeholders were enfranchised in rural districts. And here were no freeholders. So, almost all the able-bodied men of Ballycarry and a goodly portion of those of Islandmagee turned out for the '98 Rising. However, they were late for the battle at Donegore Hill and they turned back with more speed than they had turned out.[109]

And, suddenly, in Irish historiography, they and their Presbyterian counterparts elsewhere in Ulster are written out of nationalist history. Actually, they changed little. Granted, they learned a lot about unsuccessful violence: one of the sharpest anti-revolutionary poems of the nineteenth century was by a local participant, James Orr. His "Donegore Hill," is a masterpiece of a vernacular rant—"some hade, like hens in byre-neuks ..." being a fair sample of his observation of his fellow revolutionaries—which should be parsed in its entirety by anyone who generalizes about either Irish nationalism or Unionism.[110] Aside from learning the pragmatic lesson that programs of revolution hatched by the Belfast mercantile elite could backfire, the Ballycarry-Islandmagee community changed little as a consequence of 1798. The leaders went abroad for a while and came home and settled down to weaving, farming, fishing. The matters of local grievance stayed the same: tithes and rents mostly, and a skepticism of government generally. The people remained staunchly Presbyterian in their own way. (Their own way included a propensity to get drunk between the two long sermons on Sunday, a wholly understandable practice.) They remained as self-enclosed and, in that sense, self-assertive as they always had been. Why, then, are they identified as counter-revolutionaries after 1798? Not because they changed, but because the things-to-fear in the outside world changed. Crucially, the horrors of the '98 Rising in the south, which in many places was no less than a Catholic-Protestant civil war; and the rise of Daniel O'Connell and his mass mobilization of southern Catholics awakened the long-suppressed, but ever-present fear that the land settlement of Ireland would be reversed and that the Catholics would do so by direct means. The social physics were clear: the Presbyterian resentment of the Ascendancy was in considerable degree displaced by a deepening fear of resurgent Catholics.[111]

In a seminal essay on Ulster Presbyterianism in the years 1760–1860, a period that comprehends the beginning of industrialization in the linen industry and extends to full economic modernization, David W. Miller argues that Ulster Presbyterianism evolved efficiently to meet societal changes and maintained an unbroken continuity as it did so. A long-term shift occurred within Presbyterian communities generally, with a downplaying of ecclesiastical concerns and an increased emphasis upon matters conversional. In modern terms, they became more evangelical, but not overnight. What was there all the time was a sense of religious identity that provided the Ulster-Scots with a replacement for something they never could have, the myth that they were a nation. They needed something to underpin their polity. Their religious system, as it had evolved by the mid-nineteenth century, "had such remarkable staying-power in part because it helped meet the need for just such reassurance; it confirmed by modern 'empirical' standards that they were God's chosen people."[112] Thus, we can take as being reasonably probable the observations that (1) religiously framed self-perception was a central historical aspect of the Ulster-Scots world and that, whatever the "real" causality of any major set of events, religion was a viewing-lens they held very close to the eye. And (2) that, in dealing with the pre-Famine years, it would be a mistake to truncate the Ulster-Scots story: the apparently natural break at either 1776 or 1798 is merely that, apparent, not real.

When we encounter the modern literature on Ulster-Scots out-migration, we find (1) a fair degree of disagreement about migrant numbers up until the American Republic was defined and (2) after that, scarcely any interest in the topic, including the larger issue of what the Ulster-Scots pattern was after the main gate of entry to North America moved from Philadelphia and other US ports to British North America.[113]

To take the first item: the hub around which the numerical argument pivots for the American colonial period is a fine piece of old-fashioned scholarship, R. J. Dickson's monograph of 1966, which concluded that between 1718 and 1775, about 120,000 persons migrated from the province of Ulster to the Thirteen Colonies.[114] Recent debates about Dickson's work have implied reductions in numbers of Ulster out-migrants to the 70–85,000 range in the American colonial era;[115] while others suggest an increase to as high as 250,000.[116]

When one moves into postrevolutionary America, not much attention is paid. In the 1960s, Professor Maldwyn A. Jones, a pioneering scholar of American in-migration, promised a book parallel to Dickson's to cover the period 1783–1815, but the topic splayed too widely and he had to settle for an essay and the estimate that in the three decades before the War of 1812–14, "perhaps 100,000 people from Ulster" had settled in the United States.[117] The fault was not Jones's. After 1783 it was no longer possible to do a chronicle of shipping by using as entry the primarily Ulster-distributed newspapers as R. J. Dickson had done: shipping diversified quickly, with southern Irish and, increasingly, British ports becoming important, and then dominant, as the harbours for the beginning of transoceanic voyages; and, simultaneously, multiple ports of arrival, especially in British North America, supplemented, and then largely supplanted the Delaware Valley, where most early Ulster shipping had gone. Everything became too spongy and too diverse. Put simply, Dickson had not had to worry about Liverpool-to-Quebec runs or Greenock-to-St John, but by 1800 they were as large in total as the entire Ireland-US runs and after 1815, larger.

In terms that are clearer than the evidence really warrants, it appears that a parsimonious summary of the situation from 1800 to the Famine is as follows: (1) most of the estimated one million Irish migrants who sailed to North America chose British North America as their destination; what happened to them thereafter has never been satisfactorily studied. (2) More Ulster-Scots arrived in North America from 1800–45 than had arrived in the colonial period, and this holds true even if one extends the earlier period up through the end of the eighteenth century. David Noel Doyle guesstimates that as many as 450,000 Ulster out-migrants (overwhelmingly non-Catholic) shipped to North America, and this fits with cohort-depletion records derived from Irish censuses.[118] Thus, although almost totally ignored by historians of the Americas,[119] the largest migration of the Ulster-Scots to North America was in the first half of the nineteenth century and it was to British North America. Even if only two-fifths remained in British North America, the number of Ulster-Scots settlers in Canada and the Maritimes would have been roughly equal to the total of Ulster-Scots who had settled in the Thirteen Colonies.[120] (3) Unless it is proved otherwise by more than anecdotal information, I do not think that we should assume that filtration across the US-BNA border was selective by religion. As mentioned earlier, it has been suggested that Catholics, being poorer, tended more often to stay in British North America and presumably that Protestants, being better off, went to the USA in proportionately higher numbers. That is plausible but has no probative back-up. Neither does the opposite supposition that Catholics, being natural republicans, had a predisposition to cross to the United States. This has no substantive evidentiary support and runs contrary to the long-running and heroic tradition of Irish Catholic support for royalism. (4) Purely as an informed speculation, not more, I would suggest an hypothesis that future historians may be able to test. This is that in North America, considered as a whole, the proportions of Protestants (of all sorts) to Catholics in the multigenerational Irish ethnic population in the years immediately preceding the Famine was about the same as that which prevailed in the most-Irish jurisdiction in North America, Ontario: two-thirds Protestant, one-third Catholic.[121]

So, with the Ulster-Scots as with the entire Irish out-migration that preceded the Great Famine: it is the general case that unless one knows the history of the Irish in Canada, one does not know the history of the Irish in the United States; and, there is no real knowledge of the Ulster-Scots if one's historical sensibility stops at the border.

EIGHT

Finally, we should briefly observe three, almost invisible, small Protestant minorities, each of which made a tiny puncture in the overall Irish pattern of accepting life in a high-risk socio-economic zone—and also speculate about one religiously mixed minority that has as yet no history whatsoever. None of them in itself is statistically important, but, taken together, they show clearly that cultural deviation (in these cases, being a minority surrounded by a hostile majority), fuelled a propensity to migrate out of Ireland or out of their early homes in the New World.

The first group is the "Irish Palatines." These were part of a larger group of German-speaking Protestants from a medieval seigniorial jurisdiction in the southern Rhineland—usually referred to in English as "the Palatinate"—who were persecuted (or who feared they would be persecuted) for their Protestantism. Mostly they were Lutheran, with a sprinkling of pietistic souls. In 1710 approximately ten thousand were permitted to settle in the British Empire: most went to the North American colonies, some stayed in England, and about three thousand were sent to Ireland with the purpose of strengthening the Protestant interest there. About one-third of these settled in well (the rest returned to England) and formed tight communities, mostly in County Limerick, with smaller groups in Tipperary and Wexford. Being virtually pacifists, speaking a mixture of increasingly archaic German and a weird form of English, they were open to revanchist pressures from the surrounding Catholics. At the same time they were not entirely trusted by Dublin Castle, which noted, quite correctly, that they were half-way to being dissenters. Indeed, during the course of the eighteenth century they divided as between Anglicans and Methodists, and in fact were a favourite target group of John Wesley: he visited Irish Palatine communities on 13 of his pastoral trips through Ireland.[122] Small minorities such as the Irish Palatines usually are lost to history: I suspect that for every one of these rare species that historians know about, a dozen or more are now historical ciphers. We are impoverished culturally if we lose them, just as we are when a small linguistic group disappears from our collective knowledge.

Fortunately, recent scholarship by Carolyn A. Heald has preserved a good deal of the extremely complex history of this ethno-religious group. During the 1760s, the more-keenly Methodist among the Palatines migrated to New York City and there Barbara Heck and Philip Embury, from Ballingrane, County Limerick, founded a Methodist congregation. (John Street Methodist Church stands on the site of their original building.) In the nineteenth century, Barbara Heck was frequently denominated the "Mother of American Methodism." Meanwhile, other Palatines stayed in Ireland (where a small residual, but influential population remains to this day—recent generations of Irish persons are most apt to have been acquainted with the names Switzer and Teskey); and still others filtered into Pennsylvania where they merged with migrants who were arriving directly from the Rhineland Palatinate This is the kind of migration-ethnic history that inevitably is lost in the coarseness of large-number studies. But we really should remember the rivulets as well as the floods; and the Irish Palatines have yet another layer of fascinating complexity. When the American Revolution took place, the leaders among the Palatine Methodists were Loyalists—hardly surprising, considering that the Crown had sponsored their parents' escape from Germany—and they migrated yet again. This time it was to the Bay of Quinte and the St Lawrence River regions of Upper Canada. There Barbara Heck became the Godmother of Canadian Methodism. Slowly the Irish Palatines dispersed among the North American population, but they retain at least a genealogically tied identity to the present day.[123]

The Irish Palatines illustrate that the primary way small religio-ethnic entities are most apt to be preserved in modern historical literature is through study by the too-often ignored methods employed by genealogists. Bruce Elliott, one of the most proficient of professional historians to employ genealogical methods has completed a number of studies of migrant cohorts from the British Isles to New Worlds. Particularly relevant in considering how Irish migration worked in the pre-Famine period is his study of Anglican chain-migration from Counties Wexford (primarily), Wicklow, Carlow and Kilkenny. These were areas where in 1798 members of the Church of Ireland had engaged in a civil war with their Catholic neighbours. The Catholics had taken massive losses through the intervention of government troops, but hundreds, perhaps thousands of Anglicans had been killed by their neighbours, and several hundred of these through the sectarian atrocities that ran through the countryside like the stain of hematite in bedrock. Soon after the '98 Rising, the Anglicans began looking for a foreign refuge. At first, upstate New York was home for a small colony (thus suggesting that fear of Catholics, not any great loyalty to the Crown, was in play). The War of 1812–14 hindered migration, but when hostilities were terminated, members of a gentry family named Elly, from New Ross, began organizing a chain migration that centred on Brockville, Upper Canada. This also splashed into much of what is now a large sector of eastern Ontario, as far south-west as Kingston and as far north-east as present-day Ottawa. Elliott has found two lists containing 991 heads of household (representing 5,502 individuals), who in 1817 had informed the Colonial Office that they would be willing to migrate to eastern Upper Canada. Significantly, although most of these were Protestants (710 household heads), enough were Roman Catholic (281 household heads) to suggest that getting out of a potential combat zone was more important than maintaining ethno-religious purity. But here is a twist: when the Colonial Office said 'no," it would not finance free passage, most of the petitioners let the idea rest for the time being. However, soon a self-paid chain of migration, almost entirely comprised of Anglicans, began and by the mid-1820s a big portion of eastern Upper Canada (technically, the Johnstown District) was speckled with migrants from south Leinster, and this chain continued quietly and efficiently into the 1840s.[124] The total numbers are unclear, but this much is unambiguous: that these Wexford-area Protestants were large enough in number and confident enough in demeanour to be able to elbow aside the previous Tory establishment. The individual who led this putsch in 1833–34 was Ogle Gowan, by-blow of the notoriously brutal Hunter Gowan of 1798 ill-fame. As an immigrant in 1829, Ogle Gowan discovered a ready-made battalion of his fellow south-east Leinster Protestants. Gowan immediately founded the Canadian branch of the Orange Order (using a forged warrant) and in 1834 his supporters deployed fists, knives and clubs to facilitate his election to parliament. Gowan's subsequent political career was uneven and tawdry (it ended with what would today be termed child molestation). Yet, the Orange Order became the largest single voluntary organization in Ontario in the Victorian age, and left the imprint of Wexford-in-'98 upon almost the entire adult male Protestant population, Anglican, Presbyterian, Methodist, and more.[125]

An even more impressive tracing by Bruce Elliott of a not-quite-invisible ethno-religious group is his work on north Tipperary Protestants, chiefly in the three decades before the Famine. This research is valuable because Elliott traced 775 Protestant (overwhelmingly Anglican) families who were trapped on a social island that was constantly shrinking. About 17,000 descendants of Protestant colonists of the late seventeenth century farmed in north Tipperary in the early nineteenth century. They were a minority throughout this region and were under constant pressure from the resurgent Catholics. Understandably, North America seemed to offer an escape from the ever-more-claustrophobic situation they were in. What makes Bruce Elliott's study so important is that instead of dealing with aggregates, he has traced 775 families, person-by-person, generation-after-generation, as they settled in Upper Canada (or Canada West as it was named for a time) and as they moved on through several transitions in the New World. Anyone who has done even one family history knows the sheer amount of work it involves if each individual is to be documented properly, so 775 families and their successive generations is a huge endeavour. And what one finds is that a group that did not even have an agreed name ("north Tipperary Protestants" is an historian's flag of convenience), nevertheless had an empirically definable social identity in the homeland and, crucially, a set of interrelated behaviours in the New World that were dependent upon and were reticulations of their Old World ethno-religious ties. "One must remember that as a consequence of chain migration an emigrant often ended up with more relatives in Canada than he had in Ireland, and this circumstance was reinforced by the births of new generations and the deaths of old."[126]

How many more pre-Famine Irish ethno-religious subsets which today are visible only to ingenious and industrious researchers are there to be studied? Here let us try to catch the wispy outlines of one that I suspect comprises several thousand persons, but which, in the present state of research is totally unrecognized. This consists of the persons of Irish birth or of Irish parentage who were among the Loyalist population that was either forced out of the embryonic United States or chose to leave: in the latter case, to avoid republican government or to protect their personal liberty (in the case of free blacks) or to guarantee their religious freedom (in the case of Catholics). Granted, this is not directly an issue of out-migration from Ireland, but it is of direct importance because (a) the words and behaviour of the Loyalist Irish would tell us a lot about the ideology of the Irish-derived population of the Thirteen Colonies, a matter that is not revealed in any other way, and (b) since these people were notably articulate, they became a contact point for subsequent migrants from Ireland and thus formed a feedback loop into the information system on which later migrants from Ireland depended. How, one might ask, did pre-Famine migrants come to know so much about British North America, when relatively few of the early migrants had gone there? Part of the answer may be found here.

In the immediate aftermath of the American Revolution, mostly in 1784, about 40,000 Loyalists sought safety in Canada, primarily in Nova Scotia, but some in Quebec and Upper Canada. (Probably 14,000 refugees from the United States were in Upper Canada in 1791.)[127] These populations were subsequently joined by "Late Loyalists," a term for individuals from the United States who, although not victimized in the

American Revolution and its aftermath, saw British North America as a place of opportunity. Especially in Upper Canada they were able to profit from a cross-border trade and, indeed, in the War of 1812–14, family and commercial networks kept trade paths open, even while conflict was in progress. By 1811, the population of Upper Canada had grown to about 60,000 which, given that there had been very little immigration from the British Isles, suggests that citizens of the United States were prospecting there in droves.[128] Now, a signal characteristic of the Loyalists (and to a lesser degree, the Late Loyalists) is that they left more paper per person than any comparable group in eighteenth and nineteenth-century North America. They were aggrieved and they penned petition after petition to the authorities in Canada and London, describing their background, their plight, and their case for compensation. They were deprived and they wrote their old friends and relatives who remained in the United States and they tried to regain pieces of property or chattels that they had left behind. They were bereft and wrote relatives and affines in Ireland and Britain trying to suss out anything that might be going for them in the old homelands. This is not a fugitive literature. Gregory Palmer's standard biography of easily identifiable Loyalist sources, compiled in 1982, lists thousands and thousands of items that are publicly available and the number has multiplied and the ease of access increased since then.[129] Herein lies the biggest, as yet untouched, trove of material on Irish ethnic consciousness in the late colonial US, and on the character of the Irish-derived segment of the base population of the English-speaking portions of British North America. Its interrogation will necessarily involve the arduous methods demonstrated in Bruce Elliott's pioneering work. But there is a real historical entity to be sought. Its present-day invisibility is due to the refusal of historians of the Irish in America to look for it. The result of a serious interrogation of the Loyalist sources will provide not only insights into group attitudes and behaviour, but some splendid narratives as well. A good example is Fintan O'Toole's brilliant appreciation of William Johnson, the son of a modest Catholic tenant farmer from County Meath who, in the eighteenth century, became easily the most influential white person in the interior of North America. As an early settler in the Mohawk Valley and eventually the superintendent of northern Indians, he delivered the Six Nations to the British side and thus blocked the French inland conquest of North America. He became one of the richest persons in North America and, crucially, he ran his fiefdom as a Celtic estate: with a blind harper as its talisman.[130] William Johnson died on the eve of the American Revolution. His only white son, Sir John Johnson, and his Amerindian relatives and allies fought against the American Revolution and acquired massive amounts of land in both Upper and Lower Canada.[131] Father and son are part of a single narrative. When dealing with groups such as the Irish-descended Loyalists in North America, one requires successive generations for the historian to be able to see their brutality and ambition of purpose, willingness to change religious affiliation, loyalty to the Crown and their unusual ability to reach continuing accommodations with the leading indigenous groups.

Like all the pre-Famine migrant groups, the Loyalists were both the product of a complex, high-torsion set of past experiences and an indicator of the range of possibilities when the Famine flood began.

NOTES

1   William Forbes Adams, *Ireland and Irish Emigration to the New World from 1815 to the Famine* (New Haven: Yale University Press, 1932).

2   Government of Ireland, *Commission on Emigration and other Population Problems, 1948–54* [Pr. 2541] (Dublin: The Stationery Office, 1955). The highly controversial nature within southern Ireland at mid-twentieth century of emigration and its history is indicated by the majority of the commission's report being signed with 12 dissenting disclaimers. Two additional minority reports were produced by non-signatories. The central statistical portions of the report were compiled by R. G. Geary, the Irish equivalent of Gustav Sundbärg. I am grateful to Enda Delaney for helping me to understand the importance of Geary's work.

3   N. H. Carrier and J. R. Jeffery in Government of the United Kingdom, *External Migration: A Study of the Available Statistics, 1815–1950* (London: HMSO, 1953). On sectorial matters (as distinct from overall generalizations), this remains the most thorough collection of primary data and of the limits of its reliability. It is also something of a litmus-item for sorting out competence in students of nineteenth-century Irish migration. A disappointing number have no acquaintance with this crucial source, which is rather like writing nineteenth-century political history without having heard of Hansard.

4   The entire sharply compressed article is historiographically important: Cormac Ó Gráda, "A note on nineteenth-century Irish emigration statistics," *Population Studies*, vol. 19, no. 1 (1973), pp. 143–49.

5   D. H. Akenson, *The Irish in Ontario. A Study in Rural History* (Montreal and Kingston: McGill-Queen's University Press, 1984; 2nd ed., 1999), pp. 8–32.

6   D. H. Akenson, *The Irish Diaspora. A Primer* (Belfast: Institute of Irish Studies, the Queen's University of Belfast, and Toronto: P. D. Meany Co., 1993), table 11, p. 56.

7   Given the holes in the primary data, that number should be taken as, perhaps, plus-or-minus ten per cent. The latest summary of the state of Irish migration studies concludes that "we can be confident that just over a million emigrants left Ireland for North America ..." between the Union with Great Britain and the Famine. Patrick Fitzgerald and Brian Lambkin, *Migration in Irish History, 1607–2007* (Basingstoke: Palgrave Macmillan, 2008), p. 162. This excludes migrants to Australasia, Southern Africa, etc. Cormac Ó Gráda's 1989 estimate was that about 900,000 emigrated to the USA and British North America in the same period. Cormac Ó Gráda, "Poverty, population, and agriculture, 1801–45," in W. E. Vaughan (ed.), *A New History of Ireland*, vol. 5, *Ireland under the Union, I, 1801–70* (Oxford: Clarendon Press, 1989), p. 120. David Fitzpatrick in 1989 accepted the number of emigrants to North America as being one million between 1815 and 1845, with another 500,000 going to Great Britain. Fitzpatrick, "Emigration, 1801–70," in Vaughan, *A New History of Ireland, 1801–70*, p. 565. Significantly, Fitzpatrick's confidence comes from a very clever study of the depletion of the emigration-vulnerable age cohort as between the 1821 and 1841 Irish census. See Fitzpatrick, "Emigration, 1801–70," pp. 565 and 608. As an incidental point: be careful of using the annual estimated transoceanic emigration rates compiled by the commissioners of the Irish census of 1851 to cover the years 1841–51. The formula they employed works well for 1846–51 and dovetails with direct data for 1851, but yields a high overestimate for 1841–46. For the data and formula, see W. E. Vaughan and A. J. Fitzpatrick (eds.), *Irish Historical Statistics. Population, 1821–1971* (Dublin: Royal Irish Academy, 1978), table 53, p. 260.

8   Fitzgerald and Lambkin, *Migration in Irish History*, p. 162. Ó Gráda, "Poverty, population, and agriculture, 1801–45," p. 120, comes to roughly the same number, as do several others. Donald MacRaild suggests that "perhaps 500,000 had made their way to Britain," 1815–45. *Irish Migrants in Modern Britain, 1750–1922* (New York: St Martin's Press, 1999), p. 10.

9   The datum point on which all estimates are based is that of the census of Great Britain for 1841 which shows 419,256 persons of Irish birth as being "settled" in Britain. But what does this tell about total emigration from 1801–45? Some historians have simply taken the roughly 420,000 persons of Irish birth as being the total number of persons who migrated to Britain from Ireland, 1801–41; then they have added about 25,000 permanent migrants per annum, 1842–45, inclusive, and this totals roughly 500–525,000. Blind luck, but it provides about the right number.

   Actually, we need a rolling total of migrants, not a static photograph from near the end of the period. Therefore, we need a base number of Irish persons living in Ireland in 1801 and similar decennial data thereafter. In a ruminatory way, the Irish census commissioners tried to work out what the probable pattern of Irish-born persons migrating permanently to Great Britain had been between 1821 and 1831 and between 1831 and 1841—1821 and 1831 being census years in which these data were not collected. They funked the job in that they confused the probable increment in Irish-born population over each decade with the total number of persons emigrating in that decade. (People die; and some re-emigrate, and some migrate to yet another country, so the increment is net and therefore markedly less than actual total Irish migration to Great Britain.) However, without ever making the number explicit, the census commissioners worked with an inferred number for the Irish-born in Britain in 1821 and 1831, namely 314,441 for 1831 and 244,442 for 1821. Now, *if* one uses the same deflator for 1811–21 and for 1801–11 as was used for 1821–31, then the inferred number of Irish-born in Britain in 1811 would be 189,931 and that in 1801 would be 147,576. Of course the precision of all those numbers is false, but rounded to the nearest 10,000, they are serviceable. See Government of the United Kingdom, *Report of the Commissioners appointed to take the Census of Ireland for the Year 1841* [504], HC, 1843, xxiv, pp. x–xi.

To obtain an heuristic estimate of gross migration from Ireland, one would take (to begin), the increment in the Irish-born between 1801 and 1811 and add to it (a) some compensation for re-emigration to Ireland or stepwise migration to a transoceanic destination and (b) a compensation for mortality. No one has much of at notion of what "a" is—but "b" should be taken as roughly 25 per cent of the base number, in this case that for 1801. (We are here importing the actuarial figure of a lifespan being an average of 41.4 years, as shown in the Swedish population data.) Then one repeats this for each decade and aggregates. Even assuming a combined five per cent return-migration and transoceanic migration rate over each decade, when added to mortality-compensation, we obtain an heuristic total of Irish migrants who made "settlement" in Britain, 1801–41, of about 353,000. (That this is a lower figure than the Irish population of Britain in 1841 follows from their having been a significantly sized base population already present in 1801.) Add to this what one believes annual gross permanent out-migration to Great Britain was for 1842–45, inclusive—the 25,000 range is a commonplace—and one has an overall estimate of somewhat under 450,000. If stepwise transoceanic migration were taken to be markedly higher over this entire period among those permanently "settled" in Britain, then my estimate would rise to near the 500,000 standard estimate. In any case, here the chief reward of a lot of elementary accounting work is to reawaken one's occasional faith in the conventional wisdom.

10 Ó Gráda, "Poverty, population, and agriculture, 1801–45,", p. 120.

11 Adams, *Ireland and Irish Emigration to the New World*, pp. 413–14; Carrier and Jeffery, *External Migration*, p. 95; Govt of Ireland, *Commission on Emigration*, table 26, p. 314.

12 As discussed earlier, the census commissioners were flummoxed by the permanent "settlement" flow to Great Britain. If one annualizes their decennial total estimate of the flow to Britain, 1831–41, and then adds compensation for mortality, etc., at the same rate as has been done in earlier estimates, a serviceable figure is 18,500.

13 A somewhat scrubbed life is T. G. Wilson, *Victorian Doctor: being the Life of Sir William Wilde* (London: Methuen, 1942). See also James McGeachie's piece in the *Oxford DNB*.

14 William Wilde, "Table of Cosmical Phenomena, Epizootics, Ephiphitics, Famines and Pestilences in Ireland," in Government of the United Kingdom, *Report of the Commissioners of Census of Ireland for the Year 1851. Part V, Tables of Deaths* [2087–1], HC, 1856, xxix–1, vol. 1, pp. 41–333. This item is missing in several bound copies of the United Kingdom parliamentary papers that I have examined, including most importantly in the digital version of the papers put out by the UK House of Commons. However, it is in the British Library set and several others. And, happily, it is now available conveniently and in full in vol. 1 of the extremely valuable five-volume collection of contemporary material on famine and disease published in 2005, as edited by Leslie A. Clarkson and E. Margaret Crawford under the title *Famine and Disease in Ireland* (London: Pickering and Chatto, 2005). For a modern chronology of the harvest failures in the early modern era, see Raymond Gillespie, "Harvest Crises in early seventeenth-century Ireland," *Irish Economic and Social History*, vol. 11 (1984), pp. 5–18.

15 Wilde, "Table of Cosmical Phenomena," p. 104, quoting Spenser's *View of Ireland*.

16 Wilde, "Table of Cosmical Phenomena," p. 110, quoting Petty's *Political Anatomy*.

17 Clarkson and Crawford, *Famine and Disease in Ireland*, "Introduction," vol. 1, p. xvi, citing David Dickson, *Arctic Ireland; the Extraordinary Story of the Great Frost and the forgotten Famine of 1740–41* (Belfast: White Row Press, 1997), and Michael Drake, "The Irish Demographic Crisis of 1740–41," in T. W. Moody (ed.), *Historical Studies, VI* (New York: Barnes and Noble, 1968), pp. 101–24.

18 A. T. Q. Stewart, *The Shape of Irish History* (Montreal and Kingston: McGill-Queen's University Press, 2001), p. 106. In a summary table of various international families, Cormac Ó Gráda puts the national death toll of the famine in Ireland in 1740–41 at 13 per cent; and that of the Great Famine (including all deaths, 1846–52) at 12 per cent. Cormac Ó Gráda, *Famine. A Short History* (Princeton: Princeton University Press, 2009), table 1.1, p. 23.

19   In addition to Wilde, see the reprint by Clarkson and Crawford (*Famine and Disease in Ireland*, vols. 3 and 4) of Francis Barker and John Cheyne, *An Account of the Rise and Progress and Decline of the Fever lately Epidemical in Ireland*, 2 vols. (London: Baldwin, Cradock and Joy, 1821), and (*Famine and Disease in Ireland*, vol. 5), the reprint of portions of William Harty, *An Historic Sketch of the Causes, Progress, Extent, and Mortality of the Contagious Fever epidemic in Ireland during the Years 1817, 1818, and 1819* (Dublin: Hodges and MacArthur, 1820).

20   Sean J. Connolly, "The 'blessed turf:' cholera and popular panic in Ireland, June 1832," *Irish Historical Studies*, vol. 23 (May 1983), pp. 214–32.

21   Govt of UK, *Report of the 1841 Commissioners*, p. xxvi.

22   In a recent essay, François Furstenberg convincingly argues that the US control over the heartland of North America was more contingent, less secure, and more open to random upset than is usually assumed and that not until 1815 was it clear that the US now was the main imperial power in North America. François Furstenberg, "The Significance of the Trans-Appalachian Frontier in Atlantic History," *American Historical Review*, vol. 113 (Jun. 2008), pp. 647–77.

23   J. D. Gould, "European Inter-Continental Emigration, 1815–1914: Patterns and Causes," *Journal of European Economic History*, vol. 8 (Winter 1979), pp. 611–12. Gould points out the real marked difference was between sail travel of 40 days (Liverpool to New York, throughout the nineteenth century) and the roughly 14 days for the steam vessels that became common in the 1860s (p. 613). The degree to which an emigrant considered time to be a cost is, however, indeterminate.

24   I am grateful to Roderick M. MacLean for calling this to my attention. On the pre-nineteenth-century flow, see Anne O'Dowd, *Spalpeens and Tatti Hokers: History and Folklore of the Irish Migratory Labourer in Ireland and Britain* (Dublin: Irish Academic Press, 1991), pp. 1–5.

25   Mr and Mrs S[amuel] C[arter] Hall, *Ireland* (London: How and Parsons, 1841), preface.

26   Government of the United Kingdom, *Third Report from the Select Committee on Emigration from the United Kingdom*, HC, 1826–27 (237), v, p. 453, quoted in Barbara M. Kerr, "Irish Seasonal Migration to Great Britain, 1800–38," *Irish Historical Studies*, vol. 3 (Sep. 1943), p. 370. This article (pp. 365–80) is an important pioneering study on the topic. The most considered discussion of pre-Famine seasonal labour is found in David Fitzpatrick's larger discussion, "'A peculiar tramping people:' the Irish in Britain, 1801–70," in Vaughan, *A New History of Ireland, 1801–70*, pp. 623–60. A later, data-rich study is Ruth-Ann Harris, *The Nearest Place that Wasn't Ireland* (Ames, IA: Iowa State University Press, 1994). See also Ruth-Ann Harris, "Seasonal Migration between Ireland and England prior to the Famine," *Canadian Papers in Rural History*, vol. 7 (1990), pp. 363–86. There is relevant historical material in Government of the United Kingdom, *Reports, Maps, Tables, and Appendices relating to Migratory Agricultural Labourers, 1900* [Cd.341], HC, 1900, ci, pp. 5–15.

27   For the detailed tally by county of residence, port of embarkation, port of disembarkation, gender and age-category, see Govt of UK, *Report of the 1841 Commissioners*, table 3, "Showing the Number and Ages of Persons who Emigrated to Great Britain during the Summer of 1841 ...," pp. 450–51.

28   Govt of UK, *Report of the 1841 Commissioners*, p. xxvi.

29   Govt of UK, *Report of the 1841 Commissioners*, p. xxvi.

30   See notes 27 and 28 above.

31   Why a major undercount of work-migrants? As implied or stated in the text, the 1841 tally missed: (1) all who left January through April; (2) boatloads of those who left via off-shore coasters; (3) and those who embarked August through December, for non-harvesting jobs. More importantly, was (4) a big conceptual blind spot, namely, the refusal to see that Irish workers in a large number of non-seasonal occupations—railways, building, transport, unskilled urban labour, factory work—were often on a two-or-more year round of labour that eventually took them back to Ireland. They appeared to the British census commissioners to be permanent settlers, but were in fact a migrant labour force. This summary relates to note 9 above and helps to explain why I remain somewhat conservative about the level of permanent Irish migration to Great Britain.

32   Govt of UK, *Report of the 1841 Commissioners*, p. xxvi.

33   Akenson, *The Irish Diaspora*, table 11, p. 56 and table 38, p. 258 for transoceanic migrants. For migrants to Britain, the number is the Irish census takers' estimates of the incremental growth in Irish-born population 1831–41, plus 25 per cent of the 1831 Irish-born population, to compensate for mortality, return-migration, and stepwise migration overseas. See notes 2–9 above for sources.

34   Fitzpatrick, "Emigration, 1801–70," p. 581.

35   Thus, to take only two portions of British North America, 78,255 persons of Irish birth are enumerated in the 1842 census of Upper Canada. (See *Census of Canada, 1871*, vol. 4, p. 136) and 43,942 in Lower Canada in 1844 (David Noel Doyle, "The Irish in North America, 1776–1845," in Vaughan, *A New History of Ireland*,

1801–70, p. *706n1*.) A reasonable suggestion is that the majority of persons who arrived in BNA, 1801–45, did make their way to the USA, but their movements were not necessarily swift; and I suspect that at least one-quarter—and perhaps as many as four-tenths—stayed permanently in BNA. Otherwise, given the greatly reduced proportion of Famine and post-Famine sailings that went to BNA, and the known rates of fertility, it is difficult to see how the first census of the Confederation of Canada could have produced 846,414 persons whose primary ethnicity was Irish. See D. H. Akenson, *Being Had. Historians, Evidence, and the Irish in North America* (Toronto: P. D. Meany Publishers, 1985), tables 3, 4 and 7, pp. 83–88.

36   The idea put forward by Ruth-Ann Harris that most of the pre-Famine Irish migrants to Great Britain eventually went to America has gained little credence and the available census data certainly argues against this being the case. Harris, *The Nearest Place that Wasn't Ireland*.

37   Granted, the new landlords frequently were far from loved by their tenants but this does not obviate the fact that the legislation removed a major impediment to equality of access to property.

38   This explains why the seventeenth and eighteenth-century Irish migration to the European mainland (mostly military, but also clerical and commercial) is elided from the present discussion, despite a good deal of quality research on the topic having been published within the last two decades. That emigration was almost sealed off by the wars of the late eighteenth century, and only residual contacts remained, mostly among the defensive and discreet Catholic gentry class.

39   For an excellent general history, see Sean T. Cadigan, *Newfoundland and Labrador. A History* (Toronto: University of Toronto Press, 2009).

40   Fundamental to any discussion of the earliest colonizing efforts in North America by persons from the British Isles is David Quinn, *England and the Discovery of North America, 1481–1620* (London: Allen and Unwin, 1974), and *Ireland and America. Their Early Associations, 1500–1640* (Liverpool: Liverpool University Press, 1991), here esp. pp. 28–33. See also Gillian T. Cell, *Newfoundland Discovered. English Attempts at Colonization, 1610–1630* (London: Hakluyt Society, 1982), and Luca Codignola, *The Coldest Harbour of the Land. Simon Stock and Lord Baltimore's Colony in the Land, 1621–1640* (Montreal and Kingston: McGill-Queen's University Press, 1988). For a discussion of Baltimore and his colonizing heirs, see John D. Krugler, *English and Catholic. The Lords Baltimore in the seventeenth century* (Baltimore: Johns Hopkins University Press, 2004).

41   John Mannion, "The Waterford Merchants and the Irish-Newfoundland Provisions Trade, 1770–1820," *Canadian Papers in Rural History*, vol. 3 (1982), p. 179. The entire article (pp. 178–203) repays study. See also John Mannion, "Irish Migration and Settlement in Newfoundland: the Formative Phase, 1697–1732," *Newfoundland Studies*, vol. 17 (2001), pp. 257–93; and "A Transatlantic Merchant Fisher: Richard Welsh of New Ross and the Sweetmans of Newbawn in Newfoundland, 1734–1862," in Kevin Whelan and William Nolan, *Wexford: History and Society* (Dublin: Geography Publications, 1987), pp. 373–421.

42   John Mannion, *Irish Settlements in Eastern Canada: a Study of Cultural Transfer and Adaptation* (Toronto: University of Toronto Press, 1974), p. 19; Sean Cadigan, "The Moral Economy of the Commons: Ecology and Equity in the Newfoundland Cod Fishery, 1815–1855," *Labour/Le Travail*, vol. 43 (Spring 1999), p. 18. When working with the general Canadian census data, it is well to remember that Newfoundland refused to join the new Canadian confederation in 1867 and did not become part of Canada until 1949.

43   Mannion, "The Waterford Merchants," pp. 196–98.

44   For a tight, location-specific study of this and related transatlantic cultural ties, see John Mannion and Fidelma Maddock, "Old World Antecedents, New World Adaptations: Inistioge Immigration in Newfoundland," in William Nolan and Kevin Whelan (eds.), *Kilkenny: History and Society* (Dublin: Geography Publications, 1990), pp. 345–404.

45   We are here employing everyday usage and treating "West Indies" and "Caribbean" as interchangeable. Technically, they are slightly different, as the "West Indies" refers to a string of islands (the Lesser and Great Antilles and the Bahamas), and the Caribbean is the region where they are found. There is as yet no satisfactory history of the Irish in the Caribbean. For an efficient conspectus, see Nini Rodgers, "The Irish in the Caribbean, 1641–1837. An Overview," *Irish Migration Studies in Latin America*, vol. 5 (Nov. 2007), pp. 145–56. This issue of the journal focused exclusively on the Irish in the West Indies. Limitation of space prevents my dealing in detail with the matters that I am discussing in the text above; however, see D. H. Akenson, *If the Irish Ran the World. Montserrat, 1630–1730* (Liverpool: Liverpool University Press and Montreal and Kingston: McGill-Queen's University Press, 1997), which has a good deal of material dealing with all the Leeward Islands, as well as the other major English-speaking Caribbean colonies.

46   The concept of Beyond the Line came from a secret clause in the 1598 Treaty of Vervains between Spain and France where they agreed that whatever peace they might strike in European waters, they were still at war

south of the Tropic of Cancer. The term in English evolved into a reference to the unbuttoned, free-form and frequently lawless aspect of Caribbean society.

47 Nini Rodgers, *Ireland, Slavery and Anti-Slavery: 1612–1865* (Basingstoke: Palgrave Macmillan, 2007). In Irish ethnic historiography, the concept of Irish Catholics as not-white has two distinct locales: the Caribbean experience in the seventeenth and eighteenth centuries and the USA in the immediate post-Famine era. Dealing here only with the first site, the sources are the tradition of Catholic martyrology that in its application to the Caribbean began with the work of the Rev. Aubrey Gwynn, SJ, in the 1920s; and was amplified after World War II by the West Indian politician and intellectual, Eric Williams, who was wedded to the canonical Marxian historical progression and therefore, at times, merged indentured servants and African slaves as a single class entity, thus avoiding using race as the primary determinant of slavery in the European world. For these and related matters, see Akenson, *Montserrat*, passim.

48 Richard S. Dunn, "The English Sugar Islands and the Founding of South Carolina," *South Carolina Historical Magazine*, vol. 62 (1971), p. 87.

49 Akenson, *Montserrat*, pp. 83–85, 123–32; G. E. C. Coyayne, *The Complete Baronetage*, vol. 4, p. 111.

50 Akenson, *Montserrat*, pp. 52–53.

51 Akenson, *Montserrat*, p. 53, relying on the work of David W. Galenson, of Hilary Beckles and of Aubrey Gwynn.

52 Henry A. Gemery, "Markets for Migrants: English Indentured Servitude and Emigration in the Seventeenth and Eighteenth Centuries," in P. C. Emmer, *Colonialism and Migration: Indentured Labour before and after Slavery* (Dordrecht: Martinius Nijhoff Publishers, 1986), p. 33.

53 To tie this back into the Irish relationship to Newfoundland: John Mannion and Fidelma Maddock perceptively note that the labour migration of indentured servants to the colonial Americas and the permanent settlement of the Irish in Newfoundland were akin to each other—much more so than akin to the Irish migration to mainland North America after 1815. Mannion and Maddock, "Old World Antecedents," p. 353.

54 Brian McGinn, "How Irish is Montserrat—2," *Irish Roots*, no. 2 (1994), p. 16.

55 Akenson, *Montserrat*, pp. 149–50 and 243–44n113. One cannot make a judgement of whether these were merely formal conversions or not; nor whether the entire household was concerned, since oaths of religious allegiance were only required for the male head of household.

56 Louis M. Cullen, "The Irish Diaspora of the Seventeenth and Eighteenth Centuries," in Nicholas Canny (ed.), *Europeans on the Move. Studies on European Migration, 1500–1800* (Oxford: Clarendon Press, 1994), total derived from table 6.1, p. 139.

57 W. J. Smyth, "Irish Emigration, 1700–1920," in P. C. Emmer and M. Horner (eds.), *European Expansion and Migration. Essays on the Intercontinental Migration from Africa, Asia, and Europe* (New York: Oxford University Press, 1992), p. 51, cited in Fitzgerald and Lambkin, *Migration in Irish History*, p. 110.

58 Fitzgerald and Lambkin, *Migration in Irish History*, figure 1 (n.p.).

59 Nicholas Canny, "English Migration," in *Europeans on the Move*, table 4.1, p. 64.

60 None of this is helped by the instances of misreading of basic enumeration data in now-standard studies. For examples, see Akenson, *Montserrat*, pp. 201–02 and 223–24n38.

61 Cullen, "The Irish Diaspora," p. 120.

62 This is the appropriate point to mention that I am avoiding reference in the text to a toxic debate concerning the number of persons who were transported to the West Indies during the Cromwellian era. The question is a legitimate one and I have given the responsible efforts attention in my *Montserrat*, pp. 50–51, 61–65. My own guess (it can be no more than a guess on anyone's part, given the records) is that no more than ten thousand persons were shipped against their will to the West Indies in Cromwellian times. This is not far from Patrick Corish's guess that a maximum of about eight thousand may have been forcibly sent to Barbados and another four thousand to other Caribbean colonies. See Patrick Corish, "The Cromwellian regime, 1650–60," in T. W. Moody, F. X. Martin and F. J. Byrne (eds.), *A New History of Ireland*, vol. 3, *Early Modern Ireland, 1534–1691* (Oxford: Clarendon Press, 1976), p. 364. (This is a maximum-possible number, for Corish includes all of the impoverished "Irish settlers or their descendants" on Barbados.) Against these guesses are High Counting guesses (notably by Aubrey Gwynn and by Cardinal Moran) of 50–60,000. As such, they are part of the tradition of old-school Catholic martyrology and are not objectionable as long as they are not confused with historical observation. The figure of 50–60,000 is an impossible number since it would equal or exceed all Irish migration to all the Caribbean islands in the seventeenth century. Much more objectionable is an end-of-the-pier-act that is just a shade short of being hate literature: that of the journalist Sean O'Callaghan, *To Hell or Barbados. The ethnic cleansing of Ireland* (Dingle: Brandon, 2000). This opts for 50–60,000 (p. 86) and narrates the episode as the slave-taking of the virtuous Irish by the rapacious English. Anyone engaging this topic would do well to begin with the first real professional approach to the matter,

John W. Blake's, "Transportation from Ireland to America, 1653–60," *Irish Historical Studies*, vol. 3 (Mar. 1943), pp. 266–81. On the first page he sets down the fundamental problem: that of distinguishing between the several plans for transportation and the actual carrying out of the intentions.

63   Nini Rodgers, "Ireland and the Black Atlantic in the eighteenth century," *Irish Historical Studies*, vol. 32 (Nov. 2000), p. 192.

64   Rodgers, "Ireland and the Black Atlantic," p. 184.

65   Rodgers, *Ireland, Slavery and Anti-Slavery*, pp. 133–34.

66   David Noel Doyle, *Ireland, Irishmen and Revolutionary America, 1760–1820* (Cork: Mercier Press, 1981), derived from pp. 52, 61, 70, 71, 73, 74. The reader will note that the multigenerational ethnic group will be larger than the sum total of migrants from that group, given reproduction rates in the American colonies having been greater than the death rates.

67   Doyle, "The Irish in North America," p. 693.

68   Doyle's guesses are useful (and, I think, correct in their implications) because they do not pretend to excessive precision. However, if one engages in trying to infer tight ethnic proportions of the 1790 US population from the 1790 census, the results are highly misleading; and, unfortunately, they provide the kind of false precision that so beguiles historians who do not wish to examine the accounts for themselves. The basic problem is that (a) the 1790 census was a heads-of-household exercise; (b) it gave *no* direct information on national origins of the population, but (c) in the late 1920s, to facilitate the calibrating of US immigration quotas, a group of learned scholars assigned the names of the heads-of-households to a national group based upon allegedly distinct ethnic association of the various surnames. See D. H. Akenson, "Why the Accepted Estimates of the Ethnicity of the American People, 1790, Are Unacceptable," *William and Mary Quarterly*, 3rd ser., vol. 41 (Jan. 1984), pp. 102–19 and 125–29. Unhappily, even a highly admirable scholar such as David Hackett Fischer has been lulled into accepting the unreliable interpretation of the 1790 census done in the late 1920s and early 1930s as the basis for cultural models based on supposed demography. See his *Albion's Seed: Four British Folkways in America* (New York: Oxford University Press, 1989).

69   See the data in section 2 above. In the years for which there are clear pre-Famine data, the pattern is unmistakable. From 1825–30, 38.7 per cent of total transoceanic out-migration from Ireland was to the USA and 61.3 per cent to BNA; from 1831–40, it was 39.1 per cent to the USA and 59.8 per cent to BNA. This pattern held for 1846, then for 1847 each national destination was roughly equal and from 1848, the USA was preponderant, this change being consequent upon alterations in the shipping laws. See Akenson, *Irish in Ontario*, table 5, p. 32.

70   Doyle, "The Irish in North America," p. 694. I am not convinced that this was the general case; nor is the related suggestion, that the Catholics used BNA ports only as a transit base, compelling. Until proven otherwise by systematic evidence, it is best to take as the default position that between 1801 and 1845 (a) Catholics and Protestants in choosing destination-ports distributed themselves proportionally to their total flow numbers as between BNA and the USA and (b) that whether or not they stayed in Canada was also proportionally equal. In other words, do not project the post-Famine picture upon the pre-Famine situation.

71   Akenson, *Irish in Ontario*, pp. 24–26.

72   I realize that in historical studies of the Irish in the USA there is a great deal of resistance to paying attention to the Canadian data. This insularity has been particularly marked since, roughly, the end of World War II. (Previous writers, ranging from Thomas D'Arcy McGee to William Forbes Adams felt more at home in the wider North American context.) Special pleading, and a bit of American cultural imperialism, stand behind this volitional ignorance. It rather shackles the study of the Irish in the USA, not least because nineteenth-century Canadian authorities collected data on religion and ethnicity which have no parallel in the US data, and which are useful for the testing of theories about the Irish migrants and their descendants.

73   For example, between 1833 and 1835, more than 700,000 letters from New York entered the UK via the Liverpool post office; "the bulk of these were probably letters from Irish settlers." David Fitzpatrick, "Emigration, 1801–1921," in Michael Glazier (ed.), *The Encyclopedia of the Irish in America* (South Bend: University of Notre Dame Press, 1999), p. 259.

74   Fitzgerald and Lambkin, *Migration in Irish History*, p. 129; Doyle, "The Irish in North America," p. 693.

75   Leroy V. Eid, "Scotch-Irish and American Politics," in Glazier, *Encyclopedia of the Irish in America*, p. 840. See also Andrew Greeley, who correctly recognizes that at present more than half of all persons in the USA of Irish ethnicity are Protestant. Among other things, he points to Gerald Shaughnessey's 1925 estimate that over time as many as two million Irish Catholics had become Protestant in the rural south. Whatever the utility of that number, I do not think the phenomenon was limited to the south. Andrew Greeley, "Achievement of the Irish in America," in Glazier, *Encyclopedia of the Irish in America*, p. 1.

76 Three comments. (1) The study at present most required is a definition and analysis of the American penal code parallel to that of Lecky for Ireland. As instantiation of the need, until 1780 Massachusetts law proscribed Catholic priests; in fact, all the Thirteen Colonies save Pennsylvania had some sort of penal legislation. The Quebec Act, effective 1775, guaranteed religious freedom and specified an oath for public office which Catholics could take without injury to conscience, and the Constitutional Act of 1791 guaranteed full freedoms in all of British North America. The penal code in the Thirteen Colonies lingered on after the Revolution. For example, in the extreme case, Catholics were disabled from state offices in New Hampshire until 1878. I assume that the reader will infer that one reason pre-Famine Irish Catholic settlement in British North America was substantial is that there existed fewer disabilities for Catholics than in the United States. (2) The most useful collection of material on religious slippage is that of the sedulous antiquarian, Michael J. O'Brien (1870–1960), who mixed his vocation as a travelling accountant with Western Union with his avocation of hunting down fugitive records of early Irish migrants and their descendants. His slightly saddened, somewhat flummoxed studies, several of which documented or discussed Irish Catholic converts, are collected and reprinted as *Irish Settlers in America. A Consolidation of Articles from the Journal of the American Irish Historical Society*, 2 vols. (Baltimore: Genealogical Publishing Co., 1979). And (3) a valuable corrective against seeing the position of the Catholic church in early federal America as being entirely hopeless is John R. Dichtl, *Frontiers of Faith. Bringing Catholicism to the West in the Early Republic* (Lexington: University of Kentucky Press, 2008).

77 As was clear when I discussed Catholic conversions to Protestantism, I do not accept the view that Irish national identity in the homeland or Irish ethnicity in the diaspora is tied to any specific religion. This is a residual position still found in some of the backwaters of American historical writing wherein studies of "the Irish" quietly exclude Protestants. This cultural essentialism could do with a confrontation with articles 2 and 3 of the Irish constitution, as amended after the Belfast Agreement of 1998 ("… all the people who share the territory of the island of Ireland, in all the diversity of their identities and traditions …" article 3).

78 Government of the United Kingdom, *First Report of the Commissioners of Public Instruction, Ireland* (45), HC, 1835, xxiii, pp. 9–45. Roughly 19,000 were returned as unknown.

79 In this study, present-day usage is employed. In the eighteenth century and for most of the nineteenth century in Ireland, "Protestant" usually referred only to the Church of Ireland and its members: the state church until 1871. The broader pan-denominational meaning began to be ascendant in the late nineteenth century.

80 Because we are here discussing religious-based identity, I am using the term "Ulster Presbyterian," while recognizing that there were some Irish Presbyterians outside of Ulster. The term "Ulster-Scots," which at present dominates within the studies of the Irish in the homeland is a perfectly good synonym. I think it best not to use the US term, "Scotch-Irish," or the slightly scrubbed synonym, "Scots-Irish" for historiographical reasons discussed in my *Irish Diaspora*, pp. 253–56. Kerby Miller has explained convincingly why the original Irish terms—"Ulster-Scots," and the "Scottish Interest"—were replaced in the mid-nineteenth-century United States (mostly the product of an intra-Presbyterian struggle for hegemony) and was occasionally used in the twentieth century (to attract American tourists). See Kerby A. Miller, "'Scotch-Irish' Myths and 'Irish' Identities in Eighteenth- and Nineteenth-Century America," in Charles Fanning (ed.), *New Perspectives on the Irish Diaspora* (Carbondale: Southern Illinois University Press, 2000), pp. 75–92. However, there are excellent present-day scholars who are comfortable with "Scots-Irish." See, for example, Patrick Griffin's position as stated in *The People with no Name: Ireland's Ulster-Scots, America's Scots-Irish and the Creation of a British Atlantic World, 1689–1784* (Princeton: Princeton University Press, 2001), p. 176n7.

81 Sean J. Connolly, "Ulster Presbyterians: Religion, Culture, and Politics, 1660–1850," in H. Tyler Blethen and Curtis W. Wood, Jr (eds.), *Ulster and North America. Transatlantic Perspectives on the Scotch-Irish* (Tuscaloosa: University of Alabama Press, 1997), p. 31.

82 Connolly, "Ulster Presbyterians," p. 35.

83 In terms of their institutional history, the Ulster Presbyterians have been well served. A solid general survey is Peter Brooke, *Ulster Presbyterianism. The Historical Perspective, 1610–1970* (Dublin: Gill and Macmillan, 1987). Also useful is Finlay Holmes, *Our Irish Presbyterian Heritage* (Belfast: Presbyterian Church in Ireland, 1985). The standard older history is James Seaton Reid, *History of the Presbyterian Church in Ireland*, 3 vols. [vol. 3 completed by W. D. Killen] (Belfast: William Mullan, 1867). On socio-institutional relationships, see Andrew R. Holmes, *The Shaping of Ulster Presbyterian Belief and Practice, 1770–1840* (Oxford: Oxford University Press, 2006). Also valuable on Irish Presbyterianism, considered in a long time frame, is David N. Livingstone and Ronald A. Wells, *Ulster-American Religion. Episodes in the History of a Cultural Connection* (South Bend: University of Notre Dame Press, 1999). For wider denominational context, see Richard L. Greaves, *God's Other Children. Protestant Nonconformists and the Emergence of Denominational Churches*

in Ireland, 1660–1700 (Stanford: Stanford University Press, 1997) and David Hempton and Myrtle Hill, Evangelical Protestantism in Ulster Society, 1740–1890 (London: Routledge, 1992).

84   Thus, Graeme Kirkham, "Ulster Emigration to North America, 1680–1720," in Blethen and Wood, Ulster and North America, p. 86.

85   Holmes, Our Irish Presbyterian Heritage, p. 37.

86   Brooke, Ulster Presbyterianism, p. 51.

87   Holmes, Our Irish Presbyterian Heritage, p. 45.

88   The bare facts are economically provided in Sean J. Connolly (ed.), The Oxford Companion to Irish History (Oxford: Oxford University Press, 1998), p. 477.

89   The classic study which indicates the path by which the covenantal mentality interacted with evolving state forms is David W. Miller, Queen's Rebels. Ulster Loyalism in Historical Perspective (Dublin: Gill and Macmillan, 1978). Another pivotal study is Ian R. McBride, Scripture Politics: Ulster Presbyterians and Irish Radicalism in the Late Eighteenth Century (Oxford: Clarendon Press, 1998).

90   This characteristic, of being confirmed in rightness and being reinforced in group identity when outsiders attack, is typical of several covenantal cultures. See D. H. Akenson, God's Peoples. Covenant and Land in South Africa, Israel, and Ulster (Ithaca: Cornell University Press, 1992).

91   William E. H. Lecky, History of Ireland in the Eighteenth Century (London: Longmans, 1892; 2nd ed., 1913), vol. 1, p. 429.

92   The basic work (in addition, of course to Lecky), on which recent scholarship concerning anti-Dissenter discrimination is based, is James C. Beckett, Protestant Dissent in Ireland, 1687–1780 (London: Faber and Faber, 1948). Valuable concise discussions are found in J. G. Simms, "The Establishment of Protestant Ascendancy, 1691–1714," and J. L. McCracken, "The Ecclesiastical Structure, 1714–60," in T. W. Moody and W. E. Vaughan (eds.), A New History of Ireland, vol. 4, Eighteenth-Century Ireland, 1691–1800 (Oxford: Clarendon Press, 1986), respectively, pp. 1–30 and 84–104.

93   Sean J. Connolly, "Religion and History," Irish Economic and Social History, vol. 10 (1983), p. 79. This is a review essay of Patrick J. Corish's history of the Catholic community in the seventeenth and eighteenth centuries. In a stiletto-sharp continuation of the judgement quoted above, Connolly continues; "From this point of view, the most appropriate modern parallel would not be the apartheid legislation so frequently cited, but rather the policies which successive governments since 1922 have adopted towards the Irish language."

94   Holmes, Shaping of Ulster Presbyterian Belief and Practice, p. 213.

95   Beckett, Protestant Dissent in Ireland, p. 117.

96   Various sources give 1737, and others 1738. The act was passed in 1737 and given Royal assent in 1738.

97   Beckett, Protestant Dissent in Ireland, p. 122; Holmes, Shaping of Ulster Presbyterian Belief and Practice, p. 216.

98   Holmes, Our Irish Presbyterian Heritage, pp. 45 ff.; Trevor Parkhill, "With a little help from their friends: assisted emigration schemes, 1700–1845," in Patrick J. Duffy (ed.), To and from Ireland: Planned Migration Schemes c. 1600–2000 (Dublin: Geography Publications, 2004), pp. 58–60.

99   The tithe system was characterized by a good deal of complexity because of variations by local custom and according to which crops were grown. On the basic system, see D. H. Akenson, The Church of Ireland. Ecclesiastical Reform and Revolution, 1800–1885 (New Haven: Yale University Press, 1971), pp. 87–98. Some minor reforms were made in the first two decades of the nineteenth century (pp. 98–111). Further reforms and the Tithe War that occurred in the 1830s (pp. 148–59) resulted in the tithes being rolled in with the annual rent paid to the landowner. This reduced friction, but tithes remained a major grievance of both Catholics and Presbyterians.

100   Lecky, History of Ireland, vol. 1, p. 424.

101   Lecky, History of Ireland, vol. 1, pp. 424–25n4.

102   Griffin, The People with no Name, pp. 82–83.

103   Thomas Hamilton, History of Presbyterianism in Ireland (Edinburgh: T. and T. Clarke, 1887), p. 106. I treat Hamilton's report not as historical fact but as a folk belief. I am grateful to Rankin Sherling for calling this item to my attention. Hamilton's book (pp. 105–34) contains a long threnody comprised of instances of eighteenth-century, and some nineteenth-century persecutions of Presbyterians. Its value here is that the volume is itself as a late-nineteenth-century document, confirming that the tradition of Presbyterian-affliction was still a live one, well after the Famine era.

104   A beautifully crafted essay is William A. Maguire, "A question of arithmetic. Arthur Chichester, fourth earl of Donegall, 1695–1757," in Brenda Collins, Philip Ollerenshaw and Trevor Parkhill (eds.), Industry, Trade and People in Ireland, 1650–1950. Essays in Honour of W. H. Crawford (Belfast: Ulster Historical Foundation, 2005), pp. 31–50.

105 Lecky, *History of Ireland*, vol. 2, p. 51, credits this tradition. On the Steelboys and on the 1763 Hearts of Oak Boys, who in the south and west of Ulster fought landlord-dictated county cess and courvée and "small dues" owed to the Anglican church, see James Donnelly, "Hearts of Oak, Hearts of Steel," *Studia Hibernica*, vol. 21 (1981), pp. 7–73. This pioneering study is revised in Eoin F. Maginnis, "A 'Presbyterian insurrection?' Reconsidering the Hearts of Oak disturbances of July 1763," *Irish Historical Studies*, vol. 31 (Nov. 1998), pp. 165–87. Maginnis argues that despite a religiously mixed composition (including some Catholics), the leadership was Presbyterian and that the Oak Boys' "demands and propaganda seethed with resentment at the Anglican establishment of grand jurors and tithe-raising clergy" (p. 185).

106 I think the most successful attempt at defining the intra-community origins of Presbyterian elite political views and implicitly of their limits within Ulster-Scots culture, is A. T. Q. Stewart, *A Deeper Silence. The Hidden Roots of the United Irish Movement* (London: Faber and Faber, 1993).

107 Marianne Elliott, *Watchmen in Sion: the Protestant idea of liberty* (Derry: Field Day, 1985), p. 11.

108 As in the dating of many origin points, this is open to dispute. The most satisfactory discussion I have encountered is H. G. Calwell, comment in *The Non-Subscribing Presbyterian*, no. 837 (Sep. 1976), pp. 163–69. Brice, like most of the earliest Presbyterian ministers, showed no hesitancy in taking money from the Established Church and serving the dual role of Presbyterian and Anglican cleric.

109 For a clear account of the events on the ground in the '98 Rising in Ulster, see A. T. Q. Stewart, *The Summer Soldiers. The 1798 Rising in Antrim and Down* (Belfast: Blackstaff Press, 1995).

110 Orr's two volumes of collected poems are printed as *Poems on Various Subjects. By James Orr of Ballycarry with a sketch of his life* (Belfast: William Mullan and Son, 1935.). For a discussion of Orr as a social observer, see D. H. Akenson and W. H. Crawford, *Local Poets and Social History* (Belfast: Public Record Office of Northern Ireland, 1977). An appreciation of the Ulster-Scots vernacular poets of Orr's era is John Hewitt, *Rhyming Weavers* (Belfast: Blackstaff Press, 1974).

111 This instantiating case of Ballycarry and Islandmagee is taken chiefly from D. H. Akenson, *Between Two Revolutions. Islandmagee, County Antrim, 1798–1920* (Toronto: P. D. Meany, 1979).

112 David W. Miller, "Presbyterianism and 'Modernization,'" in *Ulster, Past and Present*, no. 80 (Aug. 1978), pp. 66–90. The quotation is from p. 90.

113 In discussing Ulster-Scots out-migration from the 1690s until 1845, I am completely avoiding the question of both permanent and seasonal migration to Great Britain. The void in the data and in the historical literature is too large to permit even the most hesitant guesstimates.

114 R. J. Dickson, *Ulster Emigration to Colonial America, 1718–1775* (London: Routledge and Kegan Paul 1966). A second edition, with an introduction by Graeme Kirkham, was published in 1988. In the discussion that pivots around Dickson's work, the question of the Catholics usually is left unspoken, or at best with a speculative few sentences. The problem is that at every moment, from the beginning of the plantation of Ulster right down to the present day, the largest single denomination in the historical province of Ulster has been the Roman Catholic. But, as historians, we should recognize our own ignorance: specifically, that we have no direct probative information on the Catholic proportion of the Ulster outflow at any time up to the Great Famine. On the basis of a mass of circumstantial evidence, but especially from eighteenth-century demographic data collected by Liam Kennedy and Kerby Miller (see note 116 below) and cohort-depletion data derived by David Fitzpatrick for the first half of the nineteenth century ("Emigration, 1801–70," pp. 608, 620), I am comfortable inferring that Catholics were a markedly smaller outflow than were the Presbyterians.

115 Marianne S. Wokeck, *Trade in Strangers. The Beginnings of Mass Migration to North America* (University Park, PA: Pennsylvania State University Press, 1999), pp. 167–219. Wokeck does not draw together her inferences on reducing the Ulster tally, but a total 70–85,000 seems clearly to be dictated by her research. One should note, whatever one thinks of her work on the Irish migration, that her book is a breakthrough study of the nature and extent of indentured migration from the German states. Further, she documents that the majority of migrants from Ulster ports to the Delaware Valley (the prime reception point in the colonial era) were not indentured servants, a corrective to one of the older stereotypes. Most migrants via non-Ulster ports were indentured.

116 See Liam Kennedy and Kerby A. Miller, "Irish Migration and Demography, 1659–1831," in Kerby A. Miller *et al., Irish Immigrants in the Land of Canaan. Letters and Memoirs from Colonial and Revolutionary America, 1675–1815* (Oxford: Oxford University Press, 2003), pp. 656–78. The argument between Wokeck and Kennedy-Miller rests on technical issues, and both sides necessarily employ proxy data, as migration counts had not yet begun. The issues are: (1) the accuracy of Dickson's original reporting of the number of ships; (2) the tonnage per ship; (3) the ratio of passengers carried per ton of ship. In my judgment, Kennedy and Miller win the technical argument, so at least Dickson's 120,000 is solid. Their revisionist estimate of "250,000 or more" would be incompatible with the usual interpretations of the 1790 US census, but those readings are

highly unreliable in any case. The 250,000 estimate comes from (a) an argument that Dickson's work actually understated the historical reality in all three facets mentioned above: ships, tonnage, passengers-per-ton. And (b) Kennedy and Miller present information from 19 documents from the years 1659–1834 that provide partial and quasi-censuses of religion of scattered, but site-specific, locales in Ulster. This is pioneering work and will require expansion; at present it clearly implies both a heavy dominance of Presbyterians in the American colonial migration and an overall total higher than Dickson's standard estimate.

117 Maldwyn A. Jones, "Ulster Emigration, 1783–1815," in E. R. R. Green (ed.), *Essays in Scotch-Irish History* (London: Routledge and Kegan Paul, 1969), pp. 46–68. This is repeated in Jones's article, "Scotch-Irish," in the *Harvard Encyclopedia of American Ethnic Groups* (Cambridge: Harvard University Press, 1980), p. 903. One should pay respect to Jones's *American Immigration* (Chicago: University of Chicago Press, 1960). In the migration field, he also scripted a successful Thames Television mini-series with an accompanying book, *Destination America* (London: Weidenfeld and Nicolson, 1976).

118 Doyle, "The Irish in North America," p. 704. Although this guesstimate seems sensible, I am unable to replicate Doyle's mode of calculation from the sources that he provides. Concerning the combined BNA–USA total, Doyle says that "as many as 450,000 Ulster emigrants entered North America between 1800 and 1845" (p. 704). This is a bit different from the uncited statement of Maldwyn Jones in the *Harvard Encyclopedia of American Ethnic Groups* concerning only the USA, which refers to "the Ulster emigration of 1815–1845, amounting to perhaps half a million people …"

119 An admirable, if tantalizingly brief, exception is Catharine Anne Wilson, "The Scotch-Irish and Immigrant Culture on Amherst Island, Ontario," in Blethen and Wood, *Ulster and North America*, pp. 134–45.

120 Doyle, "The Irish in North America," p. 704, sees this as "twice that of the entire eighteenth century …" Whether or not it was proportionally that large (or simply equal) depends on whether or not one accepts the flow estimates of Liam Kennedy and Kerby Miller, as I am inclined to do. If one takes the Kennedy-Miller path, then one must abandon the faith held by Doyle and others in the standard ethnic glosses on the 1790 US census, for the number of migrants, plus their natural increase, would yield an Ulster-Scots population much larger than the total that usually is inferred by using the surname information in the census.

121 This might help historians of the Irish in the United States escape from a fact that emerged during the 1990s and has upset many of them: that the majority of persons living in the United States who affirm "Irish" as their primary ethnic identity are Protestants. As I have pointed out elsewhere (*The Irish Diaspora*, pp. 219–24), this has always been the case because of pre-Famine patterns of migration and religious adhesion and also because of conversions. Here one should highlight the signal article by Michael P. Carroll, "How the Irish became Protestants in America," *Religion and American Culture*, vol. 16 (Winter 2006), pp. 25–54. As wide-lens background, see Brian Walker, "'The Lost Tribes of Ireland.' Diversity, Identity and Loss Among the Irish Diaspora," *Irish Studies Review*, vol. 15 (2007), pp. 267–82.

122 Vivien Heck, "John Wesley and the Irish Rhinelanders," in Alan Harrison and Ian C. Ross (eds.), *Eighteenth-Century Ireland*, vol. 5 (Dublin: Eighteenth-Century Ireland Society, 1990), p. 89.

123 The breakthrough study is Carolyn A. Heald, *The Irish Palatines in Ontario* (Gananoque, Ont: Langdale Press, 1994; 2nd ed., Toronto: Global Genealogy, 2009). As background, see Walter A. Knittle, *Early Eighteenth Century Palatine Emigration* (Philadelphia: Dorrance, 1937, reprinted, Baltimore: Genealogical Publishing Co., 1982); and A. G. Roeber, *Palatines, Liberty, and Property: German Lutherans in Colonial British America* (Baltimore: Johns Hopkins University Press, 1993).

124 Bruce Elliott, "Emigration from South Leinster to Eastern Upper Canada," in Whelan and Nolan, *Wexford: History and Society*, pp. 422–46 and 547–49.

125 For the life of Gowan, see D. H. Akenson, *The Orangeman. The Life and Times of Ogle Gowan* (Toronto: James Lorimer and Co.), 1986.

126 Bruce S. Elliott, *Irish Migrants in the Canadas. A New Approach* (Kingston and Montreal: McGill-Queen's University Press, and Belfast: Institute of Irish Studies, the Queen's University of Belfast, 1988). The quotation is from p. 242.

127 R. Marvin McInnis, "The Population of Canada in the Nineteenth Century," in Michael R. Haines and Richard H. Steckel, *A Population History of North America* (Cambridge: Cambridge University Press, 2000), pp. 374–77.

128 McInnis, "Population of Canada in the Nineteenth Century," p. 376.

129 Gregory Palmer, *A Bibliography of Loyalist source materials in the United States, Canada, and Great Britain* (Westport: Meckler Publications for the American Antiquarian Society, 1982).

130 Fintan O'Toole, *White Savage. William Johnson and the Invention of America* (London: Faber and Faber, 2005).

131 On both Johnsons, see the *Dictionary of Canadian Biography*.

Chapter Six

DEPRIVATION AND FAMINE

ONE

Efficiency. If not gentled by a modifier or buffered by a few sentences of qualification, it is a terribly cold word to use concerning the river of emigrants that left Sweden after the Great Deprivation; and even harsher if applied to the Great Famine out-migration and its aftermath. Yet, it is the right term. Anyone looking at human misery of dearth-triggered migration in the mid-nineteenth century has to be emotionally moved. Nevertheless, at the same time one has to appreciate the breathtaking swiftness of the sudden outpouring of human beings, unprecedented in either Swedish or Irish history. And one must recognize the subsequent changes in the *mentalité* of each nation, whereby out-migration moved from being an action that was essentially culturally dissident and transformed into something that was part of the menu-of-possibility for almost everyone who came into adulthood. In its swiftness, this cultural revolution was remarkably efficient. Painful, horrifically; but very quick and with no false starts or haverings.

This was a cultural revolution because it literally reconfigured the map of the world that was passed on from one generation to another. What lay at the end of every road was irrevocably changed; where the horizon was located was radically redefined. Distant lands and new, alien ways of making a living were no longer items of folklore, like the lands of Asgård and Tir na nÓg and their strange customs, but realistic places of opportunity, or at least refuge, for the young of each new generation. Efficiency in effecting this revolution was made possible for both Swedish and Irish societies in considerable part because of the cultural punctures discussed in chapters four and five. Those punctures formed a set of interrelated perforations, ones that both prefigured and largely determined the shape of the world which would prevail in the new *mentalité*. If Manchester and Chicago, Minnesota and Massachusetts were suddenly much closer to home than previously they had been, this was in fair degree because, in almost biblical fashion, scouts had spied out the new lands.

Still, the rapidity of this cultural revolution was changed from possibility to actuality because of a second set of phenomena: each society underwent an *axial moment of stress*. Milton Friedman, no shrinking violet when it came to altering the course of world history, once observed that "only a crisis—actual or perceived—produces real change. When that crisis occurs, the actions that are taken depend upon the ideas that are lying around."[1] In the present case, the ideas that were lying around were the experiences and attitudes of the pre-Famine and pre-Deprivation minority, those who had migrated and had sent or brought home information. And it was stress so strong that it constituted shock, which turned those ideas into change. Where one departs from Friedman is that he was primarily interested in an economic crisis providing an opportunity for a revolution in the dominant economic thought and practice. Here, the cases are that extra-economic shocks—hostile meteorology, botanic epidemic, human disease, crop failure—were independent variables that eventually of course had economic impact, but more importantly, changed the way entire societies thought and entire societies behaved along several primary axes.[2]

Sweden in the second half of the 1860s is a useful case for the historian of Ireland to consider because it can be treated as a counterfactual—or, if one prefers, a natural experiment—concerning "what would have happened if the Famine had lasted only one year, or at most two, and had been spottier in effect?" As historians of Ireland, most of us have the singularity of the Great Famine so deeply etched upon our consciousness that it is difficult to conceive that even if the crisis had been a tithe of what it actually was, the shock nevertheless could have been sufficient to produce the same long-term results that we know occurred—an emigration-culture emerged and the social configuration of land holding and family formation changed sharply in the direction of practices that yielded risk reduction. The threshold level of shock for a stressed agricultural society, situated at the edge of the European industrial revolution, may not have been very high. This is where Sweden is enlightening. Though stressed, Sweden was a bit less vulnerable than was Ireland (recall that it had about 40 per cent of the population exposed to serious risk in a one-year crop failure, as compared to 60 per cent for Ireland): which means that it should have had a higher shock-threshold than Ireland, since it had proportionately more resources to absorb extra-economic shock. In fact, as we shall see, the Great Deprivation, though it brought real pain, was not in the same league as the Great Famine. Nevertheless, the hardship triggered (not caused, triggered) a swift outflow, the emergence of an emigration-culture, and the reordering of Swedish economic life. It follows, one might argue, that Ireland (having less in the way of resources as shock absorbers) would have required less of a shock than Sweden experienced to push it along the road to a revolution in *mentalité* and social structure. It is somewhat unsettling to consider that a patchwork of two or three years of crop failure in Ireland (instead of a four-year Great Famine) well could have had the same long-term revolutionary effects and cost many, many fewer lives. This is not to diminish the tragedy of the Famine—indeed, just the opposite, for it may not have been simply tragic but also monstrously redundant. But it is to place mid-nineteenth-century Ireland where it belongs, as a central, but not solitary, volume in the library of experience compiled by poor nations on the European periphery.

The entry point to broadening the context of our understanding of the Great Famine in Ireland is the truly great Finnish famine of 1696–97. This occurred when Finland was under Swedish rule. The present volume has treated only "mainland" Sweden as its unit of study, but here reference to Finland is germane because Finland establishes one extreme of risk-realized among the main Nordic countries. Finland in the late seventeenth century possessed a population that was overwhelmingly dependent upon subsistence agriculture and at very high risk from a one-year crop failure, especially from climatic variation. The winters of the 1690s were the third coldest experienced in Europe since at least the year 1200, and for Finland were barely endurable. The entire 1690s were hard times: short of starvation, but bad enough to eat away surplus stores of food. Things were so rough by the spring of 1696 that farmers were killing off their livestock and were eating the straw and chaff themselves. In the summer of 1696, warm weather was late and a hard freeze had set in at the beginning of the second week in August, thus destroying most of the rye crop in many parishes and stunting it in most others. (Rye of course was the bread crop of all save the rich.) In the 1950s, Professor Eino Jutikkala made a careful study of every parish for which he could find the death register: he succeeded in discovering the data for parishes containing 35 per cent of Finland's population, a considerable scholarly achievement. His conclusion was that in the year 1697 an absolute minimum of 24 per cent of the population died; more likely, scholars believe, 28 per cent did so; and one-third having died (a traditional figure) is well within the range of possibility. For the moment, translate that into the conventional mode of expressing death rates—a *minimum of 240 per thousand of population* as a crude annual death rate—and this in a single year, 1697.[3] Among national cases for which there are hard data, it is a boundary figure never reached elsewhere in Europe in peacetime.

If one were mapping this Finnish famine of 1696–97, it would be seen to leech over into the north of Sweden, where agriculture was only slightly more advanced and the climate was equally severe, and then to break out in areas of hard land and significant climate exposure: such as the provinces of Närke, Småland and the island of Gotland. Unfortunately, Sweden lacks a study parallel to that of Professor Jutikkala's for Finland, and it appears that famine was spotty: a crude death rate as high as 160 per thousand on Gotland and 90 per thousand in Närke, but essentially normal in most other places.[4] This instance is a good place to point out a problem with comparing Swedish and Irish famine data: much more than Ireland, Sweden was sharply differentiated by climatic variation and agricultural possibilities. Therefore, a simultaneously nationwide famine was less likely in Sweden than in Ireland, and—crucially to the historiography—regional shortages, sharp and painful as they were, are much less apt to have attracted the attention of historians since they did not generate easily usable national data sets. That is why the Finnish case should be kept in mind. It, like the Great Famine in Ireland, is a national case.

Sweden, Ireland, and indeed, much of continental Europe joined in a single, widely spread, instance, 1739–43, of bitterly cold weather (probably caused by volcanic eruptions half a world away), crop failures, surging food prices, undernutrition and disease. Within this period most countries were hit in only two of those years, but no place, not even Italy, escaped a climate-induced rise in the death rates.[5] Sweden's crude death rate in 1743 was 43.7 per thousand of population and Finland's in 1742 was 45.6 per thousand.[6] Highlighted against this set of European background events, we see the specifically Irish boundary case. If it is true (as was discussed in chapter five), that between 13 per cent and 21 per cent of the population died in Ireland in the years 1740 and 1741, then the annual crude death rate was much higher than in the Great Famine of 1845–49.[7] In the latter event, about one-eighth of the population perished over a four-year period, indicating an annual crude death rate of about one-half to one-third of that of 1740 and 1741. Those numbers should be taken as adjectives and adverbs, not as precise demographic notations, because the early data are very spongy; they do, however, remind us that the truly hideously massive Irish Famine was not indeed that of 1845–49, but rather the now-forgotten famine of the 1740s. This eighteenth-century blur of events, unlike the Great Irish Famine of the 1840s, seems beyond our rage or direct empathy. It was not well recorded nor, after the 1840s, much remembered. I think the best we can do is to be pulled into the vortex of coruscating anger in Jonathan Swift's *A Modest Proposal for Preventing the Children of the Poor People in Ireland from being a Burden to their Parents or Country, and for Making them Beneficial to the Public* (1729). It was prophetic. Swift saw with candid eye the vulnerable world of the Irish poor, and knew that, one way or another, the brutality of their future would devour the young.

Ireland's other famine that was part of a larger European dearth occurred in 1816–19 which, as William Wilde noted (see chapter five), was a period of hunger and, especially in Ireland, epidemic. John D. Post has argued that the character of Europe's non-war-induced famines evolved rapidly from the early eighteenth century to the late nineteenth. He views the Europe-wide dearth of 1739–43 as the last old-fashioned mortality crisis: meaning, in his definition, a set of circumstances where almost every European nation experienced a subsistence crisis (read: major crop failure) that sent death rates skyrocketing. These seemingly universal and murderous spikes in mortality were gone by the end of the eighteenth century; whether by good luck or by European society's reordering itself, Post is too shrewd to say. He points instead to the Europe-wide dearth of 1816–19 and asserts that, taken as a whole, it was the worst European famine since the seventeenth century. This may be an overstatement, but certainly postwar Europe was hit by severely crimped growing seasons, consequent upon the Mount Tomboro volcanic activity. (And not just Europe; in the southern parts of Canada, frost came in August and the entire year, 1816, instead of being numbered, was known for generations thereafter as "1800-and-froze-to-death.") For whatever reason, death rates did not spike wildly throughout Europe, even though they doubled in some restricted areas. Post defines 1816–19 as "the last great subsistence crisis" of Europe in the sense that it was widespread, but nevertheless it was not a Europe-wide mortality event. And thereafter, one has famines that are vicious, but are intensely regional and not anything close to being pan-European. At a descriptive level, Post's work is useful, even if it does not explain very much: sometimes accurate description is very helpful.[8] It confirms that in dealing with mid-nineteenth-century crises such as occurred in Sweden and in Ireland, we are right to compare them as distinct entities, not as part of a massive European swatch of want, epidemic and mortality.

TWO

In Sweden, for at least two generations after the event, the Great Deprivation of 1867–69 was clearly marked in folk-memory, even if it has subsequently been ill-defined by historical scholars.[9] This is understandable, for it is a messy business from an evidentiary viewpoint, and it does not fit very closely with the style and interests of the Swedish scholarly profession. One of the problems is that the Deprivation was neither a strictly regional phenomenon nor a national one; it breaks into awkward pieces when one picks it up to examine it. In regional terms, it was severest in the five administrative counties that comprise the ancient historical region of Norrland (roughly the län of Norrbotten, Västerbotten, Västernorrland, Gävleborg and Jämtland) and also in parts of the provinces of Dalarna and of Småland. These pieces, each from a different one of the ancient three divisions of Sweden, do not fit well together. And there were shards of deprivation in Värmland, the island of Öland and isolated parishes elsewhere. Further, as we observed in detail in chapter three, the restructuring of Swedish agricultural practices was producing in the middle decades of the nineteenth century a rapid social differentiation within the agrarian population. Increasingly, a social class fragment, made up of those who were losing out in the new order of post-enclosure Swedish farming, was shoved clear of traditional forms of social support and left to float as best it could. This class fragment was not limited to any geographic region, so when the Deprivation hit, with a sharp rise nationally in basic food prices, they suffered, some badly, but mostly in a scattered fashion. Moreover, as Hofsten and Lundström have pointed out, not until 1860 were death certificates compulsory, and then only in towns. And these and other data on causes of death (such as notes made in parish registers by Lutheran pastors) are insufficiently sharp in definition to permit documentation of any widespread chain of morbidity.[10] So, if one can find scores of discussions of Sweden's adopting a bicameral Riksdag in 1867, and, in contrast, only three modern historical volumes focusing directly on the Great Deprivation, that is neither surprising nor inappropriate.[11]

Yet, in the years 1867–69 something painful indeed was going on. Assuredly, these were not famine years in the Irish sense of the term.[12] However, demotic language frequently engages hard reality and in Småland, the metrical phrase, "*det våta året, det torra året, det svåra året*" (the wet year, the dry year, the hard year) aptly summarized the sequence of near or complete crop failures.[13] In the ancient region of Norrland the term was *de stora svagåren*—the years of great want.[14] These were not skipping rhymes or advertising slogans, but were the terms by which people who were accustomed to year-after-year of barely scraping a living referred to times that were really tough. Severe weather, of course, is an exogenous force acting upon a society, but it can also be used as a predictor that something will soon go wrong: any sentient person who has watched big weather events in the twenty-first century in the developing countries and even in the strong postindustrial ones, knows that social and economic bonds have only a limited degree of elasticity. (Think New Orleans, 2005.)

Anecdotal reports, never really systematic, suggested that rural crime, mostly theft, rose in these years.[15] And begging, a massive shame in Swedish rural culture, became common in affected areas. For example, in parts of Värmland it was reported that the highways were dotted with beggars, former torpare and backstugusittare, who had abandoned their homes and were willing to work solely for food, no wages or shelter asked.[16] The same thing was happening in the province of Småland. Cottages and farms were deserted by the spring of 1869, and the new railroad stations provided a site for crowds to gather and beg.[17] Significantly, it appears that the wretched in the southern one-third of Sweden drifted towards Skåne, which was not much affected by the Deprivation and there a series of mass protest meetings (rare in Sweden in that era) tied the obvious need for food relief with pressure for land redistribution and various political reforms, including the vote for all adult males.[18] Although there is only anecdotal evidence on the rate of bankruptcy or the distressed sale of small freeholds, one pays attention to a virtually prophetic letter, written from Göteborg in 1861 by Oscar Malmborg, formerly an agent for American lands, to an America railway official, in which he describes the position of the bottom level of the freeholders (the ones who in figure 3.2 are identified as living in the high-insecurity zone):

It is the poorest who are gradually being reduced from being owners to mere labourers. Such a one who for instance owns from 25 to 50 acres, of which 4 to 6 are cultivable, though generally very stony land, a little timber and the main portion bush, slough and rock, in all worth [US] $1,500 to $3,000 cannot in the long run, after the heavy taxes are paid, support an increasing family. *One failure of crops causes his ruin at once, and in ordinary seasons he is but gradually approaching the same end* [emphasis mine].[19]

Given that almost every decade in the nineteenth century had seen a minor deprivation in Sweden (1826, 1832, 1838, 1845, 1852)[20] and given that by the 1860s the social declension caused by enclosure and the agricultural revolution was pushing the less fortunate to the brink, it is likely that everyone from small freeholders downwards on the social scale was close to serious trouble in 1867–69.

A sign that a major anomaly was occurring was the work of the publishers and evangelists of food recipes: survival prescriptions, really. The county agronomist for Kopparbergs län, travelled around in 1868, rather like a colporteur for one of the free churches, teaching the poor how to make bread with certain mosses and lichens.[21] In the far north, the local telegraph officer in Piteå, something of a botanical expert, was deputized to visit rural settlements and teach the use of mushrooms and lichens as survival foods. Indeed, the mushroom surrogate was evangelized throughout Sweden, as ten thousand copies of a booklet on edible mushrooms was published and distributed by the Royal Patriotic Society.[22] Probably the most common survival food was bark bread, most often made from pine or spruce, although elm and birch were favoured, if available. The trick was not really to use the bark, but the annual growth ring that was just beneath it. The process was laborious, requiring the debarking and then scraping of tree after tree, while being careful not to girdle them completely. The useful material had to be scraped off the inside of the bark, then baked, then dried, then scutched with a flail, then ground into flour, then kneaded into dough, preferably with a bit of grain flour.[23]

What could have been the end-pathology behind all these symptoms is shown by the case of Finland. Almost the entire 1860s had been a hard decade for Finnish farmers, but even so, 1868 saw a spike in mortality way above the norm. Studies by Kari J. Pitkänen have shown that the crude death rate was normally about 25.5 per thousand of population annually (using 1861–65 as the baseline). This rose to 82.6 per thousand in 1868.[24] In rough terms, that means that one in twelve of the population died in a single year, a rate that, had it continued for the length of time of the Irish Famine, would considerably have exceeded the Irish experience. The Finnish famine hit every age group, and although the largest numerical increase in deaths was among the very young and the very old, that is an actuarial descriptor that masks the real impact of the Finnish famine: that it sharply accelerated the real-number deaths of those we think of as least vulnerable—especially those roughly aged 20–40 and, to a lesser degree, those aged 40–64. The reality is that the famine cut a large chunk of the healthy sinew out of the Finnish body politic.[25] Given that in 1867 all regions of Finland experienced a drop in harvest yields and that a total crop failure reigned "in many parts of Finland with most farmers harvesting little or nothing,"[26] we have here an instance of the hazard that has been the centrepiece of our discussion of risk in poor agrarian societies in nineteenth-century Europe: a one-year national crop failure.

Even adjusting for the differences in political structure (Finland at this time was a grand duchy of Russia), less agriculturally developed, and open to more extreme climatic exposure than was Sweden generally, the Finnish experience could have been duplicated in the most affected parts of Sweden. But it was not: the single hardest-hit parish in Sweden in 1868, Robertsfors in Västerbotten, had a crude death rate of 84.0 per thousand, barely above the entire Finnish national level and way below the worst Finnish parishes, which had had a crude death rate well over 200.0 per thousand.[27]

So, nothing serious was happening in Sweden? Marie Clark Nelson in her admirable study of the Deprivation in Norrbotten concluded that "deaths due to starvation related diseases were not numerous and deaths due directly to starvation myths."[28] Perhaps, but this conclusion seems to verge on nominalism. To take her study area of Norrbotten, it is hard to see how a rise in the crude death rate from 17.9 in 1866 to 27.0 per thousand in 1868[29] did not involve some emaciated or fever-twisted bodies. That, as Nelson admits, parish registers did not do a very precise job of stating the cause of death and that in her study area, causes of death were rarely reported in as many as 50 per cent of the cases,[30] implies that the real problem in assessing what happened lies in the indeterminate nature of the public records. And it is perhaps obvious to suggest that the causes of death for the poor and elderly were most apt to be lost in the not-reported pile in the Established Church's spotty recording system.

One is not here saying that death by starvation or starvation-induced diseases were widespread, but neither were they negligible. On a national level, one can observe a famine-effect, but it is subtle and certainly not anything approaching Finland's in 1868 or Ireland's, 1845–49. Sweden during the nineteenth century was experiencing a slow, steady decline in the crude death rate: from 28.2 per thousand annually at the start of the century to 16.4 per cent at the end.[31] The 1860s flattened that trend-line slightly.[32] This can best be seen by comparing the crude death rate for the whole country in 1861–65 (19.8 per thousand) with that in 1869: 22.3 per thousand.[33] A very rough statement would be that the direct rise in the national death rate in a single year, 1869, represented about ten thousand human beings. Clearly the Deprivation cost lives, but reckoning which ones they were is not simple—which may be why it has not been done—and determining how those lives were lost is probably impossible.

The geographic template does not really fit very closely. Norrbottens län indeed had the highest death rate of any rural Swedish county (that is, any place outside of Stockholm) during the 1860s—a 24.8 per thousand crude death rate for the decade, compared with 20.5 for the nation. But other places where food shortages were reported to be severe were not affected in sharp mortality terms. Kopparbergs län (roughly, the province of Dalarna) and Kronobergs län and Jönköpings län (comprising the bulk of the province of Småland) had lower rates than the national average.[34] Admittedly, Kronobergs län had a bump in 1869—25.6 as compared to the national average of 22.3[35]—but this did not bring it up to the national average for the decade, as it was a limited one-year occurrence, and effectively a summary of the three hard years of 1867–69.

If, in 1867–69 Sweden we are seeing a Great Deprivation, not a famine in the Finnish mode, the primary reasons are: (1) the Gulf Stream buffered some of the climate effects in Sweden; (2) the mortality effects also were moderated by population movement, as will be indicated below; (3) Sweden possessed a larger economic surplus above subsistence than did Finland; and (4) Sweden had a civic structure that facilitated relief of want.

In this latter regard, the timing of the Deprivation was somewhat fortunate. In Sweden, ever since the mid-eighteenth century, the parish (*socken*) had been responsible for religious discipline and schooling, and for providing poor relief. During the first four decades of the nineteenth century these duties had been more sharply defined, particularly under the common schools law of 1842 and by a poor relief act of 1847 that made regular contributions by the parish a statutory obligation. Crucially, in 1862, a set of local government reforms had separated the ecclesiastical parish from the civil parish (*kommun*, usually translated as rural district). The local clergy kept control of the ecclesiastical parish, but now the freeholders and a few large tenants formed the executive board concerning such things as poor relief. This lay control, combined with an expansion of voting rights for the civic parish council to include most of those males who paid land taxes, meant that the new kommuns were more responsive to secular problems than had been their predecessors.[36] At the local level, a prophylactic against severe want had existed in many parishes since the mid-eighteenth century, the *sockenmagasin*—the parish storehouse—which was to be kept filled with grain for emergency distribution. This first line of defence was only partial in that by the 1860s only a minority of parishes in the affected regions, particularly in the north, still had these storehouses: they were emptied quickly in Norrland and also in Småland parishes in 1867. But the existence of these venerable structures was important: depots for safe storage and orderly distribution of "imported" grain were already in existence in many parishes and did not have to be created under duress.[37] As for the parishes that did not have storehouses, they had been required since 1863 to turn the equivalent amount of relief into cash reserves. Most of the affected parishes created special emergency committees and these sorted out the long-term poor (who already were on poor relief) from the able-bodied distressed. In the most distressed of the administrative counties (län), the authorities provided aid to the local parish relief committees. Usually this was in the form of monies that were converted into grains, and the food was provided to the poor, in theory on a loan basis. (The stipulations varied, parish-by-parish.) The central government sent grain ships to the north in the spring of 1868, as soon as the ice left the ports and Kalmar län, and especially the island of Öland, received a good deal of relief money, as did Kronobergs län. Part of this money went to middling farmers as secured loans, the rest as direct-grant poor relief for the underclasses. Additionally, several voluntary charity efforts raised private gifts from the unaffected Swedish provinces, from Denmark and Germany, and also from the United States.[38] A full accounting of this overlay of relief efforts has still to be done, but the certain fact is that these efforts set a floor under the potential mortality crash. Deprivation, indeed; famine no.

Still, if there was no famine, this does not mean that the Great Deprivation was not a big deal, either in the pain inflicted on a large number of individuals or in the social changes that it triggered. Paradoxically, a deprivation is harder to calibrate in historical terms than is a famine. Until a deep study is done of the years 1867–69 we can only deal in probabilistic statements about what happened in Sweden in the late 1860s. Earlier, I noted that the geographical template and the mortality template did not fit together very well. To note this is to imply that one needs to reframe the question and not focus entirely upon mortality. In the present state of the historical literature, it is more productive to speculate (1) that the deprivation effects were much more diffused than was the definition of the areas most directly affected by crop failures and (2) that this diffusion-of-pain was most acutely felt in a specific class fragment.

Recall here that in chapter three we recalibrated Nils Wohlin's extraordinary work for the Emigration Commission of 1907–13 and suggested that we avoid the once-popular idea of rural proletarianization as a descriptor of what was occurring in Sweden as a result of the various enclosure movements and of the concomitant rise of an agricultural market economy.[39] We observed that for the first two-thirds of the nineteenth century the rural world was breaking into two segments, those who were doing well out of the increasingly capitalist nature of Swedish farming, and those who were losing out. This was a deepening crease of social differentiation. The lower group—characterized as those who were on the bottom level of the condominium-of-risk in the countryside—are those who, I would suggest, experienced most of the Deprivation. That is: the landless day labourers, the servants, the torpare, the stattorpare, the backstugusittare and the small freeholders. Those who could least take a hit, were hit hardest.

To move out of the abstract, what is the real-world evidence that this rural class-fragment—as a convenient label call them "the landless," and that will include small freeholders who were in the process of losing their farms—was increasingly weak economically and therefore especially vulnerable prior to the Great Deprivation? One nicely direct observation comes from a randomized study by Lars G. Sandberg and Richard H. Steckel of the roughly 40,000 soldiers who voluntarily joined the in-country provincial regiments between 1730 and 1890, using height of recruits as an index of well-being. Generally speaking, the entry-cadre of recruits grew taller in successive intakes during the nineteenth century. However, at about 1840, a statistically meaningful change began to be apparent in one group: those who were born in the south and west of Sweden in roughly two decades, 1838–56, as compared to the preceding 20-year cohort, were a bit more than two inches shorter than their predecessors. This was exactly the area and the time in which the final and most far-reaching second stage of the enclosure movement (following the *Lagaskiftet* of 1827) and the full dominance of market agriculture were working out their effects. If we accept that these recruits were the healthy but surplus male offspring of the landless class and the younger sons of the smallest freeholders (freeholders' elder sons could expect better than a small cottage and part-time soldiering in the back of beyond), then this literal shrinkage is indicative of background deprivation in the very group we posit would later be hit hardest in 1867–69.[40]

A confirmatory, and equally direct body of data cited by Sandberg and Steckel, concerns child mortality. If we use data on the death of children above one year of age as an indicator of general well-being (or, the opposite, immiseration) of the general population, we would expect child mortality in every age group from one year up to age 19, to decrease continually from 1800 onwards for, as we saw in chapter three, the general per capita economic output of Sweden was increasing and, as discussed in the present chapter, the mortality rates for the general population were dropping in the 1850s and in the 1860s, right up to the Great Deprivation. (One screens out cholera, the one big epidemic of the nineteenth century.) However, annual child mortality was markedly higher in the 1850s than it was in the 1840s and this held both for boys and girls and for all age groups up to age 19. This child-mortality rate rose further, into the 1860s, until, like a societal physic, the Great Deprivation purged things and the child mortality rate again began to fall.[41] This probably says: (1) that among the landless class, general health was declining in the middle years of the nineteenth century, consequent upon the "agricultural revolution," and their children were the most affected, since they were the least productive part of the labour force; and (2) that most likely the entire underclass was composed of those who were literally the weakest members of society, and therefore destined to be the most affected by the rigours of the Great Deprivation.

Obviously, we are here dealing with circumstantial evidence, lots of specks of dust; but as more and more circumstantial dust coalesces, it aggregates into a constellation of probability. During the mid-1860s solid national income data began to be collected, and it was retrospected to 1861. For our purposes, the key is that in contemporary money, Sweden's national income from all sectors dropped 4.2 per cent between 1867 and 1868. Significantly, the agricultural sector decreased 13.6 per cent.[42] That fixes the sectorial location of the Great Deprivation quite firmly. The rates for day labourers in agriculture dropped 10.2 per cent between 1866 and 1869.[43] In counter-fashion, the cost of living, calculated nationally, rose 9.8 per cent from 1866 to 1868.[44]

If one really wishes to know about cost of living increases, focus on what people ate. The staples of the landless class were rye, barley and potatoes. Using 1866 as the base year, the price of rye in 1868 (the peak year) was 81.26 higher.[45] For barley, the jump in the same year was 86.7 per cent,[46] and for potatoes 73.5 per cent.[47] All of those spikes were consequential and hit the poor hard, but the most damaging was the rise in potato prices. One of the observations made by Gustav Sundbärg that has stood up well over time is that potatoes during the nineteenth century developed from a minority crop to one of the staples of the farming population. According to his estimates, per capita consumption of potatoes rose from roughly 70 pounds per inhabitant in 1800 to 620 pounds in the mid-1860s.[48] (The average included infants and children, so adult consumption was markedly higher.) Those figures are not to be taken as being precise, but the reality is that as the century progressed, the potato became more and more a staple for a large portion of the Swedish population. It was ideal for raising in a cottage garden.[49] Almost certainly the prevalence of potatoes in the everyday diet on the edge of the Deprivation was inversely related to social class: the poorer one was, the more potatoes featured as food and, at the bottom of the economic ladder, as the main food. This is salient because potatoes in some ways are a very awkward crop; they contain a good deal of water and are hard to transport in bulk, especially to areas not close to railways or canals, and long-term storage was difficult. Thus, if one observes the market price of potatoes in the mid-1860s, it is immediately clear that even in good times, potatoes had a much greater variation in price than did grain crops. For example, even in the relatively good year of 1865, the price of potatoes in Malmöhus län was 68 per cent higher than in neighbouring Kristianstad län.[50] Thus, during the big price surge of 1866–68, potato markets were much more skittish, much less national in character, than were the grain crops: potato prices in the old province of Småland doubled in those years, but those in neighbouring Blekinge rose only 52 per cent. Examples could be multiplied; the clear point is that the food source that was most closely associated with the poor was also the foodstuff that was most apt to volatize in price. If we had precise knowledge of who was most dependent upon the potato, we would have an accurate predictor of who was destined to be most hurt in the Deprivation.

Should there ever be an accurate national historical accounting of the impact of the Deprivation, it almost certainly will show two creases of vulnerability: by geographic locale and by landlessness. And where the two creases intersect, there hardship to the very edge of starvation will be apparent.

In the 1970s, Swedish government statisticians estimated that "in all, some 1,544,000 persons emigrated from Sweden during the 1851–1930 period."[51] The overwhelming majority of them migrated from 1867–1914, the pre-1867 out-migration being numerically small (albeit extremely influential in framing subsequent patterns of movement), and the post-World War I emigration being a statistical tail. Even if we accept that the contemporary official figures of registered out-migration sharply understate Swedish out-migration until the mid-1880s,[52] the flare in 1868–69 is formidable. The official registers of gross out-migration to non-European countries show the following pattern:[53]

1866	4,475
1867	5,898
1868	21,487
1869	32,060
1870	15,457
Total 1866–70	**79,377**

Thereafter, it ebbed and flowed, dropping below 3,000 in 1877 and rising to about 45,000 annually in multiple years in the 1880s.

To stay a moment longer with the 1860s, the registered numbers are somewhat understated. The official gross out-migration tally to non-European countries for the entire decade was 88,831. Gustav Sundbärg concluded that this should be increased by 20 per cent—to 106,597—to make up for such undercounts and present-day scholars see that as a minimum.[54] Where these numbers become revealing is when one compares the corrected number for gross out-migration to non-European countries to Sundbärg's estimate for Swedish net out-migration to all destinations, both in Europe and transoceanic: in rough terms, 106,000 gross out-migration to extra-European countries in the 1860s and almost 150,000 total net out-migration to all places outside of Sweden.[55] Now, obviously, those are not strictly comparable figures—the former is gross, the latter is net—but that actually loads the story against the point I wish to make: at least one-third of the out-migration in the 1860s was not part of the much-studied North American trip, but rather was the story of broke and hungry workers and their families straggling to Denmark, Germany, Norway and sometimes farther afield in Europe in search of work. Such labour migration was not always short-term. This largely unremarked aspect of the Deprivation confirms the anecdotal material about penniless labourers and bankrupt small freeholders leaving the country for neighbouring lands. It is part of a larger tranche of lost memory that needs to be recovered in greater detail.[56]

More than a generation ago, Lars Ljungmark presciently observed concerning the late-1860s' swell in migration, that it was not a direct result of famine and destitution.

Rather, those factors were mediated by the populace's calculation of the future. "What did have an impact on emigration was the general fear that crisis conditions would develop and the belief that too little progress was being made in Sweden to improve the lot of the agricultural proletariat."[57] In the terms of our present discussion, the shock of the Deprivation produced a radically different risk assessment among significant numbers of the population. This in turn yielded a willingness to adopt new, less-risky socio-economic patterns and, in consequence, also produced a virtual cultural revolution in the way subsequent generations defined the shape of their world.

To keep the big picture in mind, let us boil matters down to their most essential elements, and these are three: (1) a pre-Deprivation history of pioneer out-migration that was sharply striated by region-of-origin and, more importantly, by the ideo-cultural proclivities of the migrants; (2) a real, but very hard to assay, period of dearth, the Great Deprivation of 1867–69, which affected all of Sweden but in a sharply differential localized and class-specific fashion; and (3) a migration surge in the years 1867–70 that triggered Sweden's full-scale participation in the Great European Migration of the nineteenth century.

Viewing these three variables at an international level, Hans Norman made the following astute observations that deserve quotation in full:[58]

> The years of the crop failures in the Nordic countries, 1867 and 1868, illustrate the great significance of pioneer emigrants for continued migration. In the countries where emigration had started during the 1840s and the 1850s, there was, of course, already a tradition of emigration, and channels of communication were developed, so that emigration grew rapidly to great proportions. That was especially true for Norway and Sweden, but less so for Denmark, which did not experience any significant crop failures. In Finland, on the other hand, which suffered most during the famine years and where the death rate rose to a record high, no pioneer emigration of such importance had yet taken place which could highlight America as an alternative. Nor did Finland experience any significant emigration during the late 1860s.[59]

THREE

There: now, adjust the timeline and place Ireland on the same grid.

In making that suggestion, I am walking a knife's edge. On the one hand, I am ever-mindful of the emotional valence that surrounds the history of Irish emigration, the more so when it touches the Famine. The historical memory of those matters, however acquired, is often intensely personal. For some people it is impossible to deper-sonalize these events—even temporarily—sufficiently to permit their discussion as part of an attempt to gain a larger pan-national perspective. I do not wish to lose you as a reader, but if that is your own situation, put this book back on the shelf.

On the other side of the knife's edge, I do not intend to soften excessively my suggestion to historians of Ireland that both the massive Irish out-migration in the nineteenth century and the Great Famine's part in triggering the full flow of that migration were not unique in their pattern of occurrence (singular in magnitude yes, unique in pattern no); I believe that Ireland's historical experience of these matters in the nineteenth century—while undeniably epochal, often tragic, and often heroic—is not totally *in*comparable to that of all other European nations and, further, it is clear that the pre-Famine out-migration was central to a determination of the character of both the Famine and the post-Famine migration; people tramped where there already were footpaths.

If, after the Famine, in David Fitzpatrick's perfect phrase, *"growing up in Ireland meant preparing oneself to leave it,"*[60] that was a cultural revolution very similar to those which happened in Sweden and elsewhere. Not that everyone left: yet, for most people becoming adult in Sweden and in the British Isles in, roughly, the last two-thirds of the nineteenth century, staying at home or out-migrating were choices that were opening up to them and increasingly so as the century wore on. In both Ireland and Sweden (and in several other nations), emigration ceased to be a form of cultural and social deviation and the possibility of migration became embedded in the everyday culture of the several lands.

FOUR

The Great Irish Famine is almost as perverse in its historiography as it was in its reality: it is better served in Irish fiction than in historical writing.[61] And, despite its being one of the most recognized events in the folk memory of Europe, until the early 1990s, in book form there existed only three full-scale allegedly historical studies of the catastrophe,[62] one a vicious piece of hate literature, the second an artful novel presented in the guise of historical writing, and the third a disjointed collection of essays put together by a squabbling, if occasionally brilliant, fianna of Irish historians. The first of these was John Mitchel's *The Last Conquest of Ireland (Perhaps)*[63] of 1861 and it substituted a dark theodicy for the stunned silence that had prevailed among Famine survivors.[64] The Famine, he argued, was the embodiment of a specific evil. What appeared to be confusion and inefficiency in the relief of suffering was, in Mitchel's telling, part of an English plan. Thus, a million and half persons starved, indeed, but actually, Mitchel declared, they were slain and willful murder should have been charged against the elite of English political life. Devoid of any historical evidence though this delation may be, one can only be impressed with Mitchel's artistry, for he wrote with hot vitriol, using human skin as velum. He created a Famine that was useful as a lever to later advocates of political violence and which to this day has its followers in covens around the world. (Mitchel's skills were recognized outside the confines of Irish politics, as evidenced by his being chosen by Jefferson Davis as the propaganda master for the Confederacy, a cause he was devoted to as sincerely as he was to his form of Irish nationalism; Mitchel was also markedly articulate in opposing Jewish Emancipation.)[65]

The second major book on the Famine was the 'noir *Bildungsroman*,' sailing under the colours of history, written by Cecil Woodham-Smith, *The Great Hunger* (1962).[66] It was (and still is) the best-selling book ever written concerning Irish history either as fact or fiction. In this creation, Woodham-Smith threaded much of the serious work of Irish scholars of the 1950s onto John Mitchel's emotional and ideological framework and then—here her brilliance becomes apparent—she borrowed from novelists of the high Victorian era: she centred the story on a gradgrinding male villain, her own version of Casaubon, namely Charles Edward Trevelyan, assistant secretary to the Treasury (the chief financial civil servant in the nation) and consequently the chief administrator of relief during the worst years of the Famine. In fact, the entire Famine becomes a set of motifs that radiate around his youthful, dutiful, unimaginative, earnestly Church of England form.[67] For all Woodham-Smith's assiduous research and her mining of the work of serious historians, her book was simply updated John Mitchel, done by an English lady in pearls who wrote very nicely, like an English lady in pearls. The work fits conveniently into one form of Irish nationalism, for it seemed to blame the British, and to turn the epic and unassimilable tragedy of the Great Famine into something more easily comprehensible, mere English penny-pinching. Much of her historical material was accurate—so too was that of Ireland's most historically accurate novelist, William Carleton[68]—but shards of accuracy misaligned in a vitrine do not reconstitute a Grecian urn. Most of her readers missed the fact that Woodham-Smith's depiction of Trevelyan and of the Westminster government was mostly the disdain of a *soi-disant* patrician for the striving upper-middle classes. Woodham-Smith's apparent sympathy for the starving Irish was a bit of sackcloth around her distaste for the wrong sort of Irish: the English-born and-educated daughter of an Indian army colonel, she was a collateral descendant of Lord Edward FitzGerald of 1798 fame, the right sort of Irishman. (As the reformer of the Victorian civil service, it was C. E. Trevelyan who would soon replace aristocratic patronage by open examinations and promotion by merit, and that pretty much told what sort he was.) Relevant here is her evaluation of the character of the migrants who left Ireland because of the Famine:[69]

> The Irish famine emigration is unlike most other emigrations because it was of a less civilized and less skilled people into a more civilized and more skilled community. Other emigrations have been of the independent and the sturdy in search of wider horizons, and such emigrants usually brought with them knowledge and technical accomplishments which the inhabitants of the country in which they settled did not possess. The Irish, from their abysmal poverty, brought nothing, and this poverty had forced them to become habituated to standards of living which the populations among whom they came considered unfit for human beings.

Deep feelings, indeed.[70]

The third volume, *The Great Famine. Studies in Irish History, 1845–52* (1956) was a serious and well-documented set of essays that, taken together, provided a balanced, but not excessively detached view of the tragedy.[71] The work, however, was not promoted outside of Ireland. (The Irish government provided a subvention for printing and demanded a local publisher.) And, even within the field of Irish history, the book received less attention than it deserved. The study had begun as a brainstorm of Eamon de Valera in 1944 (he wanted the book out in 1945 for the centenary of the Famine), and had gone through two sets of editors, engendered several personality wars, and had required the ghost-writing of major sections when key figures went mute. It was a miserable experience for almost everyone concerned and served as an early indication that collaborative scholarship is not the natural metier of Irish historians. One now reads the 1956 work with admiration, but it deserved more attention in its own time.[72]

Thereafter, until the 1990s, among historians of Ireland the Great Famine was treated like a live land mine: almost no one wanted to get near it.[73] Then, in the 1990s, and the early 2000s, as the 150th "anniversary" of the Famine approached, a flood of literature appeared, some of it quite distinguished both in evidence and unfeigned empathy, and some of it merely Famine-porn.[74] Alongside several valuable local studies, were two distinguished wide-scope works. One of these, James Donnelly's collection of articles, *The Great Irish Potato Famine* (2001),[75] provides the best at-present available assessment of the most consequential and controversial issues concerning the Famine—things such as the efficacy of relief efforts, the out-shipment of grain and, crucially, how the memory of the Famine was constructed. The other volume, remarkable for its admixture of heavy economic data with deft anecdote and knowledge of Irish-language folklore, is Cormac Ó Gráda's *Black '47 and Beyond. The Great Irish Famine in History, Economy, and Memory* (1999).[76] Taken together, Ó Gráda's and Donnelly's books finally provide the secure plinth that has been so long needed for a balanced and informed discussion of the Famine. Here we will take that platform as given, if not in all details, certainly in its breadth and learning.

Therefore, in the context of the present study, I wish to shape much of our discussion of the Famine as an axial moment that triggered socio-cultural revolution, and to do so around an older and very much neglected monograph, one that does not even have the word "Famine" in its title. This is Raymond Crotty's 1966 study, *Irish Agricultural Production. Its Volume and Structure.*[77] Crotty's work is good old-fashioned economic history in that it has lots of pre-Cliometric quantitative data, a long timeline (1815 to the 1950s), a wide international scope (relevant comparisons to other nations are adduced) and a discussion of legal and social issues affecting Irish agricultural society that are elided in more recent econometric studies. And, blessedly, Crotty had dirt under his fingernails. He farmed in County Kilkenny and knew that the way Irish farmers acted never had been along the lines dictated by textbooks and that they always had been quicker than their betters (social betters in olden times, or university-based advisors in his own time) gave them credit for. Crotty's book, in a summary sentence, made one astounding assertion: *the Great Famine was not a true watershed in Irish social and economic history.*[78]

This sounds loopy, but it was not, and it deserves its day in court. Crotty had a richly textured argument, deeply rooted in qualitative as well as quantitative considerations. (1) His knowledge of early modern Irish farming systems led him to suggest that the causal base point of the problems with nineteenth-century Irish agriculture was the destruction, beginning in the early seventeenth century, of the old Celtic system of social control over agricultural resources. The ancient society had been ecologically stable and had provided a fair degree of control over family formation. "The violence of the seventeenth century destroyed or cleared away the political, cultural and religious leaders of that society, leaving a decapitated mass of people who found themselves naturally and irrevocably at war with the new alien aristocracy of land, culture, and religion."[79] (2) The old system had been largely pastoral, but as the ancient usages fell away, limitations on cereal (and later) potato acreages diminished and eventually disappeared. (3) As tillage (especially potato growing) increased, the econo-social limitations on family formation, as specified in the work of K. H. Connell, disappeared and population soared. Crucially, Crotty argues that this tillage-and-procreation boom was on its way out well before the Famine because (4) from the end of the Napoleonic Wars into the 1840s, a general deflation was occurring in the economy of the British Isles and (5) the prices paid for tillage products on the

Dublin market (a price-setter for Ireland) dropped more than for grassland products. Land for digging was harder and harder to come by, as landlords and strong farmers did their sums and encouraged forms of farming that were not labour intensive. Thence (6) "it is quite clear that by 1844 a change, which might be termed revolutionary, had taken place in marriage trends in Ireland. This was the demographic response to the changed market conditions in Britain, conditions which made capitalless tillage farming no longer profitable ... The young man who wanted to set up on his own in Irish farming after 1815 could no longer readily do so, equipped only with a cabin and a spade."[80] And "by the 1830s ... the pattern of later and fewer marriages with a consequent fall in the birth rate was well established. This falling birth rate, along with rapidly rising emigration, must have ultimately led to a falling population."[81] In sum: "the Great Famine hastened matters ..."[82] In other words, the Famine really was not necessary for the dysfunctions of early nineteenth-century Irish society to be sorted out.

Is that not the most callously dismissive viewpoint possible? Actually, quite the opposite; if anything, it is a quantum emotional leap in the definition of the Famine as a true tragedy. As discussed in chapter three, the present consensus is that pre-Famine Ireland was indeed producing sizeable agricultural surpluses, farmers were beginning to limit spade-and-potato farming and, most importantly, a reordering of the system of family formation seemed to have been in train: in sum, the transformation of Ireland from a high-risk agricultural society to a much safer one had begun. And Crotty believed that a famine was not required to get there. So his interpretation actually is the most tragic interpretation of the Great Famine possible: that it was a monumental historical redundancy.

I think Raymond Crotty was halfway right. The difficulty here is that his work has rarely been fairly parsed. One has to note that, though correct in defining the direction of pre-Famine farming and demographic trends, he stated the case more strongly than most present-day economic historians would accept. However, the deeper problem is that he has been "disproved" at an angle that is oblique to his original statements. Recall here that Crotty posited that a series of price shocks in agricultural commodity markets at the end of the Napoleonic Wars set off the chain of events he believed was occurring in the first half of the nineteenth century. To expand a quotation mentioned above: "The Great Famine was not a true watershed in Irish social and economic history; rather the change in demand conditions on the British market which was heralded by the Battle of Waterloo represented such a watershed."[83] Now, the most nimble refutation of Crotty is that by Kevin O'Rourke[84] who (a) ignores Crotty's fundamental set of price shocks, those that began in, roughly, 1815, but (b) demonstrates for the years 1845–76 that exogenous price shocks which originated in the 1840s could not of themselves have produced the same changes as did the Great Famine. This is convincing, but it refutes something Crotty did not claim, as his concern was with 1815 as the moment of the primary price shocks and those of the late 1840s were only secondary, he believed, albeit real. And (c) O'Rourke does not engage the post-1876 reforms in land tenure, which is unfortunate as Crotty's ur-argument was that everything in nineteenth-century Irish agriculture prior to the period of land reform had to be understood in terms of a landlord-tenant system that virtually refused the inherent right to the use of the land of those who were doing the actual farming. In this light, the gradual introduction of peasant proprietorship in the later decades of the nineteenth century can be perceived as the final stages of the readjustment of the Irish agricultural system.[85]

Still, Kevin O'Rourke is compelling in his demonstration that no conceivable economic shock from outside Ireland (meaning, basically, big changes in commodity prices) would have produced the same reorganization of Irish society that the Great Famine did: increased pasture farming, consolidated land holdings, limited population growth, and quantum increases in emigration. Apparently, the shock of the Great Famine was not duplicable without serious environmentally inflicted pain (such as crop failure or massively bad weather.)

Nevertheless, Raymond Crotty was right in that the Great Famine—four, or more, years of hell—was a redundancy. Not quite, however, in the way that he suggested.

Here I would suggest that the Swedish case can be used as a counterfactual, a real-world experiment. It instantiates that in a vulnerable agricultural society, quite similar to Ireland's, serious dearth could be the moment of axial stress that produced rapid and permanent change. A multiyear, full-blown famine was not a necessity (if one can use such a terrible concept). Thus far in the Swedish case, we have viewed only the swift surge in out-migration, but in later discussion we will see that Swedish society underwent a widespread set of socio-economic and *mentalité* changes, ones that were not so much caused by the Deprivation as triggered thereby.

In using the Swedish case to argue that the full hideous Irish Famine was not necessary to the transformation of Ireland into a safer, less poor country, I am implicitly doing something that is highly unprofessional in the world of academic history: quietly employing the idea of purposiveness. If one can conceive of a major consequence of the Famine to have been to translate Ireland into a less dangerous, less hungry, less risky place for human beings to spend their lives, then one inevitably is close to being wrapped into the metaphor of purpose, and into the practice of teleology. Mostly, as academic historians, we try to use a cold and antiseptic vocabulary—employing words such as "result," and "consequence," to scrub out "purpose,"—but here, in a non-theological sense, purpose is appropriate. Although I think it is imperative to avoid the hate-speech that turns the massive Irish tragedy into a mere conspiracy, it is also disrespectful (if barely conceivable) to scrub emotion from the matter. Adopting a more comfortable, risk-reduced society in the second half of the nineteenth century as a "mission" for Irish events in the 1840s, permits us to articulate the wrenching fact that, to reach that goal, the Great Hunger was so, so unnecessary.

Cormac Ó Gráda, a big and fine enough mind to be able to break out of stiff academic protocols, has dared to introduce a word that is banned from conventional historical explanations—luck:[86]

> The role of sheer bad luck is important: Ireland's ability to cope with a potato failure would have been far greater a few decades later, and the political will—and the political pressure—to spend more money to save lives greater too. If this post-revisionist interpretation of events of the 1840s comes closer to the traditional story, it also keeps its distance from the wilder populist interpretations [of genocide] mentioned earlier. Food availability *was* a problem; *nobody* wanted the extirpation of the Irish as a race.

Part of the very bad Irish luck was that the Great Famine hit at a period in United

Kingdom political development when the party structure was fragmenting and in which what would today be called neo-conservative ideology became dominant. Without being anachronistic, it is fair to say that a very close parallel to the anti-state, pro-market, pro free-trade ideology that characterized Margaret Thatcher's government in the later twentieth century and that of George W. Bush in the twenty-first, was ascendant. This, just at the time Ireland most needed state intervention. Stephen Howe has summarized the political context as follows:[87]

> In fact, no serious Irish historian has ever proposed a "genocidal" interpretation ... In reality British government reactions to the Famine were certainly not motivated by some genocidal impulse, but were at best insensitive, inefficient and ineffective. Ministers and officials were ill-informed, slow and inconsistent in their reactions, riven by internal schisms and hobbled by dogma: free market dogma which insisted that state intervention must be counterproductive, providentialist religious dogma which saw famine as punishment for sins, and cultural-cum-racial dogma which blamed the supposedly idle and feckless Irish peasantry for their own ills. Emergency relief and public works schemes were frequently a shambles, and food often did not reach those most in need. Many died, quite simply, because of bureaucracy.

Given that I have been arguing that overwhelmingly the at-risk pre-Famine Irish consciously chose to stay at home despite the avalanche of hazard that hung over them, why was the hazard's occurrence bad luck?—should they not have known that mass starvation was inevitable? Emphatically, no, for it was not even probable, and, no, they were not stupid or suicidal. The risk assessment which prevailed in pre-Famine Irish culture had been a realistic way for the Irish agricultural population (and, indeed, for governmental authorities) to look at the future, for it was anchored in a set of observations that were accurate: namely a knowledge of *one-year* crop failures. These had happened often enough in the first four decades of the nineteenth century for everyone to know that they were real hazards: they would, indeed, cost lives and economic dislocation, yet the populace would survive, injured, but mostly intact.

Where this goes all awry is that "the historical record ... indicates that many of the deadliest famines on record have been due to back-to-back harvest failures."[88] And in parts of Ireland the Great Hunger hit four years in a row.[89] Such a sequence of events is unknown in time of peace in the Irish historical record—and certainly was unknown in the folk-memory in the first half of the nineteenth century.

An unprecedented event, such as the consecutive crop failures of the Great Famine, is best looked at as a single, non-replicable event and therefore not amenable to risk assessment: this in contrast to single-year crop failures which were repetitive and were well-known to the population. The Irish people had dealt realistically with the hazard of a single-year crop failure. What they, or their governors, could not have been expected to do was to foresee the probability of a one-off event. The probability of a single unprecedented event is a meaningless concept, unless (like the predictable path of a hurtling asteroid 300 miles from the earth's surface), it has some observable trajectory. Ireland: grotesque luck indeed.

FIVE

The unprecedented character of the Great Hunger elicited a stunned response all around, not least from the assessors of the body politic. Hence, there is no comprehensive direct knowledge of how many died. Civil registration of deaths (and births and marriages) was not required until 1864. Before that date church records, especially for the Catholic population, are woefully incomplete. However, the commissioners of the 1851 census worked heroically in attempts to reconstruct the long sequence of the disaster and modern historians have tried hard to recalibrate the nineteenth-century estimates.

The population of Ireland was a bit over 8.175 million in 1841 and somewhat over 6.552 million in 1851, a loss approaching 20 per cent. This, from all causes, of which Famine-death and emigration were the most important. That, however, understates the magnitude of the loss, since the total population was growing through the year 1845 (despite the partial potato failure of that year, starvation was not yet in train), so that demographers have to make their own estimate of what the maximum population of the country was before its harsh reduction through disease, starvation and emigration began. (8.5–8.6 million is the range of the most common estimates.) After that maximum point, the crude death rate rose sharply, as did the emigration rate.

It is surely wisdom to accept that despite all of the recent work done by historians of the Great Famine, the human costs of necessity have to be defined with less than optimal precision. This because there are more unknowns than knowns in the basic algebra of the Famine, Specifically: (1) we do not know with sureness what the population of Ireland was on the eve of the Famine, late 1845, although that can be interpolated;[90] (2) as mentioned above, direct data on births and deaths in Ireland are not available until 1864; (3) the 1851 census commissioners worked hard to provide a table of total mortality, but of course death occurs in normal times, so what one really needs is a definition of the level of *excess mortality*—meaning the number who died over-and-above the number determined by the normal background crude death rate;[91] (4) that would be a straightforward issue if one knew directly and accurately how much of the population loss between 1846 and the early summer of 1851 (when the census was taken) occurred through emigration. But we do not know that with full confidence, due to the weakness of the records, although these data are stronger than those for Famine deaths; (5) therefore, the allocation of Ireland's population loss caused by the Great Famine as between emigration and Famine-caused deaths[92] is largely a product of speculation—kept on leash, fortunately, by some data that limit the imagination.

The best that can be said is that the two econometricians who have dealt most successfully with the matter in detail, Cormac Ó Gráda and Joel Mokyr, arrive at the following conclusions: Ó Gráda, working with Phelim P. Boyle, concluded in 1986 that one million Irish individuals died because of the Famine.[93] This differed somewhat from Joel Mokyr's 1983 estimates of a minimum number of excess deaths of 1.075 million— which rises to as much as 1.491 million, if unborn deaths (that is, averted births) are included.[94]

Some scholars of famines go further into detail and unless they are read carefully, unintentionally mislead us. So, first, it is sensible to be cautious of nosologies. Granted, it is important to know as accurately as possible the exact diseases that ended the lives of the hungry, and beginning with the commissioners of the 1851 Irish census, scholars have been working at this matter. The danger is that it is easy to become reductive, for very few people in any famine die directly of starvation: some nasty disease gets them first. Thus, it is useful to know that well under five per cent of Irish Famine-caused deaths were from starvation,[95] but only as perspective. In major famines, hunger is the battering ram that allows the burglars-of-life into the human body; and, further, many of the victims of famines are reasonably well-nourished individuals who contract diseases transmitted by the broken in body. Famine kills in so many ways other than starvation.

Secondly, the view, mostly associated with the work of the Nobel Prize-winning economist, Amartya Sen, that famines are a matter of distributional failure, not of real food shortages, is better as social policy prescription than it is as history description.[96] His view may apply accurately to the famines of the second half of the twentieth century, but is not automatically applicable to the eighteenth or nineteenth centuries. And, admirable as are the humanitarian motives behind Sen's analyses, in the hand of keen acolytes the distribution-approach threatens to define famines out of existence. That is: it is almost always possible to demonstrate that there is more than enough food to feed everyone in some geographic area (country, continent, or the entire world), if only it is distributed responsibly. But until that distributive equality actually happens, we still are observing famines, and renaming them is not much aid to comprehension and distracts one from the real pain-point: one million or more Irish died early.

Karl Marx said that the Famine "killed poor devils only,"[97] which is not quite right. Analysis on a barony-by-barony basis, confirms that the Famine hit hardest in the poorest baronies,[98] but death was not a fulled-cloth blanket dropped evenly upon the poor; instead, it was ill-shaped and uneven, a misshapen shroud whose shabby corners fell on some individuals of every class and every background. It is useful to note the informed speculation about the proportion of the total excess deaths caused by the Famine in each province, 1846–51:[99]

Province	Percentage
Connacht	40.4
Munster	30.3
Ulster	20.7
Leinster	8.6

Mostly, the poverty-stricken became the Famine-shriven, but not entirely. Recall that Disease is a scythe-wielding horseman riding alongside Famine. Many diseases that spread quickly in time of dearth also affect persons who are well-nourished. Tuberculosis, for example, is not primarily a disease of the malnourished, but it communicates quickly when large numbers of people are on the tramp. And cholera is not really a famine disease, but it increases in periods of hunger as hygienic practices deteriorate. Thus, of the excess deaths in the 1840s, three-quarters to four-fifths were from diseases that were either "partially sensitive" or "not very sensitive" to hunger.[100] This is not to obviate the fact that even these diseases were mostly communicated by the poor to the poor; but they spread as well into the farmstead of small landholders and to the Big House. It is hard to imagine an extended family of any size, whatever its status, that did not lose someone, although the landlords were not, in the matter of starvation, of the tortureable class.[101]

In an elegant piece of research, David Miller has reminded historians that the Great Hunger was a nastily ecumenical business. It did not strike only Roman Catholics, although undoubtedly it hit them hardest. In eastern Ulster, technological developments in the textile industries had forced down the earnings of handloom weavers and other piece-workers to subsistence levels, and the Great Famine broke many of them. Miller has recovered a set of queries that were sent to Presbyterian clergy in March 1847, asking them whether or not their flocks were suffering unusually high mortality. This was approximately the midpoint of the Famine, so the replies understate the full effect (and, also, Miller notes that the ministers underreported in that they tended to limit their replies to assessments of congregants in good standing). Even so, one-third of the 154 clergy who replied said that their people were being afflicted by the Famine.[102]

SIX

Concerning out-migration, a sensible semi-consensus estimate is that between the beginning of 1846 and the end of 1850, "somewhere around" 1.2 million people "fled Ireland."[103] Shock moved an army. If we limit our view to the point where the Famine was a causal spur beginning in 1846 (for the migration season was over when the 1845 crop problems became apparent) and the close of 1850 (an altered accounting system was introduced by the UK government for the year 1851), it is possible to deal with direct data. These are imperfect and sometimes have to be read obliquely, but they do not require suppositions about the size of the Irish population on the eve of the Famine or assumptions about normal birth and death rates, such as are required in the speculative estimates of excess mortality.

Both pattern and the total magnitude of flow are important. As a set of hard-data buffers against excessive speculation, we can employ David Fitzpatrick's compilation of Irish-born persons living in major emigrant destinations in 1850–51:[104]

Country	Number in thousands	Percentage of total
USA	961.7	48.4
Britain	727.3	36.6
Canada	227.0	11.4
Australia	70.2	3.6
Total	**1,986.2**	**100.0**

These figures exclude the small numbers in New Zealand, Southern Africa and elsewhere, but they are robust since they come from the receiver countries and therefore stand independently from the skein of suppositions required to reach excess mortality and migration figures from data generated entirely within Ireland.

Obviously, Fitzpatrick's data are not figures solely for Famine migrants: they include all those persons who had left Ireland and who still were alive abroad in 1850–51. (The US census was conducted in 1850, the others in mid-1851.) These data set some boundaries for talking about Famine migration—for example, no one could talk sensibly of two million Famine out-migrants—and they help to confirm an important shift: during the Famine exodus the pecking order of preference changed. Up to 1845 the order of emigrant preferences had been: British North America/Great Britain/the United States. With the Famine, it became: USA/Great Britain/British North America.

The shift in the North American migrants can be observed clearly. Given below is the closest set of revised figures for the North American trade, in terms of gross emigration:[105]

Year	Total to North America	To USA	Percentage to USA	To British North America
1846	109,397	68,730	62.8	40,667
1847	223,832	119,314	53.3	104,518
1848	182,282	157,473	86.4	24,809
1849	214,403	181,011	84.4	33,392
1850	210,116	183,672	87.4	26,444
1846–50	**940,030**	**710,200**	**75.6**	**229,830**

The shift from British North American to United States ports early in the Famine occurred in part because the Canadian run—which had the advantage of being cheaper—was notoriously undersupervised and dangerous as compared to the US routes: the tragedy of the Grosse Île reception station is an integral part of the narrative of the Great Famine, and the prevalence of typhus and other "immigrant diseases" at that site were known to potential travelers by mid-1847.[106] The introduction of standards comparable to those of the USA in 1848 did away with some of British North America's price advantage, as did new port entry taxes on the shippers to pay for improvements. Equally importantly, Sir Robert Peel's high-principled and politically suicidal repeal of the Corn Laws in mid-1846[107] had the immediate effect of routing American provision shipping from the USA to the British Isles and this did for US shipping what the timber trade earlier had done for the Canadian routes. Once the US vessels became dominant in the emigrant trade, economies of scale developed and US ports became the main entrepôt to North America for migrants from Ireland until the end of the Great European Migration.

My own estimates of gross out-migration from Ireland, 1846–50 inclusive, are as follows:[108]

Destination	Number in thousands	Percentage of total
United States	710	56.8
Great Britain	291	23.3
British North America	230	18.4
Australasia and other	18	1.5
Total Famine emigration	**1,249**	**100.0**

So, the conventional wisdom appears reasonable—roughly 1.25 million Irish persons left Ireland during the Famine to settle elsewhere. To clarify: this number of out-migrants should not be taken as the statistical equivalent of excess deaths, but there would have been a normal background level of out-migration in any case. Nevertheless, it is an amazing number of people to leave, unequalled in peacetime elsewhere in Europe in the nineteenth century.

Amidst all the pain of dislocation, one must be impressed with the efficiency of it all. That cruel word again, but it is the fraternal twin of the concept of self-agency. It was not the disabled who left, nor was it the very poorest. They died. The emigrants were able, no matter how battered they appeared to foreign observers. Somehow, one-and-a-quarter million of the Irish people, with precious little help from outside, navigated the matrix of information and possibility that had been mapped out for them by earlier, pre-Famine migrants. These people left on a rip tide, but they were not flotsam.

SEVEN

Taken together, a rough consensus is that the Famine-generated excess deaths of 1–1.1 million (excluding "averted births") and the Famine-era out-migration represent a total of approximately 2.3 million human beings, a remarkably large proportion (27 per cent) to disappear in five-plus years from a population that had been about 8.5 million in 1845.

This brings us to a subject that we would rather avoid, but that is central to the understanding of the direct and short-term consequences of the Famine and also to an appreciation of long-term impact: the very vexed issue, "how indeed does one arrive at the tally of the human costs of the Famine and how trustworthy is it?" In essence, this is a matter not of higher mathematics, but of accounting. The initial attempt of the Irish census commissioners was to do the equivalent of what battalion commanders send their second lieutenants to do: a body-count. The totals, when added to recorded emigration, gave initial estimates, but these forms of direct accounting have not been given much credit in the last 30 or 40 years.

Instead, the preference has been to wrap the issue of Famine mortality into some fairly complex demographic-econometric projects that (unintentionally, I think) somewhat disguise the distasteful fact that we are dealing fundamentally not with mathematical formulae, but with human bodies. That is possible not only because of the way the calculations are framed, but because the need actually to count dead bodies is obviated, as I will indicate below.

In my view, the best of these derived tallies of Famine-cost is found in the work of Cormac Ó Gráda, Joel Mokyr and, to a lesser degree, Kevin O'Rourke. The econometrics of their work is highly complex, but is found in simple expression (here using words):

Projected		**Inferred**				
						Famine emigration
Irish population in 1851	minus	Irish population in 1845	equals	The tragic residual	composed of	and
						Excess deaths late 1845 to early 1851

Actually, there are several different way to engage the basic accounting presented here, but their fundamental processes are the same.[109] There is a minor problem of asymmetry in such calculations since this method yields what is taken to be excess Famine deaths, but has no parallel concept of excess Famine emigration. Thus, all out-migration is taken to be a result of the Famine, but not all deaths are treated as Famine-caused.[110]

Yet, however one packages the demographic calculations, they all come back to fairly simple accounting methods and hinge on the very prosaic accounting concept of *fungibility*. This is an almost offensively pedestrian notion to introduce into an assessment of one of the most painful collective human tragedies of the last two centuries, but upon it depends the way we think about the component pains of the Great Hunger. Fungibility, for academics, is most often encountered by some granting body deciding on whether or not money originally allocated to one line-item of expense may be employed on another line: may the left-over money from the software purchase account be used to buy some time for a research assistant? Matters such as that. A minor concept seemingly, except that it becomes nearly thermonuclear when applied to the Great Famine. For here is the question. Are modern scholars right that the excess deaths caused by the Famine and the migration out of Ireland were fungible accounting entities?

Possibly, but we should be sharply aware that behind the complex econometrics is the simple fact (made clear above, I hope) that the several modes of tallying Famine-caused deaths through inferential means comes down to one fundamental practice: that *in this accounting mode* death and emigration from Ireland are treated operationally as equal entities and therefore they are substitutable for each other on a one-to-one basis. That is, in this form of accounting, for each person who emigrated, the number of Famine-killed is reduced by one; and for any reduction in the flow of out-migrants, the number of Famine-caused deaths increases on the final balance sheet by an identical amount.

Aside from my not having faith in the accuracy of the out-migration data at the level required by such computations, I find it unsettling that scholars of this school have not dealt with the most pivotal direct implication of their work. By virtue of one-to-one fungibility, they should be telling us that each instance of emigration must be celebrated as a triumph over death, and the entire collective emigration flow as the most profound embracing of life in Irish history. According to their formula, by emigrating, one-and-a-quarter million persons affirmed life and directly cheated death. Now, obviously this is incompatible with the dominant view in Irish historiography and folk culture that the Famine emigration was a Bad Thing, so one can see why one might wish to be *sotto voce* about it.

Kevin O'Rourke and Cormac Ó Gráda have taken a somewhat elliptical approach to this matter. They have not dealt with the central implication of fungibility in the way that it is employed in Mokyr's work or in Ó Gráda's own earlier studies, namely that, as an alternative to mega-mass death, emigration was a Very Good Thing indeed. But they have approached it by asking, in effect, how good a lifeboat was emigration, really? Their rather reluctant answer is that out-migration was a crude form of disaster relief and that more governmental money spent sending people away would have lowered the Famine death toll.[111] The limitation was that "on the whole, only those with some stake in the land could afford to emigrate, and such people were not at greatest immediate risk from starvation."[112] There was, however a knock-on effect: land that was freed up by the departure of small farmers would have been useful to the formerly landless labourers and their families.

Note here what the scholarly limitation on the effectiveness of migration-as-disaster-relief means: by establishing that although out-migration saved some lives, albeit inefficiently, Ó Gráda and O'Rourke were also establishing that, in the context of the Great Famine, death and emigration were *not* truly fungible. Which is to say, the calculations of Famine mortality of Mokyr and of Ó Gráda himself were not trustworthy in the terms in which they were stated—good guesstimates, yes, weight-bearing calculations, no.

I think the next generation's path out of this unsatisfactory situation will be to abandon faith in the fungibility of death and of emigration, and thus necessarily to give up the econometricians' technique of trading them off against each other in their indirect calculations. Instead (1) as Ó Gráda and O'Rourke briefly indicate, the work of S. H. Cousens in the 1950s and 1960s should be taken as an example, when suitably corrected, of how to use direct data—not residuals—to evaluate the excess deaths caused by the Great Famine.[113] And, in tandem (2) a full evaluation of the primary accounts of Irish emigration and of its historiography, beginning with William Forbes Adams's brilliant 1932 volume, should be assayed. (3) And these efforts *should be completely independent* of each other. This would clear the slate of one of the most vexing aspects of the residual-approach, namely that by declaring Famine emigration and excess Famine-deaths to be fungible, every error is automatically doubled. That is, in the fungible system, an overcount of emigration automatically lowers the excess deaths by an equal amount and any undercount of emigration produces an equally false increment in the derived number of Famine deaths.

Death and emigration are two independent ledger entries in the accounts of the Great Famine. Though an assiduous forensic revisiting of the original accounts would be immensely hard work, one would hope that a mode of approaching the human costs of the Great Famine that has the immediate potential of instantly reducing the magnitude of errors would have an attraction for some historians.

NOTES

1   Milton Friedman, *Capitalism and Freedom* (Chicago: University of Chicago Press, 1962), p. ix.

2   I am here paraphrasing John D. Post, *The Last Great Subsistence Crisis in the Western World* (Baltimore: Johns Hopkins University Press, 1977), pp. ix–x.

3   Eino Jutikkala, "The Great Finnish Famine in 1696–97," *Scandinavian Economic History Review*, vol. 3 (1955), pp. 48–63. The author, in a chilling comment on the lack of any real governmental aid in this period of absolute Swedish rule, notes that "death by starvation was distressing only in so far as it meant, to the monarch, the loss of so many subjects" (p. 63).

4   Jutikkala, "The Great Finnish Famine," pp. 56–57. I am skeptical of the undocumented figure of 100,000 Swedish deaths found on several advocacy websites.

5   John D. Post, *Food Shortage, Climatic Variability, and Epidemic Disease in Pre-industrial Europe: The Mortality Peak in the early 1740s* (Ithaca: Cornell University Press, 1985) is the indispensable study. See especially table 1, pp. 32–33. Here is the appropriate place to call attention to the fascinating pioneer work of Cornelius Walford, an English barrister and early chronicler of world famines. His work brings to mind both that of William Wilde (of the Irish disaster chronologies prepared in the 1850s) and, in his presentation of the work to the (soon-to-be Royal) Statistical Society, the mode of promoting such pioneering work that had been engaged by E. G. Ravenstein. See Cornelius Walford, "The Famines of the World: Past and Present," *Journal of the Statistical Society*, vol. 41 (Sep. 1878), pp. 433–535, and "The Famines of the World: Past and Present—part II," *Journal of the Statistical Society*, vol. 42 (Mar. 1879), pp. 79–265. The entire sequence of events and the various estimates of deaths are best covered in David Dickson, *Arctic Ireland: the Extraordinary Story of the Great Frost and forgotten Famine of 1740–41* (Belfast: White Row Press, 1997.)

6   Post, *The Last Great Subsistence Crisis*, p. 120.

7   Cormac Ó Gráda suggests that the total *excess* deaths (that is, over-and-above normal mortality) were 13 per cent of the total population in 1740–41 and for the Great Famine, as measured 1846–52, were 12 per cent. *Famine. A Short History* (Princeton: Princeton University Press, 2009), table 1.1, p. 23.

8   In addition to Post's books cited above, see his "Famine, Mortality, and Epidemic Disease in the Process of Modernization," *Economic History Review*, new ser., vol. 29 (Feb. 1976), pp. 14–37.

9   In the 1920s, Florence Edith Janson spent time in both Swedish and Swedish-American communities and backgrounded her archival scholarly work with oral material. She found that the Deprivation "still lives vividly in the memories of the older generation, both in Sweden and America." Florence Edith Janson, *The Background of Swedish Immigration, 1840–1930* (Philadelphia: University of Pennsylvania, 1931), p. 222.

10   Erland Hofsten and Hans Lundström in Government of Sweden, *Urval*, no. 8 (Stockholm: Statistika Centralbyrån, 1976), p. 44.

11   One of these is the semi-popular, but solid, *Ett Satans år. Norrland 1867*, by Olle Häger, Carl Torell and Hans Villius (Stockholm: Sveriges Radios Förlag, 1978). A second is very fine amateur history, distinguished by a large number of well-cited extracts from relevant documents: Ernst G. Holm and Egil Lönnberg, *Nödåren i Norra Småland, 1867–1869* (Jönköping: Länsmuseets Förlag, 1945). Most valuable is Marie Clark Nelson, *Bitter Bread. The Famine in Norrbotten, 1867–1868* (Uppsala: Acta Universitatis Upsaliensis, 1988). Also revealing is Marie Clark Nelson, "Through the Looking Glass. Report on the Famine in Norrbotten as seen through the eyes of *Norrbottens-Kurinen*, 1867–69," *Historisk Tidskrift*, vol. 104 (1984), pp. 179–204. In 1984, Ann-Sofie Ohlander and Hans Norman surveyed the literature and called for a major research project on pre-industrial episodes of deprivation and disease. The three foci were to be the town of Örebro in the 1773 famine, urban Uppsala during the 1857 cholera epidemic, and Norrbotten and four neighbouring parishes in Västerbotten in 1868. The latter segment had already been covered by Marie Clark Nelson's work, and there, apparently, things stopped. See Ann-Sofie Ohlander and Hans Norman, "Kriser och Katastrofer. Ett forskningsproject om effecterna av nöd. Svält och Epidemier i det förindustriella Sverige," *Historisk Tidskrift*, vol. 104 (1984), pp. 163–78.

12   Ulf Beijbom certainly did no one any favours in prefacing his fine study of the Swedes in Chicago with the assertion that Swedish agriculture was hit by a series of serious crop failures, 1867–69, and that "the result was mass starvation ..." One suspects he was unconsciously competing with the historians of the Irish in Chicago who, indeed, did have mass starvation as part of the backstory of their ethnic group. Ulf Beijbom, *Swedes in Chicago. A Demographic and Social Study of the 1846–1880 Immigration* (Uppsala: Studia Historica Upsaliensia, 1971), p. x.

13   Holm and Lönnberg (*Nödåren i Norra Småland*, pp. 27–42), give a meteorological chronology for 1867–69. Were this a forecast rather than an historical sequence, it would be the weather-forecast-from-hell.

14   For a weather-food memoir of the hideously long winter and spring of 1867, by a Norrland frontier farmer, see Häger, Torell and Villius, *Ett Satans år. Norrland*, p. 21.

15   Nelson, *Bitter Bread*, p. 26.

16   Ernst Lundholm, "Vedbo och Nordmakrs Härader," in Government of Sweden [editor: Gustav Sundbärg], *Emigrationsutredningen, Bilaga VIII, Bygdeundersökningar* (Stockholm: KB, 1910), p. 7.

17   *Wäktaren*, 15 April 1869, cited in G. M. Stephenson, "The Background of the Beginnings of Swedish Immigration, 1850–1875," *American Historical Review*, vol. 31 (Jul. 1926), p. 720.

18   *Wäktaren*, 6 August 1868, 26 Nov. 1868 and 1 July 1869, cited in Stephenson, "Background of the Beginnings of Swedish Immigration," pp. 720–21.

19   Oscar Malmborg to A. E. Burnside, 9 March 1861, reproduced in H. Arnold Barton, *Letters from the Promised Land. Swedes in America, 1840–1914* (Minneapolis: University of Minnesota Press, 1975), p. 90.

20   Albin Widen, "Goda år och Nödår," in Evert Wrangel, Arivd Gierow and Bror Olsson (eds.), *Svenska Folket genom Tiderna*, vol. 9, *Vid 1800-talets mitt* (Malmö: n.p., 1940), p. 257.

21   Vilhem Moberg (tr. Paul B. Austin), *A History of the Swedish People* (New York: Pantheon Books, 1973), vol. 2, p. 47. Moberg is good on this: as a child in Småland in 1868 his mother had been sent into the bush to collect hazelnuts and the buds from heather and these, with a bit of corn flour, were kneaded into dough. For a range of hunger-breads used in Småland, see Holm and Lönnberg, *Nödåren i Norra Småland*, pp. 97–101. For hunger-breads and related food preparations over several provinces, see Widen, "Goda år och Nödår," pp. 252–57. That the Swedish (and earlier, the Irish) development of famine-foods was unique in local ingredients, but not singular in its desperate creativity, is illustrated in the discussion of famine-foods in Ó Gráda, *Famine. A Short History*, pp. 73–78.

22   Nelson, *Bitter Bread*, pp. 152–53.

23   Moberg, *History of the Swedish People*, p. 45. Häger, Torell and Villius (*Ett Satans år. Norrland*, p. 14) reproduce an illustration from *Fäderneslandet*, 6 June 1867, showing a family near starvation with the father barking a tree for bread. The physiognomy of the bone-thin family members is instantly recognizable to anyone familiar with the line-drawings that were done during the Great Famine in Ireland.

24   Kari J. Pitkänen, *Deprivation and Disease. Mortality during the Great Finnish Famine of the 1860s* (Helsinki: Finnish Demographic Society, 1993), table 3, pp. 166–72. For longer-term backgrounds, see Yrjö Kaukiainen, "Harvest fluctuations and mortality in agrarian Finland, 1810–1870," in Tommy Bengtsson, Gunnar Fridlizius and Rolf Ohlsson (eds.), *Pre-Industrial Population Change. The Mortality Decline and Short-Term Population Movements* (Stockholm: Almquist and Wiksell, 1984), pp. 235–54. See also Kari J. Pitkänen, "Patterns of Mortality during the Great Finnish Famine," *Acta Demographica* (1992), pp. 81–102.

25   Pitkänen, *Deprivation and Disease*, table 2, pp. 152–64.

26   Pitkänen, "Patterns of Mortality," p. 84.

27   Nelson, *Bitter Bread*, table. 5.4, p. 94.

28   Nelson, *Bitter Bread*, p. 174.

29   Nelson, *Bitter Bread*, table 5.2, p. 82.

30   Nelson, *Bitter Bread*, p. 101.

31   Gustav Sundbärg in Government of Sweden, *Emigrationsutredningen, Bilaga V, Bygdestatistik* (Stockholm: KB, 1910), Tabeller II, table 31, p. 32.

32   Three interpretive points: (1) here I am ignoring the reduction in birth rate that occurred during the Deprivation, although it would increase any calculation of the Deprivation's full demographic effects; (2) the actual Deprivation death rate is somewhat greater than it at first appears because the impact of the Deprivation should be assessed not as a comparison with the crude death rate just before the Famine, but as a deviation from the long-term trend line, which was moving downward; (3) the national data are bloated a bit by the case of Stockholm. As I mentioned earlier, it was a septic city in the nineteenth century—in the 1860s, its crude death rate was 63.4 per cent higher than the national rate, and sepsis was fairly constant—which means that in the rural areas, the site of the Deprivation, the rise in the crude death rate was somewhat greater than is indicated in the national data. Those points granted, one still cannot convincingly argue that a Swedish famine occurred.

33   Nelson, *Bitter Bread*, p. 70; Johan Söderberg, "Interrelationships between short-term economic and demographic fluctuations in a period of crisis: south-eastern Sweden, 1866–1872," in Bengtsson, Fridlizius and Ohlsson, *Pre-Industrial Population Change*, table 2, p. 258.

34   Nelson, *Bitter Bread*, table 3.2, p. 48.

35   Söderberg, "Interrelationships between short-term fluctuations," table 2, p. 258.

36   Alberto Tiscornia, *Statens, godsens eller böndernas Socknar? Den Sockenkommunala självstyrelsens utveckling i Västerfärärnebo, Stora Malm och Jäder, 1800–1880* (Uppsala: Acta Universitatis Upsaliensis, 1992), esp. pp. 87ff.

37   Holm and Lönnberg, *Nödåren i Norra Småland*, pp. 55–87; Häger, Torell and Villius, *Ett Satans år. Norrland*, pp. 26–27.

38   Janson, *The Background of Swedish Immigration*, pp. 225–27; Nelson, *Bitter Bread*, pp. 122–50.

39   A very rigorous microstudy by Tommy Bengtsson yields the following: "The results for the period 1815–1865 confirm the conclusion that the agricultural reforms in the beginning of the nineteenth century increased the social stratification in the countryside." Tommy Bengtsson, "Mortality and Social Class in Four Scanian parishes, 1766–1865," in Tommy Bengtsson *et al.*, *Life under Pressure. Mortality and Living Standards in Europe and Asia, 1700–1900* (Cambridge: MIT Press, 2004), p. 152.

40   Lars G. Sandberg and Richard H. Steckel, "Overpopulation and Malnutrition Rediscovered: Hard Times in 19th-Century Sweden," *Explorations in Economic History*, vol. 25 (1988), pp. 1–19, esp. table 2, p. 7.

41   Sandberg and Steckel, "Overpopulation and Malnutrition Rediscovered," table 4, p. 10. Sandberg and Steckel comment that "the most likely losers in the division of increasingly scarce food, therefore, were children who had been weaned (nursing mothers were also workers) but not old enough to do meaningful work" (p. 16). Johan Söderberg has taken exception to Sandberg and Steckel's work in "Hard Times in 19th-Century Sweden," *Explorations in Economic History*, vol. 26 (1989), pp. 477–91. He finds them more "pessimistic" than are most Swedish economic historians. Crucially, he accepts their basic data (with minor reservations), but provides a "workload" hypothesis much more compatible with neoconservative economics. The keystone of his argument is that the apparent deterioration in certain geographic areas (he lumps the freeholders and the landless and avoids class analysis) was caused by these farmers' self-exploitation through a more intensive use of family and child labour, which actually raised output.

42 "The Staff of the Institute for Social Sciences, University of Stockholm," *Wages, Cost of Living and National Income in Sweden 1860–1930*, vol. 3, *National Income of Sweden, 1860–1930* (London: P. S. King and Son, 1937), part 1, table 48, p. 234.

43 Staff of the Institute, *National Income of Sweden, 1860–1930*, table 50, part 1, p. 244. Sandberg and Steckel ("Overpopulation and Malnutrition Rediscovered," table 5, p. 13) recalibrated the classic daily wage data of Lennart Jörberg, and concluded that agricultural labour wages in 1865–69 were 10.6 per cent below those of 1860–64.

44 Staff of the Institute, *National Income of Sweden, 1860–1930*, part 1, table 51, p. 247.

45 Staff of the Institute, *National Income of Sweden, 1860–1930*, part 2, table 68, p. 53. Rye per deciton rose from 11.42 kronor in 1866 to 20.70 kronor in 1868.

46 Staff of the Institute, *National Income of Sweden, 1860–1930*, part 2, table 68, p. 53. The rise was from 11.01 kronor per deciton to 20.57.

47 Staff of the Institute, *National Income of Sweden, 1860–1930*, part 2, table 68, p. 53. The rise was from 2.15 kronor per deciton to 3.73. The national figures for rye, barley and potatoes are a revision of material computed earlier and published in 1933 (see note 48), and differ somewhat from those earlier figures, although the pattern is the same.

48 Gustav Sundbärg in Government of Sweden, *Emigrationsutredningen, Betänkande* (Stockholm: KB, 1913), table 20, p. 89. Potato consumption peaked in the decade 1871–80, and then declined as an artifact of increasing prosperity in the countryside.

49 For a nice description of the ubiquity of the potato in the household gardens in Småland, taken from respondents collected by the Nordiska Museet, Stockholm, see Holm and Lönnberg, *Nödåren i Norra Småland*, p. 53.

50 "The Staff of the Institute for Social Sciences, University of Stockholm," *Wages, Cost of Living and National Income in Sweden, 1860–1930*, vol. 1, *The Cost of Living in Sweden, 1860–1930* (London: P. S. King and Son, 1933), table C.6, p. 219. These local data are a bit difficult to deal with as the reporting for most is on the basis of the län, but some of the data were reported for the historic province, and several of the regions did not report.

51 Hofsten and Lundström, *Urval*, p. 67.

52 The understatement issue has been discussed in chapter two. Hofsten and Lundström (*Urval*, pp. 64–67) provide an admirable summary of the problem: no direct data on Swedish out-migration are available before 1851; passport registers were used, 1851–60, but passport requirements were abolished in 1860; parish abstracts were used to give data, 1861–83; only from 1884 onwards did the government keep reasonably accurate direct data on out-migrants. And in all of these periods of data collection there were problems of evasion of the data net and in all eras intra-European migration was not very well recorded.

53 Sten Carlsson, "Chronology and Composition of Swedish Emigration to America," in Harald Runblom and Hans Norman (eds.), *From Sweden to America. A History of the Migration* (Minneapolis: University of Minnesota Press, 1976), table 5.1, p. 117–19.

54 See the discussion in chapter two. At the risk of *lèse majesté*, I think it likely that the Swedish government's official historical statistics on emigration (as presented in Hofsten and Lundström, *Urval*, table 4.2, p. 66) make two errors in the reading of Sundbärg's work in Bilaga IV of the Emigration Commission of 1907–13: (1) the total for registered out-migration for 1851–60 and 1861–70 are wrong, although thereafter they agree with the originals and (b) more importantly, the compilers of the modern summary table mistakenly label gross registered out-migration to non-European countries as net migration.

One needs to emphasize that the totals are for *gross* out-migration to non-European countries. Almost all of it was to the USA (Carlsson, "Chronology and Composition of Swedish Emigration to America," table 5, p. 117). In 1870 there were 97,332 Swedish-born persons reported by the US census, which marries reasonably with Sundbärg's estimate for gross out-migration to non-European countries as it is appropriately smaller than his estimate. (*Statistical History of the United States from Colonial Times to the Present* (New York: Basic Books, 1976), table C.228–95, p. 117). Of course, some Swedish in-migrants died in the USA, but one should also be aware that return-migration was also significant from a very early date in the emigration surge. This fact is lost if one mislabels gross registered out-migration as being net.

55 See chapter two for the precise numbers 1861–70.

56 As evidenced in the pioneering exhibition "The Forgotten Emigration to Denmark and Germany," mounted in 2008 by the Svenska Emigrantinstitut, Växjö. Dr Lars Hansson, then-director of the institute, was largely responsible for the innovative approach. One does not wish to imply that intra-European migration has been totally ignored, merely overshadowed by the American story. Hans Norman, for example, noted that in the 1850s more out-migrants from Kronobergs län went to Germany and Denmark than to the United States. Hans Norman, "The Emigrants and the Countries they Left," in Hans Norman and Harald Runblom,

Transatlantic Connections: Nordic Migration to the New World after 1800 (Oslo: Norwegian University Press, 1988), p. 16. Actually, Gustav Sundbärg was concerned with the matter. For 1861–70 he calculated the gross number of emigrants to European countries (as shown in official sources which he recognized was an undercount) as 33,716, which represents 27.5 per cent of the official count of out-migration of 122,447. Sundbärg, *Bygdestatistik*, Tabeller II, table 45, p. 95.

57 Lars Ljungmark (tr. Kermit B. Westerberg), *Swedish Exodus* (1965; Carbondale: Southern Illinois University Press, 1979), p. 31.

58 Norman, "The Emigrants and the Countries they Left," p. 63.

59 Norman's paradigm is also applicable within Sweden. Thus, in Norrbottens län, which had little early emigration, the rate of Deprivation-era out-migration was low as a proportion of its population, but those for the following län, which experienced sharp dearth and also had been the source of significant earlier out-migration, were the highest in the nation: Östergötland, Jönköping, Kronoberg, Kalmar. Kristanstads län, which had a strong experience of early out-migrating tradition but not much direct dearth, was a median case. So too was Kopparbergs län, which also had a strong emigration background, but where the Deprivation was spotty and was moderated by the strength of local craft and mining industries. See the län data in Sundbärg, *Bygdestatistik*, Tabeller II, table 43, pp. 43–93.

60 David Fitzpatrick, *Irish Emigration, 1801–1921* (Dundalk: Dundalgan Press Ltd, for the Economic and Social History Society of Ireland, 1984), p. 30.

61 See Margaret Kelleher's literary assessments in *The Feminization of Famine: Expressions of the Inexpressible?* (Cork: Cork University Press, 1997).

62 Because it stops with the year 1847, I am leaving out John O'Rourke's classic *The History of the Great Irish Famine of 1847, with notices of earlier Irish Famines* (Dublin: James Duffy and Co., 1874; 3rd ed., 1902). Aside from getting the operative date of the hated Gregory Clause wrong (he sets it into effect six months earlier than actually was the case, as do almost all subsequent histories of the Great Famine), Canon O'Rourke is remarkably accurate about 1847. Equally important, he deals in some detail with the earlier (and worse) famine of 1740–41. He conducted extensive interviews with survivors of the 1845–49 famine, and it is clear that he understands that the earlier famine was part of the collective folk memory of those who faced 1847 and thereafter—a fact that has since been lost.

63 John Mitchel, *The Last Conquest of Ireland (Perhaps)* (Dublin: The Irishman's Office, 1861).

64 Just as the Famine ended, Thomas D'Arcy McGee had published *A History of the Irish Settlers in North America from the earliest period to the Census of 1850* (Boston: P. Donahue, 1851). This went through several editions before Mitchel's work was published, and it helped to fix the Famine-as-genocide myth within Irish-American nationalism. It did not, however, have the international effect of Mitchel's volume. I am grateful to Professor David Wilson for his help on this matter. His definitive biography of McGee is *Thomas D'Arcy McGee, Passion, Reason, and Politics, 1825–1857*, vol. 1 (Montreal and Kingston: McGill-Queen's University Press, 2008). Vol. 2 forthcoming.

65 The shrewdest apperception of Mitchel's writing is Patrick O'Farrell, "Whose Reality? The Irish Famine in history and literature," *Historical Studies* [Melbourne], vol. 20 (Apr. 1982), pp. 1–13. Valuable on Mitchel's deep racism (which in my view is the single theme running through his anti-Jewish, anti-Black, anti-British ravenings) is Nini Rodgers, *Ireland, Slavery and Anti-Slavery: 1612–1865* (Basingstoke: Palgrave Macmillan, 2007), pp. 293–304.

66 Cecil Woodham-Smith, *The Great Hunger* (London: Hamish Hamilton, 1962, and New York: Harper and Row, 1963).

67 For a more balanced assessment of Trevelyan, see Robin Haines, *Charles Trevelyan and the Great Irish Famine* (Dublin: Four Courts Press, 2004).

68 See esp. William Carleton, *The Black Prophet* (Dublin: J. Duffy, 1847).

69 Woodham-Smith, *The Great Hunger*, pp. 206–07. The *Atlantic Monthly* gave the book prestigious entry into the American literary scene by publishing a large excerpt ("A Tale of Irish Famine," *Atlantic Monthly*, vol. 211, January 1963, pp. 67–93). The quotation above is found on p. 86.

70 Deftly, if not kindly, Elizabeth Longford in the *Oxford DNB* summarized Woodham-Smith, using the words of Noel Blakiston, one of Cecil Woodham-Smith's close literary friends, "who recalled her aristocratic appearance, high-spirited entertaining, and long hours at the Public Record Office, her arrivals and departures made in a chauffeur-driven car."

71 R. Dudley Edwards and T. Desmond Williams (eds.), *The Great Famine. Studies in Irish History, 1845–52* (Dublin: Browne and Nolan, 1956).

72 On the picaresque history of the project, see Cormac Ó Gráda's "Introduction to the New Edition" (Dublin: Lilliput Press, 1994), pp. xvii–xxvii, a reprint of his "Making History in Ireland in the 1940s and 1950s: the

Saga of 'The Great Famine,'" *Irish Review*, no. 12 (1992), pp. 87–107, also reprinted as "Making Famine History in Ireland in the 1940s and 1950s," in Cormac Ó Gráda, *Ireland's Great Famine. Interdisciplinary Perspectives* (Dublin: University College Dublin Press, 2006), pp. 234–49.

73 The chief exception came from outside of academic history and of the guild of Irish historians: the Cliometrician Joel Mokyr published *Why Ireland Starved. A Quantitative and Analytical History of the Irish Economy, 1800–1850* (London: George Allen and Unwin, 1983). For a subtle reading, in much-needed comparative perspective, of the Irish historical literature on the Famine as it existed in the early 1990s, see Ronald Rudin, "Revisionism and the Search for a Normal Society: A Critique of Recent Quebec Historical Writing," *Canadian Historical Review*, vol. 73, no. 1 (1992), pp. 30–61, esp. pp. 55–60.

74 For a considered assessment of the most noteworthy of the 1990 items, see Mary Daly, "Review Article: Historians and the Famine: a beleaguered species?" *Irish Historical Studies*, vol. 30 (Nov. 1997), pp. 591–602.

75 James Donnelly, *The Great Irish Potato Famine* (Phoenix Mill, Gloucestershire: Sutton Publishing, 2001).

76 Cormac Ó Gráda, *Black '47 and Beyond. The Great Irish Famine in History, Economy, and Memory* (Princeton: Princeton University Press, 1999).

77 Raymond Crotty, *Irish Agricultural Production. Its Volume and Structure* (Cork: Cork University Press, 1966).

78 Crotty, *Irish Agricultural Production*, p. 64.

79 Crotty, *Irish Agricultural Production*, p. 32.

80 Crotty, *Irish Agricultural Production*, p. 41.

81 Crotty, *Irish Agricultural Production*, p. 41.

82 Crotty, *Irish Agricultural Production*, p. 41.

83 Crotty, *Irish Agricultural Production*, p. 64.

84 Kevin O'Rourke, "Did the Great Irish Famine Matter?" *Journal of Economic History*, vol. 51 (Mar. 1991), pp. 1–22.

85 Crotty (*Irish Agricultural Production*, pp. 60–65) is somewhat confusing about this matter. He seems to imply that land reform was the logical outgrowth of agricultural-demographic readjustment but, simultaneously, that a revolution in land ownership could have prevented the Famine. For a balanced study of governmental policies, see Peter Gray, *Famine, Land and Politics: British Government and Irish Society, 1843–50* (Dublin: Irish Academic Press, 1999). It is useful to meld Gray's discussion of the providentialist interpretation of the Famine in some sectors of the British governing caste with Robin Haines' argument in *Charles Trevelyan and the Great Irish Famine* that Charles Trevelyan was not himself a providentialist.

86 Cormac Ó Gráda, *Ireland before and after the Famine. Explorations in Economic History, 1800–1925* (Manchester: Manchester University Press, 1988), p. 122. See also p. 35.

87 Stephen Howe, *Ireland and Empire. Colonial Legacies in Irish History and Culture* (Oxford: Oxford University Press, 2000), pp. 38–39. Both Ó Gráda's and Howe's authoritative assessments of the state of the evidence should be read in the face of the shamelessly lurid campaigns of Irish-American organizations in several states to compel the teaching of the Famine as a genocide.

88 Ó Gráda, *Famine. A Short History*, p. 31.

89 In the present study, I have used 1845–49 as the dates for the Great Famine: a partial potato failure in 1845, full in 1846, partial in 1847 and full in 1848, with continued direct impact into 1849. This is not a matter to have an academic fight over: if an historian wishes to remove 1845 (since few starved in that year), fine; and one can easily show direct demographic influence well into the year 1851.

90 Joel Mokyr notes (*Why Ireland Starved*, pp. 264–65) that he has calculated the population of each county for 1846. Unfortunately, he gives us no statement either of those county numbers or of the national total.

91 Excess deaths are defined as being the number of persons who died during the Famine "who would not have died otherwise [at that time.]" (Mokyr, *Why Ireland Starved*, p. 263). The excess mortality rate is the difference between the total death rate for the Famine and the usual crude death rate (which was running between 22.0 and 24.0 per thousand in the early 1840s). That said, the whole concept of "excess mortality" requires a bit of reflection. It is technically useful, but rhetorically misleading. Since everyone dies, the Famine spike in deaths is really an indication of early mortality, not of excess mortality. And this spike has very little meaning unless the age of death is specified and somehow reckoned cumulatively—such as in a calculation that produces the total of "human life years" lost.

92 This sets aside entirely the very complicated issue of the "unborn dead." This issue arises from the clearly observable fact that during great food shortages fewer conceptions take place and fewer conceptions come to full term. Mokyr projects these as being in excess of 400,000 for 1846–51 (Mokyr, *Why Ireland Starved*, table 9.1, p. 266).

93 Phelim P. Boyle and Cormac Ó Gráda, "Fertility Trends, Excess Mortality, and the Great Irish Famine," *Demography*, vol. 23 (Nov. 1986), pp. 543–62.

94 Mokyr, *Why Ireland Starved*, table 9.1, p. 266. Given the differences in the two estimates, the matter has not been directly joined, although Ó Gráda (*Ireland before and after the Famine*, p. 83) mildly criticized Mokyr. In 2003 they jointly authored "Famine Disease and Famine Mortality" (reprinted, Ó Gráda, *Ireland's Great Famine*, 2006, pp. 63–85), based on a paper they jointly gave in 1999, without addressing their differences, but apparently taking Ó Gráda's one million excess deaths as the right number.

95 Ó Gráda, *Famine. A Short History*, table 4.2, p. 119.

96 Amartya Sen's bibliography is large. His most influential work is *Poverty and Famines. An Essay on Entitlement and Deprivation* (Oxford: Oxford University Press, 1981).

97 Karl Marx, *Capital* (Moscow: Progress Publishers, 1954), vol. 1, p. 704, cited by Ó Gráda (*Ireland before and after the Famine*, p. 83 and elsewhere).

98 Ó Gráda, *Black '47*, p. 33. See Donnelly, *The Great Irish Potato Famine*, table 6, p. 176 for excess mortality rates by county, as derived from Mokyr's work.

99 James Donnelly, "Excess Mortality and Emigration," in W. E. Vaughan (ed.), *A New History of Ireland*, vol. 5, *Ireland under the Union, I, 1801–70* (Oxford: Clarendon Press, 1989), p. 351, citing the work of Mokyr.

100 Ó Gráda, *Famine. A Short History*, table 4.2, p. 119, employing data for Connacht and Ulster.

101 Ó Gráda, *Black '47*, p. 127, mentions that the Blake family of Renvyle, Co. Galway, were "looking forward to starvation." No citation is provided, which is unfortunate, as the Blakes were a fascinating Catholic gentry family, highly adept at survival. They were descended from late Norman (Old English) marchers who, in the 1650s, were claiming that they had never changed language or intermarried with the local Irish. The Cromwellians got them anyway, for they were Catholic. The family rebuilt its fortunes via slave plantations and the related provision trades and one family member bought the Renvyle estate in 1680. The family continued in the West Indian trade until its collapse. See *Blake Family Records* (privately printed, n.d.) and D. H. Akenson, *If the Irish Ran the World. Montserrat, 1630–1730* (Liverpool: Liverpool University Press and Montreal and Kingston: McGill-Queen's University Press, 1997), pp. 68–70.

102 David W. Miller, "Irish Presbyterians and the Great Famine," in Jacqueline Hill and Colm Lennon (eds.), *Luxury and Austerity* (Dublin: University College Dublin Press, 1999), pp. 164–67, 179. Miller's work on the Presbyterians is particularly important, as there was no religious census of Ireland between 1834 and 1861.

103 Donald MacRaild, *Irish Migrants in Modern Britain, 1750–1922* (New York: St Martin's Press, 1999), p. 33.

104 David Fitzpatrick, "Emigration, 1801–70," in Vaughan, *A New History of Ireland, 1801–70*, Appendix 2, p. 609.

105 These are derived from N. H. Carrier and J. R. Jeffery in Government of the United Kingdom, *External Migration: A Study of the Available Statistics, 1815–1850* (London: HMSO, 1953), p. 95, with revisions as specified in D. H. Akenson, *The Irish in Ontario. A Study in Rural History* (Montreal and Kingston: McGill-Queen's University Press, 1984; 2nd ed., 1999), pp. 28–32 and esp. table 5, p. 32.

106 Oliver MacDonagh's "Irish Emigration to the United States of America and the British Colonies during the Great Famine," in Edwards and Williams, *The Great Famine*, pp. 319–88, remains a major expository achievement. See esp. pp. 368–76 on British North America. A graceful recent summary of Canadian research is Mark G. MacGowan, *Death or Canada. The Irish Famine Migration to Toronto, 1857* (Toronto: Novalis, 2009). See also his "Famine Facts and Fabrication: An Examination of Diaries from the Irish Famine Migration to Canada," *Canadian Journal of Irish Studies*, vol. 3 (Fall 2007), pp. 48–55. Marianne O'Gallagher has done several significant research papers on Grosse Île. The most generally accessible is "The Orphans of Grosse Île: Canada and the adoption of Irish Famine orphans, 1847–48," in Patrick O'Sullivan (ed.), *The Meaning of the Famine* (London: Leicester University Press, 1997), pp. 81–111. See also O'Gallagher, *Grosse Île: Gateway to Canada, 1832–1937* (Ste-Foy: Carraog Books, 1984).

107 Importation Act 1846.

108 Three comments. First, the Canadian flow figures are higher than the total of Irish-born inhabitants of British North America because of many migrants landing in BNA and then moving onwards to the USA. Second, the numbers for Great Britain are inferred from noting the increment in permanent settlers in Great Britain between 1845 (which, in chapter 5, I suggested was about 450,000 in 1845 and was 727,300 in 1851). This yields 277.3 thousand settlers, which is a net migration number, as some of the migrants had died and other had returned home. Adding five per cent compensation for those factors (a purely arbitrary, but realistic figure) gives a gross out-migration for the purpose of permanent settlement in Great Britain of roughly 291,000. Third, the number to Australia, New Zealand, South Africa and elsewhere is very wobbly (but, fortunately, it is small.) It is equal to two-thirds of all migration, 1841–50, to such places as calculated in Carrier and Jeffery, p. 95, and to the Australasia total, 1847–50, reported by the Government of Ireland's *Commission on Emigration and other Population Problems, 1948–54* [Pr. 2541] (Dublin: The Stationery Office, 1955), table 26, p. 314. I suspect that David Fitzpatrick's number of 70,000 Irish-born persons living in

Australia in 1851—which he candidly admits is an estimate—is somewhat high. The matter is not central in any case.

109 Thus compare the description of Mokyr's methods in Ó Gráda and Mokyr, "Famine Disease and Famine Mortality", p. 68 and those in Mokyr's own description (Mokyr, *Why Ireland Starved*, pp. 64–65, 263–65.)

110 The question of whether or not to include averted births (that is "deaths of the unborn") further complicates the simple formula given in the text. This is both a matter of basic logic and of technical demography: if they are not to be counted, how are we to remove averted births from the calculation?

111 Cormac Ó Gráda and Kevin O'Rourke, "Mass Migration as Disaster Relief: Lessons from the Great Famine," *European Review of Economic History*, vol. 1 (1997), pp. 3–25.

112 Cormac Ó Gráda, "Making Irish Famine History in 1995," *History Workshop Journal*, no. 41 (Autumn 1996), p. 93, citing draft of Ó Gráda and O'Rourke, "Mass Migration as Disaster Relief."

113 Ó Gráda and O'Rourke, "Mass Migration as Disaster Relief," p. 13. S. H. Cousens did an impressive amount of pioneering research in the 1950s and 1960s, which is underappreciated. Especially important (and, with modifications, useful to future researchers on Famine deaths,) are Cousens, "Regional Death Rates in Ireland during the Great Famine from 1846 to 1851," *Population Studies*, vol. 14 (1960), pp. 55–74; and his "The Regional Variation in Mortality during the Great Irish Famine," *Proceedings of the Royal Irish Academy*, vol. 63, sec. C, no. 3 (Feb. 1963), pp. 127–49.

Chapter Seven

AFTER AXIAL STRESS

ONE

N ow is the time to step a bit outside of compartmentalized narrative. Up to this point, Sweden and Ireland have been discussed sufficiently in large, fairly tightly defined cells—ones that have the advantage of indicating big comparative patterns, but that inevitably have limited osmotic interchange in our consideration of the two national cases. By now, the reader should feel comfortable in swirling them together in a single discussion which takes for granted a shared knowledge of the central patterns and issues in Irish and in Swedish migration patterns to the end of the Great Famine and of the Great Deprivation.

In chapter two we presented the curve that Sune Åkerman developed and which was widely adapted to describe nineteenth and first-half of the twentieth century out-migration from almost all European countries (figure 2.1). With volume of migration on one axis and time on the other, and a reasonable amount of smoothing out of annual spikes (through, for example, the use of five-year rolling averages), the Åkerman curve is used by historians of migration, especially economic historians, to summarize efficiently the overall pattern of total net European migration from 1815 to the abrupt caesura of 1914, and for some countries of late migration the period up to World War II. The Åkerman curve can also be employed to project a country-by-country visual suggestion that, in conquering various New Worlds and creating neo-Europes therein, almost every European nation (or satrapy or region or ethnic enclave) was on to the same fundamental experience, subject chiefly to variances in the timeline. That accepted, it is easy to misread Åkerman's work as being simple-minded: after all, even when one takes each separate entity and charts the precise numbers and defines the relevant timelines, the results seems to say that, yes, almost all European regions of emigration were in the same game, but the shape of the curve itself merely shows that whatever goes up eventually comes down.

That would be unfair to Sune Åkerman, for his own work as a pioneer in Swedish emigration studies was anything but simple-minded.[1] His own primary use of the curve was to define the nature of Swedish out-migration for a specific period: 1850–1915. This is useful because once a specific point has been passed (we have here labelled it as the moment of *axial stress*), what follows is the creation of an *emigration-culture* (a term widely adopted in Swedish historiography). The moment of axial stress, in my view, was Sweden's Great Deprivation and thereafter one sees something similar to what happens in the life cycle of a gypsy moth. It moves from egg to larva to pupa to adulthood and thence to the diminution of senescence in a series of stages that are morphologically distinct. Each stage looks different from the previous one, but they are related by a code that is embedded in the genetic structure of the wee beastie. Once this code has been set down, certain limited changes in the physical environment trigger each successive stage of development.

For the years 1850–1915, the Åkerman out-migration curve fits Sweden reasonably well, for that is the shape the cloth was cut to cover. The Swedish numbers for gross out-migration to all non-Swedish destinations is given below. As the discussion in chapter two notes, the contemporary registration of gross out-migration (to all non-Swedish destinations, not just overseas) was inefficient, but unevenly so over time: thus a modern correction is helpful if not itself entirely beyond further improvement:[2]

1851–60	40,575
1861–70	157,827
1871–80	168,332
1881–90	394,886
1891–1900	259,150
1901–10	276,338
1911–20	118,275

Precisely comparable data for Ireland do not exist but, as indicated in chapter two, the pattern of gross overseas out-migration from Ireland was as follows:[3]

1841–50	1,298,394
1851–60	1,216,265
1861–70	818,582
1871–80	542,703
1881–90	734,475
1891–1900	460,917
1901–10	485,461

Accepting that the greatest gross outflow was in the second half of the 1840s and early 1850s and that the definitive tail of the curve actually is off the time-series, since it occurred after World War I, it nevertheless takes a lot of generosity to see the Åkerman curve as usefully describing both Sweden and Ireland.

Except that Sune Åkerman was much less interested in numbers than he was in socio-cultural processes, and when his work is interpreted in that vein it becomes very useful. One can rescribe the Åkerman curve so that it is not a simple quantitative time-charting of out-flow but is a venue for summarizing visually the commonality of Irish and Swedish out-migration up to World War I. In defining out-migration patterns as socio-cultural as much as economic in character, it is helpful to respecify the Åkerman curve in the terms employed in figure 7.1. Assuming that the nature of out-migration in the pioneer stage and the reality of the trauma each country experienced as an accelerant to migration have been established in earlier chapters, the question here is, what is an "emigration-culture?"

No deep theory or entangled vocabulary is required: just focus on the socialization of children and youth. Everything else follows. As I noted in chapter two, David Fitzpatrick

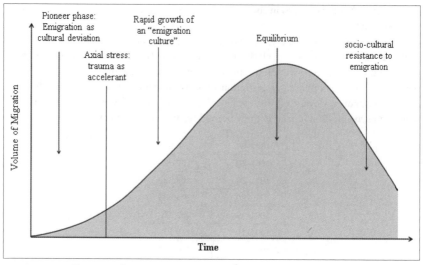

Figure 7.1. A socio-cultural reading of Åkerman's emigration curve.

brilliantly summarized the nature of socialization in Ireland in the later nineteenth and early twentieth centuries: "Growing up in Ireland meant preparing oneself to leave it."[4] He added, "One might argue that from the Famine onwards emigration was generally considered the optimum strategy for those without prospect of inheriting the family plot."[5] Not that most went away: the point is that leaving became the cultural norm to which an ambitious, but economically disadvantaged, young person was expected to aspire. The same thing happened in Sweden: out-migration changed from being a cultural deviation to being a generally considered and widely accepted mode of coping with the encramping vagaries of life. A frequently quoted report from G. Gerhard Magnusson, one of the officials of the massive Swedish emigration investigation of 1907–13, said, concerning Värmland, a jurisdiction of heavy, but not exceptional, out-migration, that every small farmer seemed to have relatives in the United States. "On the bureaus stand the American portraits of those that went over last … One can go from cottage to cottage and always find these American portraits and an assortment of American knick-knacks. Here is a lamp-shade embellished with some motto in English; here a chair-tidy bearing the names of the months in English." And on and on. "The little boy and girl grow up in this American milieu. The only beauty that comes into their lives comes through American gimcrack or American pictures; the only news they hear from the outside world comes through letters the father and mother read to them when mail comes from the older brother or sister in Illinois or Massachusetts … *They grow up and are educated to emigrate … Everything seems to be a preparation for emigration* [emphasis mine]. It is the basis of education, and it is easier to borrow money for a ticket to America than for a ticket to Stockholm."[6] Sune Åkerman, surveying the historical landscape, observed "a profound mood of departure among the majority of the Swedish population."[7] Significantly, he realized that much of Europe must be experiencing the same phenomenon, if not quite to the same degree. "From a theoretical standpoint, we ought to reconsider the rapidity with which mass emigration spread throughout Europe. Large segments of the population which did not emigrate must have been aware of this new migration alternative."[8]

Surprisingly, our redefinition of the Åkerman curve as a socio-cultural representation in figure 7.1 bounces us back to some quantitative data for Ireland and Sweden that are much more in synch with each other than are the simple out-migration flow figures—which did not track in very close harmony. Here, let us listen again to G. Gerhard Magnusson as he reports on matters in Värmland. "If one goes into a home to see how a peasant lives or to hear his opinion on emigration, one should not be surprised if he states that some or all of his children are in America."[9] The same was true of Ireland. David Fitzpatrick developed a valuable empirical set of observations that allow us to give a rough, but robust, definition to the time when an emigration-culture was ascending, when it peaked, and how rapidly or gently it began to decline. This series comprised the proportion of persons born in Ireland (or Sweden) who at any given time were living outside their homeland. These obviously are individuals who had themselves embraced out-migration as their future; they are also the brothers, sisters, children of those who remain at home; they are the tin-types or sharp-cut paper silhouettes on the wall, the ones who sometimes send letters or, better, money home.

Table 7.1, which begins with 1871 (because that is the earliest moment when worldwide data become moderately trustworthy), suggests that to understand the chronology of Ireland as an emigration-culture, it would be best not to focus solely on the dramatic stress flows of the late 1840s and early 1850s. Additionally, one should appreciate the long-term, long-deepening way that emigration cut a channel into the everyday life of most persons born in Ireland, decades after the Famine had receded. Two interpretive points in viewing table 7.1: first, as a crude baseline (it can be no better than that, given the messiness of the data), consider that Ireland had a population of roughly 6.552 million persons in 1851. In chapter six, we noted Fitzpatrick's estimate that a bit over 1,986 million Irish-born persons were alive in 1850 or 1851 in Great Britain, the USA, Canada or Australia—meaning that approximately 23.7 per cent of Irish-born persons in the world were living outside of Ireland just after the flood of the Great Famine. Compare this to the figures for later in the century, which rise continually until 1891 (38.8 per cent for the same comparative group), and then begin a long-term decline. Secondly, these figures should be read as a minimum percentage of Irish-born persons living outside of Ireland, since Fitzpatrick excluded New Zealand, South Africa and all of Asia and South America from his data set (places of interesting, but not statistically large Irish settlement). If one takes the apogee—1890—as meaning that four in ten persons who started life in Ireland decided to live it elsewhere, that is an emigration-culture at its fullest.[10]

No one would expect the Swedish curve to have the same amplitude as the Irish, but the shape of the curve is very similar. Here, alas, the Murphy's Law of transnational studies operates—almost nothing is ever comparable at the primary source level in national record-keeping systems—but one can construct an acceptable parallel to the Irish data by the simple expedient of defining a "world" Swedish population as consisting of those Swedish-born persons living in the homeland and those resident in the USA.

Table 7.1. "World" Irish Population (in thousands), 1871–1921.

Year	"World" total of Irish-born	Irish-born living in GB, USA, Canada, Australia	Percentage of Irish-born living in GB, USA, Canada, Australia
1871	8,373.9	3,067.1	36.6
1881	8,098.3	3,036.0	37.5
1891	7,484.4	2,903.0	38.8
1901	6,861.4	2,534.5	36.9
1911	6,369.7	2,136.5	33.5
1921	6,160.6	1,760.6	28.6

Table 7.2. "World" Swedish Population (in thousands), 1850–1920.

Year	Swedish "world" population	Swedish-born living in USA	Percentage of Swedish-born living in USA
1850	3,486.1	3.6	0.1
1860	3,878.5	18.6	0.5
1870	4,265.9	97.3	2.3
1880	4,760.0	194.3	4.1
1890	5,263.0	478.0	9.1
1900	5,718.4	582.0	10.2
1910	6,187.6	665.2	10.8
1920	6,529.6	625.6	9.6

Obviously this understates the extra-homeland numbers because some out-migrants did go to other transoceanic destinations and, more importantly, the numbers for Swedish-born living elsewhere in Europe is unclear. A minimum estimate would be that for every four Swedish-born persons in the USA there was one Swedish-born person living outside of Sweden, elsewhere than in the USA.[11] The useful point is that having encountered its period of axial stress roughly two decades later than did Ireland, Sweden reached its statistical high point as an emigration-culture two decades after Ireland.[12]

So, one has a resonance: a topologically similar curve of lives-lived on a world scale. Given these harmonics, a cart-load of queries legitimately follows, each question being a fining-down of the overarching concern: given a reasonable degree of comparability, how do the similarities and differences in each culture highlight features in these two migration cases that might otherwise be underappreciated?

TWO

How did the emigration out-flow interact with changes in the population characteristics of each nation? The initial and obvious answer is that if one "exports" more than 1.4 million persons from Sweden (to all destinations) in a 70-year period, 1845–1915, or roughly 5.5 million persons in the same period from Ireland (to transoceanic destinations, excluding Great Britain), there will be fewer persons in the respective socio-economic system than otherwise would have been the case—always assuming that neither large-scale in-migration nor large-scale return migration took place.

Yet the effect depends equally upon the nature of out-migration. Migration is a process that selects. Imagine a bizarre rural world in which out-migration in the form of forced exile is used to clear the society of its less productive persons: by shipping away everyone in their sixties and above. In such an instance, the effect of out-migration on the total population would be immediate (persons would be going someplace outside of the homeland to end their days), but in the longer run would be negligible (younger persons would soon replace them) and, actually, might increase the homeland population in the long run, by taking scarce resources from the old and allocating them to young men and women in the reproductive age group.

However, there is no doubt that in the era of emigration-culture, both Sweden and Ireland exported young men and women in large numbers, far larger than their portion in the respective general populations. As table 7.3[13] indicates, the majority of out-migrants were in the age of reproduction, and in the last decade of the nineteenth century and the first of the twentieth, more than 70 per cent of the Swedish emigrants and more than 80 per cent of the Irish were from ages 15 to 34, inclusive. This is usually defined demographically as the base biological breeding population of any social group. So, it was not just that young people reduced the population by leaving the country, they also took

Table 7.3. Age grouping of emigrants, 1861–1910,
Sweden and Ireland as percentage of total emigration.

Period	Age group	Irish males and females combined (%)	Swedish males (%)	Swedish females (%)
1861–70	15–24	44.4	32.2	30.6
	25–34	25.1	29.0	21.8
1871–80	15–24	46.3	40.2	38.7
	25–34	24.8	28.8	24.8
1881–90	15–24	57.2	45.2	42.9
	25–34	18.5	25.3	23.6
1891–1900	15–24	60.0	50.1	49.2
	25–34	23.7	22.0	22.3
1901–10	15–24	59.2	53.5	50.3
	25–34	24.1	22.7	21.9

with them future generations—and the children born abroad would be born American or Australian or Canadian and so on.

How sizable the loss of future generations might be is necessarily speculative. Operating on quite conservative assumptions, Kevin O'Rourke and Jeffrey Williamson suggested that in 1910 the Swedish population, through the combined influence of emigration and exported future births, was 15 per cent lower than it would have been in the absence of large-scale out-migration.[14] The missing Irish population must have been proportionally much higher, given both the higher Irish rate of out-migration and that an even higher proportion of Irish leavers were from the primary reproductive age group.

In both Ireland and Sweden, a clear long-term effect in the late nineteenth and early twentieth centuries was that these countries had a very high proportion of people over 65. The best summary of this situation is for the year 1926, and involves the Irish Free State, rather than the entire country. That said, outside of France—which lost a massive number of young people in World War I—Ireland and Sweden had proportionately the largest population of aged persons in western Europe and in the English-speaking dominions:[15]

Nation	Percentage of population over 65
France	9.4
Ireland (26 Counties)	9.2
Sweden	8.8
Norway	7.6
England and Wales	6.6
Germany	5.7
USA	4.7
Australia	4.4

Noting the larger proportion of older people in Sweden and Ireland than elsewhere does not prejudge the position of those older people in society: they may have been discarded as non-productive or, alternately, may have continued to control the productive resources of the society to such a degree that they formed a gerontocracy, or anything in-between; but certainly the social physics of nations that are heavily loaded towards the old can be expected to act differently from those with a more "normal" age distribution.

Despite the commonality as between Sweden and Ireland in the age groups which emigrated and in the shared overrepresentation of older people in the two countries, there must have been something pivotal that explains why Ireland lost total population year after year and Sweden did not. For every single year since the civic registration of births deaths and marriages was begun in Ireland, 1864, until World War I, births in Ireland exceeded deaths, and the birth rate per thousand population exceeded the death rate by between 3.0 and 8.0 year after year.[16] Therefore, on the face of things, it would seem (but only seem) that there was no problem with the Irish social system as regarding one generation producing another.

It borders on a truism to say that in Sweden natural increase in population exceeded out-migration,[17] whereas in Ireland it did not. In Ireland, the difference between the rate of natural increase and the net emigration rate was as follows:[18]

Period	Excess of net emigration rate over natural increase rate (per thousand of population)
1861–71	6.9
1871–81	4.5
1881–91	11.0
1891–1901	7.4
1901–11	2.6

Considered on the world spectrum of demographic experience, these are small numbers. An increase in the Irish rate of reproduction (as related to total population) of considerably less than one per cent would have meant that from 1861 onwards, the total Irish population would have grown, despite the heavy rate of out-migration. Thus, in fact, the true singularity of post-Famine Irish population development actually does not lie simply in emigration (and especially not in emigration considered solely as economic migration), but in the extreme and unique way that Irish society came to control matters of sexual reproduction.

THREE

To make this point, for the moment we will take the Swedish pattern at the height of the country's existence as an emigration-culture and use it as a metric device. Here our real goal is to begin to understand why biological reproduction among the majority Irish population, those who stayed at home, was not higher.

With the Deprivation of the late 1860s, Sweden's birth rate began a long period of decline. The initial drop in the late 1860s and early 1870s was due to the sudden surge of out-migrants, especially of young adults. However, thereafter, both the birth and death rates ran slowly downwards in a long period of secular decline. This was part of what is often called the European Demographic Transition, from a demographic system of relatively high fertility and death rates to a system of low birth rates and low death rates. Present-day Swedish demographers point to the 1880s as the true watershed in that transition.[19] Sweden certainly preceded Ireland in making the demographic transition to the modern arrangements—low births, low deaths—although by how long is a matter of argument.

What turns out to be the signal difference between the two countries in their era as emigration-cultures has to do with the control of the institution of marriage and its relationship to the process of producing children. In Sweden, the linkage was close, but there was a fair amount of room for variation in individual behaviour. The marital fertility rate in Sweden reached a high point in the period 1876–80 and then declined.[20] Well it would decline, would it not, if the general birth rate was declining? Probably, but not necessarily—for marriage is not required for sexual reproduction.

And here the Swedish data are fascinating. Firstly, the Swedish in their era of emigration-culture became less keen on marriage. At a flash level, this rather makes sense for, if to the table of possibilities set before a young person out-migration to a New World is added, that somewhat reduces the chances that he or she will follow the traditional pattern of family formation set down before the years of axial stress. In the mid-1870s the proportion of Swedes who married began to drop quite quickly. Yet, despite the menu-effect just mentioned, I think that it explains little: for if single people (the bulk of post-Deprivation emigrants) cleared off in large numbers, they would have left the proportion of married people at home larger, not smaller. Actually, an acceleration of a secular shift was occurring. Given below are the percentages of men and women ages 45–49, inclusive, who had never been married. Since some first-time marriages did indeed occur after age 50, the figures slightly overstate the incidence of lifelong singleness, but not by very much:[21]

Year	Percentage of men never married	Percentage of women never married
1850	9.0	12.3
1860		14.1
1870		15.5
1880		16.6
1890		18.2
1900	13.5	19.4
1910		21.5

Manifestly, this was a long-term trend (it continued until 1930).[22]

Secondly, however, a related set of data was running in just the opposite direction: the proportion of births in Sweden that were illegitimate, meaning born out of wedlock. Given below is the proportion of Swedish children born illegitimate, by this definition:[23]

Period	Percentage born out of wedlock
1851–60	9.0
1861–70	9.6
1871–80	10.4
1881–90	10.2
1891–1900	10.9
1901–10	12.7
1911–20	15.0

From the data on the increasing reluctance to marry and on the increase in extra-wedlock births, one might infer that the period in which Sweden became an emigration-culture meant that all the old values were dissolving and a headlong rush to amorality and anomie was in train. Maybe just a touch, but really the change was not as big in historical context as it appears at first.

Here we must remind ourselves of a basic point of agricultural societies which held in Europe well into the twentieth century, and certainly operated in Sweden and

Ireland throughout the nineteenth. This is that a primary task of all self-operators of farms was to breed their own labour force. In the small-farm economy, children were not much different from draught animals, save that they had a longer period of dependency before they became useful producers. Given the imperative of self-breeding this labour force, a head-of-enterprise (almost always a male) needed to be sure that the woman he married was fertile. The most efficient way to do that was to ascertain before the marriage whether or not she could have children. The dominant pattern among Swedish small farm-holders was to wait until a potential wife was pregnant. An informed rough guess is that two-thirds of the women who became pregnant for the first time were unmarried at that time.[24] And in isolated areas, the first child in what eventually became a large and stable family not infrequently was born before a marriage could be canonically celebrated. That makes sense in an agricultural society; it is much more efficient and less cruel than sending a married woman who cannot have children back to her parents, as was the sporadic practice in rural Ireland.[25] In any event, the Swedish rise in illegitimate births in the late nineteenth and early twentieth centuries, may indeed have been in some part a result of social dissolution of traditional agricultural patterns as Sweden became more urban (that is, pre- and extramarital sexual activity continued, but now the need for capturing the newborn as future workers in a farm enterprise was reduced). But it was no sexual revolution: Sweden throughout the nineteenth century always had had a comparatively high incidence of out-of-wedlock births and of non-marital sexual activity. Changing that would have been well-nigh impossible.

Thus we are at a hub issue. In the earlier nineteenth century, both Sweden and Ireland shared a potential problem: they were overwhelmingly agricultural societies with a high degree of risk exposure to single-year crop failures. After the Irish Famine and the Swedish Deprivation, the two societies quickly became emigration-cultures, which resulted in their reducing their exposure to the risk of agricultural failure quite dramatically. There were three basic ways these two societies could reduce risk. (1) They could export large numbers of their citizens. (2) They could find a mode of markedly increasing the economic carrying power of their respective countries. (3) They could enforce controls on the sexual behaviour of their respective populations and thereby reduce the size of the population in relation to available resources. Sweden chose a combination of paths "1" and "2." Ireland embraced "1" and "3"

FOUR

W hat constellation of practices and beliefs and circumstances could engage a society such as Ireland, which once had exhibited one of Europe's fastest rates of natural increase, to become the exemplar of a massive and highly successful exercise in birth reduction and thereby in population diminution? Of course in saying that "Ireland" did this or did that, I am engaged in the rhetorical convenience of personification. What "Ireland" did really was, first, the sum total of several million decisions by individual human beings and, secondly, the interactive and systemic effects these individual decisions had with each other and with institutions in the society—rather the way a lot of chemicals can pile up physically and can also interact together in a manner that is more than the sum of their individual physical characteristics. In this case, an unmistakable and unambiguous national pattern emerged.

Population limitation was achieved (let us for the moment see it as an achievement, at least as far as it reduced the risk of severe deprivation) by (1) exporting a significant sector of the most potentially prolific portions of the breeding population, the young. Persons from this tranche, if they formed sexual unions and had children, did so someplace else. Nothing singular there, for as far back as biblical times, the adventurous and fecund have been encouraged to leave situations in which resources were limited. Where Irish society was unique in modern history was (2) in efficiently preventing a large proportion of the stay-at-homes from having children.

Here a parenthetical comment is necessary. If one surveys the available historiography of Ireland on the topic of population control in the nineteenth and early twentieth centuries, one finds an inverse correlation between the amount of debate in the historiography and the actual demographic importance of the behaviour about which historians argue. No one questions that the greatest degree of population limitation was affected by exporting millions of the potentially most prolific breeders—though it rarely is expressed that way. (To describe emigration, even metaphorically, as a form of national birth control would start the plaster falling from Leinster House.) Most of the contention is about the least demographically consequential aspect of the process, namely the suppression of non-marital sexual activity and the degree to which this involved the Catholic church as an independent actor, rather than as a cat's paw for strong-farmer interests. So, in the discussion that follows, note that we are sliding down a scale, from most consequential (out-migration of youth) to secondary (reduction of those permitted to marry in Irish society) to significant, but peripheral (raised age of marriage) to ideo-religiously charged, but demographically decidedly minor matters (chiefly the reduction of illegitimacy). I apologize for the necessity of descending briefly into what must seem at moments to be an infinite regression of detail.

The Great Famine induced an increased reluctance to marry. Given below are the percentage of persons under 54 years of age in Ireland, who never married:[26]

Year	Percentage of men never married	Percentage of women never married
1841	10.0	12.5
1851	12.1	12.6
1861	14.7	14.3
1871	17.0	16.5
1881	17.1	17.1
1891	20.0	18.5
1901	23.8	21.9
1911	27.3	24.9

At the same time, the age for those who married was rising, although not at anything like the degree of acceleration or with anything approaching the demographic effect of the rise of permanent singlehood.[27]

That Ireland had any natural increase at all (that is, biological increase before the effect of out-migration) is in minor degree ascribable to improved health (no famines),[28] but mostly to those who did marry having large families by contemporary European standards. The prime piece of information that one would love to have is: how did the number of children in the *completed* Irish family evolve in the post-Famine years? That has not yet been recovered from the tattered Irish civil registration records. In the early 1970s, Robert E. Kennedy, Jr usefully pointed out that among married women the number of births (which is to say births within wedlock) was higher than in the comparator juris-diction, England and Wales:[29]

Period	Average number of legitimate births per thousand married women	
	Ireland	England and Wales
1870–72	307	295
1880–82	284	275
1890–92	287	250
1900–02	292	230
1910–12	305	191

The reality behind such numbers is well indicated by Tim Guinnane's reference to a special survey that was conducted as part of the 1911 Irish census. This showed that of Irish women who had been married 20 years or more (and thus were close to having completed the full cycle of child-bearing), roughly 50 per cent had borne five to nine children and an additional 30 per cent had given birth to ten or more.[30]

These data hint at the fact that Ireland did not make the European Demographic Transition until the 1920s (although, again, there is argument about this), but that Ireland in the later nineteenth century became increasingly unusual in Europe because it maintained its high marital fertility rate while the rate was dropping in other nations. Thus, the comments one reads in the contemporary press about large Irish families was often foreigners using the diminishing size of families in their own jurisdictions as the norm. Nevertheless, Guinnane's integration of Irish data with the overall picture produced by the European Fertility Project of the 1980s (commonly called the Princeton Project) shows that Ireland, considered as a whole, had, in 1911, the highest marital fertility of any major European country.[31]

Yet this still left Ireland's *overall* fertility rate at a level that was lower than that in England and Wales (22.4 in Ireland as compared to 29.9 in England and Wales in 1901–11.)[32] The cause: all those unmarried Irish women. "The proximate causes of Ireland's depopulation was thus heavy emigration combined with unremarkable overall birth rates," Guinnane comments. "What makes the depopulation seem more exotic is that the Irish arrived at unremarkable birthrates through a combination of large families but low marriage rates."[33]

That is a lapidary summary by a first-rate scholar. What do we make, however, of the formulation by a demographer who provides a nicely crafted formula supposedly related to both Sweden and Ireland? "A decline in proportions married will, other things equal, increase the proportion[s] of all births that occur to unmarried women."[34] Thus, June Sklar, writing on Swedish and Irish fertility patterns. Her formulation has the immediate ring of scientific profundity; then, on reflection, the hollow thunk of the merely vacuous; and, finally, the realization that in its scholarly context it is glaringly misleading. What she is saying is that *if* the overall fertility rate in a country is a constant, then that constant will be made up of legitimate births and illegitimate births, adding up to the same overall rate—which is the assumption that she began with. Presented within an essay comparing the historical record of fertility in Ireland and Sweden, the formulation might be taken to mean that, as far as the overall birthrate is concerned, it does not matter if the proportion of women who marry and have children varies, because any change will be compensated for by an alteration in the proportion of women who have children out of wedlock.

This does not even work for Sweden—the reduction of marital fertility via reduced marriage was not fully made up for by increased out-of-wedlock births[35]—and to introduce such a formula as a baseline concept concerning post-Famine Ireland is in no way helpful. In Ireland, the proportion of women who married and the incidence of illegitimacy were effectively separate, non-compensating entities. The marriage rate went down and so too did the rate of out-of-wedlock births: probably from the Great Famine onwards, but certainly from the beginning of civil registration of these matters in the 1860s.

This brings us back to the hub issue: Ireland responded to the trauma of the Great Famine by reducing future agrarian risk through exporting large portions of its potential breeding population and also by invoking tight controls on the sexuality of those who remained. Sexual reproduction outside of marriage was severely restricted and this is well substantiated by the reduction of the rate of out-of-wedlock births to norms far below those elsewhere in Europe.

An Irish behavioural weld was essayed—no marriage, then no sex—and if the bond was not completely effective, it certainly was closer to being perfectly seamless than were similar exercises anyplace else in contemporary western society.

Post-Famine only: the extremely tight control over sexuality in the second half of the nineteenth century and first half of the twentieth was not some characteristic intrinsic to Irish society, even the just-before-Famine society. It was an integral, distinctive and necessary part of the functioning of Ireland as an emigration-culture. Here we must disagree with the work of the major pioneering scholar, Kenneth Connell, in so far as it deals with pre-Famine illegitimacy. This is a reluctant necessity. His essay "Illegitimacy before the Famine,"[36] published in 1968, has nearly canonical status, but it is not a good reading of his own primary sources, and the result is that historians of Irish population and mores have seen a greater continuity between the pre- and post-Famine situations than is warranted. This has led to an implicit downplaying of the Famine as a stress-moment that torqued Irish society into new and strange configurations.

When Connell said "peasantry," he meant "Catholic peasantry." (For the moment, in discussing Connell's work, we will use "peasantry," despite its problematic meaning as discussed in earlier chapters; and, whether or not Irish Protestants had different sexual and familial patterns is not directly analysed by Connell, although he definitely had views.) And Connell had a romanticized notion of the alleged "purity" of Irish agricul-tural girls, a perspective that has a long pedigree among Marxian scholars, going back to

Friedrich Engels's own avocational interests. Connell's position was that: (1) the Irish rate of out-of-wedlock births was low by international standards decades before the Famine; (2) that what he called "illegitimate conceptions" were few: he meant babies conceived before the marriage was celebrated; (3) that there was little in the way of abortion, contraception, or of pregnant girls leaving the country; and (4) therefore pre-Famine Ireland was a remarkably pure land. This resultant phenomenon he then explained.

The problem is that Connell's work defines and explicates a non-occurrence, namely a system of sexual control that runs back from the post-Famine era into at least the 1830s and probably longer. One states the chronology that way because Connell's major stack of evidence is the information that began to be collected in 1864 through civil registration. Those data are retrospected into the pre-Famine era, but in a decidedly bent manner. "In the first complete decade of civil registration, 1871–80, illegitimate births in the 26 Counties that became the Republic were 1.63 per cent of total births."[37] Given that Connell is dealing with the first half of the nineteenth century, it is curious that as a reference point for the nineteenth-century situation, all-Ireland data are not used, rather than those for the future Republic of Ireland. By removing the 6 Counties from his work, Connell (a) preserved as part of his database the "western" and "south-western" catchment areas of the 32 Counties, as defined by the Registrar-General, the areas that had the highest post-Famine export of the young and therefore the lowest opportunity for illicit liaisons, and (b) erased the portion of the country which had significant in-migration from elsewhere in Ireland and modest urbanization, due to regional industrialization in the period from which he garners his data: the post-Famine period.[38] Not incidentally, he thereby removed most of the Protestants from his purview (perhaps a bit in overcompensation for being English Protestant of Irish descent), but without admitting what he was doing. He did rather give his tic away, however, in quoting a 1905 assessment: "As an Irish priest demonstrated (*not simply to his own satisfaction*), early in the present century, 'Orangeism and illegitimacy go together: … bastards are in proportion to the Orange lodges'" [emphasis mine].[39] Further, Connell's choice of reference dates also is peculiar. As David Miller has noted, Connell ignored the first seven years of civil registration and instead used 1871–80, when out-of-wedlock births were at an all-time low.[40] Thus, Connell tosses away 1864 (when the 26 County rate was 3.04 per cent) and uses the period 1871–80 (when the rate was 1.63 per cent) as the basis for his backward projection of the pre-Famine situation. Instead of projecting the all-time-low rate for the 1870s back to the pre-Famine period, a more reasonable suggestion would have been that illegitimacy in the early 1860s was declining from a considerably higher level that had pertained in the pre-Famine years. This fiddling becomes even clearer when one uses the all-Ireland data, rather than that for the 26 Counties. The all-Ireland rate of out-of-wedlock births in 1864 was 3.8 percent[41] nationally, and this appears to have been part of a decline from much higher pre-Famine levels—at least if the decline from 1864 to the mid-1870s has any retrospective power. (And the validity of backward projection of post-Famine data was exactly Connell's belief.) So, if the all-Ireland drop was from 3.8 per cent illegitimacy in 1864 to an all-time low of 2.3 per cent in 1875–76,[42] then a pre-Famine rate in the 5–7 per cent range is not *outré* and pretty much in the range of England and Wales in the same period.[43] David Miller's shrewd observation has too long been overlooked: "More careful scrutiny of the statistical data might just as well lead to the hypothesis that illegitimacy was really rather high before the Famine and that it dropped sharply during the succeeding generation."[44]

Tiresome as the parsing of Kenneth Connell's one piece of bad historical work may be, we have to continue, because his classic essay stands in the way of our obtaining an unobstructed recognition that the post-Famine emigration-culture was a new Ireland on earth, one that was much less risky economically and severely colder socially than its pre-Famine predecessor.

Kenneth Connell had a second major source of data, the 1833–36 Poor Law Commission, Archbishop Richard Whately's landmark enterprise, the first collection of data for all-Ireland that would today be recognized as social scientific.[45] This Connell combed in an unusual fashion. He calculated illegitimacy rates, or a near-surrogate, for 51 parishes (a non-systematic sample, but necessarily so, given the sparsity of information). Overwhelmingly, the information he used came from the local parish priest rather than from the local Anglican rector. After excluding two cases at the extreme of his collection as being untrustworthy, he had 49 cases, of which five yielded direct baptismal-register data on illegitimacy and in 44 of which he inferred the level of illegitimacy by the following method: taking various verbal reports of the annual number of illegitimate children born (as reported by priests, mostly) and then, because there were no actual baptismal registers in these cases, he calculated a local parish birth-population from the applicable county birth rate and from these two speculative figures derived an alleged rate of parish illegitimacy.[46] Curiously (1) of the 44 cases for which he did all this himself, the median level of illegitimacy was well under 2.0 per cent. But (2) on the handful for which there was actual direct data from baptismal registers, the lowest had a rate of 3.0 per cent and the remainder showed an out-of-wedlock birth rate of between 4.1 and 6.7 per cent.[47] And that without making any compensation for the undercounting of illegitimate births which undoubtedly occurred.[48]

I wish one could stop here, for one of the fugal notes of the present book is that many older works of scholarship are wrongly ignored—and my respect for most of K. H. Connell's other work is deep—but one further misprision has to be wiped away. Connell, in his almost creedal belief in Irish female virtue, had a second level of articulation that was analytically independent of his statement on illegitimacy: "We may assume (if we could [sic: can] not prove) that not only illegitimate births but illegitimate conceptions were few."[49] Strange term, "illegitimate conceptions," not widely used in historical demography, and revealing of Connell's own values. He in fact means babies conceived before the marriage of their parents was celebrated, the sort of children that we observed being common in Sweden, the product there of a normal and societally approved pattern of familial reproductive security. Even the Irish clergy of the nineteenth century were less scornful of such births than was Connell, and the tactful term "subsequent marriage" was used by them to describe the march to the altar and then, a while later, to the baptismal font. Connell cites no data whatsoever on the incidence of premarital sexual relations, so how does he argue for the supposedly nearly universal abstention from premarital coitus by the pre-Famine populace?

As Andrea Brozyna points out, he does this by (a) virtually arguing from punishment to crime and (b) by ignoring most of the consequences of female marginality in pre-Famine Irish society.[50] Connell gives sufficient quotations from the Poor

Law Commission regarding the massive disapproval of out-of-wedlock births to make it clear that bearing a bastard child undoubtedly was a serious and debilitating stain on both mother and child. (The father of the child usually got off more lightly.) However, to posit that severe punishment for a crime (if one permits that analogy), results in the act not occurring is a form of casuistry that has no probative power whatsoever. And, if one looks at the pathetic position of those women in pre-Famine Irish society who were left on the shelf, age 30, with no husband in prospect and a future of living on the scraps and handouts of siblings and cousins looming ever larger, it made sense for a "girl" to take a sexual chance. It was a survival strategy. Falling pregnant and forcing a subsequent marriage was a risky, but often successful, way to obtain a husband, child, social normalcy and thereby some degree of protection against the rigours of life in a rural subsistence economy. After the Famine, with the rise of an emigration-culture, such women had the alternative of life in Belfast, Dublin, Great Britain or North America, and they took that choice in their tens of thousands. That was later.

Given that Connell has no direct evidence for his near-total-abstinence view of pre-Famine sexuality, the best we can do is point to Sean Connolly's work with nine pre-Famine Catholic parishes which indicated that 9–10 per cent of the woman were pregnant at the time of marriage.[51] This is in addition to those who gave birth out of wedlock: so a reasonable estimate of Catholic marriages in the closely documented parishes is that in (very) roughly 14–15 per cent of the cases in which babies were born, conception either took place before a marriage was celebrated or without marriage ever taking place. And if we note that even in our own time, approximately one-third of all conceptions are spontaneously terminated; and as Angus McLaren argues, the rate was much higher in earlier times,[52] then the number of girls who came to the altar pregnant, but who subsequently lost the fetus spontaneously needs to be factored in: a doubling at least of those who gave birth before eight-and-half months after marriage. A conservative guesstimate would be that in the immediate pre-Famine era roughly one-in-five Catholic women was pregnant at the altar. This, plus the proportion of those giving birth out of wedlock suggests something less than a society of "moral purity." And if one takes note of a twentieth-century study which indicates that on average 25 to 50 acts of coitus are required for conception,[53] then one begins to realize that in the matter of sexual behaviour, pre-Famine Ireland was just another European country. Perhaps it was a touch on the controlled side, but not very.

None of this discussion would be necessary, save that unless we put aside Kenneth Connell's highly influential essay on pre-Famine sexuality, the extraordinary way in which Irish society responded to the Famine is blurred. Connell's essay fits perfectly with the way that post-Famine nationalism and post-Famine Catholicism (overlapping, but far from identical, ideological systems) wished to think of the story of the Irish people, their general culture and their religious adhesion. Despite all the romanticizing and idealizing rhetoric, pre-Famine Ireland was not a garden peopled by the primordially and preternaturally pure.

Actually, the real and demonstrable story is that in the age of post-Famine emigration-culture, Ireland experienced a pervasive sexual revolution: a sharp turn in the direction of abstinence, the special characteristic of Ireland as it modernized.

NOTES

1   For a conspectus of Sune Åkerman's own research strategies, see his chapter "Theories and Methods of Migration Research," in Harald Runblom and Hans Norman (eds.), *From Sweden to America. A History of the Migration* (Minneapolis: University of Minnesota Press, 1976), pp. 19–75; and "Projects and Research Priorities," *Historisk Tidskrift*, vol. 9 (1970), pp. 47–67; and "Toward an Understanding of Emigrational Processes," *Scandinavian Journal of History*, vol. 18 (1978), pp. 132–54.

2   Erland Hofsten and Hans Lundström in Government of Sweden, *Urval*, no. 8 (Stockholm: Statistiska Centralbyrån, 1976), table 4.7, p. 75. The major surges were 1867–73 and 1879–93, and these are smoothed out in Åkerman's model by rolling averaging. The great unresolved problem in any correction of nineteenth and early twentieth-century figures involves unregistered out-migration from Sweden to other European countries.

3   The big problem in strict comparability between these Irish data and the Swedish series is that the Irish series leaves out Irish migrants who moved permanently to Great Britain. One can list the decennial enumerations of Irish persons living in Great Britain, but whether these were really permanent out-migrations, sojourners, or stepwise migrants to transoceanic destinations is highly problematic. Hatton and Williamson, interpreting work by Cormac Ó Gráda, suggest that a lower-boundary estimate of Irish migration to Great Britain between 1852 and 1911 was one million persons. Timothy J. Hatton and Jeffrey G. Williamson, "After the Famine: Emigration from Ireland, 1850–1913," *Journal of Economic History*, vol. 53 (Sep. 1993), p. 557n2.

4   David Fitzpatrick, *Irish Emigration, 1801–1921* (Dublin: Dundalgan Press Ltd, for the Economic and Social History Society of Ireland, 1984), p. 30. Fitzpatrick's elegant operational clarity is preferable to the stolid (but nevertheless insightful) formulation by Sune Åkerman: "All this adds up to the following: *An enormous potential inclination to move, a gradual ripening of the decisions to emigrate, and strong possibilities of influence on an inter-personal level within both sending and receiving population created a situation waiting for the existing resistance to break down* [emphasis his]. When that happened the effects were sometimes quite astonishing." Åkerman, "Toward an Understanding of Emigrational Processes," p. 154.

5   Fitzpatrick, *Irish Emigration*, p. 39.

6   G. Gerhard Magnusson, "Jösse Härad i Värmland," in Government of Sweden [editor: Gustav Sundbärg], *Emigrationsutredningen, Bilaga VIII, Bygdeundersökningar* (Stockholm: KB, 1910), pp. 82–84. Translation in John S. Lindberg, *The Background of Swedish Emigration to the United States. An Economic and Sociological Study in the Dynamics of Migration* (Minneapolis: University of Minnesota Press, 1930), pp. 55–56. Substantially the same passage is translated in H. Arnold Barton, *Letters from the Promised Land. Swedes in America, 1840–1914* (Minneapolis: University of Minnesota Press, 1975), pp. 292–94, and is quoted extensively in H. Arnold Barton, *A Folk Divided. Homeland Swedes and Swedish Americans, 1840–1940* (Carbondale: Southern Illinois University Press, 1994), p. 154.

7   Åkerman, "Theories and Methods of Migration Research," p. 43.

8   Åkerman, "Theories and Methods of Migration Research," p. 43.

9   Magnusson in Lindberg, p. 55.

10 Source of table 7.1. Data in David Fitzpatrick, "Emigration, 1871–1921," in W. E. Vaughan (ed.), *A New History of Ireland*, vol. 6, *Ireland under the Union, II, 1870–1921* (Oxford: Clarendon Press, 1996), table 3, p. 640. Quite correctly, Fitzpatrick's total of Irish-born living in Ireland at the time of any given enumeration is slightly below the total Irish population, because of various forms of in-migration of persons born outside of Ireland. His numbers for 1921 are in part interpolations, as there was no Irish census between 1911 and 1926.

11 Gustav Sundbärg presented a summary of total pattern of out-migration, 1851–1910, which show 81.1 per cent going to the United States. Government of Sweden, *Emigrationsutredningen, Betänkande* (Stockholm: KB, 1913), table 68, p. 228. Besides the problematic nature of the transoceanic out-migration count (see chapter two), the number of Swedes living in Norway, Denmark, Finland and Germany almost certainly was well above official emigration notations. That granted, I am concerned to reject the notion, built widely into the English-language literature, that "between one-fifth and one-fourth of all Swedes living during this period [1851–1930] settled in North America." The source is Sten Carlsson's essay "Chronology and Composition of Swedish Emigration to America," as cited in Runblom and Norman, *From Sweden to America*, p. 129. This, as table 7.2 in the text above indicates, it is a classic case of High Counting, one that exaggerates the phenomenon under study.

12 Sources for table 7.2 are found in the source note for table 2.1, with additional material from the *Statistical History of the United States from Colonial Times to the Present* (New York: Basic Books, 1976), Series C228–95, pp. 117–18.

13   Sources for table 7.3. Joel Mokyr, *Why Ireland Starved: A Quantitative and Analytical History of the Irish Economy, 1800–1850* (London: George Allen and Unwin, 1983), table 8.1, p. 234; Hofsten and Lundström, *Urval*, table 4.3, p. 71.

14   Kevin O'Rourke and Jeffrey G. Williamson, "Open Economy Forces and late 19th-Century Scandinavian Catch-up," *Working Paper Series* (Cambridge, MA: National Bureau of Economic Research, working paper no. 5112, 1995), p. 14.

15   Source. Conrad M. Arensberg and Solon T. Kimball, *Family and Community in Ireland* (Cambridge: Harvard University Press, 1940; 2nd ed., 1968), table 4, p. 160, based on Irish Free State census, 1926.

16   For the raw data, see W. E. Vaughan and A. J. Fitzpatrick (eds.), *Irish Historical Statistics. Population, 1821–1971* (Dublin: Royal Irish Academy, 1978), table 43, pp. 244–45, and table 45, pp. 247–48. This excess of birth rate over death rate even in the later 1800s, raises the fascinating question, *if* nothing else had changed after the Famine (either in Irish family practices or in international wage rates), could Irish population growth rates have increased enough to make good the losses of 1845–59 on their own? Tim Guinnane argues "yes." Timothy W. Guinnane, "The Great Irish Famine and Population: The Long View," *American Economic Review*, vol. 84 (May 1994), pp. 303–08, esp. p. 306.

17   For birth rates, death rates, natural increase and rate of out-migration by decade, see Gustav Sundbärg, in Government of Sweden, *Emigrationsutredningen, Bilaga V, Bygdestatistick* (Stockholm: KB, 1910), Tabeller, II, Ländstabeller, table 31, p. 32. For the annual numbers, see Sundbärg. *Betänkande*, table 6, pp. 64–65.

18   Derived from Cormac Ó Gráda, *Ireland. A New Economic History, 1780–1939* (Oxford: Clarendon Press, 1994), table 9.6, p. 225. The midyear time-breaks are Ó Gráda's.

19   Hofsten and Lundström, *Urval*, pp. 21–22. They note that the Swedish birth rate even before the transition had not been high and asked "was birth control already prevalent before the 1880s?" (p. 22). Probably common if not prevalent: it is suggestive, although not conclusive, that in the only period of clear comparability, the 1860s, the Irish birth rate (which certainly was not significantly affected by birth control) was 2.5 to 5.0 per thousand of population higher than was the Swedish. Compare Sundbärg, *Bygdestatistik*, table 31, p. 32, with Vaughan and Fitzpatrick, *Irish Historical Statistics*, table 43, pp. 244–45.

20   Hofsten and Lundström, *Urval*, p. 29.

21   Hofsten and Lundström, *Urval*, table 2.6, p. 34 and table 2.7, p. 35; June Sklar, "Marriage and Nonmarital Fertility: A Comparison of Ireland and Sweden," *Population and Development Review*, vol. 3 (Dec. 1977), table 1, p. 360.

22   For the main categories of raw data on population and marriage in the eighteenth and nineteenth centuries, see Gustav Sundbärg (revised by E. Arosenius), "Demography," in Axel Johan Josef Guinchard (ed.), *Sweden. Historical and Statistical Handbook. First Part. Land and People* (Stockholm: KB, 1914), table 19, p. 129.

    Because the issue of change in the age-of-marriage will arise with Ireland, it is well to make clear here that the Swedish age-of-first-marriage was virtually constant both for men and women from 1861–1900, being 28.8 years for men for almost the entire period and dropping from 27.1 years in 1861–70 to 26.8 years in 1891–1900 for women. Lennart A. Palm, "Stormaktstidens, dolda systemskifte—från tonårsäktenskap till sena giften," *Scandia*, vol. 66, no. 1 (2000), p. 62.

23   Hofsten and Lundström, *Urval*, table 2.4, p. 31. This table corrects the errors in Sklar, "Marriage and Nonmarital Fertility," , table 2, p. 361.

24   Hofsten and Lundström, *Urval*, p. 28. The authors are a bit unclear of the time period they refer to, but their surrounding data are pre-World War I.

25   The matter of the Irish "country divorce" in the nineteenth century requires further documentation and attention. Arensberg and Kimball, who did their ethnographic field work in County Clare in the 1930s, found: (1) that local belief "still regards the woman as the offending partner in a childless marriage"; and (2) that for this fault she was especially vulnerable to domestic violence. "In the country districts they say that he may beat her and in their graphic phrase, 'bounce a boot off her now and then for it.'" And (3) that "the day of the 'country divorce.' as the farmers call it, is rapidly passing. In the old days, they say, a man might send a barren wife back to her parents, though Catholic law forbade him to marry again." However (4) they found instances in which the custom survived in an altered form. Arensberg and Kimball, *Family and Community in Ireland*. All quotations from p. 132.

26   David Fitzpatrick, "Marriage in Post-Famine Ireland," in Art Cosgrove (ed.), *Marriage in Ireland* (Dublin: College Press, 1985), table 1, p. 129. Fitzpatrick's work is especially useful for correcting the errors in Sklar, "Marriage and Nonmarital Fertility," table 1, p. 360.

27   Here, I am being intentionally unspecific. I think Ó Gráda (*Ireland. A New Economic History*, p. 215) is correct that "a rise in mean marriage age does not account for much of Ireland's post-Famine population decline … By contrast the post-Famine rise in celibacy was dramatic." My conclusion is based on simple arithmetic: it

takes a big jump in marriage age (most importantly of women) to reduce the child-bearing potential as much as is effected by complete celibacy. That said, Ó Gráda cites Fitzpatrick ("Marriage in Post-Famine Ireland," table 2, p. 130) which suggests that the mean marriage age for women rose from 26.5 years in 1841 to 27.5 years of age in 1861. And there Fitzpatrick's table stops. A separate calculation, done by Liam Kennedy and Leslie A. Clarkson, suggests that the figure for women in 1841 was 24 to 25 years and that this had risen to 28 years by 1911. No table or details are provided. Kennedy and Clarkson, "Birth, Death and Exile: Irish Population History, 1700–1921," in B. J. Graham and L. J. Proudfoot (eds.), *An Historical Geography of Ireland* (London and New York: Harcourt Brace, Jovanovich, 1993), pp. 167 and 181*n*46.

One uncontestable point is that marriage of those under the age of majority became a smaller and smaller proportion of those who did marry: 3.8 per cent of men in 1864 and 1.6 per cent in 1900. More importantly (because it reduced the time spent in the reproductive years), the proportion of not-full-age women dropped from 18.2 per cent in 1864 to 6.8 per cent in 1900. Government of the United Kingdom, *Supplement to the Forty-seventh Report of the Registrar-General in Ireland* [Cd.7121], HC, 1914, xv, p. xiii.

28   Life expectancy in Ireland rose from 49.6 years in 1870–72 (the first years for which reasonably solid data are available) to 53.6 years in 1910–12. Robert E. Kennedy, Jr, *The Irish. Emigration, Marriage and Fertility* (Berkeley: University of California Press, 1973), table 6, p. 48. One can safely infer that the key variable, age-specific mortality for females, dropped at least proportionately.

29   Abridged from Kennedy, *The Irish. Emigration, Marriage and Fertility*, table 59, p. 177.

30   Timothy W. Guinnane, *The Vanishing Irish. Households, Migration and the Rural Economy in Ireland, 1850–1914* (Princeton: Princeton University Press, 1997), p. 241.

31   Guinnane, *The Vanishing Irish*, pp. 111, 248–52.

32   Kennedy, *The Irish. Emigration, Marriage and Fertility*, table 59, p. 176.

33   Guinnane, "The Great Irish Famine and Population," p. 305.

34   Sklar, "Marriage and Nonmarital Fertility," pp. 360–61.

35   The simplest illustration of this is that from the mid-1870s through 1910, the rate of surplus births over deaths was declining, even though the death rate itself was dropping. Sundbärg, "Demography," table 10, p. 109.

36   Kenneth H. Connell, "Illegitimacy before the Famine," in his *Irish Peasant Society. Four Historical Essays* (Oxford: Clarendon Press, 1968), pp. 51–86. The volume also contains the related essay "Catholicism and Marriage in the Century after the Famine," pp. 113–61.

37   Connell, "Illegitimacy before the Famine," p. 82.

38   For the geographic definition of the original eight Registrar's divisions, see Government of the United Kingdom, *First Annual Report of the Registrar-General of Marriages, Births, and Deaths in Ireland* [4137], HC, 1868–69, xvi, pp. 18–20. These were simplified in a later report to the four provinces. When, in the 1890s, the Registrar-General's office explicitly dealt with non-marital births, they observed that "illegitimate births were proportionately more numerous in some of the districts comprising manufacturing towns." Connacht and Munster "where the rural population is more largely in excess of the town population" had markedly lower illegitimacy rates, especially Connacht. *Decennial Report and Summaries, 1891–1900, Supplement to the Thirty-Seventh Report ... Registrar-General (Ireland) ...* [Cd.2089], HC, 1904, xiv, p. 14.

39   Govt of UK, *Supplement to the Thirty-Seventh Report*, pp. 85–86. He was also upset by virtuous unmarried girls having to work as servants for landlords, where they either became pregnant after being housed with other servants or—here we notice his prurient shudder—by the landlords (lascivious Protestants, one assumes), taking advantage of them. He credits Waterford folklore about landlords' virtual droit de seigneur and of the landlord practice of taking a good-looking servant girl away and locking her up in his mansion until he had his way with her. (Govt of UK, *Supplement to the Thirty-Seventh Report*, pp. 53–54.) There is more of the same: nothing sensational, just the residual skiff of Victorian pornography.

40   David W. Miller, review of *Irish Peasant Society*, in *Journal of Modern History*, vol. 42 (Sep. 1970), pp. 387–89.

41   Govt of UK, *First Annual Report of the Registrar-General*, p. 14.

42   Government of the United Kingdom, *Supplement of the Seventeenth Report of the Registrar-General ... Ireland, containing decennial summaries for the Years 1871–1880* [C.4153], HC, 1884, xx, table VI, p. 13.

43   For England in 1851, the rate of out-of-wedlock births was 6.8 per cent of total births. *Fourteenth Annual Report of the Registrar-General ... England* [263], HC, 1840, xvii, cf. tables on pp. 8 and 10.

44   Miller, review of *Irish Peasant Society*, p. 388.

45   Connell's individual parish cases are taken from Government of the United Kingdom, *The Poor Law Inquiry (Ireland), First Report, Appendix A*, HC, 1835 (369), xxxii.

46 This procedure is even more ropey than it at first appears, because the parish boundaries of the Catholic church were frequently different from those of the Established Church and it was from information on the latter that basic parish population data was drawn.

47 Connell's table is found in "Illegitimacy before the Famine," pp. 80–81, with commentary on surrounding pages.

48 Sean Connolly did a revealing study of nine Catholic parishes and found that for 1831–50 the recorded bastardy rate was 2.4–2.5 per cent in raw numbers; and that due to systematic underreporting, the real rate was probably near to 4 per cent. Sean J. Connolly, "Illegitimacy and Pre-Nuptial Pregnancy in Ireland before 1864: The Evidence of Some Catholic Parish Registers," *Irish Economic and Social History*, vol. 6 (1979), esp. table 1, p. 8 and pp. 10–12. Where I differ with Connolly is on our guesses (that is all they can be) of the degree of undercounting. The reasons for undercounting were (1) that mothers-to-be of bastard children often cleared off rather than face the stigma of their condition; (2) children of such gone-away mothers were less apt to be baptized; (3) the pre-Famine Catholic church had a very poor system of demographic record-keeping, unlike the Established Church which was a quasi-state body; and (4) the simple fact of career protection among Catholic curates and parish priests gave them incentive to underregister illegitimate births—to report to one's bishop that one's parish was morally unregulated was not a recipe for promotion. I would be surprised if even one-half of the illegitimate births found their way to pre-Famine Catholic baptismal registers.

49 Connell, "Illegitimacy before the Famine," p. 83.

50 Andrea Ebel Brozyna, "Female Virtue and Chastity in Pre-Famine Ireland: Kenneth Hugh Connell Revisited," *Canadian Papers in Rural History*, vol. 10 (1996), pp. 117–26.

51 Connolly, "Illegitimacy and Pre-Nuptial Pregnancy in Ireland," pp. 18–21. Obviously, a systematic study of the all-too-few surviving pre-Famine parish registers is necessary. Connolly estimates the number of Catholic registers surviving as under 100 (p. 7). One has no idea how many Anglican and Presbyterian registers survive.

52 Angus McLaren, *Reproductive Rituals: The Perception of Fertility in England from the Sixteenth to the Nineteenth Century* (London: Methuen, 1984), pp. 46–47.

53 McLaren, *Reproductive Rituals*, pp. 46–47.

Chapter Eight

CONVERGENCE AS SUCCESS

ONE

Sweden and Ireland: both were success stories in that they responded to the axial trauma that each society experienced by moving quickly away from being high-risk agricultural societies—not to predominantly non-agricultural social and economic systems, but to much less risky ones. Never again would these nations be vulnerable to the swingeing vagaries of extreme rural want and its ugly paramours, the pandemic diseases of the malnourished.

Two success stories, indeed. That is just the way that the standard neo-classical economic interpretation of nineteenth- and twentieth-century European migration says things should turn out: everybody wins. This is because in the later nineteenth and early twentieth centuries migrants were not especially technically skilled, most of them coming from the agricultural sector. Without out-migration, population would have grown in the migration-sending countries and therefore the amount of agricultural resources (especially land) available per person would have declined. This would not only have dampened the wages of farm labourers and the profits of self-employed farmers, it would have lowered the entire national level of per capita income. On top of that, almost certainly the reduction in wages would have produced maldistribution effects: big landlords would have won, those lower on the scale would have lost. Hence, the millions of persons who went to the several New Worlds made everybody better off. As labourers in new lands, the migrants received higher wages than they would have earned at home; those left in the homeland had more resources (for example, larger farms to work); and the receiving countries acquired a new labour force with which to displace the indigenous inhabitants and create a neo-European economy.[1]

A nice economic story and at heart accurate, at least if one is willing to ignore that it depends for its all-ends-happily tone on the lands and natural resources of the several New Worlds being available nearly cost-free: not a story one really wants to tell the Mohawk or the Maori or anybody on the losing side of a series of transactions that made economic life so much better (in the present case) for Swedish and Irish persons, whether or not they emigrated.

Still, even if for the moment we put aside the notion that entire stolen continents and other large chunks of thieved land should appear on the liability side of the balance sheet of the Great European Migration as well as on the asset side; and even as we note that some remarkably skilful economic adaptation took place in both the Swedish and the Irish homelands, we would do well to note that in each case collateral damage was always prevalent, the gray lining inside the silver cloud.

Turning first to Sweden, the classic statement by Eli Heckscher, based on a monumental series of studies done between the two World Wars, that the major modern-izing changes in Swedish economic life occurred in the 40 years beginning around 1870 still holds.[2] A front-edge economic historian in the mid-1990s could confidently write that "Sweden's transformation from an agricultural country with large-scale production of raw materials such as timber and ore to an industrial country occurred rather late—the industrial revolution came around 1870."[3] As with all academic statements, a set of quali-fications is necessary, but these do not shake the mainframe. Yes, for example, it is true as Sture Martinius argued, the industrial revolution rose on the back of at least 40 years of agricultural reorganization and on the freeing (if such it was) of surplus agricultural labour following enclosures.[4] And, certainly the explosion of the sawn-lumber trade from midcentury onwards was part of the pre-1870 plinth for subsequent industrialization,[5] if a somewhat rough platform from the viewpoint of labour-management relations.[6] And, equally, no one questions that any generalization concerning the industrialization of Sweden must be qualified by reference to regional unevenness.[7]

Still, even if we take 1870 as a useful signal date for a sharp bend in the path of Swedish economic history, the social structure did not change overnight. Thus, the country remained overwhelmingly rural right up to World War I. Given below are the percentages of the total population that lived in urban areas, and this by a very generous definition of urban, namely in towns of two thousand or more inhabitants:[8]

Year	Percentage urban
1860	11.3
1880	15.1
1900	21.5
1913	26.3

Heckscher pointed out that as late as 1870, over 72 per cent, by his reckoning, of the Swedish population was supported by agriculture, "which again points up the virtually completely agrarian character of Swedish society."[9] Here he was typically insightful, for he realized that a good deal of the employment within small towns was really agrarian in nature, whatever the legal designation of the local jurisdiction. Keeping that insight in mind, and also noting that much of work that was categorized as industrial was basically home industry, it still is clear that a push away from primary food production was quite marked after 1870. These are the proportions of the population dependent upon the main forms of livelihood (that is, the distribution of workers and their families):[10]

Year	Agriculture & fishing	Industry (inc. mining and forestry)	Other
1870	71.9%	14.7%	13.4%
1900	55.3	27.1	17.6

In absolute terms, the total number of persons dependent upon agriculture and fishing declined from 2,996,000 in 1870 to 2,841,000 in 1900. Not a massive drop, but a harbinger of things to come. The continuing dependency upon farming and related agrarian activities as the mainstay of the economy was confirmed in a painful manner, when the depression of 1879–83 hit Sweden (in 1880 Sweden which had done so well out of free trade in both grain and primary resources, temporarily abandoned that policy). Not surprisingly, the depression markedly accelerated out-migration, particularly among rural youth.[11]

Here we return to the seminal scholarship of Nils Wohlin, which we treated in some detail in chapter three. He quietly engaged the mammoth task of recalibrating the Swedish census data of the nineteenth century, so that some very shaky categories could be stabilized and compared over time. He did all this under the hard-cast gaze of Gustav Sundbärg with whom he had fundamental disagreements, especially as portions of Wohlin's monographic work yielded somewhat different numbers than those Sundbärg was using as official governmental data.

As I made clear in chapter three, some of Wohlin's work requires accounting repairs, but nothing major. And the key point is that he recalibrated the often-skittish Swedish census records for an entire century through the medium of his own prodigious knowledge of Swedish folk life. Hence, we are getting the panoptical photo from a single lens, not as filtered through a lot of different viewpoints. My biggest change in presenting Wohlin's work is to break out and treat only the male heads of enterprises. This is explained in detail in chapter three, but here suffice it to say that the Swedish census data of the relevant period permit including women as heads of enterprises only in such an inconsistent manner that the resulting picture is heavily distorted. The male situation has the virtue of clarity and points to a crucial diminution of a class-fragment which had bulged ominously before 1860 as enclosure and the agricultural revolution had gained momentum.[12]

To catch the meaning of table 8.1, at first do not do anything involving derivatives: not even simple ratios and percentages. Instead deal with three real numbers. The first of these is the total cohort of men who were torpare, stattorpare, or backstugusittare and dependent lodgers. The overwhelming bulk of them lived in a sphere of vulnerability that became more and more acute as the Swedish agricultural revolution rolled on. (One necessarily excludes the male-servant category, vulnerable as that may have been in many instances, because the rubric was defined so as to include freeholder-sons who stood to inherit after a stint as servants; and thus the category is too heavily tainted for our purposes.)[13] The key numbers are that the men in these struggling or almost-have-not categories *decreased* between 1860 and 1900, by more than 60,000. Secondly, the number of freeholders and substantial tenants *increased* by more than 40,000 male heads-of-household. And, thirdly, an exogenous number is vital: the amount of cultivated land in Sweden *increased*—from about 2.5 million hectares in 1860 to roughly 3.7 million hectares in 1910. Here derivative numbers are not misleading: the amount of cultivated land in Sweden *increased* by about 48 per cent between 1860 and the year 1910. This was achieved through the extensive clearing of former timber lands and the reclamation of wet and waste land. Moreover, the expansion of cultivated land was accompanied by a turn towards higher-value products: hay land rose only 11.5 per cent and fallow actually dropped by 15.6 per cent.[14]

The three items when taken together make clear that a process was occurring to which we should be doubly sensitive—because it also happened in Ireland, as we shall

Table 8.1. Swedish agricultural enterprises, 1860–1900 (categorized by adult male head-persons).

Year	Commoner freeholders	Equivalent substantial tenants	Subtotal: "freeholder class"	Unspecified substantial holders	Subtotal: all freeholders & equivalent tenants	Torpare	Male servants & sons of "freeholder class" (over 15 years)	Stattorpare	Backstugusittare & dependent lodgers	Total enterprises
1860	186,880	36,229	223,109	7,792	230,901	99,815	320,879	23,815	96,514	771,924
1870	198,583	35,840	234,423	7,434	241,857	95,388	287,832	31,218	101,113	757,408
1880	209,913	39,928	249,891	6,913	256,804	92,590	308,239	34,131	83,981	775,745
1890	219,960	37,763	257,723	7,031	264,754	81,888	344,488	33,741	67,323	792,194
1900	221,479	42,763	264,242	7,252	271,494	72,252	354,836	33,351	54,238	786,171

see. This is that a *class-fragment* (here the good old Marxian concept is useful) came under severe pressure during the post-Deprivation stage of the Swedish agricultural revolution. The amount of arable land in the country increased remarkably, the number of freeholders and their equivalent large tenants grew, and the men-of-marginal-enterprises declined. The class-fragment they formed diminished steadily and, by mid-twentieth century, disappeared virtually entirely. Most emphatically, I am not here making any judgement about whether these people went to hell or to heaven; whether the class was suppressed or whether it was liberated; whether its constituents were freed to be entrepreneurial or were ground under capitalism's heel. That, for the moment is entirely in the eye of the beholder: until there is a large-sample national longitudinal study of this fragment, no one will really know what their dominant experience was. But they certainly went somewhere, and not necessarily down and out.

This post-Deprivation situation sits squarely on top of the perspective we gained earlier, in chapter three, concerning the nature of the Swedish agricultural revolution up to the 1860s. Call that Stage 1. In that stage, wide-scale enclosures and the cultivation of former waste land improved considerably the position of the freeholders. But at the same time the bulk of the benefits stopped there. *Rural social differentiation* was occurring because the agrarian population was increasing significantly, so the class-fragment of men-on-the-edge was growing, this being the inevitable result of a *bounded system* that shared out the benefits of agricultural improvements in a top-down fashion.

The major change—Stage 2 of the Swedish agricultural revolution—came when, quite rapidly, Sweden's socio-economic system changed from being a bounded one to being virtually unbounded. After the axial stress of the Great Deprivation, the emigration-culture suddenly removed the gyves and fetters of the old stasis. The men-on-the-edge could move to an industrializing locale, could leave Sweden altogether, or perhaps rise into the freeholding class, a spectrum of possibility that was unthinkable for the rural marginals in, say, 1850. Mind you, a person could just as easily slide into destitution. However, one is not being Pollyannaish in noting that the mixture of international opportunity, the continuing agricultural revolution, and the new industrial activity cast a lot of coins into the fountain. The amount of national income per capita for productive persons (an important limit, admittedly), rose by 177 per cent between 1861 and 1910, and that in constant-value currency.[15] Moreover, it appears that those on the bottom of the scale—the daily wage labourers—experienced between the later 1860s and the years 1910–13 a rise in wages between threefold (for men) to fourfold (for women). This in currency-of-the-moment in a period of time when the cost of living rose less than eight per cent, taking 1867 as a base.[16] A signal flag for how, when things worked well, the men-on-the-edge could do decently is that the län with the highest gains for male daily workers between the mid-1860s and the First World War, was Malmöhus—from whence out-migration was extremely easy and wherein industrialization in the city and large-scale cash-cropping of sugar beets in the countryside drove the wages of those who remained in the län strongly upward.[17]

The pivotal matter is that once an emigration-culture became dominant, the physics of the Swedish class structure changed markedly and apparently irreversibly and in a way that neither the continuing agricultural revolution nor early industrialization would have done by themselves. This certainly is not to endorse the almost cartoon comment that "strained relations between the different social classes in Sweden have, however, always been modified by that humanity which, as has been frequently pointed out, is a character-istic trait of the Swedes."[18] (Such was suggested not long after the Great Strike of 1909 by Dr Pontus Fahlbeck, member of the Riksdag, professor in Lund University and husband of a Finnish baroness.) But the social and economic constrictions that were loosened by the acceptance of emigration as an acceptable and readily available instrument to lance the ominously bulging carbuncle, the large class-fragment of small-hopers, reduced significantly the degree of social-class based strife.

Of course the mechanics were not simple, and I do not mean to imply that the members of the rural class-fragment simply melted away through direct foreign migration. They did not need to: they could do a stepwise exit after spending some time in an urban area; or they could settle in a town or city, and replace other urban-born labourers who left for New Worlds, all in a Ravensteinian flux. It really does not matter, as the overall result was the same. In 1970, Fred Nilsson, in the first doctoral monograph that came out of the "Sweden and America after 1860" consortium led by Uppsala University, convincingly forced migration scholars to realize that, although most Swedish migrants from 1851–1920 were indeed rural in origin, one-quarter at least passed through Swedish towns as part of their life cycle before leaving. Nilsson's monograph focuses on Stockholm. It is quite brilliant both in source-research technique and heroic in its attempt to distin-guish foreign migration by real-townies, from those who were born in the countryside and then lived in Stockholm and suburbs before making a second move. Probably about one-quarter of Stockholm's migrants to foreign lands were persons originally from the hinterlands.[19] After Nilsson's work appeared, Swedish historians worked for a time on "urban influence fields," towns and cities that attracted rural migrants and slingshot some of them into further migration.[20] None of this, however, should obscure the basic observation: all qualifications noted, the Swedish out-migration before World War I was a predominantly rural movement and the stay-home members of the ever-diminishing lower agrarian class were in general a little better off each year.[21]

TWO

Here is a similar picture of diminishing rural class-fragment, in Ireland: it is roughly the same in its shape and historical direction, but ultimately the meaning is slightly different. This picture comes from an admirable article by David Fitzpatrick on the "disappearance" (a bit of rhetorical overstatement) of the Irish agricultural labourer from 1841 to 1911.[22] It deals with the same class-fragment as the Swedish case, and does so with a baseline from before the axial stress of Famine; and it follows the working-out of the long-term effects of agricultural reorientation, as we did with Nils Wohlin's data for Sweden.

On the eve of the Famine, 1841, the Irish census can be analysed to indicate that over one-half of the adult males who were in work were hired as farm labourers, some with cottages and gardens (like the torpare), but all requiring day-work to support themselves and their families. The proportion was down to less than one-third in 1911, leading, as in the Swedish case, to the extinction of the farm day labourer as a self-conscious class-fragment by mid-twentieth century. (In Ireland, the diminution in the proportion of working males who were farm labourers was occurring at the same time as the entire working population was diminishing.) Like the Swedish case, the farm labourers became better off than they had been before the Famine: the earliest trustworthy wages are from 1860 and they were 154 per cent of that base in current coin in 1911, not as big a jump as in Sweden, but significant in an era when prices were steady or even declining.[23] And, if we accept Fitzpatrick's inference that at least from 1861 onwards the male farm labourers increasingly occupied small pieces of land, then it follows that their position was improving even more and many of them were moving out of the day labourer state. They may have been either emigrating or integrating "within the humbler strata of the farming class."[24] But in any case the decline of this vulnerable class-fragment in Ireland, as in Sweden, was actually a sign of continued successful risk-reduction in a society that still was primarily dependent upon the soil for its livelihood.

In the larger case, considering all workers, including farm owners and urban workers in Ireland, Cormac Ó Gráda has concluded that average incomes came close to trebling between 1845 and 1914.[25]

So in the Swedish and Irish cases (and, indeed, in that of the entire "Atlantic economy") we are viewing a scene that economic historians trained in neoclassical economics love. The years 1850–1914 is a favourite era: a time of increasingly liberal trade among nations (if not quite full free trade); a period of very easy labour migration, especially between the poorer countries of the European periphery and the two most dynamic economies, that of England and that of the United States of America; and a time when big money moved easily across borders.[26] The result was *convergence* of various economic variables—or, from the viewpoint of the poorer countries, of catch-up.

Given that both Ireland and Sweden were shipping out large numbers of labourers, one would expect wage rates at home to rise. And, if—to use a fanciful case—all the out-migrants went to some country that had a low growth rate, then the wages of the sending nations (Sweden and Ireland) would converge with those of the receiving country, which would be driven downward. This, however, is not what convergence usually means. Rather, it refers to a specific period of time in which productivity, wages, return to capital all go upwards, and in which the improvement in the poorer countries is greater than that in the already rich nations.

That accepted, of course actual physical mobility was central. Liam Kennedy and Leslie Clarkson put the post-Famine situation clearly and boldly:

> The Irish were advantaged—self-indulgent notions of exile notwithstanding—by ready access to the two great labour markets of the industrializing world: North America and Britain. The prospect of employment abroad, and higher earning power, persuaded many people of the benefits of mobility. Those who remained were also convinced, as uneconomic household members departed and emigrants' remittances took their place.[27]

Through their propinquity to Great Britain and their freedom of movement to English and Scottish work sites by virtue of the Union, the Irish had an advantage the Swedish lacked. Also, the Irish, because of the replacement by the 1850s of the Irish language by English as the native language of most young people, had a special advantage both in

Britain and in North America. Nevertheless, the Swedes proved almost as adaptable in their slightly later efflux to the USA.

The most vexing issue in adjudging the degree of convergence that the Irish and Swedish homelands achieved with richer economies is that in mostly agrarian countries a good deal (in some cases most) of farm income is either in-kind or is in the form of transactions that do not leave a verifiable record. Thus, the following discussion, based mostly on the work of Kevin O'Rourke and Jeffrey Williamson, necessarily is drawn from limited information: "the real urban unskilled wage rate in the home country relative to a weighted average of those real wages at the relevant destination."[28] As one comparator, O'Rourke and Williamson set real urban wages in Great Britain in 1905 as an index number 100. Below is the degree of catch-up by Sweden and Ireland:[29]

Year	Sweden	Ireland
1870	52	49
1913	98	90

That is urban labour. Agricultural labour doubtlessly followed upwards more slowly, in part because of reluctance of many farm labourers to move cityward. Thus, per capita income growth (all forms) was not nearly so impressive. Cormac Ó Gráda calculates that if one takes Britain's 1913 level of per capita income as "100," Sweden's was "61" and Ireland's was "57."[30] Among other things, these two sets of estimates, O'Rourke's and Ó Gráda's, suggest that in the half century, 1870–1914, Ireland and Sweden had very close to the same degree of economic success as measured by wage and income standards—and this despite their having taken very different paths to escape from the world of high-risk agrarian life. This will require more comment in a moment.

If the mobility of labour (emigration) accounts for a good deal of the lifting of the Irish and the Swedish populations out of the pre-Famine or pre-Deprivation high-risk zone,[31] something else was going on.[32] This something-else was two-fold. On the one hand—the clean hand in this case—widespread industrialization was occurring in Sweden and local industrialization in the north of Ireland. On the other hand—the dirty hand that the convergence economists keep out of sight as much as possible—much of what looks like an economic miracle (sometimes called "globalization") was the result of simple theft as it reverberated through an increasingly complex international economy. Kevin O'Rourke has a beautifully louche way of describing, from a Cliometrician's point of view, the European conquest of about half the world's terrestrial surface:

> The voyages of discovery were motivated by a desire for commodities that were scarce and therefore valuable. We know now that they were far more important economically than originally intended, precisely because they stumbled upon a resource so abundant that it was effectively free: New World land.[33]

Effectively free? Perhaps (to be extremely kind) "effectively free" is a term-of-art within Cliometric circles and it has only a technical meaning; even if this is the case, it merges with an endemic mindset within the larger historical community that is remarkably unconscious of economic expansion as often being a form of imperialism. However unintentionally, O'Rourke's historical description of the capture of New World resembles the cast of mind that until very recently—to take the case of Australia up until the *Mabo* decision of 1992—argued that all of Australia was terra nullius and therefore justifiably there for the taking. And so all New Worlds. Actually, in any New World, the costs to the conquerors of taking the "effectively free" lands were considerable. And the main costs—the extinction of scores of indigenous groups and the Europeanization of their land and resources—were economic "free" goods, apparently, because that side of the transaction did not count. Thus "the discoveries raised the endowment of land per European per capita sixfold," suggests O'Rourke[34] and that is as good an estimate as any other.

For Ireland and Sweden it meant that the productivity of farm labour went up sharply as many of the Irish-born and Swedish-born workforce did their labour in New Worlds, ones with masses of land and very little in the form of a landlord class. Money came home through remittances and, eventually, major items—grain being the key case— became cheaper and cheaper and therefore real wages for workers in the homeland rose through living-cost reduction as much as by demand pressure on farm labour. Land, of course was only one of the "free" (that is, stolen) primary inputs that was added to the European economy in the second half of the nineteenth century: mineral resources beyond measure and so on, few of which were acquired through a market mechanism or at anything like a market price. To continue with O'Rourke's summation of the discovery process as it worked itself out over time: "slavery, the extension of the frontier, voluntary mass migration, were part of the *vast adjustment process* [emphasis mine] that ensued. By the late nineteenth century, this adjustment process was reaching a climax, as steamships and railroads linked New World land ever more closely to the European economy."[35] That last phrase is the key: the integration of the Atlantic economy was a pivotal part—along with out-migration, population control and industrialization and agrarian improvement— in the escape of Sweden and Ireland from their earlier position as numbers on a high-risk roulette wheel.

Imperialism distributed rewards even to countries that could claim they were not formally imperialistic.[36]

To adapt an old proverb: in part, Ireland and Sweden in their era of emigration-culture were moving forward steadily because the sequestration-without-compensation of entire continents meant that they had a true luxury—the luxury of travelling on another man's wound.[37]

NOTES

1   I am grateful to Professor Frank Lewis for going through with me a bin-load of the most influential of the neoclassic texts in this tradition of interpretation.

2   Eli F. Heckscher, *An Economic History of Sweden* (tr. Göran Ohlin) (Cambridge: Harvard University Press, 1963) p. 216 (original Swedish edition 1941).

3   Tommy Bengtsson, "Introduction" in Tommy Bengtsson (ed.), *Population, Economy and Welfare in Sweden* (Berlin: Springer-Verlag, 1994), p. 4.

4   Sture Martinius, *Jordbruk och Ekonomisk Tillväxt i Sverige, 1830–1870* (Göteborg, Ekonomisk-Historiska Institutionen vid Göteborgs Universitet, 1970), esp. pp. 17–44.

5   This has been recognized in scores of studies going back to Heckscher's time. Recently, R. Marvin McInnis has somewhat rewritten the story. The usual version is that free trade in the UK gave Sweden equitable entry into the UK market and that Swedish sawn wood quickly drove out Canadian lumber. Actually, it

appears that Canadian lumber continued to dominate the UK market until at least 1870, but that Canadian producers for open-market reasons gradually turned more and more to the US market. The biggest surge in Swedish sales to the UK occurred in 1869–70, not earlier, as is usually suggested. R. Marvin McInnis, "The American Role in Swedish Industrial Development and the Canadian Connection," Lund University Economic History Seminar, Sept. 2003.

6   Anders Norbert, "Sundsvallsstrejken 1879—ett Startskoff för den stora Amerika-Unvandringen?" *Historisk Tidskrift*, vol. 98 (1978), pp. 263–82.

7   Johan Söderberg, in an admirable discussion of long-term regional variations, with worldly shrewdness adds a footnote to a conspectus of labour migration in the later nineteenth century: "The period 1860–1924 is the most thoroughly studied in Swedish economic history, and it is not difficult to find other indicators of regional economic development than those discussed here." Johan Söderberg, "A Long-Term Perspective on Regional Economic Development in Sweden, ca. 1550–1914," *Scandinavian Economic History Review*, vol. 32 (1984), pp. 1–16.

8   Gustav Sundbärg (revised by E. Arosenius), "Demography," in Axel Johan Josef Guinchard (ed.), *Sweden. Historical and Statistical Handbook. First Part. Land and People* (Stockholm: KB, 1914), table 13, p. 119.

9   Heckscher, *An Economic History of Sweden*, p. 142.

10   Pontus Fahlbeck, "Occupations and Industries. A General Survey," in Gustav Sundbärg (ed.), *Sweden. Its People and its Industries* (Stockholm: KB, 1904), table 55, p. 498.

11   Sverker Oredsson, "Statsmaktenera och den Ekonomiska Krisen i slutet ave 1870-talet," *Scandia*, vol. 33 (1967), pp. 96–174.

12   Table 8.1 is derived from Nils Wohlin in Government of Sweden, *Emigrationsutredningen, Bilaga IX, Den Jordbruksidkande Befolkningen i Sverige, 1751–1900* (Stockholm: KB, 1909), table H, p. 26 and "Råtabeller," pp. 262–303 with associated notes and also Nihls Wohlin, *Emigrationsutredningen, Bilaga XII, Jordstyckningen* (Stockholm: KB, 1911), "Tabellbilaga A," pp. 4–7, with associated notes. See also the source notes for table 3.4 in the present text and also the several source notes that precede table 3.3. Some additional comments. First, as noted in the preface to *Jordstyckningen*, Wohlin's figures do not fit precisely with the census categories for several of the years involved in table 8.1 and in table 3.4. This, frankly, is just as well, as the census tables are inconsistent over time and sometimes unyielding of basic information. The best part of a century ago, John S. Lindberg examined the census data for the 1890s concerning various agriculture sets and concluded that there were grounds to suspect that "changes have been made in the grouping without notice being given." John S. Lindberg, *The Background of Swedish Emigration to the United States. An Economic and Sociological Study in the Dynamics of Migration* (Minneapolis: University of Minnesota Press, 1930), p. 67n2. In fact, these happened throughout the century. Wohlin essentially did an historical-statistics-of-Sweden without announcing it as such and he recalibrated the nineteenth-century census data so that the categories were consistent. One suspects that the base year for his thinking about the historical statistics of Sweden from 1750–1900 was the year 1800. The 1800 census was good, but after that, enumerations for 1805–35 were weak for his purposes and the information also was sketchy for 1855 and 1860. Second, in the present table in the text, significant parts of the data for 1860 and for 1890 had to be inferred by Wohlin. His explanations make sense and the accounting is accurate, but a certain amount of faith is required. Third, from 1870 onwards, the sons-in-law of freeholders and equivalent-status tenants, are explicitly included with the servants and sons-over-15 working for a land owner or substantial tenant. Fourth, as to the vexed matter of rich persons operating their own estates: gentry are distinguishable in 1800 and thereafter: the average was 2,976 such persons from 1880–1900. See Wohlin, *Den Jordbruksidkande Befolkningen*, table E, p. 12. However, the nobility are not distinguished and they are of necessity lumped into the "unspecified' category of substantial freeholders. This requirement, that the extent and productivity of the nobility estates be disguised, seemed to be an unspoken ground rule of the Emigration Commission of 1907–13. Thus, in 1914, Dr Fahlbeck gave what can be taken as the official line when he argued that although there were no returns on the actual extent of large estates—they numbered 3,163 in 1911—it did not matter. "Everyone knows that a farm cannot advantageously cover more than, say, 400 hectares. The 3,163 greater estates, therefore, cannot occupy a very large part of the area of agricultural land under consideration." Pontus Fahlbeck, "Social Classes and Distinctions," in Guinchard, *Land and People*, p. 157.

13   This necessary elision is especially unfortunate, as Christer Lundh makes a strong case from microstudies of Skåne parishes that in the last four decades of the nineteenth century a young person's becoming a servant was less and less a simple life cycle phase and increasing a lifelong job-caste, a development that would reinforce my argument. Christer Lundh, "The Social Mobility of Servants in Rural Sweden, 1740–1894," *Continuity and Change*, vol. 14 (1999), pp. 57–78.

14   Gustav Sundbärg, *Emigrationsutredningen, Betänkande* (Stockholm: KB, 1913), table 21, p. 91. These data are not watertight, but are certainly trustworthy enough for the point being made in the text.

15   "The Staff of the Institute for Social Sciences, University of Stockholm," *Wages, Cost of Living and National Income in Sweden, 1860–1930*, vol. 3, *National Income of Sweden, 1860–1930* (London: P. S. King and Son, 1937), table 52, part 2, p. 249.

16   Staff of the Institute, *National Income of Sweden, 1860–1930*, table 51, part 2, p. 247; and "The Staff of the Institute for Social Sciences, University of Stockholm," *Wages, Cost of Living and National Income in Sweden 1860–1930*, vol. 2, *Wages in Sweden, 1860–1930* (London: P. S. King and Son, 1936), table 175, p. 137 and table 176, p. 138.

17   See Staff of the Institute, *Wages in Sweden, 1860–1930*, table 175, p. 137.

18   Fahlbeck, "Social Classes and Distinctions," p. 155.

19   Fred Nilsson, *Emigrationen från Stockholm till Nordamerika, 1880–1893. En Studie in Urban Utvandring* (Stockholm: Svenska Bokförlaget and Uppsala: Studia Historica Upsaliensia, 1970).

20   See Dudley Baines, *Emigration from Europe, 1815–1930* (London: Macmillan, 1991), pp. 54–56.

21   Even accepting the broadest definition of urban, in no period from 1861 to World War I did the urban out-migrants come close to equaling the rural ones—at least among those legally recorded. Lindberg, *Swedish Emigration to the United States*, table in note 4, p. 67.

22   David Fitzpatrick, "The Disappearance of the Irish Agricultural Labourer, 1841–1922," *Irish Economic and Social History*, vol. 7 (1980), pp. 66–92.

23   See Fitzpatrick, "Disappearance of the Irish Agricultural Labourer," table 4, p. 90 There is a long-running argument in Irish economic history about the effect of free trade in the 1840s on long-term farm wages and upon emigration. This is surveyed briefly by Kevin O'Rourke in "The Repeal of the Corn Laws and Irish Emigration," *Explorations in Economic History*, vol. 31 (1994), pp. 120–38. His own simulation for 1870 suggests that the repeal of the Corn Laws did somewhat drive down agricultural prices and thus reduce Irish agricultural wages.

24   Fitzpatrick, "Disappearance of the Irish Agricultural Labourer," p. 83. So that I do not unintentionally misrepresent Fitzpatrick's view: his general perspective is that things became worse for the farm labourers in the half-century after the Famine. I think his own data do not bear that out, and that the fact that a class-fragment can "disappear" is not always through downward mobility, much less proletarianization—my guess is that most who "disappeared" did so either by getting up (economically) or getting out (emigrating).

25   Cormac Ó Gráda, *Ireland. A New Economic History, 1780–1939* (Oxford: Clarendon Press, 1994), p. 242.

26   Without being ironic, it is fair to suggest that the period is also a favourite era because (a) some very big phenomena occurred and these are quite well documented, but (b) the filigree of data is not sufficiently fine to allow definitive determination of cause-and-effect relationships and (c) therefore, it is a great pool for the intellectually nimble Cliometrician to splash about and show dexterity without really facing strongly probative material.

27   Liam Kennedy and Leslie A. Clarkson, "Birth, Death and Exile: Irish Population History, 1700–1921," in B. J. Graham and L. J. Proudfoot (eds.), *An Historical Geography of Ireland* (London and New York: Harcourt Brace, Jovanovich, 1993), p. 176.

28   Kevin O'Rourke and Jeffrey G. Williamson, *Globalization and History. The Evolution of a Nineteenth-Century Atlantic Economy* (Cambridge: MIT Press, 1999), p. 133.

29   O'Rourke and Williamson, *Globalization and History*, table 2.1, p. 17. It is important to correct a very misleading typographical error in table 2.1, which reports the Swedish index number in 1870 at a preposterously low "28." That the correct index number is indeed "52" is repeated several times in Kevin H. O'Rourke and Jeffrey G. Williamson, "Open Economy Forces and Late Nineteenth-Century Swedish Catch-up. A Quantitative Accounting," *Scandinavian Economic History Review*, vol. 42 (1995), pp. 171–90.

30   Ó Gráda, *Ireland. A New Economic History*, p. 382.

31   O'Rourke and Williamson calculate that the impact of emigration on real wages of unskilled urban workers, 1870–1910, was 7.5 per cent for Sweden and 31.9 per cent for Ireland (*Globalization and History*, table 14.2, p. 276). It is unclear how this urban estimate relates to agrarian income, which still was the mainstay of both nations. And, to further confuse the matter, O'Rourke and Williamson state that emigration raised urban wages within Sweden, 1870–1910 by 12.3 per cent ("Open Economy Forces," p. 178) and that Swedish catch-up with Britain was 9.8 per cent, ascribable to Swedish migration (worldwide); and that of the urban wage convergence of the USA and Sweden, 1870–1914, "about half of it," was caused by migration ("Open Economy Forces," p. 180). That contrasts to *Globalization and History* (table 14.2, p. 277) where 24.6 per cent of the Swedish urban wage convergence with the USA is said to be explained by the impact of migration and "all" of the Irish convergence with the USA is thereby explained. A much more careful and data-rich

discussion is Jonas Ljungberg, "The Impact of the Great Emigration on the Swedish Economy," *Scandinavian Economic History Review*, vol. 45, no. 2 (1997), pp. 159–89. He argues not only that emigration raised urban wages through straightforward supply-and-demand factors (and with greater impact than O'Rourke and Williamson credit), but that it stimulated structural improvement in Swedish industry.

32 At this point the reader may notice that I am here staying away from the convergence-as-alchemy strand in late twentieth and early twenty-first-century economic history and thought. This world-view stitches "convergence" to "globalization" and uses both as a description of the later nineteenth-century developments and as a prescription of proper policy for the twenty-first century. Its proponents posit returns-beyond-scale when international integration of commodities, labour, capital and inputs occur without inhibition. As Cormac Ó Gráda observed, well before the full frenzy of faith in that belief hit the wall of reality in June 2007, "The implied presumption that economic integration would cause income differentials to narrow and poorer economies to 'catch up' has been the focus of a good deal of research in the last decade, not least by economic historians." He added wryly, "Theory offers other scenarios too, however," and then gives several examples of non-convergence (Ó Gráda, *Ireland. A New Economic History*, p. 271). For a discussion of economic integration (and of catch-up of poorer countries) that does not propose economic integration as superordinate over cultural and territorial matters, and which does not accept the convergence-as-alchemy approach, see Lee A. Craig and Douglas Fisher, *The Integration of the European Economy, 1850–1913* (Basingstoke: Macmillan Press Ltd, 1997).

33 Kevin H. O'Rourke, "The European Grain Invasion, 1870–1913," *Journal of Economic History*, vol. 57 (Dec. 1997), p. 775.

34 O'Rourke, "The European Grain Invasion," p. 775.

35 O'Rourke, "The European Grain Invasion," p. 776.

36 I will not here append a portmanteau note on settler culture, European emigration, colonialism and imperialism: the corpus is immense and I have read only a sand-grain of it. Two recent works seem to me to be especially thought provoking. The first is John C. Weaver, *The Great Land Rush and the Making of the Modern World, 1650–1900* (Montreal and Kingston: McGill-Queen's University Press, 2003). Weaver manages the difficult double of being monumentally erudite while still producing a manageable read. Given that land was the necessary prerequisite for the pre-emption of most other resources, this is a sensible place to start and he considers both how Europeans acquired whole continents and how they subsequently distributed these seizures among themselves. He is particularly insightful on the transformation of frontiers into assets and the conversion of land into private property. The second volume is the brilliant and brilliantly perverse *Replenishing the Earth. The Settler Revolution and the Rise of the Anglo-World, 1783–1939* (Oxford: Oxford University Press, 2009) by James Belich. The author argues—convincingly—(a) that the several variants of "Anglo-world" colonialism from which Swedes, Irish, Germans, etc., benefited became combined into a single form in the USA, Canada, other parts of the Americas, the Antipodes and southern Africa. And (b)—quite surprisingly—he does not accept that "settlerism" was a form of imperialism, although he does admit it could be quite hard on the indigene.

37 The notion that the Irish did not share any responsibility for imperialism, slavery and its adjuvants, which is in equal parts romantically nationalist and morally purblind, took a weird turn in the 1990s with a postrevisionist argument: that the Irish in New Worlds (especially the USA) were not "white" upon arrival, that they were instinctively on the side of the indigene and of the African Americans and only later became self-consciously "white" as a strategy for getting ahead in America. A stake is well-driven into this particular vampire by G. K. Peatling, "The Whiteness of Ireland Under and After the Union," *Journal of British Studies*, vol. 44 (Jan. 2005), pp. 115–33. See also the round-table discussion of the article, pp. 134–66. Also valuable is Richard Jensen, "'No Irish Need Apply:' A Myth of Victimization," *Journal of Social History*, vol. 36 (Winter 2002), pp. 405–29. Jensen shrewdly points to the English origin of the No Irish Need Apply slogan. Further work on this (ongoing by Donald MacRaild) will probably show an interesting disjuncture: that the reality of discrimination occurred in England and the mythologizing of it took place in the USA. In an apt summary of the situation (as part of a review of Nell Irvin Painter, *The History of White People* (New York: W. W. Norton, 2010), Eric Foner writes the following: "A number of books sought to explain how one or another immigrant group—Irish, Italians, Jews—'became' white as part of the assimilation process. The problem with this thesis was that these groups were white to begin with. No one had tried to prevent Irish immigrants from voting on the grounds that they were not white, hauled them into court for marrying white persons, or claimed that the law prevented them from becoming naturalized citizens [of the USA]. Immigrant groups suffered severe discrimination, but being discriminated against did not make them non-white." *Harper's*, Sept. 2010, p. 74.

Chapter Nine

A MOST CONTROLLED COUNTRY

ONE

A moment ago we observed that in the high period of emigration-culture, roughly 1870–1914, Sweden and Ireland had very close to the same degree of economic growth, as measured by improvement in one of the most basic human measures, per capita income. That is not something one would have predicted. Yes, with marked industrialization and with the completion of their agricultural revolution, Sweden could have been expected to do well, but Ireland, with significant industry limited to the northeast, might well have been expected to have lagged. The unexpected Irish effectiveness in increasing per capita income brings us out of the purely economic area and back to the socio-cultural characteristic of Ireland that in the half-century before World War I was unduplicated elsewhere in Europe: stringent population limitation. This stringency is the truly singular characteristic of Ireland in the era of emigration-culture.

Previously we have noted the dampening downward of access to the process of biological reproduction in post-Famine Irish society, and now we need to know how and why this occurred. It is very difficult to cut down sexual reproduction in a large population: *vide* the less-than-successful efforts of modern China, which possesses a strong apparatus of state interference in family matters. What permits a nation like Ireland, that had an extremely weak central government and only a flaccid reticulation of local government agencies, to create a system of biological suppression?

"System?" Yes: here an important point of disjuncture from most econometric historians and their cognate among demographers must be articulated. Granted, for many (I think most) of the men and women of Ireland the decision to limit reproduction (by emigration, by celibacy, by late marriage) was an effective way of reducing the risk they apprehended following the massive trauma of the Great Famine. Certainly, the average person was right to see some risk to life and livelihood as a continuing possibility after the Famine: 1859–64 were poor-to-critical crop years, as were 1879–81, and also three seasons in the 1890s.[1] Individual men and women made their own best guesses of how to navigate an uncertain future, but that does not mean that the resulting overall pattern was simply the sum of individual behaviours.[2] To proceed that way would be to bring back the intellectual miasma of the arch-apostle of neo-classical economics, Prime Minister Margaret Thatcher. She famously asked herself "who is society?" and then replied "There is no such thing!"[3] She meant that there was only the sum of individual egos. Now, the one thing that being alive should teach an historian is that social groups almost never behave as a simple sum of individual egos, but as a system. This sometimes is more, sometimes less than the overall sum, but certainly it is an interactive system, not an emptying of some cosmic ballot box and a chalking up of the results. (Play a team sport at a serious level; observe a clatter of drunks turn into a mob; attend a Pentecostal church; study the history of the Third Reich; anything like that should cure the Thatcherish delusion.) In what is still the single best study of rural Ireland after the Famine, Conrad Arensberg and Solon Kimball's ethnographic monograph on County Clare in the 1930s, the authors observed that there was something ineluctable lying "behind the numerical indices demographic count has yielded the census-taker. This something is of the nature of an interdependent variable. The Irish small farmers of the present day behave as they do in the matters in which we have investigated them because they are members of a social system of a certain kind."[4] And systems are in part determinative of individual behaviour. Only by recognizing that fact can one make sense, for example, of the pained observation by Cormac Ó Gráda in the mid-1990s that "The Great Famine set off a population decline unmatched in any other European country in the nineteenth century, a decline that has lasted in Ireland as a whole until the 1900s, and that *has continued in some rural areas until this day*" [emphasis mine].[5] That last phrase is important, for it could legitimately be annotated to state that, sadly, individual demographic behaviour in some rural areas continued to be determined largely by systemic patterns decades after the actions the systems determined made sense in terms of individual economic well-being. Socio-cultural systems exist, and the one that emerged in what we have called the era of "emigration-culture," was both amazing and in places surprisingly perduring.

Forty years ago or so, I could provide a clear and confident delineation of why Ireland's post-Famine demographic history took shape the way it did—almost entirely consequent upon changes in farming patterns after the Famine as they affected individual family formation. More fool me: if only it were that simple. Not only does the nature of social systems mean that things were much more complicated than I perceived, or can now explain fully, but the one thing that until recently we all avoided—academic historians, historical demographers, economic historians—was there, a big thunking reality. Almost universally, we avoided granting the Catholic church any power as an independent variable that influenced sexual behaviour. That sounds inanely impercipient in the present day, but as late as 1997, Tim Guinnane could accurately conclude that "few academic historians credit the Church with any ability to influence the demographic behaviour of Irish Catholics."[6] And he quoted Joe Lee's famous summation of the churches' (Catholic and Protestant) influence in post-Famine Ireland, namely, "The churches, however, merely reflected the dominant economic values of post-Famine rural society."[7] We were so very academic.

I now believe that the full articulation and the successful long-term maintenance of a large-scale *system* of demographic control would not have been possible without the imprinting of the ideology of reproductive suppression upon generation after generation by Holy Mother Church. As a product of its own core religious concerns, the Catholic church in Ireland had an agenda that took reproductive control well beyond what individual risk-avoidance or economic prudence would have required. Which is exactly what we should expect, given that the church was a spiritual imperium. It imposed transcendent values upon the everyday world through a set of institutions that in the century after the Famine became ever-more efficient, decade after decade. The Irish church's central religious beliefs and its institutional concerns were a single integrated phenomenon. Although I will later in the discussion analytically separate them from each other for the purpose of exposition, in everyday life as experienced by the church's adherents, they were a single existential entity.

TWO

In framing my own halting response to the question of how the post-Famine system of demographic control became so efficient, I do not intend to rush to an extreme antinomian view concerning economic "laws." In fact, economic matters must continue to be recognized as causally basic to Ireland's long reign of "moral purity," provided they are not seen as all-important.

Yet here the situation is puzzling. It is hard to understand why the single dominant economic theme of the period 1850–1914 is so rarely brought to stage-centre: namely, that Irish agriculture according to the most fundamental of metrics *became less and less productive in total.* And along some axes of assessment it actually became less efficient as well. This was a very strange, highly aetiolated agricultural revolution. It was causally contributory to the damping down of reproductive possibilities for young Irish men and women: but *not,* I now believe, enough to account fully for the remarkable biologically suppressive nature of 32 County Irish society in the era of emigration-culture—and, in the 26 Counties this held until the early 1960s generally (albeit not universally) and in some rural museum-areas until the 1990s.[8]

So, first, we need the very simple basic facts. There is indeed little intellectual dazzle in establishing the point that the Irish agrarian world produced less food in 1914 than it had in 1850 and that this was the result of a long-term trend, not of any short-term seasonal variation, but the fact is basic. As early as 1930, the Department of Agriculture of the Irish Free State was calculating that in the 26 Counties the production of starch (a sensible way of expressing the product of root and grain crops and forage in a common unit) had reached its high point in 1851–54. Thereafter it dropped into the early 1880s, after which it rose to near, but not quite, the post-Famine level on the eve of World War I.[9] That was only for the Free State and only for human consumption. A large amount of crops and forages are grown for animals, so Michael Turner in the 1990s ran a comprehensive account for the whole country and for all products of the land, employing calories as the measure of output. The result was different in detail, but led to no different conclusion. To pick just four illustrative periods from his work, the following is the total agricultural output of Ireland expressed in thousand-million calories per year:[10]

Period	Crops for human consumption	Animals for human consumption	Total
1850–54	5,710	2,050	7,760
1870–74	3,761	2,796	6,557
1890–94	3,328	2,944	6,272
1910–14	3,628	3,389	7,017

Therefore, in the 65 years after the Famine, the Irish agricultural economy, considered as a whole (a) reduced the amount of directly human-consumable crops being produced quite markedly, and (b) reduced the total food production of all sorts (including meats) noticeably and this total had not quite recovered to the early 1850s' level by 1914. It will not escape notice that an increasingly larger proportion of production over this period was in the form of the least-efficient mode of providing human nutrition: by having animals convert land-products into flesh.

In the case of certain basic items, the standards of farming practice seem to have declined significantly. The most important of these was potato culture. After the Famine, the potato remained the main food crop of most of the population. In addition, it served as the main nutriment for pigs, and the toppings and peelings were provender for poultry. Throughout the period 1851–1914, more Irish land was devoted to potato farming than to any other tillage crop except oats and tame grasses (hay), which is the way it was during the Famine years.[11] Two characteristics of post-Famine potato cultivation are interesting. First, the amount of land given over to potatoes rose though the 1850s (the high was in 1859) and then it contracted. This is the total potato-acreage at decennial intervals:[12]

Year	Total acreage
1851	868,501
1861	1,133,504
1871	1,058,434
1881	855,293
1891	753,332
1901	635,321
1911	591,259

And, second, the productivity of potato farming dropped, as measured in average tons per acre. At first, in the five years after the Famine, yields rose:[13]

Year	Total tons
1851	5.1
1852	4.8
1853	6.4
1854	5.1
1855	6.4

And then yields started to drop:

Year	Total tons
1856	4.0
1857	3.1
1858	4.2
1859	3.6
1860	2.3

Of course yields vary considerably according to weather patterns, but there is no doubt that from the late 1850s onwards productivity per unit of land of Ireland's main food crop was markedly below its demonstrated level in the first decade after the Famine:[14]

Period	Average tons per acre
1861–70	3.2
1871–80	3.0
1881–90	3.5
1891–1900	3.7

This pattern is counter-intuitive: into the later 1850s, increasing amounts of land were given over to potato production and yields per acre rose. Thereafter, the amount of potato land dropped and so did yields. In each half of that set of parallels, one would have expected the opposite to have occurred than what actually took place. In the former period, potato yields should have dropped as more marginal land was pressed into service (remember that tilled land increased throughout the 1850s) and in the later period, as marginal land was withdrawn, yields should have gone up.

What appears to have been happening was this: during the 1850s, the Irish farming community, considered collectively, was fighting a war against the Famine that had already happened. That is, they did what was best-practice before the Famine: used intensive spade labour on small holdings, applied high rates of fertilizer, seaweed, lime and sand and garnered high yields and on a greater amount of land each year. These people were not stupid but, after the massive trauma of the Great Famine, they were like a prizefighter who had been knocked out, but still was on his feet, punching away. Then, sometime in the late 1850s, they stopped fighting the Great Famine and moved into the era of the emigration-culture. That is, they reduced the land given over to potatoes—presumably retiring the marginal high-hillside and the acidic boggy lands—and eased off on the application of fertilizers and cut back on the employment of intensive labour. Not that the average farmer and cottager did not work hard, but the penny had dropped: there was no use in working-to-the-bone when the number of mouths to feed was declining. There were easier ways to farm and, as international markets opened up, more profitable ones. If one wants a useful, non-reactive indication of when the wide change in thinking occurred that characterized the emigration-culture, it is when potato production ceased to be the Holy Grail of Irish agriculture and increasingly became an arduous and oft-resented auxiliary.

To compress a helix of complex changes in agrarian practice—Ireland's version of the agricultural revolution—into a handful of indicators:[15] (1) The total amount of land given over to crops of all sorts increased until 1860 (5,970,139 acres) and then declined—incrementally: it was 4,815,265 acres in 1914. (2) Ground devoted to grain production declined almost every year from the midcentury (3,149,556 acres in 1850) to the eve of World War I: 1,247,003 acres in 1914. (3) The total of all root crops (including potatoes) dropped from a high in 1859 (1,636,432 acres) to 1,015,406 acres in 1914. (4) hay acreage began increasing immediately after the Famine. It was 1,200,124 acres in 1850 and rose almost every year and was 2,487,513 acres in 1914. (5) To the above-enumerated changes in tillage patterns must be added a related item. Pasture (meaning land where the grasses were not harvested, but were cropped by animals directly) rose from about 8,748,000 acres in 1851 to 9,932,000 in 1914. (6) Taking all that together, the Irish farmers, after about 1860 were moving away from of the business of feeding people and were moving towards feeding animals. That is a massive change, because livestock for the most part are useful only in a market economy in which there is a surplus: one does not eat bullocks, one sells them and that holds for most animals except domestic poultry and milch cows, which produce marketable secondary products (eggs, dairy products). In general, the numbers of every sort of beast were greater on the eve of the Great War than at mid-nineteenth century. (Milch cows stayed fairly steady, but in their case production is not dependent solely upon numbers-of-head, but upon genetics and upon nutritional inputs; production increased.) (7) This new market-based orientation meant that although total farm production was dropping, the financial value of farm products increased considerably: by nearly 82 per cent between 1850 and 1914, as expressed in current prices. (8) The size of the typical farm increased, although one does not want to overstate this. The main fact is that after the Famine had blasted away the poorest of the population, the land-holding situation was more stable than one would guess from the agricultural output pattern. If one defines the number of holdings as being those of any size at all—including cottages with a garden attached—the numbers declined from 1851 to 1911 by less than 7 per cent, which is hardly a revolution: from 608,066 holdings in 1851 to 566,137 in 1914. Within that total, farms of 1–5 acres dropped by 44 per cent, those of 5–15 acres by 19 per cent, those 15–30 acres declined by 12.5 per cent. Farms above 30 acres grew, but not massively: by somewhat over 9 per cent. And here is the kicker: the number of holdings under one acre grew by 170 per cent between 1851 and 1914. That is mysterious, except for the fact that most of that growth occurred in the mid-1890s and thereafter and seems to have been an alert acquisition of previously rented lands made possible by the Land Acts of 1891, 1896 and 1903. Those properties should be considered more as opportunistic freehold-acquisitions on a small scale rather than vehicles for actual farming.[16]

If, for serious farmers, the size of farms was moving slowly upwards after the Famine, it was a very slow process. Take the year 1890, before the Land Acts encouraged the creation of a slough of micro tenant-purchased holdings. In that year, the proportion of holdings was as follows:[17]

Size	Percentage
Under one acre	9.0
1–5 acres	10.8
5–15 acres	27.6
15–30 acres	23.8
above 30 acres	28.8

This was still a small-farm economy. Michael Turner suggests that in the emerging new post-Famine, strongly market-influenced economy, anything under 15 acres provided a precarious living, that of 15–30 acres was a self-sufficient family farm, and that above 30 acres a solid livelihood.[18]

What has this to do with the ideology of reproduction in post-Famine Ireland and ultimately with emigration? At a simplistic level: if one is to produce less food (as Ireland demonstrably did) *and* also fail through low capital investment to increase per capita output *and* if one wishes to improve standards of living (which definitely was achieved), *then* a tranche of the population needs to be extruded. But that was occurring anyway; the paths to the quayside were well tramped. So, instead of considering either the new lower-production Irish economy or the fact of emigration as being an independent variable, they should be seen as part of a *co-evolution* process, each train of socio-economic events reinforcing the other: young people's leaving allowed more potato land to be turned to animal raising, and more animal raising left fewer jobs for young people, who in turn concluded that they would do better elsewhere; all in a feedback spiral.

The speed-governor on the spiral of the Irish agricultural revolution was the fact that the number of farms of lands above 30 acres—the arbitrary, but realistic, nationwide cut-off point for a solid living in the market-directed, low tillage economy—grew only slowly, as noted earlier. There was no era of fire sales in Irish farming.[19] At the local level, the aggregation of land was almost as slow as the formation of a coral reef. Sometimes aggregation involved the patient acquisition of one small field after another from faltering neighbour families. But mostly it was intergenerational. For families who wished to expand their holdings, the sequence where land passed from one generation to the next intersected with a second sequence: the granting of permission-to-reproduce and the power to control the family lands. And this could be granted to one selected family member if a strategy of family land-aggregation was to succeed.

That, at least is the Ideal Type version of the now-standard story of the post-Famine Irish family. If taken with a recognition that it is an abstraction around which many real-world variations circled, it still has great value *if* one accepts that it was a form that worked economically for the new agricultural bourgeoisie, but not very well for those on the lower rungs of the agrarian ladder. This classic Ideal Type was defined by Arensberg and Kimball and by Kenneth Connell,[20] albeit in slightly different forms. Connell's discussion was mostly historical and that of Arensberg and Kimball was ethnographic, but they merge well because Arensberg and Kimball worked in a museum area and without stretching matters, it is clear that a very strong palimpsest of earlier practices can be discerned beneath their ethnography. Basically, the classic story is so simple that it needs only two words to describe it: impartible inheritance. Everything else is detail. Mind you, hard, rasping details: (1) Once a social group (call them strong farmers or the agricultural bourgeoisie) had decided for whatever reason not to subdivide land, but to aggregate it, only one member of the family could inherit.[21] (2) Intergenerational land transfer could happen at any point, but the natural social crease was at marriage of the selected male heir to a woman of another strong-farming family. (3) In some instances she brought with her land (if she had no brothers or if they had left for Britain, USA, or the colonies), otherwise cows, furniture, money. (4) These valuables paid the exit money (think of it brutally as the equivalent of severance pay) for the young man's brothers and sisters. They either left the locale or, if they stayed on, it was as third-class semi-dependents.

In historical narrative, this Ideal Type pattern has often been crystallized as a folk drama, involving a formally negotiated "Match," and these certainly did exist. Scholars argue about the generality of the Match as a ritual rural negotiation, but the central point is that whether a matchmaker was used or not, virtually every marriage among strong-farming families was based on a negotiation concerning land.

Obviously there is potential social fracture here. To be successful, this system of intergenerational transfer required very tight control by parents over children. In the Ideal Type, the males were kept in suspended animation by their parents who had complete freedom of choice about who would finally get the farm. No primogeniture, ultimogeniture or any other rigid rule prevailed. While in the state of dependence (often into their mid-30s and sometimes much longer) the "boys" and also the family's daughters had to be kept under strict sexual control. This held for the strong-farming families. The one thing that would destabilize the pattern of slow and careful aggregating of land generation-by-generation was if one of the offspring "got in trouble." In practice, the weld that held the strong-farming pattern together was marriage (whether arranged by a formal Match or not). This was the moment when two young people were licensed to reproduce. Everyone else in the family either had to stay unmarried and unsexualized (if they remained in the countryside) or, if they wished to follow a life cycle that involved having a family, to emigrate.

It worked. But only for the strong-farmers and those of the smaller landholders who were just on the edge of making it into the lower agricultural bourgeoisie. However, as I will suggest in a moment, the pattern made little sense for smallholders generally or for farm labourers. The tendency of Irish historians (including historical demographers) to generalize the later-nineteenth-century pattern of the strong farmers as if it automatically applied to the entire agrarian polity is, I think, a bit lazy. It is easy to suggest that the values of the slowly rising agricultural bourgeoisie descended gently in a Gramscian hegemonic mist upon all those below them, like snow, general all over Ireland, falling on every part of the dark central plain on ..., well, you know the rest. Beautiful, but if appropriated without real evidence, lazy history.

Instead, *a specific and very strong instrumentality* was required. This is because, in my view, the lower orders (to use a Victorian term, often associated with sexual matters) really had little reason to adopt the reproductive self-suppression practised by their betters—and therefore this is the place where the power of the churches, especially the Catholic church, enters the picture as the very item that historical demographers and Cliometricians hate: as an effective independent force whose existence and power must be recognized if Irish demography (including Irish emigration patterns) is to make historical sense.

If it was prudent for 15-acre-and-above farmers (to again use Michael Turner's break-line of the minimum self-sufficient post-Famine farm) to restrict their own children's sexuality as part of a family program of slowly aggregating land, it made little sense if a farmer were much below that line. How many generations would it take, for example, for a ten-acre farm to grow to 30 acres (the solid-livelihood line according to Turner)? We saw earlier that somewhat over 47 per cent of holdings were under 15 acres in 1890. And, David Fitzpatrick, in his study of the decline of the agricultural labourer after the Famine, calculated that one-third of the employed male workers in 1911 were farm workers.[22] These two groups are not fully meldable numerically (some of the very small holders undoubtedly were farm labourers), but one has to infer that at the very, very minimum, well over half of the rural male heads-of-family in Ireland in the half century before the Great War had no reasonable chance of seeing any of their offspring work their way up the socio-economic chain into the strong-farming class.

The situation of the majority of the population, then, was not much different from what it had been before the Great Famine, as far as prudent economic self-interest was concerned. That is, like similar rural subpopulations all around the world, children were actually a valuable potential asset. As long as they could be afforded during their non-economic years, they soon provided useful labour and ultimately an insurance policy against the vagaries of old age. It made more sense for, say, a ten-acre farmer to divide his land and let his children marry and procreate than it did to keep them all celibate and hope they would marry up the scale. And in the post-Famine era, when the British Isles, the North American mainland, and the British dominions all were open to migrants, there was a major bonus to having children: some of them probably would emigrate and send money home. (More of that later; the scale of remittances back to Ireland was quite amazing.) So, if the children stayed home, they were labour and insurance; if they left, they often were a cash source. Tim Guinnane surmises that in certain of the poorest counties such as Kerry, Galway and Mayo, "parents might have viewed children as so many tickets in a fairly generous lottery."[23]

Here the key point is that for a large portion of the population (the lower classes) a demographic system sharply different from that of the strong-farming class should have operated if simple economic self-interest prevailed. Parents should have let their children marry easily, given them a scrap of land and engendered a multigenerational branching of obligations, a network of support that would reticulate both in Ireland and overseas. And, with no hope of jumping up to strong-farmer status, there was little economic reason for a young man or woman not to spit the bit and gallop headlong into procreation; there was always someplace where they could make a living that was no worse than the prospects they faced at home if they stayed celibate. Yet, that is not the way it happened.

And the only reasonable explanation for the deviation of the reality of life-lived from the practice of simple economic self-interest, is religion. Here, religion means two things (1) an ideology; the churches call this theology—God-knowledge—but recognizing their belief systems as an ideology is all that is required here; and (2) institutions for the promulgation and enforcement of ideology. Because of its greater impact on the population than that of the Protestant churches (Ireland was 77.7 per cent Catholic, according to the census of 1861),[24] we will mostly concentrate on the Roman Catholic faith.

THREE

Gustav Sundbärg, writing on the eve of World War I, observed that talking about emigration from Sweden was the same thing as discussing Sweden in general. "There is almost nothing in the way of a political, social, or economic problem in our land that has not been conditioned in some way by the phenomenon of emigration."[25] And the converse held: virtually every major social formation affected emigration, though at varying levels of intensity. Sundbärg, as head of the monumental Swedish Emigration Commission of 1907–13, almost certainly had more knowledge about European out-migration than anyone else of his era: he collected comparative data on many countries besides the Swedish homeland. So, to interpolate his views into the Irish context is not whimsical. We must examine, in a very compressed form, the way that Irish religion (especially the Catholic church) acted as a force that by virtue of its ideology and its institutional power pounded the sexual-moral code of the strong-farmers down into the lower orders. The church's ideological and financial interests were consonant with those of the bourgeois agriculturalist class, but its force and energy in suppressing sexuality among the entire population was largely of its own making and must be recognized as that dreaded entity—an independent cultural variable. Without the church, Irish emigration would have been a very different story.

With apologies, here we need to engage a quick review of the Catholic church's ideology in the late nineteenth century. Forty years ago this would have been redundant, as most readers would have been able to list the Holy Days of Obligation, the mortal sins, all the local saints and could half-remember half of the catechism. No longer. And in another 40 years, I suspect that readers will crack open old liturgical texts or transcripts of theology lectures in Irish seminaries from the post-Famine era or read some of the turn-of-the-century tracts of the Catholic Truth Society and will say, in wonder, "most Irish people *really* believed all that?! Yes: the Faithful indeed were very faithful and their beliefs and their institutional loyalty directly affected their most fundamental everyday behaviours.

So, an extremely abbreviated ideological catalogue of the Catholic church in the era of emigration-culture: (1) God existed. (2) The Almighty had created the universe and could still intervene directly in it. (3) The visible world was a pale shadow of the invisible, for the visible world was temporary, but the invisible world was eternal. (4) All human beings possessed a soul that would exist eternally—in eternal punishment, or in union with God or, for a painful period in torment (Purgatory) before being released to heaven. (5) All human beings were structurally flawed because of Original Sin, inherited from Adam and Eve, and all therefore deserved eternal damnation. (6) However, through the church, which meted out "Grace," a person could escape from being tortured forever in hell. (7) There was no Grace, save through the church—except in certain arcane situations that had no applicability to everyday life in Ireland. (8) The visible delivery system for God's Grace was through several sacraments which were available only through the church. (9) The priests of the church were the sole custodians and administrators of the sacraments, except in rare instances, such as the lay-baptism of a nearly still-born infant. (10) The most marvellous sacrament was the Eucharist, in which the priest officiated at Mass, wherein wafers and wine were turned literally into the body and blood of Jesus Christ. (11) The sacrament that effected the most social leverage was auricular confession. That is: a person's sins could be forgiven only through confessing them aloud to a priest who would then pronounce absolution for those sins. Silent confession or formulaic group confession (as in most Protestant denominations) was not acceptable. (12) Although a person's fate through all eternity was determined primarily by the quality of his life on earth, especially adherence to the church's rules, it could be improved after death by those who were still alive engaging in specific devotions or providing subventions for specific liturgical acts. These were especially important in Irish culture for shortening a loved-one's time in Purgatory. (13) In post-Famine Irish Catholicism, the moral virtue that was most prized was sexual purity; and the sin that was most feared and denounced was improper sexual behaviour. (14) Although in a strictly rational sense, the Irish Catholic church became "a coercive organisation that curtails individual freedom,"[26]—its ultimate sanction of excommunication functionally dropped a person out of Irish society—this misses the point that the church's ideology was not simply power maximization in this world, but was anchored in a set of transcendental beliefs about an invisible world. Hence, while observing how the church operated *upon* and *within* Irish society, we must remember that the Faithful, and especially the church's administrators, would not view it as being merely *of* Irish society. Rather, it was part of an infinitely larger divine imperium.

The Great Famine made the Catholic church in Ireland into a much different societal agency from what it was prior to the Famine, and in so doing created an instrument that enforced the divinized ideology with an efficiency that was unimagined before the Famine. This historical fact was established firmly, and later built upon, by two of the most elegant and influential articles on Irish religion written in the twentieth century: that of Emmet Larkin (1972)[27] on the post-Famine "Devotional Revolution" and that of David W. Miller (1975)[28] on the major contrast between attendance to religious duties among the general population of Irish Catholics in the pre- and post-Famine periods. Of course there were continuities in the church and its adherents that bridged the two eras, but the degree of continuity professed by most earlier Catholic historians had been greatly exaggerated. That had led to some mistaken social history (as in the work of Kenneth Connell on pre-Famine sexual control that we discussed earlier). Taken together, the work of Larkin and Miller laid the basis for recognition that the social physics of the church and its adherents operated very differently within Irish society in the era of emigration-culture from earlier in the nineteenth century.

Among the many appercepctions that come out of Emmet Larkin's article (and his prodigious related work),[29] is the operation of a set of social analogies that relate to our present emigration study. Before the Famine, the church was like a 15-acre tenant farmer: it had a reasonable, albeit highly variable, income, but very little capital. Specifically, pre-Famine priests did quite well because their income came directly from saying special masses and doing baptisms and burials and for each of these they were paid directly by their parishioners. But very little money was set aside for church repair, for new buildings, much less for seminaries to improve religious education. After the Famine, the church's position quickly flipped and it became like a 50-acre strong-farmer who held a long lease: it became increasingly capital-obsessed. There was less disposable income for the individual clergy whose income dropped as population fell away and as increased central discipline limited the clergy's personal extractions. So, in accounting terms, the Catholic church became the equivalent of a strong-farmer who guarded his income flow and turned as much income as possible into capital. For the strong-farmer this was the purchase of land or of a long leasehold; for the Catholic church, it was new church buildings, improved seminaries and the strengthening of the church presence at the parish level.

Anyone who has spent much time in rural Ireland will be able to recognize visually this period in Catholic church history: it is the Era of Gray Glowering Churches, built in the common case between 1860 and 1910, usually to replace a crumbling thatched chapel: dominant, fortress-like structures, most often straddling a hill that commands a market town.

The most efficient way to summarize the progress and success of the Devotional Revolution is to look at the number of priests in service and their statistical relationship to the Irish population—priests-in-parishes being the sum-total surrogate for investment in church buildings and seminaries. The improvement was remarkable:[30]

Year	Number of priests (regular & parish)	Ratio of priests to Catholics
1840	c. 2,150	1:3,000
1849	2,574	1:1,978
1861	3,131	1:1,439
1870	n/a	1:1,250
1901	3,568	1:927

On top of this, the houses of religious orders and communities increased from 207 in 1849 to 587 in 1901, such institutions involving heavy capital and carrying costs.[31] The number of nuns grew rapidly from about 1,500 in 1850 to more than 3,700 in 1870.[32] In the usual instance, these were the daughters of strong-farmers and the dowries that would have provided for their marriages were transferred to their convents.

Along with the striking increase in institutional resources, the Catholic church in Ireland became notably more efficient—at least to the extent that one can measure the efficiency of an institution whose ultimate purpose is declared to be transcendent, by employing this-world observation. The central figure in this process was Paul Cullen (1803–78) who was an extreme adherent of Ultramontanism in his ecclesiasticism; and this he merged with something presaging Taylorist scientific management in his administrative style. After having spent most of his adult life in Rome, Cullen returned to Ireland as archbishop of Armagh in 1849, was translated to the archbishopric of Dublin in 1852 and became Ireland's first cardinal in 1866. Cullen was a complex, far from lovable, man. He distrusted Irish nationalism, viewed the secular state as the devil's handmaiden, and despised all forms and persons of Protestantism: he was proud of never having broken bread with one. In his almost three decades as the strongest figure in the Irish church, he stamped out most of the eccentricities of Irish worship (such as most pattern-days and the holding of stations for confession and mass in private houses). By his increasing control of the national seminary at Maynooth and the foundation of his own seminary for the archdiocese of Dublin, and through his strong contacts in Rome, Cullen came to control the new generation of post-Famine clergy. He developed a tight reporting structure for the clergy in both pastoral practices and in the delivery of divine service. The Irish church came to resemble the machines of the industrial revolution: virtually one product was stamped out nationwide.[33]

The natural allies of the Cullenite church—the church that lasted in Ireland at least through the 1960s—were the rural bourgeoisie, the rising tenant strong-farmers who benefited from the 1870s onward by increasing security of tenure, by government-adjudicated rent control, and, finally by state-financed mortgages so that they became freeholders. The strong-farmer class was the first tranche of the Irish population to take to the Devotional Revolution. The church offered social respectability and (as will be discussed in a moment) was keen to help control the sexual activity of the populace, which was nicely consonant with the economic strategies of the rural bourgeoisie. In return, the rising farmers had some surplus wealth and a portion of it went to the church, to build colleges and chapels.

But much more was going on than a simple class/church alliance and it is here that David W. Miller's seminal 1975 article is pivotal. He used the 1835 reports of the Commissioners of Public Instruction in Ireland to analyse a sample of parishes on which unambiguous data were available about church attendance.[34] Mass attendance averaged about 40 per cent. Not surprisingly, there has been a lot of clerical pettifogging about what this means. A nicely balanced assessment of the debate is Sean Connolly's: "On any open-minded reading it seems clear that we are looking at a pattern of religious practice quite different from the almost universal compliance first documented statistically in the 1970s, but generally assumed to have existed for the best part of the century before then."[35] Regular church attendance and the receipt of the sacraments was a post-Famine practice. The sacraments of confession, penance and attendance at Eucharist changed from a duty that was at best honoured annually, to more frequent intervals. By the late 1870s, the end of Cardinal Cullen's reign, missioners and the new generation of priests had introduced a whole range of devotions highly favoured in Rome, such as the rosary and devotion to the Sacred Heart of Jesus. Various sodalities and confraternities and "Purgatorian societies" were embedded among the laity.[36] Emmet Larkin summarized the product of the post-Famine Devotional Revolution with admirable clarity: "that the Irish were transformed as a people—men and women alike—into practicing Catholics."[37]

Thus, the Devotional Revolution involved not only a major watershed in the organizational efficiency and discipline among religious professionals; not only a quantum increase in organizational wealth; not only a thickening on the ground of priests, curates, teaching brothers, as well as orders of regular clergy and of teaching sisters; but also an acceptance of the church's discipline of devotional and of moral life by the general populace.[38]

As I implied earlier, an unspoken concordat existed between the church and the bourgeois agrarian class. Loss of chastity was the economic blunder most damaging to strong-farming families and loss of chastity was the mortal sin that the Irish Catholic church considered most spiritually damaging. Granted, there were worse transgressions on the church's scale of mortal sins—murder, blasphemy against the Holy Spirit and turning Protestant, for example—but sexual impurity was the Big Sin within the realm of everyday possibility. Here, I must emphasize that the concordat was not cynically arrived at. Each side needed only to act sincerely according to its own beliefs and a self-reinforcing system, the cultural equivalent of a cyclone, was created. On purely theological and pastoral grounds, the Irish church in the post-Famine era was committed to stamping out "impurity" and the strong-farmer class was committed to keeping their young adults on a short tether on purely economic grounds. When these two interests came together, the strong-farmers found that their protection of their own economic interests by limiting their children's rights-to-reproduction gained them credit in the invisible kingdom of the Almighty; in effect, they piled up treasure in heaven while picking up good grassland on earth. And the church, simply by preaching and enforcing its divinely dictated moral imperatives, immediately gained the staunch loyalty of the leading and most-prospering class of rural Catholics. It was a perfect covenant for each side and all the more so because it did not even need to be negotiated: seemingly, it fell full-born from the heavens.

It is impossible to read almost any collection of pastoral advice published in the high period of emigration-culture and not be stunned by the obsessive concern with imposing sexual control: take a look at the National Library's collection of early Catholic Truth Society publications. Or, more accessibly, simply read Kenneth Connell's essay on Catholicism and marriage in the century after the Famine.[39] His collage of instantiation runs from the seminary-isolation of bright young lads with a vocation, to their theology professors reserving sins-against-chastity for the students' final year, when they were able to apprehend the heaviest spiritual dangers; to the fear on the part of many parish priests of any social gathering where young men and women (or, indeed, very young boys and girls) might be alone together and thus have an "occasion for mortal sin," and on and on, with every unsupervised cross-roads dance being in need of suppression and the next week's sermon being a discourse on morality, by which was meant sexual conduct. The entire Irish population was taught that the biological alternatives for a youth were to (1) wait until a parent retired or died and then marry; (2) remain celibate all one's life; or (3) emigrate, with all the moral dangers that implied. And, as a sidebar, the moral danger of self-abuse was a matter of constant, if oblique, warning to young males. That girls and women might masturbate was beyond the possible, apparently, and extramarital relations were so unlikely that they were rarely the subject of homilies. Never mentioned in this era except among moral theologians was the sin of artificial birth control. At the pastoral level there was no sense in denouncing a sin that did not exist in practice.

In the decade 1890–1900, which Gustav Sundbärg used as the base period for his famous comparative study of European illegitimacy rates, the 32 County Irish rate of out-of-wedlock births was 2.6 per cent. This was much lower than most of the rest of Europe. The extreme upper limit was set by Portugal at 12.1 per cent. But in those Orthodox countries for which data were available, the rate was low. For Russia-proper (meaning European Russia, excluding Finland), the rate was 2.7 per cent. That of Serbia was 1.1 per cent and that of Bulgaria was 0.3 per cent.[40] The low Irish rate of illegitimacy is significant, but what it necessarily leaves unstated is the situation that almost all contemporary and historical observations accept, but which no one can conclusively demonstrate: that there was little premarital sexual congress,[41] even less adultery and very little gay sex.[42]

The triumph of the Catholic church is that although it had very strong tools of enforcement, and occasionally priests used these powers noisily, generally the church employed its powers quietly and very efficiently. Thus, quite quickly the moral (meaning sexual) code of the strong-farmers and the Catholic bishops and clergy was assimilated into the everyday life of the *entire* Catholic population. Tom Inglis, who has reflected on post-Famine Irish sexuality more than has any recent scholar, suggests that "the locus classicus for the key components of the chastity, virginity, and modesty, as well as the piety and sobriety that had taken firm hold of most Irish people, was the home with its parents (mostly mothers) and the schools with their teachers."[43]

Take first the schools. Although the Irish primary school system ("the national system of education") had been founded in 1831 as a non-denominational network, by 1850 it was clerically dominated and mostly segregated according to religion. By century's end, 88 per cent of the Catholic schools were under priestly management[44] (the rest were under Catholic gentry) and the priest appointed the school master. Catholic canon law delegated the moral supervision of each child to the local parish priest, so in Catholic locales the school catchment areas usually followed parish boundaries. By the time a child was ten years of age, he or she was literate and knew the catechism and the catalogue of sins that must be abhorred. The relatively few children who went on to secondary education (called "intermediate education,") did so in schools that were fully under clerical control and which were single-sex. Thus, in the era of emigration-culture, almost every Catholic child received a more-than-passing introduction to the key features of the faith and to the prepotent tenets of the moral code.

Parenthetically, on one matter the church fell short of its own desires in the primary schools, namely that even the youngest girls and boys should not be taught in the same school, let alone the same classroom. In 1910, the Catholic bishops stated that "apart altogether from moral considerations, we believe that the mixing of boys and girls in the same school is injurious to the delicacy of feeling, reserve, and modesty of demeanour which should characterize young girls."[45] This made explicit as episcopal policy a set of collective beliefs that long had been held by the generality of the clergy. The clergy would have liked to keep boys and girls separate even in "infant classes." However, most national schools were too small for this. Early in the twentieth century, more than 60 per cent of the primary schools were single-teacher schools having fewer than 50 pupils, so in most schools gender segregation was impractical.[46]

How one assesses Tom Inglis's second point, regarding the intra-family teaching of morality, is an historian's conundrum. Conversations, tears, beatings, arguments and parental example all left almost no evidence. What is undeniable, however, is that the Catholic church possessed a unique element of enforcement, one that infiltrated every family: the requirement for oral confession. This gave the local priest or his curate a window into the dynamics of every family. A bad (misleading or incomplete) confession was itself a mortal sin. Moreover, by a canon law theory of moral contagion, if one facilitated, even by turning a blind eye, the occasion of mortal sin, one was oneself in transgression. Functionally, by the end of Cardinal Cullen's regime, the church had a potential informant or two within every family.

Thus it was, through the instrumentality of the Catholic church, a strong and increasingly vigorous organization with a will of its own, that the moral (that is sexual) code of the agricultural bourgeoisie became the moral code of the whole Catholic people. Tom Inglis summarized the situation as follows:

> Sex became a serious subject and the church developed a monopoly of knowledge about it. Shame and guilt about sexual practices were instilled in each individual, privately, in a hushed manner, in the dark isolated space of the confessional. Sexual morality became a major issue, but it was wrapped up in a veil of silence. When it was talked or written about, it was in a vague abstract formal language which prevented the laity from developing any communicative competence about it.[47]

Of course the Catholic church was not totally against sexual activity: no sex, no Catholics.

So family life was lauded, albeit somewhat awkwardly.[48] At heart, the bishops and clergy were followers of St Paul who was notoriously conflicted about sexual matters. (What was his bedevilling "thorn in the flesh" one wonders.) St Paul stated that it was best for everyone to stay as he himself was: unmarried. "But if they cannot contain, let them marry: for it is better to marry than to burn."[49] Or, in a slightly expanded post-Famine Irish version: rather than burn eternally because of sexual impurity, it is better either to marry or to emigrate.

FOUR

W hat about the Protestants? Nobody knows definitively: but one can draw some fairly high-probability inferences. Protestants[50] composed one-quarter to one-fifth of the Irish population and though they frequently paid close attention to the actions of the Roman Catholic church, they certainly were not directly guided by it. Yet that scarcely means that they were sexually wanton. What we really would like to know is this: were Irish Protestant family patterns in the era of emigration-culture different from Irish Catholic family patterns, *other things being equal?* Important phrase. The only direct examination of this question at the requisite level of probative power that I have encountered is Cormac Ó Gráda's 1985 study of farmers and farm labourers in 22 electoral districts in Counties Londonderry and Tyrone, using the original manuscript censuses of 1901 and 1911. (These are the only two years available; earlier originals of the censuses were destroyed.) Ó Gráda's research strategy was a simple and elegantly practical keeping-other-things-equal as between the two religious groups. His finding was that for men and women who had married in the 1880s, there was no difference in age of marriage, fertility, or final family size as between Protestant and Catholics, which is to say no causally different approach to sexual morality. For those who married thereafter, a very small difference was noted, with Catholics and Anglicans having slightly larger families than Presbyterians, who tended to be slightly better off economically. In any case, the family patterns of all the denominations was very close.[51]

However, I think that after World War I (but not in the period we are here studying) Protestants began to practise birth spacing much more than did Catholics and often used what the Catholic church called "artificial" methods.[52] A litmus-date in this sequence was the Lambeth Conference of 1930 which approved family planning for Anglicans worldwide, "provided this is done in the light" of Christian principles.[53] One can probably assume that Protestants as a group probably became less strict about non-marital sex as birth control measures somewhat reduced the risk of being found out through an unwanted pregnancy. In any case, a crucial wide-data fact is that in 1971 Roman Catholic fertility in Northern Ireland was two-thirds higher than that of Protestants and, more importantly, it was high across all socio-economic levels.[54] That stands as a firm indication that cultural values (in this case religiously derived) can directly influence demographic behaviour, something that we have been arguing was also the case in the immediate post-Famine era.

But differences in Protestant-Catholic family patterns in the pre-World War I era are more apparent than real, and certainly are not clearly attributable simply to religious variance. To take one example of the apparent-vs-real character of much of the discussion, a quick look at the earliest registration of out-of-wedlock births is useful. The first report of the Registrar-General of Ireland, that for 1864, is particularly intriguing because at this early stage in their work the registration officials did not arrange their various data the way the Irish census did, according to the ancient four provinces, but rather into eight divisions that were much closer to actual socio-economic regions of the country. Here, let us examine only the four regions that show the greatest variation around the national average of out-of-wedlock births:[55]

Region	Percentage
National average	*3.8*
1. North-eastern division (Antrim, Down, parts of Londonderry, Tyrone, Armagh and Monaghan)	6.2
2. South-eastern division (Waterford, Wexford, parts of Carlow, Kilkenny, Tipperary, Limerick and Cork)	5.1
3. South-western division (Kerry, parts of Cork, Limerick and Clare)	2.4
4. Western division (Mayo, Galway, Sligo, parts of Clare)	1.9

Now, a quick reading of this information would yield the obvious fact that the area with the highest proportion of Protestants (the north-eastern division) had the most illegitimate births and that the areas with the lowest proportion of Protestants (the western division) had the lowest proportion—and from that one might conclude that sexual behaviour in Ireland varied greatly by religious faith.

Instead, take this as a basic example of multicollinearity—which is a statistician's way of saying that a lot of things can vary at once and that apparent cause is not necessarily "real" cause, and, indeed, that real cause may not in many situations be ascertainable. Ask some simple questions, all of which deal with factors other than religion that are related to reproductive behaviour and sexual "morality": which of these four areas was part of the industrial revolution of the British Isles? (Division 1); which of the areas had the highest urban concentration? (Divisions 1 and 2); which of the four areas was most exposed to foreign cultural influences by virtue of extensive seaborne trade? (Divisions 1 and 2); which area had the highest rate of cohort depletion—meaning, in this case, that it sent the highest proportion of its young people to other Irish counties, to Great Britain or to a transatlantic destination? (Division 4); and which of the four areas that we are dealing with received the most in-country migrants from other parts of Ireland? (Division 1).[56]

That is a simple exercise intended to illustrate that many of the attributes associated with religion (which follow, for example, from being Catholic in Mayo) may have no causal relationship to the apparently virtuous posture of the local population on the illegitimacy issue: a disproportionate share of the Mayo young left and therefore had children (if at all) elsewhere, whether in or out of wedlock. A dozen or so factors cross-hatch with religion and, given the destruction of almost all nineteenth-century Irish manuscript census records, one doubts if the question ever will be sorted out fully. Still, let us return to the province of Ulster for the 1901–11 period, because that is where the one glimmer of certainty is found, as established by Cormac Ó Gráda's 1985 study: his key point being that there was only the slightest difference in family patterns between rural Protestants and rural Catholics. The following are the out-of-wedlock rates by province (unfortunately the original eight-division method of reporting had been abandoned), covering the ten years 1901–1910:[57]

Province	Percentage
National average	2.6
Connacht	0.7
Munster	2.3
Leinster	2.7
Ulster	3.4

What interpretive facts are potentially relevant? First, that despite the commonplace assumption, the largest denomination in the historical province of Ulster was Catholic and by a long shot: 44 per cent in 1901, as compared to 27 per cent Presbyterian, the next largest group. And if one goes back early in the emigration-era, as late as 1861 an absolute majority of the Ulster population was Catholic.[58] This basilisk-like fact, when combined with Ó Gráda's comparative study, makes it hard to ascribe Ulster's apparent immorality (if such it was) to either major group. Second, Ulster, 1910, had the highest proportion of marriages that involved minors (7.5 per cent of all females who married), while Connacht had the lowest (3.6 per cent for females).[59] This seems to imply that in Ulster, the general population was more resistant than elsewhere in Ireland to the raising of the marriage age, which had been increasing every year since figures were first kept in the 1860s. Thirdly, this resistance relates directly to Ulster's having the largest urban population of any province, urban being defined as registrars' districts of ten thousand or more persons. If the main economic force behind the unique Irish demographic revolution had to do with rural land-holding, then such a force would have less impact in urban areas. Fourthly, urban areas in Ireland had demonstrably different marriage patterns than did rural areas: both higher marriage rates and higher rates of illegitimacy which, taken together, suggest a less-suppressed range of sexual behaviour.[60] None of this, however, relates directly to potential differences in the moral code as between Catholics and Protestants.

Nevertheless, one small piece of the Registrar-General's bundle of numbers speaks to a difference that I would present less as a proof of differences than as the basis of a midrash on nascent possibility. Specifically, there are two urban centres in Ulster that often are taken as being the prototypical civic-social embodiments of the two faiths, often to the point of caricature: Ballymena and Newry, "Prod" and "Mick" to the core, respectively. Now, in 1910, the rate of marriage in the two registrar's districts that enclosed these centres was virtually identical: 5.3 per thousand of the population in Newry district and 5.4 in Ballymena district. However, the rate of out-of-wedlock births was 6.3 per cent in Ballymena and 2.5 per cent in Newry.[61] Maybe they did have more fun in Ballymena, or at least enjoyed more guilt.

My own best guesses would be that (1) sexual suppression in rural areas was almost identical as between Catholics and Protestants for the period between the Famine and the Great War, whenever other things were equal. (Again, that important phrase.) (2) That in urban areas, which were far from being dominant—17 per cent of the Irish population lived in towns (about two thousand persons in 1851) and the proportion was still as low as 33.5 per cent in 1911[62]—there was beginning to be a wedge of divergent behaviour between the two groups. This was not statistically very important before World War I, but was predictive of a phenomenon that would expand in the 1920s and thereafter. Overall, however, in the era of emigration-culture, Protestants and Catholics, when in the same socio-economic situation, acted pretty much the same.

There: have I not just destroyed my own argument about there being an important causative cultural variable that it is necessary to recognize in order to explain the sexual control—and thus to explain in part the high emigration rate—of the Irish people: namely the ideological commitment and institutional efficiency of the majority faith in the Roman Catholic church? Actually, no.

Recall that my argument is that one can get to grips with the Irish emigration—culture, and with its physics of extruding so many people and totally suppressing the reproductive activities of about one-quarter of those who did not emigrate, only through a very simple equation, both variables of which are necessary:

$$\text{Reproductive control} \quad = \quad \begin{array}{c} \text{Rural embourgeoisement} \\ \textit{plus} \\ \text{religious indoctrination projected into all class levels} \end{array}$$

Although split among more subgroups than were the Catholics, the Protestant population was shaped according to the same formulaic simplicity. My suggestion is that the Protestants came out almost (but not quite) as suppressive of sexuality in the era between the Famine and World War I as did the generality of Catholics, but by a slightly different route. Specifically (1) the "rural embourgeoisement" portion of the equation was stronger among the Protestant population generally than it was among the Catholic population. This held throughout the country, but was especially demographically important in the north of Ireland where the bulk of the Protestants lived. It is crucial not to overstate this difference, however: most rural Protestants were small farmers and labourers, just as were the Catholics. It is only that the Protestants were moving into the middle class somewhat more quickly, and this was particularly the case among the Presbyterians.[63] (2) The surplus of force on this half of the formula (the economic half) compensated for a somewhat less tight control of their flocks by the clergy of the Protestant denominations (the religious half of the formula).

However, the massive blind spot in the literature on Irish reproductive control and suppression is that it has focused almost entirely on Catholics: Connell, and Arensberg and Kimball set a pattern that has yet to be broken. In fact, the Protestant churches between the Famine and the Great War were in a period of group energization in which communal religious affirmations grew stronger, both as far as strictly spiritual matters were concerned and as far as group social control was involved. As a collective phenomenon, this has not received the study it deserves. But if one puts together such things as the Great Revival of 1859, the disestablishment of the Established Church in 1871 (which actually increased social cohesion and spiritual devotion among the Anglican laity), and the sense of pan-Protestant religious identity that developed in the north from 1886 onwards, as the fear of Home-Rule-and-Rome-Rule raised its head—then one recognizes that something akin to the Devotional Revolution among Catholics occurred among Protestants. Paler, but real.

Tom Inglis is right to see "Victorian prudery" as a phenomenon that runs through both Catholics and Protestants in the era of emigration-culture, a time of ever-increasing "respectability." As long as one does not reify the concept—it refers to a bundle of attitudes not to a specific countable entity—he is right:

> To understand Irish attitudes to sexuality it is necessary to place them within the wider context of Victorian attitudes to women, marriage, and the family. Victorians were accustomed to thinking of sex in terms of sexual emotions. Sex was about dark, primeval forces, anarchic and explosive instincts that knew no values, possessed no morality, and had no sense of good and evil. Unless it was controlled rigorously, sex would overthrow all the finer sensibilities.[64]

And, while this background of "Victorianism" applied both to Protestants and Catholics, the Protestants, being slightly more bourgeois, embraced the cult of respectability somewhat earlier and more fully.

One matter we should not misperceive is that neither the Protestant clergy nor the laity were warm and cuddly on the sex issue. From pulpit denunciations of fornication (ah, how the sermons made that four-syllable word into a four-letter word), to pursed-lipped discussion of "impropriety" in vestry meetings, the clergy were the flag-bearers of rectitude. Of course, the laity in the congregations acted as enforcers of the moral order. Among most rural Presbyterian groups, the custom still was for notorious sinners, as named by the clergy and lay leaders, to sit in a special pew of shame, facing the congregation. This punishment would be imposed on a couple who had been detected in fornication and for those couples who came to the marriage altar with the girl being pregnant. Exactly how effective this was requires more data than we have to hand, but at one time I went through the church registers of the two Presbyterian churches on Islandmagee, County Antrim, one of the foundation-locations of Presbyterianism in Ireland and in some ways a Weberian Ideal Type of a Presbyterian community. Despite the fact that the place had possessed a bit of a rough image for sexual impropriety in the years before the Famine,[65] the baptismal record of the Second Islandmagee Presbyterian Church between 1854–1920 shows an illegitimacy rate of only 1.6 per cent. This from a total of 1,338 baptisms.[66] Obviously, this could be explained by a sinning couple's being run off the parish, but other factors make it seem not. In fact, what appears to have been the case is the couple who fell-into-trouble, took their lumps of social disapproval and then married. Of the 200 women married in the First Islandmagee Presbyterian Church from 1845–67, inclusive, 13.5 per cent were pregnant at the altar. Clearly, several hundred comparable studies of Protestant and Catholic parish registers are necessary before any firm conclusion can be drawn.

However, Joseph Lee's judgement of a generation ago stands as wisdom. "In the comparative context, the similarities and marital mores of Irish Catholics and Protestants were far more striking than the local difference on which polemicists loved to linger."[67] If I am inclined to see Catholic enforcement of strict sexual control as being slightly stronger in the period of emigration-culture than was Protestant, it is because the instrument of compulsory oral confession gave the Catholic church a Stasi-like entry into virtually every family. That really worked.

FIVE

Sweden and Ireland, considered as nation-wide entities, dealt with similar problems and in each case by 1914 had found their way out of the previous century's long winter of deprivation. Quite justifiably, both nations have been described as being, in the first half of the nineteenth century, inhabitants of the "poor European periphery." Each had been a poverty-washed agricultural country characterized by a high degree of risk in the face of potential crop failures. Each experienced a sharp agricultural trauma, a moment of axial social and economic stress. Thereafter, each society rearranged itself so as to reduce to a negligible level the damage that would follow from further agrarian failure.

Each nation in the 50 years prior to World War I became an emigration-culture. This term refers not only to the continued out-flow of a significant number of those born in each country but, crucially, to a cultural development that was bigger than the mere sum of individual decisions. Now each society reared its young to be prepared to leave it, and that is about as big a collective cultural change as any society can make.

Within the demographic arc of the full-blown emigration-culture—roughly, 1870–1914—both Sweden and Ireland exported a lot of young people. "Exported" is a neutral term: perhaps the homeland made money on the transaction, perhaps the societal loss was greater than the benefit. The adamantine fact, though, is that hundreds and hundreds of thousands left, most for ever.

By the development of industry, each country moderated the need to export its young. This was quite dramatic in Sweden, but in Ireland was much less impressive, being essentially a regional development in Belfast and its periphery.

Both countries experienced the fruition of an agricultural revolution in the era of emigration-culture. Both of these "revolutions" forced out a large shard of one of the major class-fragments, the small tenant farmers and the landless labourers. Where they went is not entirely clear.

However, the Swedish agricultural revolution and the Irish one were very different indeed. The Swedish agrarian reordering increased the total amount of land being farmed, considerably raised total production, especially of arable crops, and increased productivity through the consolidation of freeholds. The Irish agricultural revolution had created by 1914 a nation of freeholders or, alternately, very secure tenants (this through United Kingdom legislation). But what accompanied these improvements was a change that, over a 50-year period, turned Irish farming patterns almost upside down. Intensive tillage was reduced; arable grains and legumes were planted in ever-smaller quantities. Hay, grass, cattle and other animals became the main crops. Animal products were profitable, as they could be sold in the ever-growing market in industrial England and Scotland in the form of meat or dairy products. But what a strange agricultural revolution: most agrarian revolutions in western society have increased production, increased efficiency and ultimately reduced the number of farmers and farm labourers required. This one reduced production, reduced efficiency (at least as far as land utilization was concerned) and reduced the number of people who could live on the land at a standard they saw as acceptable. Paradoxical as it may seem, the collective response of Irish rural society to the Great Famine was, from about 1860 onwards, to produce less food, a very consequential decision for an overwhelmingly agrarian society, particularly one that showed no hint of a national industrialization process.

So, Sweden was able to escape from being a risky, poverty-stricken society by (1) increasing industry on a widespread basis; (2) augmenting agricultural production; and (3) exporting people. It did not attempt to introduce any new limits on sexual reproduction.

Ireland escaped high-risk poverty as well, and the contrast to the Swedish route is valuable for highlighting the uniqueness of Ireland's socio-economic trajectory between the Famine and the Great War. Ireland's success as an emigration-culture pivoted entirely on one collective decision, one so monumental that, in my opinion, no aspect of subsequent Irish history up until at least the mid-1960s, makes full sense without understanding what was decided. The formula for the post-Famine rebalancing as between population and available resources could have been written on a postcard: *only about half of the population must be permitted to reproduce*. Nobody ever wrote that down, but that is what the socio-economic-religio system decided, and it was indeed a system.

The numbers are a bit slippery because of possible double-counting, but the overall result is unambiguous. Remember that in 1901, 36.9 per cent of persons born in Ireland and still alive were living in the USA, Great Britain, or the main British dominions (see table 7.1), so, considering additional locations not concluded in those figures, some 38–40 per cent of the Irish-born were living outside of Ireland. That is to say, they had (in the usual case) not been permitted to procreate in Ireland, or, less often, had decided to raise the families they had started in Ireland someplace else in the world. In either case, they were removed from the reproduction-base of the homeland. And, of the 61.9 per cent of the Irish-born (worldwide) who remained in the homeland, we noted earlier that in 1901, of men and women aged 45–49 inclusive, 13.5 per cent of the men and 19.4 per cent of the women had never married—and few of these people ever would marry and very, very few would have children. Therefore, only a moiety of those who came of age in the era of emigration-culture—call it "half" and be done with niggling—were part of the Irish system of human biological reproduction.[68]

Of course, such a system of biological limitation had its psychic costs, but we should not project into our own evaluation of those costs in post-Famine Ireland the values of the twenty-first century. Here I wish to distance myself most emphatically from those commentators who seem to believe that any historical culture wherein young people did not behave like, say, UCD undergraduates in our own time, was necessarily pathological. The psychic costs need to be articulated in the terms of the historical period,—which is not to minimize them, but it is to refuse to turn them into psychobabble. A sympathetic and realistic summary of the contemporary psychic costs of the post-Famine system was provided by Kevin Danaher, who had studied more Irish folklore than almost anyone of his generation:

> Irish tradition did not regard the attainment of a particular age by an individual as conferring any particular status on that individual. "Coming of age at twenty-one" was a legal concept which meant very little to the ordinary people. On the other hand, marriage brought an important change of status. On marriage both the man and the woman reached full status, irrespective of their age, *while the unmarried person, of any age, was still regarded as a lesser being* [emphasis mine].[69]

That is how Ireland successfully escaped from being a high-risk society, by joining collective socio-moral values and individual incentives—and disincentives. Systemically, it gave every young person a fifty-fifty chance of becoming a full human being under the nation's collective system of values. Every young person had to guess whether they were likely to be in the winning or the losing half of their age group and to act accordingly.

Irish demographers and economic historians like to point out that, really, Irish demographic patterns were not so very different than those of the rest of Europe.

They are so very wrong.

NOTES

1   In the discussion below I shall rely for crop output data mostly on the work of Michael Turner, *After the Famine. Irish Agriculture, 1850–1914* (Cambridge: Cambridge University Press, 1996). This is an extraordinary piece of scholarship, providing corrected production series for all the major Irish crops from the beginning of reliable numbers up to the beginning of World War I. Its presentation has the virtue of being accessible both to academic historians and employable as a database for Cliometricians.

2   Tim Guinnane has put forward the most plausible version of this viewpoint in his *Vanishing Irish*. "My approach to population change after the Famine ... is based on thinking about demographic patterns as the outcome of individual behaviors motivated by Irish men and women's efforts to try to make their way in the world ... Why focus on individuals or couples? Because, quite simply, aggregate demographic patterns reflect the decisions of individuals." Timothy W. Guinnane, *The Vanishing Irish. Households, Migration and the Rural Economy in Ireland, 1850–1914* (Princeton: Princeton University Press, 1997), p. 16.

3   Interview with Douglas Keay, *Woman's Own*, 23 Sept. 1987.

4   Conrad M. Arensberg and Solon T. Kimball, *Family and Community in Ireland* (Cambridge: Harvard University Press, 1940; 2nd ed., 1968), p. 300.

5   Cormac Ó Gráda, *Ireland. A New Economic History, 1780–1939* (Oxford: Clarendon Press, 1994), p. 213.

6   Guinnane, *The Vanishing Irish*, p. 74.

7   Joseph J. Lee, *The Modernization of Irish Society, 1848–1918* (Dublin: Gill and Macmillan, 1973), p. 5. A useful historiographic study could be made of why, from roughly 1950 to the end of the century, two generations of well-trained Irish historians blinkered ourselves to the possibility that the Church could have been an effective *force majeure* in influencing Irish sexual behaviour.

8   For a summary of his own innovative work, see Tom Inglis, "Origins and Legacies of Irish Prudery: Sexuality and Social Control in Modern Ireland," *Eire-Ireland*, vol. 40, nos. 3 and 4 (Winter 2005), pp. 9–37.

9   Government of Ireland, Department of Industry and Commerce, *Agricultural Statistics, 1847–1926* (Dublin: The Stationery Office, 1930), pp. 6–13, cited in Turner, *After the Famine*, pp. 139–40.

10   Turner, *After the Famine*, table 5.8, p. 145.

11   See Turner, *After the Famine*, Appendix 1, Part A, pp. 227–31. Here a word about the vocabulary of the time. "Arable crops" by convention are taken to mean various grains (wheat, oats, barley, rye etc.) and legumes (peas, beans, other pulses). "Tillage" includes all these and also tame grass land that is cut at least once annually for hay. Grassland used solely for pasturage is not included in tillage.

12   Turner, *After the Famine*, pp. 230–31.

13   Turner, *After the Famine*, Appendix 2, p. 245, and D. A. E. Harkness, "Irish Emigration," in Walter Willcox (ed.), *International Migrations*, vol. 2, *Interpretations* (New York: National Bureau of Economic Research, 1931), p. 271.

14   Harkness, "Irish Emigration," p. 271.

15   The following data are taken from Turner's annual tables (*After the Famine*, pp. 227–54) and pasturage numbers, p. 15. Annual currency values from table 4.2, p. 108.

16   In addition to Turner's tables, his chapter on land occupation (*After the Famine*, pp. 65–94) is valuable, not least because it makes clear that any generalization has to be qualified by reference both to local (sometimes he says, parish-by-parish) and year-by-year factors. That granted, overall patterns did exist; they are not as sharp, however, as the rhetoric around land usage often suggests. In the future, a basic empirical study, involving several parish microstudies, is needed in order to discover exactly who was acquiring the large number of very small holdings (under one acre) under the Land Acts.

17 Derived from Turner, *After the Famine*, pp. 250–52. Incidentally, in using Turner's data, it is best to focus on landholders, as these become confused rather easily with his report on occupiers of land, which is close, but not quite the same thing.

18 Turner, *After the Famine*, pp. 84–85. This post-Famine summary is worth comparing to my visual suggestion of pre-Famine risk according to farm size (figure 3.1). Accepting the change in the crop-mix between the two periods, the two views correlate nicely.

19 The one period of mass liquidation may have been in the immediate wake of the Famine, when it is possible that the holdings of emigrated or deceased families were grabbed by neighbours. This is something quite different from acquisitions from old landlords under the Encumbered Estates Act of 1848, and understandably it is not a subject that has been attractive to Irish scholars.

20 Arensberg and Kimball, *Family and Community in Ireland*; Kenneth H. Connell, *Irish Peasant Society. Four Historical Essays* (Oxford: Clarendon Press, 1968), esp. "Catholicism and Marriage in the Century after the Famine," pp. 113–61.

21 For an illuminating discussion of how the Irish pattern of impartible inheritance operated in the twentieth century, see Liam Kennedy, "Farm Succession in Modern Ireland: Elements of a Theory of Inheritance," *Economic History Review*, new ser., vol. 44 (Aug. 1991), pp. 477–99. The study is particularly useful in showing how the closed system of family transactions reduced the full force of the market economy and "agrocapitalism."

22 David Fitzpatrick, "The Disappearance of the Irish Agricultural Labourer, 1841–1922," *Irish Economic and Social History*, vol. 7 (1980), p. 84.

23 Guinnane, *The Vanishing Irish*, p. 268. See also Turner, *After the Famine*, p. 94.

24 Government of the United Kingdom, *Census of Ireland for the Year 1861*, part 4, vol. 1 [3204-III], HC, 1863, lix, pp. 30–33.

25 Gustav Sundbärg in Government of Sweden, *Emigrationsutredningen, Betänkande* (Stockholm: KB, 1913), p. 653.

26 Tom Inglis, *Moral Monopoly. The Catholic Church in Modern Irish Society* (Dublin: Gill and Macmillan, 1987), p. 6. This pioneering sociological study of the modern Irish church has been late to receive adequate respect from historians. Although I disagree with Inglis's belief that Irish Catholics followed the church's teaching only for reasons of "rational, instrumental calculation of means toward more immediate, specific material ends," (p. 6) Inglis's collection of data is invaluable and, one should add, that he is better informed about church history than are most Irish historians.

27 Emmet Larkin, "The Devotional Revolution in Ireland, 1850–75," *American Historical Review*, vol. 77 (Jun. 1972), pp. 625–52.

28 David W. Miller, "Irish Catholicism and the Great Famine," *Journal of Social History*, vol. 9 (Autumn 1975), pp. 81–98.

29 In this discussion, I am informed in considerable degree by the series of books Emmet Larkin has written on the Catholic church in the nineteenth century (and the surrounding decades of the eighteenth and twentieth centuries). Particularly helpful is the information and discussion found in the following: *The Making of the Roman Catholic Church in Ireland, 1850–1860* (Chapel Hill: University of North Carolina Press, 1980) and *The Consolidation of the Roman Catholic Church in Ireland, 1860–1870* (Chapel Hill: University of North Carolina Press, 1987).

30 Guinnane, *The Vanishing Irish*, pp. 69–71; Larkin, "The Devotional Revolution in Ireland," pp. 627, 544; Connell, "Catholicism and Marriage," Appendix, p. 160.

31 Connell, "Catholicism and Marriage," p. 152*n*5.

32 Larkin, "The Devotional Revolution in Ireland," p. 644.

33 Cullen served in Ireland at the perfect moment in church history for his style of administration. The reign of Pius IX (1846–78) saw the almost total decline in the temporal power of the papacy and, in compensatory countercurrent, a sharp increase in top-down ecclesiastical discipline and in new dogmas. These matters included the declaration of the Immaculate Conception of the Blessed Virgin Mary (1854), the promulgation of the Syllabus of Errors (1864), and the acceptance of the Infallibility of the Pope when speaking *ex cathedra* on faith and morals (1870). Within a year of that last event, the Vatican lost its final temporal jurisdiction and quietly put its one remaining battle frigate up for sale.

34 In addition to his "Irish Catholicism and the Great Famine," see Miller's "Mass Attendance in Ireland in 1834," in Stewart J. Brown and David W. Miller (eds.), *Piety and Power in Ireland, 1870–1960. Essays in Honour of Emmet Larkin* (Belfast: Institute of Irish Studies, the Queen's University of Belfast, 2000), pp. 158–79. Despite its title, the education report was a de facto census and also a trove of nationwide information about religious behaviour. This was because the purely educational queries were supplemented by a

round of interrogatories that required the clergymen of each denomination to indicate for his parish the number of adherents and also the average number who attended weekly service. Thus this investigation into education became one of the most important systematic sources of information on religion of the pre-Famine population. See Government of the United Kingdom, *First Report of the Commissioners of Public Instruction, Ireland* (45 and 46), HC, 1835, xxxiii, and *Second Report* (47), HC, 1835, xxxiv.

35   Sean J. Connolly, "The Moving Statue and the Turtle Dove: Approaches to the History of Irish Religion," *Irish Economic and Social History*, vol. 31 (2004), p. 12. The statistical documentation Connolly is referring to showed that, in 1974, 91 per cent of Catholics in the Irish Republic attended Mass at least weekly (Inglis, *Moral Monopoly*, p. 27).

36   Larkin, "The Devotional Revolution in Ireland," pp. 644–45.

37   Larkin, "The Devotional Revolution in Ireland," p. 651. Larkin here was being just a little triumphalist. In fact, "the Irish" in the 32 Counties included well over a million Protestants throughout the years between the Famine and World War I. Moreover, the proportion of Protestants in the Irish population grew from over 22 per cent in 1861 (the first direct religious census) to over 26 per cent in 1911 (W. E. Vaughan and A. J. Fitzpatrick (eds.), *Irish Historical Statistics. Population, 1821–1971* (Dublin: Royal Irish Academy, 1978), table 13, page 49), most probably because the Catholics left Ireland in proportionately higher numbers than did Protestants. For not-ungenerous caveats concerning Larkin's views of pre-Famine levels of devotion and of subsequent post-Famine changes, see Donal A. Kerr, *'A Nation of Beggars'? Priests, People and Politics in Famine Ireland, 1846–1852* (Oxford: Clarendon Press, 1994), pp. 318–25. These comments should be placed in the context of Kerr's chapter, "The Roman Catholic Church in Ireland by 1844," in his *Peel, Priests and Politics. Sir Robert Peel's Administration and the Roman Catholic Church in Ireland, 1841–1846* (Oxford: Clarendon Press, 1982), pp. 1–67.

38   I fully accept Connolly's point that the Devotional Revolution has to be accepted as a reality, and that, simultaneously, it is wisdom not to become too imaginative in positing major changes in mentalities in the second half of the nineteenth century ("The Moving Statue and the Turtle Dove," p. 15). For our purposes, all that is necessary is to note the logarithmically increasing influence of the church upon the entire Catholic populace, rich to poor, and the imposition of ever-stricter definitions of official religious culture and of the devotional and moral requirements this placed upon the laity.

39   Connell, "Catholicism and Marriage," pp. 113–61. The massively important pioneering study by John H. Whyte, *Church and State in Modern Ireland, 1923–1970* (Dublin: Gill and Macmillan, 1971) has a good deal of relevant material from the early period of the Free State which, if read carefully, projects a light back into the pre-World War I period.

40   Gustav Sundbärg, *Aperçus, Statistiques Internationaux* (Stockholm: Imprimerie Royale, 1908), table 84, pp. 136–37. This is still the base source of international comparative illegitimacy rates. Much of this pioneering material found its way into the 1907–13 Swedish commission on emigration that Sundbärg headed. Interestingly, Connell ("Catholicism and Marriage," p. 83) misstates Sundbärg's research in claiming that Ireland had Europe's lowest illegitimacy rate.

41   There was no equivalent in pre-World War I years of the "PFI" flow to Great Britain of the 1960s and thereafter. This was the London social worker's code for Pregnant from Ireland. June Sklar has calculated that, for 1871, the number of Irish girls who became pregnant in Ireland and gave birth in England was 235 and that for 1911 was 72. June Sklar, "Marriage and Nonmarital Fertility: A Comparison of Ireland and Sweden," *Population and Development Review*, vol. 3 (Dec. 1977), p. 365.

42   Arensberg and Kimball (again, in the 1930s and in the Free State) made two passing observations that are germane. First, in discussing rural morality they used this phrase, "people's attitude toward illegitimacy and premarital intercourse, *one and the same to them …*" (*Family and Community in Ireland*, p. 209, emphasis mine). And they observe that "both rural expressions and rural standards of conduct seem to reflect the attitude that only the married have a sex life or, if others have it, they should not (p. 211).

43   Inglis, "Origins and Legacies of Irish Prudery," p. 10. For a strong argument that it is often necessary to think in terms of national sexual cultures (as Inglis has done), see Dagmar Herzog, "Syncopated Sex: Transforming European Sexual Cultures," *American Historical Review*, vol. 114 (Dec. 2009), pp. 1287–1308. One should here mention a book that is very insightful into aspects of the post-1922 period in the 26 Counties: Diarmaid Ferriter, *Occasions of Sin. Sex and Society in Modern Ireland* (London: Profile Books, 2009). Unfortunately its discussion of 1845–1922 (pp. 11–99) is handicapped (as the author seems to realize) by the fact that he adopts as his primary theoretical framework Michel Foucault's focusing on sexual acts as "transgressive," "resistant," or "alternative" discourses against state or communal oppression. That may—just may—work for the Irish Republic in the mid-twentieth century, and certainly does for the last one-third of that century, but from the Famine to the Great War, all that Ferriter produces is Charles Stewart Parnell, James Joyce, a farmer

buggering his cow, some child-seducers, Roger Casement, prostitutes at the Curragh military camp, and urban incest. To adduce this as evidence of a pervasive subculture of transgressive and therefore subversive sexual expression would require a vivid imagination.

44   Government of the United Kingdom, *Sixty-seventh Report of the Commissioners of National Education in Ireland, for the year 1900* [Cd. 704], HC, 1901, xxi, pp. 9, 12, 13.

45   "Statements and Resolutions of the Irish Hierarchy at the Maynooth Meeting, June 21," *Irish Ecclesiastical Record*, 4th ser., vol. 27, no. 7 (Jul. 1910), p. 92.

46   D. H. Akenson, *Education and Enmity. The Control of Schooling in Northern Ireland, 1920–50* (Newton Abbot: David and Charles, for the Institute of Irish Studies, the Queen's University of Belfast, 1973), pp. 12–13.

47   Inglis, *Moral Monopoly*, p. 141.

48   For what is actually an excellent summary of the canon-law relationship of the church to the family in the late nineteenth century, see the articles relating to family life in the 1937 constitution of the 26 Counties.

49   I Corinthians 7:9.

50   The term Protestant is being used in this context to refer to Anglicans, Presbyterians, Quakers, Methodists, Baptists and all other denominations of the Reform tradition—rather than in the sense that the term was used in official documents until 1871, to refer only to the Established Church.

51   Cormac Ó Gráda, "Did Ulster Catholics always have Larger Families?," *Irish Economic and Social History*, vol. 12 (1985), pp. 79–88.

52   This would seem to be the implication of later work done by Ó Gráda and Walsh, but the whole situation is complex. Protestants seem to have take up birth control more quickly than did Catholics, but the fertility gap which opened in the post-World War I years, disappeared in the Republic of Ireland in the 1980s. It remained of significant magnitude, however, in Northern Ireland as late as the 1990s. The whole matter is complicated by the underreporting of religious affiliation in the north. See Cormac O'Grada and Brendan Walsh, "Fertility and Population in Ireland: North and South," *Population Studies*, vol. 49 (Jul. 1995), pp. 259–79.

53   "The Life and Witness of the Christian Community—Marriage and Sex," resolution no. 15, *Report ... Lambeth Conference, 1930* (London: SPCK, 1930).

54   Ó Gráda, "Did Ulster Catholics always have Larger Families?," p. 79.

55   Government of the United Kingdom, *The First Annual Report of the Registrar-General of Marriages, Births, and Deaths in Ireland* [4137], HC, 1868–69, xvi, pp. 14 and 18–21.

56   Nothing presented in this exercise is controversial. If one wishes back-up information, consult Vaughan and Fitzpatrick, *Irish Historical Statistics*, or David Fitzpatrick, "Emigration, 1871–1921," in W. E. Vaughan (ed.), *A New History of Ireland*, vol. 6, *Ireland under the Union, II, 1870–1921* (Oxford: Clarendon Press, 1996), pp. 606–52.

57   Government of the United Kingdom, *Supplement to the Forty-seventh Report of the Registrar-General in Ireland* [Cd. 7121], HC, 1914, xv, table VI, p. xiv.

58   Vaughan and Fitzpatrick, *Irish Historical Statistics*, table 16, p. 53 and table 21, p. 68.

59   Govt of UK, *Supplement to the Forty-seventh Report of the Registrar-General*, p. xiii.

60   Nationally, for 1910: urban unions had a rate of 6.4 marriages per thousand of population, rural unions 4.4 per thousand. And the urban rate of out-of-wedlock births was 3.1 per cent, while that of the rural areas was 2.3 per cent. See Govt of UK, *Supplement to the Forty-seventh Report of the Registrar-General*, table VIII, p. xv.

61   Govt of UK, *Supplement to the Forty-seventh Report of the Registrar-General*, table VIII, p. xv.

62   Vaughan and Fitzpatrick, *Irish Historical Statistics*, table 9, p. 27.

63   For the earliest relevant data, see *Census of Ireland for the Year 1861*, part 4, vol. 3 [3204-III], HC, 1863, lxi, p. 62. Two interpretive points: (1) the census table requires some arithmetical corrections and (2) it is necessary to realize that the "no occupation" category actually consisted mostly of farm labourers and cottagers.

64   Inglis, "Origins and Legacies of Irish Prudery," p. 11.

65   "Ordnance Survey Memoir of the Parish of Islandmagee," vol. 1, p. 95. (Original in the Royal Irish Academy. It has since been reprinted in somewhat abridged form by the Institute of Irish Studies, the Queen's University of Belfast.)

66   D. H. Akenson, *Between Two Revolutions. Islandmagee, County Antrim 1798–1920* (Toronto: P. D. Meany, 1979), pp. 122–23.

67   Lee, *Modernization of Irish Society*, p. 6.

68   My estimate may be too conservative. David Fitzpatrick, the only scholar who has worked seriously on cohort-depletion in the late nineteenth century (meaning the proportion from any standard age group that goes missing from Ireland between any two dates) has summarized his work for the era of emigration-culture: "The assumption that half of each cohort would depart was built into the politics of the family ..."

David Fitzpatrick, "Emigration, 1801–1921," in Michael Glazier (ed.), *The Encyclopedia of the Irish in America* (South Bend: University of Notre Dame Press, 1999), p. 262. If Fitzpatrick is right (and only a bit more than one-fifth of those who remained in the cohort married), then more than 60 per cent of those who came of age in the half-century before the First World War were not permitted to be part of the Irish system of reproduction. Fitzpatrick's cohort-depletion method is, I think, more accurate in its implications than is the inference one picks up by simply looking at the Irish worldwide and where they were living. That method, which I used in the text, tilts the picture because it includes in the Irish totals all those children below emigrating-age and thus understates the degree of biological limitation inherent in the Irish system. Thus, in the text above, as has been my practice throughout this book, I am loading any variance in the data or in its interpretation so that it reflects against my own case.

69 Kevin Danaher, "Marriage in Irish Folk Tradition," in Art Cosgrove (ed.), *Marriage in Ireland* (Dublin: College Press, 1985), pp. 99–100.

Chapter Ten

OPEN VERDICTS

ONE

There is a revealing scene in one of Walter Macken's short stories in which a young man danders along an Irish beach on a pleasant morning. He feels the eyes of passers-by on him. "What is a young fellow like that doing on the sand on a Monday morning?" he imagines them thinking. "Why isn't he working or emigrating?"[1]

One can parse that tiny lapidary text in a number of ways, of which two are relevant to our present purpose. Holistically, Macken gives us a small, but complete social system: a young man, his perception of the community that surrounds him and of its most salient attitudes, pitched on a specific geographic setting, a beach that is the boundary of one national culture and, simultaneously, the edge of the great sea avenue to the entire rest of the world.

At the other interpretive extreme, one can read it with a determined superficiality as saying that in Ireland the societally accepted determinants of a young man's life were simple: he was expected to go where the money was best; his not buying into that game would be to excise himself from the normative culture. And there is a great deal to be said for hard-edged superficiality. At the beginning of chapter four, I suggested that if one were limited to dealing only with one explanatory factor for the Great European Migration during the years 1850–1914, then projected differences in economic well-being would be the right choice. In fact, if forced to be determinatively narrow, one could go farther. As Jeffrey G. Williamson put it: "It should be stressed that late nineteenth-century mass migrations *can be explained largely by the size of the wage gaps between the sending and receiving countries*" [emphasis mine].[2] That is an extremely efficient summary of more than three decades of work by Williamson and various colleagues, notably Kevin O'Rourke and Timothy Hatton. (The major studies have been discussed in earlier chapters.)

This formulation certainly saves a lot of time and one wonders why most academic historians of migration give it, and similar recipes, a passing nod and then go on to look at other things. It is not because of technical failings. Granted, Williamson *et al.* have used the long-outdated compendium of Willcox and Ferenczi (1929)[3] for their basic migration data; and their use of urban wage differentials is less than compelling when applied to migrations that were mostly rural in origin. Those are weaknesses, but do not tip over the basic strength of their demonstration that Europeans who migrated went to places where there was more money to be had than at home. Indeed, when one takes the wage-differential model a couple of decades into the twentieth century, when southern European migrants began big-number labour visits to North America and Australasia, the model has an even tighter fit with the empirical reality.

One of the reasons that most historians of migration in the nineteenth century shy away from this model is the hubris in the way it is presented. In one corner of the academy it has become what Francis Bacon called "an idol of the tribe."[4] That idol, like most votive objects, encompasses *a* truth and, by the constant affirmation on the part of its perfervid believers, it is embraced as *the* truth. The hubris that is necessary to keep the faith intact is rather off-putting to the general run of mainline historians. And our trade often is too critical of any seemingly apodictic statement and is certainly excessively skeptical of attempts at generalized discussions of human behaviour.[5] (Pick up a recent issue of any of the first-line historical journals, read any "nuanced" or "theoretically informed" essay and try to find a statement of generalization or summary-of-results which is not so hedged about with qualifications that one has to use a corkscrew to unspiral the actual intent of the author.)

Both sides are at fault. Yet, before discussing differences, we should note what the two disciplines have in common: namely, that they both face the intractable Black Box problem. The Black Box is the human mind. No matter how much one knows about what happens before any given human decision is made and about the subsequent reportage of why the decision was made, and no matter how accurately one can assay the apparent consequences of that decision, the reason why the actual decision was made is forever unknowable. What we have is limited to observable behaviour and observable circumstances. Heaven only knows what really goes on inside the Black Box. Granted, in rare cases we have chartings of neurological patterns, but even these are merely descriptive. The causality of human decision-making is imputed by the observer. And, yes, there exist minutely detailed personal diaries kept by introspective individuals, but these are fundamentally no different from any other form of behaviour, for they only come into existence by the physical act of someone writing and then preserving that writing. Indeed, this form of behaviour, crafted as it so often is for the unseen audience of posterity, is potentially much less useful than are other, allegedly less revealing forms of behaviour. Good historians are aware of both the limits of each form of evidence and of the bigger limitation: ultimately, we are only engaged in guessing (smart guessing, one hopes) about what went into any human decision.

Part of the problem academic historians have in embracing fully Cliometric discussions of the sort engaged in by Jeffrey Williamson and confrères, concerning the Great European Migration, is epistemological in the most basic sense. Quite unconsciously, most Cliometricians' underlying framework posits effect as determining cause. That is, the data on wage differentials in the Great European Migration deals entirely with effect: people went to places where wages were higher and, mostly, earned higher wages themselves. But to present that increased-wage effect as the cause of their migration— even considered on a mass-data scale—requires just a bit more rhetorical modesty (such as the recognition that other variables could be primary for many individuals) and a lot more historical context than usually is provided. Most mainline historians would demand a good deal of probatively strong material on motive-for-leaving, in the form of data that is independent of the final measure of effect, before asserting that an accounting calculation concerning relative wage rates was why the Great European Migration took place. And, for the most part, the Cliometricians are deeply allergic to the hard graft of finding and evaluating the myriad primary sources that are productive of independent information on the motives for leaving.[6] Of course, no one left home and ventured into strange lands simply to make less money. Yet it was altogether possible for migrants to leave home searching for a *mélange* of desiderata and to achieve several of them, of which only one was higher wages.

Thus, the Williamson *et al.* model is viewed with skepticism by mainline historians because *it seems to adopt the simple logical error that the consequences of a decision is the cause of that decision.* As a small example of the way this error in thought can affect the historical study of migration, take the fictive case of an Irish milliner who in 1870 migrates from Dublin to New York City. Before leaving, she has been beaten twice or more weekly by her husband and recently he has been threatening to kill her. So, despite her fear of starting life over in a strange world, she escapes, sets up a small milliner's shop in Brooklyn and eventually becomes a fashionable women's clothier. She had left Ireland because of a vicious domestic situation, but because she fortuitously had improved her economic lot in the dominant econometric literature she is designated as having migrated for reasons of wage improvement.[7]

Why, then, do I still believe in the high value of the work of econometric historians in their dealing with the Great European Migration? It is, firstly, because in the period in which there are systematic data they show with immense analytic power the commonalities found among large, very large, numbers of instances of human behaviour. And, secondly, because whatever the expressive failings of many econometricians (words fail many of them, literally) and despite the unreflective epistemology of some, those deficits can be dealt with by bringing the econometric material into the larger matrix of wide-lens historical research. We gain an awful lot by paying attention.

If there is a Prime Directive for dealing with the Great European Migration, it is the imperative for humility and for continual puzzlement. This has a long and distinguished intellectual pedigree. It goes back roughly 2,500 years when Heraclitus of Ephesus recognized the unbridgeable reality that limits all of humanity's observations of itself. *Everything is in constant flux and movement ... nothing is abiding. When I step into the river for the second time, neither I nor the river are the same.*[8] If Heraclitus's observation is correct, then it follows (1) that all generalized historical explanations are transient, for they splash about in the same ever-moving river as does any pattern of thought; and (2) that individual human memory—take a personal memoir as an example—is itself forever inaccurate, because of the simple impossibility of the author's exact re-entry into the flowing river of time. Embracing these cruel realities is not something historians enjoy, but doing so reduces the temptation to intellectual hubris by reminding us how transient and fragile any historical explanation actually is.

So too does the principle of complementarity, which demands that we accept the daunting fact that two (or more) divergent perceptions may be simultaneously true. Vexingly: equally true, but impossible to express in a single explanatory system.

The Great European Migration of the "true nineteenth century" must be understood as a generalized experience that was part of a cultural-social swirl that involved large numbers of individuals over a big swatch of time and space. Thus, it was a communal experience, shared in its main outlines across cultures and linguistic groups. And this commonality was a fact that the people of the time understood, even if later nationalistic historians forgot. To put it tangibly: anyone, from any nation, who passed through the nexus of the port of Liverpool, as did most Irish and Swedish transatlantic migrants, learned of the commonality of the migration experience.

Yet, each of these migration-events was also individual. In cases where enough documentation has been left to us, the historian can construct an explanation for a set of personal migration decisions that is equally as strong as is the explanation-from-large-numbers. Indeed, case studies are often probatively stronger than are mass generalizations, because they are able to be more precisely anchored in specific contexts of class, religion, family structure and culture. So, as historians, we need to keep both of the main sorts of depiction—generalization and individual agency—in our story simultaneously. A difficult job.

This brings to mind a fascinating piece of nineteenth-century drawing-room entertainment. It was provided by an ingenious little machine, a variant of the stereoscope, called a "thingumatrope." (Spellings vary, as they should with such an eccentric device.) It consisted of two separate images and a spindle that made the images revolve.[9] As the speed of the device increased, the two separate images, though still viewed individually, were merged by the wonderful perceptual apparatus of the human brain and made into one complete picture.

That, in migration studies is our job, to see simultaneously the collective and the individual; and to recognize both the integrity of individual agency and the power of society-wide cultural systems.

TWO

In earlier chapters, I suggested that both Sweden and Ireland experienced an early nineteenth-century pioneering stage of out-migration, followed in each case by a period of axial stress; and then by an era of emigration-culture in which each society redefined where it fitted in the world's geography and, most importantly, what the possible futures were for the nation's children. The distance in existential time between, say, 1840 and 1860 for Everyman living in Ireland, and between, say, 1860 and 1880 in Sweden, was a quick-fled century or more. They passed rapidly from an old world into a new, albeit one not necessarily better. For largely agricultural societies, in which change traditionally had been incremental, the quantum jump and torque of the societies moving from the periphery of Europe to the main sea lanes of the transoceanic world was massive.

Yet, while as historians we try to retrospect ourselves empathetically into their trans-formational mental experience, we should at the same time recognize that, in the long view, a great deal about out-migration and about the emigrants changed only partially between the later pioneer period, the time of axial stress, and the period of emigration-culture. These continuities are as much a reality as are the variations: just less dramatic and harder to document.

For example, at the simplest level, choices of destinations for out-migrants were quite stable over time. If one takes the pattern of Irish emigration at the year 1848 (when the USA decisively replaced Canada as the first choice) and the pattern of Swedish migration at the year 1868 (when the spate began full-flow), not a great deal alters before World War I in terms of the big picture. The Swedes continue to go towards inland North America (to the very cheap land the Homestead Act had opened in the American Midwest in 1862) or, alternately, engage in labour-migration to nearby European countries. The Irish chose the USA first, then Great Britain, and then various dominions or colonies of the British Empire, and that pattern continued.[10] Of course the filigree is fascinating, both as regards the character of the out-going population and the evolution of their preferred destinations; yet the overall pattern changed only slowly and certain minority phenomena changed only very, very slowly. These are often nudged aside when the big story is told. We should not lose sight of such things as: the Free Church population in Sweden continued to be over-represented in the emigration stream (more of that later); the permanent presence of Irish Protestants as a major component of the post-Famine migrant flow (roughly one-fifth or more);[11] and that seasonal work-migration to Great Britain continued well into the twentieth century. It was replaced by a form of "seasonal migration" that now lasted for two or three years, not two or three months. But temporary it was, despite the way it was tallied in the UK censuses.[12] There is no conflict between the picture of sophisticated adjustment between international labour supply and demand that is characteristic of the era of emigration-culture and the continued influence of the patterns set earlier in the pre-Famine and pre-Deprivation periods by those who in those earlier times left their homelands. We might well think of the earlier migrants as much as researchers as pioneers. And as researchers, they did their work extremely well.[13]

THREE

There was, I believe, a qualitative aspect of the Swedish and Irish migration patterns that is just as real as is the quantitative picture, and it is here that a whole series of open verdicts must be recognized. After the Famine and after the Deprivation, Irish and Swedish migrants indeed were more responsive to economic factors than they previously had been—that is a fundamental part of the emigration-culture which in each country replaced the limpet-like stay-at-home predilections of the pre-Famine and pre-Deprivation populaces. Yet, when one tries to grasp motive in real people, not humans as economic aggregates, one feels as if one is trying to grasp a handful of cloud. Usually the motives of the average migrant were either contradictory in the vexingly paradoxical way that almost all human motives are. Most people, when one learns much about them, seem often to be at an angular relationship with themselves, wanting one thing, but often doing another. Yes, one can grant that from the end of the Famine and of the Deprivation, migrants were no longer simply fleeing hardship, but were taking the time to do some shrewd economic calculations: hence, the compelling data on their going places where wages were better. Nevertheless, when one encounters individual lives and finds evidence of motive, it very often is expressed both in terms of tangible and of intangible benefits. Making more money and reducing the risk-quotient in everyday life were important; yet, the tangible improvements in life's standards were part of something rather larger: an enhanced status as individual human beings.

This cannot be proven (by me or by anyone), but instantiation is not hard to find. To take an accessible set of examples, Swedish government officials in conducting their massive emigration investigation, 1907–13, made the quite sensible decision to contact

Swedish-born persons who had left the country and asked them why they left and how it all had worked out. These fill half of a densely printed 260-plus-page volume and are an example of how sometimes doing something merely sensible produces a result that is quite wonderful. (Sadly, this common-sense approach was not adopted by the Irish government when it conducted a major study of emigration in the late 1940s and 1950s.)

The easiest way to think about what the Swedish Emigration Commission did is to imagine that you have been given a full-time job teaching at a community college for adult learners. Your task for the year is to teach several sections of a course in life-writing; by the end of the year, you are to have each of your 400-plus students produce a thoughtful and honest memoir of how they themselves got here (wherever that is) and what this shows about how the world works. The results are at first sight disappointing: two out of three are so off-topic or semi-literate that they need a heavy rewrite or, mercifully, binning. As for the rest, even after a full year of tutoring, some of your students will barely be able to muster 500 words; yet others will write a memoir the size of a novella; and still others will surround their own life-stories with observations that are reflective, shrewd, resentful, self-pitying and stoic in about equal measure. Now, that big stack of final papers is similar to what Sweden's Emigration Commission elicited as a soft-data summation of the era of emigration-culture, an unapologetic parallel to the masses of hard statistical data that it also generated. What the commission did was to advertise widely in Swedish-American newspapers for responses to a large question— "what have been the causes of the Great Emigration from Sweden?" and then, effectively, "how does your own life-history fit into that pattern?" One hundred and nineteen of the respondents' answers were then collated and published as part of the 20 research appendices to the emigration report.[14] One does not need to be a cynic to reckon that the published versions of the life-narratives were open to all sorts of potential biases. The most damaging was the underrepresentation of women emigrants. There is no question that we are reading a government-financed publication and that editing took place along a number of axes.[15]

But before going all righteous on the matter of methodological purity, ask whether or not several score life-narratives written by Irish migrants at a single period in the era of emigration-culture, say in 1910, might not help us to understand better how their world was shaped and how they navigated it? If only we had an Irish exercise to lay besides the Swedish one.

The stack of emigrant life-narratives was arranged by the commission in the order of the birth-date of the émigré (the earliest was born in 1828) and this was roughly the order of their emigration. Only two of the migrants had taken themselves out of Sweden before the Deprivation; seven during it. If one reads the memoirs in their published order, one gains a layer-by-layer picture of the outflow in terms that are specific to each individual. The memoirists often generalize about emigration, but it is always about a phenomenon they have themselves been through as participants, not merely as observers. The self-biographies of the older emigrants often are incredibly rich in their detail and thoughtful in reflections on the whole matter of Swedish transoceanic migration.

The one motif that runs through every life story is this: work counts. Almost everyone uses successive forms of employment as the metre stick by which time is measured. To some degree, this is a result of the way the Emigration Commission asked for information, but there is more to it than that. Except for a few who had simply pulled up stakes and went a-roaming, these people understood that their own lives necessitated a series of economic quests: for many of them, there were more important things in life, but there was no life without the economic quest. A somewhat jaded, but very successful farmer-cum-US government employee surveyed the various reasons for emigration from Sweden and then pronounced. 'I believe that 90 per cent of the emigrants travel here for economic reasons. Were there prospects for their own home and livelihood in Sweden, then emigration would stop all by itself."[16] An early-twentieth-century migrant, a man with a clearly expressed affection for Sweden, explained that he had left because it was an economic dead-end. He had no chance whatsoever of owning his own farm and so he left for the USA, though reckoning it was "the lesser of two evils."[17] That rural-formed decision is typical: since it was only in the last five years before World War I that migrants from urban areas equalled in number those from the countryside,[18] the matter of urban wage differentials between Sweden and North America should not be calibrated too finely. Most of the potential migrants in the period of the emigration-culture viewed the river of information they received from overseas through the broad and grainy perceptual aperture of rural poverty.

"Mother Sweden can be compared to a mother who has had too many children; she is too poor to clothe and feed them," was the poetic way a Wisconsin farmer, originally from Dalarna, summarized the entire Swedish emigration-culture.[19] The depth of poverty and the brutish labour conditions it produced are hard to fathom in our own time. What does one make of the children of torpare who commonly began full-time employment (or, too often, full-time underemployment) as early as age ten or twelve, under terms that frequently required work from 5 AM to 8 PM, or an equivalent amount of time?[20] The memory of these experiences clearly affected many out-migrants for the rest of their lives. Mention of large families—six to eight siblings being common—is frequent, and one understands why the parents had to set their children to labour. One matter that comes through with clarity is confirmation of the point argued in chapter eight, that the class of small landowners and especially the customal renters (torpare) who paid most of their rent in labour, was diminishing noticeably: some rose on the social scale, but those represented in these life-narratives were part of the class fragment that was often trapped—"one who starts out as a day-labourer [literally, day-churl] usually ends up as a day-labourer"[21]— and, frequently immiserated. Consequently, many of their offspring left Sweden.[22]

All that is very general. What is most fascinating to me in the bundle of life-narratives is (1) the indications of actual moments-of-decision to emigrate and (2) the clear statements that money was not the whole picture and that the migrants had been influenced, often strongly, by non-financial factors.

Consider first the moment-of-decision, the catalytic instant when potential emigration (always on the menu of life-possibilities in the half-century before World War I) became actual. These moments often are beautifully basic. For example, several of the self-biographies contain the memory of a cathartic take-this-job-and-shove-it event. Thus: a sail-making apprentice in Småland, working from 5 AM each day in a 12' x 12' room with five other apprentices and six journeymen, had a very bad day. For whatever reason, his boss returned from the midday meal and, dissatisfied with the work completed, took a darning-last and thumped the apprentice. The apprentice took up the same tool and bashed the master and in an ensuing mêlée was badly beaten up by the journeymen. That night he went to his father who told him to "Go back and tell them that you don't work there anymore; and I'll be up in the morning." The articles of apprenticeship were dissolved and the day after that the young man was on a ship for Germany and the start of a world-roaming career.[23] A quieter epiphany occurred to a 30-year-old day labourer who tried with a couple of his fellow day labourers to sublet some land instead of doing day-work. The land-holder told them that his practice wouldn't run to such a measure. And from that day onward, the day labourer set his mind on going to America.[24]

Some emigration decisions were those of necessity crystallized as opportunity. A Skaraborg lad at age 13 was taken by a bone disease that resulted in his being sent to a lasarett and having both legs amputated. Almost miraculously for the time, he survived and regained health and got a job with a bootmaker. He could barely make enough to support himself, however. So, he decided there was no future in Sweden, went to Canada and subsequently owned a shop and boarding house in Chicago.[25] Rather less dramatic were the blocked careers that decided theologically inclined young people to leave Sweden and try the New World. Five of the life-biographies related that poverty, sickness and (in one case) reservations about the Swedish Established Church, resulted in their following their spiritual vocation by completing their education in the USA and being ordained in the Augustana Synod form of Lutheranism in the new country.[26]

Massive amounts of pro-emigration propaganda floated around the countryside in the last quarter of the nineteenth century (and, actually, quite a bit of anti-emigration material), and of course it had an effect. One admires the simple candour of a Skåne respondent who explained. "I got a hold of a book and read about America and so I got what they call America-Fever."[27] The very simplicity of the explanation for a major life-decision gives authenticity. One suspects that thousands and thousands of emigrants made one of the most important decisions in their lives on the basis of social contagion, the fever of fashion gone viral.

In the collection of life-narratives, far and away the most common enabling influence was family: usually family members who sent tickets or money from the far side of the Atlantic, and that represents the pattern in Sweden throughout the era of emigration-culture. This transatlantic family aid can be fairly quantified, and is discussed later. Here the interesting thing is to watch internal family dynamics on their own, as they lead a potential migrant to turn possibility into reality. An 1880 emigrant recalled that after the visit of an uncle back from America, nothing would keep him from going to America.[28] An extended-family-conversation-cum-negotiation catalysed the out-migration in the summer of 1870 of a young man and his father from Kronobergs län. He, his brother and his father worked intensively three stone-pocked acres and had always had a hard time making a go of things: previously, the father had to work as a labour-migrant in Denmark and the older brother in Germany. One day in 1870, the young man and his father were helping the father's brother work on his cowshed and the father blurted out, "Brother Anders-Daniel, help me get to America!"

"Dear one, I can't do that. I don't have any money."

"All that I want is that you go surety for me."

"I'll do it."

And soon thereafter the young man and his father were on the boat.[29]

A lovely, if morally spavined family arabesque, comes from the life-narrative of the man whom I mentioned earlier had provided the formulation that 90 per cent of all Swedish emigration was for economic reasons. He was a large land-owner's son (four thousand acres in woodland, but only five acres of crops) and had a secondary school education to age 15. He was, he says in his memoir, quite satisfied with the religious and political scene in the homeland and was convinced that Sweden had the best system of government in the world. It was his mother, he recalls, who most contributed to his decision to emigrate. Over the will of her husband, she convinced her darling son to escape the life of the northern Swedish woodlands, which she described as being permanent serfdom. So, barely age 18, he arrived in Duluth, Minnesota and after a few years' farm and carpentry work, in May 1877 took himself to Rapid City in the Dakota Territory. This was not long after General Custer's bad day and the subsequent suppression of the Sioux. Among other profitable employments (architect, mechanical and civil engineer), our man became deputy state surveyor. He did quite well out of the seizure of native lands: a 1,600-acre ranch, which he reported was fully stocked with cattle and modern machinery, plus some town properties and $3,000 in the bank. He had no debts, he said proudly. And apparently no guilt, for he had done what his mother wanted: although he had helped to visit thralldom upon the indigene, he had indeed escaped it for himself.[30]

Every single one of the life-narratives in the collection formed by Sweden's Emigration Commission could be granted factual accuracy, but nevertheless questioned for emotional veracity. After all, the individual stories were written following the events that led to the writers' out-migration from Sweden and there is such a thing as retrospected memory. But, then, it is rather difficult to ask someone to remember an event before it actually happens. Assuming one does not take skepticism to the point of parody, one of the things that gives the collection as a whole a texture of believability is the way so many of the memoirists intermingle their own self-biographies with observations concerning the general reasons for the Swedish outflow in the era of emigration-culture. This congeries of complaint is remarkably consistent over the body of the 119 self-biographies; and the discontent is interlaced with expressions of affection for Sweden as a land, and for the Swedish as a folk, in exactly the sort of mixed emotion one gets in people who are being honest with themselves. The migrants' sense of being somehow cheated comes down to a phrase perfectly expressed by Robert L. Wright in his collection of Swedish emigrant ballads. Of course money counted, but "all dreams were not of wealth," Wright observed. "*Some concerned the size of the shadow cast by a man*" [emphasis mine].[31]

In the view of the writers of the emigrant life-narratives, there were three collar-rasping, unnecessarily humiliating limits on a man's shadow in Swedish society in the period of the emigration-culture: a social structure so stiff as to nearly exhibit post-mortem rigor; a political system representative excessively of privilege, and a state church whose professional administrators were irritatingly officious even towards their most obedient adherents.[32] (All this is their view, not necessarily reality.)

Examples of the first category of intangible-deprivation (intangible because they are not talking about lack of wages, but lack of respect), are not complex. "The upper classes scorn manual labour and its practicioners," was one of the four basic reasons that was listed by one memoirist for the high level of Swedish emigration.[33] In a long response, one near-60-year-old from Kalmar län became rhetorical. "Another thing, how has the aristocratic element in so-aristocratic Sweden treated and used the simple and homely, but honourable, upright and industrious country people, the folk that now one wants to keep at home?"[34] He followed his query with examples of how clergy and priests were often so forbidding that the lower classes did not dare go near them. This man had been back to Sweden twice since leaving in 1868 and he admitted that things were getting better, but then ended with a now well-known statement. "Here [in America] we have rich men; here we have bosses; here we have clever men; here we have straw-bosses who may work us like dogs—but *masters* we have none."[35] That last statement indicates a conundrum: did the writer (and those like him) acquire his resentment of the Swedish class system before he left or was it mostly the product of attitudes picked up after migration? Given the ubiquity of pro-emigration propaganda and also of letters back to Sweden, a contagion-effect almost certainly heightened sensitivity to social-class rigidity. The vision of America was a lens that magnified any imperfections the potential migrant saw or felt concerning Swedish society.[36]

A similar puzzlement holds for the frequently expressed opinion in the collection of life-narratives that excessive political inequality was a contributory cause of high emigration. Undeniably, the USA from the end of the Civil War onwards possessed a wider system of representative government at every level—from federal down to the parish/township level—than did Sweden. The Swedish Riksdag was reshaped from the seventeenth-century system of four "Estates" into a bicameral structure only in 1867. The franchise was extended for males in 1907 so that the electorate rose from 9.5 per cent to 19 per cent of the whole adult population, and in 1918 almost universal adult suffrage was granted.[37] Now, the keenness for political equality was one of the general characteristics of the early Swedish emigrants: they were strongly anti-slavery, joined the Union army in surprising numbers, viewed Abraham Lincoln as something close to the fourth member of the Trinity, and became overwhelmingly Republican in politics. (In these matters lies much of their subsequent distance in American life from the Irish Catholic immigrants to the USA.) When an emigrant wrote in his memoir that "I am a citizen of the United States and when I vote it is worth as much as the vote of a millionaire," he was talking more about the New World than remembering accurately how he had felt in the Old.[38] Still, there were more reflective views, ones that suggested that a greater civic involvement would have ameliorated some of the class hostility of Swedish society and reduced the sense of exclusion from power of the majority of the population.[39] This granted, it appears that political equality was a desideratum more frequently of significance to the later migrants than to those of the 1870s and 1880s.[40]

Surprisingly, the item that runs through the collection of Swedish life-narratives with the most plangency is the matter of the state church. Complaints about it seemed to tie together the other grievances. This is surprising, because only five of the memoirists were Baptists; in fact, almost everyone else had been at least a nominal member of the Established Church and yet, right alongside social snobbery, it was the (non-economic) reason for emigration that was most often mentioned. I suspect what one is hearing is the equivalent of a big lint-brush of grievance: because church officials were also governmental officials, they were an obvious focus of vexation at bureaucracy; because they were members of the ruling classes (however marginally in some cases), they were resented for imputed snobbery; and no one enjoyed paying taxes to local officials even if they claimed to be God's vicars on earth. So, the church was a constantly chafing collar. Except for extreme Free Church adherents, the state church was not the sole cause of many individuals leaving Sweden, but it was the cartoon-like embodiment of much that most vexed men and women who had been raised in an emigration-culture, the sort of irritant that tipped their decisions towards leaving. In a notably unspiritual, but revealing, fashion, a Malmöhus emigrant noted that religious freedom in America meant that he was not forced to pay the salary of a state clergy, but could put as much, or as little, in the offering plate as he wished.[41] That fairly summarizes the populace's relationship with an Erastian church.[42]

Earlier I suggested that we should be sensitive to continuities that bridged the great axial rift in Swedish and Irish societies before the pre-emigration period and the era of emigration-culture. In Sweden one tendril of such continuity was that Baptists especially (and Free Church adherents in general) were still over-represented in the outflow from Sweden. This cannot be proven comprehensively because the Swedish government did not retain out-migration records according to religion, although they had the basic data in their local records: one suspects that the tendency of Free Church adherents to get away from Sweden was sufficiently embarrassing to church and state so as to induce archival amnesia on this issue. The Baptists in the collection of life-narratives were pungent in their commentary, but too small in number to make an evidentiary splash.[43] And, in compiling his final report for the Emigration Commission, Gustav Sundbärg accepted that, in addition to economics, the desire for "the pure way of life" (a Baptist phrase for escaping the state church) had motivated some emigrants;[44] but he localized the effect of religion to the 1860s.[45] Fortunately, the historian of the Baptists in the USA, A. G. Hall, compiled an annual tally (through the mid-1890s) of the total numbers of Baptists in Sweden and of those who emigrated.[46] When compared with the national emigration rate,[47] this showed that Baptists had a higher propensity to migrate than did the general population, 1869–95, with the exception of 1875 and 1876 when the 1873 relaxation of religious pressures was being tested. In most years, the Baptists' rate of out-migration was two to three times that of the general population, too high to be ascribed solely to socio-economic factors. One is dealing (as with other Free Church groups) with people who were on a mission based on the belief that in leaving the rule of the state church behind them they would obtain effectually what they asked faithfully.[48]

In themselves, the Baptists are not of great moment—perhaps ten thousand transoceanic migrants in the last three decades of the nineteenth century[49]—but they are a solid instantiation of a wider phenomenon. This is that *given a reasonable assurance of economic success*, potential migrants often left for reasons that were cultural, not material, and often were anchored in values and beliefs concerning intangible benefits to be found in the New Land.[50]

This formulation, illustrated here chiefly by the collection of life-narratives collected by Sweden's Emigration Commission is, I believe, metonymic of a wider situation characteristic of most of the Great European Migration of the nineteenth century. We have (1) accepted that the most widely documentable probable cause of migration was economic; and (2) also have granted that a lot of men and women left for overseas for reasons that were personal and idiosyncratic, and sometimes frivolous: a fight with a boss, being dumped by a lover, getting in trouble with the law and just plain being bored to death. But (3) we have illustrated that any interpretation of the Great Migration which does not take into account non-tangible matters—no matter how hard they may be to define operationally—is reductive to the point of volitional ignorance. The truism that people migrate for a better life is merely silly if a better life is defined solely in economic terms.

The verdict that one must leave open in this debate is the assessment of the power and valence in any given historical society (or class, or religious body, or ethnic group) of the preference for being better off in material terms or better off in terms of non-tangible self worth—*the size of the shadow cast by a man.*

FOUR

If there is a single question that I would like to know the answer to, it is this: what did the mechanics of the Great European Migration do to families? Not the obvious things, such as removing members from the family hearth, but rather how was the shape of the family in certain societies twisted and stretched, rather like the malleable surfaces that topologists deal with? In the cases of Ireland and of Sweden, one must be impressed with the way many families and kinship groups were able to stretch, sometimes the world around. In recent years, historians who work with emigrant correspondence have become more and more aware both of the tensile strength and the plasticity of links in some families. My own eyes were opened to this when working through correspondence of the Australia-New Zealand Irish and being struck by how well-informed family members at home were about their relatives abroad. The enlightening case to me was the Quinns, a Falls Road, Belfast family who carried on a triangular flow of information as between the family in Belfast and two brothers, one an underground mine manager in Australia who retired in New Zealand; and the other a gum digger, general bush-man and heavy drinker in New Zealand. The perhaps-mythical power of the Irish Mother showed clearly here, for brother William took to tattling on his hard-living brother to Mother, who was clearly still She Who Must be Pleased.[51] From such cases, one becomes aware that although many men and women were lost forever to the homeland, a counter-theme emerges: the amazing degree to which some families kept in contact with each other. This meant, among other things, that in some ways the people we think of as isolated inhabitants of the European periphery actually had a remarkably cosmopolitan sense of world geography, not as an empty map, but as a series of sites where their family, kin, friends, acquaintances lived. From his immersion in the study of the Dalarna-Minnesota migration, Robert Ostergren came to the conclusion that "by the time the exodus finally ceased, nearly every Swede could claim to know someone in America."[52]

The simplest way to show the continuity of contact—without in any way judging its intensity or emotional robustness[53]—is to note the flow of mail.[54] Nothing mysterious here: each letter was a unit of information sent through intentional action by one human being to another. Sune Åkerman stated that "we know that in the 1880s about 500,000 letters reached Sweden from North America every year."[55] In 1883, a Swedish journalist waxed poetic: he said that "Thousands, millions of such letters fall like flakes from a snow cloud over the entire land from Skåne to Lapland."[56] The letter-flow to Ireland was probably at least twice as large as that to Sweden—a reasonable estimate for 1854 was that more than one million letters were sent to Ireland from the USA alone, never mind other countries.[57] (Actually, there is a small mystery here—why have so relatively few of the Irish migrant letters survived, as compared to the Swedish ones—but that is a side issue.)[58]

A common and accurate observation is that after the Famine and after the Deprivation, emigrants were mostly young and unmarried. For example, as table 7.3 in an earlier chapter indicated, in the 1890s, 60 per cent of the Irish emigrants and 50 per cent of the Swedish emigrants were in the 15–24 age group and they were leaving before the usual marriage age in their respective societies. From an evidentiary point of view, it is worth noting that as far as Ireland is concerned, the assertion that the majority of emigrants were unmarried cannot be based on direct data: but the circumstantial evidence is compelling, mainly the age-data and the number of marriages reported by the Registrar-General and, for Sweden, these are the direct data:[59]

Unmarried persons in total emigration (including children).

Period	Migrants to Europe (%)	Transoceanic migrants (%)	All destinations (%)
1871–80	74.7	57.8	63.3
1881–90	73.2	63.1	64.5
1891–1900	66.8	70.6	70.0
1901–08	61.4	74.0	72.3

Sweden, and especially Ireland, were unusual in the proportion of women (mostly young women) in the flow. This was the Swedish situation:[60]

Females in Swedish out-migration.

Period	Migrants to Europe (%)	Transoceanic migrants (%)	All destinations (%)
1871–80	47.1%	43.2%	44.4%
1881–90	52.9	43.7	45.0
1891–1900	57.3	47.6	49.2
1900–08	55.8	42.8	44.5

For Ireland the proportion of females was even more noteworthy:[61]

Females in Irish out-migration to all destinations.

Period	Percentage
1852–60	48.8
1861–70	44.7
1871–80	45.1
1881–90	48.7
1891–1900	53.5
1901–10	50.2

For comparison, note that in the years 1906–10, migrants from all national groups into the USA were only slightly more than 30 per cent female.[62] For the Swedish and Irish migrants, the reasonably balanced sex-ratio of their emigrants meant that in most places where they settled, potential marital partners could be found within the ethnic group.[63]

In any case, the key interpretive point is not to see these young men and women as so many atomistic particles. Actually, the various New Worlds, which once had been a frightening void, now were sprinkled with brothers and sisters, cousins and other people from the old home parish. Potential spouses of similar backgrounds were there for both Swedish and Irish persons. Leaving home indeed was a wrenching decision, and homesickness often an achingly real illness of the heart for these young people, but the reality of the extended-family support networks must be recognized.

The density of the flow of letters from previous migrants suggests the reality of continuing contact with home and with base identity in the Old World. The frequency of transoceanic passages being prepaid by those who went before confirms the continuing strength of family ties. Thus, to take a representative sample, of the Swedish out-migrants in 1883–85 on the ten largest shipping lines, somewhat over half travelled on prepaid tickets.[64] The Irish figures were higher: in 1868 the amount of prepaid passages was enough to pay for 75 per cent of the emigrants, at least if somewhat spongy data are trustworthy. The most common transaction was the support of a brother or sister's emigration, although spouses sometimes sent money to bring their partners over. The flow of funds in general was from men to women.[65] More trustworthy data, for 1904–15, indicate that in that period one-third of all Irish passengers who travelled steerage to the United States did so on tickets prepaid stateside.[66] In the usual case these were paid for by family members, but sometimes a family member would broker a ticket from a future employer of the potential emigrant. (This was more often the case with young girls going into domestic service than among any other group.) We need not assume that these passages were a free gift—one suspects that cousins usually wanted payback, and that brothers and sisters may have done so as well. But the systemic and familial nature of the transactions is noteworthy.

The tensile strength of both the Swedish and the Irish bonding to their parents in the homeland is further indicated by the level of remittances: meaning money sent home that could be used for any purpose, unlike prepaid tickets. These monies may have been employed to send yet another family member overseas, but could just as well pay the rent or buy a heifer. The totals sent are quite astounding. A study of American banks revealed that in 1882 nearly $3 million was sent to the Swedish homeland. That is roughly $15 per head for each Swedish-born person in the USA, including children and other dependents.[67] To go somewhat outside our usual timeline, it is worth noting that the average annual sum for the years 1922–27 was $9.45 million: old-age pensions paid by the Swedish government (which had been introduced in 1913) were almost equalled in total amount annually by the remittances from North America.[68] The Irish figures were similar, although slightly harder to grab accurately, as remittances to Ireland were tallied as part of the flow of remittances to the entire United Kingdom.[69] Cormac Ó Gráda estimates that the Irish receipts for 1907 were about $15 million from all remittance sources, meaning about $11 sent for each Irish-born person in the United States.[70] This total amount was equal to 2–3 per cent of Irish national income on the eve of World War I.[71]

Each of the items I have mentioned—the flow of letters, the high level of prepaid passages, the stream of remittances and the gender-balanced emigration—can be taken as indicating both strength and plasticity in family patterns on the part of Swedish and Irish societies. If that is the case, why then would I suggest that the entire matter of evolving transnational family patterns is of necessity a case that leads to an open verdict? Not because we do not have enough data to draw some conclusions: of course historians never have enough information to be absolutely 100 per cent sure about anything, but to hide behind that fact is simply to hide, an occupational disease that really should be resisted. No, the reason I am positing an open verdict is that *almost everything we know about the Swedish and the Irish family in the era of emigration-culture has a double meaning.* The very plasticity of the emigrant family structures is the problem. A transnational social network that is stretched and twisted so forcibly as that of Sweden and of Ireland develops big holes and rips. People drop right out; and what looks like admirable flexibility in familial arrangements that span oceans often conceals creases that pinch and sometimes irrevocably injure individuals.

The existence of holes in the fabric is well documented by Ruth-Ann Harris who spent a decade or more collecting Irish missing-persons advertisements in the *Boston Pilot*, a leading Irish Catholic newspaper. These were small ads, and it was usual to have a column given over at least weekly to attempts to pleas for help in getting in touch with someone, most often on the part of a relative in Ireland or in North America, but sometimes by lawyers in Ireland who needed a signature for property transfer or for inheritances. The standard advertisement gave name and age, home parish, where the person was last known to have been, and often a wrenching short plea from a brother or sister or parent for any information.[72] Much the same project could be done for Swedish-American newspapers. As any historian knows, the most elusive pieces of evidence to uncover are those that indicate a lack of something. The useful aspects of all those small advertisements, all those indications of families that had lost trace of each other, is that they help just slightly to overcome the way that the evidentiary table is tipped—emigrant letters, remittances, prepaid tickets all testify to continuing functioning family ties. When the ties snap, however, the usual case is that they leave nothing behind, not even a smudge on history's great wall. Sometimes people drop into the gone-missing category because of illness, drink, economic failure, and sometimes because they really had no more use for their relatives and family. Necessarily, one has to multiply by some unknown exponent the relatively few cases we do discover, such as the long run of information in the *Boston Pilot* that yields positive evidence of tattering in the fabric of family.

Another indication that family ties were not quite so gloriously strong for either the Irish or the Swedish folk was the (apparently) low proportion of emigrants who decided to come home.[73] "Return-migration"—also called "reverse-migration" and "re-migration" in some studies—is the very devil of migration history and for the Great European Migration it is a special problem. Nobody, no nation during the Great Migration, no scholar since then, has gotten even one country's nineteenth and early twentieth century's actual return-migration defined solidly, and I doubt it if ever can be done.[74] Instead of actual return-migration rates, we must settle for *proxy return-migration rates.* This is useful as long as the rates are labelled clearly as proxies, not the real thing (they rarely are) and are calculated sensibly (they sometimes are). The only time a realistic set of proxies covering several European countries becomes possible is at the very end of what we have denominated as the Great European Migration, the years just before World War I, and even then the data only involve migrants to the USA and return-migration from there.

In 1907 US officials began collecting information not only on people coming into the United States on a permanent basis, but also on those who upon leaving stated that they were going away permanently. The most sensible (and ingenious and clearly labelled) way of dealing with this material has been that of J. D. Gould who reworked the USA data by introducing one major piece of exogenous information specific to the early twentieth century: that the average period of stay in the USA for "temporary European migrants" (meaning those who did not remain permanently, whatever their original intention) was about four years.[75] Gould then lagged the earliest US immigrants-return data, covering the years 1907–14, and compared it with the US permanent in-migrant data for 1904–11 (while keeping tourists, business visitors etc., out of the equation). His results give a Proxy Return Migration Rate (which he called a "repatriant ratio") whose highlights are as follows:[76]

Country	Proxy Return Migration Rate (%)
Bulgaria/Serbia-Montenegro	68.5
Greece	63.4
Italy	57.9
Germany	21.7
Scotland	13.1
England	11.6
Sweden	9.6
Norway	6.7
Ireland	6.3
Wales	–1.4

Two comments. All of these proxy rates were higher than they (almost certainly) would have been a decade earlier, because in 1907–08 the US was in an economic recession. Second, even the lower pre-1907 rate seems to have been following a previous jump in 1893–94, related to the US economic crisis of 1893. Where things were before 1890, much less where they were in 1870, is purely speculative, but certainly they were markedly lower for both Sweden and Ireland. My own guess is that the Proxy Return Migration Rates (using Gould's method) were not above five per cent for either country before 1890, and lower still before 1870. After 1890, as Sweden industrialized, labour migrants began to treat North America as just another stop on the itinerary of job sites, and the proportion making the circuit back to Sweden certainly rose, to ten per cent or above.[77] Mind you, that is for the proxy rate.[78] One still longs for real data on the simple questions, such as "where did the men and women who left Ireland and Sweden in the year 1870 spend the last days of their lives?"[79]

What comes out of the fog of the information on return-migration is the fact that no one has seriously disputed that neither Irish nor Swedish transoceanic migrants very often returned home permanently before the 1890s.[80]

To return to the matter of remittances, two questions linger. The first of these is: did the monies sent home by emigrants ultimately hurt the people at home—and is the answer the same for both counties? Concerning Ireland, David Fitzpatrick has suggested that "the twin effects of emigration were to ameliorate poverty in the short term, and to discourage radical economic and social transformation by facilitating the maintenance of large families, small farms and other 'archaic' but homely elements of Irish life."[81] And that, although there may have been some economic benefits to the agrarian structure, on balance emigration "placed severe constraints on agricultural development."[82] The strength of this argument is not clear concerning emigration as a general phenomenon (would a markedly larger rural population really have helped agricultural development?), but it has a certain remorseless realism concerning remittances sent home by emigrants. That is: the monies sent to parents on small farms allowed them to pay the rent and keep on with their mode of life; whereas if there had been no remittances, a brutally Darwinian harrowing would have cleared the old folks and stay-at-home siblings off the land quickly and speeded up the conversion to larger and larger pasture farms.

In Sweden, remittances from abroad *may* have had the opposite effect in general. That is: made farming slightly more efficient. Anecdotal reports by observers to the Emigration Commission of 1907–13 suggested that frequently farmers had been able to clear themselves of debt and some to purchase more land because of money sent by children from abroad.[83] If this were the general result, it means that some of the Swedish remittance money was going to investment, not to pure rents. That well may have been the case because, as discussed in chapters eight and nine, the Swedish and the Irish agricultural revolutions were very different indeed. The Swedish agricultural revolution increased the amount of cultivated land by 47.6 per cent (from 1860 to 1910) and turned the agrarian structure away from hay and pasturage and towards arable activities. When this was combined with the abolition near the end of the nineteenth century of restrictions in inheritance laws on the sale of freehold land, it is clear that it became significantly easier to acquire a small, but viable, freehold unit.[84] This relates to the phenomena noted in Nils Wohlin's work, as tallied in table 8.1, showing that during the agrarian revolution the numbers of freeholders and substantial tenants increased, while that of the small renters and the labourers decreased. A considerable degree of economic discomfort was involved in this set of transactions, but some torpare became freeholders. And some small freeholders became larger. And, given the expansion of available land and the cultivation of more high-value crops, it is sensible to infer that a portion of emigrant remittances were turned into agricultural investment and improvement. Still, the macro-economic effect of remittances in both Sweden and Ireland is an open question.

The second lingering question concerning remittances is one that has sometimes been approached in academic language, but rarely has been phrased in simple words, for it borders on the unthinkable: should we not see the remittance payments to parents in the Old Country by children living in one of the New Worlds as being the pay-off in a system of baby-farming? Thus, Kerby Miller notes "Irish parents' calculating attitudes toward their sons' and daughters' departure had potential dangers that threatened the very interests that their migration was designed to promote."[85] Reflecting on the costs to parents of rearing children, David Fitzpatrick observes that "the emigrants amply repaid their rearing costs ..." This was "often within the 'moral economy' of their widely scattered families."[86] And T. W. Guinnane, approaching the family as a micro-economic unit, notes that "the desirability of emigration for young people meant that Irish parents could spend less on each child than would other European parents ..." That was the case because "Irish parents also knew that for the price of passage to Britain, North America, or Australia they could settle their children in any of several robust economies with a large Irish community." Guinnane continues. "For the poorest couples, children might not have been just cheap, but were one way to ensure that the rent would be paid and that there would be an income in old age."[87]

What is being described here for Ireland, holds for rural Sweden but with slightly less force—because, considered as a social system, Sweden had not limited the right to biological reproduction the way the Irish socio-economic-cultural system had done. Recall that in chapter nine we demonstrated that in the era of emigration-culture only about half (or less) of the Irish population was permitted access to biological reproduction. Thus, having children was a limited-licence privilege and the limitation on the right of reproduction made the children of the franchisees (to use a really cruel term) more valuable than if everyone could have had kids. For couples on the bottom rungs of the agrarian ladder, it was much more profitable to rear a child to emigration age than it was to bring annually a couple of bullocks to stocker size. Viewing this situation, T. W. Guinnane concluded that "in my view, high emigration rates altered the costs and benefits of rearing children, and so gave some Irish couples an incentive to continue to have large families long after the practice had ceased in many parts of Europe."[88] In other words, baby-farming.

That is offensive, is it not? Cruel, reductive, dismissive, presentist, elitist, judgemental, and a lot more. Actually, no, as long as the microsituation of the family is viewed within the macro-structure of the emigration-culture. Specifically (1) Farmers of small holdings throughout Europe had always bred their own labour force and thus shored up their insurance for old age. Is there really any difference between a subsistence-farming couple, say, small renters in Småland or in Mayo, having children in 1840 and expecting some of the children to work off-the-farm and bring home a few pennies and to take care of mother and father in old age—and in 1880 rearing some of the children to work off-farm—in Chicago, say—and send money home? The only significant difference is that it is hurtful to the vanity of the emigrants and especially of their descendants in the New World to see their own roots in such a cold light. (2) The marginal economic position of the farm couple in each case makes their actions both sensible and, probably, necessary. Their behaviour should not be judged primarily as an issue of ethics or morality. The poor-with-family were in a socio-economic system which dictated that rearing children for emigration was one of the most promising paths for their own survival as a couple and for an old age with a warm hearth and the occasional pipe of tobacco. (3) Crucially, as I emphasized earlier, almost everything to do with emigration-culture has a double meaning. The material left on the historical record is totally ambiguous, and failing any new probative material, we should accept emotional indeterminacy as the default conclusion: so, some parents were callous, while others were regretful about the nature of their world and how they had to treat their children. Many parents were conflicted within themselves about what was happening: the loss of children being balanced by the expectation of material comfort. The children themselves can only have been torn emotionally by the knowledge that from New South Wales or California or Minnesota they were expected to send money home. This expenditure of hard-won money was either an inconvenience or, worse, a bar to saving and getting on in the world. The entire moral economy formed by the remittance system is not something about which one should either become romantic or, alternately, condemnatory.

Near the end of the era of emigration-culture, two Irish writers left memoirs or fictionalized autobiographies that show the mixed feelings of young people around the expectations that they would provide for their parents.[89] Both cases are of seasonal migrants, Paddy ("the Cope") Gallagher (1873–1964) and Patrick MacGill (1881–1963). Both were born in the harsh parts of County Donegal and were members of large families (9 children in Gallagher's case, 11 in MacGill's) of farmers who held small bog-and-rock farms. Gallagher was sent out by his mother to the hiring fair at Strabane when he was 10 years of age and MacGill was posted to be a full-time hired labourer at age 12. Both men eventually took to labouring in Scotland, Gallagher at age 16, MacGill at 14. They began with potato harvesting and, like so many seasonal labourers, stayed longer and longer in Britain as the years passed before finally packing in the migrant labourer's life: Gallagher to farm and organize one of the first co-ops in Ireland (hence his name, Paddy the Cope) and MacGill to soldiering and then to becoming a full-time writer in England and, later in life, in the USA. Both posted money home to Donegal from Britain and sometimes brought it home in person.

Paddy Gallagher was the less reflective of the two, but not without self-awareness. Thus, in his autobiography he reveals four facets of his own relationship to the remittance system: (1) he sent money when he was doing well, but when he could not save any money he stopped writing home—sending a remittance was a signal that he was being at least a modest success; (2) at times, his parents had to send him several letters in order to make him disgorge a pound note or two to them; (3) there was a quiet theatre of intra-family blackmail involved: when one of his sisters who was still at home told him that his parents would go out of their wits if he did not return, he made up his mind to send the parents some money, but not to go back to the old place; (4) but when there was real trouble at home—a shopkeeper demanding payment of a long-running debt— Gallagher sent £5 to his father and continued sending him money until the debt was cleared.[90] In these matters, Gallagher showed not much sign of love for his parents, but a willingness to honour a set of moral obligations that he found inconvenient, but nevertheless unavoidable.

Patrick MacGill was much more articulate. Though now almost entirely forgotten, MacGill in his time was a highly successful vernacular poet[91] and a witness to aspects of Irish rural life that the improvers of the Irish Literary Revival worked with a will to avoid seeing—and with good reason, for the Irish potato-hokers and the navvies on the roads and job sites of Great Britain were not a pretty sight. MacGill had experienced a fair slice of the menu of jobs that Irish labour-migrants performed in Great Britain—farm labourer, railway navvy, drainage digger, plate-layer—so his *Children of the Dead End. The Autobiography of a Navvy* (1914) was nothing if not well-informed. And in the preface, he emphasized that the novel was mostly autobiographical and that he had witnessed first-hand nearly everything he wrote about. That granted, one does not have to accept MacGill's fictional alter-ego ("Dermod") as a typical Irish migrant labourer—but one has to grant authenticity to his voice as one of the spectrum of possible responses to the remittance system. For Dermod recognizes clearly the basic physics of being a young person born to parents of a marginal small holding, and he resented the reality which he learned early. After his first six-month stint away from home as a young labourer, still in Ulster, he sent £4.5s to his parents for the landlord and the priest and kept only the remaining 15 shillings of his six-months' wage for himself.

> I never for a moment thought of keeping all my wages for myself. Such a wild idea never entered my head. I was born and bred merely to support my parents, and great care had been taken to drive this fact into my mind from infancy. I was merely brought into the world to support those who were responsible for my existence. Often when my parents were speaking of such and such a young man I heard them say: "He'll never have a day's luck in all his life. He didn't give every penny he earned to his father and mother."[92]

Dermod took to labouring in Scotland and there, as when he had worked around Ireland, he received a monthly letter from his parents. His conflicted reaction to those letters is an unusually clear articulation of what I think was the reaction of many emigrants to missives from home:

> Now and again I got a letter from home, and my people were very angry because I had sent so little money to them during the summer months. For all that, I liked to get a letter from home, and I loved to hear about the people whom I had known since childhood. On the farm [in the Scottish lowlands where he was employed] there was no one to speak to me or call me friend.[93]

That is cartoon-like in its clarity, but I think basically accurate: most letters from home to emigrants probably were at least implicitly a nudge to send some money. And, inevitably the letters had a resonance that went back to the emigrants' childhood. Thus they asserted that the proper centre of the emigrant's emotional world was in the old homeland, where remembered friendships were warmer and more comforting than the cold and lonely harshness of a strange land.[94]

That an emigrant inevitably would be deeply riven in a way that could be self-recognized but nevertheless was difficult to escape is clear:

> For myself I wanted to make some money and send it to my own people in Glenmornan. I reasoned with myself that it was unjust for my parents to expect me to work for their betterment. Finding it hard enough to earn my own livelihood, why should I irk myself about them? ... [B]ut strangely inconsistent with this train of thought, I was eager to get on to Kinlochleven and make money to send to my own people in Glenmornan.[95]

Certainly this picture by Patrick MacGill hit a chord among the less-than-literary audience at which it was aimed—the first print run of ten thousand copies sold out in the first ten days, according to the publisher.[96] That was in the British Isles.

On a world scale, the depth of the emotional tearing, the frequency of communication, the proportion of migrants who actually sent money home, the periodicity of those remittances, all of that is unknowable. But Patrick MacGill certainly got the story right for many: loyalty besprinkled with resentment. Clearly, one aspect of the emigration-culture of Ireland and Sweden is that—given the amount of remittances sent back to each homeland—parents were remarkably successful in inculcating social controls over their children that for many offspring lasted well into their adult years and these controls remained robust over thousands of miles. Call it love, call it cold loyalty, call it exploitation. Cases of each can certainly be instanced. Our primary operational definition of emigration-culture has been a society that teaches most children, of all classes and religions, that as adults they have the possibility of emigration. The schools, the newspapers, the chain of letters from abroad all helped to prepare young Irish and Swedish boys and girls to emigrate if they so desired. Manifestly, what myriad families also taught was that the obligations of family membership did not stop at the sea coast.

Ultimately, over time individuals became more and more distant from their parents and, as the older generation passed away, the ties of extended kinship weakened. Finally, in one, two, or more generations, diaspora in the biblical sense (which implied a possible return to the homeland), was replaced by diaspora in the narrow sense of the Greek word—permanent dispersal, as a seed before a wind.

Eventually, Irish men and women, and Swedish men and women, ceased being Irish or Swedish and became American or Canadian or British or Australian or whatever. Of course, they conceived of themselves as being, for example, American-with-a-difference, but so too did every ethnic group. Here is one of the most heart-wrenched, yet keenly apperceptive summaries of the final stages of a diaspora. It is by the pioneer scholar of Irish Studies in the USA, John V. Kelleher. One can substitute "Swedish" for Irish and the meaning stays true; and one can substitute "Australian," "Kiwi" or any other diaspora location for "America." It still preserves, as if in amber, a truth that we can hold up to the light and see with certainty, albeit inevitably slightly dimmed by time's imperfect coating: an enhulling that always makes historical depictions less clear to us than to those who were there at the time and to whom none of this had to be explained:

> Is there, then, nothing to show for all that century-long struggle of the Irish to become American? Practically nothing. They became American, and that was it. There is no point talking about this or that people's contribution to America. The only contribution any people consciously make is what they want for themselves, and, predictably, in America that has always been what other Americans of older vintage already possess. When the newcomers get this, they throw away what they had to content themselves with before. Or, another way of putting it is, the Irish contribution was their grandchildren, no longer Irish.[97]

In the final reckoning, perhaps this is what most diasporas are all about.

NOTES

1   Walter Macken, "The Coll Doll," in *The Coll Doll and Other Stories* (Dublin: Gill and Macmillan, 1969), pp. 8–9.
2   Jeffrey G. Williamson, "Economic Convergence: Placing Post-Famine Ireland in Comparative Perspective," *Irish Economic and Social History*, vol. 21 (1994), p. 20*n*26.
3   Walter F. Willcox and Imre Ferenczi, *International Migration*, vol. 1, *Statistics* (New York: National Bureau of Economic Research, 1929).
4   Francis Bacon, *Novum Organum* (1620), 1:41.

5   In 1978, Sune Åkerman wrote, concerning migration research in general and Swedish research in particular, that "there exists no real communication and interaction between economic and demographic research on the one hand and behavioural research on the other." Sune Åkerman, "Toward an Understanding of Emigrational Processes," *Scandinavian Journal of History*, vol. 18 (1978), p. 133n3. Sadly, the fields are even less close at present than they were in 1978.

6   Here, a qualification of the sort that we academic historians often make: in my reading, I find that Swedish economic historians are much more willing to engage in research into primary records and to work at the assessment of their value, than are those in the English-language tradition. Within the North American academy, I particularly respect the digging in primary material as antecedent to Cliometric exercises in the work of R. Marvin McInnis and Frank Lewis, whose work serves as a template of the way a serious reworking of primary quantitative sources, econometric methods and cultural argumentation can produce major results: for example, in their case for a complete negation of the concept of the widely held belief that nineteenth-century Catholic Quebec was agriculturally inefficient because of cultural backwardness. See: Frank Lewis and R. M. McInnis, "The Efficiency of the French-Canadian Farmer in the Nineteenth-Century," *Journal of Economic History*, vol. 40 (1980), pp. 497–514; R. M. McInnis, "A Reconsideration of the State of Agriculture in Lower Canada in the First Half of the Nineteenth Century," *Canadian Papers in Rural History*, vol. 3 (1982), pp. 9–49; Frank Lewis and R. M. McInnis, "Agricultural Output and Efficiency in Lower Canada, 1851," *Research in Economic History*, vol. 9 (1984), pp. 45–87. For an Irish illustration that econometric concepts can be melded with sophisticated cultural and social constructs, see *The Economic and Social Implications of Emigration*, composed by the National Economic and Social Council of Ireland (Dublin: National Economic and Social Council, 1991).

7   Although the instance mentioned is heuristic, rural Ireland could be a cruelly abusive place for a married woman. For an extreme case see Angela Bourke, *The Burning of Bridget Cleary. A True Story* (London: Viking Penguin, 2000).

8   Heraclitus, *On the Universe* (tr.), frag. 41.

9   Some models worked on a vertical axis, others horizontally. A particularly good example of the latter is found in the Film Museum, Kristianstad.

10   These statements reprise material presented earlier in the text. For a more detailed review, see D. H. Akenson, *The Irish Diaspora. A Primer* (Belfast: Institute of Irish Studies, the Queen's University of Belfast, and Toronto: P. D. Meany Co., 1993); the articles by David Fitzpatrick, by Patrick O'Farrell and by David Noel Doyle in W. E. Vaughan (ed.), *A New History of Ireland*, vol. 6, *Ireland Under the Union, II, 1870–1921* (Oxford: Clarendon Press, 1996), pp. 606–763; Harald Runblom and Hans Norman (eds.), *From Sweden to America. A History of the Migration* (Minneapolis: University of Minnesota Press, 1976).

11   Direct data on the religious composition of the full flow of Irish out-migrants does not exist, although one finds relevant data in the censuses of Canada, Australia, New Zealand. Kerby Miller guessed, realistically, that "at least 75 per cent" of the 1871–1921 migrants to the USA were Catholics. (Kerby A. Miller, "Assimilation and Alienation: Irish emigrants' responses to industrial America, 1871–1921," in P. J. Drudy (ed.) *The Irish in America: Emigration, Assimilation, and Impact* (Cambridge: Cambridge University Press, 1985), p. 88. Given that a slightly higher proportion of Protestants went elsewhere than the USA, a boundary set of estimates for Protestants would be 75–80 per cent of out-migrants in an average year. The base religious population of the 32 Counties was 77.7 per cent Catholic in 1861, reducing gradually to 73.9 per cent in 1911. Both major groups, it must be emphasized, were reduced in absolute numbers. (Akenson, *The Irish Diaspora*, table 5, p. 29; detailed county data is found in W. E. Vaughan and A. J. Fitzpatrick, *Irish Historical Statistics. Population, 1821–1971* (Dublin: Royal Irish Academy, 1978), tables 13–21, pp. 49–68.

     The volatile question that cannot be assayed here is to what extent a significant proportion of the Protestants were pushed out. One raises this issue because Peter Hart's belief (see chapter 11, note 9) that small violent acts have a large effect on populations that see themselves as isolated, has a resonance in the 1861–1914 period. It relates to a phenomenon one infers when looking at the parish-by-parish religious census data for the nine counties of the historical province of Ulster, which one picks up, case by case, when collecting "soft" data on the Irish diaspora. This is that the plantation of Ulster was being rolled back by the once-conquered Catholics, townland by townland, from at least 1861 onwards. The isolated outcroppings of the plantation were being amputated, one after another. This process has continued right down to the present day. The topic deserves a thorough study.

12   The classic study is Cormac Ó Gráda, "Seasonal Migration and the Post-Famine Adjustment in the West of Ireland," *Studia Hibernica*, vol. 13 (1973), pp. 48–76. Ó Gráda argued that seasonal migration to Great Britain did not begin to diminish until the late 1860s or early 1870s. He posited an annual migration in the mid-1860s of 60,000, which was roughly the same level as in the pre-Famine period. He concluded that the

numbers dropped sharply between the early 1880s and the 1910s, when it was below 20,000 annually. For an example of the continuing seasonal migration culture into the mid-twentieth century in a virtual museum area, see Brian Coughlan, *Achill Island tattie-hokers in Scotland and the Kirkintilloch Tragedy, 1937* (Dublin: Four Courts Press, 2006). For the larger perspective, see David Fitzpatrick, "The Irish in Britain, 1871–1921," in Vaughan, *A New History of Ireland, 1870–1921*, pp. 653–702. A valuable collection of essays is Donald M. MacRaild (ed.), *The Great Famine and Beyond. Irish Migrants in Britain in the Nineteenth and Twentieth Centuries* (Dublin: Irish Academic Press, 2000).

13 This is an adaptation of the formulation by J. D. Gould, "European International Emigration: The Role of 'Diffusion' and 'Feedback,'" *Journal of European Economic History*, vol. 9 (Fall 1980), p. 314.

14 Government of Sweden [editors: Gustav Sundbärg and Nils Wohlin], *Emigrationsutredningen, Bilaga VII, Utvandrarnes egna Uppgifter* (Stockholm: KB, 1908). To avoid possible confusion, note that this volume also has 170 bare-bones observational biographies of men and women who emigrated in 1907 which were collected by the staff of the commission. The letters from Swedes in America (including Canada) are items 171–289. The circular asking for information was signed by Sundbärg and Wohlin and was informal, almost avuncular, in tone. It was quite leading, however, in mentioning the topics that might well be covered in the life-narrative. (See pp. 27–28.)

15 The most obvious weaknesses of the collection of life-narratives: (1) The published memoirs were only semi-blinded. That is, they give the initials of the respondent, his or her present residence, the year of emigration and the person's home base in Sweden. Almost all the memoirs carry more precise details concerning the individual's family patterns, religion etc. This semi-blinding is much less than is usually required by present-day academic ethics committees that oversee research projects with "live subjects." However, the incomplete blinding may actually have increased accuracy because there was an implicit check-process in operation. The collection was widely circulated and anyone whose views were misrepresented by the Swedish government's publication could raise trouble in the Swedish-American press. (2) Out-migrants to places in Europe were ignored. Some of the respondents gave details of temporary labour migration to Denmark, Germany, etc., but this was incidental. (3) H. Arnold Barton notes that "many of the respondents suspected the government's Commission on Emigration of being in league with self-interested opponents of emigration from [among] the upper classes." H. Arnold Barton, *Letters from The Promised Land. Swedes in America, 1840–1914* (Minneapolis: University of Minnesota Press, 1975), p. 323n25. Barton is correct in that this suspicion is expressed in several memoirs; nevertheless, I think that the emigrants' suspicion was not well founded. Taken as a whole, the life-stories give a harsh shellacking to the Swedish social and political elite. Matters that are not directly treatable in the officially derived data (remember Nils Wohlin's not being able to do an accounting of nobility estates, much less royal ones) are treated in some of the memoirs. (4) Before being published, the life-narratives were edited into standard Swedish by Gerhard Magnusson, an employee of the commission. Not high Swedish: but expressions and forms that were unique to a single Swedish dialect (no small problem) were "translated" into the general language and Svinglish for the most part was weeded out, although a Creole was probably the home language of most Swedish-Americans by the beginning of the twentieth century. The editing enraged Vilhelm Moberg (quite a few things did, actually). "In the *Emigrationsutredningen* were reprinted several hundred America-letters that unfortunately enough have been paraphrased in standard Swedish and from which the *svensk-amerikanska* thus is weeded out. I consider this procedure to be a great mistake; due to the paraphrasing, the originality and colloquial tone of the letters have, to a large extent, been lost." Vilhelm Moberg, *The Unknown Swedes. A Book about Swedes and America, Past and Present* (Carbondale: Southern Illinois University Press, 1988, tr. Roger McKnight from the original ed., 1950; 2nd ed., 1968), p. 48. (5) A more pressing problem was the simple matter of self-selection. Responding to the Commission on Emigration's appeal for information required not just literacy (nearly, but not quite universal among Swedish out-migrants), but a sense of selfhood: whether as a success or as an aggrieved person forced by circumstances from the homeland. And (6) the 119 published life-narratives may—or may not—represent the totality of those that were received. Of the degree of operation of that potential bias, one has no idea. For a reading of these letters that is straight description, see Emory Lindquist, "Appraisal of Sweden and America by Swedish Emigrants: The Testimony of Letters in Emigrationsutredningen (1907)," *Swedish Pioneer Historical Quarterly*, vol. 17 (1966), pp. 78–95.

16 Sundbärg and Wohlin, *Utvandrarnes egna Uppgifter*, no. 189, p. 163, em. Jämtland, 1871.

17 Sundbärg and Wohlin, *Utvandrarnes egna Uppgifter*, no. 252, p. 238, em. Halland, 1903. See longer translated excerpt in Lars Ljungmark (tr. Kermit B. Westerberg), *Swedish Exodus* (Carbondale: Southern Illinois University Press, 1979), p. 28.

18 Ljungmark, *Swedish Exodus*, p. 29.

19 Sundbärg and Wohlin, *Utvandrarnes egna Uppgifter*, no. 209, p. 181, em. Kopparberg, 1881.

20 For example, Sundbärg and Wohlin, *Utvandrarnes egna Uppgifter*, no. 172, p. 133, em. Östergötland, 1869; no. 173, p. 134, em. Östergötland, 1868; no. 183, pp. 153–54, em. Gäveleborg, 1870; no. 188, p. 160, em. Skaraborg, 1872; no. 203, p. 175, em. Skaraborg, 1886.

21 Sundbärg and Wohlin, *Utvandrarnes egna Uppgifter*, no. 185, p. 157, em. Östergötland, 1880; see also no. 208, p. 180, em. Örebro, 1882.

22 Fully one-third of the memoirs contain evidence of the pinching down on the agrarian lower classes. For example, see letters number: 172, 174, 176, 182, 186, 195, 202, 204, 206, 218, 237, 238, 241, 242, 243, 250, 256.

23 Sundbärg and Wohlin, *Utvandrarnes egna Uppgifter*, no. 177, pp. 144–54, em. Kalmar, 1870. He ended his career as Chicago's representative in the national letter carriers federation.

24 Sundbärg and Wohlin, *Utvandrarnes egna Uppgifter*, no. 211, pp. 181–84, em. Gåveleborg, 1882.

25 Sundbärg and Wohlin, *Utvandrarnes egna Uppgifter*, no. 204, pp. 176–77, em. Skaraborg, 1887.

26 Sundbärg and Wohlin, *Utvandrarnes egna Uppgifter*, no. 182, p. 153, em. Värmland, 1869; no. 184, pp. 156–57, em. Södermanland, 1880; no. 202, pp. 174–75, em. Älvsborg, 1884; no. 228, pp. 213–14, em. Jämtland, 1896; no. 231, pp. 217–18, em. Norrbotten, 1893. The over-representation of Lutheran clergy in the collection reflects the involvement of Augustana Synod officials in recruiting respondents, but does not invalidate the actual life-narratives.

27 Sundbärg and Wohlin, *Utvandrarnes egna Uppgifter*, no. 178, p. 150, em. Malmöhus, 1869.

28 Sundbärg and Wohlin, *Utvandrarnes egna Uppgifter*, no. 185, p. 157, em. Östergötland, 1880.

29 Sundbärg and Wohlin, *Utvandrarnes egna Uppgifter*, no. 175, pp. 135–37, em. Kronoberg, 1870.

30 Sundbärg and Wohlin, *Utvandrarnes egna Uppgifter*, no. 189, pp. 161–63, em. Jämtland, 1871.

31 Robert L. Wright, *Swedish Emigrant Ballads* (Lincoln: University of Nebraska Press, 1965), p. 3. This is a brilliant collection and is valuable as a primary source to compare to the emigrant ballads of other countries. For a collection of ballads, with music, see Knut Brodin, *Emigrantvisor och andra Visor* (Stockholm: Åhlén och Åkerlunds Förlag, 1938).

32 As triangulation and as an indication that the attitudes expressed early in the twentieth century were not products of any recent adventitious events: after reading five printed collections of Swedish emigrant letters written in the 1870s and published in the 1880s, Franklin D. Scott summarized as follows: "Repeatedly, the writers of the 1870s and 1880s struck the same chords, emphasizing always the social and political equality in America and the lack of a state church." Franklin D. Scott, "Sweden's Constructive Opposition to Emigration," *Journal of Modern History*, vol. 37 (Sep. 1965), p. 309.

33 Sundbärg and Wohlin, *Utvandrarnes egna Uppgifter*, no. 229, pp. 214–15, em. Västernorrland, 1893.

34 Sundbärg and Wohlin, *Utvandrarnes egna Uppgifter*, no. 176, pp. 137–44, quotation, p. 144, em. Kalmar, 1868.

35 Sundbärg and Wohlin, *Utvandrarnes egna Uppgifter*, p. 145. The phrase became well known through Lars Ljungmark's use (Ljungmark, *Swedish Exodus*, p. 36).

36 Ljungmark makes this point convincingly (*Swedish Exodus*, p. 36). The majority of life-narratives contain indications of social-class resentment, and there is no profit in listing them all. One item, however, is particularly worth quotation: "When I related in America that in Sweden a farm servant must hold his hat in his hand when speaking to his householder, one can not even get an Irishman to believe that, even though landlord oppression in Ireland surpasses that in Sweden." Sundbärg and Wohlin, *Utvandrarnes egna Uppgifter*, no. 193, pp. 167–68, em. Södermanland, 1882.

37 Franklin D. Scott, *Sweden. The Nation's History* (Minneapolis: University of Minnesota Press, 1977), pp. 407–08.

38 Sundbärg and Wohlin, *Utvandrarnes egna Uppgifter*, no. 225, p. 209, em. Malmöhus, 1895.

39 Thus a Värmland migrant to Canada who said that the political immaturity of Sweden drove him out. Sundbärg and Wohlin, *Utvandrarnes egna Uppgifter*, no. 277, pp. 257–58, no date given for his emigration.

40 For examples, see: Sundbärg and Wohlin, *Utvandrarnes egna Uppgifter*, no. 214, pp. 187–88, em. Uppsala, 1891; no. 225, pp. 207–10, em. Malmöhus, 1895; no. 244, p. 231, em. Småland, 1902 (anti-monarchy); no. 248, p. 233, em. Blekinge, n.d.; no. 263, p. 248, em. Västerbotten, 1907 (anti-monarchy).

41 Sundbärg and Wohlin, *Utvandrarnes egna Uppgifter*, no. 225, p. 208, em. Malmöhus, 1895.

42 For other pragmatic references, see Sundbärg and Wohlin, *Utvandrarnes egna Uppgifter*, no. 224, p. 207, em. Malmö, 1893; no. 229, pp. 214–15, em. Västernorrland, 1893; no. 238, pp. 225–26, em. Jönköping, 1893; no. 239, pp. 226–28, em. Jönköping, 1906; no. 270, p. 254, em. Göteborg, n.d.; no. 282, p. 260, em. Västernorrland, n.d.

43 The clearly outspoken Baptists' life-narratives are Sundbärg and Wohlin, *Utvandrarnes egna Uppgifter*, no. 181, pp. 152–53, em. Värmland, 1862; no. 194, pp. 168–69, em. Södermanland, 1881; no. 227, pp. 212–13, em. Värmland, 1893; and probably no. 218, pp. 190–96, em. Jönköping, 1891.

44   Gustav Sundbärg, in Government of Sweden, *Emigrationsutredningen, Betänkande* (Stockholm: KB, 1913), p. 659.

45   Sundbärg, *Betänkande*, p. 858.

46   A. G. Hall, *Svenska Baptisternas Historia under en Tid af femtio År, 1848–1898*, 2 vols. (Chicago: A. G. Halls Förlag, 1900). The emigration data are in vol. 1, p. 221.

47   See John S. Lindberg, *The Background of Swedish Emigration to the United States. An Economic and Sociological Study in the Dynamics of Migration* (Minneapolis: University of Minnesota Press, 1930), table 2, p. 42.

48   On the Free Church groups that relate to out-migration, see Hall, *Svenska Baptisternas Historia* and the standard work, George M. Stephenson, *The Religious Aspects of Swedish Immigration. A Study of Immigrant Churches* (Minneapolis: University of Minnesota Press, 1932). Useful primary material is found in Gunnar Westin (ed.), *Emigranterna och Kyrkan. Brev från och tell Svenskar i Amerika, 1849–1892* (Stockholm: Svenska Kyrkans Diakonistyrelses Bokförlag, 1932); *Svenska Baptism genom 100 År. En Krönika i Ord och Bild* (Stockholm: privately printed, 1958).

As far as catching the interaction of "Primitive Christianity" and the call to migrate—in this case to make *aliyah*—Selma Lagerlöf's *Jerusalem* is too often ignored. (1901–02; first Engl. tr., London: W. Heinemann Ltd, 1903.) These pilgrims were not unique in the Christian periphery—witness the Afrikaner "Jerusalemgangers," on whom see J. P. Claasen, *Die Jerusalemgangers met besondere verwywysing na J. A. Englsin* (Silverton, RSA: Promedia-Publikasies, 1981) and Antjie Krog, *Jerusalemgangers* (Capetown: Human and Rousseau, 1985). The Swedish story is told in Olaf Fahlen, *Nåsbönderna i Jerusalem. Berättelsen om en märklig Utvandring* (Stockholm: Wiken, 1988) and the US side by Bertha Spafford Vester, *Our Jerusalem. An American Family in the Holy City, 1881–1949* (Jerusalem: The American Colony, 1950). See also: Anders Olsson, "Utvandringen från Nås till Jerusalem och dess bakgrund," in Bjorn Hallerdt (ed.), *Emigration från Dalarna* (Falun: Dalarnes Forminnes och Hemsbygdsförbund, 1966), pp. 139–54; Paul Elmen, "The American-Swedish Kibbutz," *Swedish Pioneer Historical Quarterly*, vol. 32 (Jul. 1981), pp. 205–18. These items are of general value because they provided a pointed illustration of emigration as acts of geopiety, something that was a more diffused phenomenon in North America generally. Ruth Kark, "Sweden and the Holy Land: pietistic and communal settlement," *Journal of Historical Geography*, vol. 22 (1996), pp. 46–67.

The phenomenon of geopiety, mixed with the more general considerations of out-migrant behaviour, is discussed in Robert C. Ostergren, *A Community Transplanted. The Trans-Atlantic Experience of a Swedish Immigrant Settlement in the Upper Middle West, 1835–1915* (Madison: University of Wisconsin Press, 1988) which deals with a North American immigrant community whose origins in Dalarna were similar to those of the Jerusalem-goers. The records of the South Isanti County, Minnesota Baptist church are found in the Minnesota Historical Society. Related material includes: *"On the Banks of the Rum:" Centennial Story of Cambridge, Minnesota, 1866–1966* (Cambridge, MN: Cambridge Centennial Committee, 1966); P. Ryden, *Svenska Baptisternas i Minnesota Historia: Från 1850-talet till 1918* (Cambridge, MN: Historiska Kommitte, Statskonferens Minnesota Baptisternas, 1918), pp. 160–68.

49   Lindberg, *Swedish Emigration to the United States*, p. 42. The succeeding italicized phrase is Lindberg's, p. 44.

50   There exists a question within Swedish historiography concerning a further putative cause of emigration—compulsory military service. Compulsory military service requirements were the one major barrier to free emigration of males after 1860. Training requirements for 20-year-olds rose from 30 days in the 1860s to 92 in the 1890s and then jumped to 240 days in 1901 when Sweden's defence force moved towards a non-professional military, with the basic manpower coming from compulsory service. Among the life-narratives of those who left in the 1890s and thereafter, compulsory military service was named as a general cause of Swedish emigration by the majority of writers. And Gustav Sundbärg's influential view in the report of the Emigration Commission was that this compulsory service spurred emigration. In contrast, historians in the 1970s argued that it did little except affect the timing of when a young man left. For the strongest argument along these lines, see Ann-Sofie Kälvemark, *Reaktionen mot Utvandringen* (Uppsala: Studia Historica Upsaliensia, 1972), pp. 64–111.

51   On the Quinn family correspondence, see D. H. Akenson, "Reading the Texts of Rural Immigrants: Letters from the Irish in Australia, New Zealand, and North America," *Canadian Papers in Rural History*, vol. 7 (1990), pp. 396–98.

52   Ostergren, *A Community Transplanted*, p. 111.

53   For discussions of modes of interpreting in European emigrant letters, see the essays in Bruce S. Elliott, *et al.* (eds.), *Letters Across Borders. The Epistolary Practices of International Migrants* (Basingstoke: Palgrave Macmillan, 2006). Concerning the interpretation of post-Famine Irish emigrant letters, see: David Fitzpatrick, "Ambiguities of 'Home' in Irish-Australian Correspondence," in his *Home or Away: Immigrants in Colonial Australia* (Canberra: Australian National University, 1992). Concerning the interpretation of

post-Deprivation emigrant letters, see H. Arnold Barton, "As They Tell it Themselves: The Testimony of Immigrant Letters," in his *The Old Country and the New: Essays on Swedes and America* (Carbondale: Southern Illinois University Press, 2007), pp. 128–36, and his research note on "Neglected Types of Correspondence as Sources for Swedish-American History," *Swedish-American Historical Quarterly*, vol. 33 (1982), pp. 76–78.; Eva St Jean, "'Letters from the Promised Land': Interpreting Ambiguities in Immigrant Letters," *Swedish-American Historical Quarterly*, vol. 46 (2006), pp. 93–125.

54 For collections of letters sent home to Sweden, mostly in the post-Deprivation period, see: Barton, *Letters from the Promised Land*; Westin, *Emigranterna och Kyrkan*. For a listing of smaller printed collections, see Barton, *Letters from the Promised Land*, pp. 328–30. Useful for catching tone and style is a set of 20 blinded letters, selected for their purported cultural typicality (and in their uncorrected original spelling and dialect) in Government of Sweden [editors: Gustav Sundbärg and Nils Wohlin], *Emigrationsutredningen, Bilaga II, Utvandringsväsendet i Sverige* (Stockholm: KB, 1909), pp. 153–70. Although focusing on pre-Deprivation material, Larson's fine inventory of printed and ms material contains some later material. Esther Elisabeth Larson, *Swedish Commentators on America, 1638–1865. An Annotated List of Selected Manuscript and Printed Materials* (New York: New York Public Library, 1963).

For collections of letters from Irish migrants in the post-Famine period, see: David Fitzpatrick, *Oceans of Consolation: Personal Accounts of Irish Migration to Australia* (Cork: Cork University Press, 1995); Angela McCarthy, *Irish Migrants in New Zealand, 1840–1937* (Woodbridge, Suffolk: Boydell Press, 2005); Lawrence W. McBride, *The Reynolds Letters: An Irish Emigrant Family in Manchester, England, 1878–1904* (Cork: Cork University Press, 1999); Patrick O'Farrell, *Letters from Irish-Australia, 1825–1929* (Belfast: Ulster Historical Foundation, 1990).

55 Sune Åkerman, "Projects and Research Priorities," *Historisk Tidskrift*, vol. 9 (1970), p. 53.

56 Ernest Beckman, *Amerikanska Studier* (Stockholm, 1883), vol. 1, p. 174, quoted in Barton, "As They Tell it Themselves," p. 133.

57 EMILE [Early Emigrant Letter Stories], http://www.emigrantletters.com/IE/output.asp?CategoryID=6579, accessed on 18 January 2010.

58 As primary material for his monumental *Emigrants and Exiles. Ireland and the Irish Exodus to North America* (New York: Oxford University Press, 1985), Kerby A. Miller did an extraordinarily industrious search for Irish emigrant letters in public and private collections, both pre- and post-Famine. He found over five thousand letters in 73 institutions and 146 private collections. That is prodigious individual research. However, even if one assumes that later research will unearth an additional five thousand letters, the total would be remarkably small in relation to the number of letters sent home.

And it is small as compared to the Swedish situation. Through Svenska Emigrantinstitutet in Växjö one has access to well over 50,000 emigrant letters. The national archives (*Riksarkivet*) and the nine major county archives all contain significant collections. For a useful, but now somewhat dated guide, see Thomas Aurelius (ed.), *Svensk Arkivguide* (Uppsala: Institutet för Ortshistoria, 1990). The emigration records, including letters, for Karlstad are now available electronically, and, to take an example, from Kinda Kommun in Östergötland about 2,500 emigrant letters are available electronically. There is no question that as early as the 1907–13 Emigration Commission, emigrant letters were viewed as being valuable both culturally and as sources of socio-economic data. As we observed earlier, the Emigration Commission solicited letters from migrants and also published a sample of the typical emigration letter to family. That 20-letter sample was preceded by two important assertions: (1) that there should be a worldwide call for Sweden's cultural historians to use the letters to acquire knowledge of the everyday and ordinary communication between Sweden and its emigrants, and (2) that emigrant communications are certainly preserved in their hundreds of thousands in Swedish cottages. The Emigration Commission asserted that such letters were preserved in multifarious ways, lovingly and carefully. Further, the Commission said, their signification concerning the development of the Swedish folk-outlook in the last half of the nineteenth century makes them an efficient cultural metric. Sundbärg and Wohlin, *Utvandringsväsendet i Sverige*, pp. 151 and 152.

Contrast that valuing of emigrant letters and preserving them as physical artefacts in the early twentieth century with the situation described by Kerby Miller: "Many families burned their children's letters as soon as they read them, and the receipt of an 'empty American letter' (that is, one that contained no remittances) was rarely admitted." Kerby A. Miller, "Paddy's Paradox: Emigration to America in Irish Imagination and Rhetoric," in Dirk Hoerder and Horst Rössler, *Distant Magnets. Expectations and Realities in the Immigrant Experience, 1840–1930* (New York: Holmes and Meier, 1993), p. 284. No documentation is given for this assertion; nevertheless, I think Miller is on to something culturally important, at minimum the failure of the Irish to treasure and preserve their children's letters with anything like the enthusiasm of the Swedish recipients of similar correspondence.

59 Derived from Gustav Sundbärg in Government of Sweden, *Emigrationsutredningen, Bilaga IV, Utvand-ringsstatistik* (Stockholm: KB, 1910), table 57, p. 166. The cautions about official underreporting mentioned in earlier chapters are worth remembering.

60 Derived from Sundbärg, *Utvandringsstatistik*, table 57, p. 166.

61 Derived from Government of Ireland, *Commission on Emigration and other Population Problems, 1948–1954* [Pr.2541] (Dublin: The Stationery Office, 1955), table 28, pp. 318–19. The cautions in earlier chapters about the reporting of migration to Great Britain apply.

62 J. D. Gould, "European Inter-Continental Emigration. The Road Home: Return Migration from the USA," *Journal of European Economic History*, vol. 9 (1980), p. 53.

63 The question of whether or not single women who emigrated followed homeland customs in terms of economic and reproductive behaviour, or were in some way liberated from them, is beyond the scope of the present argument. However, they clearly had a wider menu of opportunity and of choice than in the homeland.

On Swedish female emigrants, see: Ulf Beijbom, *Utvandrarkvinnor. Svenska Kvinnaöden i Amerika* (Stockholm: Norstedts, 2006). Also see: Ann-Sofie Kälvemark, "Utvandring och Självständighet. Några synpunkter på den kvinnliga emigrationen från Sverige," *Historisk Tidskrift*, vol. 103 (1983), pp. 140–74; Joy K. Lintelman, "'She did not whimper or complain': Swedish-American Female Charity Cases in Minneapolis, 1910–1930," *Swedish-American Historical Quarterly*, vol. 45 (Jan. 1994), pp. 5–23; Kerstin Moberg, *Från Tjänstehjon till Hembiträde* (Uppsala: Uppsala Universitet, 1978); Marie-Christine Vikström, "Vi vågade oss också västerut! Kisakvinnornas utvandring till Nordamerika, 1845–1915," in Sören Edvinsson *et al.* (eds.), *Befolkningshistoriska Perspectiv. Festskrif till Lars-Göran Tedebrand* (Umeå University: Report no. 24, Demographic Data Base Project, 2004), pp. 229–56.

For a wide conspectus of the historical issues on Irish women, see the essays in the following collections: Anthony Bradley and Maryann Valiulis (eds.), *Gender and Sexuality in Modern Ireland* (Amherst: University of Massachusetts Press, 1997); Margaret Kelleher and J. H. Murphy (eds.), *Gender Perspectives in 19th-Century Ireland: Public and Private Spheres* (Dublin: Irish Academic Press, 1997); Patrick O'Sullivan (ed.), *Irish Women and Irish Migration* (London: Leicester University Press, 1995). For basic data, see the chapter "Women and the Irish Diaspora: the Great Unknown," in my *Irish Diaspora*, pp. 157–58.

64 Kristian Hvidt, *Emigrationen fra Norden* ... (Copenhagen, 1971), pp. 132–33, cited in Barton, *Letters from the Promised Land*, p. 320n2.

65 David Fitzpatrick, "Emigration, 1801–70," in W. E. Vaughan (ed.), *A New History of Ireland*, vol. 5, *Ireland under The Union, I, 1801–70* (Oxford: Clarendon Press, 1989), pp. 601–13, esp. note 5, and also table 9, p. 616. Trevor Parkhill notes that in the north of Ireland a similar pattern was in operation as early as the 1830s. The surveyor for Faughanvale, Co. Londonderry, reported that "a constant correspondence is kept up and each emigrant is generally furnished with his outfit by another who has gone before him." Ordnance Survey for Faughanvale, Co. Londonderry, quoted in Trevor Parkhill, "Pre-Famine Protestant, post-Famine Catholic," in Brenda Collins, Philip Ollerenshaw and Trevor Parkhill (eds.), *Industry, Trade and People in Ireland, 1650–1950. Essays in Honour of W. H. Crawford* (Belfast: Ulster Historical Foundation, 2005), p. 159. The post-Famine system was much more generalized and was made possible by the development of international postal orders and bank cheques.

66 David Fitzpatrick, "Emigration, 1801–1921," in Michael Glazier (ed.), *The Encyclopedia of the Irish in America* (South Bend: University of Notre Dame Press, 1999), pp. 261–62.

67 B. J. Hovde, "Notes on the Effects of Emigration upon Scandinavia," *Journal of Modern History*, vol. 6 (Sep. 1934), p. 259. Cf. *The Statistical History of the United States, from Colonial Times to the Present* (New York: Basic Books, 1976), Series C.228–95, p. 117.

68 Hovde, "Notes on the Effects of Emigration," pp. 259–60, citing the work of A. Lilienberg.

69 Through no fault of his own, Arnold Schrier's pioneering work, showing that a total of about $260 million was sent from the USA to the United Kingdom, 1848–1900, has frequently been seized upon as the Irish total, something quite different. Arnold Schrier, *Ireland and the American Emigration, 1850–1900* (Minneapolis: University of Minnesota Press, 1958), p. 41.

70 Cormac Ó Gráda, *Ireland. A New Economic History, 1780–1939* (Oxford: Clarendon Press, 1994), p. 228; *Statistical History of the United States*, Ser. C.228–95, p. 117.

71 Ó Gráda, *Ireland. A New Economic History*, p. 228.

72 For a summary of the project, see Ruth-Ann M. Harris, "Searching for Missing Friends in the *Boston Pilot* Newspaper, 1831–63," in Andy Bielenberg (ed.), *The Irish Diaspora* (London: Longman, 2000), pp. 158–75. The advertisements ran 1831–1916. Harris edited four volumes of the material (Boston: New England

Genealogical Society, 1989–94) and other editors added four subsequent volumes. The entire project is a nice case of using an unpromising source to produce some intriguing data.

73   For background discussions, all of which deal with data at the tail-end or after the end of the Great European Migration, see Ewa Morawska, "Return Migrations: Theoretical and Research Agenda," in Rudolph J. Vecoli and Suzanne M. Sinke (eds.), *A Century of European Migrations, 1830–1930* (Urbana: University of Illinois Press, 1991), pp. 277–92; Theodore Salaoutos, *The Greeks in the United States* (Cambridge: Harvard University Press, 1964); Mark Wyman, *Round-Trip to America. The Immigrants Return to Europe, 1880–1930* (Ithaca: Cornell University Press, 1993).

74   Here is the problem and it explains why good guesstimates of pre-twentieth-century return-migration rates are all that we can reasonably expect. Beneath the usual irritants of habitual undercounts in official records and of migrants going in and out of the home country whilst lying to officials, is a systemic methodological matter. This is that the phenomenon of return-migration is a longitudinal concept, requiring information on individual personal histories. But all that any nation possessed in any depth is information on aggregates and then only at single points in time. We want to know, for example, how many Irish or Swedish migrants who left their homeland in the year 1870 had returned home permanently by, say, 1880, 1890, or 1900, or never. The only true measure of return-migration is an accounting of what members of a given group of people actually did over the course of their lifetime. The trouble is that this very basic question cannot be answered, because the name-bearing records of the recipient nations and of the home countries are not strong enough to answer the question even in the sketchiest of ways. If one employs aggregate data, the easiest way to go astray is to take the number of returned-emigrants to a given country for a given year—say 1875 when Sweden began trying to keep track of returnees—and to divide it by the number of out-migrants in that year and to declare that this is the rate of emigrants who return. It is nothing of the sort, since the people returning in 1875 had left Sweden in any year except 1875. Using ten-year collections of data (the Swedish government's official method) slightly moderates the problem but, mostly, merely disguises it.

75   Gould, "Return Migration from the USA," pp. 41–112, esp. pp. 55–56. Gould's exogenous data were from (a) somewhat crude US Department of Labor data; (b) an Italian governmental emigration inquiry; and (c) Swedish data which were also fairly wobbly. The Swedish information requires comment. The four-year period of Swedish return-migrants originated in the doctoral these of Lars-Göran Tedebrand, *Västernorrland och Nordamerika, 1875–1913. Utvandring och Återinvandring* (Uppsala: Studies Historica Upsaliensia, 1972). This was an admirable work, but portions were later blown out of context. It has been used to suggest that the average Swedish emigrant who returned did so in four years. In fact, Tedebrand found that those who reverse-migrated to Västernorrland from North America had in most cases been gone four years or less (table 68, p. 254). Later this was read to mean that persons who emigrated to the USA and returned to Sweden did so on average in four years or less in most cases. The problem is reverse-migration to Nörrland was to a region that was atypical for (a) industrializing very fast in the later nineteenth century; (b) for not having been the source of much earlier out-migration, which had been much stronger from the south; and (c) for the population's having doubled between 1860 and 1900. The sort of person choosing to return to this boom area was scarcely a national profile-figure of return-migrants, either in age or in intent.

76   Gould, "Return Migration from the USA," table 2, p. 57. The negative Welsh return rate is somewhat problematical. Another analysis of the 1908–14 data, which did not lag the in- and out-migration material, calculated an Irish return rate of 8.7 per cent and a Swedish return rate of 11.2 per cent. Walter D. Kamphoefner, "The Volume and Composition of German-American Return Migration," in Vecoli and Sinke, *A Century of European Migrations*, table 13.2, p. 300.

77   For the official raw Swedish reverse migration data, see Lars-Göran Tedebrand, "Remigration from America to Sweden," in Runblom and Norman, *From Sweden to America*, table 8.2, p. 209. The entire essay (pp. 201–27) is important. Also, Lars-Göran Tedebrand, *Historia och Demografi. Valda Texter* (Umeå: Johan Nordlander, 1999), pp. 1–27. Here one must point out that the US government data and the Swedish government data do not come anywhere close to each other for the years for which they overlap, just before World War I. The US data, as calibrated by Gould (using a four-year lag), gives Swedish proxy remigration rates of 9.6 per cent and the Swedish aggregate data for 1901–10 (unlagged) yield 20.1 per cent, and for 1911–20 yield 45.6 per cent. There is no simple way to bridge this chasm. Because the US data involved several national groups, it has had more impact on the European historical literature than has the Swedish material. The intriguing matter here is that the major Swedish historians of migration have resolutely ignored the widely reported US data (the Uppsala Project is a good example of that), while Gould, who was well acquainted with Tedebrand's work, paid attention to Tedebrand on turnaround times and ignored the aggregate Swedish data except in a passing footnote. That, in miniature, is what the state-of-play is: two sets of scholars walking past each other without making eye contact.

78 The worry one has about the quick interpretation of the Swedish data is that the return-rate is artificially high before the early twentieth century: to indicate why, forget Tedebrand's four-year lag. The official Swedish data are unlagged. Thus, for example, the percentage for 1881–90 (5.8 per cent in the official reckoning) is actually a comparison of out-migration for 1881–90 with the summation of everyone who returned in that period after having originally migrated anytime from 1850 or so, onwards. That would not be an insuperable problem except that it is almost certain that the early migrants who did come home did so after much longer intervals than those in the labour-migration of the later period. Therefore, since the average length of time before return-migration occurred was constantly reducing, it follows that a log-jam effect was occurring in any given tally period. Both the 1881–90 proxy rates (5.8 per cent) and those for 1891–1900 (23.5 per cent) were being raised by this jamming effect; plus, out-migration was relatively low in the 1890s and that further artificially raised the Swedish government's version of the proxy remigration rate. Simply put, like is not compared to like in the governmental data cited as authoritative. (See governmental data reproduced in Tedebrand, *Västernorrland och Nordamerika*, table 59, p. 224). In contrast, Gustav Sundbärg, whose viewpoint was formed by the data collected for the 1907–13 Emigration Commission, declared that "only 6 per cent of the emigrant Swedes have returned from the United States, though the percentage has considerably risen during recent years." Gustav Sundbärg (revised by E. Arosenius), "Demography," in Axel Johan Josef Guinchard (ed.), *Sweden. Historical and Statistical Handbook* (Stockholm: KB, 2nd ed., 1914), p. 143.

79 Gould's table 3 ("Return Migration from the USA," p. 60) indicates that the age profile of the Irish and the "Scandinavian" reverse-migrants just before World War I was close to that of the southern Italians (a quick-turnaround group), so this implies that by then (relatively late in the Irish and Swedish migration to North America) there were not a lot of old people going home among either the Irish or the Swedes. Actually, it was French, Portuguese and English who seem to have had the greatest proportion of (to be anachronistic) Old Age Pensioners going home in their sunset years. One suspects the difference is because almost all of the old people who had cleared off following the Great Famine and the Great Deprivation were already back in the homeland or dead long before this pre-war data-set was compiled.

80 The data for return-migration to Ireland from Great Britain and those concerning return from European countries to Sweden are not close to even the level of reliability of the transoceanic data. They are best left aside.

81 Fitzpatrick, "Emigration, 1801–1921," p. 262.

82 Fitzpatrick, "The Irish in Britain, 1871–1921," p. 627.

83 Sundbärg, *Betänkande*, pp. 307, 335, 410, 422, discussed in H. Arnold Barton, *A Folk Divided. Homeland Swedes and Swedish Americans, 1840–1940* (Carbondale: Southern Illinois University Press, 1994), p. 151.

84 Maria Ågren, "Individualism or self-sacrifice? Decision-making and Retirement within the early modern marital economy in Sweden," in Maria Ågren and Amy Louise Erickson, *The Marital Economy in Scandinavia and Britain, 1400–1900* (London: Ashgate, 2005), p. 231.

85 Miller, "Paddy's Paradox," p. 282.

86 Fitzpatrick, "The Irish in Britain, 1871–1921," p. 628.

87 Timothy W. Guinnane, *The Vanishing Irish. Households, Migration and the Rural Economy in Ireland, 1850–1914* (Princeton: Princeton University Press, 1997), p. 269.

88 Guinnane, *The Vanishing Irish*, p. 269. Two comments: (1) This was "an incentive," and not the only one, for the church in this period had a strong ideological commitment to large families. And (2) as noted in chapter seven, by the later nineteenth century, Swedish farm families show evidence of birth spacing. Not so in Ireland.

89 I am grateful to Roderick W. MacLean for guiding me to these writers.

90 Patrick Gallagher, *My Story* (London: Jonathan Cape, 1939), esp. pp. 66–70.

91 While still railway-navvying, MacGill sold his first volume of self-published poems, *Gleanings from a Navvy's Scrapbook* (1910) door-to-door in Greenock and Glasgow and it was later claimed that eight thousand copies were sold. That is hard to believe, but certainly he did well enough to do another self-published book of verse, *Songs of a Navvy* (1911), which was then picked up and republished by a commercial publisher as *Songs of the Dead End* (London: The Year Book Press, 1913).

92 Patrick MacGill, *Children of the Dead End. The Autobiography of a Navvy* (London: Herbert Jenkins, 1914), p. 48.

93 MacGill, *Children of the Dead End*, p. 107.

94 The evidentiary problem here is insuperable. If (as I pointed out in note 58 above), the number of surviving letters from emigrants is small, and in the case of Ireland minuscule; the situation is even worse for letters to emigrants from home. That number is microscopic compared to the actual flow, which is hardly surprising, given the emigrants were on the move and did not have safe places to keep such vulnerable items.

95   MacGill, *Children of the Dead End*, pp. 173–74. MacGill's actual home was in Glenties, Co. Donegal.
96   That, according to the frontispiece blurb for MacGill's next novel, *The Rat-Pit* (London: Herbert Jenkins, 1915). That novel deals with labour migration to lowland Scotland of 1905 and after and is more fictional than MacGill's first narrative work.
97   John V. Kelleher, "Irishness in America," originally published in the *Atlantic Monthly*, vol. 208 (Jul. 1961), pp. 38–40, reprinted in Charles Fanning (ed.), *Selected Writings of John V. Kelleher on Ireland and Irish-America* (Carbondale: Southern Illinois University Press, 2002), p. 154.

Chapter Eleven

EPILOGUE

ONE

T he Great European Migration is one of those rare phenomena in which the conventional periodization of history and the reality on the ground actually coincide. The "true" nineteenth century, 1815–1914, is firmly, if nastily, framed by the end of one European bloodbath and by the beginning of another. Between those epic attempts at self-destruction of each other on their home turf, the nations of Europe did an extremely effective, if slightly off-hand, job of taking over most of the usable and colonizable land of planet earth, outside of the heartland of Asia. Neo-Europes were created throughout South America, North America, Australia, New Zealand, parts of Africa and on islands in both the Atlantic and Pacific. This occurred in places of whose very names Europeans had not even agreed upon at the beginning of the nineteenth century. A few locales which had been valuable possessions in the eighteenth century, but were now useless, were dropped—the Swedish government's comic attempts to get rid of St Barthélemy in the mid-nineteenth century is a diverting example—but mostly, settler imperialism pressed constantly onward. No case was bigger than the creation of the United States as a vast sea-to-sea imperium, an outcome that could scarcely have been predicted at the time Napoleon Bonaparte was engaged in his multifront world war. Nor could the settler-colonization of the Canadas, Australasia and New Zealand have been considered predictable. The people we have been discussing, the Irish and the Swedes, settled overwhelmingly in the British or in the US empires, but we should remember that neo-Europes were also expanding south of the Rio Grande River in the western hemisphere; and there were some ambitious attempts at European settlement in Africa.

The Great European Migration is best considered to be over in 1914. The War-to-End-All-Wars is a natural cincture. It effectively stopped European transoceanic migration for half a decade. But, more importantly, it coincided with the last remnants of the so-called "free" land being grabbed. The prepotent characteristic of the Great Migration was the seizure and occupation of land and of resources (timber, iron, gold and later, petroleum) from their previous indigenous "owners" (use whatever synonym you deem appropriate for the aboriginal holders; they were pillaged in any case). For every nation that participated, the simple unavoidable fact of the entire enterprise was that the Great European Migration required as a precondition the willingness to victimize the indigene. And the reason that this translation of large populations across great distances and their overspreading of immense terrestrial spaces will never again be repeated, save through near-apocalyptic wars, is that Planet Earth has almost run out of habitable land to despoil.

After the Great War ended, migration from Europe began again. However, it was qualitatively of a vastly different sort than during the Great Migration. Mostly it consisted of labour-migrants whose intention upon arrival in their new homelands was to stay for a while and then return home: although they often remained in their new land for most of their lives or permanently. They tended to be more urban and more industrial than the earlier migrants and, to the horror of some, especially in the USA, came largely from southern Europe. They formed a highly consequential population movement, but it was substantively different in mode and intent from the settler-conquest that had been the leitmotif of the nineteenth-century migration. To use an analogy from medieval history, they were engaged in the process of subinfeudating the conquests made by the previous century's marcher-lords.

TWO

N either the history of Swedish emigration nor of Irish emigration ended with the Great War: both histories run continuously to the present day. However, after World War I the context and meaning of out-migration changed, as did the volume. Now migrants from both countries were part of Europe's general flux of labour-migration. The primary destinations changed and the annual volume of transoceanic migration became markedly less than in the previous century. Thus, to take the Swedish case first, given below are the basic data on gross out-migration (assume, as usual, an underreporting of intra-European migration):[1]

Period	Within Europe	Outside Europe
1916–20	16,785	22,658
1921–25	13,166	59,438
1926–30	9,462	46,579
1931–35	7,959	4,400
1936–40	8,820	4,584
1941–45	10,277	1,261
1946–50	28,335	21,849

That information is admirably clear. Not so for Ireland. The country was partitioned in 1921 and reliable information on a whole variety of social and economic matters became a scarce commodity. As the leading expert on post-1921 emigration has noted, before the 1980s, the level of gross out-migration "is essentially a matter of conjecture."[2] Still, we can put together some data for gross transoceanic migration for a few years. It is rather awkward in form:[3]

Period	Northern Ireland	Irish Free State/ Eire	Total
1924–27	41,674	106,446	148,120
1928–31	33,208	62,921	96,129
1932–35	3,779	2,781	6,560
1936–39	5,356	2,331	7,687

But that is only gross transoceanic migration. What about movement to Great Britain? Given the porous borders between the 26 Counties and the 6 Counties, the unrecorded migration between Northern Ireland and Great Britain, and the incompleteness of migration data from the 26 Counties to Great Britain even during World War II, it is all guesstimates. Even after the contretemps of 1948–49 when the 26 Counties declared themselves to be the Republic of Ireland and the United Kingdom in response guaranteed the Britishness of Northern Ireland, the borders still were highly permeable: indeed, the UK Citizenship Act of 1949 stated that the new Irish Republic was not to be regarded as a foreign country, nor were citizens of the Republic to be treated as aliens when they entered the UK.[4] A solid study has suggested that from the 1930s onwards about three-quarters of emigrants chose Great Britain, one-eighth the United States, with Canada, Australia and New Zealand taking the other one-eighth.[5]

One possible reason for the reduction of Swedish and Irish transoceanic migration and for the bending of the remaining migrant stream away from transoceanic destinations is plausible but not real: namely the introduction of US in-migration restrictions. During the early 1920s, a strong wave of restrictive sentiment gained strength, and in May 1924 an immigration act was passed that aimed both to reduce immigration generally and to filter the flow so that the "better" sort of immigrants would be privileged. The better-sort were those of the ethnic groups who were already in the USA, so both the Irish and the Swedish nations were favoured. Each had a quota set in 1924 and then subsequently reduced in 1929. But neither group ever filled its quota, so US restrictions did not directly influence matters—although a general sense of unwelcome to migrants may have cast a vague penumbra of foreboding about the possibility of entering the USA.

For Ireland, the intuitively attractive idea that the achievement of independence for the 26 Counties would have reduced emigration and even engendered a good measure of return-migration has no traction. Far from it. The Irish civil war of 1922–23 turned the Free State into a very sour place. Moreover, emigration immediately after Independence actually increased because of two syndromes of sectarian bigotry. One of these, in Northern Ireland, took the form often called "the Belfast Pogroms." The term is somewhat excessive (they were neither on a Czarist scale nor government-initiated), but the events were nasty enough. In the summer-rioting and house-burning of 1920 and 1921 in Belfast, at least 68 persons were killed, mostly Catholics, and a sharp set of housing boundaries was drawn. These events in themselves did not drive many Catholics from Northern Ireland, but they presaged a new government that systematically disadvantaged Catholics; the long-term result was that although Catholics in the 1920s to 1960s had a larger natural increase than did Protestants, the Catholic proportion of the Northern Ireland population stayed remarkably constant. That was because Catholics emigrated in higher proportions than did Protestants. One infers that they went to Britain, mostly, or farther abroad, but relatively rarely to the 26 Counties, which in those years was an economic shambles.[6]

The other set of bigotries operated in southern Ireland and is much less often discussed. This is that the Protestant population was pushed out: not just Dublin Castle officials and military officers, but ordinary citizens who, in the first instance in the early 1920s, were either attacked or intimidated by republican extremists or, from the mid-1920s onwards, were disadvantaged by governmental policies, including the juridical imposition of Roman Catholic family law upon the entire population of the 26 Counties. At present, in Irish historiography there is a sharp debate about Protestant victimization after Independence. The flashpoint is Peter Hart's argument that the Protestant minority fell by over 30 per cent after Independence. "It represents easily the single greatest measurable social change of the revolutionary era. It is also unique in modern British history, being the only example of the mass displacement of a native ethnic group within the British Isles since the seventeenth century."[7] Hart's statement relates mostly to the era of the burning of Protestant big-houses and the intimidation of small farmers and shopkeepers in the 1920s and is based on his assertion (with which I agree) that small violent acts do have a large effect on isolated populations, way out of proportion to the actual direct impact of the violence. A continuation of this question of sectarianism concerns the Irish Free State and its successors essentially locking out of governmental offices the Protestant community and the imposition of cultural norms upon that community which were alien to its heritage. That is too complex an issue to summarize here, but the simple fact is that the Protestant proportion of the 26 Counties dropped by 45 per cent between 1929 (the first year that good information is available) and 1961.[8] Thus, in the 26 Counties "down to the 1950s, emigration was the main cause of the decline of the southern Protestant population."[9] This at a time when the Catholic population was also dropping through out-migration, although not as rapidly. Thus, the sum-total of the achievement of Irish Independence in the 26 Counties in 1921 was not what one would intuitively have guessed. Certainly, when the entire 32 Counties are considered, southern Independence did not decrease the propensity for out-migration and, in all probability, increased it.[10]

There were, however, some developments that contributed directly to the overall reduction of both Swedish and Irish emigration and to the redirection of that which did occur. One of these was simply the working out of the long-term impact of the phenomenon we saw as causally crucial to the last half-century of pre-World War I emigration: wage differentials as between countries and their convergence. As we noted in chapter eight, urban wages in the USA were not so much higher by 1914 than those of Sweden or other northern European countries, or Great Britain and Ireland. So, the wage advantages of migrating to North America in 1920 were considerably less than they had been in, for example, 1870. One could gain almost as much in wages, while avoiding the expense and inconvenience of long-distance travel, by moving to England or to Germany or to Denmark. That was the result of convergence-as-catch-up on an international level. Then, in the 1930s, the US hit such a deep economic slough that there were no jobs to be had and convergence-as-levelling-down took over. The effect of each of these two forms of wage convergence was to direct the migration flow to continental Europe in the Swedish case and to Great Britain in the Irish.

Another long-term development influenced Sweden, but barely affected Ireland. This was the reduction in both the overall birth rate and the marital fertility rate through family planning. This had begun by the 1870s, but became most marked in the early twentieth century. The Swedish marital fertility rate (that is, the number of births related to the total number of married women) shows this pattern very clearly: it dropped by 18.9 per cent between 1901–10 and 1911–20, and in subsequent decades dropped by 26.2 per cent and then 27.1 per cent from that of the previous decade, thus cumulatively cutting the marital fertility rate in half between 1901 and 1940.[11] In adopting this course, Swedish couples were following the prescription of the pioneer Swedish student of emigration, Knut Wicksell, who intertwined his analytic scholarship with some practical advice. "If we want for the future to reduce emigration ... we must cease to breed emigrants."[12] He did not mean by abstinence.

The case of Ireland could scarcely have been more dissimilar. In the 26 Counties, the general birth rate (considered as live births in relation to the total population) was higher in 1950 than it had been in 1921 and even slightly higher in 1970 than in 1950. The Northern Ireland rate came down somewhat over the same period but, considered on a 32 County basis, the Irish national birth rate actual rose in the first 50 years after Independence.[13] Most importantly, for Catholics, birth control remained a mortal sin and the state did what it could to keep them from sinning. Under the Irish Free State's censorship act of 1929, advocating the use of artificial birth control (at that time condoms and diaphragms, and later, the contraceptive pill) was illegal and was enforced mostly by the Customs Service with help from local vigilantes.[14] This led to some interesting cases, as when the report of the United Kingdom government's Royal Commission on Population was banned from Ireland because it recommended birth control as a necessary means of population limitation. This particular form of thought-policing was overturned only in 1976 when the Supreme Court of the Irish Republic allowed a book by the Irish Family Planning Association to be sold to the general public. As for contraceptives, they were illegal under the 1935 Criminal Amendment Act, and only in 1979 did it become legal for married couples (and only married couples) to purchase contraceptives, if given a prescription by their doctor.[15]

THREE

I f we accept that, as a wide-frame international phenomenon, the Great European Migration was over by World War I, it still is fair to ask: at what dates can we say that the era of emigration-culture in Ireland and Sweden had wound down to the point where it could be considered to be just another one of the ripples in each nation's socio-cultural life, rather than a dominant characteristic?

Here is one possible hard-headed indicator: when in-migration to the nation became larger than out-migration, at that date the emigration-culture had been well and truly subsumed. For Sweden that year was 1930; for Ireland, 1996.[16]

That seems a bit stringent for Ireland. It is more accurate, given Ireland's special characteristic as the only European country to lose population by natural means (that is, excluding warfare) during the era of the Great European Migration, to enquire when it ceased losing its bone and sinew, year after year. For Northern Ireland, the population was growing ever since it was set up as a separate jurisdiction. For the area that eventually became the Republic, the population finally began to increase in the period between the censuses of 1961 and 1966. Taken together, the 32 Counties had begun to grow just a bit earlier, in the 1961–66 period.[17]

Nevertheless, the receding emigration-culture was still noteworthy. In the 1950s, remittances sent from England and Scotland to the Republic of Ireland were approximately equal to the sum the government spent on old-age pensions. In 1952, remittances from Great Britain were 2.5 per cent of the Irish Republic's national income and, as the economy of the British Isles improved in the early 1960s, rose to 3.2 per cent.[18] This, from an Irish-born population in Great Britain that was reckoned at over one million in 1961, and at a time when the combined population of the 32 Counties was somewhat above 4.2 million persons.[19]

FOUR

As this study said at its very beginning, Jacob Burckhardt was right to remind us, concerning every historical era, that many things everyone knew at the time went unrecorded and were lost as shared knowledge to later generations, including historians. Which is one reason we should walk modestly.

H. Arnold Barton, ground-breaking historian of Swedish culture as it interacted with Swedish-American life, acquired something close to Burckhardt's wisdom by his own route. Having spent much of his scholarly life chronicling Swedish emigrants, he began to trace his own ancestors, and after he had found their old homestead in Småland, he became increasingly romantic about it. One August day in 1971 he was driving through the countryside with a very shrewd Danish friend, an art historian. As they passed along the countryside, Barton recalls, "I fell into a state of sweet yet melancholy reverie under the powerful spell of the passing landscape. How could my forebears have left all this for the windswept prairie frontier out in Iowa?"

His friend understood Barton's preoccupied silence and punctured forever the false nostalgia for the land the emigrants had left.

"Yes," he said, "it is very beautiful to us. But do we really understand how it looked to them?"[20]

NOTES

1   Government of Sweden, *Historisk Statistik för Sverige*, vol. 1, *Beforlkning, 1720–1950* (Stockholm: Statistiska Centralbyrån, 1955), table B. 17, p. 64.

2   Enda Delaney, *Irish Emigration since 1921* (Dundalk: Dundalgan Press, 2002), p. 4.

3   Derived from W. E. Vaughan and A. J. Fitzpatrick (eds.), *Irish Historical Statistics. Population, 1821–1971* (Dublin: Royal Irish Academy, 1978), table 57, p. 267, and Government of Ireland, *Commission on Emigration and other Population Problems, 1948–54* [Pr.2541] (Dublin: The Stationery Office, 1955), table 88, p. 118.

4   On the unique relationship of the juridical entities within the British archipelago and how they related to citizenship and migration after 1921, see Mary E. Daly, "Irish Nationality and Citizenship since 1922," *Irish Historical Studies*, vol. 32 (May 2001), pp. 377–407.

5   P. J. Drudy, "Migration between Ireland and Britain since Independence," in P. J. Drudy (ed.), *Ireland and Britain since 1922* (Cambridge: Cambridge University Press, 1986), pp. 107–23, cited in Delaney, *Irish Emigration since 1921*, p. 7. This conclusion fits comfortably with the net emigration data for the 26 Counties presented in Govt of Ireland, *Commission on Emigration*, tables 86 and 87, and the gloss thereon, pp. 115–16. If anything, these 26 Counties' data imply that the proportion going to Great Britain was even higher than the Drudy study suggests.

6   The physics of this whole process and the data upon which the description is based are found in more detail in D. H. Akenson, *Education and Enmity. The Control of Schooling in Northern Ireland, 1920–50* (Newton Abbot: David and Charles, for the Institute of Irish Studies, the Queen's University of Belfast, 1973), pp. 25–38.

7   Peter Hart, "The Protestant Experience of Revolution in Southern Ireland," in Richard English and Graham Walker (eds.), *Unionism in Modern Ireland. New Perspectives on Politics and Culture* (Basingstoke: Macmillan, 1996), p. 81. See also Leigh-Ann Coffey, *The Planters of Luggacurran, County Laois. A Protestant Community, 1879–1927* (Dublin: Four Courts Press, 2006).

8   D. H. Akenson, *A Mirror to Kathleen's Face. Education in Independent Ireland, 1922–1960* (Montreal and Kingston: McGill-Queen's University Press, 1975), table (unnumbered), p. 116. On cultural issues, see the chapter "Protestantism Abashed," pp. 109–34. See also John Oakley, "Religion, ethnic identity and the Protestant minority in the Republic," in William Crotty and David E. Schmitt (eds.), *Ireland and the Politics of Change* (London: Longmans, 1998), pp. 86–106.

9   J. J. Sexton, "Emigration and Immigration in the Twentieth Century: an overview," in J. R. Hill (ed.), *A New History of Ireland*, vol. 7, *Ireland, 1921–84* (Oxford: Oxford University Press, 2003), p. 807. For a nicely balanced discussion of the minority-and-emigration issue as it existed prior to World War II, see Enda Delaney, *Demography, State and Society. Irish Migration to Britain, 1921–1972* (Liverpool: Liverpool University Press; Montreal and Kingston: McGill-Queen's University Press, 2000), pp. 69–83. Delaney agrees with Peter Hart, *The IRA at War, 1916–1923* (Oxford: Oxford University Press, 2003), p. 226, that just over 100,000—34 per cent—of the Protestant population of the 26 Counties emigrated between 1911 and 1926. Hart suggests this happened mostly between 1921–23 and—here he differs from Delaney—was primarily the result of harassment and intimidation.

10   Matters of space preclude discussing the way in which governmental policy of the 26 Counties in the late 1920s and especially in the 1930s (the era of the "Economic War" of 1932–38 with Britain) impoverished the country and, ironically, actually increased movement to Great Britain over what it otherwise would have been.

11   Erland Hofsten and Hans Lundström in Government of Sweden, *Urval*, no. 8 (Stockholm: Statistiska Centralbyrån, 1976), table 6.17, p. 111.

12   Knut Wicksell, *Om Utvandringen* (Stockholm: 1882), in Franklin D. Scott, "Sweden's Constructive Opposition to Emigration," *Journal of Modern History*, vol. 37 (Sep. 1965), p. 310, and in Franklin D. Scott, "Changing Swedish Attitudes toward America and Emigrants," *Swedish-American Historical Quarterly*, vol. 35 (Jul. 1984), p. 302.

13   See Vaughan and Fitzpatrick, *Irish Historical Statistics*, table 46, pp. 249–50 and table 49, pp. 254–55. A succinct, transparent discussion of the major differences in demography between the north and south of Ireland is Liam Kennedy, *People and Population Change. A Comparative Study of Population Change in Northern Ireland and the Republic of Ireland* (Dublin and Belfast: Co-operation North, 1994).

14   Irish Free State Act 1929/16, with amendments in 1930, 1941 and 1946.

15   Diarmaid Ferriter, *Occasions of Sin. Sex and Society in Modern Ireland* (London: Profile Books, 2009), pp. 190–91, 422–23.

16   Govt of Sweden, *Historisk Statistik för Sverige*, vol. 1, table B. 17, p. 64; Martin Ruhs, "Ireland: From Rapid Immigration to Recession," Migration Information Service, http://www.migrationinformation.org/Profiles/display.cfm?ID=740, accessed on 29 January 2010.

17   Vaughan and Fitzpatrick, *Irish Historical Statistics*, tables 3, 4 and 5, pp. 3–4.

18   Enda Delaney, *The Irish in Post-War Britain* (Oxford: Oxford University Press, 2007), p. 42.

19   Kevin Howard, "Constructing the Irish of Britain: Ethnic Recognition and the 2001 UK Censuses," *Ethnic and Racial Studies*, vol. 29 (2006), p. 110; Vaughan and Fitzpatrick, *Irish Historical Statistics*, table 3, p. 3.

20   H. Arnold Barton, *The Search for Ancestors. A Swedish-American Family Saga* (Carbondale: Southern Illinois University Press, 1979), p. 13.

SELECT BIBLIOGRAPHY

This bibliography consists of studies that I have found most directly useful for the comparative study of Irish and Swedish structural, cultural and mobility patterns in the era of the Great European Migration. The list is selective: a comprehensive bibliography of all potentially relevant material would fill a book in itself. Many of the more recent items in my selection are accessible electronically. The others should be easily available from any university library that participates in an interlibrary loan consortium.

(1) THE GREAT EUROPEAN MIGRATION

Akenson, D. H., *God's Peoples. Covenant and Land in South Africa, Israel, and Ulster* (Ithaca: Cornell University Press, 1992).

Akenson, D. H., *Some Family. The Mormons and how Humanity keeps track of itself* (Montreal and Kingston: McGill-Queen's University Press, 2007).

Allen, Robert C., Tommy Bengtsson and Martin Dribe (eds.), *Living Standards in the Past* (Oxford: Oxford University Press, 2005).

Baines, Dudley, *Emigration from Europe, 1815–1930* (London: Macmillan, 1991).

Belich, James, *Replenishing the Earth. The Settler Revolution and the Rise of the Anglo-World, 1783–1939* (Oxford: Oxford University Press, 2009).

Blegen, Theodore C., *Norwegian Migration to America, 1825–1860* (Northfield: Norwegian-American Historical Association, 1931; 2nd rev. ed., 1940).

Brubaker, Rogers, "In the Name of the Nation: Reflections on Nationalism and Patriotism," *Citizenship Studies*, vol. 8 (Jun. 2004).

Canny, Nicholas (ed.), *Europeans on the Move. Studies on European Migration, 1500–1800* (Oxford: Clarendon Press, 1994).

Cell, Gillian T., *Newfoundland Discovered. English Attempts at Colonization, 1610–1630* (London: Hakluyt Society, 1982).

Chayanov, Alexander V., *The Theory of Peasant Economy*, tr. and ed. Daniel Thorn, *et al.* (Chicago: Irwin, 1966).

Cipolla, Carlo M., *Literacy and Development in the West* (Harmondsworth: Penguin Books, 1969).

Codignola, Luca, *The Coldest Harbour of the Land. Simon Stock and Lord Baltimore's Colony in the Land, 1621–1640* (Montreal and Kingston: McGill-Queen's University Press, 1988).

Craig, Lee A., and Douglas Fisher, *The Integration of the European Economy, 1850–1913* (Basingstoke: Macmillan Press Ltd, 1997).

Dichtl, John R., *Frontiers of Faith. Bringing Catholicism to the West in the Early Republic* (Lexington: University of Kentucky Press, 2008).

Dunn, Richard S., "The English Sugar Islands and the Founding of South Carolina," *South Carolina Historical Magazine*, vol. 62 (1971).

Elliott, Bruce S., *et al.* (eds.), *Letters Across Borders. The Epistolary Practices of International Migrants* (Basingstoke: Palgrave Macmillan, 2006).
Emmer, P. C. (ed.), *Colonialism and Migration: Indentured Labour before and after Slavery* (Dordrecht: Martinius Nijhoff Publishers, 1986).
Emmer, P. C. and M. Horner (eds.), *European Expansion and Migration. Essays on the Intercontinental Migration from Africa, Asia, and Europe* (New York: Oxford University Press, 1992).
Erickson, Charlotte, *Leaving England: Essays on British Emigration in the Nineteenth Century* (Ithaca: Cornell University Press, 1994).

Fischer, David Hackett, *Albion's Seed: Four British Folkways in America* (New York: Oxford University Press, 1989).
Friedman, Milton, *Capitalism and Freedom* (Chicago: University of Chicago Press, 1962).
Furstenberg, François, "The Significance of the Trans-Appalachian Frontier in Atlantic History," *American Historical Review*, vol. 113 (Jun. 2008).

Gabaccia, Donna R., "Is Everywhere Nowhere? Nomads, Nations and the Immigrant Paradigm of United States History," *Journal of American History*, vol. 86 (Dec. 1999).
Gjerde, Jon, *From Peasants to Farmers. The Migration from Balestrand, Norway, to the Upper Middle West* (Cambridge: Cambridge University Press, 1985).
Gould, J. D., "European Inter-Continental Emigration, 1815–1914: Patterns and Causes," *Journal of European Economic History*, vol. 8 (Winter 1979).
Gould, J. D., "European Inter-Continental Emigration. The Road Home: Return Migration from the USA," *Journal of European Economic History*, vol. 9 (Spring 1980).
Gould, J. D., "European International Emigration: The Role of 'Diffusion' and 'Feedback,'" *Journal of European Economic History*, vol. 9 (Fall 1980).

Hafen, LeRoy R. and Ann W. Hafen, *Handcarts to Zion. The Story of a Unique Western Migration, 1856–1860* (Glendale, CA: Arthur H. Clark Co., 1976).
Haines, Michael R. and Richard H. Steckel, *A Population History of North America* (Cambridge: Cambridge University Press, 2000).
Hammond, J. L. and Barbara, *The Village Labourer* (London: Longmans Green and Co., 1912).
Harrison, K. David, *When Languages Die: The Extinction of the World's Languages and the Erosion of Human Knowledge* (New York: Oxford University Press, 2007).
Harvard Encyclopedia of American Ethnic Groups (Cambridge: Harvard University Press, 1980).
Hatton, Timothy, "A Model of UK Emigration, 1870–1913," *Review of Economics and Statistics*, vol. 77 (Aug. 1995).
Hatton, Timothy J., and Jeffrey G. Williamson, *The Age of Mass Migration: Causes and Economic Impact* (New York: Oxford University Press, 1998).
Hoerder, Dirk, *Cultures in Contact. World Migrations in the Second Millennium* (Durham: Duke University Press, 2002).
Hoerder, Dirk, and Horst Rössler, *Distant Magnets. Expectations and Realities in the Immigrant Experience, 1840–1930* (New York: Holmes and Meier, 1993).
Homans, George C., *English Villagers of the Thirteenth Century* (Cambridge: Harvard University Press, 1941).

Knittle, Walter A., *Early Eighteenth Century Palatine Emigration* (Philadelphia: Dorrance, 1937, reprinted, Baltimore: Genealogical Publishing Co., 1982).
Krugler, John D., *English and Catholic. The Lords Baltimore in the seventeenth century* (Baltimore: Johns Hopkins University Press, 2004).

Lewis, Frank, and R. M. McInnis, "The Efficiency of the French-Canadian Farmer in the Nineteenth-Century," *Journal of Economic History*, vol. 40 (1980).
Lewis, Frank, and R. M. McInnis, "Agricultural Output and Efficiency in Lower Canada, 1851," *Research in Economic History*, vol. 9 (1984).
Lippman, Walter, *The US War Aims* (Boston: Little Brown and Co., 1944).

Marx, Karl, *Capital* (Moscow: Progress Publishers, 1954)
McInnis, R. M., "A Reconsideration of the State of Agriculture in Lower Canada in the First Half of the Nineteenth Century," *Canadian Papers in Rural History*, vol. 3 (1982).
McLaren, Angus, *Reproductive Rituals: The Perception of Fertility in England from the Sixteenth to the Nineteenth Century* (London: Methuen, 1984).
Merseyside Maritime Museum, *Liverpool and Emigration in the 19th and 20th Centuries* (Sheet no. 64, 2008).
Mitchell, B. R., *European Historical Statistics, 1750–1970* (New York: Columbia University Press, 1975).
Morawska, Ewa, "Return Migrations: Theoretical and Research Agenda," in Rudolph J. Vecoli and Suzanne M. Sinke (eds.), *A Century of European Migrations, 1830–1930* (Urbana: University of Illinois Press, 1991).

O'Rourke, Kevin H., "The European Grain Invasion, 1870–1913," *Journal of Economic History*, vol. 57 (Dec. 1997).
O'Rourke, Kevin, and Jeffrey G. Williamson, *Open Economy Forces and the late 19th-century Scandinavian Catch-up* (Cambridge: National Bureau of Economic Research, HIER Discussion Paper, no. 1709, 1995).
O'Rourke, Kevin, and Jeffrey G. Williamson, *Globalization and History. The Evolution of a Nineteenth-Century Atlantic Economy* (Cambridge: MIT Press, 1999).
O'Rourke, Kevin, and Jeffrey G. Williamson, "Around the European Periphery 1870–1913: Globalization, Schooling, and Growth," *European Review of Economic History*, vol. 1 (Sep. 2006).

Painter, Nell Irvin, *The History of White People* (New York: W. W. Norton, 2010).
Palmer, Gregory, *A Bibliography of Loyalist source materials in the United States, Canada, and Great Britain* (Westport: Meckler Publications for the American Antiquarian Society, 1982).
Post, John D., "Famine, Mortality, and Epidemic Disease in the Process of Modernization," *Economic History Review*, new ser., vol. 29 (Feb. 1976).
Post, John D., *The Last Great Subsistence Crisis in the Western World* (Baltimore: Johns Hopkins University Press, 1977).
Post, John D., *Food Shortage, Climatic Variability, and Epidemic Disease in Pre-industrial Europe: The Mortality Peak in the early 1740s* (Ithaca: Cornell University Press, 1985).

Quinn, David, *England and the Discovery of North America, 1481–1620* (London: Allen and Unwin, 1974).

Roeber, A. G., *Palatines, Liberty, and Property: German Lutherans in Colonial British America* (Baltimore: Johns Hopkins University Press, 1993).

Rudin, Ronald, "Revisionism and the Search for a Normal Society: A Critique of Recent Quebec Historical Writing," *Canadian Historical Review*, vol. 73, no. 1 (1992).

Salaoutos, Theodore, *The Greeks in the United States* (Cambridge: Harvard University Press, 1964).
Sen, Amartya, *Poverty and Famines. An Essay on Entitlement and Deprivation* (Oxford: Oxford University Press, 1981).
Statistical History of the United States from Colonial Times to the Present (New York: Basic Books, 1976).

Thistlethwaite, Frank, "Atlantic Partnership," *Economic History Review*, 2nd ser., vol. 7, no. 1 (1954).
Thistlethwaite, Frank, "Migration from Europe Overseas in the Nineteenth and Twentieth Centuries," in *Rapports V. Histoirée Contemporaine* (Stockholm: Sixteenth International Congress of the Historical Sciences, 1960).

Vester, Bertha Spafford, *Our Jerusalem. An American Family in the Holy City, 1881–1949* (Jerusalem: The American Colony, 1950).

Walford, Cornelius, "The Famines of the World: Past and Present," *Journal of the Statistical Society*, vol. 41 (Sep. 1878).
Walford, Cornelius, "The Famines of the World: Past and Present—part II," *Journal of the Statistical Society*, vol. 42 (Mar. 1879).
Weaver, John C., *The Great Land Rush and the Making of the Modern World, 1650–1900* (Montreal and Kingston: McGill-Queen's University Press, 2003).
Willcox, Walter F. and Imre Ferenczi, *International Migration*, vol. 1, *Statistics* (New York: National Bureau of Economic Research, 1929). The second volume (1931) was a collection of interpretive essays by various scholars and Willcox was sole editor.
Wokeck, Marianne S., *Trade in Strangers. The Beginnings of Mass Migration to North America* (University Park, PA: Pennsylvania State University Press, 1999).
Wyman, Mark, *Round-Trip to America. The Immigrants Return to Europe, 1880–1930* (Ithaca: Cornell University Press, 1993).

(2) IRISH SOCIETAL AND MIGRATION PATTERNS

Adams, William Forbes, *Ireland and Irish Emigration to the New World from 1815 to the Famine* (New Haven: Yale University Press, 1932).
Akenson, D. H., *The Irish Education Experiment. The National System of Education in the Nineteenth Century* (London: Routledge and Kegan Paul and Toronto: University of Toronto Press, 1970).
Akenson, D. H., *The Church of Ireland. Ecclesiastical Reform and Revolution, 1800–1885* (New Haven: Yale University Press, 1971).
Akenson, D. H., *Education and Enmity. The Control of Schooling in Northern Ireland, 1920–50* (Newton Abbot: David and Charles, for the Institute of Irish Studies, the Queen's University of Belfast, 1973).
Akenson, D. H., *A Mirror to Kathleen's Face. Education in Independent Ireland, 1922–1960* (Montreal and Kingston: McGill-Queen's University Press, 1975).
Akenson, D. H., *Between Two Revolutions. Islandmagee, County Antrim 1798–1920* (Toronto: P. D. Meany, 1979).
Akenson, D. H., "Why the Accepted Estimates of the Ethnicity of the American People, 1790, Are Unacceptable," *William and Mary Quarterly*, 3rd ser., vol. 41 (Jan. 1984).

Akenson, D. H., *Being Had. Historians, Evidence and the Irish in North America* (Toronto: P. D. Meany, 1985).

Akenson, D. H., *The Orangeman. The Life and Times of Ogle Gowan* (Toronto: James Lorimer and Co., 1986).

Akenson, D. H., "Reading the Texts of Rural Immigrants: Letters from the Irish in Australia, New Zealand, and North America," *Canadian Papers in Rural History*, vol. 7 (1990).

Akenson, D. H., *The Irish Diaspora. A Primer* (Belfast: Institute of Irish Studies, the Queen's University of Belfast, and Toronto: P. D. Meany Co., 1993).

Akenson, D. H., *If the Irish Ran the World. Montserrat, 1630–1730* (Liverpool: Liverpool University Press and Montreal and Kingston: McGill-Queen's University Press, 1997).

Akenson, D. H., *The Irish in Ontario. A Study in Rural History* (Montreal and Kingston: McGill-Queen's University Press, 1984; 2nd ed., 1999).

Akenson, D. H. and W. H. Crawford, *Local Poets and Social History* (Belfast: Public Record Office of Northern Ireland, 1977).

Andrews, J. H., "A Geographer's View of Irish History," in T. W. Moody and F. X. Martin (eds.), *The Course of Irish History* (Cork: Mercier Press, 1967).

Arensberg, Conrad M., and Solon T. Kimball, *Family and Community in Ireland* (Cambridge: Harvard University Press, 1940; 2nd ed., 1968).

Beckett, James C., *Protestant Dissent in Ireland, 1687–1780* (London: Faber and Faber, 1948).

Belchem, John, *Irish, Catholic and Scouse. The History of the Liverpool-Irish, 1800–1939* (Liverpool: Liverpool University Press, 2007.)

Bew, Paul, *Ireland. The Politics of Enmity, 1789–2006* (Oxford: Oxford University Press, 2007).

Bielenberg, Andy (ed.), *The Irish Diaspora* (London: Longman, 2000).

Blake, John W., "Transportation from Ireland to America, 1653–60," *Irish Historical Studies*, vol. 3 (Mar. 1943).

Blethen, H. Tyler, and Curtis W. Wood, Jr (eds.), *Ulster and North America. Transatlantic Perspectives on the Scotch-Irish* (Tuscaloosa: University of Alabama Press, 1997).

Bourke, Angela, *The Burning of Bridget Cleary. A True Story* (London: Viking Penguin, 2000).

Bourke, P. M. Austin, "The Visitation of God?", in Jacqueline Hill and Cormac Ó Gráda (eds.), *The Potato and the Great Irish Famine* (Dublin: Lilliput Press for *Irish Historical Studies*, 1993).

Boyle, Phelim P., and Cormac Ó Gráda, "Fertility Trends, Excess Mortality, and the Great Irish Famine," *Demography*, vol. 23 (Nov. 1986).

Bradley, Anthony, and Maryann Valiulis (eds.), *Gender and Sexuality in Modern Ireland* (Amherst: University of Massachusetts Press, 1997).

Brooke, Peter, *Ulster Presbyterianism. The Historical Perspective, 1610–1970* (Dublin: Gill and Macmillan, 1987).

Brown, Stewart J., and David W. Miller (eds.), *Piety and Power in Ireland, 1870–1960. Essays in Honour of Emmet Larkin* (Belfast: Institute of Irish Studies, the Queen's University of Belfast, 2000).

Brozyna, Andrea Ebel, "Female Virtue and Chastity in Pre-Famine Ireland: Kenneth Hugh Connell Revisited," *Canadian Papers in Rural History*, vol. 10 (1996).

Cadigan, Sean, "The Moral Economy of the Commons: Ecology and Equity in the Newfoundland Cod Fishery, 1815–1855," *Labour/Le Travail*, vol. 43 (Spring 1999).

Cadigan, Sean, *Newfoundland and Labrador. A History* (Toronto: University of Toronto Press, 2009).

Carleton, William, *Traits and Stories of the Irish Peasantry*, 2 vols. (Dublin: William Curry, 1830), expanded version, 3 vols. (Dublin: W. F. Wakeman, 1833).

Carleton, William, *The Black Prophet* (Dublin: J. Duffy, 1847).

Carroll, Michael P., "How the Irish became Protestants in America," *Religion and American Culture*, vol. 16 (Winter 2006).

Clark, Samuel, *Social Origins of the Irish Land War* (Princeton: Princeton University Press, 1979).

Clarkson, Leslie A. and E. Margaret Crawford (eds.), *Famine and Disease in Ireland* (London: Pickering and Chatto, 2005).

Coffey, Leigh-Ann, *The Planters of Luggacurran, County Laois. A Protestant Community, 1879–1927* (Dublin: Four Courts Press, 2006).

Collins, Brenda, Philip Ollerenshaw and Trevor Parkhill (eds.), *Industry, Trade and People in Ireland, 1650–1950. Essays in Honour of W. H. Crawford* (Belfast: Ulster Historical Foundation, 2005).

Connell, Kenneth H., *The Population of Ireland* (Oxford: Clarendon Press, 1950).

Connell, Kenneth H., *Irish Peasant Society. Four Historical Essays* (Oxford: Clarendon Press, 1968).

Connolly, Sean J., "Illegitimacy and Pre-Nuptial Pregnancy in Ireland before 1864: The Evidence of Some Catholic Parish Registers," *Irish Economic and Social History*, vol. 6 (1979).

Connolly, Sean J., "Religion and History," *Irish Economic and Social History*, vol. 10 (1983).

Connolly, Sean J., "The 'blessed turf:' cholera and popular panic in Ireland, June 1832," *Irish Historical Studies*, vol. 23 (May 1983).

Connolly, Sean J., *Religion, Law, and Power: The Making of Protestant Ireland, 1660–1760* (Oxford: Clarendon Press, 1992.)

Connolly, Sean J. (ed.), *The Oxford Companion to Irish History* (Oxford: Oxford University Press, 1998).

Connolly, Sean J., "The Moving Statue and the Turtle Dove: Approaches to the History of Irish Religion," *Irish Economic and Social History*, vol. 31 (2004).

Cosgrove, Art (ed.), *Marriage in Ireland* (Dublin: College Press, 1985).

Coughlan, Brian, *Achill Island tattie-hokers in Scotland and the Kirkintilloch Tragedy, 1937* (Dublin: Four Courts Press, 2006).

Cousens, S. H., "Regional Death Rates in Ireland during the Great Famine from 1846 to 1851," *Population Studies*, vol. 14 (1960).

Cousens, S. H., "The Regional Variation in Mortality during the Great Irish Famine," *Proceedings of the Royal Irish Academy*, vol. 63, sec. C, no. 3 (Feb. 1963).

Crawford, W. H., "Landlord-Tenant Relations in Ulster, 1609–1820," *Irish Economic and Social History*, vol. 2 (1975).

Crawford, W. H., "The Evolution of the Linen Trade in Ulster before Industrialization," *Irish Economic and Social History*, vol. 15 (1988).

Crotty, Raymond, *Irish Agricultural Production. Its Volume and Structure* (Cork: Cork University Press, 1966).

Daly, Mary E., "Review Article: Historians and the Famine: a beleaguered species?" *Irish Historical Studies*, vol. 30 (Nov. 1997).

Daly, Mary E., "Irish Nationality and Citizenship since 1922," *Irish Historical Studies*, vol. 32 (May 2001).

Delaney, Enda, *Demography, State and Society. Irish Migration to Britain, 1921–1972* (Liverpool: Liverpool University Press; and Montreal and Kingston: McGill-Queen's University Press, 2000).

Delaney, Enda, *Irish Emigration since 1921* (Dundalk: Dundalgan Press, 2002).

Delaney, Enda, *The Irish in Post-War Britain* (Oxford: Oxford University Press, 2007).

Dickson, David, *Arctic Ireland; the Extraordinary Story of the Great Frost and the forgotten Famine of 1740–41* (Belfast: White Row Press, 1997).

Dickson, David, Cormac Ó Gráda and Stuart Daultrey, "Hearth Tax, Household Size and Irish Population Change, 1671–1821," *Proceedings of the Royal Irish Academy*, sec. C, vol. 82 (1982).

Dickson, R. J., *Ulster Emigration to Colonial America, 1718–1775* (London: Routledge and Kegan Paul, 1966). Second edition, with an introduction by Graeme Kirkham, 1988.

Donnelly, James, "Hearts of Oak, Hearts of Steel," *Studia Hibernica*, vol. 21 (1981).

Donnelly, James, *The Great Irish Potato Famine* (Phoenix Mill, Gloucestershire: Sutton Publishing, 2001).

Doyle, David Noel, *Ireland, Irishmen and Revolutionary America, 1760–1820* (Cork: Mercier Press, 1981).

Drake, Michael, "The Irish Demographic Crisis of 1740–41," in T. W. Moody (ed.), *Historical Studies, VI* (New York: Barnes and Noble, 1968).

Edwards, R. Dudley, and T. Desmond Williams (eds.), *The Great Famine. Studies in Irish History, 1845–52* (Dublin: Browne and Nolan, 1956; 2nd ed., Dublin: Lilliput Press, 1994).

Elliott, Bruce, "Emigration from South Leinster to Eastern Upper Canada," in Kevin Whelan and William Nolan, *Wexford: History and Society* (Dublin: Geography Publications, 1987).

Elliott, Bruce, *Irish Migrants in the Canadas. A New Approach* (Kingston and Montreal: McGill-Queen's University Press, and Belfast: Institute of Irish Studies, the Queen's University of Belfast, 1988).

Elliott, Marianne, *Watchmen in Sion: the Protestant idea of liberty* (Derry: Field Day, 1985).

Elliott, Marianne, *The Catholics of Ulster: A History* (Harmondsworth: Penguin, 2000).

Elliott, Marianne, *When God Took Sides. Religion and Identity in Ireland* (Oxford: Oxford University Press, 2009).

Ferriter, Diarmaid, *Occasions of Sin. Sex and Society in Modern Ireland* (London: Profile Books, 2009).

Fitzgerald, Patrick, and Brian Lambkin, *Migration in Irish History, 1607–2007* (Basingstoke: Palgrave Macmillan, 2008).

Fitzpatrick, David, "The Disappearance of the Irish Agricultural Labourer, 1841–1922," *Irish Economic and Social History*, vol. 7 (1980).

Fitzpatrick, David, *Irish Emigration, 1801–1921* (Dundalk: Dundalgan Press Ltd, for the Economic and Social History Society of Ireland, 1984).

Fitzpatrick, David, *Home or Away: Immigrants in Colonial Australia* (Canberra: Australian National University, 1992).

Fitzpatrick, David, *Oceans of Consolation: Personal Accounts of Irish Migration to Australia* (Cork: Cork University Press, 1995).

Foster, Roy F., *Modern Ireland, 1600–1972* (Harmondsworth: Penguin, 1988).

Foster, Roy F., *Paddy and Mr Punch. Connections in Irish and English History* (Harmondsworth: Allen Lane, 1993).

Freeman, T. W., *Pre-Famine Ireland. A Study in Historical Geography* (Manchester: Manchester University Press, 1957).

Gallagher, Patrick, *My Story* (London: Jonathan Cape, 1939).

Geary, Frank, "The Act of Union. British-Irish Trade and Pre-Famine Deindustrialisation," *Economic History Review*, new ser., vol. 48 (Feb. 1995).

Gillespie, Raymond, "Harvest Crises in early seventeenth-century Ireland," *Irish Economic and Social History*, vol. 11 (1984).

Glazier, Michael (ed.), *The Encyclopedia of the Irish in America* (South Bend: University of Notre Dame Press, 1999).

Goldstrom, J. M. and Leslie A. Clarkson (eds.), *Irish Population, Economy, and Society. Essays in Honour of the late K. H. Connell* (Oxford: Clarendon Press, 1981).

Government of Ireland, Department of Industry and Commerce, *Agricultural Statistics, 1847–1926* (Dublin: The Stationery Office, 1930).

Government of Ireland, *Commission on Emigration and other Population Problems, 1948–54* [Pr. 2541] (Dublin: The Stationery Office, 1955).

Government of the United Kingdom, *Third Report from the Select Committee on Emigration from the United Kingdom*, HC, 1826–27 (237), v.

Government of the United Kingdom, *First Report of the Commissioners of Public Instruction, Ireland* (45 and 46), HC, 1835, xxxiii, and *Second Report* (47), HC, 1835, xxxiv.

Government of the United Kingdom, *The Poor Law Inquiry (Ireland), First Report, Appendix A*, HC, 1835 (369), xxxii.

Government of the United Kingdom, *Report of the Commissioners appointed to take the Census of Ireland for the Year 1841* [504], HC, 1843, xxiv.

Government of the United Kingdom [author: William Wilde], "Table of Cosmical Phenomena, Epizootics, Ephiphitics, Famines and Pestilences in Ireland," in *Report of the Commissioners of Census of Ireland for the Year 1851. Part V., Tables of Deaths*, vol. 1 [2087–1], HC, 1856, xxix–1.

Government of the United Kingdom, *Census of Ireland for the Year 1861*, part 4, vol. 1 [3204-III], HC 1863, lix.

Government of the United Kingdom, *The First Annual Report of the Registrar-General of Marriages, Births, and Deaths in Ireland* [4137], HC, 1868–69, xvi.

Government of the United Kingdom, *Reports, Maps, Tables, and Appendices relating to Migratory Agricultural Labourers, 1900* [Cd. 341], HC, 1900, ci.

Government of the United Kingdom, *Sixty-seventh Report of the Commissioners of National Education in Ireland, for the year 1900* [Cd. 704], HC, 1901, xxi.

Government of the United Kingdom, *Supplement to the Forty-seventh Report of the Registrar-General in Ireland* [Cd. 7121], HC, 1914, xv.

Government of the United Kingdom [compilers: N. H. Carrier and J. R. Jeffery], *External Migration: A Study of the Available Statistics, 1815–1950* (London: HMSO, 1953).

Gray, Peter, *Famine, Land and Politics: British Government and Irish Society, 1843–50* (Dublin: Irish Academic Press, 1999).

Greaves, Richard L., *God's Other Children. Protestant Nonconformists and the Emergence of Denominational Churches in Ireland, 1660–1700* (Stanford: Stanford University Press, 1997).

Green, E. R. R. (ed.), *Essays in Scotch-Irish History* (London: Routledge and Kegan Paul, 1969).

Griffin, Patrick, *The People with no Name: Ireland's Ulster-Scots, America's Scots-Irish and the Creation of a British Atlantic World, 1689–1784* (Princeton: Princeton University Press, 2001).

Guinnane, Timothy W., "The Great Irish Famine and Population: The Long View," *American Economic Review*, vol. 84 (May 1994).

Guinnane, Timothy W., *The Vanishing Irish. Households, Migration and the Rural Economy in Ireland, 1850–1914* (Princeton: Princeton University Press, 1997).

Guinnane, Timothy W. and Ronald I. Miller, "Bonds without Bondsmen: Tenant-Right in Nineteenth-Century Ireland," *Journal of Economic History*, vol. 56 (Mar. 1996).

Haines, Robin, *Charles Trevelyan and the Great Irish Famine* (Dublin: Four Courts Press, 2004).

Hall, Mr and Mrs S[amuel] C[arter], *Ireland* (London: How and Parsons, 1841).

Hamilton, Thomas, *History of Presbyterianism in Ireland* (Edinburgh: T. and T. Clarke, 1887).

Harris, Ruth-Ann, "Seasonal Migration between Ireland and England prior to the Famine," *Canadian Papers in Rural History*, vol. 7 (1990).

Harris, Ruth-Ann, *The Nearest Place that Wasn't Ireland* (Ames, IA: Iowa State University Press, 1994).

Harrison, Alan, and Ian C. Ross (eds.), *Eighteenth-Century Ireland*, vol. 5 (Dublin: Eighteenth-Century Ireland Society, 1990).

Hart, Peter, "The Protestant Experience of Revolution in Southern Ireland," in Richard English and Graham Walker (eds.), *Unionism in Modern Ireland. New Perspectives on Politics and Culture* (Basingstoke: Macmillan, 1996).

Hart, Peter, *The IRA at War, 1916–1923* (Oxford: Oxford University Press, 2003).

Hartwell, R. M., "Kenneth H. Connell: An Appreciation," *Irish Economic and Social History*, vol. 1 (1974).

Hatton, Timothy J., and Jeffrey G. Williamson, "After the Famine: Emigration from Ireland, 1850–1913," *Journal of Economic History*, vol. 53 (Sep. 1993).

Heald, Carolyn A., *The Irish Palatines in Ontario* (Gananoque, Ont: Langdale Press, 1994; 2nd ed., Toronto: Global Genealogy, 2009).

Hempton, David, and Myrtle Hill, *Evangelical Protestantism in Ulster Society, 1740–1890* (London: Routledge, 1992).

Herzog, Dagmar, "Syncopated Sex: Transforming European Sexual Cultures," *American Historical Review*, vol. 114 (Dec. 2009).

Hewitt, John, *Rhyming Weavers* (Belfast: Blackstaff Press, 1974).

Hill, J. R. (ed.), *A New History of Ireland*, vol. 7, *Ireland, 1921–84* (Oxford: Oxford University Press, 2003).

Hill, Jacqueline, and Colm Lennon (eds.), *Luxury and Austerity* (Dublin: University College Dublin Press, 1999).

Holmes, Andrew R., *The Shaping of Ulster Presbyterian Belief and Practice, 1770–1840* (Oxford: Oxford University Press, 2006).

Holmes, Finlay, *Our Irish Presbyterian Heritage* (Belfast: Presbyterian Church in Ireland, 1985).

Howard, Kevin, "Constructing the Irish of Britain: Ethnic Recognition and the 2001 UK Censuses," *Ethnic and Racial Studies*, vol. 29 (2006).

Howe, Stephen, *Ireland and Empire. Colonial Legacies in Irish History and Culture* (Oxford: Oxford University Press, 2000).

Inglis, Tom, *Moral Monopoly. The Catholic Church in Modern Irish Society* (Dublin: Gill and Macmillan, 1987).

Inglis, Tom, "Origins and Legacies of Irish Prudery: Sexuality and Social Control in Modern Ireland," *Eire-Ireland*, vol. 40, nos. 3 and 4 (Winter 2005).

Jensen, Richard, "'No Irish Need Apply:' A Myth of Victimization," *Journal of Social History*, vol. 36 (Winter 2002).

Kelleher, John V., "Irishness in America," orig. pub. *Atlantic Monthly*, vol. 208 (Jul. 1961), reprinted in Charles Fanning (ed.), *Selected Writings of John V. Kelleher on Ireland and Irish-America* (Carbondale: Southern Illinois University Press, 2002).

Kelleher, Margaret, *The Feminization of Famine: Expressions of the Inexpressible?* (Cork: Cork University Press, 1997).

Kelleher, Margaret, and J. H. Murphy (eds.), *Gender Perspectives in 19th-Century Ireland: Public and Private Spheres* (Dublin: Irish Academic Press, 1997).

Kennedy, Liam, "Why Ireland Starved: An Open Verdict," *Irish Economic and Social History*, vol. 11 (1984).

Kennedy, Liam, "Farm Succession in Modern Ireland: Elements of a Theory of Inheritance," *Economic History Review*, new ser., vol. 44 (Aug. 1991).

Kennedy, Liam, *People and Population Change. A Comparative Study of Population Change in Northern Ireland and the Republic of Ireland* (Dublin and Belfast: Co-operation North, 1994).

Kennedy, Liam, and Leslie A. Clarkson, "Birth, Death and Exile: Irish Population History, 1700–1921," in B. J. Graham and L. J. Proudfoot (eds.), *An Historical Geography of Ireland* (London and New York: Harcourt Brace, Jovanovich, 1993).

Kennedy, Robert E., Jr, *The Irish. Emigration, Marriage and Fertility* (Berkeley: University of California Press, 1973).

Kerr, Barbara M., "Irish Seasonal Migration to Great Britain, 1800–38," *Irish Historical Studies*, vol. 3 (Sep. 1943).

Kerr, Donal A., *Peel, Priests and Politics. Sir Robert Peel's Administration and the Roman Catholic Church in Ireland, 1841–1846* (Oxford: Clarendon Press, 1982).

Kerr, Donal A., *'A Nation of Beggars'? Priests, People and Politics in Famine Ireland, 1846–1852* (Oxford: Clarendon Press, 1994).

Larkin, Emmet, "The Devotional Revolution in Ireland, 1850–75," *American Historical Review*, vol. 77 (Jun. 1972).

Larkin, Emmet, *The Making of the Roman Catholic Church in Ireland, 1850–1860* (Chapel Hill: University of North Carolina Press, 1980).

Larkin, Emmet, *The Consolidation of the Roman Catholic Church in Ireland, 1860–1870* (Chapel Hill: University of North Carolina Press, 1987).

Lecky, William E. H., *History of Ireland in the Eighteenth Century* (London: Longmans, 1892; 2nd ed., 1913), 5 vols.

Lee, Joseph J., *The Modernization of Irish Society, 1848–1918* (Dublin: Gill and Macmillan, 1973).

Livingstone, David N., and Ronald A. Wells, *Ulster-American Religion. Episodes in the History of a Cultural Connection* (South Bend: University of Notre Dame Press, 1999).

MacGill, Patrick, *Gleanings from a Navvy's Scrapbook* (self pub: 1910)

MacGill, Patrick, *Songs of a Navvy* (self pub: 1911), reissued as *Songs of the Dead End* (London: The Year Book Press, 1913).

MacGill, Patrick, *Children of the Dead End. The Autobiography of a Navvy* (London: Herbert Jenkins, 1914).

MacGill, Patrick, *The Rat-Pit* (London: Herbert Jenkins, 1915).

MacGowan, Mark G., "Famine Facts and Fabrication: An Examination of Diaries from the Irish Famine Migration to Canada," *Canadian Journal of Irish Studies*, vol. 3 (Fall 2007).

MacGowan, Mark G., *Death or Canada. The Irish Famine Migration to Toronto, 1857* (Toronto: Novalis, 2009).

Macken, Walter, *The Coll Doll and Other Stories* (Dublin: Gill and Macmillan, 1969).

MacRaild, Donald (ed.), *The Great Famine and Beyond. Irish Migrants in Britain in the Nineteenth and Twentieth Centuries* (Dublin: Irish Academic Press, 2000).

MacRaild, Donald, *Irish Migrants in Modern Britain, 1750–1922* (New York: St Martin's Press, 1999); 2nd rev. ed., *The Irish Diaspora in Britain, 1750–1939* (Basingstoke: Macmillan, 2010).

Maginnis, Eoin F., "A 'Presbyterian insurrection?' Reconsidering the Hearts of Oak disturbances of July 1763," *Irish Historical Studies*, vol. 31 (Nov. 1998).

Mannion, John, *Irish Settlements in Eastern Canada: a Study of Cultural Transfer and Adaptation* (Toronto: University of Toronto Press, 1974).

Mannion, John, "The Waterford Merchants and the Irish-Newfoundland Provisions Trade, 1770–1820," *Canadian Papers in Rural History*, vol. 3 (1982).

Mannion, John, "A Transatlantic Merchant Fisher: Richard Welsh of New Ross and the Sweetmans of Newbawn in Newfoundland, 1734–1862," in Kevin Whelan and William Nolan, *Wexford: History and Society* (Dublin: Geography Publications, 1987).

Mannion, John, "Irish Migration and Settlement in Newfoundland: the Formative Phase, 1697–1732," *Newfoundland Studies*, vol. 17 (2001).

Mannion, John, and Fidelma Maddock, "Old World Antecedents, New World Adaptations: Inistioge Immigration in Newfoundland," in William Nolan and Kevin Whelan (eds.), *Kilkenny: History and Society* (Dublin: Geography Publications, 1990).

McBride, Ian R., *Scripture Politics: Ulster Presbyterians and Irish Radicalism in the Late Eighteenth Century* (Oxford: Clarendon Press, 1998).

McBride, Lawrence W., *The Reynolds Letters: An Irish Emigrant Family in Manchester, England, 1878–1904* (Cork: Cork University Press, 1999).

McCarthy, Angela, *Irish Migrants in New Zealand, 1840–1937* (Woodbridge, Suffolk: Boydell Press, 2005).

McGee, Thomas D'Arcy, *A History of the Irish Settlers in North America from the earliest period to the Census of 1850* (Boston: P. Donahue, 1851).

Miller, David W., "Irish Catholicism and the Great Famine," *Journal of Social History*, vol. 9 (Autumn 1975).

Miller, David W., "Presbyterianism and 'Modernization,'" in *Ulster, Past and Present*, no. 80 (Aug. 1978).

Miller, David W., *Queen's Rebels. Ulster Loyalism in Historical Perspective* (Dublin: Gill and Macmillan, 1978).

Miller, David W., "Irish Presbyterians and the Great Famine," in Jacqueline Hill and Colm Lennon (eds.), *Luxury and Austerity* (Dublin: University College Dublin Press, 1999).

Miller, Kerby A., "Assimilation and Alienation: Irish emigrants' responses to industrial America, 1871–1921," in P. J. Drudy (ed.), *The Irish in America: Emigration, Assimilation, and Impact* (Cambridge: Cambridge University Press, 1985).

Miller, Kerby A., *Emigrants and Exiles: Ireland and the Irish Exodus to North America* (New York: Oxford University Press, 1985).

Miller, Kerby A., "Paddy's Paradox: Emigration to America in Irish Imagination and Rhetoric," in Dirk Hoerder and Horst Rössler, *Distant Magnets. Expectations and Realities in the Immigrant Experience, 1840–1930* (New York: Holmes and Meier, 1993).

Miller, Kerby A., "'Scotch-Irish' Myths and 'Irish' Identities in Eighteenth- and Nineteenth-Century America," in Charles Fanning (ed.), *New Perspectives on the Irish Diaspora* (Carbondale: Southern Illinois University Press, 2000).

Miller, Kerby A. *et al.*, *Irish Immigrants in the Land of Canaan. Letters and Memoirs from Colonial and Revolutionary America, 1675–1815* (Oxford: Oxford University Press, 2003).

Mitchel, John, *The Last Conquest of Ireland (Perhaps)* (Dublin: The Irishman's Office, 1861).

Mokyr, Joel, "Irish History with the Potato," *Irish Economic and Social History*, vol. 8 (1981).

Mokyr, Joel, *Why Ireland Starved: A Quantitative and Analytical History of the Irish Economy, 1800–1850* (London: George Allen and Unwin, 1983).

Moody, T. W., F. X. Martin and F. J. Byrne (eds.), *A New History of Ireland*, vol. 3, *Early Modern Ireland, 1534–1691* (Oxford: Clarendon Press, 1976).

Moody, T. W., and W. E. Vaughan (eds.), *A New History of Ireland*, vol. 4, *Eighteenth-Century Ireland, 1691–1800* (Oxford: Clarendon Press, 1986).

National Economic and Social Council of Ireland, *The Economic and Social Implications of Emigration* (Dublin: National Economic and Social Council, 1991).

Oakley, John, "Religion, ethnic identity and the Protestant minority in the Republic," in William Crotty and David E. Schmitt (eds.), *Ireland and the Politics of Change* (London: Longmans, 1998).

O'Brien, Michael J. [posthumous collection], *Irish Settlers in America. A Consolidation of Articles from the Journal of the American Irish Historical Society*, 2 vols. (Baltimore: Genealogical Publishing Co., 1979).

O'Dowd, Anne, *Spalpeens and Tatti Hokers: History and Folklore of the Irish Migratory Labourer in Ireland and Britain* (Dublin: Irish Academic Press, 1991).

O'Farrell, Patrick, "Whose Reality? The Irish Famine in history and literature," *Historical Studies* [Melbourne], vol. 20 (Apr. 1982).

O'Farrell, Patrick, *Letters from Irish-Australia, 1825–1929* (Belfast: Ulster Historical Foundation, 1990).

Ó Gráda, Cormac, "Seasonal Migration and the Post-Famine Adjustment in the West of Ireland," *Studia Hibernica*, vol. 13 (1973).

Ó Gráda, Cormac, "Did Ulster Catholics always have Larger Families?," *Irish Economic and Social History*, vol. 12 (1985).

Ó Gráda, Cormac, *Ireland before and after the Famine. Explorations in Economic History, 1800–1925* (Manchester: Manchester University Press, 1988).

Ó Gráda, Cormac, "Making History in Ireland in the 1940s and 1950s: the Saga of 'The Great Famine,'" *Irish Review*, no. 12 (1992).

Ó Gráda, Cormac, *Ireland. A New Economic History, 1780–1939* (Oxford: Clarendon Press, 1994).

Ó Gráda, Cormac, "Making Irish Famine History in 1995," *History Workshop Journal*, no. 41 (Autumn 1996).

Ó Gráda, Cormac, *Black '47 and Beyond. The Great Irish Famine in History, Economy, and Memory* (Princeton: Princeton University Press, 1999).

Ó Gráda, Cormac, *Ireland's Great Famine. Interdisciplinary Perspectives* (Dublin: University College Dublin Press, 2006).

Ó Gráda, Cormac, *Famine. A Short History* (Princeton: Princeton University Press, 2009).

Ó Gráda, Cormac, and Kevin O'Rourke, "Mass Migration as Disaster Relief: Lessons from the Great Famine," *European Review of Economic History*, vol. 1 (1997).

O'Grada, Cormac, and Brendan Walsh, "Fertility and Population in Ireland: North and South," *Population Studies*, vol. 49 (Jul. 1995).

O'Neill, Kevin, *Family and Farm in Pre-Famine Ireland. The Parish of Killaashandra* (Madison: University of Wisconsin Press, 1984).

O'Rourke, John, *The History of the Great Irish Famine of 1847, with notices of earlier Irish Famines* (Dublin: James Duffy and Co., 1874; 3rd ed., 1902).

O'Rourke, Kevin, "Did the Great Irish Famine Matter?" *Journal of Economic History*, vol. 51 (Mar. 1991).

Orr, James [posthumous collection], *Poems on Various Subjects. By James Orr of Ballycarry with a sketch of his life* (Belfast: William Mullan and Son, 1935.).

O'Sullivan, Patrick (ed.), *The Irish World Wide* (Leicester: Leicester University Press, 1992–97), 6 vols.

O'Toole, Fintan, *White Savage. William Johnson and the Invention of America* (London: Faber and Faber, 2005).

Parkhill, Trevor, "With a little help from their friends: assisted emigration schemes, 1700–1845," in Patrick J. Duffy (ed.), *To and from Ireland: Planned Migration Schemes c. 1600–2000* (Dublin: Geography Publications, 2004).

Peatling, G. K., "The Whiteness of Ireland Under and After the Union," *Journal of British Studies*, vol. 44 (Jan. 2005).

Quinn, David, *Ireland and America. Their Early Associations, 1500–1640* (Liverpool: Liverpool University Press, 1991).

Reid, James Seaton, *History of the Presbyterian Church in Ireland*, 3 vols. [vol. 3 completed by W. D. Killen] (Belfast: William Mullan, 1867).

Rodgers, Nini, "Ireland and the Black Atlantic in the eighteenth century," *Irish Historical Studies*, vol. 32 (Nov. 2000).

Rodgers, Nini, *Ireland, Slavery and Anti-Slavery: 1612–1865* (Basingstoke: Palgrave Macmillan, 2007).

Rodgers, Nini, "The Irish in the Caribbean, 1641–1837. An Overview," *Irish Migration Studies in Latin America*, vol. 5 (Nov. 2007).

Schrier, Arnold, *Ireland and the American Emigration, 1850–1900* (Minneapolis: University of Minnesota Press, 1958).

Sklar, June, "Marriage and Nonmarital Fertility: A Comparison of Ireland and Sweden," *Population and Development Review*, vol. 3 (Dec. 1977).

"Statements and Resolutions of the Irish Hierarchy at the Maynooth Meeting, June 21," *Irish Ecclesiastical Record*, 4th ser., vol. 27, no. 7 (Jul. 1910).

Stewart, A. T. Q., *A Deeper Silence. The Hidden Roots of the United Irish Movement* (London: Faber and Faber, 1993).

Stewart, A. T. Q., *The Summer Soldiers. The 1798 Rising in Antrim and Down* (Belfast: Blackstaff Press, 1995).

Stewart, A. T. Q., *The Shape of Irish History* (Montreal and Kingston: McGill-Queen's University Press, 2001).

Turner, Michael, *After the Famine. Irish Agriculture, 1850–1914* (Cambridge: Cambridge University Press, 1996).

Vaughan, W. E. (ed.), *A New History of Ireland*, vol. 5, *Ireland under the Union, I, 1801–70* (Oxford: Clarendon Press, 1989).

Vaughan, W. E. (ed.), *A New History of Ireland*, vol. 6, *Ireland under the Union, II, 1870–1921* (Oxford: Clarendon Press, 1996).

Vaughan, W. E., and A. J. Fitzpatrick (eds.), *Irish Historical Statistics. Population, 1821–1971* (Dublin: Royal Irish Academy, 1978).

Walker, Brian, "'The Lost Tribes of Ireland.' Diversity, Identity and Loss Among the Irish Diaspora," *Irish Studies Review*, vol. 15 (2007).

Wall, Maureen [née McGeehin], *Catholic Ireland in the Eighteenth Century: Collected Essays of Maureen Wall*, ed. Gerard O'Brien and Tom Dunne (Dublin: Geography Publications, 1989).

Whyte, John H., *Church and State in Modern Ireland, 1923–1970* (Dublin: Gill and Macmillan, 1971).

Williamson, Jeffrey G., "Economic Convergence: Placing Post-Famine Ireland in Comparative Perspective," *Irish Economic and Social History*, vol. 21 (1994).

Wilson, Catharine Anne, *A New Lease on Life. Landlords, Tenants, and Immigrants in Ireland and Canada* (Montreal and Kingston: McGill-Queen's University Press, 1994).

Wilson, David, *Thomas D'Arcy McGee, Passion, Reason, and Politics, 1825–1857*, vol. 1 (Montreal and Kingston: McGill-Queen's University Press, 2008). Vol. 2 forthcoming, 2011.

Wilson, T. G., *Victorian Doctor: being the Life of Sir William Wilde* (London: Methuen, 1942).

Woodham-Smith, Cecil, *The Great Hunger* (London: Hamish Hamilton, 1962, and New York: Harper and Row, 1963).

(3) SWEDISH SOCIETAL AND MIGRATION PATTERNS

Note: The entries in this section are listed according to Swedish alphabetical order. That is, "z" is followed sequentially by "å," "ä," and "ö." The conventions employed concerning punctuation, placement of quotation marks, and capitalization are those of English-language usage which are slightly different from Swedish protocols.

Alwall, Jonas, "Religious Liberty in Sweden: An Overview," *Journal of Church and State*, vol. 42 (2000).

Barton, H. Arnold, *Letters from the Promised Land. Swedes in America, 1840–1914* (Minneapolis: University of Minnesota Press, 1975).

Barton, H. Arnold, *The Search for Ancestors. A Swedish-American Family Saga* (Carbondale: Southern Illinois University Press, 1979).

Barton, H. Arnold, "Neglected Types of Correspondence as Sources for Swedish-American History," *Swedish-American Historical Quarterly*, vol. 33 (1982).

Barton, H. Arnold, *A Folk Divided. Homeland Swedes and Swedish Americans, 1840–1940* (Carbondale: Southern Illinois University Press, 1994).

Barton, H. Arnold (ed.), *Peter Cassel and Iowa's New Sweden* (Chicago: Swedish-American Historical Society, 1995).

Barton, H. Arnold, *Northern Arcadia. Foreign Travelers in Scandinavia, 1765–1815* (Carbondale: Southern Illinois University Press, 1998).

Barton, H. Arnold, *Sweden and Visions of Norway. Politics and Culture, 1814–1905* (Carbondale: Southern Illinois University Press, 2003).

Barton, H. Arnold, *The Old Country and the New: Essays on Sweden and America* (Carbondale: Southern Illinois University Press, 2007).

Beijbom, Ulf, *Swedes in Chicago. A Demographic and Social Study of the 1846–1880 Immigration* (Uppsala: Studia Historica Upsaliensia, 1971).

Beijbom, Ulf, *Utvandrarkvinnor. Svenska Kvinnaöden i Amerika* (Stockholm: Norstedts, 2006)

Bengtsson, Haldan, "The Temperance Movement and Temperance Legislation in Sweden," *Annals of the American Academy of Political and Social Sciences*, vol. 197 (May 1938).

Bengtsson, Tommy (ed.), *Population, Economy and Welfare in Sweden* (Berlin: Springer-Verlag, 1994).

Bengtsson, Tommy, *et al.*, *Life under Pressure. Mortality and Living Standards in Europe and Asia, 1700–1900* (Cambridge: MIT Press, 2004).

Bengtsson, Tommy, and Martin Dribe, "New Evidence on the Standard of Living in Sweden during the Eighteenth and Nineteenth Centuries: Long-Term Development of the Demographic Response to Short-Term Economic Stress," in Robert C. Allen, Tommy Bengtsson and Martin Dribe (eds.), *Living Standards in the Past* (Oxford: Oxford University Press, 2005).

Bengtsson, Tommy, Gunnar Fridlizius and Rolf Ohlsson (eds.), *Pre-Industrial Population Change. The Mortality Decline and Short-Term Population Movements* (Stockholm: Almquist and Wiksell, 1984).

Brodin, Knut, *Emigrantvisor och andra Visor* (Stockholm: Ählén och Åkerlands Förlag, 1938).

Bäck, Kalle, "Lagaskifte och torpbebyggelsen i Östergötland, 1827–65," *Historisk Tidskrift*, vol. 108 (1988).

Carlson, Benny, "Eli Heckscher and Natural Monopoly: The Nightmare that Never Came True," *Scandinavian Economic History Review*, vol. 40 (1992).

Edvinsson, Sören, *et al.* (eds.), *Befolkningshistoriska Perspectiv. Festskrif till Lars-Göran Tedebrand* (Umeå University: Report no. 24, Demographic Data Base Project, 2004).

Elmen, Paul, *Wheat Flour Messiah. Eric Jansson of Bishop Hill* (Carbondale: Southern Illinois University Press, 1976).

Elmen, Paul, "The American-Swedish Kibbutz," *Swedish Pioneer Historical Quarterly*, vol. 32 (Jul. 1981).

Ericsson, Tom, and Börje Harnesk, "'Disputationsmöten och öfningsfält för tankekrafter.' Läseriet i övre Norrland in 1800-talets början," *Historisk Tidskrift*, vol. 113 (1993).

Fahlen, Olaf, *Nåsbönderna i Jerusalem. Berättelsen om en märklig Utvandring* (Stockholm: Wiken, 1988).

Floren, Anders, and Göran Ryden, "Protoindustri och tidigkapitalism," *Historisk Tidskrift*, vol. 112 (1992).

Fält, Helmer, *Separatismen i Orsa, 1850–1860* (Stockholm: Diakonistyrelsens Bokförlag, 1967).

Gelfgren, Stefan, "Väckelse och Sekularisering. Exemplet Umeås Evangelisk-Lutherska Missions-förening, 1850–1910," *Historisk Tidskrift*, vol. 123 (2003).

Government of Sweden, *Emigrationsutredningen* (Stockholm: KB, 1907–13). This consists of a massive main report (*Betänkande*) and 20 appendices, several of which are monographs in themselves. Most, but not all, of the material is identifiable by its main editor or author and this information is specified in my citations. The key persons for our purposes were Gustav Sundbärg and Nils Wohlin.

Government of Sweden, *Historisk Statistik för Sverige* [multi-volume] (Stockholm: Statistiska Centralbyrån, 1955).

Government of Sweden [authors: Erland Hofsten and Hans Lundström], *Urval*, no. 8 (Stockholm: Statistika Centralbyrån, 1976).

Gårestad, Peter, *Industrialisering och Beskattning i Sverige, 1861–1914* (Uppsala: Acta Universitatis Upsaliensis, 1987).

Hall, A. G., *Svenska Baptisternas Historia under en Tid af femtio År, 1848–1898*, 2 vols. (Chicago: A. G. Halls Förlag, 1900).

Hallerdt, Bjorn (ed.), *Emigration från Dalarna* (Falun: Dalarnes Forminnes och Hemsbygdsförbund, 1966).

Harnesk, Börke, *Legofolk. Drängar, Pigor och Bönder i 1700- och 1800-talens* (Umeå: Acta Universitatis Umensis, 1900)

Hasselberg, Yiva, "Networks and Scientific Integrity: Eli Heckscher and the Construction of Economic History in Sweden, 1920–1950," *Scandinavian Economic History Review*, vol. 54 (2006).

Hatton, Ragnhild (ed.), *Captain James Jefferyes's Letters from the Swedish Army, 1707–1709* (Stockholm: P. A. Norstedt and Söner, 1954).

Heckscher, Eli F., "The Place of Sweden in Modern Economic History," *Economic History Review*, vol. 4 (Oct. 1932).

Heckscher, Eli F., *An Economic History of Sweden* (tr. Göran Ohlin) (Cambridge: Harvard University Press, 1963).

Hofsten, Erland, *Svensk beforkningshistoria. Några grunddrag i utvecklingen från 1750* (Stockholm: Raben and Sjögren, 1986).

Holm, Ernst G., and Egil Lönnberg, *Nödåren i Norra Småland, 1867–1869* (Jönköping: Länsmuseets Förlag, 1945).

Håger, Olle, Carl Torell and Hans Villius, *Ett Satans år. Norrland 1867* (Stockholm: Sveriges Radios Förlag, 1978).

Hörsell, Anne, *Borgare, Smeder och Änkor. Ekonomi och Beforkning i Eskilstuna gamla stad och fristad, 1750–1850* (Uppsala: Acta Universitatis Upsaliensis, 1983).

Isacson, Matts, and Lars Magnusson, *Proto-industrialisation in Scandinavia. Craft Skills in the Industrial Revolution* (Hamburg: Berg, 1987).

Janson, Florence Edith, *The Background of Swedish Immigration, 1840–1930* (Philadelphia: University of Pennsylvania, 1931).

Johansson, Rolf, "Registrering av Flyttare. En Källkritisk Granskning av Svensk Kyrkobokboksmaterial, 1840–1890," *Scandia Tidskrift för Historisk Forskning*, vol. 42 (1976).

Jutikkala, Eino, "The Great Finnish Famine in 1696–97," *Scandinavian Economic History Review*, vol. 3 (1955).

Kark, Ruth, "Sweden and the Holy Land: pietistic and communal settlement," *Journal of Historical Geography*, vol. 22 (1996).

Kent, Neil, *A Concise History of Sweden* (Cambridge: Cambridge University Press, 2008).

Kälvemark, Ann-Sofie, *Reaktionen mot Utvandringen* (Uppsala: Studia Historica Upsaliensia, 1972).

Kälvemark, Ann-Sofie, "Utvandring och Självständighet. Några synpunkter på den kvinnliga emigrationen från Sverige," *Historisk Tidskrift*, vol. 103 (1983).

Lagerlöf, Selma, *Jerusalem* (1901–02; 1st Engl. tr., London: W. Heinemann Ltd, 1903).

Larson, Esther Elisabeth, *Swedish Commentators on America, 1638–1865. An Annotated List of Selected Manuscript and Printed Materials* (New York: New York Public Library, 1963).

Larsson, Margareta, "1800-talets Sociala Förändringar ur Folkmängdstabellens Perspectiv," *Historisk Tidskrift*, vol. 109 (1989).

Lindberg, John S., *The Background of Swedish Emigration to the United States. An Economic and Sociological Study in the Dynamics of Migration* (Minneapolis: University of Minnesota Press, 1930).

Lindquist, Emory, "Appraisal of Sweden and America by Swedish Emigrants: The Testimony of Letters in Emigrationsutredningen (1907)," *Swedish Pioneer Historical Quarterly*, vol. 17 (1966).

Lintelman, Joy K., "'She did not whimper or complain': Swedish-American Female Charity Cases in Minneapolis, 1910–1930," *Swedish-American Historical Quarterly*, vol. 45 (Jan. 1994).

Ljungberg, Jonas, "The Impact of the Great Emigration on the Swedish Economy," *Scandinavian Economic History Review*, vol. 45, no. 2 (1997).

Ljungmark, Lars (tr. Kermit B. Westerberg), *Swedish Exodus* (1965; Carbondale: Southern Illinois University Press, 1979).

Lovell, Briant Lindsay, *Scandinavian Exodus. Demography and Social Development of 19th-century Rural Communities* (Boulder: Westview Press, 1987).

Lundh, Christer, "The Social Mobility of Servants in Rural Sweden, 1740–1894," *Continuity and Change*, vol. 14 (1999).

Magnusson, Lars, "Drinking and the Verlag System, 1820–1850: The Significance of Taverns and Drink in Eskilstuna before Industrialisation," *Scandinavian Economic History Review*, vol. 34 (1986).

Magnusson, Lars, "Försnilling, Smyghandel och Fusk. Förlaggssystem och hantverkskultur i Eskilstuna vid början av 1800-talet," *Historisk Tidskrift*, vol. 86 (1986).

Magnusson, Lars, *An Economic History of Sweden* (London: Routledge, 2000).

Martinius, Sture, *Jordbruk och Ekonomisk Tillväxt i Sverige, 1830–1870* (Göteborg, Ekonomisk-Historiska Institutionen vid Göteborgs Universitet, 1970).

Mattson, Hans, *Reminiscences. The Story of an Emigrant* (Saint Paul: D. D. Merrill Co., 1892).

McInnis, R. Marvin, "The American Role in Swedish Industrial Development and the Canadian Connection," Lund University Economic History Seminar, Sept. 2003.

Miller, Roger, and Torvald Gerger, *Social Change in Nineteenth-Century Swedish Agrarian Society* (Stockholm: Acta Universitatis Stockholmiensis, 1985).

Moberg, Kerstin, *Från Tjänstehjon till Hembitrade* (Uppsala: Uppsala Universitet, 1978).

Moberg, Vilhelm, *Utvandrarna* [*The Emigrants*] (Stockholm: Albert Bonniers Förlag, 1949).

Moberg, Vilhelm, *Invandrarna* [*Unto a New Land*] (Stockholm: Albert Bonniers Förlag, 1952).

Moberg, Vilhelm, *Nybyggarna* [*The Settlers*] (Stockholm: Albert Bonniers Förlag, 1956).

Moberg, Vilhelm, *Sista Brevet till Sverige* [*Last Letter Home*] (Stockholm: Albert Bonniers Förlag, 1959).

Moberg, Vilhelm, *The Unknown Swedes. A Book about Swedes and America, Past and Present* (Carbondale: Southern Illinois University Press, 1988, tr. Roger McKnight from the original ed., 1950; 2nd ed., 1968).

Moberg, Vilhem (tr. Paul B. Austin), *A History of the Swedish People*, 2 vols. (New York: Pantheon Books, 1973).

Moller, Jens, "The Landed Estate and the Landscape: Landownership and the Changing Landscape of Southern Sweden during the 19th and 20th Centuries," *Geografiska Annaler. Series B. Human Geography*, vol. 67 (1985).

Montgomery, G. A., *The Rise of Modern Industry in Sweden* (London: P. S. King, 1939).

Mulder, William, *Homeward to Zion. The Mormon Migration from Scandinavia* (Minneapolis: University of Minnesota Press, 1957).

Murdoch, Steve, and Alexia Grosjean, "Irish Soldiers in Swedish Service, 1609–13," *The Irish Sword*, vol. 24 (Winter 2004).

Nelson, Marie Clark, "Through the Looking Glass. Report on the Famine in Norrbotten as seen through the eyes of *Norrbottens-Kurinen*, 1867–69," *Historisk Tidskrift*, vol. 104 (1984).

Nelson, Marie Clark, *Bitter Bread. The Famine in Norrbotten, 1867–1868* (Uppsala: Acta Universitatis Upsaliensis, 1988).

Nilsson, Fred, *Emigrationen från Stockholm till Nordamerika, 1880–1893. En Studie in Urban Utvandring* (Stockholm: Svenska Bokförlaget and Uppsala: Studia Historica Upsaliensia, 1970).

Norbert, Anders, "Sundsvallsstrejken 1879—ett Startskoff för den stora Amerika-Unvandringen?" *Historisk Tidskrift*, vol. 98 (1978).

Nordbäck, Carola, *Samvetets Röst. Om mötet mellan Luthersk ortodoxi och konservativ Pietism i 1720-talets Sverige* (Umeå: Department of Historical Studies, Umeå University, 2004).

Norman, Hans, and Harald Runblom, *Transatlantic Connections: Nordic Migration to the New World after 1800* (Oslo: Norwegian University Press, 1988).

Norström, Thor, "Real Wages. Alcohol Consumption and Mortality in Sweden, 1861–1913," *European Journal of Population*, vol. 4 (1988).

Ohlander, Ann-Sofie, and Hans Norman, "Kriser och Katastrofer. Ett forskningsproject om effecterna av nöd. Svält och Epidemier i det förindustriella Sverige," *Historisk Tidskrift*, vol. 104 (1984).

Ohlsen, Karin, and Eva Olander, *Orsaord* (Orsa: Orsa-Skattunge Hembygdsförenings, 2010).

Olsson, Carl-Axel, "Eli Heckscher and the Problem of Synthesis," *Scandinavian Economic History Review*, vol. 40 (1992).

Olsson, Mats, "Manorial economy and *corvée* labour in southern Sweden, 1650–1850," *Economic History Review*, new ser., vol. 49 (2006).

Olsson, Nils William, *Swedish Passenger Arrivals in New York, 1820–50* (Chicago: Swedish Pioneer Society, 1967).

Olsson, Nils William, *Swedish Passenger Arrivals in US Ports (except New York)* (Stockholm: Acta Stockholmiensis, 1979).

Olsson, Nils William, with Erik Wiken, *Swedish Passenger Arrivals in the United States, 1820–1850* (Stockholm: Acta Stockholmiensis, 1995).

"On the Banks of the Rum:" Centennial Story of Cambridge, Minnesota, 1866–1966 (Cambridge, MN: Cambridge Centennial Committee, 1966).

Oredsson, Sverker, "Statsmaktenera och den Ekonomiska Krisen i slutet ave 1870-talet," *Scandia*, vol. 33 (1967).

O'Rourke, Kevin H., and Jeffrey G. Williamson, "Open Economy Forces and Late Nineteenth-Century Swedish Catch-up. A Quantitative Accounting," *Scandinavian Economic History Review*, vol. 42 (1995).

Ostergren, Robert C., *A Community Transplanted. The Trans-Atlantic Experience of a Swedish Immigrant Settlement in the Upper Middle West, 1835–1915* (Madison: University of Wisconsin Press, 1988).

Palm, Lennart, "Household Size in Pre-Industrial Sweden," *Scandinavian Economic History Review*, vol. 47 (1999).

Palm, Lennart, "Stormakstidens, dolda systemskifte—från tonårsäktenskap till sena giften," *Scandia*, vol. 66, no. 1 (2000).

Pettersson, Lars, "Reading and Writing Skills and the Agrarian Revolution: Scandinavian Peasants during the Age of Enclosure," *Scandinavian Economic History Review*, vol. 44 (1996).

Pitkänen, Kari J., "Patterns of Mortality during the Great Finnish Famine," *Acta Demographica* (1992).

Pitkänen, Kari J., *Deprivation and Disease. Mortality during the Great Finnish Famine of the 1860s* (Helsinki: Finnish Demographic Society, 1993).

Proeschold, Kevin, "The Prolific Pen of George M. Stephenson: An Annotated Bibliography," *Swedish-American Historical Quarterly*, vol. 52 (Apr. 2002).

Quigley, John Michael, "An Economic Model of Swedish Emigration," *Quarterly Journal of Economics*, vol. 86 (Feb. 1972).

Runblom, Harald, and Hans Norman (eds.), *From Sweden to America. A History of the Migration* (Minneapolis: University of Minnesota Press, 1976).

Runeby, Nils, *Den Nya Världen och den Gamla. Amerikabild och Emigrationsuppfattning i Sverige, 1820–1860* (Uppsala: Studia Historica Upsaliensia, 1969).

Ryden, P., *Svenska Baptisternas i Minnesota Historia: Från 1850-talet till 1918* (Cambridge, MN: Historiska Kommitte, Statskonferens Minnesota Baptisternas, 1918).

Sandberg, Lars G., and Richard H. Steckel, "Overpopulation and Malnutrition Rediscovered: Hard Times in 19th-Century Sweden," *Explorations in Economic History*, vol. 25 (1988).

Sandewall, Allan, *Separatismen in Övre Norrland, 1820–1855* (Uppsala: Svenska Kyrkhistoriska Föreningen, 1952).

Sandewall, Allan, "Konventikelplakatets upphävande—ett gränsar i Svensk Religionsfrihetslagstifning?" *Kyrkohistorisk Årsskrift*, vol. 58 (1957).

Scott, Franklin D., "Sweden's Constructive Opposition to Emigration," *Journal of Modern History*, vol. 37 (Sep. 1965).

Scott, Franklin D., *Sweden. The Nation's History* (Minneapolis: University of Minnesota Press, 1977),

Scott, Franklin D., "Changing Swedish Attitudes toward America and Emigrants," *Swedish-American Historical Quarterly*, vol. 35 (Jul. 1984).

Selling, Olof H., "Dahlkarlar skulle kunne med nytta tages i stort från Sverige," *Dalarnas Hembygdsbok, 1966* (Falun: Dalarnas Fornminnes och Hembygdsförbund, 1968).

Soltow, Lee, "The rich and the destitute in Sweden, 1805–1855: a test of Tocqueville's inequality hypotheses," *Economic History Review*, new ser., vol. 42 (Feb. 1989).

"The Staff of the Institute for Social Sciences, University of Stockholm," *Wages, Cost of Living and National Income in Sweden 1860–1930*, 3 vols. (London: P. S. King and Son, 1933–37).

Stattin, Jan, *Hushållningssällskapen och Agrarsamhällets Förändring—utveckling och verksamhet under 1800-talets första hälft* (Uppsala: Acta Universitatis Upsaliensis, 1980).

Stegeby, E. Kenneth, "An Analysis of the Impending Disestablishment of the Church of Sweden," *Brigham Young University Law Review*, vol. 51 (1999).

Stephenson, George M., "The Background of the Beginnings of Swedish Immigration, 1850–1875," *American Historical Review*, vol. 31 (Jul. 1926).

Stephenson, George M., *The Religious Aspects of Swedish Immigration. A Study of Immigrant Churches* (Minneapolis: University of Minnesota Press, 1932).

St Jean, Eva, "'Letters from the Promised Land': Interpreting Ambiguities in Immigrant Letters," *Swedish-American Historical Quarterly*, vol. 46 (2006).

Sundbärg, Gustav (ed.), *Sweden. Its People and its Industry. Historical and Statistical Handbook* (Stockholm: KB, 1904).

Svenska Baptism genom 100 År: En Krönika i Ord och Bild (Stockholm: privately printed, 1958).

Svensson, Gunnar, *Folket i Nasareths* (Väröbacka: Häralds, 1993).

Svensson, Patrick, "Peasants and Entrepreneurship in the Nineteenth-Century Agricultural Transformation of Sweden," *Social Science History*, vol. 30 (Fall, 2006), pp. 387–429.

Söderberg, Johan, "A Long-Term Perspective on Regional Economic Development in Sweden, ca. 1550–1914," *Scandinavian Economic History Review*, vol. 32 (1984).

Söderberg, Johan, "Hard Times in 19th-Century Sweden," *Explorations in Economic History*, vol. 26 (1989).

Söderlund, E. F., *Swedish Timber Exports, 1850–1950. A History of the Swedish Timber Trade* (Stockholm: Almqvist and Wiksells, 1952).

Tedebrand, Lars-Göran, *Västernorrland och Nordamerika, 1875–1913. Utvandring och Återinvandring* (Uppsala: Studies Historica Upsaliensia, 1972).

Tedebrand, Lars-Göran, *Historia och Demografi. Valda Texter* (Umeå: Johan Nordlander, 1999).

Tiscornia, Alberto, *Statens, godsens eller böndernas Socknar? Den Sockenkommunala självstyrelsens utveckling i Västerfarärnebo, Stora Malm och Jäder, 1800–1880* (Uppsala: Acta Universitatis Upsaliensis, 1992).

Unionius, Gustaf E. M., *Minnen från en sjuttonårig vistelse in nordvästra Amerika*, 2 vols. (Uppsala: W. Schultz, 1861–62).

Westin, Gunnar, *George Scott och hans Verksamhet i Sveriga* (Stockholm: Svenska Kyrkans Diakonistyrelses Bokförlag, 1928–29), vol. 1, *Akademisk Avhandling* and vol. 2, *Handlingar, Tal och Brev*.

Westin, Gunnar (ed.), *Emigranterna och Kyrkan. Brev från och till svenskar i Amerika, 1849–1892* (Stockholm: Svenska Kyrkans Diakonistyrelses Bokförlag, 1932).

Westin, Gunnar (ed.), *Ur den Svenska Folkväckelsens Historia och Tankevärld. Brev fran och till den Svenska Baptismens Banbrytare, 1850–1855*, 2 vols. (Stockholm: B.M:s Bokförlags, 1933–34).

Widen, Albin, "Goda år och Nödår," in Evert Wrangel, Arivd Gierow and Bror Olsson (eds.), *Svenska Folket genom Tiderna*, vol. 9, *Vid 1800-talets mitt* (Malmö: n.p., 1940).

Winberg, Christer, *Folkökning och Proletarisering. Kring den sociala Structuromvandlingern på Sveriges landsbygd under den agrara revolutionen* (Göteborg: Historiska Institutionen i Göteborg, 1975).

Winberg, Christer, "Familj och Jord in tre Västgötasocknar. Generationsskiften bland självägande bönder, c. 1810–1870," *Historisk Tidskrift*, vol. 101 (1981).

Wohlin, Nils, "Jorddelningsväsendet i Sverige och statistiken," *Ekonomisk Tidskrift*, vol. 9 (1907).

Wohlin, Nils, "Torpkommissionens Betänkande," *Ekonomisk Tidskrift*, vol. 13 (1911).

Wright, Robert L., *Swedish Emigrant Ballads* (Lincoln: University of Nebraska Press, 1965).

Ågren, Maria, *Jord och Gäld: Social skiftning och rättslig konflikt i södra Dalarna c. 1650–1850* (Uppsala: Acta Universitatis Upsaliensis, 1992).

Ågren, Maria, and Amy Louise Erickson, *The Marital Economy in Scandinavia and Britain, 1400–1900* (London: Ashgate, 2005).

Åkerman, Sune, "Projects and Research Priorities," *Historisk Tidskrift*, vol. 9 (1970).

Åkerman, Sune, "Toward an Understanding of Emigrational Processes," *Scandinavian Journal of History*, vol. 18 (1978).

INDEX

abstinence, sexual
  see population limitation
Act of Indemnity (1719ff) 115
Adams, William Forbes 25*n*31, 25*n*33, 93, 94,
  160
age structure
  in European countries (1926) 174
Agricultural Revolution, Ireland
  farm size 205–08
  post-Famine 202–08, 220–21
  pre-Famine 29–30
Agricultural Revolution, Sweden 50–55,
  189–93, 220–21, 243
Åkerman, Sune 4–6, 168–71, 184*n*1, 238,
  248*n*5
Åkerman curve 5, 168–72
American Baptist Publication Society 83,
  92*n*61
American Civil War 84, 236
Andrews, J. H. 14
Anglicans
  see Church of Ireland
Anglo-Irish
  see Church of Ireland
Anthony (Captain) Thomas 107
Anti-Conventicle Act 73–74, 78, 80, 82
arable crops
  definition 222*n*11
Arawak 107
Arborelius, Olof Ulrik 79
Arensberg, Conrad 201, 206, 218
Argentina 99
arrendator 44, 46
"artificial" birth control 213, 215
  see also population limitation
"Atlantic Community" 4–6, 21*n*6
Augsburg Confession 73
Augustana Synod 84
Australia 10, 99, 156–57, 166*n*108
Avalon Peninsula 105

  see also Newfoundland
"averted births" 154–55, 158, 165*n*92, 167*n*110
axial stress 152, 168, 172, 230
  as concept 136–37
  see also Great Deprivation; Great Famine

"baby farming" 207–08, 244–45
Bäck, Kalle 64*n*96
backstugusittare 45–6, 48, 54, 190–93
Bacon, Francis 228
"bad luck" 152–53
Ballingrane 122
Ballycarry 119–20
Ballymena 217
Baptists 69, 75–85, 104, 237, 250*n*43, 251*n*48
  see also Readers
Barbados 107
bark bread 141
barony
  definition 14
Barthélemy, Saint 257
Barton, H. Arnold 8, 86*n*12, 249*n*15, 262
Beckett, James C. 116, 133*n*92
Beijbom, Ulf 161*n*12
Belchem, John 86*n*10
Belfast 29, 118, 220
"Belfast Pogroms" 259
Belich, James 199*n*36
Bengtsson, Tommy 61*n*75, 162*n*39
Beyond the Line 129–130*n*46
birth rate
  Ireland 17, 32–34, 174–75, 179–80, 185*n*19,
  261
  Sweden 17, 42, 60*n*61, 175–77, 185*n*19,
  260–61
Bishop Hill, Illinois 82
"Black Box" 228
Blake family 166*n*101
Blegen, Theodore C. 22*n*11
"blessed turf" 97–98

Bohemian Brethren 88*n*23
Bonaparte, Napoleon 99, 257
bonde
    as concept 28
Bourke, P. M. Austin 33, 37, 57*n*32, 58*n*40
Boyle, Phelim P. 154
Brazil 99
British North America 102–03, 110, 111, 121,
    128–29*n*35, 131*n*72, 156–57, 166*n*108
    see also Canada; Maritimes; Newfoundland;
    Ontario; Quebec; Upper Canada
Brubaker, Rogers 6–7
Bulgaria/Serbia-Montenegro 242
Burckhardt, Jacob 1, 52, 262
Bush, George W. 153

Calvert, George (cr. baron Baltimore, 1625) 104
Canada 156–57, 166*n*108
    see also British North America
Carib 107
Caribbean 106–10, 129*n*45, 130*n*62, 156–57,
    166*n*108
Carleton, William 27, 149
Carrier, N. H. 24–25*n*31, 25*n*33, 94, 126*n*3
Carroll, Michael P. 135*n*121
catch-up
    see convergence
Cassel, Peter 81–82, 87*n*17
Catechism of 1810 75–76
Catholic Apostolic Church
    see Irvingites
Catholic Church (Roman), Ireland
    belief system 209–11
    emancipation 104, 120
    institutional strength 211–15
    membership 113, 211
    oral confession 214, 219
    see also devotional revolution; population
    limitation
Catholic Church (Roman), Sweden 72–73, 76,
    88–89*n*25
Catholic Truth Society 209, 213
Charles XV 79
Chayanov, Alexander V. 52, 64*n*98
Chichester, Arthur 117
Chile 99
Chomsky, Noam 93
Church of Ireland 72, 81, 88*n*21, 104, 113–22
    passim, 123–24, 215–20, 225*n*50
    see also population limitation

civil liberties, Sweden 79–85, 88*n*21, 88–89*n*25,
    90–91*n*49
Clark, Samuel 35, 57*n*35
Clarkson, Leslie A. 31–32, 127*n*14, 186*n*27,
    194
class-fragment
    as concept 192
Clause, Gregory 164*n*62
clergy, Swedish 68, 69, 70, 75–85
    see also Swedish State Church
cliometricians
    see economic historians (as group)
Coleridge, Samuel Taylor 39
common freehold village, Swedish 51
    see also enclosure, Swedish
communications, internal
    pre-Deprivation Sweden 68
    pre-Famine Ireland 30
comparative history
    as concept 7–8
Conacre 36–39, 58*n*40
condominium of risk 43, 47, 62*n*78
    as concept 37
Connell, Kenneth H. 31–34, 56*n*20, 57*n*31,
    150, 180–83, 186*n*39, 206, 213, 218
Connolly, Sean J. 97–98, 113, 115, 133*n*93, 183,
    187*n*48, 187*n*51, 212, 224*n*35, 224*n*38
conscription (Swedish)
    see military service, Sweden
contraception
    see population limitation
convergence 188–96, 198*n*29, 198–99*n*31,
    199*n*32, 227–29, 260
    as concept 188
    as alchemy 199*n*32
copyholders 35–37
cost of passage
    to Great Britain 98–102
    to North America 99–100, 128*n*23
counties, Irish definition 13–14
counties, Swedish
    see län
"country divorce", Irish 185*n*25
Cousens, S. H. 160, 167*n*113
Crawford, E. Margaret 127*n*17
Crawford, W. H. 56*n*8, 57*n*37
Criminal Amendment Act (1935) 261
Cromwell, Oliver 114, 130*n*62
Crotty, Raymond 150–52, 165*n*85
Crown estates, Swedish 61*n*66

crude death rate
  see death rate
Cullen, Louis 108
Cullen, Paul 211–12, 214, 223n33
cultural punctures 85, 93, 94–95, 100–25 *passim*
  as concept 71
currency system, Swedish 49

Dakota Territory 235
Dalarna 52, 79, 82, 83, 87n19, 139, 142, 233, 238
Danaher, Kevin 221
Danish emigration 147
day labourer
  Irish 36–39, 193–94, 198n24, 207–08, 233
  Swedish 45–55, 144, 145, 190–94
  see also landless labourers
de Valera, Eamon 149
death rate 60n61, 142–43, 144–45, 154, 162n32
  see also excess death rate; fungibility; Great Deprivation; Great Famine
deindustrialization 28–31, 40–41
Delaney, Enda 126n2, 263n9
Delaware Valley 108, 121, 134n115
Denmark 8
  see also intra-European migration, Swedish
"Dermod"
  see MacGill, Patrick
"devotion"
  see cultural puncture
Devotional Revolution 210–15
  see also Larkin, Emmet; Miller, David W.
Dickson, David 31–32, 160n5
Dickson, R. J. 120–21, 134n114, 134n116
disease, famine 142, 151–55
Dissenter Relief Acts
  Irish 116
  Swedish 80–81
Dissenters, Irish
  see Methodists; Presbyterians
Dissenters, Swedish 73–85
  see also Baptists; Free Church; Methodists
distress foods 161n21
  see also bark bread
Donegall, successive earls of, 117–18
Doyle, David Noel 110–11, 121, 135n118, 135n120
dräng 45–55, 197n13
Dribe, Martin 61n75
Duluth 235

economic historians (as group) 2–3, 65–66, 188–89, 195–96, 227–30, 248n6
Elliott, Bruce 123–25
Elliott, Marianne 118
Embury, Philip 122
emigrant demography (1861–1910), 173–75
  gender 239–40, 253n63
  marital state 239
emigrant letters 238, 239, 240, 251–52n53, 252n54, 252n58, 255n94
Emigration Commission (Irish, 1948–54) 93–94, 126n2, 262n5
Emigration Commission (Swedish, 1907–13) 24n29, 42–43, 61n69, 62–63n84 144, 170, 197n12, 208–09, 231–38, 243, 252n58, 255n78
emigration culture
  Åkerman's concept 168–71
  decline 261–62
  figure 170
  Fitzpatrick's definition 8, 148, 169–70, 247
  summary 220–22
emigration
  motives 65–66, 71–85, 94–95, 99–100, 116, 158, 227–38 *passim*
enclosure, Swedish 44, 50–55
Encumbered Estates Acts (1848–49) 104
Engels, Friedrich 181
enskiftet 51
  see also enclosure, Swedish
Erickson, Charlotte 21n6
Established Church, Irish
  see Church of Ireland
European Demographic Transition
  as concept 175–77
  Ireland 179
  Sweden 175–77
European Fertility Project 179
evangelicalism
  as concept 89n32
excess death rate
  as concept 165n91
  see also fungibility; Great Famine

Fahlbeck, Pontus 193, 197n12
Famine, Irish (1739–41) 97, 127n18, 160n5
Famine, Irish (1845–49)
  see Great Famine
famines, European 137–42
  see also Great Deprivation

farm size, Irish
  post-Famine 204–06
  pre-Famine 37–38
  see also agricultural revolution, Ireland; land
    acts
Faughanvale (Co. Londonderry) 253*n*65
Ferenczi, Imre 18, 21*n*3, 24*n*31, 227–30
Ferryland 105
fertility rates
  pre-Famine Ireland 31, 32–34
  see also population limitation
Finland 9, 141
  emigration 147
  famines 137–38, 141–42
First Dissenter Act (Sweden, 1860) 80
Fitzgerald, Edward 149
Fitzgerald, Patrick 108, 126*n*7
Fitzpatrick, David 8, 126*n*7, 128*n*26, 148,
  167*n*108, 169–72, 186*n*27, 193, 198*n*24,
  207, 225–26*n*68, 243, 244
"floating bridge" 101–02
  see also seasonal migrants to Great Britain
Foner, Eric 199*n*37
frälse 44
Franchise Act (Irish, 1850) 119
Francke, A. H. 88*n*23
Free Church 77–85, 231, 237, 251*n*48
  see also Baptists; Readers
freeholders
  Swedish 42–55
  Irish 35, 119, 190–93
  see also agricultural revolution; *bonde*; land
    acts
"free" land 195–96
Freeman, T. W. 56*n*5, 57*n*37
Friedman, Milton 136–37
fungibility
  as concept 159–60

Gabaccia, Donna 6
Gahn, Henric 87*n*19
Gallagher, Paddy ("the Cope") 245
Gävle 68, 70, 82
Gävleborg 139
Geary, R. G. 126*n*2
Germany 8, 23*n*27, 242
  see also intra-European migration, Swedish
Gjerde, Jon 92*n*69
globalization
  see convergence

godsägare 43–44
Goodhue County 82
Göteborg 68, 78
Göthar (Goths) 12
Gould, J. D. 99, 128*n*23, 242, 254*n*75, 254*n*77
Gowan, Ogle 123–24
grassland
  definition 222*n*11
Gray, Peter 165*n*85
Great Britain 156–57, 166*n*108
  see also Liverpool; seasonal migrants to
    Great Britain
Great Deprivation (Sweden) 21, 136–42,
  231–38
  as axial stress 136–37
  crude death rates 142–45
  emigration 146–47
  locales 139–44
  poor relief 143
  price effects 145–46
  as test case 152
  vulnerable class 144–45, 162*n*41
Great European Migration
  as concept 4–6, 257–58, 261
  and "nation" 6–7
  and "poor European periphery" 8–10
  size of 16–21
Great Famine (Ireland) 16–17, 21, 136–37,
  138–39, 148–60, 204, 231–38
  averted births 154–55, 158, 165*n*92,
    167*n*110
  "bad luck" 152–53
  calculation of human loss 156–60
  crude death rate 154
  emigration 156–60
  excess death rate 154
  historiography 148–53, 164*n*61
  land sales 223*n*19
  not genocide 152–53
  population loss 154–60
  Presbyterians 156
  price shocks 151–52
Great O'Neill 104
Great Revival (Irish, 1859) 218
Great Strike (Sweden, 1909) 193
Greece 242
Greenock 121
Griffin, Patrick 117, 132*n*80
gross European emigration 18–19

gross Irish emigration 19, 21, 94–96, 102,
    110–13, 121, 126n7, 169, 258–59
    see also Ó Gráda Paradox
gross Swedish emigration 18–20, 21, 66–67,
    86n6, 86n9, 146, 169, 258
    see also net migration; Ó Gráda Paradox
Grosse Île 157
Guinchard, Axel Johan Josef 23n23
Guinnane, Timothy W. 57n37, 185n16, 201,
    208, 222n2, 244
Gulf Stream 8, 10, 142
Gwynn, Aubrey 130n47

Hälsingland 82
Hansson, Lars 163n56
härad 22n21
    definition 14
Harris, Ruth-Ann 241
Hart, Peter 248n11, 260, 263n9
Hasselquist, T. N. 84
Hatton, Timothy J. 21n2, 24–25n31, 227
hazard (Irish) 96–100
    agricultural definition 35
    as concept 34–35
    summary 57–8n39
    see also risk assessment
Heald, Carolyn A. 122–23, 135n123
hearth-tax 31–32
Hearts of Oak Boys 134n105
Heck, Barbara 122
Heckscher, Eli 40, 58n48, 188–89
Hedberg, Fredrick Gabriel 82, 83
hemmansägare 44, 46
    see also bonde
hemmansbrukare 44
Heraclitus 229
Herrnhutism 88n23
Hoerder, Dirk 22n8
Hofsten, Erland 140, 163n52, 163n54, 185n19
Holy Communion, Sweden 75–85
Holyhead 101
Homans, George C. 60n63
Homeland Evangelical Mission Society 77
Homestead Act (1862) 231
Howe, Stephen 153
Hull (England) 68, 82
husförhörslängd 74

"Ideal Type"
    see Weber, Max

illegitimate births
    see out-of-wedlock births
Immaculate Conception, BVM 223n33
impartible inheritance
    see farm size, Irish
imperialism
    as concept 6
indentured labourers 107–08, 112, 134n115,
    134–5n116
India 10
indigene 112, 235
indigenous dispossessed 6, 188, 195–96
industrialization
    Ireland 220
    Sweden 40–41, 189–91, 221
Inglis, Tom 213–14, 219, 222n8, 223n26
inheritance, impartible
    see farm size, Ireland
inheritance, Swedish 61n72, 61n73
inhyseshjon 45–55 *passim*
    see also rural social differentiation
intra-British Isles migration, Irish
    see Irish migration to Great Britain
    see also seasonal migrants to Great Britain
intra-European migration, Swedish 69–70,
    87n19, 146–47, 163n54, 163–64n56,
    184n11, 258–59
Irish civil war 259
Irish Family Planning Association 261
Irish migration to Great Britain 94–96,
    126–27n7–9, 184n3
    see also seasonal migrants to Great Britain
Irish national system of education 213–14
Irvingites 81
Isanti County (Minnesota) 251n48
Islandmagee 119–20, 219
Italy 8, 23n27, 242

Jamaica 107
Jämtland 139
Janson, Florence Edith 22n21, 161n9
Jansson, Eric 82, 83
Jeffery, J. R. 24–25n31, 25n33, 94, 126n3
Jefferyes, James 9–10
Jennings, John 10
Jensen, Richard 199n37
Jews 88n25
Johansson, Rolf 25n36
Johnson, John 125
Johnson, William 125

Johnstown District 123
Jones, Maldwyn A. 120–21, 135*n*118
Jönköping 142
Jutikkala, Eino 138, 160*n*3

Kalmar 143, 236
Kandiyohi County 82
Karlskrona 82
Kelleher, John V. 247
Kennedy, Robert E., Jr. 179
Kennedy, Liam 56*n*14, 134*n*114, 134–35*n*116, 135*n*118, 135*n*120, 186*n*27, 194, 263*n*13
Kimball, Solon 201, 206, 218
Kingston (Ontario) 123
kommun 22*n*21
    definition 14
Konventikelplakat
    see Anti-Conventicle Act
Kopparberg 141, 142
Kristianstad 84, 145
Kristianstad Tract Society 83–84
Kronoberg 142, 234

Lagan Valley
    see Belfast
lagaskiftet 144
    see also enclosure, Swedish
Lagerlöf, Selma 91*n*58, 251*n*48
Laggan Presbytery 114
Lake Siljan 85
Lambkin, Brian 108, 126*n*7
län
    definition 12–14, 22*n*20
Land Acts, Irish 27–28; 1891 205; 1896 205; 1903 205
landless labourers
    Irish 35–49 *passim*, 193–94, 198*n*24
    Swedish 45–55 *passim*
    see also backstugusittare; inhyseshjon; Irish seasonal labourers; *lösa daglönareklassen*; rural social differentiation; rural social structure
land tenure, Irish 35–39
    see also land acts
land reclamation
    see agricultural revolution, Sweden
landskap
    see provinces, Swedish definition
Lapland 238
Larkin, Emmet 210, 212, 223*n*2, 224*n*37

see also Devotional Revolution
Läsare
    see Readers
Late Loyalists 124–25
Latter-day Saints
    see Mormons
leaseholds, Irish 35–38
leases, Swedish 43–47
Lee, Joseph J. 31–32, 201, 219
Lewis, Frank 248*n*6
life expectancy
    Ireland 186*n*28
life narratives 231–38, 249*n*15, 250*n*36
Lincoln, Abraham 236
Lindberg, John S. 87*n*16, 197*n*12, 199*n*31
Lippman, Walter 4–5, 21*n*5
literacy 59*n*58, 214
Liverpool 10, 68, 82, 86*n*10, 99, 101, 121
"lives" 35–38
    see also land acts; leaseholds, Irish
Ljungberg, Jonas 23*n*25
Ljungmark, Lars 146–47
lösa daglönareklassen 45–46
    see also day labourers, Swedish
Longford, Elizabeth 164*n*70
Loyalists 122–23
lumper 33
Lundh, Christer 197*n*13
Lundström, Hans 140, 163*n*52, 163*n*54, 185*n*19
Lutheranism
    see Augustana Synod; State Church of Sweden

MacDonagh, Oliver 166*n*106
MacGill, Patrick 245–46, 255*n*91
Macken, Walter 227
MacLean, Roderick M. 128*n*24, 255*n*89
MacRaild, Donald 126*n*8
Magnusson, G. Gerhard 171, 249*n*15
Magnusson, Lars 54, 63*n*87, 63*n*93
Maguire, William A. 133*n*104
male heads of enterprises
    as concept 46–47, 190
Malmborg, Oscar 140
Malmöhus 145, 237
Malthus, T. H. 35, 57*n*34
Mannion, John 105–06
manors 42, 43, 51
mantal 62*n*76

Maori 188
marital age
  Ireland 178–79, 185–6n27
  Sweden 185n22
marital fertility
  England 179
  Ireland 179, 244–45, 260–61
  Sweden 179–80, 185n19
  Wales 179
  see also population limitation
marital rate
  Ireland 178
  Sweden 175–77
  see also population limitation
Maritimes 103
Martin, F. X. 22n22
Marx, Karl 155
Maryland 105
Mass attendance 210, 212, 224n35
  see also Devotional Revolution
"match" 206–07
  see also population limitation
Mattson, Hans 84, 85, 92n68
Mattson's Settlement (Vasa, Minn.) 84
Maynooth Seminary 211
McBride, Ian R. 133n89
McGee, Thomas D'Arcy 164n64
McGinn, Brian 108
McInnis, R. Marvin 195–96n5, 248n6
McLaren, Angus 183
Methodists 78, 81, 122–23, 225n50
  Sweden 76–77, 83
  see also Scott, George
Mexico 99
military service
  Sweden 69–70, 251n50
Miller, David W. 120, 133n89, 156, 166n102,
  181–82, 210, 212, 223n34
  see also Devotional Revolution
Miller, Kerby 132n80, 134n114, 134–35n116,
  135n118, 135n120, 243–44, 248n11,
  252n58
missing relatives 241
Mitchel, John 148, 149, 164n65
Moberg, Vilhelm 91n58, 161n21, 249n15
"Modest Proposal" 139
Mohawk 188
Mohawk Valley 125
Mokyr, Joel 30, 55, 57–58n39, 154, 158–60,
  166n94

Montreal 68, 82
Montserrat 108
Moody, T. W. 22n22
moral purity
  see population limitation
  see also Connell, K. H.
Moravian Brethren 88n23
Mormons 69, 90n49
Mount Tomboro 139

Napoleonic Wars 99, 101, 150, 151
Närke 79
natural increase
  definition 17
  see birth rate
  see also death rate
Nelson, Marie Clark 142–43, 161n11
net Swedish emigration 66–67
New Brunswick 111
Newry 217
New York 68, 103
New Zealand 10, 238
Newfoundland 99, 104–06, 109–10, 130n53
Nilsson, Fredrik Olaus 78–79, 83, 193
nobility-gentry estates, Swedish 43–44, 46,
  61n74, 197n12
Norelius, Andrew 92n60
Norelius, Erik 92n60
Norman, Hans 147, 164n59
Norrbotten 139, 142
Norrland 75–76, 82, 139
Norway 8, 22n11, 242
  see also intra-European migration
Norwegian emigration 8, 147
Nova Scotia 124–25

Ó Gráda, Cormac 27–28, 30, 57–58n39, 94,
  126n7, 150, 152, 154, 158–60, 161n7,
  166n94, 186n27, 194, 201, 215, 240,
  248–49n12
  see also Ó Gráda Paradox
Ó Gráda Paradox 27–8, 34–35, 55, 93–96,
  99–100, 102, 104, 109, 112
O'Brien, Michael J. 132n76
O'Connell, Daniel 120
O'Farrell, Patrick 164n65
Öland 140
Olsson, Nils William 86n4
Ontario 110, 111, 121
oral confession, Catholic 209, 214, 219

Order of Divine Service
  Sweden (1693) 76
  Sweden (1811) 75–85
O'Rourke, John 164*n*61
O'Rourke, Kevin 8, 18, 21*n*2, 151–52, 158–60,
  195–96, 227
Orr, James 119
Orsa 79, 83, 92*n*61, 92*n*69
  see also Ostergren, Robert C.
Orsa-Läseriets 79
Östergötland 68–69
Ostergren, Robert C. 85, 92*n*69, 238, 251*n*48
O'Toole, Fintan 125
Ottawa 123
out-of-wedlock births 213, 225*n*60
  Bulgaria 213
  Finland 213
  Ireland 180–83, 186*n*38, 187*n*48, 216–17
  Portugal 213
  Russia 213
  Serbia 213
  Sweden 176–77
  sources 224*n*40
  see also Connell, K. H.

Palatines, Irish 122–23
Palmer, Gregory 125
Palmquist, Gustaf 84, 92*n*68
Palmqvist, Per 79
papal infallibility 223*n*33
Parkhill, Trevor 253*n*65
Paul, Saint 215
peasant
  as concept 27–9, 180–81
Peatling, G. K. 199*n*37
Peel, Robert 157
penal code
  American 132*n*76
  Irish 72, 88*n*20, 104–10, 114–16
  Swedish 71–83 *passim*
Petty, William 97
"PFI" 224*n*41
Pietists 71–72, 73, 88*n*23
piga 45, 61*n*72, 197*n*13
Pitkänen, Kari J. 141–42
Pius IX 223*n*33
"poor European periphery" 8, 220
Poor Law Commission (1833–36) 182–83
population limitation

Catholic Church 207, 209–15, 216–17, 218,
  222*n*7
  and economics 201–08, 212–13, 218
  in Ireland 178–83, 200, 221–22, 223*n*21,
    225–26*n*68, 261
  Protestants 215–20
  as a system 200–01, 222*n*2
  in Sweden 60*n*61, 185*n*19, 259–60
population total, Ireland 17, 31, 38, 154, 158
  see also "world" Irish population
population total, Sweden 17, 41–42
  see also "world" Swedish population
Portugal 8, 213
Post, John D. 139, 160*n*2, 160*n*5
potato 153, 163*n*48, 163*n*49, 203–04, 206
  Ireland 33–34, 39
  Sweden 145
  see also Great Famine
poverty trap 96
pre-marital pregnancy rate
  see population limitation
prepaid tickets
  see remittances
Presbyterians 113–22 *passim*, 132*n*80, 215–20,
  225*n*50
  clergy 114–17
  and marriage 115–16
Princeton project
  see European fertility project
Profanation Clause 78, 80
Protestants, Irish 231, 259–60, 263*n*9
  definition, 132*n*79
  see also Church of Ireland; Methodists;
    Presbyterians
Protestants, Swedish
  see also Baptists; Free Church; Methodists;
    Mormons; State Church of Sweden
provinces
  Irish definition 13–14
  Swedish definition 12–13, 22*n*20

Quebec 82, 103, 111
Queen Elizabeth 104
Quigley, John Michael 65, 86*n*1
Quinn family, Belfast 238
Quinte, Bay of 123–24

Ravenstein, E. G. 5, 8, 160*n*5, 193
Readers 75–85, 87*n*18, 89*n*26, 89*n*28, 89*n*29,
  90*n*36, 92*n*60, 92*n*69, 92*n*72, 104

regium donum 114
religious composition
  of Ireland (1834) 113
  of North America 111–12, 131n75
  of Upper Canada (1842) 111–12
religious conversion 108–09, 112–13, 130n55,
  131n75, 132n77, 134n113, 135n121
re-migration
  see return migration
remittances 240–1, 243, 246, 253n69, 262
return migration 241–43, 254n74, 254n75,
  254n77, 255n78, 255n79
reverse migration
  see return migration
Revised Hymnal (1819) 75–76
Riksdag 140, 236
Rising (1798) 119, 123–124
risk assessment 100–101, 221, 222, 223n18
  as concept 34–35
  Ireland 137, 153
  Ireland, pre-Famine 35–39, 55, 96–100,
    137, 141, 153
  Sweden, pre-Deprivation 39–55, 137
"Rob Roy" 101
Rodgers, Nini 106–10
Roman Catholic Church
  see Catholic Church (Roman)
Rosenius, Carl Olov 77, 83
Royal Patriotic Society 141
Runeby, Nils 70
"rural embourgeoisement"
  see agricultural revolution, Irish
rural proletarianization
  see rural social differentiation
rural social structure
  pre-Deprivation Sweden 39–55
  pre-Famine Ireland 35–39
rural social differentiation
  Ireland 193, 198n24, 207–08
  Sweden 54–55, 64n96, 144–45, 162n39,
    189–94
rural/urban proportions
  Ireland 28
  Sweden 39, 59n50, 189, 198n21
  Russia 9, 10

Sacramental Law (1855) 80
Sandberg, Lars G. 144–45, 162n40
Sandewall, Allan 75, 80, 89n27
säteri 44

Scotch-Irish
  as concept 132n80
  see also Presbyterians
Scotland 242
Scott, George 76–77, 83
seasonal migrants to Great Britain 98–103
  passim, 128n31, 231, 245–47, 248–49n12,
    262
Sen, Amartya 155
Six Nations 125
Skåne 43, 51, 197n13, 238
Skaraborg 234
Sklar, June 180
slave economy
  see slavery, African
slavery, African 107–10, 130n47, 195–96
Småland 79, 139, 140, 145, 233
Smyth, W. J. 108–09
sockenmagasin 143
Söderberg, Johan 162n41, 197n7
Soltow, Lee 50, 62n81
South America 99
Spain 8
Spenser, Edmund 97
St John (New Brunswick) 121
St. John's (Newfoundland) 105–06
Stapleton, William 107
State Church of Sweden 72–85 *passim*, 234,
  236–38, 250n32
stattorpare 45–55 *passim*, 190–93
  see also rural social differentiation
Stayer, James 88n23
Steckel, Richard H. 144–45, 162n40
Steelboys 118, 134n105
Stephenson, George M. 88n24
Stewart, A. T. Q. 97
Stockholm 79, 162n32
storskiften 51
  see also enclosure, Swedish
"strong" farmers 36
"subsequent marriage" 182–83
  see also population limitation
Sundbärg, Gustav 18–20, 23n23, 23n24, 24n29,
  25n38, 26n42, 43, 66–67, 145, 146, 190,
  208–09, 213, 224n40, 237
Svear (Swedes) 10, 11
Swedish Established Church
  see State Church of Sweden
Swedish State Church
  see State Church of Sweden

Swift, Jonathan 139
Switzer family 122
Syllabus of Errors 223*n*33
Synge, Archbishop Edward 117

Tedebrand, Lars-Göran 254n77
temperance movement 76–77, 89–90*n*34
tenant-right 35–36, 57*n*37
   see also land acts
terra nullius
   doctrine 196
Teskey family 122
Test Act (1704), 115
Thatcher, Margaret 153, 200
"thingumatrope" 230
Thirteen Colonies 110, 111, 121, 124
Thistlethwaite, Frank 5, 21*n*2, 21*n*5
tillage
   definition 222*n*11
Tipperary Protestants 124
tithes
   Irish 117, 119, 133*n*99
   Swedish, 81
torp
   see torpare
torpare 44–55, 190–93
   see also rural social differentiation
Trans-Appalachian Frontier 128*n*22
Treaty of Limerick 104
Trevelyan, Charles Edward 148–49, 164*n*67
Turner, Michael 202–208 *passim*, 222*n*1
Tyrone, Wars 9

Ulster Custom 35–36, 57*n*37
Ulster-Scots
   as concept 132*n*80
   see also Presbyterians
Unionius, Gustaf E. M. 91*n*54
United States censuses 131*n*68, 131*n*72
   nature of 110–11
United States of America
   famine migration 156–57, 166*n*108
   migration restrictions, 259
   see also cost of passage; Loyalists; return

migration; Thirteen Colonies; "world" Irish
   population; "world" Swedish population
Upper Canada 110, 111, 123

Värmland 140
Vasa (Minn.) 84
Vasa, Gustav 79, 84
Västerbotten 139, 142
Västernorrland 139
Västmanland 69
Venezuela 99
von Zinzendorf, Count 88*n*23

wage rates
   see convergence
Wales 242
Walford, Cornelius 160*n*5
War of 1812–14 123
Weber, Max 119, 206, 219
Wentworth, Thomas (Earl of Strafford) 114
West Indies
   see Caribbean
Whalley, Buck 9
Whately, Richard 182
"whiteness" and Irish debate 112, 130*n*47,
   199*n*37
Wiberg, Anders 83, 85, 92*n*68
Wicksell, Knut 261
Wilde, William 96–97, 139, 160*n*5
Willcox, Walter F. 18, 21*n*3, 24*n*31, 227
William III 114
Williams, Eric 130*n*47
Williamson, Jeffrey G. 8, 18, 21*n*2, 227–29
   passim
Wilson, Catharine Anne 92*n*69
Wilson, David 164*n*64
Winberg, Christer 60*n*61
Wohlin, Nils 24*n*29, 42, 43, 60*n*65, 62*n*84, 144,
   190, 193, 197*n*12, 243
Wokeck, Marianne S. 134*n*115, 134*n*116
Woodham-Smith, Cecil 148–49, 164*n*70
"world" Irish population 171–72, 184*n*10, 221
"world" Swedish population 171–72, 184*n*11
Wright, Robert L. 235, 250*n*31